Second Edition

Educational
PSYCHOLOGY FOR
EFFECTIVE TEACHING

Kenneth T. Henson

The Citadel

Ben F. Eller

The University of Alabama

Kendall Hunt
publishing company

Book Team

Chairman and Chief Executive Officer Mark C. Falb

President and Chief Operating Officer Chad M. Chandlee

Vice President, Higher Education David L. Tart

Director of Publishing Partnerships Paul B. Carty

Editorial Manager Georgia Botsford

Development Editor Melissa M. Tittle

Vice President, Operations Timothy J. Beitzel

Assistant Vice President, Production Services Christine E. O'Brien

Senior Production Editor Laura Bies

Permissions Editor Renae Horstman

Cover Designer Jenifer Fensterman

Web Project Editor Sheena Reed

Cover image courtesy of Ken Henson.

www.kendallhunt.com
Send all inquiries to:
4050 Westmark Drive
Dubuque, IA 52004-1840

Dedication

This book is dedicated to the day when all children of the world are blessed with a nurturing, caring family and wise, understanding teachers.

Brief Contents

Contents

PART 1

HOW STUDENTS DEVELOP

PART 3

MAJOR LEARNING THEORIES AND HOW THEY ARE USED IN TEACHING

CHAPTER 8

PART 4

INSTRUCTIONAL METHODS FOR EFFECTIVE TEACHING

CHAPTER 9

CHAPTER 10

PART 5

MOTIVATING STUDENTS AND MANAGING THE CLASSROOM ENVIRONMENT

CHAPTER 11

CHAPTER 12

PART 6

GRADING AND ASSESSING STUDENT PERFORMANCE

CHAPTER 13

Most Common Problems Faced by First-Year Teachers		
1940	**1986**	**2010**
1. Talking	1. Use of drugs	1. Lack of financial support
2. Chewing gum	2. Lack of discipline	2. Lack of discipline
3. Making noise	3. Lack of financial support	3. Use of drugs

Source: Clement, M. C. (1998, April 8). *Beginning teachers' perceptions of their stress, problems, and planned retention in teaching*. Paper presented at the meeting of the Midwest ATE, Urbana, IL. Johnson, W. J. (1985). Education on Trial (p. 20). San Francisco: 1(5 Press), Phi Delta Kappa Poll 2010.

BECOMING AN EXCEPTIONAL, PROACTIVE TEACHER . . .

Provide your students another tool to reach this goal!

Offering an unparalleled combination of theory and application, this motivational text emphasizes the theme that exceptional teachers are *proactive*. In every chapter, students learn to plan ahead and prepare for the many and varied situations they will encounter in today's classrooms.

The experiences of many of the country's finest K-12 teachers and the writing of educational psychologists, Dr. Kenneth T. Henson and Dr. Ben F. Eller advise and instruct aspiring teachers concerning the skills and knowledge they will need to make appropriate classroom decisions. The result? Your students come away from this book saying "Yes,

I can do this! I can use those proactive steps to become the teacher I want and need to be!"

Preface

When we began our writing of *Educational Psychology for Effective Teaching*, we committed ourselves to those who would be our nation's school professionals. We determined to present our worthy readers a book of academic distinction; a lucid presentation of the value and importance of educational psychology in the school environment; a contemporary presentation of research in educational psychology; and an enjoyable, readable text.

Our efforts were guided by three major goals: (1) to enhance our readers' understanding and ability to apply the principles of educational psychology to the classroom environment, (2) to provide a succinct explanation of what is known about student learning, (3) to present explanations and examples of how future teachers and other school professionals can proactively prepare and successfully address the academic and social issues of today's students.

By facilitating teacher understanding of students' cognitive, academic and social behavior, educational psychology provides aspiring teachers the tools to analyze situations and make appropriate choices. Our text emphasizes proactive preparation for teaching, recommending teachers and other school professionals plan for academic presentation, student diversity and potentially difficult academic and social situations. As part of our approach, we sought out academicians and recognized teachers throughout the country for consultation and participation in our efforts. Each chapter includes the invaluable contributions and advice of professors, school professionals, and teachers who have been honored as "Teachers of the Year" in their respective states. ∎

Organization

The text is organized in a clear and easy-to-use format. Each chapter begins with a list of learning objectives followed by an introduction, then presents content and concludes with a recap of major ideas.

The writing style is straightforward, avoiding excess jargon. Important new terms are set in **bold type** and are listed in a quick reference guide in the **Key Terms** section at the end of each chapter. The terms are defined in their respective chapters and in the **Glossary** at the end of the book.

The seven main topics covered in the text are:

- The contributions and importance of educational psychology in the school environment

- How students develop mentally, academically and socially
- Student diversity in the classroom
- Major learning theories and how they affect teaching
- Instructional methods for teachers
- Motivating students and managing the classroom
- Grading and assessing student performance

Features

We believe you will enjoy and benefit from learning how successful school professionals cope with challenges in today's classrooms. In this second edition, additional features have been added to take advantage of their expert advice and reflection on defined classroom situations. These features include:

- **A Teacher's Class** profiles teachers who have won the prestigious 'Teacher of the Year' award in their respective states. Found in every chapter, this feature provides students firsthand counsel from the country's best K-12 teachers, all recipients of their respective states' "Teacher of the Year" awards.

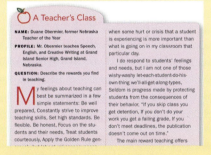

- **Todd Williams** is an on-going hypothetical narrative of a first-year teacher's experiences. This engaging case study begins in Chapter 1 and continues throughout the book, giving your students firsthand glimpses of the everyday challenges and rewards of a new teacher. They witness as teacher Todd Williams begins his first day, and in each subsequent chapter,

they follow Todd through significant experiences relating to each chapter's theoretical and application topics.

- **A View from the Field** relates interviews with educational psychology professors on specific topics relevant to chapter content. Found in every chapter, these "Views" expose students to the perspectives of other educational psychologists and professional educators. They respond to questions on key chapter topics, providing students alternative insights into application of the major theories and methodologies discussed within the chapter.

- **INTASC Standards**, where applicable, are noted within each chapter. *Please see a concise list of these standards at the end of this Preface.

INTASC Standard 2 Learner differences.

- Decision-making skills in the classroom as teachers work with students, families, fellow teachers, and administrators.
- An awareness of the special problems faced by non-English speaking students, minorities and developmentally delayed students. This implies that language skills, understanding concerning the norms of subcultures and student cognitive and social development patterns are critical to learning. Education can and should be a great equalizer; a means of upward mobility for students, regardless of race, economic background, or geography (Farr, 2011, p. 23).
- Skills necessary to solve the more traditional problems in today's classrooms include classroom management, enhancing cognitive development, motivation, and appropriate evaluation.
- Other factors, such as economic conditions and technology, will have a major impact on future schools and will require new methods of learning delivery systems.
- As the complexity of our society increases, so will the need for teachers to have a thorough background in theories of learning, development, and cognition. According to Guyton and Fielstein (1991, p. 207), "Although information is necessary, it cannot be expected by itself to modify learned attitudes."

- **What Would You Do** boxes provide the opportunity to brainstorm what you would do in the academic and social situations presented.

WHAT WOULD YOU DO?

In every state, education reform programs are increasing the pressure on teachers to increase the achievement scores of students. Suppose you have a student who is highly admired by his or her classmates and yet this student thinks it's cool to cruise along and earn Cs and Ds. One such student actually responded to just enough test items to earn a C or C minus, leaving the rest of the questions blank. He didn't want to be thought of as a 'nerd' by his peers. Is it feasible to use another student as a model to reverse the behavior of this student?

Emphasizing planning for classroom situations, the text offers the following:

- **Proactive Teaching** in every chapter describes specific classroom situations followed by proactive options and alternatives. For example, *Proactive Teaching* from Chapter 4 suggests

alternatives for facilitating the acceptance and understanding of multiculturalism in today's classrooms.

 **PROACTIVE TEACHING**

Throughout this text we define methods and techniques educational psychology provides the proactive teacher. Our proposed solutions will be based on research that has examined successful methodologies used by teachers in the classroom environment. Typical problems you will face in your teaching career are listed under "Classroom Situations" with "Proactive Alternatives."

CLASSROOM SITUATION	**PROACTIVE ALTERNATIVES**
You hope to stimulate an interesting, relevant learning climate in your classroom. A sense of community in the classroom encourages students and builds a sense of confidence (Redman & Redman, 2011). In addition to the typical textbook instructional material, you want to add contemporary information related to subject matter.	Plan to use easily accessible, contemporary material on topics related to curriculum content. A good example is current news items and reports. Current news is accessible and relevant topics can be used to enhance and stimulate classroom instruction. Selected TV programs and field trips can be used to demonstrate relevance and importance of subject matter.

- **Proactive Exercises** are provided to help you anticipate and constructively address classroom situations *before* they occur. By students working through problematic and typical classroom situations, they gain understanding through choosing appropriate, proactive responses to the variety of realistic scenarios they'll face in their teaching careers.

PROACTIVE EXERCISE

Table 1.1 lists techniques offered by educational psychology that can have a positive impact on the confidence, pride and self-reliance of minority and immigrant students, students from economically poor backgrounds, and students with impairments.

- **Further Applications** suggests ways to apply chapter content to the classroom environment. At the end of each chapter, these innovative exercises offer opportunities to explore major themes of the chapter in greater depth.

FURTHER APPLICATIONS

1. Develop a daily lesson plan that includes a menu of both primary and secondary reinforcers.
2. For a lesson in your own chosen subject and grade level, choose between using ratio scheduling and interval scheduling. Write a rationale to defend your choice.
3. Choose a complex concept in your future teaching curriculum, and show how you can break it down into many simple parts, using shaping or chaining.
4. Behavioral learning theorists contend that considerable student behavior is a result of classical, or respondent conditioning. Consider the following incidents in a typical elementary and/or secondary classroom.

- **Case Studies** are integrated throughout chapters and drawn from actual classroom experiences. Woven into textual material, they offer specific classroom examples to illustrate theoretical discussion. For example, in Chapter 6, "Behavioral and Social Learning," a case study investigates Renee, a fourth grader, in terms of student learning, teacher impact on learning, and the relationship of student behavior and learning.

CASE STUDY

A new middle school was to be constructed in Cross Creek. The funding had been secured by public vote on bonds. The town council had appointed a committee to recommend structure, environment, climate, and school policy for the new school. Several committee members were committed to having the "best" middle school possible for their community.

However, during the first committee meeting, there was confusion about how best to proceed. Some wanted to hire consultants; others suggested using school building plans of neighboring towns. The debate continued for two hours. Finally, Nell Gray, a former school counselor, now retired and respected throughout the community for her honesty and candor, rose to speak. "I sense the committee truly wants to make our new school the best possible. Perhaps, an appropriate beginning would be asking pertinent questions. Despite press reports that often suggest the opposite, many schools in our state and nation are truly outstanding. Why not take advantage of their success? We could identify a number of these schools and simply study their characteristics. We could search out answers to the most obvious questions: What are the characteristics of effective schools? What do they emphasize academically? What is the climate of such schools? How do they maintain discipline? How are effective schools organized in terms of class size? What are their policies on grading and retention? What is the management style of their administrators? What teaching methods are used by their teachers? What are the social and academic characteristics of their students?"

Technology in the Classroom as a learning resource, is a unique feature of our text. Current trends suggest technology will continue to have a dramatic impact on the classroom and student learning. To this end, two sections are included at the conclusion of each chapter to facilitate your effective use of technology in the learning process.

- **Technology in the Classroom** describes how technology can be used to complement chapter content. Featuring the use of technology in the classroom, these sections are alternative ways of using technology in the classroom. For example, "Technology in the Classroom" from Chapter 2 focuses on cognitive and language development, offering suggestions for multimedia, and other software sources for preschool, elementary, middle, and high school.

TECHNOLOGY IN THE CLASSROOM

As you consider the applications of technology to the subject material in each chapter, we suggest that you avail yourself of the vast amount of information and advice available on the Internet.

We suggest that you begin with the U.S. Department of Education homepage (**http://www.ed.gov/**). This homepage offers information and houses the "National Center for Education Statistics," which publishes a document that contains a comprehensive review of education statistics publications, including the "Conditions of Education." This annual report includes information on enrollment rates, dropout rates, and trends in academic achievement and education spending.

- **Surfing the Web** provides websites and other resources related to chapter subject material. With this innovative feature, students can pursue chapter-related topics using the Web. The authors list website addresses related to chapter material, describing the content of each site.

SURFING · THE · WEB

'Strengthening Teaching' is the major focus of a website furnished by the U.S. Department of Education. (**http://www.ed.gov/pubs/teaching**). A resource for student learning is the National Research Center on Student Learning at the University of Pittsburg (**http://www. lrdc.pitt.edu**).

The Department of Education also offers (**http://www.ed.gov/pubs/parents.html**). Another resource for teachers, counselors, and parents is the Administration for Children and Families website (**http://www.acf.dhhs.gov**). This is an excellent resource of vital information that brings together a range of federal programs, including Aid to Families with Dependent Children, At-Risk Child Care, Child Welfare Services, Community Services Block Grants, Foster Care and Adoption Assistance, Head Start, and the National Center on Child Abuse. ■

At the end of each chapter four features summarize major themes, provide suggestions for discussion and introduce content of the next chapter. These features include:

- **Recap of Major Ideas** summarizes the major concepts of the chapter for quick review.

RECAP OF MAJOR IDEAS

1. Educational psychology in the school environment is the study of applying the methods and theories of Psychology to student development, behavior, cognition and learning processes.
2. A growing percentage of our nation's children face obstacles inhibiting their becoming successful learners. Effective teachers find ways to help these 'at-risk' students succeed.

- **Further Applications** suggests ways to apply chapter content to classroom situations.

FURTHER APPLICATIONS

1. Develop a daily lesson plan that includes a menu of both primary and secondary reinforcers.
2. For a lesson in your own chosen subject and grade level, choose between using ratio scheduling and interval scheduling. Write a rationale to defend your choice.

- **Key Terms** provides a list of the major terms introduced in the chapter.

KEY TERMS

learning	unconditioned reinforcer
behavioral learning theory	conditioned reinforcer
extinction	pairing
modeling	continuous reinforcement
classical conditioning	reinforcement schedule
stimuli	interval schedule
neutral stimulus	fixed interval schedule

- **Looking Ahead** offers a brief preview of the next chapter.

LOOKING AHEAD

Chapter 6 emphasized how the teacher and the classroom environment affect the behavior of students. Behavioral approaches to teaching and learning is an extremely important topic and complements our next two chapter topics, the cognitive development of students. Contemporary educational psychologists have long stressed the importance of student creativity, perception, memory, thinking, and problem solving. These mental or cognitive functions are the major topics of the next two chapters. ■

In addition, a fully integrated student and instructor website for this text is available. The Web access code is included on the inside front cover of this textbook. Look for the Web icons in the text's margin to direct you to various interactive tools to enhance your learning experience. The site includes:

Instructor Resource Manual

Test Bank

PowerPoint® slides

Study Guide

Poll Questions

Glossary of Key Terms

You are to be commended for your pursuit of becoming a teaching professional. We congratulate you for choosing the career that undergirds all other professions. As such, you will shape the lives of many young people. Such responsibility requires education, commitment and dedication. We designed this text to help you achieve such worthy goals.

INTASC (Interstate New Teacher Assessment and Support Consortium)

The certification, licensure requirements and demonstration of subject mastery by new teachers varies from state to state. Therefore, it is often difficult for new teachers to satisfy such requirements in states other than where their degree was earned. *INTASC*, a program of the Council of Chief State School Officers, is developing a new licensing examination, *Test for Teaching Knowledge*, in an attempt to establish common standards for the certification and licensing of teachers.

In addition to NCATE (National Council for Accreditation of Teacher Education), many university and college teacher programs across the nation have implemented the ten standards developed by INTASC into curriculum goals and content. The certification and licensure requirements of future teachers will continue to be an important issue for prospective teachers. Therefore, applicable INTASC

standards are noted in each chapter where proceeding chapter content addresses standard. The ten core standards of INTASC are:

Standard 1 – Teacher mastery and knowledge of subject matter.

Teacher understands central concepts, tools of inquiry, and structure of discipline(s) he/she teaches and can create learning experiences making these aspects of subject matter meaningful to students.

Standard 2 – Teacher knowledge of human development and learning.

The teacher understands how children develop and learn and provides learning opportunities supporting student intellectual, social and personal development.

Standard 3 – Teacher ability to adapt instruction for individual student needs.

The teacher understands how students differ in their approaches to learning and creates instructional opportunities that adapt to the diversity of learners.

Standard 4 – Multiple instructional strategies.

The teacher understands and can use a variety of instructional strategies to encourage students development of critical thinking, problem solving, and performance skills.

Standard 5 – Classroom motivation and management skills.

The teacher uses his/her understanding of individual and group motivation and behavior to create a learning environment encouraging positive social interaction, active engagement in learning, and self-motivation.

Standard 6 – Teacher communication skills.

The teacher uses knowledge of effective verbal, nonverbal, and media communication techniques to foster student active inquiry, collaboration, and supportive interaction in the classroom.

Standard 7 – Instructional planning skills.

The teacher plans instruction based on knowledge of subject matter, students, the community and curriculum goals.

Standard 8 – Assessment of student learning.

The teacher understands and uses formal and informal assessment strategies to ensure the continuous intellectual, social, and physical development of the learner.

Standard 9 – Professional commitment and responsibility.

The teacher, as a professional educator, continually evaluates the effects of his/her choices and actions on others (students, parents, and other professionals in the learning community) and who actively seeks out opportunities to grow professionally.

Standard 10 – Partnerships.

The teacher fosters relationships with school peers, parents, and agencies in the community to support students' learning and well-being.

Source – http://www.ccsso.org/projects/interstate-New-Teacher-Assessment-and -Support-consortium/#resource

The Interstate New Teacher Assessment and Support Consortium (INTASC) standards were developed by the Council of Chief State School Officers and member states. Copies may be downloaded from the Council's website at http://www.ccsso.org.

Council of Chief State School Officers. (1992). Model standards for beginning teacher licensing, assessment, and development: A resource for state dialogue. Washington, DC: Author. ■

Acknowledgments

There are many to whom we owe a debt of gratitude for their efforts during the writing of this text. We cannot overemphasize the support and professionalism provided by the Kendall/Hunt staff throughout this project. Thank you Developmental Editor Melissa Tittle, Senior Web Project Editor Sheena Reed, Senior Production Editor Laura Bies, and Senior Permissions Editor Renae Horstman. Your tireless and impeccable work to make our text a success is sincerely appreciated. We are honored the artwork of Professor K. A. Henson, Cincinnati Art Academy, graces our book cover. These individuals brought their creative ideas to our text and remained cheerful contributors throughout the project.

We also want to express our sincerest appreciation to the following former State Teachers of the Year who allowed us and our readers to enter their classrooms and share in their remarkable work.

Ms. Constance Cloonan, New Jersey

Ms. Renee Coward, North Carolina

Mr. James Ellingson, Minnesota

Ms. Sandra Gifford, Texas

Ms. Marilyn Grondel, Utah

Ms. C. C. Lancaster, Washington

Ms. Susan Lloyd, Alabama

Mr. Duane Obermier, Nebraska

Ms. Shirley Rau, Idaho

Mr. Howard Selekman, Pennsylvania

Mr. John Snyder, Nevada

Ms. Nancy Townsend, South Carolina

Ms. Bea Volkman, Alabama

The professors who provided "A View from the Field" enabled us to go beyond our own perspectives. We appreciate the sharing of their expertise.

Dr. Li Cao, University of West Georgia

Dr. Lori Flint, East Carolina University

Dr. Mary A. Davis, (Strubbe) – Northern Arizona University

Dr. Edmund T. Emmer, University of Texas at Austin

Dr. Daphne D. Johnson, Sam Houston State University

Gregory J. Marchant, Ball State University

Dr. Jan Moore, Eastern Kentucky University

Dr. Sheila A. Pemberton, Tennessee Tech University

Dr. H. S. Pennypacker, University of Florida

Dr. John Stone, East Tennessee State University, President–Education Consumer Foundation

*Dr. Elizabeth E. Thrower, Montevallo University

Dr. Jules A. Troyer, Valdosta State University

Dr. Paul A. Wagner, University of Houston, Clear Lake

Dr. Steve Wininger, Western Kentucky University

*The advice and contributions of Dr. Thrower were invaluable in this second edition. Her revisions of chapters 5, 13 and 14 were exemplary and sincerely appreciated. In addition, Dr. Thrower was invaluable in the designing of our PowerPoint presentations for the chapters.

Finally, we were fortunate to have had many excellent reviews of our manuscript. We were guided by the reviewers' efforts and appreciate the many improvements that resulted directly from their suggestions.

REVIEWERS

Dr. Kathleen Everling
University of Texas at Tyler

Dr. Jocelyn Holden
Ball State University

Dr. Mark Lewis
University of Texas at Tyler

Dr. Shelia Pemberton
Texas Tech University

Dr. Rebecca Martinez Reid
Indiana University –
Bloomington

Dr. Jill Shurr
Austin College

Dr. Cecil Smith
University of Alabama

Dr. Elizabeth Thrower
Montevallo University

Dr. Jules Troyer
Valdosta State University

Dr. Sheila Webb
Jacksonville State University

About the Authors

DR. KENNETH T. HENSON is a former public school science teacher who received his B.S. from Auburn University, M. Ed. from the University of Florida, and Ed. D. from the University of Alabama. He is both a National Science Foundation Academic Year scholar and a Fulbright scholar. His grant proposals have earned over 100 million dollars enabling the design and implementation of several innovative teacher education programs. These programs have received best program statewide and national awards. His AT&T technology grant was the largest funded in 1991. He received the Association of Teacher Educator's Distinguished Teacher Educator Award in 2000 and the Text and Academic Authors Franklin Silverman Lifetime Achievement Award in 2008. He is author or coauthor of more than 50 books and over 300 articles published in national journals. For the past decade he has served as Professor of Education at The Citadel in Charleston, South Carolina.

DR. BEN F. ELLER is Professor Emeritus, University of Alabama. He taught Educational and School Psychology and founded the university's Educational Technology program. He received his B.S. from Milligan College and completed his graduate studies at the University of Tennessee. Dr. Eller has published extensively and presented papers, nationally and internationally, in both educational psychology and educational technology. His research in educational psychology focused on maladaptive student behavior in the classroom, the emotionally impaired student, abandoned and abused children, and the delinquent adolescent. He has been recognized for his work designing academic and social programs for such students in the school and home environment. His research in educational technology emphasized the impact of technology on contemporary and future classrooms. He has served on numerous editorial and directorial boards and currently writes and consults.

Educational Psychology for Effective Teaching

Educational Psychology and the Learning Environment

LEARNING OBJECTIVES

Upon completing this chapter, you should be able to:

1 Identify three ways educational psychology relates to today's and tomorrow's classroom environment.

2 Explain the concept of *proactive teaching*.

3 Compare and contrast the qualities of effective teachers with the teaching skills contemporary educational psychology research suggests will be necessary for future teachers.

4 Describe three environmental factors in the classroom that impact student learning.

5 List four recent changes in U.S. culture and population that will define the characteristics of our nation's future students.

6 Explain how the three major national education reform acts, Rosa' Law, Race to the Top, and No Child Left Behind impact contemporary and future classrooms.

7 Relate three major characteristics of future students and explain how teacher awareness of these characteristics can assist in preparing for classroom instruction.

8 Compare and contrast the "artistic" and the "scientific" characteristics of "good" teachers.

9 Explain the importance of applying the findings of educational psychology research to the school environment.

INTRODUCTION

Within their classrooms, teachers have always been the critical factor determining the academic and social success of students. From the time they arrive at school until they leave, teachers impact the lives of their students. Effective teachers recognize the importance of their influence and they prepare long before they arrive at school as they plan each lesson and they continue preparing after the school day ends as they consider teaching methodologies, methods of minimizing disruptive behavior, and design of future lesson plans to fit the diverse needs of their students.

Two generations ago Flanders (1990, pp. 86–87) aptly articulated the challenge of today's teachers.

> We must be living in a new era when good intentions alone are not enough. One major change in this decade is that teachers are now being held accountable for the quality of learning in their classrooms more rigorously than in the past. Honor may be bestowed only on those who can combine good intentions with effective performance. We may have reached a point at which honor only becomes effective teachers.

Two major goals of this text are to explain how educational psychology can help prospective teachers prepare and facilitate the academic achievement and the social success of their future students.

EDUCATIONAL PSYCHOLOGY TODAY AND TOMORROW

Educational psychology is a field of tremendous variety. In this section, we look at the responsibilities common among today's school professionals and expected trends that will impact tomorrow's classrooms.

Defining the Discipline

As a discipline, educational psychology has been around for more than a century. As early as the 1880s, Louisa Parsons Hopkins wrote about recognizing the importance of psychology in education:

> It would be as absurd for one to undertake to educate the young with no knowledge of . . . psychology, as for one to attempt to produce a sonata while ignorant of the phenomena of sound. (Hopkins, 1886, p. 3, as cited in Glover & Bruning, 1990)

Despite the early insight of Hopkins, many still debate the relationship of education and psychology and, thus, the definition of educational psychology. Several factors complicate the task of defining educational psychology.

> " Upon the subject of education . . . I can only say that I view it as the most important subject which we as a people can be engaged. "
> ABRAHAM LINCOLN

First, it includes two disciplines: education and psychology. Clifford (1984) argues that combining education and psychology is appropriate. He defines educational psychology as applying the methods of psychology to studying the process of education. Others define educational psychology as knowledge gained from psychology and applied to the classroom (Grinder, 1981). Therefore, *educational psychologists* are often defined as those who apply the principles of psychology to education and who devote their professional lives to understanding learners, the learning process, and the instructional strategies that enhance learning.

Educational psychologists perform many different roles. Some design curriculum content and evaluate the impact of curriculum changes on student behavior and academic achievement; others are involved with computer-managed and computer-assisted instruction in the classroom. Many educational psychologists teach in university and college teacher-preparation programs. Their responsibilities are typically divided among teaching and researching the variables determining:

- the effectiveness of teaching methodologies
- how students learn
- how teachers can effectively interact and communicate with students, families, and other teachers
- how best to teach others.

The "scientific methodologies" (discussed later in the chapter) educational psychologists have used to answer these complex questions have been fruitful and, on many issues, answers are still being pursued.

Research in educational psychology has been ongoing for generations and, as a result, an accumulated knowledge base (or body of knowledge concerning the 'science' of teaching and learning) has been established (Biddle, Good, & Goodson, 1996; Christensen, 1996). This knowledge base includes such factors as:

- the environmental and cultural influences on the learner
- the cognitive functioning of students
- managing the classroom
- how students learn, and how all of these variables relate to teachers and teaching.

The problems of tomorrow's teachers and the role of educational psychology will be more complex than in the past.

Educational psychology's data base of information provides many options and suggestions on becoming a successful teacher (Clark, Hong, & Schoeppach, 1996). A major purpose of this text is to acquaint you with the research findings that can foster effective teaching.

Current trends in educational psychology indicate that the following skills will be necessary for future teachers and other school personnel:

INTASC Standard 2   Learner differences.

- Decision-making skills in the classroom as teachers work with students, families, fellow teachers, and administrators.

- An awareness of the special problems faced by non-English speaking students, minorities and developmentally delayed students. This implies that language skills, understanding concerning the norms of subcultures and student cognitive and social development patterns are critical to learning. Education can and should be a great equalizer; a means of upward mobility for students, regardless of race, economic background, or geography (Farr, 2011, p. 23).

- Skills necessary to solve the more traditional problems in today's classrooms include classroom management, enhancing cognitive development, motivation, and appropriate evaluation.

- Other factors, such as economic conditions and technology, will have a major impact on future schools and will require new methods of learning delivery systems.

- As the complexity of our society increases, so will the need for teachers to have a thorough background in theories of learning, development, and cognition. According to Guyton and Fielstein (1991, p. 207), "Although information is necessary, it cannot be expected by itself to modify learned attitudes."

Two key elements for student learning are: 1) Teacher/student communication. 2) Very specific, well-defined rules for student behavior in the classroom.

As Erasmus (1989, p. 274) aptly expressed,

> Teachers must be able to reach beyond their worlds to touch that of their students and assist students to do the same. . . . [W]e (teachers) must learn to listen and listen to learn.

The need for "real world" teacher skills suggests that educational psychology is of prime importance in addressing contemporary and future needs of our nation's teachers. Therefore, let us begin with a discussion of a "good teacher" and defining today's and tomorrow's student learner.

THE TEACHING PROFESSION

What makes a teacher good? Is the teacher an artist or a scientist? And why teach? What are the advantages? These are the issues in this section.

A "Good" Teacher

As we ponder our educational careers, most of us can remember exceptional teachers. Think about your favorite teacher(s). Can you remember their teaching techniques or what they did in class that made them special? If you remember characteristics such as friendliness, good management skills, knowledge of subject matter, were academically demanding yet their classes were interesting and fun, then you agree with the research literature in Educational Psychology.

Will you be happy with your chosen profession? A recent poll found that most of today's teachers are happy with their profession. And beginning teachers are critically important as they continuously revitalize and bring enthusiasm to our schools (Ingersoll & Merrill, 2010; Ripley, 2010). Seventy percent of Americans would support their children becoming teachers (Bushaw & McNee, 2009).

Despite the myth "some people are born teachers," prospective teachers become "good" teachers through hard work, study and experience. Contemporary Educational Psychology has identified the typical characteristics of good and/or effective teachers.

"In fact, we know more about effective teaching than ever; unfortunately much more than we use" (Hersh, 2009).

How can you best prepare to become a good teacher? Are there implications for the types of courses you should pursue in your academic curriculum? Can you identify a number of positive factors or indicators for future teachers? In short, what does it take to be a good teacher? It takes an individual who cares enough about students to invest the time and energy needed to become an expert manager of the classroom, subject content, and student learning.

In the play *A Man for All Seasons*, an ambitious young man named Richard Rich asks Sir Thomas More for help in getting a government job. The chancellor urges him instead to become a teacher, saying, "You'd be a fine teacher, perhaps even a great one."

"And if I were, who would know it?" the aspiring politician complains. To which More rejoins, "You, your pupils, your friends, God. Not a bad public, that."

Many young people, like you, are ready for the challenge; they are excited about their future teaching careers. "Todd Williams," whose development we will follow throughout the text, exemplifies such enthusiasm.

TODD WILLIAMS...

was beginning his career as a teacher. He was convinced that teaching eighth-grade history was going to be an exciting, yet challenging, task. The principal, Ms. Wickersham, was showing him around his new working environment, Thomas Jefferson Middle School. "Todd, I'd like you to meet some of your fellow teachers."

They chatted as they walked through the halls until Ms. Wickersham knocked on a door. The door was labeled with a sign that read "Through This Door Walk Some of the Brightest Students in the County. Welcome." Ms. Stephens opened the door and exchanged pleasantries. Many of Ms. Stephens' comments stood out in Todd's mind: "I've got a good, hard-working group this year. I'm very proud of them. Jim and Pat are a little behind but they are coming along. The class is excited about the plans for the district computer fair."

Todd noticed the class. The students were busy, hardly noticing the visitors. Some were working with computers; others were discovering "real" and "imaginary" numbers from problems on the board. Yes, there was noise, but it was healthy noise, the noise of students going about their tasks—learning, being excited, asking questions. The heading on the board, "Einsteins for Today," had 10 students' names beneath it. They had 100 percent correct answers on today's homework assignment.

As they approached Mr. Humphrey's Advanced History Class, Todd and Ms. Wickersham could overhear comments coming from the open classroom door. "Well, it seems that you feel that it was wrong for such a man as Galileo to be persecuted by the inquisitorial court for his opinions?"

"Yes," a student shot back, "it was wrong of the court because Galileo was right."

"Yes, Gino," responded Mr. Humphrey, "Galileo was right in believing his astronomical discoveries and for saying the earth did move. But would you be so quick to defend a racist who discovered a cure for cancer?"

There was silence, until a student asked, "What's that got to do with anything, especially Galileo?"

Mr. Humphrey replied, "Well, how many things did Galileo personally believe that were wrong? Did he not share the ignorance of his time? Did he not believe in the divine right of kings, in slavery, in the permanent servility of serfs and women? Would he not, by our standards, be labeled a bigot?" There was silence. Mr. Humphrey prodded his students. "Think, where is the discrepancy in my logic?" Just as a student was about to respond, Mr. Humphrey noticed his visitors and, smiling, walked to the door; Todd yearned for the class to continue.

As Todd and Ms. Wickersham were returning to the office, she commented, "Todd, we are like most middle schools, where teachers and students are concerned. We have teachers whom I consider to be the best, the very best—and we have some who need summer workshops to improve their skills, and a few who perhaps shouldn't be teachers. We have students who are three and four years ahead in achievement—writing sophisticated computer programs, producing plays, and like Mr. Humphrey's class, debating world issues—and we have some in special classes who are working on basic skills. But, that's what we're here for—to educate all our students. I hope you enjoy it here. I know I do."

PROACTIVE EXERCISE

Table 1.1 lists techniques offered by educational psychology that can have a positive impact on the confidence, pride and self-reliance of minority and immigrant students, students from economically poor backgrounds, and students with impairments.

> " Tomorrow's teachers must be risktakers, innovators. There can be no complacency. The students that we encourage to teach should be those who sometimes step over the boundaries of what is acceptable, Students who question grades, who question methods, who force us to rethink our ideas—those students should be teachers. "
> SHIRLEY RAU, FORMER IDAHO TEACHER OF THE YEAR

Like Todd and his new principal, Ms. Wickersham, many of today's educators remain optimistic about the future of the teaching profession. They realize that their effectiveness is important to students' lives (Semadeni, 2010). This optimism is fueled by the fact that today's social scientists can predict with a great deal of certainty many future educational trends. You can use these trends to prepare for your teaching career. Future teachers will face many of the same challenges that teachers have faced in the past. These perennial challenges include motivating students; maintaining discipline; and working with families, fellow teachers, and administrators, all with unique personalities and expectations.

However, future challenges for teachers like Todd also will include the continued increase in the number of minority and immigrant students, including non-English-speaking students; an increase in the number of students with learning disabilities; integration of technology into the classroom; and a dramatic increase in the number of older students in higher education. What alternatives does educational psychology suggest for teaching students who are labeled "bright," "creative," "minority," "learning impaired," or "non-English-speaking"?

These specific issues will be discussed in later chapters, but there are many other decisions that you, as a teacher, will have to make regardless of where you teach. As Shirley Rau, former Idaho Teacher of the Year, suggests, your success as a teacher, counselor, or other education specialist will hinge on your ability to recognize these issues and apply your innovations and skills to make decisions that resolve or reduce the magnitude of the problems.

INTASC Standard 7   Planning for instruction.

TABLE 1.1

Techniques to Aid Special-Needs Students

Student	Suggested Activities to Enhance Confidence and Self-Reliance among Students
Minority	1. Design class activities that include various cultures, For example, you might have assignments requiring studies of famous people of various cultures and races. Such people might include Martin Luther King, Gandhi, Mother Teresa, Lech Walesa, Nelson Mandela, and Liu Xiaobo. 2. Show films and videos portraying the cultural history of various races and cultures and invite minority guest speakers who can be viewed as role models to facilitate positive feelings of students about themselves and their classmates.
Students from economically poor backgrounds	Use academic reinforcers suggested in Chapters 6 and 12. Additionally, as with all your students, include these students in leadership activities, Serving as teacher assistant for a day or week, class officer, class representative, editor of the class paper, or student council representative illustrates to students and peers they can succeed. Familiarize yourself with your school's services for such students. Many schools offer 'free breakfast and/or lunch programs, as well as pre and after school care.
Physically disabled	Remember that physical disability does not imply mental or social impairment, Typically, the same social and academic activities can be used with these students as with your other students. Also, include physically impaired students in physical activities. Make modifications and use other students as substitutes to provide the opportunity for students who are impaired to participate in games and sports. Students' self-reliance and confidence can be adversely affected by exclusion. Provide students who are mentally impaired with academic material that ensures success. More detailed examples of techniques for students with special needs will be discussed in Chapter 5.

The Teacher as Artistic Scientist

Effective teaching is **contextual**, meaning that the success of any teacher behavior depends on the immediate situation (Christianbury, 2011, p. 48) and teachers must adapt their approaches to fit each classroom. As you recall your exceptional teachers of the past (or present), their artistic attributes might have included personality, spontaneity, and positive display of emotions. Teaching, obviously, engages the "artistry" of the individual who teaches and produces the "works of art"—students who will become successful academically, socially, and in their chosen field. Yet, when you consider the act of teaching, teachers use the methods of science to instruct, question, counsel, evaluate, or produce a work of art. The goal of this text is to provide you with teaching skills generated by the science of educational psychology. The artistry will be, in large part, your creativity and personality and the enthusiasm you bring to the teaching profession. This suggests that teacher and student "curiosity" and "innovation" are critical to the learning process.

> " Teaching may be the greatest of all arts since the medium is the human mind and spirit "
> JOHN STEINBECK

Curiosity and Innovation

Effective teachers are always looking for better ways to teach (Highlighted & Underlined, 2010). The good news is that the practice of teaching is learnable (Ball & Forzani, 2011). The bad news, as previously noted, is that we know a lot more about effective teaching methods than we are using (Hersh, 2009). For example, when the level of noise in a classroom interferes with learning, some teachers respond by trying to shout over the noise. Although this is a common response, it seldom works. Effective teachers are willing to explore different approaches. For example, instead of raising their voices, these teachers may pause, using eye contact to quiet their class. Other teachers may use **proximity control**, which simply means that they walk to the noisiest part of the room and stay there until the noise level subsides (discussed in detail in Chapter 12).

These methods may not work with all groups; there may be methods that work better, as we will explore in later chapters. This is why curiosity, experimentation, and risk-taking are so important to teachers. Throughout their careers, successful teachers continue to learn (Rothman, 2009). Teachers who reflect on their experiences increase the likelihood that their teaching will improve and they will become productive members of their learning community (Reames, 2010). But to challenge students to explore their capabilities, effective teachers, like Ms. Stephens and Mr. Humphrey, whose classes Todd visited, are willing to take risks, such as challenging students to "compete in the district computer fair" or raising such issues as the reactionary beliefs during the time of Galileo. As Friday (1990, p. 99) describes, effective teachers find a way to touch and shape lives.

> It has long been clear to me that teaching is at once the most difficult and the most honorable of professions. We have all been touched by the example, guidance, and motivation of a teacher whose often reluctant pupils we were. We can each recall a moment of insight or truth when caught in the act of learning. None of us owes larger debts for whatever we may have become, for whatever we may have been able to accomplish, than we owe to teachers in our past lives whose total devotion to young people

Effective teachers educate and address the problems of students at all levels.

and to their discipline has been their chief reward and the reason we honor teachers and the teaching profession.

The characteristics of those teachers who form special bonds with their students are difficult to measure but fortunately we have a considerable body of research in educational psychology literature. The findings to date focus more upon classroom organization, time management, and student/teacher interactions, which can be more easily quantified than such personal qualities as warmth and individual concern. However, Charles Sposato, former Massachusetts Teacher of the Year, whom we quote in the sidebar, notes that students are very aware of these issues. What are the results of the research to date? Can educational psychology prescribe techniques that will guarantee success in the classroom? Let us quickly rephrase our question. Can educational psychology offer recommendations and/or techniques that will maximize the likelihood of your being successful in the classroom and becoming that special teacher? The answer is a resounding "yes." Chapter 9 will discuss in detail the characteristics of such teachers, but briefly summarized, the research to date (Armstrong, Henson, & Savage, 2009) indicates the following:

- The effective teacher plays a central, dominant role in the classroom but involves students in planning and organization.
- Successful teachers set high academic standards and communicate those standards to students.
- Effective teachers work mostly with the entire class but often with small groups, sometimes providing independent work.
- Effective teachers maintain a brisk lesson pace, requiring overt student participation.
- Effective teachers use little criticism, shape student responses so that they are correct, hold students responsible for their work, and treat students equitably.
- Effective teachers set and maintain clear rules for students' academic and social behavior.

What implications do the characteristics of successful teachers have for prospective teachers? How do teachers feel about their profession; and perhaps most important, how will you feel about your chosen profession after teaching for a year? Let us relate the advice of Duane Obermier, former Nebraska Teacher of the Year.

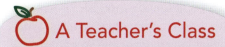

A Teacher's Class

NAME: Duane Obermier, former Nebraska Teacher of the Year

PROFILE: Mr. Obermier teaches Speech, English, and Creative Writing at Grand Island Senior High, Grand Island, Nebraska.

QUESTION: Describe the rewards you find in teaching.

My feelings about teaching can best be summarized in a few simple statements: Be well prepared. Constantly strive to improve your teaching skills. Set high standards. Be flexible. Be honest. Focus on the students and their needs. Treat students courteously. Apply the Golden Rule generously, but let natural consequences happen.

I firmly believe in treating students like fellow human beings who have feelings just like I do. They don't appreciate being embarrassed or humiliated or confronted with problems in front of their peers. But they do respond to kindness, encouragement, a friendly tease, and a smile. I try to teach manners in my classroom by being mannerly to my students. "John, I never interrupt you when you're speaking. Please don't interrupt me." Also, I believe that working and learning at school can and should be fun. I joke and laugh frequently with my students. In addition, I believe that there may well

be times when some hurt or crisis that a student is experiencing is more important than what is going on in my classroom that particular day.

I do respond to students' feelings and needs, but I am not one of those wishy-washy let-each-student-do-his-own-thing we'll-all-get-along-types. Seldom is progress made by protecting students from the consequences of their behavior. "If you skip class you get detention. If you don't do your work you get a failing grade. If you don't meet deadlines, the publication doesn't come out on time."

The main reward teaching offers me is the hundreds and hundreds of relationships I've had the opportunity to develop. I thoroughly enjoy seeing and visiting with former students and I don't just mean those who have graduated. It's fun to walk the halls during passing periods and see juniors and seniors whom I had in class as sophomores. It's interesting to me that a friendly relationship can be maintained even with the students who didn't do well in the class . . . even those who failed. Here's an example from last summer: I was jogging near my home and a student from second semester swung in next to me riding his bicycle. This student was definitely "at risk" in our school and had been anything but academically successful in my class. I sent him to the office a couple of times for not doing his work; he had trouble with the spelling exams, and he ended up with a failing grade. As I jogged and he pedaled we talked, laughed a little, and I encouraged him to be back in school in the fall. He is back, he's in my class again, and I'm confident that he'll pass this time. In fact, the improvement in his work has permitted me to send his guardian an "up" slip just a couple of days ago.

The other relationships that teaching has provided me are with my co-workers at Grand Island Senior High and with teachers from other schools. What a great bunch of people! Words like talented, dedicated, creative, dynamic, sensitive, and caring are appropriate descriptions for my colleagues. I feel privileged to be a part of them. ■

Why Teach? The Advantages

Like Duane Obermier, many teachers report that they love teaching and have no regrets concerning their career decision. If you question teachers about why they teach, the response will often be "I value the profession and the responsibility". The average teacher's salary today for high school teachers is just over $56,000 and the average for middle-level teachers is just over $52,000 a year [salaries retrieved on Feb 20, 2011 at www.payscale.com/research/us/all_k-12_teachers/salary]. The average starting salary is about $36,000.

Hopefully your future students will describe you the same way you describe the best teachers you had in your educational career. Let us now turn to the characteristics of your future students and the teacher/learner relationship.

> "Teachers who stay in the profession value interpersonal relationships and working with other people. On balance, most teachers find their careers satisfying, enjoy students, and the challenges teaching affords them and their students" (Carter & Doyle, 1996, p. 133).

MYTH: Students are about the same today as they were in the past and will be in the future.

THE STUDENTS OF TODAY AND TOMORROW

Changes in society affect our schools in important ways. Today's changes are dramatically altering the characteristics and nature of our student population. For example, we are entering an era in which young people will be in short supply. Since 1983, and for the first time in our nation's history, the population of people over 65 is greater than the population of teenagers; and the difference is growing. It will challenge us to find new ways to involve this large segment of our population in efforts to improve our schools. Immigration is another important factor currently impacting American education. More than 5 million children of immigrants entered U.S. public schools between 2000 and 2010. Approximately 3.5 million of these children are from homes where English is not the first language. During the same time period, 150 languages were represented in our nation's schools. Today, one out of every three Americans is a member of a minority, one in six U.S. residents are

Hispanic, and in less than a decade there will be no majority or ethnic group in the United States. Every American will be a member of a minority group, (U.S. Department of Education, 2010).

Think about the many ways that these changes affect teachers. For example, cultural values and language can become barriers as you work with families and students from other cultures. But, along with such challenges come new opportunities. For example, having culturally diverse classes can be a definite advantage because it affords you and your students opportunities to examine the contributions each group has made to the development and enrichment of our nation (Henson, 2010).

> REALITY:
> Our student population is experiencing dramatic changes.

Educationally At-Risk Students

Our educational system faces a challenge in attempting to educate the increasing number of "educationally at-risk" students. Educationally at-risk students are defined as those children whose chances for graduating from high school are small. In America, almost 7,000 students drop out every day (Bushaw & McNee, 2009). In African American communities and in some Latino communities and Native American communities, the dropout rate is almost 80 percent (Azzam, 2009).

Having culturally diverse classes can be a definite advantage because it affords teachers and students opportunities to examine the contributions that each group has made to the development and enrichment of our nation." (Henson, 2011)

One of the largest groups of poor students, and often the most neglected group is rural children. According to the National Center for Education Statistics (Provasnik et al., 2007), 35 percent of rural students live below the national poverty level. Another 26.3 percent live just barely above the poverty line. Poverty is defined as an income of $25,000 or less for a family of four (U. S. Department of Health and Human Services, 2006).

Why is it that in a society that has one of the highest living standards in the world, we continue to experience an increase in the number of educationally at-risk students? A number of social factors contribute to this dilemma.

Poverty, language barriers, children born to young unmarried females, and students with impairments add to the school-age at-risk population. Poverty is more common among children than among any other age group (Reed & Sautter, 1990). In the next decade, the number of children in poverty will increase, as will the number of youths eligible for Head Start programs. James Bryant Jr. (2011) has noted the inequitable treatment of rural schools. Furthermore, recent education policies from NCLB (No Child Left Behind) to R2T (Race to the Top), both discussed later in the chapter, seem to be urban centered (Dillon, 2010). The United States leads all the industrialized nations in its rate of adolescent pregnancy, a significant factor in the level of poverty among children. Adding to this list are the 1 million student-age run-aways each year (Banks, Kopassi, & Wilson, 1991).

The Classroom Environment

The relationship and interactions among students, teachers, and the school environment have direct effects on learning and behavior. School climate and policy significantly impact on the academic and social activities of students and teachers in and out of the classroom. The following case study demonstrates one town's attempts to define and create a learning environment in its new school.

CASE STUDY

A new middle school was to be constructed in Cross Creek. The funding had been secured by public vote on bonds. The town council had appointed a committee to recommend structure, environment, climate, and school policy for the new school. Several committee members were committed to having the "best" middle school possible for their community.

However, during the first committee meeting, there was confusion about how best to proceed. Some wanted to hire consultants; others suggested using school building plans of neighboring towns. The debate continued for two hours. Finally, Nell Gray, a former school counselor, now retired and respected throughout the community for her honesty and candor, rose to speak. "I sense the committee truly wants to make our new school the best possible. Perhaps, an appropriate beginning would be asking pertinent questions. Despite press reports that often suggest the opposite, many schools in our state and nation are truly outstanding. Why not take advantage of their success? We could identify a number of these schools and simply study their characteristics. We could search out answers to the most obvious questions: What are the characteristics of effective schools? What do they emphasize academically? What is the climate of such schools? How do they maintain discipline? How are effective schools organized in terms of class size? What are their policies on grading and retention? What is the management style of their administrators? What teaching methods are used by their teachers? What are the social and academic characteristics of their students?"

Gray paused, and, after several seconds, a ninth-grade teacher, Otis Webb, spoke. "I noticed an article in a teaching journal just yesterday that summarizes the characteristics of schools considered to be outstanding. I'll bring copies to our next meeting." Sharon DeRidder reminded the committee of the outstanding reputation of Roosevelt High in Loudon County and suggested some committee members should visit to glean ideas.

The committee meeting continued with renewed enthusiasm.

We wish Cross Creek well in its efforts to build a "good" school. We feel they are off to a good start.

This description of planning for Cross Creek Middle School provides one example of the classroom fraternity-the congregation of teachers, counselors, students, families, administrators, and other school professionals who determine and define activities within a school environment. Nell Gray was correct; this country benefits from an abundance of excellent schools and teachers (Berliner & Biddle, 1997). Recent research on successful school environments focuses on teacher behavior in the classroom and how schools design curriculum and manage students, both academically and socially.

Births among very young mothers are dramatically illustrated by the fact that every day in America, 40 teenage girls give birth to their third child." (U.S. Dept. of Education, 2010)

The research demonstrates that the activities of teachers, schools, and students are critical. They significantly impact student social and academic progress (Berliner, 1990, Gronlund & Wough, 2009).

EFFECTIVE SCHOOLS

Some schools are more effective than others, and the school students attend can make a significant difference in level of academic achievement. This section presents the characteristics of effective schools in the areas of instruction, evaluation, communication and training, climate, and discipline.

> Effective schools emphasize the basic skills of reading, writing, and math.

Instructional Emphasis

In reviewing the research on effective schools, one of the most consistent findings is that effective schools emphasize instruction. The instructional focus is pervasive and understood by faculty, students, and school administrators.

The curriculum of effective schools is planned and purposeful but offers some electives for students. Most of the school day is devoted to academics, and there is an emphasis on acquisition of basic skills (reading, writing, and math). Although learning tasks in effective schools are planned at the appropriate level of difficulty for students, effective schools typically have high and uniform standards of academic achievement, and school activities are focused toward well-defined academic objectives.

Study and homework are important in effective schools and are typically coupled with immediate teacher feedback. Most homework is assigned by teachers, and because the impact of homework on learning is affected by the extent students complete homework assignments, and because teachers have limited control over student behavior outside the classroom, teachers must establish clear policy communicating the consequences for failure to do assignments. However, failure to complete homework might result from external factors outside student control. Therefore, teachers should monitor, be aware, consult with students and families and, when necessary, adjust expectations and policy.

Evaluation

Effective schools use systematic evaluation procedures to determine student progress. Student progress is continually assessed to diagnose, evaluate, and provide feedback. Student progress is typically recognized by the public and governmental agencies via achievement test scores, graduation rates, academic awards, and other official recognitions of accomplishment. Effective schools accept responsibility for the outcomes of instruction and use achievement measures for program evaluation.

Academic Expectations

Students and families in effective schools are aware of instructional requirements and know students are expected to meet high academic expectations (Duke & Jacobson, 2011). Teachers communicate to students that mastery of learning tasks is expected and includes evaluation demonstrating mastery. Principals of effective schools attend to the quality of instruction and stress the importance of continually improving instruction. The principal consistently communicates to teachers, students, staff, and families, the school's commitment to academic achievement.

Staff training is important in effective schools. Teachers work collaboratively (Louis & Wahlstrom, 2010). Development activities examine alternative teaching methods to provide teachers with new techniques to use in the classroom. Staff training is also used to maintain and promote successful learning outcomes. Both principals and teachers in effective schools act on the assumption they can solve their school's problems.

Instructor
Manual

Effective schools use evaluation to measure student progress and to promote learning. Effective teachers work together to provide an orderly and safe school environment.

School Climate

Several factors in the school environment influence student achievement (DuFour, 2011; Gronlund & Waugh, 2009). Effective schools maintain an orderly and safe climate conducive to learning and teaching (Kraft, 2010). Teachers provide appropriate opportunities for students to discuss social and academic issues (Duplechain et al., 2008). Typically, there is a well-defined goal of making learning pleasurable (Yelon, 1996). There is also a sense of community. Most students in effective schools willingly participate in the educational process and engage in extracurricular activities provided by the school.

Principals and teachers in effective schools have a sense of responsibility to their students (Jones, 1990). They are empathetic, have personal interactions and enjoy rapport with students. Teachers feel they have authority and support from administration and they can use their judgment when dealing with problems. Effective schools use staff developmental activities to promote a positive school climate and immediately address undesirable staff attitudes. Staff development programs focus on teachers sharing successful methods (Louis & Wahlstrom, 2011).

Discipline

Research shows that 'good' schools have fair but well-defined rules concerning discipline (U.S. Department of Education, 2010). Effective schools can be very small, very large, or somewhere in between. Teachers, families, and students are made aware of school rules concerning discipline. For example, absences have been found to decrease in those schools who immediately notify families of students' absences (U.S. Department of Education, 1994). Personnel in good schools learn to be firm but fair. However, firmness is not to be construed as harshness. Instead of punitive discipline, teachers provide respectful directives. For example, a teacher may tell students "please take your seats now" (Hanny, 1994).

> Effective teachers maintain discipline in their classrooms.

School and Class Size

There appears to be no relationship between the size of schools and school achievement. As stated previously, effective schools can be very small, very large, or somewhere in between. Perhaps there is no relationship between school size and achievement because both small and large schools can have positive characteristics. Large high schools usually have more diverse curricular offerings. Small schools typically have more social cohesiveness, teacher cooperation, and positive interactions between teachers and students.

The relationship between class size and student achievement is not well defined. There is no relationship between class size and achievement when class size is within a range of 20 to 40 students (Rutter, 1983). However, class

> Research studies on the effectiveness of class size on achievement are inconclusive.

sizes below 20 students have been found advantageous for remedial students, impaired students, disadvantaged students, and students in the early grades. Carson and Badarack (1989) reported small achievement gains in small classes, and Johnston (1990) reported improved teacher morale. After several years of studying the effects of class size, Nye et al. (1994, p. 4) reported that "small is far better" maintaining class size is often associated with increased student achievement. However, the practices teachers employ are as important as the size of the class. In future chapters, we address those teacher practices.

Student Study
Guide

PROACTIVE TEACHING

Throughout this text we define methods and techniques educational psychology provides the proactive teacher. Our proposed solutions will be based on research that has examined successful methodologies used by teachers in the classroom environment. Typical problems you will face in your teaching career are listed under "Classroom Situations" with "Proactive Alternatives,"

CLASSROOM SITUATION	PROACTIVE ALTERNATIVES
You hope to stimulate an interesting, relevant learning climate in your classroom. A sense of community in the classroom encourages students and builds a sense of confidence (Redman & Redman, 2011). In addition to the typical textbook instructional material, you want to add contemporary information related to subject matter.	Plan to use easily accessible, contemporary material on topics related to curriculum content. A good example is current news items and reports. Current news is accessible and relevant topics can be used to enhance and stimulate classroom instruction. Selected TV programs and field trips can be used to demonstrate relevance and importance of subject matter.

NATIONAL EDUCATIONAL ISSUES

This chapter began with a discussion of the teaching profession and the specific traits of successful schools: students and teachers. The following examines national issues presenting challenges to future teachers, including laws impacting educational reform, racial prejudice, sex discrimination, drug abuse, sex education, and AIDS awareness education.

Racial Prejudice

Despite the dearth of interracial interaction in some classrooms, interaction between races is the norm in many schools. As a teacher, you have a unique opportunity to impact students' attitudes about racial prejudice. By helping students realize that interracial interaction merits your approval, you increase the probability of students feeling comfortable with interracial friendships and experiences.

Students can be exposed to positive models via visitors to the class, public media, and literature. Students should be exposed to African Americans, whites, Latin Americans, Native Americans, Asians, and other nationalities who interact positively with each other in a variety of vocational and social settings.

One area that is extremely difficult to manage is the role modeling among peers. In many classrooms, identifying peers who can serve as models of interracial interaction for other students is difficult. However, appropriate role models can be very important. You might begin with your potential as a role model. Students, especially younger students, respond to a member of another race as they see their teacher responding to that person. It is thus imperative that you respond consistently and positively to members of all racial and ethnic groups. Many teachers have a tendency to be more paternalistic, protective, defensive, or reinforcing in their responses to one race or minorities. Something as innocuous as shortening a student's name, calling students by nicknames, and touching students may be looked upon as paternalistic or discriminatory if confined to one group. Your approval is a major means of demonstrating acceptance. For that reason, and for ethical reasons, no group should enjoy a greater measure of your approval than another.

Sex Discrimination

During the last decade, there has been a great deal of concern about sexual stereotyping in our society. Despite progress, social norms often continue to condition females to behave in a dependent, submissive, and cautious manner. This, despite the fact approximately 80 percent of working age women in our society are in the workforce and the number are growing. The evolution of how women have been and continue to be stereotyped is illustrated by the following:

Lifestyle Patterns for Females		
1950s	**1990s**	**2010**
· Get married	· Get a job	· Try to find a job
· Have children	· Get married or stay single	· Pay off education bills
· Be a 'housewife'	· Perhaps have children	· Get married or stay single
	· Continue a career, become a home-maker or both	· Perhaps have children
		· Continue a career, share home-making chores or both

Group assignments and compliments on group progress can promote racial acceptance.

Your behavior toward students can and will affect the behaviors of your students toward each other.

Teacher praise and role playing are effective methods for teaching students to respect differences in gender, ethnicity and race.

Race—A social group identified by its ancestry.

Minority— A group of people historically defined as being less in number but more recently is often characterized as being disadvantaged.

Ethnicity— A social group sharing a cultural heritage.

On the other hand, males are conditioned to conceal emotion, be tough and compete. One way to help minimize sex discrimination is for teachers to make deliberate but appropriate attempts to reinforce students for behaviors that are antithetical sexual stereotyping. Girls, in particular, should be encouraged to take leadership roles, choose unconventional academic activities, and accept new challenges. We are encouraged when we hear teachers saying, "Sharon, I'm glad you're thinking about a career in law," "Tamarie, I like the way you provide leadership in student council," "Stan, you have an ability to show compassion for others," "Calvin, the social skills you're developing in your enrichment course will be very useful in the future."

Another avenue for encouraging atypical sex-role behavior is role-play. Suppose you want to reinforce unconventional sex-role behaviors in students. You could simulate different types of vocational situations and have students assume non-stereotypic roles in those situations (for instance, a female department head interviewing a male for a staff position; a female doctor working with a male nurse in diagnosing a male's medical problem. You could use these occasions to recognize appropriate, vocational behaviors of students.

Drug Abuse

In asking "What knowledge is of most worth?" the nineteenth-century philosopher Herbert Spencer grouped human activities under five headings and then arranged them in order of importance. At the top of the list he put those activities directly related to self-preservation.

"Above all," Spencer wrote, "man needs knowledge to guard himself against the incapacities and slow annihilation that his own bad habits bring him."

Many topics dramatically illustrate the importance of values among students; but perhaps none more than *drug abuse*. The first 15 years of the Gallup Poll of the American Public's Attitudes toward Public Schools found the public considered discipline the major problem in our schools. In 1986, drug abuse replaced discipline as the number one problem in the schools and continues to remain so (Elam, Rose, & Gallup, 1996). If you teach secondary students, and unfortunately even elementary, the chances are very good you will face drug issues among your students. The adage, "there are two kinds of drug abusers among our youth—boys and girls" is much more painful than humorous. Just how serious is drug abuse among our youth? The U.S. Department of Education (2010) provides the following statistics:

- Children are beginning alcohol use at an early age; the average beginning age is 12 years.

- One-half of high school students are classified as regular drinkers, one in three drinks heavily at least once a week, and one in four has a serious drinking problem. Approximately 4 million youths under the age of 17 are alcoholics, and children as young as 9 are being treated for alcoholism.

- Teen drinkers account for nearly 50 percent of all fatal automobile accidents.

- Some 80 percent of high school seniors have used marijuana, and two-thirds of American students will have used an illicit drug other than marijuana and alcohol before they graduate from high school.

As a future teacher, drug use among students will provide you with many challenges. In Chapter 12 you will learn that an effective strategy for dealing with classroom discipline is through preventive efforts. Although there is indisputable evidence that a greater return is given on money spent on preventing drug abuse than on money spent treating drug abusers, Americans have been reluctant to invest in drug prevention. The average American who does not have a drug habit will pay between $850 and $1000 next year to treat our society's drug and alcohol abuse problems. Yet, during the same time, Americans will spend only about $1.75 on each child to prevent drug abuse (U.S. Dept. of Health & Human Services, 2010). As a proactive teacher, it is important to take advantage of any prevention programs offered by your school environment and to be an advocate of such programs.

AIDS Education

By 1991, 270,000 Americans had been diagnosed as having contracted acquired immunodeficiency syndrome (AIDS). In 1996 this number exceeded 513,000 (Blake, 1996). In 2011 this number had increased to over one million with 56,000 new cases being reported yearly (www.wncap.org). Approximately 35 million adults and 1.5 million children worldwide are currently living with AIDS. About one-fifth of all AIDS victims are in their twenties. Because the incubation period may be five years or more, we know that some AIDS victims contracted the disease while in high school and college.

As a future school professional, you will share the responsibility for educating about the spread of AIDS and for assisting the school and community to cope with its presence. The following classroom learning experiences are suggested by (Woodring, 1995):

- Answering imaginary letters from early adolescents with questions about AIDS in the form of a newspaper advice column.

- Writing about, or participating in, a group discussion on teacher and student attitudes concerning the social-ethical issues involved in AIDS prevention.

- Simulating a community task force that is charged with developing policy for assisting a person with AIDS in the school.
- Practicing using the AIDS National Hotline telephone service.
- Writing an editorial for the school or community newspaper on the need for an AIDS education program.
- Serving on a student committee to write a brochure to disseminate facts about prevention of AIDS.
- Serving on a student committee to review audiovisual materials on AIDS appropriate for use in schools.

As you continue to prepare for your new career, we encourage you to take advantage of every opportunity to learn more about AIDS. Your awareness of the policies in your school concerning teaching and advising your students concerning AIDS awareness and prevention is essential.

NATIONAL LAWS IMPACTING TODAY'S CLASSROOMS

Rosa's Law

The many factors related to becoming an effective teacher are dramatically illustrated by recent national laws. Some like **Rosa's Law**, signed into law by President Barack Obama in 2010 legitimately reflect the concern in updating and clarifying terminology used in defining the mental abilities of students. Rosa's Law replaces the term *mental retardation* with *intellectual disabilities* in all federal articles related to education. Most educational institutions, academic journals and textbooks, as well as a number of states, have already adopted the new terminology.

No Child Left Behind

Other laws such as **No Child Left Behind (NCLB)**, signed by former President George W. Bush on January 8, 2002 have had a dramatic impact on the governance of schools, individual classrooms, teachers and other educational professionals. The NCLB act was passed primarily as a result of the school reform reports of the 1990s concluding that our nation's educational system needed major reformation (Kochan & Herrington, 1992). Initially, NCLB requires all students in grades 3 through 8 take standardized achievement tests in math and reading every year. In 2007 a yearly standardized science test was added and now math, reading, and science achievement tests are required of all students grades 3 through 5, 6 through 9, and 10 through 12.

NCLB also requires reporting on **adequate yearly progress (AYP)** meaning that math, reading and science achievement test scores will determine if schools are making adequate progress. In addition, NCLB requires schools to develop separate AYP goals and scores for students with disabilities, students

In February of 2012, ten states will not be required to pursue school reforms associated with "No Child Left Behind". At least 28 more states are expected to follow (discussed in chapter 5).

from low-income families, racial and ethnic minority students, and non-English speaking students.

Race to the Top

More recently, as part of the 'American Recovery and Reinvestment Act of 2009, President Barack Obama, announced on July 24, 2009 a new education initiative, **Race to the Top (R2T, RTTP)**. R2T is a $4.35 billion U. S. Department of Education program designed to address the needs of teacher and school effectiveness and student learning. The R2T program is designed to facilitate reforms in state and local districts (K through 12), through a state completion for funding (R2T Website: http.//www2.ed.gov/programs/racetothetop/index.html). RT2 is an attempt to persuade states to adopt 'common standards' in assessing and measuring student achievement. These common standards were developed by the National Governors Association and the Council of Chief State School Officers. The criteria for the state funding competition are outlined in Table 1.2.

TABLE 1.2
Criteria for R2T State Funding
Great Teachers and Leaders (138 points)
In this section states are required to provide plans for improving teacher and principal effectiveness, ensuring equitable distribution of **effective** teachers and principals, and providing alternatives and paths for success for aspiring teachers and principals. In addition, states must show that they support teachers and principals and plans to improve teacher and principal preparation programs within their state.
State Success Factors (125 points).
The State Success Factors requires states to explain their education agenda, how they plan to implement and sustain their proposed plans, and how they will demonstrate progress in raising student achievement scores.
Standards and Assessments (70 points).
In this section, states are required to relate plans for developing and adopting common standards for measuring student achievement and school progress, how they will support the transition to higher standards and assessments for students and teachers. In addition, the defining and the process of implementation of assessment measures are required.
General Selection Criteria (55 points)
The General Selection Criteria requires states to define how they will maintain conditions for high-performing schools, including charter schools, and how they will make education a high funding priority.

(Continued)

TABLE 1.2 (CONTINUED)
Criteria for R2T State Funding

Data Systems to Measure and Support Instruction (47 points)

Data Systems to Measure and Support Instruction requires states to define how they will or are currently Implementing a common statewide longitudinal data system and how they will access and use data collected to improve instruction.

State prioritization of Science, Technology, Engineering, and Math (STEM), worth another 15 points, was added to the above points, for a possible total of 500 points.

Improving the Lowest Achieving Schools (50 points)

In this section states must define how they will improve student achievement, faculty and administrative performance in their lowest-achieving schools and other positive interventions will be undertaken in the lowest achieving schools.

Summary

In March, 2010 the first state R2T winners and awards were announced. The states were: District of Columbia, $75 million; Delaware, $100 million; Florida, $700 million; Georgia, $400 million; Hawaii, $75 million; Maryland, $250 million; Massachusetts, $250 million; New York, $700 million; North Carolina, $400 million; Rhode Island, $75 million; and Tennessee, $500 million.

(Race to the Top Program Executive Summary, http://www2.ed.gov/govprograms/racetothetop/index.html).

Programs for International Student Assessment (PISA)

Although it is too early to determine the success or failure of NCLB and R2T, the latest global rankings of high school achievement test scores by **PISA** (Program for International Student Assessment) demonstrate the challenges faced by our nation's educational system. PISA is an international evaluation of 15-year-old student achievement in reading, math, and science. The program began in 2000 and is sponsored by the Organization for Economic Co-operation and Development (OECD). Tests are administered every three years and the 2009 results were reported in 2010. Table 1.3 shows the ranking of U.S. students.

TABLE 1.3			
PISA - U. S. Student Rankings			
Year	**Math**	**Reading**	**Science**
2003	22nd	18th	21st
2006	35th	*	34th
2009	31st	15th	23rd
* (not available)			

(OECD, 2003, 2006, 2009 PISA databases, (http://pisa2009.acer.edu.au/multidim.php))

Although there is yet little research evidence as causes of the differences among countries, it is interesting to note that among the 2009 international leaders: Shanghai, China; Finland; South Korea; and Hong Kong, China some common teaching trends emerge. These trends include disciplined students, highly qualified teachers, a well-defined curriculum, and prompt attention and treatment to learning problems. (Official PISA site data. (http://pisa2009. acer.edu.au/multidim.php) "Executive Summary" (http://www.oecd.org/ dataoecd/54/12/46643496.pdf)

Although the reforms, discussion, and debate on teacher effectiveness and student achievement continues, teachers still have considerable freedom and influence on their students. But as illustrated by Rosa's Law, NCLB, R2T, state, and federal laws are significantly influencing the decisions teachers must make about their classrooms.

INTASC Standard 10   Leadership and collaboration

Social Responsibility and Teaching: A Teacher's Contributions to Social Progress and the Global Community

Interactions between teachers, students, and the school environment are critical to academic success; but how does the educational community affect social progress? What is the relationship of education and global progress? A primary goal of any educational endeavor should be the enhancement of human life. As teachers, we must concern ourselves with what happens to students once they complete their formal education. Do they have the skills, attitudes, and behaviors necessary to successfully engage in the "pursuit of happiness" and become productive citizens?

As suggested earlier in the chapter, poverty exists in every city, small town, and rural area in this country. Ironically, some of the areas of highest per-capita income have some of the worst pockets of poverty. Yet, because of the relatively high standard of living enjoyed by so many, American students often find it difficult to conceptualize the economic crises many nations of people continually face. For example, many American students are not aware of the famine that struck Africa in the mid-1980s and 1990s and in some areas continues today. Nor do many realize some countries have been at war for literally decades or that currently an entire African population is threatened by the AIDS virus.

Conditions of these magnitudes threaten the global community. Certainly, our school curricula cannot afford to ignore such information, and surely our schools must take some responsibility for helping future generations develop a responsibility toward troubled people of all nationalities.

As a teacher, strive to develop among students a sense of world and national citizenship. Make periodic group assignments and tasks requiring cooperation as part of the lesson plans. Few classroom events could have a more profound impact on your students' respect for other nations than inviting someone from another country to visit your class. If you teach near a university, the international organization on campus can help identify foreign students who would be willing to meet with your class. These visits can enable your students to understand the social norms and values in other societies. Such international issues reflect the importance of the issues facing our national educational system.

PROACTIVE TEACHING

With the national and international issues facing teachers in the classroom, how should they approach their chosen profession? This brings us to a major theme of this text: **proactive teaching**, In the simplest of terms, proactive teachers anticipate and prepare for classroom problems and situations *before* they occur, Helping teachers become proactive is a major focus of this text, Consider the situations and alternatives described in the following sections;

CLASSROOM SITUATION	PROACTIVE ALTERNATIVES
■ You anticipate that several students in your classes will lag significantly behind their peers academically.	■ Have remedial materials prepared *prior* to the beginning of classes. ■ Prepare for peer tutoring in advance by examining the past academic records of students to determine who could be tutors and who may need assistance.
■ You anticipate that some of your students will excel academically.	■ Have accelerated materials and projects prepared prior to the beginning of classes to challenge academically advanced students. ■ Prepare "team" oriented material that provides the opportunity for students to work together.
■ You will be asked for your opinion on types of punishment for disciplinary action in your school.	■ Prepare in advance the disciplinary measures you will use in your classroom and communicate these measures to students at the beginning of the school year.

- Some students will seem to take delight in disrupting your class, and the remainder of the class might reinforce their behavior.

- You will most likely encounter one or all of the following:

  a. You will suspect that one of your students is a victim of abuse.

  b. A senior-high female student will confide in you that she is pregnant.

  c. You will become aware that one of your students has a drug problem.

- Familiarize yourself with school rules concerning discipline.

- Through the study of Chapter 6, discover alternatives and ramifications of punishment.

- Have written class rules prepared to discuss with your students the first day of class, (Chapters 6 and 12).

- The rules should stipulate very specifically:

  a. appropriate academic and social student behavior; and

  b. inappropriate academic and social student behavior; and the consequences of both types of behavior.

- Familiarize yourself with your school's counseling and referral services.

- Discuss with a counselor, school psychologists, and/or administrator of your school the legal responsibilities of teachers concerning child abuse, pregnancy, and drugs.

> The phrase "proactive teacher" is defined as the ability of teachers to anticipate problems and opportunities and therefore make quality decisions, both personal and professional, that will promote students' social and academic success.

As our classroom situations suggest, the decisions you will be making as a teacher will be varied and complex. Therefore, the process you use to make decisions is extremely important. Reactive teachers can be problem solvers; proactive teachers are also problem solvers, but in addition they make decisions that *shape* their classroom environment. They prepare themselves, their students, and the classroom environment for student success. They attempt to maximize the likelihood of students' social and academic success by *acting on* the classroom environment. Additionally, they possess an abundance of efficacy; they believe they and their students will succeed.

A VIEW FROM THE FIELD
A VIEW FROM THE FIELD

PROFILE

Dr. Daphne D. Johnson (Ph.D. in Educational Psychology and Individual Differences from the University of Houston—University Park) is Chair of Curriculum and Instruction at Sam Houston State University where she teaches undergraduate and graduate courses in human growth and development, instructional strategies, and classroom management.

Dr. Johnson's research interests include critical thinking and effective strategies for online instruction. She has been published in *Instructional Leader, Interactive Technology and Smart Education, New Teacher Advocate, TechEdge, Learning and Leading with Technology, Kappa Delta Pi Record*, and *American Secondary Education Journal*. Dr. Johnson is co-editor of the journal *Inquiry: Critical Thinking Across the Disciplines*.

Dr. Johnson has written grants designed to increase the retention of students to graduation; and more recently summer study for students 4th through 8th grades, focusing on logic and critical thinking skills.

QUESTION: What advice would you give to beginning teachers?

Over Planning! It is important to critically consider their room arrangement, rules and procedures, discipline plan, family communication plan, and the diverse needs of the learners who will occupy their classrooms. The more planning completed before the school year begins, the more successful the teacher will be.

Planning procedures, I believe, is the most important part of over planning. Procedures are the backbone of a well-run classroom. When procedures are taught, practiced, and enforced, they become invisible. Teachers should plan how students will enter the classroom, where they turn in homework, get missed work when they are absent, and get the teacher's attention, along with hundreds of other classroom procedures.

QUESTION: How can teachers use educational psychology to instill in students "the joy of learning"?

Children are born with an innate curiosity and love of learning. Teachers who know this and draw upon this knowledge can teach a child almost anything. Learning should be fun! Yes, it is difficult sometimes but difficult does not have to mean boring.

Educational Psychology offers so much information about our brains, how we learn and process information at all ages, and provides us ideas on how to motivate all types of children. Over the last 10 years, I have asked pre-service teachers about their favorite learning experience in school. In that time, not one pre-service teacher ever said her favorite experience was a worksheet. Think about it . . . what was your favorite learning experience in school?

Most responses are group activities where the learners were required to use their curiosity and love of learning to solve, create, or analyze something. Most responses were hands-on activities that involved some degree of research, and required discussion, collaboration and compromise. Learning to plan these types of experiences for your students begins with getting a firm grasp on the research base offered in Educational Psychology. ■

We have explored several national issues challenging future teachers. Now, let's examine how the research findings of educational psychologists and technology can be applied to improve teaching.

APPLYING EDUCATIONAL PSYCHOLOGY RESEARCH IN THE CLASSROOM

As we have discussed, many social factors (nationally and internationally) will influence the classroom environment in the twenty-first century. Does the past and contemporary research in educational psychology have implications for addressing the student/teacher educational issues we have discussed in this chapter? The activities discussed in Table 1.1 indicate contemporary research in educational psychology offers alternatives to teachers facing such issues. Obviously, many other factors will influence the school environment in the coming years, such as technology, the anticipated teacher shortage, and an unpredictable economy, just to name a few. The variables determining the effectiveness of teaching methodologies, how students learn, how best to interact with students, their families and your peers are critical yet, exceedingly complex. The research educational psychologists have undertaken to answer such questions has been difficult and painstaking. However, the knowledge gleaned over the years, through research, can assist you tremendously as you strive to become an effective teacher.

Traditionally, educators have addressed research by focusing on the view that only empirical, quantitative research was acceptable. However, **qualitative research**, such as **case studies** and journal keeping, can have unique potential for addressing some classroom issues. Qualitative research allows the study of how people describe events and defined experiences. In recent years, qualitative research methods have made an increasing impact in education and especially in special education (Ferguson & Halle, 1995). We will be offering case studies throughout the text.

As a future teacher, you face a variety of challenges: You will be part motivator, counselor, negotiator, disciplinarian, and, yes, teacher. The study of educational psychology will be an important part of your preparation for the diverse role you will have as teacher in one the most complex of all occupations (Silva, 2010).

Knowledge of research generated by educational psychologists is essential for those preparing to be teachers.

YOUR GOALS AND EDUCATIONAL PSYCHOLOGY

Perhaps the most important issue pertaining to a career in education is individual goals, namely yours. Enumerating your goals might offer some contrast to the political, social, and economic goals for education advocated by groups and other individuals. You may have a goal of becoming a millionaire (good luck!), or you may have a goal of pursuing a graduate degree in night school as you pursue you career teaching elementary school (many have done this, so good luck on this one also). Goals that include students enjoying your classes, maximizing student achievement, and establishing good rapport with your students and fellow teachers are goals we hope you will embellish.

A Bit of Advice

What is the best advice an educational psychologist can give you as a prospective teacher? Candidly that's a tough question but let's begin with you as a human being. One of the first lessons you will learn when you begin your career as a teacher is that you are very human. After you have been in the classroom for a few months or less, you will find that how your students' respond to you as a teacher will have a dramatic personal impact on you both inside and outside the classroom. If you are having a difficult time in the classroom; your students are not responding in class, your students are not learning, your classes are behaviorally out of control, or you don't get along with your peer teachers—such career problems will affect you negatively inside and outside the classroom. Such problems can affect your relationships with your family and your friends and can impact your feelings about yourself. Conversely, if you are successful as a teacher, you enjoy teaching, your students like you and you them, your students learn, and you get along with your peers. The chances are very good such career success will affect you positively inside and outside the classroom. This includes your relationships with your family, your friends, and how you feel about yourself.

TECHNOLOGY IN THE CLASSROOM

As you consider the applications of technology to the subject material in each chapter, we suggest that you avail yourself of the vast amount of information and advice available on the Internet.

We suggest that you begin with the U.S. Department of Education homepage (**http://www.ed.gov/**). This homepage offers information and houses the "National Center for Education Statistics," which publishes a document that contains a comprehensive review of education statistics publications, including the "Conditions of Education." This annual report includes information on enrollment rates, dropout rates, and trends in academic achievement and education spending.

"Elementary and Secondary Statistics at a Glance" (**http://edreform.com/pubs/edstats,htm**) offers a useful snapshot of public education in America. Do you want to compare your school or district with the national average? This is the place to come. U.S. information on schools, enrollment, teachers, student-teacher ratios, expenditures, salaries and wages, and overall funding is readily available.

An excellent source of educational publications can be found at **www.edweek.com**.

Other resources include the American Psychological Association, or APA (**http://www,apa,org**) and the National Association for School Psychologists, or NASP. (**http://nasp,web.org**).

In the forthcoming Technology in the Classroom sections, we will provide web addresses for additional information that relates to subject material covered in the chapter. ■

RECAP OF MAJOR IDEAS

1. Educational psychology in the school environment is the study of applying the methods and theories of Psychology to student development, behavior, cognition and learning processes.

2. A growing percentage of our nation's children face obstacles inhibiting their becoming successful learners. Effective teachers find ways to help these 'at-risk' students succeed.

3. Effective proactive teachers have specific qualities which can be defined and learned.

4. Teachers have a responsibility to educate students, regardless of their social, economic, or physical limitations.

5. The environments of the school and classroom significantly impact student learning and socialization.

6. The increasing complexity of our national educational issues accentuates teachers' needs for effective teaching methodologies and classroom skills and an understanding of educational psychology research findings applicable to such issues.

Characteristics of Effective Schools

- Instruction is emphasized.
- Curriculum is planned and purposeful.
- The school day is devoted to academic activities.
- Homework is given.
- Systematic evaluation procedures are used.
- High achievement is expected and recognized.
- Principals provide instructional leadership.
- Teachers effectively use instructional time.
- The climate is safe and orderly.
- Principals and teachers have a sense of responsibility to students.
- Discipline procedures are fair and consistent and punishment is infrequent. (Armstrong, Henson, & Savage, 2009)

Characteristics of Well-Managed and Organized Classrooms

- Classroom rules are put into effect the first day of class.
- Classroom rules are communicated to students.

- Expectations are made clear to students.

- Teachers monitor student behavior.

- Teachers consistently, systematically, and quickly follow through on rules.

- Students know they must work on academic activities.

- Students are accountable for their work.

- Academic activities run smoothly with brief transition times.

- Teachers spend little time on misconduct.

- Instructions are clear.

- Lessons are well organized. (Armstrong et al., 1989)

FURTHER APPLICATIONS

1. *Teaching minority students.* The number of minority students in American classrooms is growing at an unprecedented rate. Unfortunately, some teachers are not prepared for the diversity these students bring to the classroom. Those teachers who are insightful and prepared can use this unique opportunity for their students and themselves to learn more about the many cultures that make up our population.

   Examine your own prejudices. How long has it been since you have chosen to collaborate on a project with a member of another culture? Can students be taught to better understand the behaviors of other ethnic and racial groups? Do you agree there are just as many differences among individuals within groups as there are between groups?

   Prepare a set of three activities that you can use in a multicultural class to help your students learn to understand and appreciate members of other ethnic and racial groups. Justify your selection of these activities by basing them on knowledge about multiculturalism that you have gotten from this chapter and other sources.

2. *Teaching at-risk children.* Increased poverty, changes in work patterns, and changes in the family structure are among the many concerns in our society that have made the attainment of a good formal education difficult for many American children. The number of at-risk students is rapidly increasing. As a future teacher, you will need to prepare yourself to identify these children and provide ways of helping them succeed.

Make a list of several categories of at-risk students. For each category, briefly describe the effects these conditions may have on young people in the classroom. List three recommendations a teacher could make to the parents of at-risk students.

3. *Using teacher effectiveness research*. Think back to your elementary or secondary school days. Can you recall a teacher or teachers as being your favorite?

   a. How would you describe this teacher? Make a list of adjectives that come to mind.

   b. Examine your list. How many of these entries involve feelings, emotions, or values?

   c. How serious was this teacher about achievement? Was this a teacher who held high expectations for students?

   d. List four ways you can use the methodologies of this teacher in your career.

      What will be the characteristics of your teaching and your classroom? Will they reflect the changes that are predicted for future classroom environments?

4. *Addressing contemporary educational issues*. Examine the issues raised in the National Educational Issues section. What issues do you believe should be addressed in the classroom and how should this be done?

KEY TERMS

school reform legislation
effective teachers
educational psychology
knowledge base
proximity control
educationally at-risk
effective schools
racial prejudice
sex discrimination

acquired immunodeficiency syndrome (AIDS)
Rosa's Law
No Child Left Behind
Race to the Top
proactive alternatives
reactive teachers
proactive teachers
efficacy

LOOKING AHEAD

Chapter 1 set forth a major goal for this text: To help prospective teachers facilitate the academic and social achievement of their future students. These responsibilities require an understanding of student developmental processes. Over the years, educational psychologists have collected valuable information concerning these processes, forming theories to explain their relationships. Paramount among these are theories of cognitive and language development. Chapter 2 examines these developmental theories. ■

Part 1

How Students Develop

Chapter 2

Cognitive and Language Development

LEARNING OBJECTIVES

Upon completing this chapter, you should be able to:

1

List the stages in Piaget's theory of cognitive development and describe the typical characteristics of children in each stage.

2

Explain Piaget's concepts of readiness and equilibrium and the influence each has on student learning.

3

Define Vygotsky's theory of cognitive development and explain how a student's "zone of proximal development" and "inner speech" relate to the teacher/learner relationship.

4

List alternative strategies for using Piaget's theories in the classroom and be able to defend or challenge criticisms of Piaget's theories.

5

Provide four guidelines for teachers who want to apply knowledge of cognitive development to improve student learning.

6

Define *phonology, morphology,* and *semantics as* basic components of language.

7

Outline the "milestones" in language development from birth to 4 years.

8

State four ways teachers can enhance the language development of students.

INTRODUCTION

As children grow older, they experience and learn more and begin to think in different ways. Becky, a preschool child, is not able to understand that two straight strings of equal length are still equal in length when one is formed into the shape of a circle. Terrill, a fifth grader, can add a long series of numbers but cannot discuss geometric concepts, whereas Freida, a high school senior, can write perceptive short stories about life in the twenty-third century. **Cognitive development** is a process whereby individuals acquire a more sophisticated and complex knowledge of the world around them (Craig, 1986). No one knows precisely how the brain matures, but psychologists have developed some very plausible theories. This chapter will discuss theories of cognitive development and the implications they have for the proactive teacher. Jean Piaget and Lev Vygotsky developed two of the leading theories of cognitive development; both theories, in addition to language development will be analyzed in this chapter.

The development of language is one of the best examples of how thoroughly and dramatically cognitive development impacts learning in children. The development of language skills among preschoolers and school-age children will be discussed, with an emphasis on the implications of language development for teachers. As you read about the theories of Piaget and Vygotsky, ask yourself these questions:

- How can teachers facilitate the cognitive and language development of their students?

- Does cognitive development vary among children?

- As children mature, how does this impact their capacity to learn?

TODD WILLIAMS...

was visiting Ms. Tracie Tomlinson's first-grade class. She had a great reputation as a teacher. Todd was interested in observing her teaching skills and in their dinner plans for the evening. As Todd observed, he became intrigued by the differences in the way the first graders went about their learning tasks.

During math period, most students performed very well when asked to count, recognize, and print numbers. Although it was early in the academic year, several students were comfortable with adding and subtracting single-digit numbers. However, some students became confused when Tracie began a drill asking them to identify the larger or smaller of two single-digit numbers on the two cards she held up. Even some of the students who could add and subtract had difficulty. Then Todd discovered that several first graders were confusing the size of the cards with the value of the numbers. Several students picked the largest card as the largest number.

Tracie had purposely made the cards various sizes. However, it took considerable explanation and practice before many of the students understood that the size of the card did not relate to their number's value.

Tracie circulated throughout the class, praising students for independent work yet encouraging and facilitating the work of those who needed assistance. She also encouraged those students who were working together in group activities.

Todd noticed that students who were comfortable working independently would often "talk" themselves through tasks. Although comfortable with working alone, Angela started her art lesson with a series of questions and statements to herself. "This is fun. What color should I use for the heart? Who got my crayons? I believe this is going to be good. Uh oh. . . . how can I fix it? Not that color. . . . maybe this one!" Other students were more inclined to work with their classmates, seeking

their approval and support and often requesting help from Ms. Tomlinson.

Two of Tracie's students seemed withdrawn and reluctant to participate in class activities. Tracie provided them extra attention and encouragement. Todd learned later that neither of the disengaged students spoke English. Their non-English speaking families had just migrated from Vietnam. Fortunately, Tracie found two community members, also from Vietnam, who volunteered to act as interpreter for two hours every other day.

Trent interrupted class with the following question, "Ms. Tomlinson, my mother got voted alderwoman. She said we live in a democracy. I thought we lived in a house.

"What's an alderwoman?" quizzed So Ling.

Todd was curious about, yet impressed with, Tracie's answer. She did not try to specifically define the words but rather used a classroom example. She reminded the class of how they voted Christina to represent the class on the school paper. The class discussed voting and how Christina was their representative and Terry's mother was an alderwoman because they received the most votes.

Todd's observations raise several questions. Why did so many of Ms. Tomlinson's first graders have a difficult time understanding the size of the cards did not relate to the value of the numbers printed on them? Should she encourage independent work as she did, or should she encourage students to work together, as she also did? When Angela "talked" herself through her art lesson, was that a "productive" learning process, or should she be required to work quietly? Should Ms. Tomlinson have attempted to specifically define a democracy to her first graders?

CAUSAL FACTORS OF HUMAN DEVELOPMENT—NATURE VS. NURTURE

Most educational psychologists agree that human development begins at conception and is the physical, social, and cognitive adaption to one's environment as they age. Educational psychologists also agree that the source and causal factors of development are *heredity* and *environment* but have been debating for decades which has the most influence (Berk, 2001; Fabes & Martin, 2000). This debate is labeled **Nature vs. Nurture** (Overton, 2006).

Heredity, or nature, is defined as the genes, physical traits, intelligence and maturation capabilities you inherit from your parents. **Nurture**, or environment, is defined as the culture you live in; your home, society, parents, friends, religion, all your past and current experiences. Which do you consider the most important? Consider the following.

CASE STUDY

Dr. Thrower stood before her 201 Ed. Psych class at Statesville University. "We defined and discussed heredity and environment in our last class session. So, which is more important, your heredity or your environment? We've agreed our environment shapes so much of what we are . . . current and past experiences both good and bad, your family, your friends, the schools you've attended, your faith, if you have a faith, and where you've lived and live. Environment is so important to you that you are spending your present life and a considerable amount of money trying to control what your environment will be in the future; getting a degree, a job, and building a life for yourself. But let me ask, what if you had been born in Darfur, North Korea, or Iraq? If you had been born, raised, and now lived in one of those environments would you be wearing the same clothes, had cereal and milk for breakfast this morning, speak English? Do you really think you'd have the same religious and political beliefs you now have?

A few of Dr. Thrower's students sat up, their bodies shifted, and two of three stopped texting as she continued.

"Obviously, environment is important but what about heredity? What if you had been born with an IQ of 200? Maybe someone in here was. If so, what if you had been born with an IQ of 40? What if you had been born male instead of female, or female instead of male? What if you had inherited from your parents a condition that limits your physical activity, or if you inherited a body that makes you a great athlete?"

Dr. Thrower leaned toward her students. "I hope you begin to understand the reason for the debate among social scientists about which is more important, heredity or environment. So, your assignment for next class is a three-page paper of your opinion on 'heredity vs. environment'." Groans followed Dr. Thrower as she smiled and turned on her PowerPoint.'

PIAGET'S THEORY OF COGNITIVE DEVELOPMENT

(Miller, 2002), offers the following solution to the debate; "heredity and environment can't be separated. Human behavior is determined 100% by heredity and 100% environment." Despite the debate, you are going to be teaching language and cognitive skills to your students. The *cognitive* aspects of developing student thinking and problem-solving skills has been the topic of considerable research in educational psychology. Few have influenced the thinking about cognitive development more than psychologist Jean Piaget (Armstrong et al., 1997). Piaget (1952, 1960, 1963, 1964, 1969, 1970, 1972) provided one of the most detailed theories of children's cognitive development. Piaget offered an account of human mental processes that is coherent and systematic and provides a plausible, comprehensive explanation of the power, complexity, and organization of thinking (Case, 1984). However, not all educational psychologists accept Piaget's ideas; making the study of his work both interesting and controversial. Since his death in 1980, his theories have been the subject of extensive research and debate.

As stated earlier, much of Piaget's theory was developed through his research with his own three children. Samples this small are generally considered too small to be reliable, and Piaget has been criticized for this limitation. However, his observations of his children were very comprehensive. He spent years observing and questioning them, and having them perform structured, intellectual tasks. He used insights gained from these observations to develop theories about how children think and learn. Additionally, his institute repeatedly tested his theories on hundreds of other children.

> Piaget is criticized because much of his early research was limited to his three children. However, his theories were later tested repeatedly in his institute with hundreds of children.

The Active Role of Children in Learning

Piaget maintained that children attempt to understand their world by adapting and interpreting the objects and the events they experience. He focused on the *active role* of children in development. Ms. Tomlinson's first graders are a good example; she encouraged her first graders to be active in the learning process. Piaget reasoned that children are not merely passive recipients of information in their environment. Their thoughts are formed in the environment

According to Piaget, children actively interpret new experiences and adapt them to what they already know.

as they interpret new experiences and adapt them to what they already know, then act accordingly. Piaget also believed children develop both physically and mentally at different rates. Some children grow faster and larger than others and some are more athletic. Some mature faster intellectually, socially, and emotionally. The development of social and emotional awareness varies with intelligence and a child's environment. He also believed children develop gradually but in the order of his (Piaget's) developmental stages. Children coo and babble before they say words. Phrases and sentences follow words; walking follows crawling.

An attractive feature of Piaget's theory is his explanation for the concept of *readiness* (Case, 1984). Children cannot learn from experiences until they have reached the cognitive level of thought that allows them to understand those experiences. A good example is Ms. Tomlinson not expecting her first graders to understand the intricacies of a democracy. Piaget used the term **readiness** to mean the level of mental development necessary to benefit from experiences.

For example, Dalphine, age 3, experiences the taste of ice cream. As she grows older and acquires the ability to discern taste, texture, and color, she acts accordingly. When asked her favorite, she can demonstrate readiness by choosing among many flavors. Her favorite, by the way, is double fudge, chocolate ripple.

Strategies for Problem Solving

According to Piaget, the actions of children, such as choosing their favorite color, do not occur haphazardly or randomly. Piaget maintained that children develop strategies and rules to solve problems. These strategies are called *operations*. The development of operations, in turn, leads to the development of *mental structures,* **which** Piaget called *schemata*. Schemata are memories, thoughts, and understandings gained by the child through experience. For instance, Tyler, age 4, may have a schema for understanding birds. In Piaget's developmental theory, Tyler may have a schema for birds that consists of his pet parakeet. As Tyler grows older, his schema for birds may change to "things that fly." As Tyler grows even older, his schema may change to "animals with feathers, some that fly and some that don't." Although some of Ms. Tomlinson's first graders were confused by the concepts of the size of cards and the values

As children mature, their schemata must be revised to understand their environment. This is labeled the drive for equilibrium.

of numbers, as they grow older and mature mentally they will develop better strategies and rules for determining the greater of two numbers.

Another common use of schemata in the classroom is solving problems. Academically, a schema can be as elementary as a preschooler reaching for a ball or as complex as a secondary student conjugating verbs or solving algebraic equations. A language student with the assignment of translating a French sentence into English activates schemata, which includes recognizing both the French and English language, developing procedures for translating, and arriving at a solution.

Striving for Equilibrium

The development of schemata involves another important Piagetian concept, **equilibrium**, which Piaget believed was very important to cognitive growth. Equilibrium is the process of maintaining balance, or an understanding of the environment with the individual's current schemata.

Most of us are comfortable with order in our lives. We have general routines we follow to get up, get to work or school, have meals, study, and so forth. However, spontaneous and unique experiences happen and are important in life. Piaget maintained that people, especially children, have an innate need to maintain a sense of order and predictability in their lives. Piaget labeled this need *striving*, or the drive for equilibrium.

When the current schemata are inadequate, or unclear to the individual, **disequilibrium** occurs and changes must be made in the schemata. For instance, if Tyler has a schema for birds that consists of his pet parakeet and he goes to the park and is told that the brown pigeon he sees is also a bird, Tyler must conceptualize this inconsistency in some way. If he is developmentally ready to experience disequilibrium about this event, then some change must be made in his schemata to achieve equilibrium. When Tyler was younger, he dealt with this inconsistency by disregarding the new information; the pigeon is also a bird. But Tyler has since matured, and now he must find a way to make this new information fit with what he already knows about birds. Until he does, he will experience disequilibrium. He may solve this problem (change his schema for birds) in one of many different ways. For instance, he might change his schema of birds to include both his pet parakeet and the pigeon.

Equilibrium is an evolving state because there is always a better equilibrium (Wadsworth, 1978). You may encounter an unfamiliar word as you are reading this chapter and experience disequilibrium. You achieve equilibrium by finding the definition of the word, but the next day you may experience disequilibrium again when you hear the same word used in an entirely different context. According to Piaget, disequilibrium results in motivation to learn and seeking out methods of handling disequilibrium.

> As children grow older they become better problem solvers if they can maintain equilibrium.

Adaptation through Assimilation and Accommodation

Achieving equilibrium is not always an easy task. It occurs through a process that Piaget referred to as **adaptation**. Adaptation consists of either changing a response to the environment or changing one's schemata to reconcile what is experienced in an environment. Disequilibrium prompts people to adapt, and adaptation results in establishing a state of equilibrium.

With children, **assimilation** occurs when their current schemata influence their responses to new experiences. For example, Anna may have a schema for horses that consists of "large, four-legged animals," but she doesn't have one for elephants. When seeing an elephant for the first time, she assimilates this experience into her schema for horses and calls the elephant a "horse."

Accommodation alters schemata. If Anna develops a new schema for elephants, perhaps one for "large, four-legged animals with trunks," accommodation takes place. While developing a schema for elephants, she may also change her schema for horses to "large, four-legged animals that do not have trunks." Schemata will continue to change as she experiences other four-legged animals.

Piaget used the key concepts of operations, schemata, equilibrium, adaptation, assimilation, and accommodation to discuss how children move from one stage of cognitive development to the next (illustrated in Table 2.1). However, it is important to remember that other factors influence cognitive development, including social interaction, learning, and maturation (Eggen & Kauchak, 1992).

SOCIAL INTERACTION

Piaget discovered that **social interaction** was a critical factor in the cognitive development of children. Ms. Tomlinson encourages her students to socially interact during class group activities. Although social interaction among children is typically stressed in preschool and elementary school environments, interaction by children with adults is also very important. A good example is Ms. Tomlinson circulating throughout her class interacting with, praising, and encouraging her students.

TABLE 2.1	
Piaget's Concepts of How Children Move from One Stage of Cognitive Development to the Next	
Concept	**Skill Developed**
Operations	Plans, strategies, and rules of problem solving
Schemata	Memories, thoughts, and understandings
Equilibrium	State of balance achieved when schemata are adequate

Concept	Skill Developed
Adaptation	Altering the environment or schemata to achieve consistency
Assimilation	Altering responses to the environment to be consistent with schemata
Accommodation	Altering schemata to be consistent with the environment

Social Interaction and Learning: Lev S. Vygotsky

Lev S. Vygotsky (1896–1934), an eminent Russian psychologist, offered an expanded view of the role of social and cultural influences on the cognitive development of children. Although Vygotsky's work has not had the impact on education and psychology as Piaget's, his work has been recognized and acclaimed (Wertsch, 1985; Glassman, 2001).

Unfortunately, Vygotsky died at age 38 of tuberculosis and his work was suppressed by the Soviet Union until 1956 (Goetz, Alexander, & Ash, 1992). Although Vygotsky was influenced by Piaget's work, he maintained that culture, social institutions, and customs were dominant factors in a child's cognitive development, especially thought and language.

According to Vygotsky, the process and complexity of adaptation among children is influenced significantly by such factors as home environment, peer relationships, diet, clothing, and mastery of language. This agrees that the changing social characteristics of our future students discussed in Chapter 1 (minority, students from impoverished home environments, immigrant and non-English speaking) can impact on their cognitive development.

Vygotsky astutely emphasized cultural factors influencing cognitive development, suggesting that social changes affecting children are critically important to their cognitive functioning. Tyler may be capable of modifying his schema for birds, or Anna of an elephant, but this learning process can be altered dramatically by Tyler, Anna or any child experiencing the trauma of parental divorce, rejection by peers, or sometimes just the process of moving to another home and/or school environment. Achieving equilibrium is not always an easy task, especially for children.

Student Proximal Development

Vygotsky's instructional processes emphasized teacher/student cooperation, teachers supporting their students, and the language development of students. According to Vygotsky, students have a **zone of proximal development**. He defined this zone as the degree or amount students can and have learned on their own compared with what they have the potential to learn with assistance from an adult or teacher—"the distance between the actual developmental level as determined by independent problem solving and the level of potential development as determined through problem solving under adult guidance and under the direction of more capable peers" (Vygotsky, 1978, p. 86). A fourth-grade student may be proficient in the basics of math (addition, subtraction, multiplication, and division) yet have the capability of mastering logarithms, percentages, and fractions with the help of her teacher.

According to Vygotsky, "What the child can do in cooperation today he can do alone tomorrow." Therefore, good instruction defines and leads a student's cognitive development; "instruction must be oriented toward the future, not the past" (Vygotsky, 1962, p. 104).

Vygotsky would agree that Angela's process of "talking herself" through the art lesson in Ms. Tomlinson's class is a healthy developmental process. He termed the process of children using language to guide themselves through learning tasks, *inner speech*. This process of "thinking out loud," according to Vygotsky, provides children a method of verbally accessing the task at hand and relating prior knowledge and skills needed to accomplish the task.

Children often use inner speech (thinking aloud) to guide themselves through tasks.

However, classroom application of Vygotsky's concepts is limited by lack of definition and detail (Wertsch, 1985). How much assistance, for example, should a teacher or adult provide students to process in their *zone of proximal development*? Does the environment impact both independent student learning and teacher-facilitated learning? Does the amount of instruction needed vary among students? These questions can be partially answered by the rate of development of individual students. The application of Vygotsky's theories is discussed further in Chapter Eleven.

In the Classroom

Suppose you are teaching a secondary Social Studies/English class. You have introduced a simulation game to help students develop advocacy skills needed to address concerns in their legislative district. The students are enjoying the freedom to express opinions on political issues but a brother and sister, whose family immigrated from Mexico, lack English skills and are confused.

A teaching alternative might be to divide the class into small groups and assign the newcomers to a group of students who encourage and include the new students in group discussions. Occasionally, monitor this group to ensure the new students are learning the concepts. Encourage the group members to be patient as their new classmates gradually grasp concepts. As Martinez (1998, p. 609) says, "Anxiety is a spoiler in the problem-solving process." Encourage the new students to write and/or articulate their opinions on government issues when they are comfortable with the concepts.

Maturation

A child's ability to learn and socially interact, regardless of assistance from adults, peers, and teachers, is tempered by the child's rate of **maturation**. Maturation in children is defined as the physiological changes resulting from heredity, nutrition, and environment. Maturation is also defined as a gradual, orderly unfolding or developing of human behavior as a result of heredity (Rathus, 1990). Educational psychologists study, research, and debate the importance and impact of a child's environment and heredity on maturation. However, educational psychologists agree that heredity, nutrition, and the environment are the determinants of a healthy and normal maturation. Within the biological parameters of maturation, both Vygotsky and Piaget emphasized the importance of social interaction and experience.

Consider the following experience of Ms. Frye. Think about the differences in cognitive development and maturation of Ms. Tomlinson's first graders as they discussed voting, in contrast to Ms. Frye's eleventh graders as they debate international issues on East/West relations.

INTASC Standard 7   **Planning for instruction**

CASE STUDY

Ms. Frye's 11th-grade Advanced Political Science class was having a heated discussion on the Middle East. Pam argued that the Western world had no business in the area. Ali was trying to convey the importance of religion to the people of the Middle East, and Jamal was disagreeing with everybody. Finally, Rich announced, "Heck, if we need the oil we should go take it. We are the biggest and strongest. We outnumber them 10 to 1 and we shouldn't take any lip off any little piss ant country." Several of the students moaned, and Pam was livid in disagreeing.

Ms. Frye tolerated the chaos briefly then called the class to order. She had been waiting for this opportunity because a recent teacher workshop on "enhancing the cognitive functioning of students" had provided her with some good ideas.

"Okay, our discussion has raised several interesting points and quite a bit of disagreement. I think it is now time for a quiz covering the Middle East topic." Groans exuded from the class as she continued. "But today we're going to do something a bit different. To date our quizzes have been multiple-choice format, but I'm not sure that is the appropriate test format for addressing such issues. Therefore, this is a take-home quiz, and is to be returned Monday. Rich just argued that 'we' are the biggest and strongest and 'we' outnumber 'them' 10 to 1. But are we and do we? Let's take a look at the quiz." Ms. Frye passed out the following quiz:

Quiz 4

Advanced Political Science, 11th grade Ms. Frye

The following is an excerpt from an issue of *World Development Forum*.

1. If our world were a village of 1,000 people, what would its ethnic and religious composition be?

2. In the village would be 564 Asians, 210 Europeans, 86 Africans, 80 South Americans, and 60 North Americans.

3. There would be 300 Christians (183 Catholics, 84 Protestants, 33 Orthodox), 175 Muslims, 128 Hindus, 55 Buddhists, 47 Animists, and 210 atheists or people without any religion.

4. Of these 1000 people, 50 would control half the total income, 500 would be hungry, 600 would live in shantytowns, and 700 would be illiterate.

Based on this information, you are to write a paper (about five pages) that advises the United Nations on alternatives for improving race relations throughout the world.

Please use the following guidelines.

1. Identify, collect, and present resource material (I suggest the library and online resources) that supports your position.

2. You are encouraged to recommend strategies that are unique and creative.

3. Think about your task of persuading UN representatives to accept your viewpoint. Remember the UN represents almost all nations of the world, with a great diversity of opinions and beliefs.

Ms. Frye added, "I will grade your papers but in addition, all papers will be judged by a student-elected, five-member 'UN' team. One paper will be selected as the 'best solution,' and one paper will be selected as the 'most creative solution.' These two papers will be entered in the County Contemporary Issues Competition."

CRITICAL THINKING

Take a moment to analyze the events that occurred in Ms. Frye's classroom. Express your interpretation of these events by responding to the following questions:

1. What evidence can you offer suggesting that Ms. Frye's 11th grade students are, or are not, mature enough to benefit from this type of activity?

2. Will Ms. Frye enhance the cognitive functioning of her students, and does the controversial nature of the issue increase such a possibility?

3. Was Ms. Frye's moving on to another topic, at the peak of discussion, appropriate?

4. The information sought on Ms. Frye's quiz would undoubtedly contrast with some of her students' current values and beliefs. How does the use of her test relate to Piaget's theory of disequilibrium?

5. What social issues are raised by such activities in any classroom?

PIAGET'S STAGES OF CHILD AND ADOLESCENT DEVELOPMENT

Inspired by information gleaned in a workshop, Ms. Frye challenged her students with an assignment requiring considerable understanding and analysis. Although creative problem-solving assignments that challenge students should be an integral part of curriculum planning, Piaget would caution that students must be developmentally ready for such academic tasks. Piaget defined the term **developmental learning stages** by outlining the periods children pass through during their early formative years (Table 2.2).

Characteristics of Piaget's Developmental Learning Stages

- Child development has four distinct stages.

- All children pass through these stages of development regardless of race or culture.

- All children go through the stages in the same order, **but** they do not necessarily pass through them at the same age.

- Passing through the earlier stages of development is a prerequisite for the later stages.

- Many individuals never reach the highest cognitive level. (Piaget, 1952, 1960, 1963)

Initially, children only react to their environment, but by about age 2 they begin reacting to their own thinking.

Piaget's Learning Stages Defined
Sensorimotor Period (Ages 0–2)

As noted in Table 2.2 *Piaget's Four Stages of Development*, the sensorimotor period occurs from birth to about age 2. During this stage, children begin to see the relation between goals and the means to attain the goals, and they begin to use symbolic thought. The major accomplishment of this stage is the development of the child from a reflexive to a reflective organism. At birth, the child's only behaviors are reactions to the environment, but by about age 2 most children begin to react to their own thinking. This stage is characterized by what Piaget called **object permanence**. Object permanence is the knowledge that objects exist even though they are out of sight. Piaget had an interesting method for measuring the attainment of this level of growth. During the early months of the sensorimotor period, children will not search for objects once they are taken out of view (or hidden), implying that they do not recognize their existence when the objects are out of sight. However, during the latter months of the sensorimotor period, children will search for objects that are shown to them and then hidden.

Preoperational Period (Ages 2–7)

Piaget refers to the second period of cognitive development as the **preoperational period**. If you plan to teach preschool children, you will be especially interested in this stage because it covers the age span of about 2 to 7 years, the age of preschool and primary grade school children. The major characteristic of children during this period is the development of symbolic modes of representation, meaning children no longer have to have objects present to understand them. This comprehension allows them to use language, imitate others, engage in symbolic play such as playing house, and draw representations of objects and illustrations of current and past experiences. Toward the conclusion of this stage of development, children are able to engage in intuitive problem solving, such as placing blocks together to copy a design.

However, during the preoperational period, children's thinking is still characterized by **egocentrism, irreversibility**, and **centration**. From the years 2 to about 7, children are typically unable to see things from another person's perspective. They view the world internally and are limited to their perceptions and environment. This characteristic is called egocentrism. For example, if you watch a group of young children talking and playing, you will notice they often play by themselves, even though they are in a group. Often when they talk, even if the talk is directed to another child, they talk as if they are the only person listening. Remember Angela talking herself through Ms. Tomlinson's art lessons?

During the preoperational period, children develop the ability to use symbols and engage in intuitive problem solving.

At the preoperational stage, children are unable to conserve.

TABLE 2.2

Piaget's Four Stages of Development

Stage	Ages	Characteristics
Sensorimotor	Birth to 2 years	Develop from reflexive infant with focus on sensory and motor experience to reflective child with ability to use symbolic thought and understand object permanence.
Preoperations	2 to 7 years	Child develops symbolic modes of representation. Thought is limited by egocentrism, irreversibility and centration.
Concrete operations	7 to 11 years	Child develops the capacity to perform first order operations and can think deductively. Thinking is characterized by decreased irreversibility, egocentrism, and centration.
Formal operations	11 to 15 years and older	Characterized by the ability to perform second-order operations. Thinking is flexible, abstract, and systematic.

Although children at this stage are able to solve problems, they typically cannot retrace their steps. This characteristic is called **irreversibility**. For instance, a preoperational child may be able to take a ball of clay and roll it into a long "stick" shape, but the same child often has problems if asked to make the stick back into a ball.

At the preoperational stage, children also are unable to focus on more than one dimension of a problem. This is called **centration**. One aspect of centration is preoperational children's lack of conservation skills, or their inability to recognize that when one dimension of a problem changes, all other dimensions may or may not change. This inability to conserve is illustrated in Figure 2.1.

For example, a preoperational child is shown two identical glasses with identical amounts of juice in each glass. Juice from one of the glasses is poured into a taller, thinner glass. When asked which of the two glasses contains more juice, the short glass or the taller glass, the preoperational child will most often point to the taller, thinner one, not recognizing that the change in the height of the glass did not change the amount of liquid in the glass. The child has centered on the *height* of the glass.

You might recall that Ms. Tomlinson's first graders confused the size of cards with the value of the numbers. This has implications for attempting to teach abstract concepts to preschoolers and even early elementary students. Brain development and maturation are still in process with these children, significantly influencing their learning of concepts. Understanding a

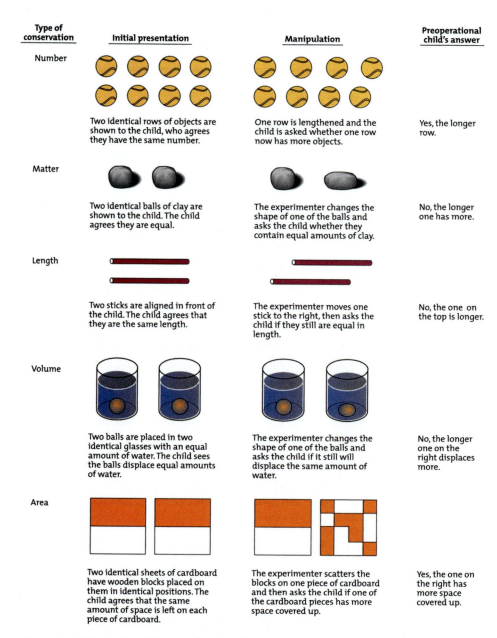

Type of conservation	Initial presentation	Manipulation	Preoperational child's answer
Number	Two identical rows of objects are shown to the child, who agrees they have the same number.	One row is lengthened and the child is asked whether one row now has more objects.	Yes, the longer row.
Matter	Two identical balls of clay are shown to the child. The child agrees they are equal.	The experimenter changes the shape of one of the balls and asks the child whether they contain equal amounts of clay.	No, the longer one has more.
Length	Two sticks are aligned in front of the child. The child agrees that they are the same length.	The experimenter moves one stick to the right, then asks the child if they still are equal in length.	No, the one on the top is longer.
Volume	Two balls are placed in two identical glasses with an equal amount of water. The child sees the balls displace equal amounts of water.	The experimenter changes the shape of one of the balls and asks the child if it still will displace the same amount of water.	No, the longer one on the right displaces more.
Area	Two identical sheets of cardboard have wooden blocks placed on them in identical positions. The child agrees that the same amount of space is left on each piece of cardboard.	The experimenter scatters the blocks on one piece of cardboard and then asks the child if one of the cardboard pieces has more space covered up.	Yes, the one on the right has more space covered up.

Figure 2.1 Examples of Conservation Problems

Source: From John W. Santrock, *Children* 2nd Ed., © 1990 Wm, C. Brown Communications "democracy" involves understanding concepts, so Piaget would agree that Ms. Tomlinson was probably correct in discussing the meaning of voting with a classroom example while not expecting her first graders to understand the concept in depth.

In another example, a preoperational child is first shown two rows of sticks with equal numbers. When the bottom row is spread out and the child is asked, "Which row has the *most* sticks?" most preoperational children will indicate the bottom row, not recognizing that changing the length of the row of sticks does not change the number of sticks, as Ms. Tomlinson's first graders focused on the size of the cards rather than on the size of the number.

Concrete Operations Period (Ages 7–11)

Prospective elementary teachers will be especially interested in Piaget's third level of development, the concrete operations stage. This stage covers the elementary school child's development from about ages 7 until 11. According to Piaget, during this stage, children are able to perform first-order operations, or *operations on objects.* They begin to think deductively and solve problems such as, "If all ducks are birds, is Donald, your pet duck, a bird?" Concrete operational children have the ability to use more logic and objectivity in solving problems than preoperational children; they also have better *classification* skills. According to Piaget, the major limitations of concrete operational children is that they typically can only perform first-order operations; meaning they solve problems based on past experiences or on concrete objects that are present. For instance, they can solve the problem "If Jan is taller than Tina, and Tina is taller than Juanita, who is the tallest?" much better if they can see pictures of the three girls or if they actually know them.

Formal Operations Period (Ages 11–15 and Older)

Piaget's fourth and final stage of development is the formal operations stage, which can begin at age 11 or 12. During this stage, children begin to perform second-order operations. This means they can use concepts they have never encountered in their experiences, and can begin to use objects they cannot actively manipulate. For instance, a formal operational child can solve the problem "If all dogs have four legs, and Rambo is a dog, how many legs does he have?" We recall a middle school teacher's comment that "Nathan, one of my brightest students, catches on quickly to the abstract ideas we discuss in history, like democracy and capitalism." Thus, formal—operational children's thinking becomes more **flexible, abstract**, and **systematic**. Ms. Frye's home-

> At the formal operations stage, children can work with abstractions without the use of concrete objects.

work assignment requiring her students to "advise the UN on alternatives for solving the Middle East crisis" is a good example.

Note that even though formal operational thinkers can understand abstract concepts, they still learn better when concrete evidence is presented (Hetherington & Parke, 1986). A fifth-grade teacher notes:

> One thing I've learned, though, is regardless of their level, they learn better when I give them activities they all can work on. When discussing Columbus, something I do is spread a big map of the world on the floor and let them use wooden ships to trace the routes used to discover North and South America.

At the formal operations level, children can draw inferences and make predictions.

PROACTIVE EXERCISE

Suppose your first teaching job is in a state experiencing considerable education reform. You realize that some students in your classes are academically and developmentally behind. Your state has mandated that schools will be held accountable for students performing at a minimum achievement level. You have been asked to serve on a teacher committee charged with making curriculum recommendations. What would you suggest?

Children in the concrete operations period can sort objects on the basis of many combinations of dimensions.

In summary, Piaget's theory of cognitive development suggests that children use the process of *adaptation* to achieve equilibrium, or a state of balance. Adaptation occurs when children change the environment to fit their current schemata (**assimilation**), and when children change their schemata to fit the environment (**accommodation**). As children achieve equilibrium, they achieve higher levels of thought, which allows them to move through four stages of development. As summarized in Table 2.2, children begin as reflexive organisms, or organisms that focus on sensory and motor experiences. As they grow older, they are able to think symbolically and solve problems deductively. The final outcome of their cognitive development is the ability to reason and to think abstractly. (Piaget's concepts in the four stages of development are summarized in Table 2.3.)

TABLE 2.3
Concepts in Piaget's Four Stages of Preoperational Cognitive Development

Concept	Definition
Object permanence	Knowledge that objects exist even when they are out of sight
Egocentrism	Inability to see things from another person's point of view
Centration	Focus on just one dimension of an object and inability to look at other dimensions
Conservation	Ability to recognize that when one dimension of a problem changes, other dimensions remain unchanged
Part-whole relationships	Understanding the relationship between the subsets of a group of objects and the entire set

A VIEW FROM THE FIELD

PROFILE

Paul A. Wagner, Ph.D., University of Missouri—Columbia; Visiting appointments at the Department of Philosophy, Yale University, Center for Moral Development, Harvard University, Institute for the Mathematical Study of the Social Sciences, Stanford University. Author of over 100 publications including articles in the journals; Cognition and Brain Theory, Cognitive Science, The Clearing House, Multicultural Perspectives, Interchange, The Educational Forum and Science Education. With Douglas Simpson, Wagner was co-author of Ethical Decision-making in School Administration (Sage, 2009). He has served on the National Ethics Committee for the 40,000 member American Association of Public Administrators. He has served as consultant on six major educational psychology textbooks.

QUESTION: What do teachers need to know about brain functioning and student learning?

Dr. Wagner: Certainly since Noam Chomsky's review of B. F. Skinner's Verbal Behavior in the New York Review of Books in 1957, the processing that takes place inside the human brain has been an important and unavoidable topic for anyone concerned about human learning and thinking. Noble Laureates and economists Herbert Simon and Kenneth Arrow demonstrated that human behavior cannot be understood simply by looking to past experience and self-interest.

Nobel Laureate and psychologist Daniel Kahnemann has demonstrated that people use many heuristic techniques to solve many problems of practical importance. So again, what goes on inside the brain—mindfulness—proves critical to understanding human nature including learning, thinking, planning, preference, and so on.

Cognitive scientists imagine the brain as a type of computer hardware (wetware as they are fond of saying) and the mind as the software the brain uses to process data input. Evolutionary psychologists and neuroscientists add that these internal workings must be established to understand why humans learn as they have come to learn over successive generations. Humans don't just associate ideas, rather they seem to be wired from birth to be language users, relatively cooperative and relatively responsive to aesthetic evaluations. When a child thinks, that child is not just etching on a blank slate. Rather, the child is employing data using available software. Learning, then, becomes adding data and learning to accommodate additional software to think through challenges of various sorts.

QUESTION: How is the study of cognitive development important to teachers?

Gestalt psychologists William Wundt recognized that there is more to human experience than just the sum of perceptual parts. Developmental psychologists such as Jean Piaget and Lawrence Kohlberg recognized that children develop incrementally to more sophisticated ways of figuring out the world around them. Social psychologists (and each a past president of the American Psychological Association) such as Albert Bandura, and Martin Seligman respectively, have noted the role of human learning through role modeling and in the satisfaction of becoming more fully engaged in the surrounding world. Cognitive science recognizes the role each of these thrusts in orchestrating the mind of learners at every stage of development.

Cognitive scientists try to draw upon each of these areas to build a model of mind that will help teachers understand more extensively why children learn as they do. Children do not learn in each case simply because they find an experience rewarding. Children seem inclined by evolution to taxonimize the world around them in certain ways and then to figure out pragmatic strategies for fulfilling a host of natural instincts. For example, could it be that children learn as they do because they have an evolutionarily evolved instinct to search for truth. It may also be the case that children learn as they do simply to optimize survival or increase production of satisfying neurochemicals.

Modeling how a child naturally thinks is part and parcel of figuring out how the child learns. Figuring out how the child accommodates and assimilates new data through participation in a zone of proximal development tells the teacher what resources to employ, how to employ them and when to employ them to advance learning in the life of each child. ■

Criticisms of Piaget's Theory

As a pioneer in the systematic study of children, Piaget's insights have provided important information about the way children think and develop. As articulated by Flavell (1985, p. 2). "That Piaget's stage theory has made an enormous-indeed, unmatched-contribution to the field of cognitive development obviously needs no arguing."

However, Piaget's theory is not without criticism. Following are some of the more common criticisms of his work.

Criticisms of the Sensorimotor Stage (Ages 0–2)

At the sensorimotor stage, it is argued that infants may know more than Piaget was able to infer by watching their motor actions (Flavell, 1985). As you will recall, Piaget's method of investigation primarily consisted of observing his three children. When his children were infants, Piaget observed their actions and their motor responses to objects. Of course he couldn't observe the complexity of their language development when they were infants. Therefore, any insights he made about the thinking of young children were made on rather limited observations of a few types of behavior.

Criticisms of the Preoperations Stage (Ages 2–7)

Piaget may have underestimated the importance of experience and the effects training can have on cognitive development. For example, researchers have been able to train young children in tasks of conservation (Miller & Brownell, 1975; Murray, 1979), but it is difficult to tell whether children can be trained to constantly perform at this level. One argument is that children trained in conservation tasks often repeat what they have been taught, without actually believing or understanding.

> The exact ages for cognitive development vary among children.

Criticisms of the Concrete Operations Stage (Ages 7–11)

The ages of the concrete operations stage appear to be influenced by cultural variation. The capacities of concrete operations may not be universal and acquired at the same time, and concrete operations often do not appear in the same order in children of different cultural environments (Gardner, 1982). The cognitive structure proposed by Piaget does not fully explain cognitive development during the concrete operations period (Klausmeier & Sipple, 1982).

> Piaget may have underestimated the value of experience in learning.

Criticisms of the Formal Operations Stage (Ages 11–15 and Older)

One of the most enduring aspects of Piaget's theory is that adolescents do reason differently than young children, but criticism has been directed at Piaget's

> Piaget's theory lacks specificity in addressing the effect of cultural climates on cognitive development.

formal operations period (Gardner, 1982). First, some suggest that formal operational thinking can be taught to children who are still in the concrete operations period. Some research suggests that children as young as 8 or 9 can understand many of the principles of formal operations.

A second limitation of Piaget's formal operations period is that not all adolescents and adults reach the formal operational level of thinking. Individuals who have limited educational experiences may acquire formal operations later than Piaget indicated or they may never reach this level (Gardner, 1982). (Capon & Kuhn, 1979; Grinder, 1975). Piaget (1972) also concluded that formal operations may not be found in some cultures, but education can influence the acquisition of formal operational thought. Also, some consider Piaget's definition of the formal operations period incomplete; there may be a level of thinking more advanced than formal operations.

Adolescents in the formal operations period become engrossed in pondering the possibilities of life.

The criticisms of both Vygotsky's and Piaget's views are not without merit. However, it is very important to remember that Vygotsky was Russian and Piaget Swiss. The majority of Piaget's research was done during the 50s, 60s, and 70s, and all Vygotsky's work was done during the 20s and 30s in Russia. Neither had any way of knowing the degree of developmental distraction children in the United States (and globally) would face with language, race, single-parent families, poverty, and the labels of "minority" and "non-English speaking." Recent studies demonstrating the cultural factors of language, prejudice, family conflict, and other risk factors can significantly impact the cognitive development of children is a tribute to their insight and conclusions.

The first part of this chapter examined Piaget's theory of cognitive development and the effect of social interaction on learning as perceived by Vygotsky. We will now consider implications these theories have for the teacher's in the classroom.

As evidenced by the comments of Howard Selekman, the following are some principles and cautions when using Piaget's theories in the classroom.

> Formal operational thinking may be totally absent in some cultures.

INTASC Standard 1   **Learner development**

Implications of Cognitive Development for Classroom Teaching

Many attempts have been made to apply Piaget's theory to education, with varying levels of success. One purpose of theory is to guide our thinking which, in turn, affects our behavior (Knovac, 1993). Therefore, rather than using Piaget's theory (or that of any other theory) in a step-by-step prescriptive fashion, a more viable option might be to transform theories into general principles and use these principles to affect educational practice. Consider the comments and suggestions of Howard R. Selekman, former Pennsylvania Teacher of the Year.

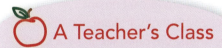 A Teacher's Class

NAME: Howard R. Selekman, former Pennsylvania Teacher of the Year

PROFILE: Mr. Selekman teaches English Literature in middle school.

ADVICE TO ASPIRING TEACHERS: My best teaching occurs when my

Students are lighting the way through their cooperative discussion and problem solving, and I am a learner.

- Students are writing daily, and I am writing with them.

- Students are talking more than I am.

- Students at risk do not have to be the recipients of anger and yelling.

- Students are grouped heterogeneously.

- Opportunities to meet, talk, plan, implement, and evaluate with my colleagues are frequent.

- Students are attempting to discover connections among the disciplines they are studying.

- Students' parents are engaged in the issues and themes their children are working with.

- Professional opportunities allow me to participate in shared decision making.

- Feeling of having fun is at a maximum.

QUESTION: How can contemporary teachers developmentally prepare today's students for our global society?

At the root of the teaching profession are the basic human needs to make a bond, a link with others. Teachers seek to establish many connections, connections that are meaningful to us and our students, connections that help us meet our common needs for freedom, for fun, for belonging, for control and power, for fulfilling our need to be all that we can be, and for discovering how we can enrich our lives by doing more than just surviving. In my work as an English teacher of middle-level students, I use literature as a grand opportunity for my students and me to learn about the human condition and to learn how critical it is to be able to make connections in the global community in which we all will live. Central to the success of connection making in my classes are the intensive writing and sharing of writing that become a nurturing way of life for all my students, fast learner and slow learner alike, and for me. Writing about human conflicts that are reflected in literature becomes the tool by which my students and I engage with the world in a socially conscious manner.

My work in fostering the concept of connection making operates at a number of levels simultaneously. There is the nurturing and warm connection that I seek to establish between my students and me. I work hard at validating the "voice" of each student as an individual. We keep journals, and we write freely in them. We write at the beginning of class, in the middle of class, at the end of class. Sometimes we write with complete sentences; sometimes we don't. When appropriate, we write over an extended period of time, revising, listening, and conferencing with one another, editing, sharing, even publishing. We write what we have learned, what our opinions are, what our questions are, what our predictions are. We write about what we know, and what we don't know. We reflect on our many experiences in our writing. We write about the connections among the various subjects we are learning. These will be the moments when we discover our own voice, learning to develop and enrich it by sharing, taking risks, and experimenting with words, points of view, styles, and Working to make my students feel comfortable taking those risks, always being there for them to say, "You're doing fine, but let's take it a step further or a step in a different direction": these are the focus of my making a supportive connection with my students. What gives the process validity for my students is that I also write; I also take risks and experiment along with them. I share and open my writing up, often feeling the same tenuousness as my students feel when they are asked to reveal and share their writing. When last week we were writing letters to be mailed to editors of various newspapers and magazines, businesses, government agencies, and other institutions, I, too, wrote my letter, in my case to the editor of the Arts and Leisure sections of the *New York Times*, and my letter was opened to the class for suggestion and response.

Teachers are more successful when we learn how powerful our own modeling is for our students, and when we brave the waters that show them that we, too, have our vulnerable spots.

There is the equally important task of helping students make connections with their fellow students. Students of diverse backgrounds do not always find it comfortable making connections with one another. Yet, coming to terms with diversity must be one of my deepest concerns because I know that these early experiences are the foundations for success in the very different kind of world in which my students will live out their adult lives. I also know that appreciating diversity is an asset that will help my students develop their own self-esteem and sense of belonging with much greater power. Carefully, gradually bringing the rich diversity of students in my classes together in quartets, trios, and duets of writing; discussion; problem solving; word processing; reporting; and a host of other interaction activities begins each student on a journey to the discovery of self and others-the journey that will bring them directly on route to the very global challenges of the twenty-first century. Meeting the global challenges of the next century will begin with all the nourishment of a kind word and the kindness of words as we present ourselves to others, participate in collective decision making, and partake of structured academic controversy in my classroom. I never use the reference to "one day in the real world," with my students. We are in the real world in my classes. We are in the business and pleasure of becoming lifelong learners, and I model the behaviors of a lifelong learner to give credibility to my role as teacher—and to give myself personal credibility as a professional. ■

> One of Piaget's and Vygotsky's primary messages to teachers: The key to students' learning is their active participation in the process.

The Key to Learning Is Activity

The key to student learning is their activity was one of Piaget's and Vygotsky's primary messages to teachers (Wadsworth, 1978). Teacher activities are critically important also, but student learning depends primarily on students' actively participating in the learning process (Kowalski, Weaver, & Henson, 1994). However, as early as 1984 Goodlad reported, on average 75 percent of high school class time is devoted to instruction via the teacher relating information to students. Contrary to Piaget's and Vygotsky's advice, the same is true today (Henson, 2011).

Consider the following list of principles of teaching that employ a general approach to using Piaget in education.

Student Study Guide

1. Create an environment in which children can be active and will be able to initiate and compare their activities. Howard Selekman (former Pennsylvania Teacher of the Year) offered "My best teaching occurs when my students are lighting the way through their cooperative discussion and problem solving."

2. Teachers who are willing to admit their mistakes and laugh at themselves foster a safer climate for their students to take risks (Graseck, 2009; Wagner, 2009–2010). Allow children to go through stages of being wrong. Again quoting Selekman, "Working to make my students feel comfortable taking those risks, always being there for them to say, "You're doing fine, but let's take it a step further or a step in a different direction.""

3. Remember that learning can take place through students' interacting with other students.

Allowing students to make connections with their fellow students can facilitate learning. Students of diverse backgrounds do not always find it comfortable making connections with one another. Yet, coming to terms with diversity must be one of my deepest concerns because I know that these early experiences are the foundations for success in the very different kind of world in which my students will live out their adult lives. (H. R. Selekman)

4. If you want students to learn, teach directly, engage student activities, and reinforce their learning.

A key word in human growth is adaptiveness. Being human means having a truly adaptive response to the rich differences among individuals, among cultures, while recognizing that we all share a fundamental humanity and a fundamental dignity. (H. R. Selekman)

INTASC Standard 4   Content knowledge

Matching Instruction to Developmental Level

One of the ways Piaget's theory has traditionally been used in education is to match instruction to children's developmental levels. This implies that teachers should not expect or assign academic material to students before they have developed the cognitive ability to complete such tasks. However, it is a fundamental error to assume that students at a certain developmental level will perform all tasks at that level equally well. Students may be at different developmental levels in various academic areas (Klausmeier, Klausmeier, & Sipple, 1982).

Rather than attempting to design curricula with distinct tasks assigned at particular levels, it is more appropriate to teach academic content that is within a student's capabilities. It is important that teachers be aware this range may be quite broad and could be different for various subject areas (Berlinger & Yates, 1993). Mr. Selekman provided a good example of designing a flexible curriculum for students' ranges of capabilities:

Central to the success of connection making in my classes are the intensive writing and sharing of writing that become a nurturing way of life for all my students, fast learner and slow learner alike, and for me. Writing about human conflicts that are reflected in literature becomes the tool by which my students and I engage with the world in a socially conscious manner.

Determining the range of students' capabilities may be the result of trial and error (Ross, Bondy, & Kyle, 1993). A child's range of capabilities could, in fact, change over time. A teacher indicated to us that her second-grade students "are at so many different levels that I spend most of my time planning about 10 different lessons for each day." A more useful approach of Piaget's developmental level is to modify curriculum in line with knowledge of the developmental stage, without placing undue emphasis on the stages (Klausmeier, 1988).

The Learning Disabilities Association of America offers the following strategies for encouraging development:

Age 2 to 3	· Repeat new words
	· Verbally describe what you are doing and thinking
	· Expand what the child says, such as, "more milk", you respond with "Jill wants more milk."
Age 3 to 4	· Assist the child when they explain or tell stories with pictures, drawings, and stories
	· Allow the child to finish what they are explaining or telling without interruption
	· Encourage the child to play with others
	· Talk to the child about new places they will be visiting
Age 4 to 5	· Teach the child how to use the phone and introduce them to computers
	· Encourage the child to talk about their daily activities, friends and interests
	· Reinforce the child's imagination and verbal creativity of their stories and experiences
Age 5 to 6	· Listening and encouragement is essential when children of this age begin to talk about their thoughts and feelings
	· Carry on conversations with them as though they were adults
	· Children of this age typically love to be read too. Read age-appropriate books, sing songs, rhymes every day if possible. As they gain reading skills have them read to you.

A child may be at different levels of development from one discipline or subject to another.

Children of every age	· Listen and allow the child to talk with interruption as you carry on conversation
	· Ask questions and encourage the child to do the same
	· Reading to and by the child cannot be overemphasized and should encouraged and praised
	· As the child gains writing skills encourage them to write about their feelings and experiences then have them talk about what they wrote

Instruction for Enhancing Student Logic and Problem Solving

Much of the application of Piaget's theories in education has focused on training formal operational thought, perhaps because so many studies have shown that large percentages of adolescents and adults do not reach this stage of development. Since the passage of NCLB and R2T, discussed in Chapter 1, teachers have been pressured to structure instruction toward teaching the "basics' and "meeting competencies" designed so students can pass defined levels of achievement. This emphasis has resulted in students being taught facts rather than learning to think abstractly or to engage in systematic reasoning and other characteristics that Piaget prescribed for the formal operational stage. Piagetian theory suggests that instruction in middle and senior high schools should be geared to teaching students not only basic facts but how to think logically and abstractly, solve problems, and to develop and test hypotheses. Ms. Frye's UN assignment is an example of challenging students to think logically and abstractly.

Piaget's first goal for education is to prepare students to do things they've never done before.

Piaget (1964) proposed two goals of education that are most applicable for adolescents and adults. His first goal for education is to prepare students to do things they have never done before, thereby hopefully educating children to invent, discover, and create. Vygotsky believed that such student preparation can be facilitated best through teacher assistance and direction. Piaget's second goal for education is to develop students who can think logically and reason. Thus, proactive curriculum planning concerned with students' academic and social development is essential for successful teaching. Consider the proactive alternatives in the Proactive Teaching section.

Piaget's second goal for education is to prepare students to think logically.

Classroom Situation	Proactive Alternatives
You anticipate that some of your students will be self-directed and independent and will be able to complete most academic assignments with a minimum of explanation, However, you know you will encounter students who have ability but are unsure of themselves, lack confidence, and need extensive teacher attention and explanation to complete the most elementary assignments.	· Elementary students—At the beginning of each academic task verbally explain to students your expectations. Encourage students to complete academic tasks with a minimum of teacher attention, and praise students who are able to do so. However, there will be students who require more explanation and attention. Encourage students to work both independently and in groups, when appropriate. · Secondary and middle school students—Plan to give assignments via board, handouts, or PowerPoint with explicit, detailed explanations of academic tasks to be completed. Beginning with your first assignment, refer students to written explanations if their questions can be answered by those explanations. As with elementary students, praise and encourage students for independently completing tasks. However, it is critical that teachers be aware of students lacking in reading or language skills. With such students' teacher attention, verbal explanation and patience are essential.

2. You are aware that you have interesting contrasts among your students. Some can memorize facts, dates, and places but have difficulty relating such facts to abstract issues, whereas other students seem to thrive on judging and analyzing issues but lack the interest or motivation to learn the facts related to issues.	· Plan to have assignments that require learning important facts, dates, and places that relate to understanding and explaining issues and strategies.
	· Plan class discussions that detail the relationship of facts to issues. Your plans should include extensive student involvement. Example issues might include:
	
	  a. The relationship of population and pollution.
	
	  b. The pros and cons of nuclear energy
	
	  c. Ms. Frye's Middle East assignment and Mr. Selekman's "writing connections"

So far, this chapter has examined Piaget's theory of cognitive development, Vygotsky's view of the effects of social interaction on learning, and the implications these theories have on the classroom teacher's instruction role. Language development is inextricably linked to cognitive and social development. The next part of the chapter explores these relationships and their application for teaching.

THE DEVELOPMENT OF LANGUAGE

Basic Components of Language

Piaget viewed language as a means of communicating thought. Both he and Vygotsky agreed that a major component in a child's cognitive development and functioning was *linguistic* or *language* development.

Language	Age
"Mama." or "Dada."	9 months
"I hungry."	18 months
"Daddy, pick me up."	2 years
"Pa-Paw took me to the zoo.	
We saw the animals.	
	3 years

Such remarks from children are the result of the remarkable attainment of language acquisition. Within a period of 2 to 3 years, normal children develop speech that is characterized by beginning with one-word utterances and progressing to descriptive more complex sentences.

Many cognitive psychologists agree that language acquisition is one of the most extraordinary of human accomplishments (Colledge et al., 2002; Matlin, 1989). A normal 6-year-old has a vocabulary of 14,000 words. To achieve such a vocabulary, a child must learn approximately nine new words a day beginning about age 9 months (Carey, 1979). Most adults attempting to learn a new language would find this very difficult, if not impossible.

The basic components of language includes **phonology** (meaning sounds), **morphology** (defined as units of meaning), and **semantics** (the meanings of words and groups of words) (Rathus, 1990). Phonology refers to the basic sounds (signed languages used by the deaf are exceptions) within a spoken language. The English alphabet has 26 letters, but the English language comprises a set of approximately 40 sounds or phonemes (Gleason, 1989).

Two major tasks in language development are learning to discern the differences between the phonemes and, consequently, learning to articulate them appropriately. Often, this is difficult in the English language because the same letter can be used to produce a different phoneme or sound. For example, the o in the word "to" is a different phoneme from the o in the word "occur." The ability of young children, as early as 8 to 12 months, to begin to develop and understand the complexities of a language is a remarkable accomplishment in cognitive functioning.

Within the English language, the same letter can be used to produce a different sound, yet children as young as 8 months are able to understand and learn such complexities.

Morphemes are the smallest unit of language. Morphemes consist of one or more phonemes that constitute words, meaningful prefixes and suffixes (for example pre, ion), verb tenses, and plural connotations. For example, the morpheme "pre" is an appropriate prefix for *preface*; the morpheme "ment" is an appropriate suffix for *development*. An "ed" morpheme at the end of a verb such as *trained* suggests past tense.

Preschool Language Development

Past and contemporary research has demonstrated that infants have an innate capability to recognize, learn and use human speech (Colledge et al., 2002; Coltheart, 1987; Emas, 1985).

Infants, and even newborn babies, demonstrate a remarkable propensity for language development. The verbal interactions between parents, adults, and infants begin very early and can be a source of intimacy, stimulation, and the beginnings of language acquisition (Glover & Bruning, 1990). Examples of such verbal interaction are many. A father may pick up his infant son when the baby babbles "dw . . . dw . . . dw" and then imitate his son with "da . . . da," perhaps reinforcing sound and language. A mother often affectionately 'coos' and talks to her baby or responds when her baby cries.

Levy (1988) suggests that crying in early infants is an integral part of two periods when infants develop speech: the **pre-linguistic** (birth to 1 year) and **linguistic** (after 1 year). Table 2.4 traces language development during the pre-linguistic period into the linguistic stage and provides milestones in language development with approximate age.

Table 2.5 indicates that vocalization and language among children is well established by age 4. Therefore, it is very important for parents and preschool teachers to proactively respond to the child's language development process. The following lists language development tools for parents and preschool teachers.

Vocalization and language of child	Family/Teacher Tools
1. Responding to infant vocalizations	Talking encourages infants and children to vocalize and provides the opportunity for children to model and identify words with action, their environment, and individuals.
2. Fostering the verbal and conversational skills of children	Provide opportunities for the child to verbalize. Ask children to explain their experiences, places, and ideas and allow them to express themselves without interruption. Be very patient with the conversational skills of children. The vocabularies of younger children are typically limited and correct grammar and syntax is a slow developmental learning process. Children communicating with other children is important but an adult taking the time to converse with a child is essential.

(Continued)

Vocalization and language of child	Family/Teacher Tools
3. Fostering the reading skills of children	The reading skills of children can be enhanced and encouraged by reading to them and providing the opportunity and time for them to read. Typically, children enjoy reading and especially being read to. Interesting and exciting children's books at age and developmental level should be used. Also, be very patient with the reading skills of children. As explained earlier, because of maturation, environment, interest, and motivation, children will vary in their rate of learning, especially reading.

Literacy and Language

Table 2.5 suggests, under normal conditions, most of the essentials of language have been developed by age 4. By this age, children normally have an extensive vocabulary and can communicate in sentences with adults, and grammatical syntax is beginning to formalize. This means children are ready to learn to read and comprehend written language. This process of learning to read and write competently is the beginning of **literacy** (Goetz et al., 1992).

With most children, learning to read and write is a natural developmental learning process. However, the development of literacy depends on the opportunities a child has to develop its language, reading, and writing skills (Teale & Sulzby, 1986). When provided encouragement, opportunity, verbal interaction with peers and adult instruction, literacy skills can develop at incredible rates.

However, the classroom teacher often encounters students whose language development is influenced by such factors as students' dialects, students who speak no English, or children who speak English as a second language. A **dialect** is defined as a variation of standard English that is notable in vocabulary, grammar, or pronunciation (Eggen & Kauchak, 1992).

TABLE 2.4	
Early Speech Development with Infants of Normal and Above Mental Ability	
Prelinguistic Period	**Birth to Approximately 12 Months**
Crying	Begins at birth and is earliest form of infant vocalization, usually signaling discomfort and/or hunger. Crying is common among infants and has a biological base.
Cooing	Cooing normally indicates a pleasant state for the infant and often occurs in response to family or guardians' soothing vocalizations.
Babbling	Typically, babbling occurs at about six months and is defined as playful infant speech. Babbling is a "universal language" across nationalities and even deaf babies babble almost identically (Rodda & Grove, 1987).

Prelinguistic Period	Birth to Approximately 12 Months
Linguistic Period	9 to 12 Months through Language Development
First words	"First words" by infants is defined as progressing from babbling to sound making that is meaningful. Infants' first words are most often given generalized meanings, such as "pretty" for bright colors, "Da Da" or "Ma Ma" are often mispronounced, First words are often associated with behavior such as waving "bye-bye."
First sentences	Following meaningful single-word vocalizations, children will begin to converse in simple sentences, Usually children develop two-word sentences, such as "more milk," "big ball," and "my daddy" (Braine, 1987). Once children begin to make sentences, sentence use accelerates while single-word use decreases.
Literacy	When children become literate, they are able to apply their knowledge of language to understanding, identification and problem solving.

TABLE 2.5	
Milestones in Language Development	
Approximate Age*	**Vocalization and language**
Birth	**Cries**
12 weeks	Markedly less crying than at 8 weeks; often responds to talk and gestures with smiles, followed by squealing-gurgling sounds usually called cooing, which is vowel-like in character and pitch-modulated; sustains cooing for 15–20 seconds
16 weeks	Responds to human sounds more definitely; turns head; eyes seem to search for speaker; occasionally some chuckling sounds
20 weeks	The vowel-like cooing sounds begin to be interspersed with more consonantal sounds; acoustically, all vocalizations are very different from the sounds of the mature language of the environment
6 months	Cooing changes into babbling resembling one-syllable utterances; neither vowels nor consonants have very fixed recurrences; most common utterances sound somewhat like "ma", "mu", "da", or "di"
8 months	Reduplication (or more continuous repetitions) becomes frequent; intonation patterns become distinct; utterances can signal emphasis and emotions
10 months	Vocalizations are mixed with sound play such as gurgling or bubble blowing; appears to wish to imitate sounds, but the imitations are never quite successful
12 months	Identical sounds sequences are replicated with higher relative frequency of occurrence, and words (mamma or dad-da) are emerging; definitely shows signs of understanding some words and simple commands ("Show me your eyes")

(Continued)

TABLE 2.5 (CONTINUED)	
Milestones in Language Development	
Approximate Age*	**Vocalization and language**
Birth	**Cries**
18 months	Has a definite repertoire of words-more than 3 but less than 50; still much babbling but now of several syllables with intricate intonation pattern; no attempt at communicating information and no frustration for not being understood; words may include items such as "thank you" or "come here," but there is little ability to join any of the items into spontaneous two-item phrases; understanding is progressing rapidly
24 months	Vocabulary of more than 50 items (some children seem to be able to name everything in environment); begins spontaneously to join vocabulary items into two-word phrases; all phrases seem to be own creations; definite increase in communicative behavior and interest in language
30 months	Fastest increase in vocabulary, with many new additions every day; no babbling at all; utterances have communicative intent; frustrated if not understood by adults; utterances consist of at least two words, although many have three or even five words; sentences and phrases have characteristic child grammar—that is, they are rarely verbatim repetitions of an adult utterance; intelligibility is not very good yet, though there is great variation among children; seem to understand everything that is said to them
3 years	Vocabulary of some 1,000 words; about 80 percent of utterances are intelligible even to strangers; grammatical complexity of utterances is roughly that of colloquial adult language, although mistakes still occur
4 years	Language is well established; deviations from the adult norm tend to be more in style than in grammar.

*The ages in this table are approximations. Families and teachers should not assume children have language problems if they are somewhat behind.

In the Classroom

Suppose your first teaching assignment is to team teach a class of 35 second-grade students. You and your co-teacher have begun teaching a reading unit. Most of the students are reading as well as you had expected, and a few are very advanced. However, you notice that a few tend to withdraw and are behind in reading skills.

As you and your fellow teachers attempt to resolve this problem, one of the first considerations should focus on the levels of opportunities these children have experienced. Their passive behavior may signal little encouragement or help in learning to read or write. While you investigate their records, you can begin encouraging these students to express their ideas more often, first orally then writing. Be aware of students who do not speak English or who speak English as a second language.

Language Diversity in the Classroom

As described in Chapter 1, our nation's students represent a complex mixture of languages and ethnic dialects. Examples of dialect can include Spanish-American, Italian-American, Asian, black English, and even regional dialects, such as "southern" and "New England Yankee."

PROACTIVE EXERCISE

Dr. Jaime Curtis (2010) at the University of Texas, Pan American uses bilingual cognitive mapping to help his limited Limited-English-Proficient (ELP) students learn English while learning mathematics. A **bilingual concept map** is a metacognitive tool for planning and assessing the content knowledge of students with limited English skills. The students put the concept being studied in the center of the page, circle it, and then surround the concept with relating words they can identify. Students explain the concept/word connections. Dr. Curtis has found this provides his ELP students better understanding when compared to memorization.

Bilingual Language Acquisition – Teaching Alternatives

Advocates of a bilingual education and teaching English to non-English speaking students suggest that similar approaches can be used with non-English-speaking students and students who speak English as a second language (Diaz, 1983; Genesee, Paradis, & Crago, 2004).

The following bilingual guidelines for teachers are offered for teaching English and/or a second language.

Chapter Modules

- The process of students learning, speaking, reading, and writing English, or any language, should be fun and enjoyable. Teachers can facilitate such behavior by using high-interest reading materials and allowing students to use reading material of their choice. This includes students being read to.

- To prevent non-English speaking students from falling behind academically, teach non-English speaking students in their native language until they are proficient in English. This will prevent them falling behind academically because of a language barrier.

- Do not pressure children to immediately eliminate dialect and language. This is most often a gradual process and, again, it should be enjoyable.

- Design English or other language reading, writing, and language material ensuring student success. Material should be readily mastered by students and should leave students with feelings of accomplishment.

- Provide language-development material familiar to students. This could include material in a native student language with English translation, cultural material native to student family background, or material student has mastered.

- Encourage families of students to actively promote reading, writing, and use of English or other language in the home environment.

- Be very patient with the progress of language development among students, emphasizing success rather than errors and mistakes. This implies proactive planning, practice, and feedback that rewards accomplishment.

The advantages of children at any grade learning a second language are well documented.

- Bilingual children learn and say their first words at the same rate as monolingual (one language) children.

- There are no significant differences in size of vocabulary when comparing bilingual and monolingual children.

- Very young (birth to 5 years) children who learn or are taught two or more languages develop mentally and socially at the same rate as monolingual children. (Crago, 2004, Pearson, 1998)

> The advantages of children learning a second language are well documented.

> "There's a revolution being waged by thousands of ordinary people doing extraordinary things with words, images, and sounds over the Internet. Using little more than their own talent and a few electronic tools, these individuals are creating, day- by-day, a new media for the twenty first century. There's a simple name for the revolutionary new media. . . . it's called the Web. . . ." Gagnon, 1996, p.3

TECHNOLOGY IN THE CLASSROOM

The following websites can be valuable tools for teachers seeking out information on the cognitive and language development of students.

www.reading.org – International Reading Association

www.ncss.org – National Council for the Social Studies

http://www.srcd.org/ – The 'Child Development Journal' published by Society for Research in Child Development

http://www.piaget.org/ – The journal 'Cognitive Development' published by Jean Piaget Society. ■

SURFING • THE • WEB

This chapter emphasizes the critical role that parents play in the cognitive and language development of children, The U.S. Department of Education is an excellent source for families, teachers, and school administrators. Available on their website is their "Helping Your Child" series, 12 hypertext pamphlets specifically aimed at parents (**http://www.ed.gov/pubs/parents.html**). ■

RECAP OF MAJOR IDEAS

1. As children mature mentally and socially, they pass through developmental stages.

2. When learners detect discrepancies in their understandings, disequilibrium is created and they are prompted to resolve the conflict. According to Piaget, this motivates such students to learn.

3. Vygotsky believed that teacher support and direction enhance student learning processes.

4. When using open inquiry, the teacher should not interfere with student activity but should act as a catalyst.

5. Learners may reach one level of cognitive development in one content area while remaining at a lower level in other content areas.

6. Students can improve their learning skills by understanding their own personal traits, the nature of each task to be mastered, and the learning process.

7. Students often systematically develop their own learning strategies.

8. Infants and children demonstrate a remarkable propensity for language development.

9. Language development has become a major concern in our society's schools because of dialect, the growing number of non-English-speaking students, and students who speak English as a second language.

10. The teaching of language should be enjoyable and non-threatening and can begin at a very early age.

11. The advantages of bilingualism are well documented.

FURTHER APPLICATIONS

1. Piaget's theories reflect his keen concern for the significant role that a child's environment and level of cognitive development play in learning.

   Develop three techniques that you can use to teach a particular concept for a defined subject and grade level that you plan to teach. For example, a PowerPoint presentation or a three-dimensional model could be used. Next, develop a dialogue that you can use to explain the relationships between each image and the content of the lesson.

2. According to Piaget's developmental theory, students pass through the same sequence of stages, although some may never reach the highest stage.

   Outline one alternative that you could use for students who are developmentally and as a result academically, deficient in a defined subject area.

3. Many concepts taught in middle and secondary level classrooms require abstract, formal thinking, yet many students in these classes are not developmentally ready to handle this level of mental operations.

   Select a complex concept in a content area that you plan to teach and devise a teaching strategy you could use when teaching this concept.

KEY TERMS

cognitive development
readiness
operations
schemata
equilibrium
disequilibrium
motivation
adaptation
assimilation
accommodation
social interaction
zone of proximal development
inner speech
maturation

developmental learning stages
sensorimotor period
reflexive
reflective
object permanence
preoperational period
symbolic modes
egocentrism
irreversibility
centration
conservation
concrete operations
first-order operations
logic and objectivity

formal operations
second-order operations
flexible
abstract
systematic

language acquisition
phonology
morphology
semantics
dialect

LOOKING AHEAD

Chapter 1 stated that a major goal of this text was to help future teachers and other school professionals prepare to guide the *academic* and *social development* of their future students. Such an ambitious and honorable undertaking requires an understanding of theories explaining how students develop socially and academically. The next chapter examines three additional areas of development critical to learning: emotional, social, and moral development. ■

Chapter 3

Emotional, Social, and Moral Development of Students

LEARNING OBJECTIVES

Upon completing this chapter, you should be able to:

1 List three environmental determinants of the social, moral, and emotional development of students.

2 Define and evaluate three implications of Erikson's theory for teachers.

3 Define the five ecological *systems* of Bronfenbrenner's Bioecological Model of Development.

4 Relate five ways social cognition can influence the classroom.

5 Define an appropriate and legal teacher response to suspected student physical and sexual abuse.

6 State two teacher alternatives to student bullying and cyber-bullying.

7 Define the relationship between maturation and student achievement.

8 List and discuss Kohlberg's six stages of moral development.

9 Explain how teachers can use simulations and "current events" to discuss and teach moral issues.

INTRODUCTION

As students advance through grade levels they change in many ways. As related in the previous chapter, the development of students has been the subject of Educational Psychology research for generations and today provides valuable insights into how the classroom environment can impact the emotional, social and moral development of students. This chapter discusses the major theories of such development.

EMOTIONAL AND SOCIAL DEVELOPMENT

As you observe a group of students in a classroom, you become aware of the different ways students interact. Some students appear shy and withdrawn while others are outgoing and socially active. Adults exhibit similar characteristics. How do *you* behave in social situations? As you talk, laugh, and interact with others you feel emotions, exhibit social skills and personality traits much like the students you will teach.

The emotional and social characteristics your students will exhibit are the result of their innate abilities and life experiences resulting in their ability to express thoughts, feelings, attitudes and social skills (Lerner, Theokas, & Bobek, 2005). These emotional and social characteristics affect how students treat others and, in turn how others treat them. This is also true of student/teacher relationships. For example, students who exhibit appropriate, positive social classroom behavior are often perceived by their teachers to be more academically competent, and often they are, but sometimes they are not (Byrne & Gavin, 1996).

> How we interact with others is based on our past experiences, which include learned personal beliefs and social skills.

TODD WILLIAMS...

was finishing his meal at the PTA banquet, held annually in the school cafeteria. The food was delicious. Todd leaned toward Marie, sitting next to him, and suggested the cooks should be hired for the school cafeteria. Marie smiled and said, "It's the same cooks." As Todd was protesting, "No way," the banquet speaker, Ms. Peak, was introduced.

A social worker known for her accomplishments with school-age young people, Ms. Peak paused, then began: "It's 7:00 am, the beginning of a typical school day and week. The following students are getting ready for the school day.

Marshall, age 16, is a sophomore from an upper-middle-class family. His father is a successful businessman and his mother is an attorney. As Marshall's father leaves for work, he once again reminds Marshall to "keep his grades up" if he wants to attend an Ivy League university; "B's and C's won't get it." His mother, also leaving, reminds him how well his sister is doing at Princeton. Marshall frowns, says he is trying, and has breakfast alone. As he plays with his food, Marshall reviews for a chemistry exam. He checks chemistry formulas written on a note card. Before he leaves for school, he folds the note card around his arm and secures it with a rubber band. Marshall's shirtsleeve hides the card containing the formulas he will need for the exam.

Serena, age 10, is a fourth grader from a middle-class family. The last words she hears from her mother as she leaves from school are slurred: "Get your breakfast at school." As her teacher, you notice she has become sullen and withdrawn and you are concerned about the repeated bruises about her arms and legs.

Toni, age 17, is an eleventh grader and twice you've smelled alcohol as you walk by his desk. You've talked to Janie, a 7th grader, repeatedly about looking on the papers of others during quizzes and she just turned in a paper copied from the Internet. Viana, a tenth grader, is obviously pregnant.

Ms. Peak paused and scanned the teachers in the audience, then continued:

"Ladies and gentlemen, your students' emotional, social, and moral development is primarily dependent upon their environment and family backgrounds. You already know that, and there's something else we know that makes us special in their lives. Regardless of their background we, as counselors, administrators, and teachers can have an impact, a very significant impact on their development and lives. We have our troubled students in class, 50% of their waking hours. We can make a difference." Ms. Peak hesitates and holds up a paper. "What I just related are examples of student problems we teachers face every day. There are other problems listed on this handout. I'm going to pass out copies and divide you into groups. Your assignment is to brainstorm solutions, share your experiences and discuss teacher options to each of the problems listed. When you finish we'll share and discuss our ideas."

ERIKSON'S THEORY OF PSYCHOSOCIAL DEVELOPMENT

As Marshall, Toni, Viana, and Serena mature into young adults, they may emerge as socially healthy or unhealthy individuals. One of the leading traditional theories of social development is E. H. Erikson's (1959, 1963, 1968) **theory of psychosocial development**. Erikson's theory concentrates on the development of healthy, positive behavior patterns. Erikson suggests that a healthy personality is developed through individuals' ability to love and work and the personal satisfaction they get from these activities.

Erikson's theory centers around eight developmental stages. During each stage, a person must face, and ultimately resolve, a central *crisis*. As a person progresses through each stage, a new psychosocial value, such as hope, will, or fidelity, is developed. *Resolution*, or resolving the crisis, at each stage is a prerequisite for advancing to the next stage. Thus, each new stage draws from the earlier stages as new levels of psychosocial functioning are learned.

According to Erikson, the resolution of a crisis during any stage of development is never absolutely positive or negative. Thus, a child will carry both positive and negative characteristics into each new stage, but Erikson emphasizes that a ratio of higher positive to negative is important for the development of a healthy personality.

Erikson's Eight Stages of Psychosocial Development

The heart of Erikson's theory is his eight stages of psychosocial development. During each stage, people face and resolve a crisis. A specific value is gained by the person who successfully progresses through a developmental stage. Table 3.1 summarizes Erikson's eight stages.

Stage I (Infancy: Ages 0–1)

The first stage, *trust versus mistrust*, takes place during infancy, and developmentally healthy children leave this stage with the value of *hope*, meaning they come to believe their wishes and needs will be met. Trust, which plays a role in later stages by forming a sense of identity, is related to parental care. To help an infant acquire trust, parents must respond willingly, lovingly, reliably, and quickly to the infant's needs, especially the primary needs of hunger, thirst, and shelter. How do we know when infants have acquired trust? Trust is first exhibited by infants who do not become distressed when their parents leave the room or move out of sight. Trust is not damaged when parents restrict their infants, if they do so consistently and with a sense of caring. For example, the parents of Tommy, an 8-month-old infant, will not allow him to touch the fire in the fireplace, even though Tommy is curious. According to Erikson, this will not affect Tommy's trust.

Sidebar notes:

All individuals experience both positive and negative resolutions of conflicts. According to Erikson, a ratio of higher positive to negative resolutions is a prerequisite for healthy personality development.

According to Erikson, resolving crisis is essential for healthy psychosocial developmental.

Families help infants develop trust by responding lovingly, consistently, and willingly to their needs.

Families can help their children develop a sense of autonomy by providing guidelines for appropriate decision making.

Infants resolve the crisis of the first stage with mistrust if their parents fail to meet their social needs or if their parents are abusive.

Stage II (Early Childhood: Ages 2–3)

During the second stage, children or toddlers face the crisis **of** *autonomy versus doubt* and obtain the psychosocial value of *will*. The second stage involves achieving a sense of independence, or autonomy, in the guidance of bodily functions and learning self-control. Children in this stage learn to walk and run and become toilet trained. Experimentation and exploration to determine what they can do and where they can go by themselves are key characteristics of children at this stage. At this stage, children should learn self-control in positive, effective ways rather than withdrawing or becoming hostile. They also should begin to develop the ability to appropriately control emotions and bodily functions, including toileting.

Families and caregivers of children play important roles in crisis resolution. According to Erikson, families and caretakers should encourage children in their search for independence while establishing protective guidelines.

Stage III (Preschool: Ages 4–5)

During Erikson's third stage of psychosocial development, preschool children face the crisis of *initiative versus guilt* and acquire the psychosocial value of *purpose*. If children have positively resolved the crises of the previous two stages, they enter the third stage with a sense that they are people separate and apart from others. During the preschool years, children are typically active and continually on the move, exploring the world around them. As they positively resolve the crisis of initiative versus guilt, they develop the ability to plan and initiate behavior. They learn to cooperate with others and exhibit appropriate behavior toward others.

Families and teachers of preschoolers should provide children opportunities to be active and explore. Expect mistakes and refrain from excessive scolding and punishment. For preschoolers, mistakes are part of active exploration. When mistakes occur, families and teachers should provide guidance and suggestions.

Stage IV (Elementary School: Ages 6–12)

During the elementary school years, children face the crisis of *industry versus inferiority*. With a positive resolution of the crisis in this fourth stage, children gain competence in themselves. In addition to play, elementary schoolchildren begin to exhibit more productive activities and gradually learn to engage in academic tasks. Children also place emphasis on people outside the family, in contrast to the earlier three stages, and discover that being recognized outside the family is important. They learn that the attention of teachers, peers, and others has value.

> Families can help children develop a sense of security by providing opportunities to explore within a caring, nurturing home environment.

The preschool and elementary school years are characterized by physical activity, high energy, maturation and physical growth.

Stage V (Adolescence)

The teenage years are characterized by the crisis in Erikson's fifth stage, *identity versus role confusion*, and positive resolution leads to the value of *fidelity*. During this stage, the four previous crises (trust versus mistrust, autonomy versus shame, initiative versus guilt, and industry versus inferiority) are resurrected. According to Erikson, teenagers attempt to integrate the earlier crises with their feelings, past learning, and future expectations. For example, Ms. Peak suggested that Marshall thought he had to cheat to live up to his parents' expectations. Simultaneously, teenagers must deal with a rapidly maturing body while facing the challenges of expected adult tasks and behavior. They can easily become preoccupied with their peers and the desire to be popular. In Erikson's fifth stage, adolescents often seek identity in their appearance and through their friends while sometimes ignoring other aspects of their lives such as academics.

The positive resolution of the fifth crisis requires role experimentation and exploration of the range of life opportunities. Teenagers face what Erikson calls an *identity crisis*, or a period of time when they can be confused about their roles. A negative resolution of the crisis may result in *identity confusion*, or delays in making commitments.

Stage VI (Young Adulthood)

The first crisis of young adulthood, *intimacy versus isolation*, occurs in Erikson's sixth stage. Positive resolution of the crisis leads to the value of *love*, or mutual devotion. After emerging from the adolescent years with a strong sense of identity, Erikson argued that people are challenged to develop a shared relationship with others and make commitments to meaningful affiliations and partnerships.

Stage VII (Adulthood)

Erikson's seventh stage occurs during adulthood and involves the crisis of *generativity versus stagnation*; positive resolution results in the psychosocial value of *care*. The positive resolution of this crisis involves concern for the next generation. According to Erikson, failure to resolve this crisis means an inability to guide others and approaching the future with uncertainty.

Stage VIII (Maturity)

The final crisis that individuals must face in their lives is *ego integrity versus despair*, which occurs in later life. The positive resolution of this crisis leads to the value of *wisdom*. At this stage, adults should be able to accept their lives, find them satisfying and ideally face old age with a feeling of order and satisfaction.

Teachers of elementary school-age children can help them develop a sense of industry and competence by assigning tasks that require interacting with others.

The final crisis that individuals face is the realization of aging, which is resolved through wisdom. Wisdom, according to Erikson, is possible when people feel their lives have been worthwhile and meaningful.

Though generally accepted, Erikson's theory is sometimes criticized for lacking a sound research base.

An examination of Erikson's eight stages shows that others play significant roles in the development of an individual's personality. In the first three stages, children's families play important roles in establishing trust, independence, and initiative. In the fourth stage, industry versus inferiority, peers and teachers join the family in critical roles. The "significant others" during the crisis of "identity versus role confusion" are family, teachers, and same-sex and opposite-sex peers. During the last three stages, society and a new family (spouse and offspring in addition to parents and siblings) become important.

Criticisms of Erikson's Theory

Erikson's theory of psychosocial development is popular and generally accepted but his theory, like Piaget's theory of cognitive development, is not without criticisms. Like Piaget, most of Erikson's theory is based on his own personal experiences rather than on extensive research data. Although he did attempt to validate his theory with groups of subjects, the samples he used were not extensive enough to satisfy requirements for sound research.

Another concern with Erikson's theory is that it focuses on males, which is explained by the fact that Erikson's own life formed the foundation for his theory (Gilligan, 1982). For example, the fifth stage, identity versus role confusion, appears to pertain to males only; however, females may display types of identity formation inconsistent with Erikson's theory. Some women may skip the stage entirely, or may return to the stage in their adult years after having children. Women in western cultures typically have the freedom to choose among traditional or contemporary opportunities, and therefore, may not make career and parenthood decisions on the time tables described by Erikson, and in today's society the same is true for men (Nucci, 2006).

> Even during the preschool years, teachers should provide students opportunities to make choices.

Implications of Erikson's Theory for Classroom Teaching

Erikson's theory of psychosocial development has many implications for teachers as they interact with their students. The theory suggests ways proactive teachers can assist students in resolving psychosocial conflicts in a positive manner. At each of Erikson's stages, teachers can positively impact how children experience and resolve crises.

Teachers can guide and encourage preschool children to make appropriate choices. For example, allow children to independently choose games and books, where they sit, and who they wish to have as their friends. If a child cannot choose a toy or wants to play with all the toys, direct the child's attention to making a choice. Compliment the child for choices made and for sharing.

	TABLE 3.1			
	Erikson's Eight Stages of Psychosocial Development			
Stage	Critical Environmental Factors	Psychosocial Value	Description	Significant Others
I. Infancy	Nurturing family environment	Hope	Healthy Psychosocial Development if family or caregiver responds to infant's needs. Mistrust, self-doubt and guilt may develop if family does not respond to infant's needs in a consistent and nurturing manner.	Family and/or caregiver
II. Early childhood	Opportunity for independent behavior and toilet training	Will	Emphasis on physical development, play and control of bodily functions. Shame and doubt could be issues if inappropriately criticized, punished and controlled.	Family, Siblings
III. Preschool	Language development and appropriate social interaction	Purpose	Child begins to learn responsibility and direction, and completing tasks. A negative environment can result in child's guilt about actions.	Family, siblings
IV. Elementary school	Academic and social expectations of school environment	Competence	Children should lean to cope with demands of academic tasks and expectations. Feelings of inferiority may result if child fails.	Family, siblings, peers, teachers

Stage	Critical Environmental Factors	Psychosocial Value	Description	Significant Others
V. Adolescence	Sexuality and peer relationships	Fidelity	Adolescents must be able to make appropriate choices concerning peer relationships, sexuality, and career choices. Negative resolution may result in identity confusion and/or prolonged delay in making commitments.	Family, siblings, teachers, same-sex and opposite-sex peers
VI. Young Adulthood	Career choices, Intimacy, marital decisions and children	Love	Positive resolution allows person to develop shared relationships with family and friends. Negative resolution results in isolation and self-absorption.	Spouse, children, workplace, society
VII. Adulthood	Family, friendship, career	Care	Positive resolution allows adults to establish and guide the next generation.	Family, parenting workplace, society
VIII. Maturity	Family, friendship, retirement	Wisdom	Individuals should be able to establish a feeling of order, a sense of accomplishment and satisfaction about their lives.	Family security

Make sure children are provided opportunities to experiment and explore. Encourage free play, creativity, and make-believe games. When students make mistakes trying to do something on their own, provide guidance, be tolerant and understanding.

As students in elementary school face the responsibilities of learning and interacting with teachers and friends, they need to experience success in

Teachers can help children resolve the industry versus inferiority crisis by providing opportunities in which children can be successful.

According to Erikson, teachers can help students resolve feelings of inferiority by providing tasks where students can be successful.

Elementary and secondary teachers should give students challenging tasks, encourage them, and praise them when they are successful.

Middle school teachers should be tolerant and flexible but establish clear, well-defined expectations for student behavior.

completing academic tasks. While providing opportunities for these experiences, urge students to set and work toward realistic goals. When students successfully accomplish tasks, provide positive feedback for their accomplishments.

Middle school teachers should be tolerant of the many role conflicts pre-teen and teenage students experience. This means being tolerant of fads, peer relationships and conflicts, coping with their sexuality and, sometimes, perplexing behavior. Show respect for their opinions and decisions, but at the same time, establish well-defined rules for academic and social behavior in the classroom, communicate these rules to students and their families, and provide systematic feedback about their academic and social accomplishments and deficiencies.

According to Miserandino (1996, p. 208),

> "Children who have their needs met . . . will come to hold positive beliefs about their competence and autonomy."

As our proactive alternatives suggest, social cognition, social problem solving, and social skills are critical factors in the classroom environment and

INTASC Standard 8   Instructional strategies.

PROACTIVE TEACHING

CLASSROOM SITUATION

1. You anticipate having students such as Renee, a 13-year-old eighth grader, who feels she is unattractive and no one likes her. Such students often withdraw, and their grades suffer.

PROACTIVE ALTERNATIVES

· Familiarize yourself with counseling services provided by your school and/ or school system for student referrals.

· Prior to classes beginning, plan class activities and privileges that can promote appropriate student behavior and enhance student/peer interaction. Examples of privileges for elementary students might be collecting assignments, cleaning the board, running

2. You will have students such as Justin, a 15-year-old, who is small and immature for his age. As a result, Justin attempts to get the attention of his peers by acting out in class, making funny remarks, and "showing off" at inappropriate times.

3. Steve, a 10-year-old fourth grader, has developed prematurely. He is larger than his peers, captain of the football and basketball teams; is loud and boisterous; and has a tendency to bully other students when he doesn't get his way. He disrupts class, and some of the other students reinforce his behavior by laughing and imitating.

errands to the office, being the teacher's assistant or playground captain, having choice of seating in class, and tutoring other students. Examples for secondary students might be being the leader for group assignments, planning a class social or field trip, having a choice of seating in class, judging a class debate or exhibit, and tutoring or being tutored by peers.

· As we recommend in Chapter 6, class rules concerning inappropriate behavior should be explained and discussed with students the first week of class. It is a good idea to have rules in writing to distribute to students and families.

· Plan part of the discussion with students concerning inappropriate behavior to include appropriate student responses when someone else misbehaves. Emphasis should be placed on students ignoring such behavior.

> Puberty has been defined as:
> a. The beginning of adolescence
> b. Hormones spurring rapid growth
> c. "A mess"

> Allowing time for students to interact and discuss feelings with each other can facilitate the development of social cognition.
>
> Through the use of role playing, identifying and explaining desired behaviors, and allowing students to discuss appropriate peer interactions, teachers can help students learn to exhibit appropriate social behaviors.

thus become an important part of what proactive teachers should understand about the socialization of students. In addition to learning academic material, students also learn a great deal from the social environment of the classroom. Teachers should make efforts to incorporate the teaching of social cognition into daily classroom activities. Arrange the social environment of the classroom to encourage appropriate student interaction, ask questions, and feel comfortable about themselves and others.

URIE BRONFENBRENNER'S BIOECOLOGICAL MODEL OF DEVELOPMENT

More recently, (Bronfenbrenner 1989, 2000, 2005) offered a model of human development that includes the hereditary and biological (Bio) traits of an individual, such as inherited ability, race, and intelligence. How such traits interact within the **social contexts** (ecological) where individuals live and have lived forms the basis of their development Social context includes the major components of an individual's environment. Examples are family, friends, religion, neighborhood, schools attended, the country, and society in which the individual lives.

Imagine the differences environment has on the developmental of children born in Chicago as compared to rural Appalachia, or Los Angeles in contrast to Bangladesh. Supposed you had experienced a different set of friends as you grew up, attended different schools, or been raised in a different culture. Bronfenbrenner maintained the development of individuals from childhood through adolescence is dependent on their interaction within the **microsystem, mesosystem, exosystem, macrosystem**, and **chronosystem** in which they live. The following are definitions.

- Microsystem—The current environment of an individual and the individual's interaction with such as family, home, school, friends, and peers.

- Mesosystem—The mesosystem combines and links microsystems such as peers and friends, family and local culture, teacher, individual, and family.

- Exosystem—An individual's exosystem is the linking or interaction of two or more environments within their microsystem. A child's development is affected but often the child has no control of interaction. A family may move to a different environment. The child's father, mother, or caretaker may lose a job, get divorced, or separate, impacting the child's development, outside the child's control.

- Macrosystem—Includes the broader interactions within the microsystem of an individual such as characteristics of the culture, moral beliefs, and customs. Within the macrosystem, Bronfenbrenner emphasized the particular characteristics and stresses impacting the individual such as poverty, violence, and access to (or lack of) educational and social opportunities.

- Chronosystem—As time passes, an individual's environmental mores evolve and change. A child's community grows or shrinks, governance continually changes, the family moves to a new home, the values and/or ethnicity of the community changes, views on divorce, sex, and other social issues evolve. How individuals interact with this evolution in values and environment significantly impacts their development.

Bronfenbrenner's bioecological model offers a very succinct defining of human development, especially childhood through adolescence. His inclusion of both hereditary and environmental factors offers an inclusive view of how children develop. Since the major tenets of Bronfenbrenner's model were developed in the late 1980s and 1990s, he was acutely aware of the contemporary environmental factors influencing human development. The following is how such environmental factors impact teaching and student development within the school environment.

ENVIRONMENTAL DETERMINANTS OF THE EMOTIONAL, SOCIAL, AND MORAL DEVELOPMENT OF STUDENTS

In this chapter, both Erickson and Bronfenbrenner have argued that developing the personality, social skills, and self-concept of students are critical issues within the classroom environment and are significantly influenced by student/teacher interaction.

A national poll (Bushaw & McNee, 2009) found that Americans consider such issues very important in the school environment, and school professionals agree. Additionally, there is considerable agreement among educational psychologists and other school professionals that education can and should be involved in the emotional, social, and moral development of students.

Despite recent budget cuts, many schools have managed to maintain mental health programs, counselors, and school psychologists who are available to students with emotional and behavioral problems and to students experiencing personal and/or family crisis. Many schools have programs to combat drug and alcohol abuse, and some schools have developed classes for the personal growth in areas such as self-concept and social skills.

In the preface of this text the authors stated: *THIS BOOK IS DEDICATED TO THE DAY WHEN ALL CHILDREN OF THE WORLD ARE BLESSED WITH A NUTURING, CARING FAMILY AND WISE UNDERSTANDING TEACHERS.* Our reasoning for the dedication is simple. The research and data are very clear. Children of all ages, who are fortunate to have families that are nurturing, caring, understanding and motivate their children to do well in school **while setting limits and enforcing explained rules**, are significantly more likely to develop emotionally, socially, morally, and succeed academically (Henson, 2010; Hoffman, 2001). This is true regardless of family structure; traditional family units (mother and father present in family), families where there are stepparents, single parent families, a family unit where child is being raised by a family member other than parents or guardian and in adoptive family units (U. S. Department of Education, 2010; U. S. Department of Health & Human Services, 2010). This is also true across ethnic and racial types. As Bronfenbrenner's Bioecologial Model so aptly

> Despite budget cuts, most schools have been able to maintain some mental health services for students.

emphasized, the importance of a nurturing, caring, loving environment to a child's development and consequent academic success cannot be overstated.

Other environmental factors critical to the development of the emotional, social, and moral well-being of your future students are; community setting, economic status, relationship with peers, religious influences, ethnicity, and very important -the schools they attend (Lerner, Theokas, & Bobel, 2005; Bronfenbrenner & Evans, 2000).

Consider the developmental challenges of a child born in poverty vs. wealth, or a child born to an abusive family as opposed to a nurturing family. As noted in chapter one, your students will have diverse environmental backgrounds. Many of your students will live in single-parent homes. Some will come from families of wealth, most will not. Some will have been and/or are being physically and/or verbally abused. Within the school environment, you will have students who are very popular with their peers and some who are not. You will encounter students with alcohol and other drug problems.

More than 30% of teenage girls and 40% of teenage boys are sexually active. Sixty-one percent of these teenagers say they do not use birth control preventatives. Thirty-nine of every 1000 births in the United States are to teenage girls' ages 15–19 (U. S. Department of Health and Human Services, 2009). Six percent of adolescent girls and 8% of adolescent boys identify themselves as lesbian (girls) or gay (boys) or bisexual (having feelings for both sexes) (U. S. Department of Education, 2010).

We continue our discussion of environmental factors critical to the emotional, social, and moral development of students with the one most psychologists agree is the most important—the home environment.

Home Environment

The home environment of U.S. children has changed dramatically over the past forty years. (Amato, 2006) reports that half of U.S. children are now being raised in single- parent families. Often this results in the children being cared for by grandparent(s), other family member(s) or guardian(s) as the single parent works. Divorce can be traumatic for everyone involved, especially for children, regardless of age.

Children witness and experience the turmoil and strife between parents leading to separation from one parent. Moving to a new area, enrolling in a new school, separating from friends, and facing the challenge of finding new ones are traumatic challenges for children of divorce. The amount of trauma brought on by divorce is primarily dependent on the parents' concern and behavior toward the child prior to, during, and immediately following divorce and separation. This is especially true during the first months after the divorce. Understanding, listening, explaining and nurturing by parent(s), teachers, guardians, and other family members with such children during this crisis are critical to their emotional well-being (Lerner. Theokas & Bobek, 2005).

Teacher awareness of the trauma that can and will occur among their students suggests communication with families can be critically importance. How can teachers interact and open lines of communication with the families of their students? Consider the following.

INTASC Standard 10   **Leadership and collaboration.**

Communicating with the Families of Students

- Within most schools, there are Family/Teacher organizations and/or planned periodic meetings with teachers, family and students. Be sure the time, place and date of such meetings are communicated to families of your students in ample time frames for family planning.

- Establish teacher-family contact via email, notices, and telephone calls. At the beginning of the school year, one of the first tasks for any teacher is to establish emergency contacts for all students. This should include student address, phone numbers (both work and school), an alternate contact, and family physician, if possible. Such a list should include relevant health issues of students. If language is a barrier, check with peer teachers, school administration, or counselor for options.

- Make sure families are provided contact information for both you and the school.

- Inform your students' families they are welcome to make scheduled visits. Plan activities that include family involvement. Plan and encourage scheduled family class days.

- Obviously, serious behavior and academic problems should be communicated to the student's family. Periodically informing students' families about their successes and outstanding work is just as important, yet, is rarely done (Landrum, Lingo, & Scott, 2011). A friend of the authors, a fifth grade-teacher, uses a monthly family checklist to make sure she reports, at least once a month, something positive about each of her students. In 2008, she was selected "Outstanding Teacher" in her county.

DETERRENTS TO STUDENT DEVELOPMENT

Unfortunately, there are many deterrents to a child's development that can occur within their family unit and school environment. One of the most dramatic and destructive is **abuse (physical** and **sexual)**. According to the U. S. Department of Health and Human Services (2010), more than three million abuse and neglect offenses are reported yearly. More than a third of these are confirmed. The potential of such abuse to impede the emotional and social development of children, regardless of age, cannot be overstated. Following are some characteristics of physical and sexual abuse and alternatives for the teacher.

Physical and Sexual Abuse

Characteristics of physical abuse:

- Unexplained bruising, burns, and lacerations.
- Often such injuries are repeated as indicated by various stages of healing.
- Student is either withdrawn, or aggressive and hostile.

Characteristics of Sexual Abuse

Physical signs can be:

- pain by victim in genital area.
- Blood on clothing, especially underclothing.
- Bruising about genital area.
- Student is sullen, withdrawn, or very hostile and aggressive.
- Student may display inappropriate sexual behavior or be fearful of close contact.

Excellent information concerning legalities and appropriate format for reporting abuse can be found by calling the Child Help National Child Abuse Hotline at 1-800-4-A-CHILD.

Concerning teacher response, first and foremost, teachers and all other school professionals are required by federal law (Keeping Children and Families Safe Act of 2003 (P.L. 108-36)) to report suspected cases of abuse. In almost all school environments, there are teacher orientations that explain the requirements, ramifications, and liabilities of reporting and failing to report suspected physical and/or sexual abuse of students. Acquaint yourself with your state laws and school policy. If you, as a teaching professional, suspect abuse, or if one of your students reports being abused, document the date, time, and nature of the abuse and report this to your school administration immediately.

Bullying

Another very common deterrent to a child's academic development is **bullying**. Bullying is one of the most neglected problems in our public schools today. In a study that surveyed over 40,000 teens ages 15–18, Josephson Institute of Ethics (2010) reported the following:

- In the past 12 months, 50% of teens reported they had bullied or teased another student
- 47% stated they had been bullied

- In the past 12 months, over half of teens reported hitting someone in anger.

Cyber-bullying

According to (Garbarino & deLara, 2002) as many as 160,000 children a day avoid attending school for fear of being bullied.

Cyber-Bullying is now a defined problem, as technology (blogs, YouTube, email, and texting) is now a means to intimidate and humiliate (Weinstein, 2007). Lies, pictures, slander, and rumors are being used via technology to victimize. The Pew Internet and American Life Project (2007) reported that almost a third of teens have been victims of *cyber-bullying*. Consider the following alternative for teachers facing the problems of bullying, cyber-bullying and aggressive behavior.

Bullying

At the beginning of the school term, communicate very clearly to students, the meaning, rules and ramifications of bullying, cyber-bullying, fighting, and violent behavior. It is very important that this information is also communicated to families of students.

- Praise students when they cooperate and work together, especially when differences are settled appropriately. Encourage and be a model of showing respect and courtesy. Students should be taught methods and techniques of resolving potentially volatile situations such as remaining calm, counting before responding, or walking away.

- Provide students avenues of addressing and discussing issues of lying, dishonesty, teasing, gossiping, and rumors. Student discussions and role playing concerning such issues can be constructive.

- When bullying occurs, families of the students should be contacted immediately. Often if the families can be brought together and the issue discussed and counseled, resolution is possible.

- Deal with intimidation and threats immediately, calmly, and firmly. If a student reports a physical threat and it is confirmed, this should be reported to administration and legal authorities immediately.

Cyber-bullying

- If a student informs you about a cyber-bullying incident and you find it is true, report it to the administration and secure information on appropriate format for contacting the student's family.

- Teachers and families should advise students to never provide personal information over the Internet or other cyber device.

- Students should be advised to report threats, intimidation, and rumors they receive, regardless of format, to their families and teachers.
- Students can be taught never to open messages from an unknown person and how to block unwanted messages.
- Guest authority figures such as law enforcement officers can be persuasive with all ages of students in addressing the laws concerning bullying, cyber-bullying and other forms of aggressive behavior.

Aggressive Behavior

It is important for teachers to proactively plan for aggressive situations such as fighting and/or out-of-control behavior. If you encounter a fight, or if a student is physically out-of-control:

- Approach calmly but keep a safe distance.
- Never try to physically restrain.
- If possible, immediately send another student(s) for an adult and try to get observing students away from aggressor(s).
- Calmly, but firmly, address the students, giving them options for their behavior, such as "Tim, I want you to return to your seat" or "Quinton, I want you and Romano to walk away from each other, NOW!" Also, articulate the consequences of their behavior. "If you don't, the Principal and your family will be informed of your behavior."
- Do not be drawn into an argument with such as "Well, he started it" or "I don't care what you do". Simply, state what you want the students to do and the consequences if they do not comply.

Many of the deterrents of student development discussed are very relevant to students during their adolescence. This brings us to our next topic, contemporary adolescent issues.

CONTEMPORARY ADOLESCENT ISSUES

Puberty

Adolescence has two distinct periods: pubescence, or preadolescence, which consists of the two years preceding puberty and the beginning of the adolescence growth spurt, and puberty, which is distinguished by certain marks of sexual maturity (Rogers, 1982). This period is typified by steady growth, high energy, and maturation of nerve and muscle tissue (Minuchin, 1982). These activities are essential for skillful and coordinated physical activity. *Puberty* is defined as the period of early adolescence during which hormones spur rapid physical development. One of the major physiological characteristics of sexual maturity is the production of live sperm cells in males and the first menstrual period in females. The sexual maturing of males is characterized by the growth of the testes, scrotum, and penis; the appearance of facial, underarm, and pubic hair; ejaculation of semen; and a deepening voice. Sexual maturity of females is characterized by breast development and underarm and pubic hair growth. Girls usually enter puberty earlier than boys, as many teachers will attest, "There's a big difference between the levels of development of boys and girls."

Such development has a dramatic impact on the behavior of these students and, consequently, their teachers. Middle and secondary teachers should be aware of the physical and emotional changes that occur with students during puberty. The "child becoming an adult" at the age of puberty often becomes less dependent on parents, teachers, and other adults. Additionally, peer relationships change dramatically. During this period of development, the issue of acceptance and popularity among peers cannot be overemphasized. Peer relationships, if negative, can have a devastating impact on emotional development. Another critical issue is that sex drives begin to conflict with social norms and personal values.

Gender Differences

Boys and girls mature differently, but maturation rates also differ among members of the same sex (Rogers, 1982). Some adolescents mature early, reaching puberty a year or more earlier than other members of the same sex. Others reach maturity later than their peers of the same sex.

Teachers should be sensitive to a number of student problems that can occur during this developmental period. Slower-maturing students can experience feelings of inadequacy and inferiority. During this period, use praise, compliments, and other social rewards that are too often inadvertently reserved for those who mature early. Other changes include the female students entering the age of menarche, the beginning of menstruation. This development can cause shyness, irritability, and a need for emotional support.

PROACTIVE TEACHING

Let's examine the profiles of four typical early- and late-maturing boys and girls, all 14 years of age:

Marcie is an early-maturing female. She is 5 feet 5 inches tall, weighs 135 pounds, and is considerably larger than most of her female classmates. Her menstrual periods began 3 years ago and her breast development is at an adult level. Marcie lacks poise and confidence and feels conspicuous about her appearance. She has a greater interest in boys than other girls her age, and boys often take an interest in her. This causes problems of jealousy with many of her girl friends.

Jaslyn is a late-maturing girl. At 5 feet and 93 pounds, she is just beginning to develop breasts and recently began her menstrual periods. Jaslyn feels good about herself, and her self-confident, outgoing nature makes her popular with both male and female classmates, as well as teachers.

Cyrus is an early-maturing boy. At a height of 5 feet and 11 inches and a weight of 185 pounds, he is one of the largest boys in his class. He has adult pubic, underarm, and facial hair. Cyrus's friends look up to him, and he was recently elected student council president. He is also one of the stars of the school football team and is a natural and confident leader.

Hasean is a late-maturing male. At 5 feet 2 inches and 110 pounds, he is known as the "shrimp" of his class. He has no pubic or underarm hair but keeps a disposable razor ready for the day when he can begin shaving. Although he is energetic and bouncy, he is also seen as the class clown, and many of his classmates and teachers find his attention-seeking tactics disruptive.

List three options for teachers of such students?

The contemporary adolescence problems of drugs, teenage pregnancy, school dropouts, and unemployment continue to be critical issues in the educational environment. However, by displaying an understanding of the developmental changes that adolescents experience, proactive teachers can help these students, especially early-maturing girls and late-maturing boys who often have difficulty. Support can be provided to adolescents, or any student, through praise and attention. Also remember, there are exceptions. You will encounter some early-maturing girls and late-maturing boys who are poised, confident, and popular.

Be aware of resources for assisting adolescent students. Such resources include the school psychologist, school counselor, referral and community agencies and the administrative staff. Schools often provide programs that address the special needs of students experiencing puberty. Such assistance includes sex education programs, drug and substance abuse programs, and crisis counseling.

> Adolescents go through a series of periods in developing self-identity. Each period may become a terminal point for adolescents.

MARCIA'S FOUR PERIODS OF IDENTITY SEARCH

J. E. Marcia (1966, 1967, 1980) elaborated on Erikson's identity stage, providing additional information about adolescent experience as they commit to roles, careers, and beliefs. Marcia identified **crisis** as a major factor in the adolescent's attainment of **identity**. Crisis involves those times in adolescence when teenagers are actively involved in choosing among alternatives such as college or occupation, friends, and social and moral beliefs.

Marcia also described four periods that adolescents go through in their search for identity, as seen in Table 3.2. Adolescents may experience all four periods or may become stagnated at a particular period. During the first period, **diffusion**, adolescents lack commitment to their future occupation or their current beliefs. They often lack self-direction, are disorganized, tend to be impulsive, and probably avoid getting involved. During the second period, **foreclosure**, adolescents have yet to experience an identity crisis. They accept and endorse parents' positions on occupational choices and values.

During the third period, **moratorium**, teenagers are experiencing a crisis often characterized by dissatisfaction with their current status, daydreaming a great deal, and questioning their family's values. Adolescents seeking independence often conflict with their parents over such issues as sex, curfews, and money (Sebald, 1986). They may openly defy their parents, or their rejection of their parents' wishes may be more discreet. Marshall, the sophomore in the earlier scenario who was preparing to cheat on his exam is an example of a teenager rejecting parental values. However, adolescent conflict with parents typically dissipates during middle adolescence and later declines during young adulthood.

The final period is **achievement**. Teenagers in this period have passed through crises, exploration, and questioning and have made a commitment that they have selected for themselves. The period of achievement in adolescence is followed by young adulthood, Erikson's stage VI.

TABLE 3.2	
Marcia's Four Periods of the Search for Identity	
Period	**Description**
Identity diffusion	No commitment and no concern about lack of commitment
Foreclosure	Acceptance and endorsement of families' positions
Moratorium	Dissatisfaction with current status but haven't made a commitment
Identity achievement	Passed through crises and made own commitment

DEVELOPMENT OF SOCIAL COGNITION AND AWARENESS

Both Erikson and Bronfenbrenner provided guidelines of how people develop their personality traits by defining how people interact in their social environment. Erikson defined **social cognition** as the way people reason about themselves and others in social situations. It results from people's interactions and their skills within the social environment. Social cognition is very much related to psychosocial development; it changes dramatically as children grow older (Eisenberg & Harris, 1984). Flavell (1979, p. 43) defines social cognition as;

> Our conceptions, knowledge, and observations concerning our own and other people's feelings, perceptions, thoughts, personality traits, social interaction, moral and other norms (social, legal), and numerous other contents of our social world.

The cultural diversity of students in today's classrooms (discussed in Chapter 1) makes the following aspects of social cognition and social skills essential as they relate to psychosocial development: self-understanding, friendship, and self-concept.

Self-Understanding

Self-understanding is an important aspect of social cognition because an understanding of one's self in social situations is essential for understanding others (Eisenberg & Harris, 1984; Marlowe, 1986; Pellegrini, 1985). However, there are many differences between self-understanding and understanding others. Understanding of self involves differentiating one's self from others in society (Damon & Hart, 1982).

The development of such values begins as children cognitively develop an understanding of their personal characteristics, such as their personality and physical features. They also become aware of their mental and physical capabilities and their preferences and options. During late childhood, children begin to compare themselves with others as they acquire knowledge of their place in peer groups and in the family. Early adolescence is characterized by students' increasing understanding of their personality; older adolescents realize that personal social traits and beliefs affect their social behavior.

As children mature, their understanding of self grows. When we asked Brian, a 4-year-old, to tell us about himself, he first told us, "I'm 4 years old." He said he liked to play on swings and he didn't like Stu, a boy in his class. When we asked him if anyone didn't' like him, he egocentrically replied, "Of course not!" Brandy, age 10, described herself as the best speller in class and a generally "okay" person. Juanita, age 13, described herself as a good leader; her friends know "she gets things done." Pol-San, age 17, gave the most detailed description of himself. He said that he was "sometimes shy, but usually warmed up and could eventually feel comfortable with people." Some of the other students at school don't like him because they think "he's a nerd," and although this bothers him, he continues to earn good grades. He sees himself as a caring, sensitive person and believes that some people like him because they find him trustworthy.

Student Study Guide

In late childhood, children begin to acquire knowledge of their place in peer groups and in their families.

What do you understand about yourself? When asked in Chapter 1, what you expect to get from your profession, did you have a good answer? Self-understanding is something that eludes many many students but some are certain about their feelings and reasons for their actions. For example, some students are aware they feel comfortable around certain people and feel uncomfortable around certain others. They may or may not understand why others don't feel the same.

In the Classroom

Regardless of age or level of maturity, students rarely see themselves as others see them. In the classroom, teachers at all levels can help by providing students opportunities for self-reflection. Because some students are not happy with the person they perceive themselves to be, they have difficulty focusing on their positive features. Unfortunately, this can lead to devastating consequences. Matthew Selekman (2009/2010) attributes student self-harm to emotional disconnections and failure to fit in. Teachers can help by providing opportunities for self-growth and by giving frequent encouragement and reassurance while students are developing their self-images. Consider the following teacher options.

- Focus on student behavior. Acknowledge the display of appropriate behavior and improvements in behavior.

- Avoid criticizing students in the presence of their peers, and do not permit students to ridicule each other. At the beginning of the school year, set and enforce classroom policy forbidding ridicule.

Friendship

Another aspect of social skills is **friendship**, or having personal, close relationships with peers. Friendships are very important, but often students' ideas about friendships differ from adults. Students' friendships change with age, changing from a concrete, behavioral level to an abstract, psychological level. Friendship evolves as students mature from a self-centered view of friends as people who satisfy needs to a view of friendship as a reciprocal and mutual relationship (Eisenberg & Harris, 1984).

Preschool and primary grade children define friends as playmates with whom they have fun (Eisenberg & Harris, 1984). Students of this age often do not clearly differentiate between friends and best friends but can identify the people they like and dislike. Elementary students see friends as people who assist and support one another. Their view of friendship includes sharing physical activities and materials to being kind and helpful. During adolescence, the view of friendships, once again, changes from simply being close to another person to relationships allowing individuality. At this time, exclusivity of friendships becomes less important, but emotional support and acceptance become much more important.

The developmental nature of friendship is easily seen when children are asked, "Who are your friends and why are they your friends?" For example, Seth, a 6-year-old, listed names of several friends and indicated they are his friends because they play together after school. Ola, a 10-year-old, said, "Beau and Madelyn are my best friends because we play 'gameboys' and we like each other." Felice, a 16-year-old, names her group of closest friends and notes, "We're friends because we don't give each other a hard time. We're there for each other during good times and bad." One adolescent we interviewed described her friends as "people I can always talk to. We feel the same way about a lot of things, but when we don't, I can count on them to tell me the truth."

Summary of the Development of Social Cognition

Social cognition requires understanding ourselves and others, and knowing the rules of social interactions. As with cognitive development, children's social cognition and values change dramatically as they grow older. Table 3.3 summarizes the developmental changes in social cognition.

Self-understanding begins with children's understanding of their personality and physical characteristics. As children grow older, self-understanding becomes more abstract as they become more aware of social traits and how those traits affect their beliefs and behavior. Social knowledge or interpersonal understanding, changes from knowledge of traditional "good manners" or what is correct and incorrect to consideration of others and awareness of the subtleties of social interactions.

Role and perspective taking in younger students is often egocentric, which implies that young students may not always be aware or able to understand what another person is thinking, feeling, or intending. Older students are increasingly able to understand the perspectives of others.

> Social cognition means knowing the rules of social interactions and requires a degree of understanding of one's self and others.

TABLE 3.3

Summary of Developmental Changes in Social Cognition

Cognition	Change
Self-understanding	Infants and young children gain an understanding of their physical features and capabilities.
	Older children develop an awareness of their place in their family and their peer group.
	Young adolescents begin to focus on their relationships and social personalities.

Cognition	Change
	Older adolescents begin to understand that social traits affect social behavior and beliefs affect actions.
Friendship	Preschool children see friends as people to play with.
	Elementary schoolchildren see friends as kind, helpful, and supportive.
	Adolescents see friends as those who provide emotional support and allow individuality. This is true regardless of the nature and complexity of their problems.

SELF-CONCEPT

Self-concept or **self-esteem** is individuals' perceptions of themselves, or how they feel about themselves and their abilities. Students' self-concepts, both positive and negative, are formed through the experiences with their environment. Self-concept is an important attribute for teachers to understand about their students (Scott et al., 1996). Research suggests that self-concept and academic achievement are positively correlated (Beane, 1982). Self-concept influences students' performance in the classroom, and such performance also influence self-concept.

Mack and Ablon (1983) specified five stages for the development of self-concept, summarized in Table 3.4.

During phase 1, infants learn the rudiments of positive self-concept through their relationships with family and other significant people in their environment. Infants gradually learn to distinguish themselves from others and learn that they can do things on their own.

Phase 2 encompasses the toddler period. Children in this phase continue to rely upon family and others' attitudes and opinions, but their ability to accomplish more on their own increases. They look to family for positive reactions to accomplishments, learn to value praise, and feel pride in what they do.

Phase 3 involves preschool children. During this period, people other than family, enter children's lives, and the opinions of those people who are valued and trusted by children become important. Children in phase 3 encounter many new and often stressful situations and build their self-concepts by mastering these stressful events.

During the elementary school years, or phase 4, three sources of self-concept become integrated: the opinions of others, children's own competencies, and children's opinions of themselves. For example, praise from another person, such as a teacher, enhances a child's self-esteem only if the child feels competent. Although self-concept grows a great deal during this

> Students' self-concepts and levels of academic achievement are closely related.

> Talent and potential will be wasted unless children believe they possess ability and have the freedom to use and develop their talents (Miserandino, 1996, p. 210).

phase, children continue to feel that the ultimate truth about themselves lies in others, not themselves.

The final phase 5, occurs in adolescence. Many radical changes occur in self-concept from the elementary school years to the adolescent years. At this time, adolescents' self-concepts are radically changed by physical, cognitive, and social changes. They must construct a new body image as a result of puberty. They are able to think abstractly, or to think about what they are going to do in the future.

TABLE 3.4	
Development of Self-Concept	
Stage	**Description**
Infancy	Learn basics of self-concept from family
Early childhood	Learn to feel pride in accomplishment
Preschool	Learn the importance and trust of others outside family
Elementary	Opinions of others and self competencies become integrated
Adolescence	Self-concept changes as new body image is constructed and abstract thinking is developed

Enhancing Student Self-Concept in the Classroom

Fostering the self-concept of students is beneficial both academically and socially. As indicated earlier, academic achievement and self-concept are positively correlated, so enhancing self-concept may increase school performance, while successful classroom experiences may increase self-concept. Yet, according to Scott and colleagues (1996, p. 286), most self-esteem programs used in schools have historically consisted of superficial activities; thus self-esteem is seldom addressed at the conceptual level. The following are suggested for enhancing the self-concepts of students in the classroom:

- Avoid hasty judgments about students' self-concepts. Carr and Kurtz-Costes (1994) found that teachers' ratings of students' self-concepts are often incorrect.
- Miserandino (1996) suggests helping students find personal meaning in their academic studies.
- Help students set reasonable goals for themselves.
- Remind students of their academic, social, and personality strengths.
- Teach students how to appropriately praise others.
- When praising students' work, make specific and accurate comments.

- Assign tasks that challenge students and yet are within their ability to complete, and give them the autonomy required to complete the tasks (Scott et al., 1996).

- Teach students to develop self-evaluation skills and to make realistic evaluations of themselves and their academic work.

The research on the impact teachers have on student self-esteem has been exhaustive. Results indicate that teacher support and encouragement of student autonomy are associated with higher student self-esteem (Scott et al., 1996, p. 287). One effective way to build students' self-esteem is through classroom discussion. Participation in class discussions can enhance a stronger sense of self-confidence. For those students who are reluctant to participate, a good method for increasing participation is a process called frontloading. **Frontloading** is the process of providing shy students with information prior to a discussion that will encourage them to speak up (Feather, 2012).

MORAL DEVELOPMENT

In recent years, educators and families of students have expressed considerable concern about student morality. Schools are not only being asked but expected to address this issue. Oana (1993, p. 5) expresses the complexity of this problem: "The problem is, today's schools, no matter how much they change, they cannot cope with all the social ills its clients bring to their doors each day."

However, our schools have always been inextricably connected to the local community and to society at large. Apple (1990, p. 526) notes that schools have always played an important role in societal issues, "Whether we recognize it or not, curriculum and more general educational issues in the U.S. have always been caught up in the history of class, race, gender, and religious relations."

Lounsbury (1991, p. 5), a longtime leader in the National Middle School Association, states what he considers the school's role in moral development.

> We need classrooms in which beauty is savored, truth honored, compassion practiced, and fellowship honored; classrooms where creativity is encouraged, where youngsters are assisted in dreaming of a better life; classrooms that are laboratories of living rather than places where teachers stand and talk and students sit and listen. . . . the school must not attempt to dictate a particular set of values but must assist young adolescents in exploring their values, attitudes, and standards.

The moral development of students has a rich foundation in educational psychology literature.

Kohlberg's Theory of Moral Development

Kohlberg's (1958, 1969, 1978, 1984) theory states there are six stages of moral development contained within three levels of morality, as illustrated in Table 3.5. He identifies three characteristics in his six stages. First, children always go through the stages in the same order **(invariant)** regardless of culture or background. Second, children's moral behavior at each stage is **cross-sectional**; meaning their level of behavior at any point in time doesn't vary with different situations. Third, the stages are **hierarchical**; the development of characteristics at the earlier stages are prerequisites for the development of the characteristics at the later stages, and once individuals progress to later stages, the behaviors of the earlier stages are displaced. This does not imply that everyone reaches the highest stage; many never do. Entire cultures or individuals within cultures may become fixed at a lower stage (Kohlberg, 1958, 1981).

Kohlberg's Six Stages of Moral Development
Level 1

The first level of Kohlberg's developmental theory is **preconventional morality** and is comprised of two stages. The first is **heteronomous morality**. During this stage, children do what is "right" to avoid punishment. Children at this stage are egocentric; they are not morally mature enough to consider ethics in their behavior. For example, Samantha, a six- year-old at the heteronomous morality stage, refrains from copying others work because she's afraid the teacher will catch her, not because she thinks cheating is wrong.

The second stage of preconventional morality is **individualism and exchange**. During this stage, individuals follow rules to serve their needs. Although primarily egocentric, they are aware that other people are important, and while acting to meet their own needs and interests, they can let others do the same. Individuals at this stage feel "what's right is what's fair," or what is a compromise between the individual and another person. Quinton appears to be at Kohlberg's second stage of moral development. When confronted by the teacher about copying Anna's exam, Quinton answers, "So what, Anna doesn't care."

TABLE 3.5		
Kohlberg's Six Stages of Moral Development		
Level	**Stage**	**Description**
1. Preconventional morality	1. Heteronomous morality	Do what's right to avoid punishment.
	2. Individualism, purpose, and exchange	Do what's right because it's fair.

Level	Stage	Description
2. Conventional morality	3. Mutual interpersonal expectations, relationships, and interpersonal conformity	Do what's right because it's expected by family, teachers, and peers.
	4. Social system and conscience	Do what's right because of duty or to follow laws.
3. Postconventional morality	5. Social contract or utility and individual rights	Do what's right because of the welfare and protection of people.
	6. Universal and ethical principles	Do what's right because of self-chosen ethical principles.

Level 2

The second level is **conventional morality**. Stage 3, the first stage at this level, is *mutual interpersonal expectations, relationships, and interpersonal conformity*. At this stage, individuals do what is expected of them in an effort to please others such as member of their family, teachers, and peers. It is important to "be good" and for this reason, this stage might be called the "good boy and good girl" stage. Being good to people at this stage means showing concern for others, and group feelings take precedence over individual feelings. The reasons for being good include a personal need to be good in the person's own eyes as well as the eyes of others. People at this stage support rules that society defines as good behavior.

Stage 4, the second stage in conventional morality, is *social system and conscience*. In this stage, people do what is right because of a sense of duty, because there are laws, or because of contributing to the order of society. They believe that everyone should follow social rules because the societal system would break down if everyone violated the rules. Following the moral norms of society is important.

> At the postconventional level, people must understand how others are affected. When in conflict, certain rights are as important as civil laws.

Level 3

The third level is **postconventional morality**. Stage 5, **social contract** *or utility and individual rights*, is the first stage at this level. People should obey the rules and laws of society "because it's the law" and because it is necessary for protecting the rights of citizens. People at this stage believe that laws and duties should be based on the benefit of the greatest number of people. People at this stage are aware that other people hold a variety of opinions and values but feel that rules should be followed. However, they recognize the conflict between moral and legal issues and

During the heteronomous morality stage, students may not understand that cheating on a test is ethically wrong.

are often conflicted when these do not agree. Stage 6 is called **universal and ethical principles**. People at Kohlberg's last stage base their judgment of what is right on self-chosen ethical principles. Although they may feel that many laws are based on such principles, they act in accordance with their principles when it conflicts with the law. They believe in principles such as justice, equality of human rights, and the respect for the dignity of individuals.

Criticisms of Kohlberg's Theory

Kohlberg's theory has been criticized from several standpoints. One area of criticism has been directed at Kohlberg's contention that his six stages are invariant, or that individuals move to the next highest stage rather than regressing to previous stages or skipping stages. Evidence suggests that stages of morality do not follow the rigid course described by Kohlberg.

Woolfolk (1987) suggested that Kohlberg's stages are culturally biased. Specifically, she criticized stage 6 as being biased in favor of Western ideas of individualism, liberty, and justice. Kohlberg did concede that his theory is biased toward the Western culture. The cultural diversity of today's and future U.S. students, noted in Chapter 1, indicates that teachers must be cautious and patient when interpreting and shaping student emotional, social, as well as moral development. This does not suggest a teacher's role in the moral development of students is diminished. Kohlberg suggests that harshness and rigidity be replaced by patience and understanding, in addition to high moral and academic expectations.

There are no sex differences when the development of moral reasoning occurs.

Another major criticism of Kohlberg's theory is from a feminist perspective. Gilligan (1982) pointed out that Kohlberg's theory was originally developed using a sample of male subjects. She pointed out that females responding to questions about moral dilemmas are more likely to use an orientation of care and responsibility whereas males are more likely to speak of rights and justice.

However, other studies have shown no sex differences in Kohlberg's stages. Walker (1984), for example, reviewed several studies investigating sex differences in moral reasoning and found that there are no significant sex differences.

PROACTIVE EXERCISE

Suppose you teach second graders and you have noticed some of your students copy the work of others. Does Kohlberg's six steps of moral development address this issue? If so, how? Fifty-two percent of students admit to using the Internet to cheat on academic assignments. Does Kohlberg's moral development address this issue?

MORAL DEVELOPMENT TEACHING MODELS

Research concerning instruction on moral issues have been fruitful and provide guidelines for teachers (Hersh, Paolitto, and Reimer,1979; Nucci, 2001; Cook & Cook, 2005). The following are some of those guidelines.

- Children from families providing moral guidance are likely to reflect such guidance in their behavior.

- Developmentally, the nature of moral conflict, changes as children age.

- The ability of teachers to understand the perspective of students is critical when dealing with moral issues in the classroom.

- Discussing moral and hypothetical issues in the classroom environment is important.

- Develop a proactive plan for moral issue you will encounter in the classroom. For example, have plans for dealing with cheating and lying.

- A classroom environment that is accepting of students' input and discussions concerning moral issues and dilemmas is important in fostering listening and communication skills and as serving as a basis for moral reasoning.

- As a teacher, be aware of peer pressure concerning moral issues, especially during adolescence.

INTASC Standard 9   Professional learning and ethical practice.

In summary:

- Prepare topics in advance for class discussions on moral issues. These might include such topics as respect for others and their belongings, compromising, interaction with peers, and how students want to be treated by others.

- Be prepared to involve families concerning such issues. Your school counselor or school psychologists could advise you

- Understand the nature of moral conflict from a developmental perspective and recognize that students of different ages react differently to moral conflicts.

- Elements that promote moral growth include the teacher's ability to take the perspective of students when dealing with moral issues and the students' ability to understand the perspectives of others.

- Develop an awareness of the moral issues students face. Develop a variety of hypothetical and real issues to discuss in the classroom and recognize the issues actually occurring in the classroom.

- Develop strategies for questioning students about their moral reasoning. For instance, in classroom discussions emphasize the moral issue involved, ask "why" when students give responses to moral dilemmas. Broaden the scope by assigning students to take the roles of others.

- Create a classroom atmosphere that is conducive to discussions about moral issues. For example, be receptive to students' spontaneous discussions of moral dilemmas, when appropriate. Foster listening and communication skills in students, and encourage student interactions.

- Anticipate possible difficulties. For example, be aware that peer pressure influences the responses students have to issues or hypothetical moral dilemmas being discussed.

- Be very cautious not to impose your personal and/or religious beliefs on your students.

> Simulated or real-life situations can be used to facilitate instruction in moral issues.

As suggested, one alternative to stimulating class discussion of moral issues is presenting to students real and/or hypothetical issues. The following classroom situations are typical issues that occur in the classroom and can be proactively presented for class discussions:

- A student finds personal belongings missing from his or her desk or locker.

- A student bullies another.

- A group of students spreads rumors about another.

- A student uses profanity in the classroom.

- A ninth-grade male student makes sexually suggestive remarks to a female student.

Other issues may be teacher oriented and require advice from the school counselor, school psychologist and/or administration, such as:

- Parent(s) recommend banning certain books from the library.

- Students confide in you that they are taking and selling drugs.

- Three members of your fifth-grade class ask your permission to have prayer every day in class.

- Two eleventh graders (boyfriend and girlfriend) ask your opinion of living together before marriage.

You may have more examples of real-life situations that may present themselves in the classroom. You will encounter many such classroom situations offering opportunities for moral discussions.

Facilitating the discussion of moral issues

Current events can provide opportunities for moral discussions. The political world offers many examples such as the illegal activities of political and religious leaders, and the treatment of minorities and human rights activists.

School curricula also provide many opportunities for moral discussions. Some of the topics in history, science, art, literature, and other subjects present very valuable moral dilemmas for classroom discussion. For example, in history, Gandhi's rebellion against the British rule in India, and in literature, the activities of Tom Sawyer and Huckleberry Finn provide excellent opportunities for discussion.

Current events provide opportunities for moral discussions.

TECHNOLOGY IN THE CLASSROOM

The educational demographics discussed in Chapter 1 outlining the characteristics of future U.S. students demonstrate the need for technology as a tool for addressing the moral development of students. First, on a national scale, how can future technology assist teachers with the social and moral development of students? Consider the following:

1. Software should be available in numerous languages.

2. Hardware should be developed that converts teacher instruction to various languages as per student needs. The United Nations has been doing this for more than three decades.

3. For one-parent households, future educational software should be developed for the home environment that emphasizes interaction with only the mother *or* father *or* foster parent.

4. Schools should continue to find ways to make educational technology available prior to and after normal school hours. If students of any socioeconomic level have the time and interest to use technology other than during school hours, it should be made available.

5. Few educational software vendors have attempted to address the social issues of contemporary and future students. Suppliers and vendors of future educational software must not shy away from such issues as drug addiction, dropouts, divorce, sex, and AIDS education. Such relevant software will be a tremendous asset, if not a necessity, for future teachers and students.

6. Hardware and software for "interactively" teaching the physically and mentally impaired must become a priority budget item in our nation's schools. Today, touch- and sight-sensitive monitors and adaptive input devices such as voice input could be invaluable teaching tools if available for use and equipped with appropriate software. Future hardware and software should adapt such innovations as holograms and three-dimensional simulations. Additionally, adaptive technology for the physically impaired should be designed to replace crutches, braces, and wheelchairs.

7. Interactive Distance Learning should continue to evolve as an integral part of our nation's elementary and secondary curriculum. Technology is now available to teach 'interactively' in the remotest rural or urban school classroom anywhere on the planet. Technology vividly illustrates that education can be delivered on a global basis. ■

RECAP OF MAJOR IDEAS

1. As students age and pass through levels of psychosocial development, their moral values change.

2. According to Erickson, adolescents often experience an identity crisis during puberty.

3. Individuals experience both positive and negative resolutions of conflict. A ratio of higher positive than negative resolutions is a prerequisite for healthy personality development.

4. According to Bronfenbrenner, the inherited traits of an individual, interacting with the individual's environment is instrumental to development.

5. As children mature, they become less egocentric.

6. Teacher behavior impacts the mental, moral, and social development of students.

7. Teachers are required by law to report suspected cases of student physical and sexual abuse.

8. Bullying and cyber-bullying are serious problems in the classroom environment.

9. A student's self-perception is often inaccurate.

10. As children mature, they should increasingly be able to see events from other persons' perspectives.

11. Teachers can help students develop interpersonal problem-solving skills.

12. Students' self-concepts, school success, and their achievement levels are closely related.

13. Models for teaching moral issues are available for teachers.

14. Real and simulated situations are useful in teaching moral issues.

15. When discussing values and moral issues, teachers should be careful not to impose their own personal values.

FURTHER APPLICATIONS

1. Student cheating is a perennial problem for teachers at all grade levels. Suppose you are administering a quiz and, although you have reminded students of their responsibility not to look on each other's papers, Janen, one of your best students, is openly allowing Toni to copy her answers. What would you do?

2. Teachers and positive classroom experiences can positively impact the emotional, social, and moral development of school-age young people. Consider the following classroom situations:

   a. You discover four of your ninth graders using the Internet to copy classroom assignments. What are your alternatives as a teacher?

   b. Your twelfth-grade history class wants to discuss religious history. You are aware that your students are diverse in their religious beliefs—Protestant, Catholic, Jewish, or agnostic—and you are not sure about some foreign students' religious beliefs. How will you handle the religious diversity of your students?

c. You have been asked to serve on a teacher committee charged with the responsibility of designing a course on "marriage and family planning for ninth graders." What would you recommend?

d. You are aware that certain students in your sixth-grade class are very popular, whereas others lack self-confidence and interpersonal skills. How can you, as a teacher, enhance the social skills of such students?

3. Students often become dissatisfied with school and begin the identity crisis all over again. To illustrate Marcia's four periods of identity, let's take a look at four typical teenagers:

a. Sonja, a junior in high school, is in Marcia's period of identity diffusion. She knows that her parents and teachers want her to be more serious about her life, but she is having too much fun with cheerleading, parties, and her friends to be concerned. During the past year, her school grades have dropped to C's and D's because she studies very little and she seems satisfied with her low grades. When her teachers question her about her low grades, her typical response is, "These are my last years in high school and I want to have fun. I'll get serious after high school—when I'm married or have a job."

b. Ramon is in Marcia's period of foreclosure. He studies hard and usually makes good grades. Like his older brother, he is in the school band. He is planning to attend the university where his older brother is enrolled. His parents are physicians, and Ramon plans to become an engineer. He attends church regularly with his family. Ramon plans to pursue pre-med at college.

c. Malcolm is in Marcia's period of moratorium. He is highly intelligent and popular. Malcolm's parents are both engineers, but he wants to be a musician, or perhaps a carpenter. He has taken music and carpentry classes in high school but changed to other classes because he didn't like the teachers. Last summer, he shaved his head and began smoking pot, to the despair of his parents. This summer, he plans to form a rock band and play at parties. He told his parents that if the band is successful he may quit school for a while and take the band on tour.

4. Theresa is in Marcia's stage of identity achievement. Although she was rather disorganized her first year of high school, she soon settled down and concentrated on her studies. Last summer, she took classes at the local community college and plans to enroll as a drama major at the state university after high school graduation. The local theater

group awarded her a scholarship and she plans to work part time to pay for the rest of her college tuition. She has been going steady with her boyfriend for 2 years but realizes that their relationship may have to be put on hold while she concentrates on her studies in college.

How would you, as a concerned teacher, advise these four teenagers? What would you recommend to their families? Compare your answers with those of your classmates.

KEY TERMS

psychosocial development

bioecological model of development

psychosocial value

resolution

trust versus mistrust

autonomy versus shame

will

initiative versus guilt

industry versus inferiority

competence

identity versus role confusion

identity crisis

identity confusion

intimacy versus isolation

generativity versus stagnation

ego integrity versus despair

wisdom

pubescence

puberty

menarche

crisis

commitment

diffusion

foreclosure

moratorium

achievement

social cognition and self-understanding

social knowledge

role and perspective taking

friendship

self-concept

self-esteem

Kohlberg's theory of moral development

preconventional morality

heteronomous morality

instrumental purpose

conventional morality

postconventional morality

social contract

universal and ethical principles

social convention

LOOKING AHEAD

This chapter discussed the emotional, social, and moral development of students. The theories studied will help you understand and hopefully predict students' classroom behavior. Chapter 4 discusses the social and academic issues in culturally diverse classrooms. ■

Part 2

How Student Differences Affect Teaching

Chapter 4

Cultural Diversity in the School Environment

LEARNING OBJECTIVES

Upon completing this chapter, you should be able to:

1

Name and describe four culturally diverse groups of students commonly found in today's classrooms.

2

Explain the racial and ethnic changes that will occur in the United States over the next two decades.

3

Identify four cultural influences currently impacting today's educational environment.

4

Explain *cultural discontinuity* and its significance for multicultural education.

5

Contrast *cultural assimilation* and *multicultural* education.

6

Compare and contrast the ethnic, racial, and economic differences often occurring between students and teachers.

7

Explain how poverty, gender differences, and prejudice impact the school environment.

8

Relate two methods teachers can use to make their classes culturally compatible for Hispanic American, African American, Asian American, and gifted minority students.

INTRODUCTION

"Education was free . . . it was the only thing my father was able to promise us when he sent for us; surer, safer than bread or shelter. On our second day I was thrilled with the realization of what this freedom of education meant. A little girl from across the alley came and offered to conduct us to school. My father was out, but we five, between us, had a few words of English by this time. We knew the word "school." We understood this child—who had never seen us until yesterday, who could not pronounce our names, who was not much better dressed than we—was able to offer us the freedom of the schools of Boston. No application made, no questions asked, no examinations, rulings, exclusions, no machinations, no fees. The doors stood open for everyone of us." (Mary Antin [1912, p. 186]; the child of European immigrants, about starting public school in Boston without being able to speak English).

In this chapter we use the term **diversity** to mean those human characteristics that have the potential to either enrich or limit a student's capacity to learn within the school environment. Some of the characteristics may refer to individuals; others may refer to groups. Diversity among students can provide teachers a catalyst for student learning, the development of relevant curricula, and an opportunity to expand teaching repertoires (Davidson & Phelan, 1993, p. 4). An excellent example of how such opportunities can be applicable to today's diverse classrooms is Ferriter's (2010) suggestion of requiring students to write their autobiographies then discuss and share with their peers.

STUDENT DIVERSITY: IMPLICATIONS FOR THE CLASSROOM TEACHER

As early as 1986, Harold Hodgkinson Demographic Projections predicted the student diversity we find in our classrooms today. More than thirty percent of students in the United States are minorities, and each of the nation's 24 largest city school systems has a minority majority. By 2020 more than two-thirds of all school age children will be African American, Hispanic, Asian or Native American (Drake, 1993; Steinberg, 2005). More than 5 million children of immigrants entered U.S. public schools between 2000 and 2010 (Children's Defense Fund, 2010). Let us review what was said in Chapter 1 about what this student diversity brings to the classroom:

- 4 million schoolchildren come from homes where English is not the first language.

- More than 150 languages are spoken in our nation's schools.

- In 7 states, 25 percent or more of students are language minorities.

> " America's call for excellence and equity cannot be answered except in a diverse and culturally rich environment. "
> DRAKE, 1993, P. 264

- In 2010, 75 percent of language-minority students were Hispanic and 1 in 6 U.S. residents were Hispanic (U. S. census, 2010).

This diverse population of students has well- defined **multiracial** and **multiethnic** attributes. While African Americans are lumped into a single racial grouping, they come from a diversity of cultural and social backgrounds. Puerto Ricans, Cubans and Mexicans are all labeled 'Hispanic' but are from very different cultures. This implies that teachers of today and tomorrow will not only have to be sensitive to "minority" needs but also to the cultural diversity found among minorities. Families and teachers are the key to the academic and social development of ulturally diverse students. However, creating the most favorable learning climate for culturally diverse students is a challenge. Todd is seeking a way to accomplish this.

Teachers must be aware of cultural diversity among students.

TODD WILLIAMS...

being African American himself, was very aware of the problems of student minorities. Several students from one particular class had approached Todd about minority and ethnic problems. Todd decided to take class time to discuss the issues that concerned these students. He wanted maximum class input and discussion, so he decided to solicit class input through a survey. Prior to class discussions, he had students respond to the following:

- When someone gets loud and obnoxious and that someone is a member of another ethnic or racial group, are you as tolerant of their behavior as you would be if that person were of your race or ethnicity?
- Do you have friends of different races and/or ethnic groups?

- Do you have friends who were born outside the United States?
- Do you have friends you consider prejudiced?
- When a crime is committed, do you usually suspect that the culprit is a member of a minority group even though there is no evidence to suggest this?
- When a person whose background differs from your own is caught committing a crime, do you often think, "That's the way those people always act"?
- When a member of your own race commits a crime, do you hope the culprit will avoid getting caught?
- Do you ever find yourself more critical of members of other groups for saying or doing things that you would ignore among members of your own group?

- Are you intolerant of people who find it difficult to speak your language?
- If your first language is English, have you ever said or thought, "This person deserves to be ignored until he or she learns to speak English and be an American."

Answers to such questions extend beyond ethnic and racial differences to include feelings toward members of the opposite sex, people of other religious faiths, people of wealth and poverty, and people from other geographic areas.

In the classroom, feelings of resentment, aggression, suspicion, and envy can inhibit learning and social growth. A major teacher goal is a classroom environment with a minimum of obstacles and disruptions. This requires teachers to establish and maintain a classroom atmosphere that encourages positive attitudes and relationships among students of all racial and cultural groups. This chapter is designed to help you succeed with the challenge of creating such positive relations among the many diverse students who will occupy your future classes. Consider the teaching of democracy by Mary Bicouvaris, former NEA national teacher of the year.

A Teacher's Class

For more than 25 years, Ms. Bicouvaris taught the values of democracy. Her dedication and service exemplified the importance of public education. She stressed the importance of voting by giving her students examples of countries whose citizens were denied the right to vote or to even voice their political opinions and political beliefs. She gave extra credit to students who worked on political campaigns for candidates of their choice.

During her tenure, Ms. Bicouvaris organized the school's model United Nations program to "expand students' horizons and give them a sense of America's place on the world stage."

Ms. Bicouvaris' ability to captivate students with stories was one of her teaching strengths. "The smartest students love story-telling," she stated. "The weakest ones worship it. You can be as stiff as you want as you teach about the Panama Canal or you can tell them a story and they will never forget."

Students were required to be active participants in Bicouvaris classroom. "I believe we must make greater efforts to prevent student failure." If a student failed to complete an assignment,

Bicouvaris entered a zero in her grade book but she would be looking for the assignment the next day. "I won't give up until I see the assignment," she explained. "This tells my students I'm not going to give up on them either."

Mary Bicouvaris says that the smartest students love storytelling and the weakest students worship it.

Springer (2009) and Lemke and Coughlin (2009) agree with Ms. Bicouvaris, stating that the digital age has now brought storytelling into mainstream classrooms. Students can now record, edit then tell, listen and share their storytelling with their peers. Let us continue our discussion of the role of the classroom in multicultural education. ■

Role of the School

Historically, Americans have viewed the role of the school as that of helping children of other cultures learn how to adjust or fit in with the American way of life. This process is called **assimilation**. The goal of assimilation is to enable the minority student to blend into the U.S. mainstream way of life. Another approach to addressing the needs of cultural groups is to help minority students honor their own cultures while learning to succeed in the culture of this country. As Janzen (1994, p. 10) explains, "Multiculturalism should not only develop appreciation for the perspectives of others, but should sustain a value—tolerant acceptance of diverse cultural understandings, belief systems, customs, and (perhaps) sociopolitical traditions."

Each generation has its own unique art, dress, values, and educational environment.

Which approach should our schools take, assimilation or multiculturalism? Perhaps a prerequisite question is; should schools do anything different in educating minority students? Proponents of multicultural education argue that we must offer special help to minority students. To fail to address this problem is to contribute to unemployment, poverty, and crime. Banks (1994, p. 4) argues,

> Our society has a lot to gain by restructuring institutions in ways that incorporate all citizens. People who now feel disenfranchised will become more effective and productive citizens, new perspectives will be added to the nation's mainstream institutions. The institutions themselves will then be transformed and enriched.

Let us begin by examining cultural diversity in addressing the question of assimilation or multiculturalism.

Culture

The attitudes, behaviors, and values of a group are collectively known as **culture**. Cultures differ from one group of people to another and, over time, many attributes of a culture change. For example, the 1950s, 80s, and 90s in America had their unique art, dress, and values. All societies and nationalities have cultures, and culture has many different attributes. It is the social glue that holds a society together.

Most societies have an established way of passing its values and customs from one generation to the next. Culture plays an important role, even in the most primitive societies. Often in primitive societies, the senior members spend time with the youth to ensure they develop the skills, attitudes, and values needed to become citizens who contribute positively to the good of their culture. In industrialized nations the family, schools, and religious institutions are the guardians and caretakers of this responsibility.

As we will see in Chapters 6 and 12, peer pressure and family environment can positively or negatively affect student academic achievement and social behavior. The classroom environment and the attitudes of teachers, peers, and families affect a student's motivation to interact socially and succeed academically. Clearly, students need to be aware and capable of coping with social changes in their lives (Bandura, 1986).

PROACTIVE EXERCISE

Suppose you are leading a class discussion on what should be planted in a time capsule that reflects their generation. What types of objects would best portray today's culture to a future generation? What criteria would you use to guide the selection of objects to put into the time capsule?

Cultural Discontinuity

From the moment of birth, children begin to learn about their environment. In the process, the child is also learning how to cope. Because the environment is continuously changing, individuals must continuously change and learn. Such learning by urban dwellers may be, to a degree different from rural folks. Northerners sometimes speak and behave differently than southerners. As we move from one part of the country or even from one part of town to another, often we find various ethnic and racial communities, each with its own set of values and expectations.

Family involvement is essential for maximum student achievement (Barton & Coley, 2009/2010); however, students who attend a school whose cultural

> " Race: A group of people who share common biological traits that are seen as self-defining by the people of the group.
>
> Minority group: A group of people who have been socially disadvantaged—not always a minority in actual numbers. "
> WOOLFOLK, 1995, P.165

climate differs significantly from that of their community, experience a unique set of challenges. Suddenly teachers and administrators have expectations that may be foreign to what such students have experienced at home or even in previous schools. This is especially true of immigrant students. Some of these expectations may conflict with past established personal values and behaviors. Environmental situations making conflicting behavioral expectations can produce a condition known as **cultural discontinuity**. Glatthorn (1993, p. 381) explains:

> The best way to think about these children and youth is not to consider them "disadvantaged" nor "culturally deprived," but to see them as individuals experiencing cultural discontinuity. As used by contemporary scholars, cultural discontinuity is the clash of two cultures: people with a particular set of cultural values and norms find themselves in an alien world with very different values and norms.

The differences among cultures and the degree they affect students vary. Students, especially young students are often not able to leave their personal lives outside the classroom (Duplechain, 2008). Teachers must recognize such differences in students' perspectives (Ball & Ferzani, 2011). For example, a student may come from a home environment where education is not a priority or where people outside the family unit are not to be trusted.

A common problem faced by members of some minority groups is lack of English skills. U.S. schools have a poor history of educating students in other languages; yet, most of the rest of the industrialized world is bilingual. Sizer (1992) recommends that students be proficient in a minimum of two languages. Some argue a second language interferes with one's native language, but there is no support for such a belief. In fact, (Ovando, 1994) and Bialystok, Majumder, and Martin (2003) report that bilingualism increases cognitive functioning and creativity. Students who learn a second language, at any age, appear to gain a better understanding of the printed word and the rules of grammar.

CULTURAL DIFFERENCES BETWEEN STUDENTS AND TEACHERS

In this country, teaching has a history of being a profession white middle-class citizens choose as a career (Ducette, Sewell, & Shapiro, 1996). As illustrated by Table 4.1, even today the teaching profession remains a profession dominated by middle-class white European-American teachers. In 1971 and 1994

In the United States, there are often significant cultural, ethnic and racial differences between teachers and students.

Today's students face many problems that are causes for concern, among them are poverty, gender bias, and ethnic and racial discrimination.

respectively, women made up 66 and 73 percent of teachers in public elementary and secondary schools, and 88 and 87 percent were non-Hispanic whites. Between 1971 and 1994, the total number of these teachers increased 25 percent. Yet, throughout the past four generations, the student population has become increasingly minority. During the twenty-first century, the majority of the population of this country will be people of color with non-English-speaking backgrounds and many with low incomes (Gomez & Smith, 1991). Additionally, the school environment has other major cultural diversity differences. Unfortunately, today's teachers and students face many problems that are causes for concern, among them are poverty, gender bias, and ethnic and racial discrimination.

CAUSES FOR CONCERN

Poverty among Students

At the same time ethnic and racial differences between students and teachers are increasing, students are bringing other problems to the classroom environment, impacting their learning, including poverty (LeRoy & Symes, 2001). Poverty among children (as noted in Chapter 1) can have a devastating effect on learning. The by-products of poverty, such as malnourishment, homelessness, inadequate opportunities, and an impoverished view of self can be devastating to anyone, especially school-age children. Neuro-scientists have found that stress brought on by living in poverty can impair language development and memory (Krugman, 2008). By the end of fourth grade, impoverished students of all races are typically two years behind their peers in both reading and math achievement (Rebell, 2008). The United States has the highest rate of poverty among children of all developed countries. Today, more than one in five children lives in poverty (Poverty is defined as a family of four with an annual income of less than $25,000) (U.S. Department of Health and Human Services, 2010). Those figures increase among Hispanic American and African American children; approximately 36 percent and 44 percent, respectively, live in poverty.

Characteristics of Impoverished Students

- High Mobility—Students who live in poverty may live in places that rent by the day or week, or live in a homeless shelter, or are homeless.

Moving often may be a necessity; looking for work or escaping an abusive parent.

- Attendance is irregular—Frequent absenteeism is often a problem with highly mobile students. Additionally, teachers often have limited access to achievement level resources.

- School Behavior—The behavior of impoverished students can range from hostility and aggression to subdued and withdrawn. Their behavior is dictated by their treatment in their family structure.

- Academic behavior—Their academic behavior is often characterized by failing to complete academic tasks, lack of interest and motivation. **However, it is important to note that many students from impoverished backgrounds are excellent students**. Many impoverished students have the talent and resilience to succeed, but too often, that is not the case. The attributes of poverty are powerful distracters to academic success (Haycook, 2001).

TABLE 4.1					
Selected Characteristics of Public School Teachers from Spring 1961 to Spring 2011					
	1961	**1971**	**1981**	**1991**	**2001**	**2011 (Projected)**
Number of teachers (thousands)	1,408	2,055	2,185	2,398	2,681	2,988
Sex (%)						
Men	31.3	34.3	33.1	27.9	26.0	23.9
Women	68.7	65.7	66.9	72.1	74.0	76.1
Race (%)						
White	-	88.3	91.6	86.8	86.1	84.0
Black	-	8.1	7.8	8.0	7.8	8.1
Hispanic	-	-	-	-	4.4	4.6
Other	-	3.6	0.7	5.2	1.7	3.3

SOURCES: National Education Association. *Status of the American Public School Teacher, 1990–2011*, and *Mini-Digest of Education Statistics, 1995*.

Compare Table 4.1 percentages with the U.S. population percentages in Table 4.2.

TABLE 4.2	
U. S. Population Percentages – 2010	
Race	**Percent**
Caucasian	63.7
African American	12.6
Hispanic	18.3
Asian	4.8
*Other	6
*(Native American, Native Hawaiian, Pacific Islander)	

U. S. Census, 2010

Consider the following suggestions for teachers who have students living in poverty.

PROACTIVE TEACHING

CLASSROOM SITUATION

Many of your students come from impoverished backgrounds.

PROACTIVE ALTERNATIVES

- Take advantage of preschool and afterschool programs, and advise families of such programs.
- Arrange tutorial programs for students in need, especially with a friend or peer.
- Check with family/teacher organizations, school counselors, and school psychologists for information on community resources available for students from such backgrounds.
- Encourage families to get involved in family- related school activities.
- As with all your students, be alert to their academic skills and talents, including athletics.
- Acquaint yourself with breakfast and lunch programs for such students. Your school counselor, fellow teachers, or

principal can advise. Other programs providing school materials may be available. If no such programs exist, don't hesitate to be an advocate. Often, family/teacher organizations are a good place to start.

· In today's classrooms, a sense of respect must include honoring the differences among students (Black & Toreilo, 2012). A study of several teachers who were highly successful, although they taught in poorly-performing urban schools (Poplin et al., 2011) found these teachers had a profound respect for their students.

Gender Bias in the Classroom

Another cause for concern is the gender inequity that exists in many school environments. Repeatedly, the National Assessment of Educational Progress (NAEP) exam finds that girls perform better than boys on reading tasks, and boys perform better than girls in math (US Department of Education, 2005). These differences have appeared repeatedly on every annual NAEP exam that has been given. The Program for International Student Assessment (PISA) (Else-Quest, Hyde, & Linn, 2010) reports similar gender gaps. On the NAEP tests given to third graders, 20 percent of the girls outscore boys in reading. By eighth grade, this gap has increased to 38 percent. By high school, the math gap increased to 47 percent. During the 1990's, gender inequity had become such a concern that the Association for Supervision and Curriculum Development declared it a national problem (Sears, 1993). Examine the following "Kindergarten Awards."

> " While sex refers to biological differences, gender refers to judgments about masculinity and femininity. "
> DEAUX, 1993

Kindergarten Awards	
Boys' Awards	**Girls' Awards**
Very Best Thinker	All-Around Sweetheart
Most Eager Learner	Sweetest Personality
Most Imaginative	Cutest Personality
Most Scientific	Biggest Heart

This awards list appeared in a *Wall Street Journal* report about a kindergarten graduation in June of 1994 (Divan, 1994). According to Freeman and Boutte (1996, p. 24), "Even in the 90s, schools rewarded boys for being energetic, clever students and girls for being attractive and sociable friends."

When students begin preschool at age 4 or 5, boys are developmentally behind their female peers (Streitmatter, 1994). At this age, girls are better at speaking, reading, and counting. Traits such as competition, problem solving, and achievement for boys and caretaking skills, socialization, and supportive behavior for girls are reinforced by both families and teachers (Jewett, 1996). According to Jewett, developmental psychologists find few differences in the behavior of infant boys and girls, but families interact and raise them differently.

Despite the fact that boys and girls are typically educated together from preschool to secondary school graduation, they do not enter postsecondary schooling with equal educational benefits (Freeman & Boutte, 1996). In the late 1990s the average science proficiency for boys and girls age 9 was approximately the same, but by age 13 a performance gap, favoring boys, becomes evident (Blake, 1993). Many educational psychologists believe the differences stem from what girls are taught, academically and socially, by parents, peers, and teachers.

However, during the past decade, as females have become much more involved in the "hard sciences" the gender gaps on the SAT and on other achievement scores have been diminishing. Males continue to score higher than females on tests of general knowledge and mechanical reasoning. Females score higher on language skills, including reading and writing (ETS, 2008). Although females typically mature earlier than males and are ready for such skills as math and verbal skills at a younger age, too often school curricula are not designed to meet the needs of these gender differences.

Neuroscientist Lise Eliot (2010), who is an expert on gender differences in children's brains, says that neuroscientists have identified very few reliable differences between boys' and girls' brains. But, according to Eliot, PISA scores show that female math performance also correlates with gender equity, from country to country. She concludes that "No mental ability or ability difference is "hardwired" into the brain" (p. 33). Rather, mental abilities grow out of socio-cultures.

Eliot states the gaps can be traced back to childhood, when boys played with more active toys (like trucks and balls) and girls played with verbal-relational toys, like dolls. She concludes

> In the past 15 years, claims about hardwired differences between boys and girls have propagated virally, with no genuine neuroscientific justification. In reality, culture, attitudes, and practices influence boy-girl academic gaps far more than prenatal testosterone does.

The sooner teachers open their eyes to such influences, the sooner we can bring out the best in every child. (p. 36)

In March 2010, the Center on Educational Policy examined state test scores from all age groups in all 50 states and found girls are doing as well as boys in mathematics but boys' reading scores still lag behind girls' scores by over 10 percent (Chudowsky & Chudowsky, 2010).

INTASC Standard 2   **Learning differences**

Ethnic and Racial Issues

An **ethnic group** is people who share a similar culture. Sharing a similar culture means sharing an environment with a unique history, community behavior, beliefs and sometimes language. Within **racial groups**, people share biological traits, such as hair and skin color (Betancourt & Lobez, 1993). Often an individual's ethnicity and race overlap but because ethnicity is environmentally determined while race is based on heredity, in today's educational environment they can be very different. Our society and school population have become a mix of ethnicity and race. In addition, adoptions and marriage between races and ethnic groups have resulted in a rich 'melting pot' in our society and schools. In 1954, "separate but equal" schools for African American children were ruled unconstitutional and inherently unequal by the U.S. Supreme Court in *Brown vs. The Board of Education of Topeka*. However, segregation and racial discrimination remain serious problems in American education. Furthermore, African American students attend more segregated schools than Caucasian students, and Latinos are more likely than African Americans to attend segregated schools (Gandara, 2011). In 2005–06, more than 60 percent of Latinos living in urban areas in the Western U.S. attended schools that were 90–100 percent non-white (Orfield & Frankenberg, 2008).

Minority students are also segregated within schools, a practice with the same disadvantages of inter-school segregation (Gandara, 2011). Although the increase in education and salaries of Latino families should have closed the gender gap, the practice of increased segregation has cancelled out most of those gains (Berends & Penaloza, 2010).

Decades of research on desegregation demonstrates integration is not a cure-all for abolishing prejudice and racial inequality or for providing equal opportunity for education (Schofield, 1991). More than six decades have passed since segregation became illegal in our country, yet today approximately two-thirds of African American students attend schools where "minorities" make up 50 percent or more of the student body.

As early as 1992, Garibaldi provided an excellent example of the failure of our school system and society to address the problems facing African

American students. She chaired a task force of community leaders and educators whose charge was to review the status of African American males in the public city schools of New Orleans. The committee found the following:

- In an urban school system where 87 percent of the 86,000 students are African American, African American males account for 58 percent of non-promotions, 65 percent of suspensions, 80 percent of expulsions, and 45 percent of the dropouts—even though they represent only 43 percent of the school population.

- African American females fared somewhat better, but data suggest alarming trends. These young women represent 44 percent of the school population but accounted for 34 percent of non-promotions, 29 percent of suspensions, 20 percent of expulsions, and 41 percent of the dropouts.

- More than 800 of the 1,470 non-promotions in the first grade and more than 1,600 of the 2,800 non-promotions in the sixth through eighth grades were African American males. (p. 5)

Unfortunately, New Orleans is not an isolated case. Since Garibaldi's report, Prince George County, Maryland, and Milwaukee, Wisconsin, have reported similar findings on the academic and social status of African American students.

It is important to point out that the vast majority of students of all races and ethnic groups want to be successful in their academic endeavors (Carter & Wilson, 1991). Further, note that *achievement*, however measured, academically or socially, relates not to race, color, or ethnic grouping but to socioeconomic status (Gleitman, 1991).

He compared students from different ethnic and racial groups at the same socioeconomic level and found no significant differences in achievement level.

Sex and Sexual Identity Issues in the Classroom Environment

Consider the following:

- By age 16, more than 60 percent of boys and 40 percent of girls have experienced sexual intercourse. More than 30 percent of teenagers, age 16 and above report to being sexually active.

- Four children in ten, born in the U. S. are born to unmarried parents.

- One in twenty adolescents define themselves as gay or lesbian (attracted to same-sex partners) (Steinberg, 2005).

Teachers who teach adolescents will inevitably face some of the issues listed above. Teachers must be aware of school policy and legal liability concerning such issues. School counselors and school psychologists are good resources for such information and referral. Table 4.3 offers some guidelines.

Issue	Teacher Options
Pregnancy	1. Be supportive and a willing listener. As with any student, often just allowing them to discuss issues they are dealing with in their lives can be helpful. A tactful referral to a professional is not a dismissal of responsibility and may be best for the student.
	2. Require student to perform academically as any other student.
	3. Physical activities should not be required. Be aware of emergency procedures and personnel and how to contact the student's family.
	4. Inappropriate comments and teasing from other students should not be tolerated.
Abortion & birth control	1. It is imperative you be aware of school policy concerning advising or discussing with any student the issues of birth control and abortion.
	2. Repeating; be proactive and seek out advice on appropriate action from other school professionals.
	3. Do encourage student to stay in school as long as possible. Include family of student in discussions of such issues.
Gay & lesbian issues	1. Be supportive and a willing listener. Again, a tactful referral may be the best for the student.
	2. Require student to perform academically as any other student.
	3. Focus of setting aside biases you may have on such student issues while concentrating on their academic, social and emotional well being.
	4. Harassment, verbal or physical, should not be tolerated and dealt with immediately.
	5. As with all your students with any issue, follow-up is very important.

How should teachers address challenges created by such issues as minority status, language barriers, poverty, gender, and student sexual issues? The remainder of the chapter discusses options for teachers.

Former first lady Hillary R. Clinton created a controversy during 1996 with her book and statement of belief that "It takes a village to raise a child." Do you agree or disagree? What implications does this have for the school environment?

Instructor Manual

INTASC Standard 2   Learning differences

Fostering Culturally and Socially Compatible Classrooms

An adage in real estate says there are three factors determining the value of property: (1) location, (2) location, and (3) location. Most educational psychologists would agree that the problems of our educational system and our society discussed in this chapter (racial injustice, sex discrimination, immigration, and language differences) should be addressed by three things: (1) family and education, (2) family and education, and (3) family and education. Educational psychologists tell us that for education to be successful parents, community, government, teachers, and students must be active, viable participants. As you continue reading, note how often this theme repeats itself.

Boutte and McCormick (1992) say that understanding, respecting, and teaching your students are the keys to creating **culturally and socially compatible class rooms**. They stress the following;

- All students are similar in that they have the same basic needs such as water, food, shelter, respect, and love.

- Different groups fulfill some of these needs in different ways (different types of houses, religions, diets, and so on). Thus, similarities and differences can be assets in the classroom.

Boutte and McCormick recommend the following as basic components for enhancing the cultural and social environment in classrooms:

- *Modeling by teachers*. If teachers demonstrate that they value persons of differing characteristics and backgrounds, children will sense and emulate this attitude.

- *Curricular inclusion of multicultural heritage*. The curriculum should include customs, music, art, and literature representing various cultures. For example, not all students celebrate Christmas. Some students celebrate Kwanzaa, Hanukkah, and other holidays.

- *Multicultural literature*. Teachers should use literature featuring gender diversity and children with differing racial characteristics and home environments.

- *Multicultural experiences*. By supplementing the curriculum with colloquial and non-English expressions, the teacher can teach students the value of language diversity. Bialystok, Majumder, & Martin (2003) report that bilingualism correlates with increased cognitive abilities in concept formation, creativity, cognitive flexibility and a better understanding of how language works. This is especially true in early childhood.

- *Resource persons from different cultures.* Teachers should take advantage of the varying ethnic and cultural backgrounds within the community. Willing parents and other members of the community can be invited to class to share their cultures.

MOTIVATING STUDENTS OF VARIOUS CULTURAL GROUPS

As you read these suggestions, remember that while school should adapt to learner culture and backgrounds, there is danger in overgeneralizing about cultural effects. Such generalizations can lead to stereotyping students from different backgrounds. For example Hawley and Nieto (2010), caution that "Students of color are often more dependent on school for learning how to learn than are more economically advantaged students who may have more varied learning opportunities" (p. 68).

Hispanic American Students

Hispanic students are characterized by a sense of loyalty to family and friends, value harmony in interpersonal relationships, and are respectful of those in authority (Garcia, 1992). They tend to prefer activities where they can achieve academic and social goals in cooperation with others rather than in competition with others. They also value role models (Vasquez, 1990). Therefore, teachers of Hispanic students should stress group activities, involve families, and provide role models.

A Teacher's Class

Consider the family issues raised in Rachel Moreno's class. Ms. Moreno is a former 'Teacher of the Year' in Arizona. In Ms. Moreno's Spanish classes at Flowing Wells High School outside Tucson, Arizona, every student has three "primos" (cousins).

Together they form a "familia." Familia members, Ms. Moreno says, "sit together, rejoice together, and support one another." Ms. Moreno believes that kids learn better with a support system.

The focus on "la familia" is a reverberation from Ms. Moreno's earlier career teaching "Home Economics." She now teaches Spanish.

"Home economics focuses on the family, plus I can't stand a classroom where the kids don't know one another," she explains.

"If I touch kids' hearts in some way," she adds, "then I'm doing what I'm supposed to. And they, in their turn, will do something similar for someone else."

To teach Spanish culture as well as language to her mostly non-Hispanic students, Ms. Moreno uses an activity-based cultural approach. The biggest activity is a two-way student exchange with a Mexican community in the state of Sonora.

Every spring, 40 Flowing Wells students go to Sonora for a 4-day exchange. They stay with families in five villages where the children attend a vocational agriculture school. Two weeks later, the Mexican students come to Arizona.

"La familia" is a theme in Sonora, too. "For some of my students, their Mexican family is the most real family they've seen in a long time," Ms. Moreno says. "And they don't want to leave it."

Moreno's cultural emphasis has shifted a bit from Mexican and Mexican-American to Spanish. She was honored with a trip to Spain as a recipient of a 'King Juan Carlos Fellowship' honoring the Quincentennial of the Kingdom of Spain. ■

Role models can have a dramatic impact on the academic success of students.

African American Students

Garibaldi (1992) offers a very logical formula for teaching African American students.

> When we publicly recognize the successful academic experiences of young African American students, we simultaneously raise their self-concept, self-esteem, and academic confidence. (p. 7)

First, African American students, like all other students, can succeed. Through appropriate feedback, families and teachers must motivate their children and students to engage in behaviors that lead to academic success. Teacher-family interaction can be very important to the academic success of students. As with all ethnic and racial groups, teacher-family interaction is critical to the success of African American students (Barton & Coley, 2009). In addition, Pressley, Raphael, Gallagher, and DiBella (2004) and Garibaldi (1992) suggest the following:

- Encourage African American students, like all other students, to resist peer pressure when it is detrimental to academic success.

- Systematic motivation should be paired with high expectations.

- Modeling is important. Try to recruit African American college students as tutors, speakers and teacher aids for your students. As role models, they can have a positive impact on the academic and social behavior of elementary and secondary students.

- Foster team activities and cooperative learning paired with praised for accomplishments.

- Beginning in the earliest grades, enlist families to encourage their children to pursue college and postsecondary education.

Getting families of students involved with schools is a difficult challenge, yet well worth the efforts. Their reluctance is often the inability to speak English, poverty, and/or low education levels. Fewer than half of Latino mothers in the United States are high school graduates (Hawley & Nieto, 2010), leaving many feeling estranged and unwelcome. Often this tendency to stay away from school is misinterpreted as a lack of caring. But, according to Hawly and Nieto, "In fact, in general, African American, Latino, American Indian, and Pacific Island families have a great deal of respect for education and view it as the best way out of poverty and hopelessness (p. 71).

Technology can help. Donna DeGennaro (2010) explains how through a program titled "Tech Goes Home" the city of Boston has provided computers to over 5,000 poor families in 43 Boston schools. Each family must attend 25 hours of classes, after which it can purchase the computer for $50. The students get rigorous training and, in turn, teach their family members additional skills. Through this process, families are becoming computer-wise and are expanding their knowledge of the world while also becoming familiar with their schools. Each family has an email account, enabling family members to talk to their child's teacher anytime and keep up with how their child is doing in school. Participating in this program jumpstarts parent-student discussions on the student's schoolwork. Additional information about the Tech Goes Home Program can be found at http://tgh.lgfnet.org.

Asian American Students

Little research is available on the learning styles of Asian American students, partly because of the perception of their academic success (Caplan, Choy, & Whitmore, 1992). The perception that Asian American students are successful in school is not without empirical evidence. Caplan and his associates surveyed Asian American families in five urban areas: Orange County, California; Seattle; Houston; Chicago; and Boston. Examining the academic success of Asian American children, they found that

- Asian American students' mean GPA was 3.05 on a 4.0 scale.
- 27 percent had a GPA in the "A" range.
- 52 percent had a GPA in the "B" range.
- 17 percent had a GPA in the "C" range.
- Only 4 percent had a GPA below a "C" range.

Even more striking were their math scores. Almost 50 percent earned A's in math; another third earned B's. This means that four out of five Asian American students earned an A or a B in math.

Caplan, Choy, and Whitmore (1992) and Chen and Stevenson (1995) attribute the success of Asian American students to their families, who place a very high value on education and hold high expectations on their children. For example, Caplan and colleagues found that homework for Asian American children was often a family event. Parents and children typically gather at a table and work together until homework assignments are completed. This suggests that teachers working with Asian American students should encourage such values and work to establish a good relationship with these students' families (as with all students).

However, Yee (1992) cautions that not all Asian American students are outstanding, hardworking model students, and stereotypes suggesting they are can be very detrimental to their academic and social development.

Gifted Minority Students

The study by Caplan, Choy, and Whitmore emphasized a very important point concerning minority students. Giftedness presents a source of diversity in the classroom (Ducette et al., 1996). Teachers can serve these students better by shifting their focus from "being gifted" to "the development of gifted behaviors" (Renzulli & Reis, 1991). Many minority students and students considered "at-risk" are academically and socially gifted. Yet, many are living below the poverty level, having language barriers, have immigrated from Third World countries, and have experienced prejudice throughout their life (Harris, 1991). Harris recommends the following in addressing the needs of gifted minorities:

- Provide limited English proficiency students who are perceived as "not ready" for gifted programs some form of linguistic enrichment until their language skills become proficient. For example, you might institute "research" activities with the students, using books in their native language. Explain the concept of gifted programs to the families of gifted students.

- When possible, involve outreach workers familiar with and have the language skills for the particular minority culture. The use of peers is often successful in communicating with families fearful of school authority.

- Place and identify gifted minorities according to educational background, potential, and academic success rather than chronological age.

- Ensure the evaluator who screens and selects gifted minorities has the cultural knowledge and testing skills to appropriately evaluate.

TEXTBOOK AND TEACHING MATERIAL BIAS

In this country, prior to the 1920s, textbook authors largely ignored minority groups (Garcia, 1993). Once they began including minorities, many portrayed them in ways that promoted and magnified stereotypes. Once educators became sensitive to the effect textbooks were having on the ways this affected minorities and on how other students perceive minorities, efforts were made to produce multicultural materials designed to reverse bias and stereotypes.

Garcia and Garcia (1980, 1993) developed a system for classifying multicultural materials designed to promote more positive images of minority groups. As you examine the four levels of materials, note the methods the creators suggest teachers use each level of materials.

- *Level I Materials.* These are relatively simplistic materials designed to portray the achievements of ethnic groups. These materials often lack credibility because they sometimes exaggerate. (Garcia and Garcia, 1993) recommend that teachers use their discretion and use these materials sparingly.

- *Level II Materials.* These depict authentic or true experiences of ethnic and racial groups. However, they often blame the mainstream population for minorities' problems. The Garcias caution teachers against overuse of such materials.

- *Level III Materials.* These give the historical experiences of several minority groups and then focus on one of these groups. Although there is usually more variance in behaviors within a culture than between two cultures, Level III materials often fail to show the behaviors and experiences common to more than one group. Teachers are also cautioned to limit the use of these materials.

- *Level IV Materials.* These are the most complex materials and are designed around broad content generalizations. Unlike the other levels, materials on this level identify experiences common to several groups. Unlike other materials that give overly simplistic conclusions, these materials require students to critically analyze content.

Incorporating multiculturalism into lessons is an excellent way to positively address tolerance. Ebron and Lamb (1995, p. 91) describes one program that successfully showcases diversity as an asset.

> Nappy hair, milky-white skin and almond-shaped eyes attract the attention and curiosity of children as young as 3 years old. How kids interpret these differences depends upon the meaning families and teachers attach to them.

A tool today's educators are using to foster open-mindedness is the award-winning "Teaching Tolerance" material, developed by the Southern Poverty Law Center in Montgomery, Alabama. Materials include video kits on topics such as the Civil Rights movement and a semiannual magazine that profiles multicultural innovations like La Escuela Fratney, a Milwaukee school whose 380 pupils learn the three R's in Spanish and English on alternate days.

> The material goes beyond race and ethnicity, dealing with gender, sexual orientation, ageism, religion and physical disabilities as well". As the program's implementer, Rita Tenorio, points out, "It's a good way for students to understand differences."

The following is a list of resources for textbook and other multicultural materials:

> The National Assessment and Dissemination Center for Bilingual Bicultural Education (385 High St., Fall River, MA 02720) has Spanish, Portuguese, Asian, Native American, Greek, Italian, and French materials.

> The Dissemination Center for Bilingual/Bicultural Education (6504 Tracor Lane, Austin, TX 78721) has Spanish, Navajo, Portuguese, and French materials. Another center funded by the National Institute of Education (NIE) and the Educational Products Exchange Institute (EPIE) has published informative volumes (EPIE Institute, 453 West St., New York, NY 10014).

> *Child of UNICEF*. Eight children, each from a different country, tell of their experiences with UNICEF in separate booklets.

> *Africa: An Annotated List of Printed Materials Suitable for Children*, Information Center on Children's Cultures, United States Committee for UNICEF, 331 East 38th St., New York, NY

10016. An evaluation of all in-point English-language materials for children on the subject of Africa.

The Proactive Teaching box suggests alternatives for facilitating multiculturalism in the classroom.

PROACTIVE TEACHING

CLASSROOM SITUATION	PROACTIVE ALTERNATIVES
· Prior to the start of the school year, your class rolls suggest that you will be teaching a culturally diverse class. You view your class diversity as an academic and social asset. At the beginning of the school year, what activities could you use to facilitate your students viewing class diversity as a learning experience?	· Prepare to use role models from the community who reflect the diversity of the class. For example, an African American MD, a Hispanic teacher or a successful business woman would demonstrate opportunities across groups. · Plan activities that positively display the diversity and similarities of your students. For example, compare students' differences and similarities—an African American, a Hispanic, and an Asian all are members of the same school, the same classroom, like to "text," and think Lebron James is the greatest.

New Discoveries Lead Scientists to Rethink Racial Differences

Thanks to spectacular advances in molecular biology and genetics, most scientists now reject the concept of race as a valid way to divide human beings into separate groups.

Contrary to widespread public opinion, researchers no longer believe races are distinct biological categories created by differences in the genes that people inherit from their parents. Genes vary, they say, but not in ways that correspond to the popular notion of black, white, yellow, red or brown races.

"Race has no basic biological reality," said Jonathan Marks, a Yale University biologist. "The human species simply doesn't come packaged that way."

Instead, a majority of biologists and anthropologists, drawing on a growing body of evidence accumulated since the 1970s, has concluded that race is a social, cultural, and political concept based largely on superficial appearances.

"In the social sense, race is a reality; in the scientific sense, it is not," said Michael Omi, a specialist in ethnic studies at the University of California in Berkeley.

Luigi Cavalli-Sforza, an eminent professor of genetics at Stanford University, agreed. "The characteristics that we see with the naked eye that help us to distinguish individuals from different continents are, in reality, skin-deep," he said. "Whenever we look under the veneer, we find that the differences that seem so conspicuous to us are really trivial."

Scientists concede that people do look different, primarily because of the varied environments in which their ancestors lived. And they agree that as a social concept, race matters a great deal. The color of a person's skin, the texture of his hair, or the shape of her eyes can be sources of love, pride and partnership—or fear, hatred, and injustice.

The idea that races are not the product of human genes may seem to contradict common sense.

"The average citizen reacts with frank disbelief when told there is no such thing as race," said C. Loring Brace, an anthropologist at the University of Michigan. "The skeptical layman will shake his head and regard this as further evidence of the innate silliness of those who call themselves intellectuals."

The new understanding of race draws on work in many fields.

"Vast new data in human biology, prehistory and paleontology have completely revamped the traditional notions," said Solomon Katz, an anthropologist at the University of Pennsylvania.

This is a switch from the prevailing scientific dogma of the 19th and much of the 20th century. During that period, most scientists believed that humans could be sorted into a few inherited racial types (Boyd, 1996, *Ashville Citizen Times*).

A SUGGESTED BEGINNING

Teachers have many options as they plan to prepare to address the diversity they will face in their classrooms. Let us reiterate our opening chapter comments. We view diversity as an opportunity teachers have to capitalize on the differences among their students. Gullnick and Chinn (1994) offer the following suggestions:

- Place students, regardless race or ethnicity, at the center of the teaching and learning process.

- Promote human rights and respect for cultural differences.

- Assume all students can learn.

- Acknowledge and build on the life histories and experiences of students' micro-cultural memberships.

- Critically analyze oppression and power relationships to understand racism, sexism, classism, and discrimination against the disabled, young, and aged.

- Use current events to discuss society, social justice and equality.

These efforts engage the teacher with the elements of diversity, and engagement is a good starting point. Because teachers are role models, such efforts demonstrate to students the teacher's confidence and commitment to the development of the potential of students regardless of background. There is good news: efforts to reduce social inequities between minority and mainstream students have been working. Differences in the scholastic achievement (SAT) scores between mainstream students and African American students have declined and since The National Assessment of Educational Progress (NAEP) has been in use, these differences have been cut in half. A Los Angeles teacher discovered an effective way to mentally and physically engage poor-performing students in classroom discussions. Before weighing in on controversial discussions, her students were required to preface their comments by referencing the previous speaker's comments. This encouraged them to listen more carefully to their classmates (Poplin et al., 2011).

Teachers can also use the arts to demonstrate to students more about the cultures represented in the classroom. While increasing cultural awareness, a study of Harlem renaissance that made connections with street murals supported student academic achievement (Bode & Fenner, 2010).

TECHNOLOGY IN THE CLASSROOM

A VIEW FROM THE FIELD

PROFILE

Dr. Tammy Graham is an Assistant Professor of Education at The Citadel, where she teaches courses related to special education and educational psychology. Her research interests include differentiated instruction, college students with disabilities, and teacher efficacy and attitudes. She earned her Ed.D. in Educational Leadership from Cambridge College. She also holds degrees in special education administration, mild learning handicaps, and learning disabilities. Dr. Graham is

co-author of a book chapter on e-learning. Additionally, she has presented in conferences sponsored by the American Educational Research Association; the Learning Disabilities Association of America; and the Council of Exceptional Children, Teacher Education Division.

QUESTION: How can teachers use the current knowledge base on various cultures to create effective learning environments for these students?

Dr. Graham Teaching about student differences is one of my favorite activities. As a child, I sometimes witnessed others inaccurately judge my father's intelligence level due to his dialect. These experiences awakened a desire in me to teach the importance of respecting various cultures and the value of getting to know students as individuals. Public schools continue to increase in diversity, and teachers and their students often come from different cultural backgrounds. As a result, young learners may enter kindergarten with norms and values that are different than those stressed by the school. If we ignore these differences, we may limit our abilities to form personal connections with our students, which may impede their education.

It is imperative that teachers show students they care about them as individuals by taking time to learn about their backgrounds. Additionally, it is essential that teachers model an appreciation for all cultures, foster a community of respect in their classrooms, and teach tolerance for differences. Furthermore, varying teaching styles to meet all learners' needs, incorporating opportunities for cooperative learning activities, integrating information and examples from various cultures into lessons, and having high expectations for all students should be the norm rather than the exception. ■

SURFING • THE • WEB

An abundance of information is available on the web concerning student diversity in the classroom. The following are excellent resources:

1. The website for the National Clearinghouse for Bilingual Education (**http://www.ncbe.gwu.edu**)

2. The website for "The Globe Program (Global Learning and Observations to Benefit the Environment)" (**http://globe.fsl.noaa.gov/**)

3. "Countries Where Volunteers Serve." Divided by regions (Africa, Interamerica, Asia-Pacific, and Eastern Europe and the Mediterranean), the country profiles and links to other Internet resources about each country are available, (**http://www.peacecorps.gov/www/io/Countryl.html**) ■

Resources

Althelstan

P.O. Box 802; La Jolla, Calif. 92038; (619) 689–1757

Publishes a free quarterly on technology and language learning; a yearbook provides updated lists of vendors that produce technology-based language learning products.

TESOL

1600 Cameron, Alexandria, Va. 22314

Publishes *CALL* (Computer Assisted Language Learning) *Interest Section Software List*, an annual booklet that lists software used by ESL (English as a Second Language) teachers. Groups programs according to language skill area.

RECAP OF MAJOR IDEAS

1. Within the classroom environment, teacher and student diversity can either enrich or limit learning.

2. American expectations of minorities have shifted from demanding they drop their customs to having schools help minorities take pride in their heritage.

3. Often more differences can be found within cultures than among cultures.

4. Minority students sometimes face conflicting expectations at school and with peers.

5. Even though the percentage of minority students has rapidly increased, the percentage of minority teachers has not.

6. Gender inequity became a major concern in the 1990s and continues today.

7. Respecting all students is an important factor in establishing multicultural classrooms.

8. Gifted students come from all ethnic and cultural backgrounds.

9. Fostering multicultural classrooms begins by teachers believing in the potential of all students.

FURTHER APPLICATIONS

1. What do the following have in common?

    a. Dr. Charles Drew

    b. Frederick Jones

    c. Otis Boykin

    d. Granville T. Woods

    Answer: They were all inventors, and they were all African American.

    a. Dr. Charles Drew developed ways of preserving blood plasma.

    b. Frederick Jones invented the portable X-ray machine, truck refrigerator systems, and the self-starting gasoline motor.

    c. Otis Boykin invented the control unit used in the pacemaker, chemical air filters, and many other electronic devices.

    d. Granville T. Woods invented the electric incubator, the automatic air brake, and the telephone receiver.

    Compile a list of Hispanic American and Asian American artists and/or inventors to provide examples of role models for future culturally diverse students.

2. Develop a list of activities you would like to use to familiarize your future students with the scientific and social contributions of various minority cultural groups. These might include assignments featuring the contributions of different groups in the fields of:

    a. Teaching

    b. Philanthropy

    c. Medicine

    d. Government

KEY TERMS

diversity	cultural discontinuity
assimilation	culturally compatible classrooms
culture	holistic academic atmosphere
ethnicity	socially gifted
race	multicultural materials
minority group	

LOOKING AHEAD

This chapter examined the concerns and potential of culturally diverse students. Chapter 5 will focus on the concerns and potential of exceptional students who have specific learning abilities, disorders and impairments. Such students include the gifted and students with physical challenges (such as hearing and vision impairment). Communication disorders, emotional/behavioral disorders, and mental impairment will also be discussed. ■

Exceptional Students: Teaching Learners with Special Needs

LEARNING OBJECTIVES

Upon completing this chapter, you should be able to:

1

Describe five categories of students who have special needs.

2

List three essential factors to be considered when teaching students who have special needs.

3

Explain the requirements of individualized education programs (IEP's) as set forth by Public Law 94-142.

4

Provide two definitions of "gifted students" and define of one alternative strategy for teaching these students.

5

Explain why the length of time a specific disability has existed is important academically.

6

List three characteristics of students with intellectual impairments.

7

Identify and describe students with behaviorally based disorders.

8

Name three rights Public Law 94-142, IDEA, NCLB, and ESEA Flexibility provide for students who are labeled as special needs or disabled.

9

Explain the characteristics of an individualized education program for a student who has a special need.

10

Define mainstreaming and explain why earlier attempts to mainstream special students failed.

11

Develop two alternative strategies for soliciting the cooperation of students and families during IEP planning and implementation sessions.

12

Define the teacher's role in seeking services for students with special needs.

During our nation's early history, society tried to isolate and ignore students with special needs but now our schools are committed to providing for their unique learning needs.

INTRODUCTION

Throughout this book we have examined how students develop and behave socially, emotionally, and mentally. You have learned that environment, developmental maturity, and academic experiences affect student behavior. We know that each student perceives the academic environment in a unique way, filtering observations through the individual's *perceptual screen*—previous experiences which give meaning to new experiences. For example, middle-school student Carlos, whose older brother has just bought his first car, may become quite curious when his science teacher introduces a unit on internal combustion. But his classmate, Trent, who has no older siblings may find the same unit boring. Angela, whose family spent a week vacationing in Mexico may be interested in learning Spanish; whereas, some of her classmates may find the topic dull.

Ms. Barnes's seventh graders (see the Todd box on pages 153–154) were very comfortable with their fellow mainstreamed students; whereas, other classes not privy to Ms. Barnes's expertise may have been less at ease. The heredity and/or environment of the life outside of school of some students may be so different from their classmates' their ability to perform academically may require special help. As Ms. Barnes related to Todd, education for students with special needs should be a primary goal of formal education.

EDUCATING STUDENTS WITH SPECIAL NEEDS

During our nation's early history, those students who were noticeably different from their peers were often viewed with suspicion and even disdain. In many instances, individuals who had special needs were literally locked away from the rest of society. The concern was not for helping these individuals, but for protecting "normal" people from them.

But, as psychologists and society learned more about these "special" people, their educational needs slowly began to be developed and recognized. By the middle of the century, classes for exceptional students became a reality. Unfortunately, the results of these special classes were often more negative than positive, and student differences were magnified. Often, the least-experienced and least- prepared teachers were assigned to teach exceptional students.

Additionally, the method of putting all impaired students together had a negative effect: it drew attention to students who were different, and their problems amplified. Such results led to efforts that placed students with disabilities in the classrooms with nondisabled students.

TODD WILLIAMS...

received word that three new students would be enrolling in his classes at the start of the second term. Two of the new students were to be "mainstreamed" from special classes they had been attending. The principal, Ms. Wickersham, informed Todd that one of the students was confined to a wheelchair but was a B student academically. The second student was hearing impaired and made average grades. The third student had an IQ of 148, but her grades were poor. When Todd expressed concern about his limited experience teaching such students, Ms. Wickersham suggested he visit Ms. Barnes's seventh-grade math class.

When Todd entered Ms. Barnes's class early the next day for his appointment to observe and glean information, he saw three students, one sitting quietly in a wheelchair and two in loud disagreement. "No, it's my turn," insisted Leona.

"No, it's my turn," argued Chuck. Before the argument got any louder, Ms. Barnes interceded. "Chuck, it is Leona's turn; you are scheduled for tomorrow." Chuck shrugged and wandered to his seat as Leona grinned and wheeled Mario, the student in the wheelchair, to his desk. Todd noticed that Mario's desk was a small table that was tall enough to fit over the wheels of his wheelchair.

As Ms. Barnes greeted the class, she passed written instructions to two students sitting in the front row. Todd later discovered that these two students were hearing impaired. As the class continued, Todd noticed Leona turning textbook pages for Mario and sharing her notes. Occasionally, a student would tap the shoulder of one of the hearing-impaired students to point out something noted on the board. Todd was very curious about something else. Every 30 minutes, Ms. Barnes placed a token in a cup on the desk of a large, red-haired student (Ralph).

Two hours into the class, and for no apparent reason, Ralph let out a high-pitched scream, then laughed as he pounded his hands on his desk. Todd was startled by the sudden noise and very surprised by the lack of a class response. The students, who were working on fractions at the time, did not respond at all. There was no laughter; no one even looked in Ralph's direction. The students continued to work as if nothing had happened. Ms. Barnes responded by walking to Ralph's desk and removing two tokens from the cup. Ralph's muttering of "I don't care" was totally ignored as Ms. Barnes walked away. However, when 30 minutes passed, a token was placed in Ralph's cup.

When time came for lunch, Leona continued to help Mario, putting up his books, pushing him to the lunchroom, helping him through the lunch line, and sitting with him. Todd was full of questions as he followed Ms. Barnes. "Leona is mature and considerate to help Mario as she does. What were she and Chuck arguing about earlier?

"Oh, they were just arguing over whose turn it was to be Mario's assistant for the day. The students take turns helping Mario by being his assistant. They look forward to this; they really like him. He's a very popular class member," explained Ms. Barnes.

"But how did you get the students to be so cooperative and supportive?" questioned Todd.

Ms. Barnes continued, "Well, I usually have three or four students every term who are challenged or impaired; so during the first week in class, I spend some time talking with the class about student differences, but mostly about how students are alike.

I am very open and honest with my students and when I ask for their help, they respond. It is voluntary but I do provide some incentives. For example, Mario's daily assistant gets to be first in line for activities outside the classroom."

Todd was impressed and inquired, "What are the tokens with Ralph all about and why did he suddenly yell in class?"

Ms. Barnes smiled and answered, "Ralph has a behavior problem. He has outbursts that can be disruptive in class; therefore, I put him on a token program. He earns a token for every 30 minutes he does not disrupt. He can cash in his tokens for privileges he and I agreed on."

"What kind of privileges?" quizzed Todd.

"Well, 20 tokens earn 30 minutes of his choice of creating T-shirt art, reading sports magazines, or doing computer activities. We had to start with a token every 5 minutes at the beginning of school. I hope to phase out the tokens before the term ends. He's doing much better."

"But none of the students paid any attention to him when he yelled," responded Todd.

"Yes, I know," replied Ms. Barnes. "I'm so proud of them. I talked with the students in Ralph's absence and asked for their help. I asked them to completely ignore Ralph when he disrupted class. At the first of the year, they laughed and gave him lots of attention, and Ralph loved that. The class earns privileges by ignoring Ralph and completing their assignments. I want Ralph to learn that he can get attention by behaving in class and performing academically."

"Doesn't it take a lot of class time to provide for students with special needs?" asked Todd.

Ms. Barnes smiled, "Todd, do you know that Alexander the Great suffered from epileptic seizures; Franklin D. Roosevelt was confined to a wheelchair throughout his presidency; and Steven Hawking, one of the most brilliant minds of our time, is disabled by Lou Gehrig's disease. Further, Tom Cruise and Cher are LD (learning disabled). Todd, I had the opportunity to attend a performance by the "Famous People Players" last week. This play group is internationally known for its remarkable performances. All but 3 of the 30 plus cast are developmentally impaired. So many of the students with disabilities we have the privilege to teach are bright and creative. I am delighted to have the opportunity to spend class time with them."

Todd looked admiringly at Ms. Barnes for a time then finally asked, "Do you suppose you could help me develop a system for my class?"

Mainstreaming

The process of putting students with disabilities in class with nondisabled students is called **mainstreaming**. But, like special classes, mainstreaming has its limitations. One primary problem with mainstreaming was the manner it was initially implemented; most teachers lacked the special preparation needed for teaching, managing, and motivating students with special needs (Stern, 1992). Imagine your feelings of inadequacy if you had no training to teach students with impairments, but several such students were in your classes. Imagine the feelings of the students with impairments.

The result was many students placed in mainstreamed classes were ignored. Not knowing how to teach students with disabilities, many teachers could not make the needed adjustments. It was hoped by placing them with nondisabled students, students with disabilities would feel less different and be able to perform academically. But over time it became clear that the disabling conditions of students rarely fade by simply associating with others. Something more was needed that resulted in federal legislation commonly known as Public Law 94-142 (the Education for All Disabled Children Act of 1975).

Public Law 94-142

In 1975, President Gerald Ford signed into law the Education for All Disabled Children Act, commonly known as **PL 94-142**. Because of the failure of attempts to fulfill the needs of students with disabilities through the provision of services in the regular education special classroom, PL 94-142 was amended in 1990. The word handicapped was replaced by disabled, and PL 94-142 was retitled as the **Individuals with Disabilities in Education Act (IDEA)**. PL 94-142 ensures a free and appropriate public education for all students with disabilities. This legislation calls for the "least restrictive environment" that will allow students with special disabilities to be placed in regular education classes if those students are not restricted when placed with nondisabled students. The intent of the law was to keep students with disabilities in the classroom with students with no disabilities, as opposed to grouping and isolating them.

Research findings and demographic data leading to the enactment of Public Law 94-142 help us understand the need for this legislation:

- There are more than 8 million children who have disabilities in the United States today.
- The educational needs of children with disabilities are not being fully met.

> Thomas Edison was withdrawn from school at an early age because his teacher thought he was incapable of learning. Fortunately, his mother, a teacher, recognized his genius and educated young Tom at home.

> Neither isolating special students nor mainstreaming them without providing special instruction has been an effective way to meet their academic needs.

The 1990 Individuals with Disabilities Act enabled students with disabilities to be placed in regular education classes.

- More than half the children who have disabilities do not receive appropriate educational services.

- One million children with disabilities are excluded entirely from the public school system.

- There are many students in regular programs whose impairments are undetected.

- Because public school systems lack adequate services, families often must find other services at their own expense (or sue the school system), although schools are *legally* required to provide these services!

- With appropriate funding, state and local educational agencies have the expertise and the methods to provide effective special education and related services.

- State and local educational agencies have the responsibility to educate students with disabilities, but they have inadequate financial resources to do so.

- Helping state and local educational agencies provide programs to meet the educational needs of children with disabilities facilitates equal protection of the law.

Americans Disabilities Act

In 1990, President George W. Bush signed into law the **Americans Disabilities Act (ADA, PL 101-336)** avowing, "Let the shameful wall of exclusion finally come tumbling down" (George Bush Presidential Library and Museum, 2011). Many consider ADA to be the most significant legislation pertaining to the civil rights of individuals with disabilities (Gargiulo & Metcalf, 2010). ADA goes beyond the classroom walls, prohibiting discrimination against persons with disabilities in both the public and private sector. ADA also broadened the traditional view of who was considered disabled to include, for example, "people with AIDS, individuals who have successfully completed a substance abuse program, and persons with cosmetic disfigurement. Further, any individual with an impairment substantially limiting a major life activity is covered (Gargiulo & Metcalf, 2010, p. 19). ADA requires communities to focus not only on appropriately educating children with disabilities, but on ensuring all buildings, facilities, and communication devices are nondiscriminatory. Consider the positive effect ADA has had for student with disabilities, specifically adolescents transitioning from high school to the public sector. ADA has provided hope and opened doors for students with disabilities as they progress beyond the K-12 classroom.

No Child Left Behind Act of 2001

The Elementary and Secondary Education Act was reauthorized by congress in 2001 and signed into law in 2002 by President George W. Bush (PL 107-110). This legislation became known as the **No Child Left Behind Act (NCLB)**. As stated in Chapter 1, this law was primarily enacted to address the school reform reports of the 1990s. As it relates to students with special needs, this law proposed that all students, including those in special education, will be proficient in reading and mathematics, and later in science. Required annual testing in Grades 3–8 and at least once in Grades 10–12 is included in NCLB and the testing does not exclude special education students. The hoped benefit being that "assessment results will directly translate into instructional accommodations, further aligning special education and general education into a unified delivery system responsible for serving all learners" (as cited in Gargiulo & Metcalf, 2010, p. 20). NCLB further mandates that all teachers be "highly qualified" and schools make "adequate yearly progress" toward the end result of schools being 100% proficient by year 2014. These mandates led to greater emphasis on "high-stakes testing" and to more general education curriculum being provided to special education students. It also changed how colleges and universities train teachers to ensure that graduates are considered highly qualified.

Individuals with Disabilities Education Improvement Act of 2004

In 2004, President George W. Bush signed into law a new version of IDEA (PL 108-446), commonly known as the **Individuals with Disabilities Education Improvement Act of 2004 (IDEA 2004)**. A major objective of this amendment was to align IDEA with the NCLB Act. For example, Individual Education Plans (IEPs) written for students with special needs, were required to address students' "educational progress," but this terminology changed to "academic and functional performance" after IDEA 2004 to more closely align with NCLB (Gargiulo & Kilgo, 2011). IDEA 2004 also addressed additional requirements for IEPs that schools must adhere. The writing and requirements for IEPs will be addressed later in this chapter.

Elementary and Secondary Education Act Flexibility of 2011

On September 23, 2011, President Barack Obama introduced flexibility to specific requirements in the Elementary and Secondary Education Act or NCLB. Recognizing that NCLB has led to school improvement but also recognizing that NCLB has failings, President Barack explained,

"The goals behind No Child Left Behind were admirable. . . . Higher standards are the right goal. Accountability is the right goal. Closing the gap is the right goal. And we've got to stay focused on those goals. But experience has taught us that, in its implementation, No Child Left Behind had some serious flaws that are hurting our children instead of helping them. Teachers are too often being focused to teach to the test. Subjects like history and science have been squeezed out. And, in order to avoid having their schools labeled as failures, some states, perversely, have actually had to lower their standards in a race to the bottom instead of a Race to the Top." (The White House, 2011)

Termed the **Elementary and Secondary Act Flexibility (ESEA Flexibility)**, each state's education agency can request flexibility in specific requirements of NCLB "in exchange for rigorous and comprehensive state-developed plans designed to improve educational outcomes for all students, close achievement gaps, increase equity, and improve the quality of instruction" (U.S. Department of Education, 2011b). According to the U.S. Department of Education (2011c), a provision included is that states that adopt higher standards are allowed to apply for waivers of the NCLB 2014 proficiency deadline. Schools may also apply for waiving the NCLB requirement of being labeled a failing school by not meeting adequate yearly progress. Further, schools can ask for more flexibility in the way they make use of their funding. However, it is stressed that the flexibility will not be granted in exchange for nothing. The schools are expected to "maintain rigorous accountability, including for subgroups of students" (U.S. Department of Education, 2011c). The impact of ESEA Flexibility on the nation's education systems and on how schools will adapt to educate students with special needs will unfold in the years to come.

Keeping abreast of current legislation and laws governing education is difficult but imperative for today's classroom teacher. Penalties for not following guidelines in legislation can lead to loss of federal funding, civil and criminal law suits, and even loss of a teacher's job. However, proactive teachers are aware that mandated legislations, with the purpose of benefiting students, can increase their effectiveness in the classroom. Despite the many changes to the laws and court challenges of the legislation, certain components have remained constant: students are afforded the right to a free, appropriate public school education, students with disabilities are to be educated in the least restrictive environment, students with disabilities are entitled to an IEP, assessments of students are to be nondiscriminatory, and families have the right to participate and to due process (Gargiulo & Metcalf, 2010). If a child is being considered for special education, the family must be offered,

Parents of special students have many rights to ensure the design and use of an effective IEP.

1. Notice of the proposed action

2. The right to a hearing prior to final action

3. The right to counsel at that hearing

4. The right to present evidence

5. The right to full access to relevant school records, including the right to purge information that is inaccurate, misleading, or discriminatory

6. The right to compel attendance of and to confront and cross-examine officials or employees who might have evidence of the basis for the proposed action

7. The right to an independent evaluation

8. The right to have the hearing open or closed to the public at the parent's option

9. The right to an impartial hearing officer

The hearings are to be held at a place and time convenient to family. In other words, students and their parents/family have a right to question the appropriateness of IEPs or plans developed for them and to demand educational plans that address the unique learning needs of the individual involved.

> As noted in chapter 1, in February of 2012, ten states were granted permission to pursue school reform outside the requirements of 'No Child Left Behind'. Many more states are expected to be granted the same permission.

INTASC Standard 1   Learner development

The Teacher's Role

As Todd learned, illustrated by Ms. Barnes's class, if you work in the educational environment, you will be directly involved in complying with the guidelines set forth in state and national legislation. This will include developing a program plan each year demonstrating how your school is meeting legislative requirements. Your responsibility as a teacher will be to help educate students with disabilities and, like your other students, get the instruction and support they need. The process to accomplish this task is well defined by federal legislation.

Facilitating Individualized Education Programs

A meeting to develop an educational plan for each student with a disability is required within 30 days of the diagnosis of the disability but before the placement recommendation. At a minimum, those required to attend this meeting include a representative of the local school district who is knowledgeable in the area of the student's disabling condition, an individual skilled in interpreting the educational implications of the evaluation, the student's teachers (including a regular education teacher and a special education teacher), and a parent/guardian of the student. Teachers are responsible for seeing that the services planned are implemented. Furthermore, teachers are required to evaluate the program for students with disabilities in their classes. Federal laws require at least one progress review each year and a complete reevaluation every three years. The state where you teach may require more comprehensive reevaluation procedures.

Teachers and families should work together sharing their concerns for the welfare of the student; by working together they better serve the student. Unfortunately, some parents/families are unlikely to be motivated to attend or participate in individualized education program meetings. Because some families are intimidated when faced with a room full of professional educators, the best approach to IEP meetings is a simple, friendly, jargon-free one in which teacher and families participate as equal partners. As McNamara (1986,) explained, "Being clear, precise and up-front with parents will pay high dividends in [your] ability to assist in carrying out the educational plan."

Each individualized educational plan must contain, as a minimum, these statements and projections:

- The child's current level of academic functioning
- Annual instructional goals accompanied with their instructional objectives
- The specific educational services to be provided
- The extent to which the child will be able to participate in normal classroom activities
- The plans for how the services will be initiated and the length of the services provided
- Annual, objective criteria for evaluation and a schedule for determining whether instructional objectives are being achieved

> Before holding an IEP conference, teachers should carefully plan a strategy to gain the cooperation of all parties concerned.

Although any member of the planning team can make the initial draft of the IEP, responsibility for ensuring that the plan is implemented belongs to the teacher(s). Proactive teachers should view the IEP as an organized approach to providing the educational experiences needed by students with disabilities. We suggest that teachers and school professionals work with families prior to their first meeting for forming IEPs: For example, we suggest the following:

- Encourage families to bring questions.
- A week or two before the meeting, ask involved family members to think about long- and short-term educational goals for their child.
- Involve families in prioritizing goals for the year.
- Ask what motivators have been effective at home.
- Make a follow-up phone call or contact to ensure that involved family members clearly understand goals identified for their child and the steps to be taken to reach these goals.

The "A View from the Field" box offers further suggestions to teachers for seeking help for students with special needs.

A VIEW FROM THE FIELD

A VIEW FROM THE FIELD

PROFILE

Dr. Lori Flint is an Assistant Professor in the Department of Curriculum & Instruction at East Carolina University. Teaching both graduate and undergraduate students, she earned her doctorate from the University of Georgia in Educational Psychology and a Master of Education in Talent Development from Ashland University. Dr. Flint serves on boards of several national and local organizations related to improving schools and student experiences. An active advocate for children at the local, state, and national levels, she has experience teaching and parenting gifted and creative children and adults, focusing on their needs from birth through adulthood. Her research interests include increasing student achievement and motivation, especially through the specific teaching of skills needed for school and real-life survival; gender; social and emo-tional areas; and individual differences such as gifted students with learning disabilities.

QUESTION: What services or resources are available in the schools to help teachers who have students with special needs?

Dr. Flint—When students exhibit characteristics or learning differences setting them apart from others, uncovering the basis for these differences can be challenging. Good educators need to be good problem solvers, using all available resources to unlock the talents inherent in every child. Teachers can start to better understand students by looking to special area teachers, such as health, physical education, business education, art, and music to gather clues about students' performance outside the "regular" classroom. If, for example, a student performs well in physical education, is it the teacher who makes the difference, or is the fact the student is able to move about during class time rather being constrained at a desk all day? In addition, the student's permanent record or cumulative folder often contains a wealth of overlooked information. Taking the time to sit down and examine trends of student behavior over time can provide a great deal of information.

QUESTION: Whom should a teacher ask for help?

The first and foremost important thing to keep in mind here is to ask for help. Too often, when children fail, educators simply give up, or even blame them for lack of success. Other places to turn for assistance are the gifted education specialist, the special education teacher, and the guidance counselor, depending on the specific needs/behaviors of the student. Parents or caregivers can also shed light on student behaviors, including both strengths and challenges. Finally, there are outside resources, such as district personnel in various areas, as well as university faculty-researchers who can shed light on those children who are puzzles to us. Doing all this detective work is vitally important for the student's success in school, and it is immensely gratifying for the teacher who helps a child turn around. ■

INTASC Standard 3   Learning environments

Inclusion

Inclusion is a dominate practice in our nation's schools as they strive to meet legislative requirements pertaining to the least restrictive environment. Gargiulo and Metcalf (2010) define inclusion as "the movement toward, and the practice of, educating students with disabilities and other learners with exceptionalities in general education classrooms alongside their typical peers with appropriate supports and services provided as necessary" (p. 446). Figure 5.1 illustrates that the majority of students with special needs (54%) are placed in the regular education classroom.

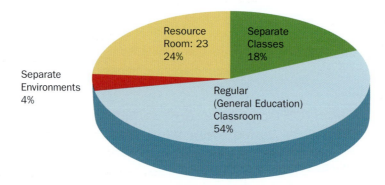

Figure 5.1 Percentages of Students with Disabilities Served in Various Educational Settings

Adapted from Gargiulo, R. M., & Metcalf, D. (2010). *Teaching in today's inclusive schools. A universal design for learning approach*, p. 6. Belmont, CA: Wadsworth Cengage.

Notes: Data are for students ages 6–21 enrolled in special education during the 2006–2007 school year. Information based on data from the 50 states, District of Columbia, Puerto Rico, and the outlying areas. Separate environments include students receiving an education in residential facilities, separate schools, or hospital/homebound programs.

Source: Adapted from U.S. Department of Education. (2008). *IDEA data*. Available at https://www.ideadata.org/PartBReport.asp

The length of time spent in the normal classroom setting defines whether the student with a disability is designated to receive *partial inclusion* or *full inclusion*. Partial inclusion indicates that the student is in the regular classroom part of the day; and, full inclusion states the student is in the regular classroom the entire day. Inclusion is not meant to be a one size fits all approach to educating students with disabilities. The intent is not to place every student with a disability in the regular classroom for the entire day. Nor is it the intention to expect regular classroom teachers to have the knowledge and expertise to appropriately educate all students with disabilities. Rather, the expectation is that the special education teachers and other experts attend the students' classrooms and assist the regular classroom teachers in meeting the students' needs. However, due to the short supply of special education teachers and lack of funding, many regular classroom teachers are left with much of the responsibility of educating students with disabilities. Unfortunately, some teachers feel overwhelmed and ill-prepared to attend to the needs of students with severe disabilities.

Research has indicated that approximately one-third of teachers who leave their position to teach at other schools or who leave the profession list mainstreaming as their primary reason for dissatisfaction (Morrison, 2009). Many pre-service teachers are concerned they will begin their teaching responsibilities without the skills they need to work in classrooms that include children with disabilities. Therefore, inclusion practices have created both supporters and critics.

Criticisms of inclusion argue that the time teachers must spend with students with disabilities takes time away from the nondisabled students. Critics are also concerned that teachers might lower academic standards to accommodate students with severe disabilities. However, when comparing inclusive to non-inclusive classrooms, there are no conclusive research data to indicate academic disadvantages in inclusive classrooms (Savich, 2008). The cost of educating students with disabilities in the regular education setting is also a concern. According to the U.S. 2005 Special Education Expenditure Program (as cited in Savich, 2008), it costs 1.6 times more to educate students with disabilities than those without. However, this expenditure is still less than what it costs to educate students with disabilities in a separate, special education classroom (Savich, 2008).

Proponents for inclusion practices point to the social and academic benefits inclusion has shown for students with disabilities. Research indicates social and cognitive gains (Savich, 2008) and an increase in self-esteem and self-concept (Wolfberg & Schuler, 1999) in children with disabilities. Furthermore, an inclusive classroom fosters a community valuing diversity and acceptance.

A major role of teachers is to help students feel they are an important part of their classes. Williams (1997) studied the effects of placing students with disabilities in the classroom with regular students and reported, "Interestingly, students in both rural and urban schools felt that they were members of a few classes and did not feel like members of others" (p. 139). Yet, feeling a part of the class affects both students' levels of motivation and academic achievement (Goodenow, 1993). Students with a high sense of belonging were found to be more academically engaged than their counterparts who had a low sense of belonging (Goodenow & Grady, 1994).

Janny and Snell (1996) reported that teachers with students with disabilities in their classrooms work to promote the idea that each of these students is just another student. Certainly, such teachers do not dote over these students; neither do they ignore them. Instead, they expect students with disabilities to follow routines and roles and participate in class activities as much as possible. Participation in class activities is especially important because classroom participation is associated with feeling a part of the class. As Williams (1997) explained, "Since class participation appears to be crucial to membership, students with severe disabilities need to be taught to acquire skills that will promote their active participation" (p. 149). Williams also reported that when teachers practiced fairness by sharing their attention among all students and involving all students in class activities, after being in class with disabled students for a year, the other students viewed their classmates equally.

When successfully implemented, the benefits of inclusion practices outweigh the disadvantages. Classroom teachers and special education teachers should collaborate to ensure that all students experience the benefits inclusion can bring. Table 5.1 provides a summary of key elements needed for full inclusion.

TABLE 5.1
Key Elements of Full Inclusion Models

· **"Homeschool" attendance**. Defined as the local school the child would attend if not disabled.

· **Natural proportion at the school site**. The percentage of children with special needs enrolled in a particular school is in proportion to the percentage of pupils with exceptionalities in the entire school district; in general education classes, this would mean approximately two to three students with disabilities.

· **Zero rejection**. All students are accepted at local schools, including those with severe impairments; pupils are not screened out or grouped separately because of their disability.

· **Age/grade-appropriate placement**. A full-inclusion model calls for serving children with special needs in general education classrooms according to their chronological age rather than basing services on the child's academic ability or mental age.

· **Site-based management or coordination**. Recent trends in school organizational reform suggest a movement away from central office administration for special education programs to one where the building principal (or other administrator) plays a large role in planning and administering programs for all children in the school.

· **Use of cooperative learning and peer instructional models**. Instructional practices that involve children learning in a cooperative manner rather than in a competitive fashion and using students to assist in the instruction of classmates with disabilities can be effective strategies for integrating exceptional learners in the general education classroom.

Source: R. M. Gargiulo & D. Metcalf, *Teaching in Today's Inclusive Classrooms. A Universal Design for Learning Approach*. (Belmont, CA: Wadsworth Cengage Learning, 2010, p. 11).

PROACTIVE TEACHING

CLASSROOM SITUATION

Unless you teach in very unusual circumstances, you will have students with special needs in your classes. Some of these students will be physically disabled or sensory impaired. Some will demonstrate academic, behavioral, or social difficulties due to intellectual impairments,

PROACTIVE ALTERNATIVES

· Check available school records for information on the needs of your students and the services they have received or are receiving. Read the assessment reports, IEPs, health records, attendance reports contained in these files.

emotional disturbance, or learning impairments. Others may be gifted and talented. Your preparation for meeting the educational needs of these students is critical to your success as a teacher.

· Check with your school psychologist, guidance counselor, or someone in administration for information on related services available for exceptional students. Confer with previous teachers concerning the interests, abilities, and special needs of your students.

· Confer with previous teachers about what has worked in meeting the needs of these students in their classrooms.

· Talk to your students about how they view their school-related successes and failures and together work out a plan for a successful school year.

· Make plans for meeting with families early in the school year. Prepare in advance the kind of information you need from families and the information you can provide for them.

· Relax. Plan to look for the good in your students. Most students with special needs served in regular education settings are more like than unlike their peers!

· Realize that even your best students have the potential to fail. When what you attempt fails, regroup, re-plan, and try again.

THE NATURE OF SPECIAL NEEDS CONDITIONS

Although there are several common categories of impairment-physical, mental, emotional, sensory, and neurological-these categories often have considerable overlap. IDEA classifies disabling conditions using the following categories: autism, developmental delay, emotional disturbance, hearing impairments (including deafness), intellectual disabilities, learning disabilities, orthopedic impairments, other health impairments, speech or language impairments, traumatic brain injury, and visual impairments (including blindness). A developmental delay is defined as impairment in one or more of the following: adaptive development, cognitive development, communication development, physical development, or social or emotional development. Approximately 10% to 12% of students in the United States have a disability and receive some type of special education service (Morrison, 2009). Table 5.2 indicates the percentages of children served under IDEA. Even students belonging to the same category differ because of three critical factors: (1) the *degree* of impairment (mild, moderate, or severe), (2) the *length* of time the student has been disabled or impaired, and (3) the *stability* of the condition.

TABLE 5.2	
Children with Disabilities Ages 3 to 21 Served under IDEA	
Category	**Percentage Served**
Learning Disabilities	44%
Speech or Language Impairments	22%
Intellectual Disabilities	9%
Emotional Disturbance	7%
Other Health Impaired	6%
Developmental Delay	4%
Autism	2%
Multiple Disabilities	2%
Hearing Impairments	1%
Orthopedic Impairments	1%
Visual Impairments	<1%
Deaf-Blindness	<1%
Traumatic Brain Injury	<1%

Source: U.S. Department of Education (2005). Office of Special Education and Rehabilitative Services, Office of Special Education Programs, *26th Annual Report to Congress on the Implementation of the Individuals with Disabilities Act, 1*, Washington, DC.

STUDENTS WITH PHYSICAL DISABILITIES

People have a tendency to underestimate the abilities of individuals with physical disabilities.

Students with physical disabilities can qualify for special education services via three potential categories: multiple disabilities, orthopedic disabilities, and traumatic brain injury. If a student has a disabling health condition, they may qualify for services under other health impaired laws. When students have two or more disabling conditions requiring services in more than one special education area, they can be classified as multiple disabled. Orthopedic disabilities include individuals who typically have an impairment interfering with the normal functions of the bones, joints, or muscles, including internal organs and systemic malfunctions. These impairments range from congenital (lifelong) conditions and deformities—such as limb absence, heart defects, hemophilia, cerebral palsy, epilepsy, and spina bifida—to traumatic conditions, such as amputations or burns. Individual with traumatic brain injury have often suffered an external brain injury, for example, a brain injury due to an automobile accident. Traumatic brain injury does not include injury to the brain caused before or during birth.

The needs of students with physical disabilities are often intensified if the student has had the disability for a considerable length of time. For example, if the cause was congenital (birth defect), such as cerebral palsy, the student may have had limited educational experiences. Visual and speech defects are common; poor facial muscle control may cause drooling, giving the false impression of an intellectual disability, and causing teachers and other school personnel to underestimate the abilities of these students.

Teachers can help students with physical disabilities succeed by providing a climate of success, by accepting and including them in the social activities of the school, and by setting realistic, demanding expectations. Remember Mario, the student in a wheelchair in Ms. Barnes's class? He is a good example of not only succeeding academically in a regular education setting but also being accepted as a popular member of his class.

STUDENTS WHO ARE INTELLECTUALLY DISABLED

Students who are intellectually disabled have significantly sub-average intellectual functioning and adaptive behavior than their chronological- or grade-age peers. Below average intellectual functioning is often defined as an IQ of 70 or lower. The onset of an intellectual disability must occur before the age of 18. According to the American Psychiatric Association's (APA) Diagnostic and Statistical Manual of Mental Disorders, there are four levels of severity pointing toward intellectual functioning:

Classification	IQ
Mild	55-69
Moderate	40-54
Severe	25-39
Profound	24 and below

Those who are mildly intellectually disabled often are similar to normal classmates in height and weight, but closer observation often reveals they are lacking in strength, speed, and coordination. They also tend to have more health problems (Henson 1996, p. 176).

Students who are mildly intellectually disabled may experience frustration when expected to function socially and/or academically at their chronological age. Typically, they have short attention spans and are unable to concentrate for extended periods of time. Antisocial, disruptive, and inappropriate classroom behavior can often be attributed to the students' disability. Expectations to perform beyond their abilities sometimes results in frustrations manifesting in inappropriate social behaviors, such as acting out in class or refusing to attempt or complete class work.

Moderate Intellectual Disability

Because the level of intellectual development for students who are moderate is typically 25 to 53 percent lower than students of average intelligence, students with moderate intellectual disabilities often respond slowly to education and training. But, when given appropriate educational opportunity, many of these students can be educated for jobs requiring exceptional skills.

Students who lack memory skills, ability to generalize, language skills, conceptual and perceptual abilities, and creative abilities should be given tasks that are attainable, brief, relevant, sequential, and designed for success.

INTASC Standard 7 & 8   Planning for instruction & instructional strategies

Teaching Alternatives for Students Who are Intellectually Disabled

To learn more about your future role as a teacher of students with mental disabilities, consider the following questions:

1. What are the duties of administrators and support personnel?
2. What are the techniques available to school personnel to diagnose learners who have mental disabilities?
3. Are there examples of individualized education programs available for teachers?
4. How can I prepare my nondisabled students for the entry of students who are disabled into the classroom?
5. How can I prepare my learners with disabilities for entry into the classroom with learners who are nondisabled?
6. Where can I get help in learning how to evaluate learners with disabilities so that I will be demanding, yet fair, in my expectations of these students?
7. Where can I conduct low-anxiety, nonthreatening meetings with students with disabilities and their families?

Students Who Have a Behaviorally Based Disability

The diagnosing of certain disabilities is dependent upon symptomatology specifically related to abnormal, disabling behaviors. This includes attention-deficit/hyperactivity disorder, autism disorder, Asperger's Syndrome, and

Most students who exhibit apathy or hostility should not be classified as behaviorally disordered.

emotional disturbance. Students with these disorders are typically perceived as behaviorally confused or bewildered, often do not understand social stresses, and feel unaccepted in their efforts to resolve them (Love, 1974). These students are more at risk for being either hostile or apathetic. Those with serious behaviorally based disorders often require psychological services.

Most students who exhibit apathy or hostility should not be classified as disabled. The key elements with identifying these students are the intensity, duration, and frequency of such behaviors. For example, the student who occasionally disrupts class or yells at a classmate is probably not disordered, but the one who twice daily over a period of time has a violent, prolonged temper tantrum may have a behavioral disorder. Key in the diagnosis of a disabling condition is whether the behavior is significantly impairing the child's ability to learn and achieve in the classroom. At any grade level, especially the middle and secondary levels, students with behaviorally based disorders often show oversensitivity to criticism. Some may exhibit depression. Again, it is the frequency, duration, and intensity of the behavior that indicates the seriousness of the condition.

Prior to 1975, children with behaviorally based disorders, like other children with disabilities, were assigned to classes taught by specially trained teachers. After the enactment of PL 94-142, the method used to evaluate such children was changed. Many students with behaviorally based disorders are now educated, at least for part of the school day, in regular educational settings.

> Teachers should arrange for behaviorally based disordered students to have successful experiences and provide a climate free of threat and fear.

Children who have behaviorally-based disorders often have limited ability to make independent decisions and are often significantly influenced by their peers. Ironically, and unfortunately, children who have behaviorally- based disabilities are sometimes socially rejected by their classmates, which can affect their academic progress. According to Bender and Evans (1989), "These students exhibit attention disorders and other problem behaviors which further hinder their academic progress" (p. 89).

Attention-Deficit/Hyperactivity Disorder

Jamie, age 3, was expelled from preschool for frequent fights with other children. When Jamie played with other children, he would escalate the play into aggressive behavior and fighting. Examples of aggressive behavior included his throwing sand in the faces of other children and hitting them with toys. When the fighting became so aggressive that Jamie's teacher feared for the safety of the other children, she asked his mother to remove him from preschool. Jamie's parents were shocked by the teacher's request. They admitted that Jamie was an aggressive child, difficult to discipline, subject to frequent temper tantrums, and had a short attention span. Jamie had displayed such behaviors since infancy. His parents believed he would "outgrow" such behaviors, and that his teacher simply did not understand or know how to cope with Jamie. They believed another preschool would provide the educational environment Jamie needed (Campbell, 1988). Jamie suffers from *attention-deficit hyperactivity disorder* (ADHD).

Students diagnosed with ADHD are eligible for special education services under the category of other health impaired. **ADHD** is described as a set of symptoms reflecting excessive inattention or hyperactivity and impulsivity, within the context of what is developmentally appropriate for the child's age and gender (APA, 2000; Landau & McAninch, 1993). ADHD is found in 3 to 7 percent of children (APA, 2000). The disorder is much more prevalent in males; "with the male-to-female ratios ranging from 2:1 to 9:1 depending on the type" (APA, 2000). An individual can be diagnosed with ADHD by displaying symptoms related only to inattention or only to hyperactivity and impulsivity; or, a diagnosis can involve symptoms in both inattention and hyperactivity/impulsivity.

Symptoms of ADHD

The symptoms of ADHD are characterized by a child's inability to sustain a response long enough to accomplish assigned tasks. Therefore, the descriptions of "doesn't listen, can't concentrate, work independently, or complete assignments" (Barkley, 1990) are often correct.

According to APA's (2000) *Diagnostic and Statistical Manual of Mental Disorders*, the symptoms necessary for diagnosis are as follows:

Inattention

- lacks attention to details or makes careless mistakes
- has difficulty sustaining attention
- does not seem to listen when spoken to
- does not follow through on instructions and fails to finish schoolwork or other duties
- difficulty organizing
- avoids, dislikes, or is reluctant to engage in tasks requiring mental effort
- often loses things necessary for tasks or activities
- is easily distracted
- often forgetful

Hyperactivity

- fidgets or squirms
- leaves seat in classroom or in situations in which being seated is expected
- runs or climbs excessively in inappropriate settings (in adolescents or adults, restlessness is experienced)
- has difficulty playing or engaging in leisure activities quietly
- is "on the go" or acts as if "driven by a motor"
- talks excessively

Impulsivity

- blurts our answers before questions are completed
- has difficulty awaiting turn
- interrupts or intrudes on others (APA, 2000, p. 92)

APA (2000) further clarified that the symptoms must interfere with the student's ability to function in the classroom and in other settings. The symptoms must have been evident before age 7, persisted for at least 6 months, and present in two or more settings. If the individual presents six or more symptoms under inattention and six or more symptoms under hyperactivity/impulsivity, the diagnosis is ADHD Combined Type. If six or more symptoms are present under inattention but less than hyperactivity/impulsivity, the diagnosis is ADHD Predominately Inattentive Type. And if six or more symptoms only under hyperactivity/impulsivity but less than six under inattention, the diagnosis is ADHD Predominately Hyperactivity Impulsive Type.

Because of their behavior, ADHD children face many social and academic problems in the classroom. Their behaviors may include stealing, lying, being aggressive, and violating rules. Additionally, their peers reject them because of their aggression, bossiness, intrusiveness, and low toleration for others. Academically, ADHD children are at high risk for underachievement, exhibiting such actions as being noisy and disruptive, being frequently out of their seats, and not completing homework and schoolwork (McGee & Share, 1988).

Treatment and Teacher Alternatives

The treatments for ADHD include medication, behavior management plans, and a combination of both medication and behavior management. Medication is the most prevalent treatment (Barkley, 1990). Concerta, Dexedrine, and Ritalin are common medications prescribed for individuals with ADHD. These medications increase the production of neurotransmitters in the brain. A large majority of children respond to medication and often experience improvement in attention and memory, are less disturbing to others, and have better relations with parents, teachers, and friends (Barkley, 1990). For children who do not respond to medication, the National Association of School Psychologists (1992) suggested that teachers' interventions should include the following:

- Classroom modifications to enhance attendance, academic production, and social adjustment (Chapters 6, 8, 9, and 12)

- Behavioral management systems to reduce problems most likely to be affected by attention deficits (Chapters 6 and 12)

- Direct instruction in study strategies and social skills (Chapters 2 and 8)

- Consultation with families to assist in behavior management in the home (Chapters 6 and 12)

- Working collaboratively with community agencies that provide medical and related services to students and families

Autistic Disorder and Asperger's Syndrome

Autism is sometimes first recognized by a child's family or guardians due to the child's lack of interest in social interaction. Individuals diagnosed with autism display "markedly abnormal or impaired development in social interaction and communication and a markedly restricted repertoire of activity and interests" (APA, 2000, p. 70). APA's (2000) diagnosis criteria specifies that delays occur before age 3 in at least one of the areas: language used in social communication, in social interaction, and in play activities. The majority of children diagnosed with autism also have an associated diagnosis of an intellectual disability that can range from mild to profound. The reported cases of autism range from 2 to 20 cases per 10,000 individuals. The behavioral characteristics of individuals with autism include aggressiveness, hyperactivity, impulsivity, self-injurious behaviors, short attention span, and temper tantrums, especially in young children. In describing behaviors of autism, APA (2000) indicated,

> There may be odd responses to sensory stimuli (e.g., high threshold for pain, oversensitivity to sounds or being touched, exaggerated reactions to light or odors, fascination with stimuli). There may be abnormalities in eating (e.g., limiting diet to a few foods, Pica) or sleeping (e.g., recurrent awakening at night with rocking). Abnormalities of mood or affect (e.g., giggling or weeping for no apparent reason, an apparent absence of emotional reaction) may be present. There may be a lack of fear in response to real dangers, and excessive fearfulness in response to harmless objects. A variety of self-injurious behaviors may be present (e.g., head banging or finger, hand, or wrist biting). (p. 72)

Asperger's Syndrome (AS) is a disorder also marked by severe and sustained impairments in a child's social interactions. It is a separate disorder from autism due to differences in speech and language development. Children with Asperger's do not show severe delay in speech by age 2 as do children with autism. Further, individuals with Asperger's develop appropriate "spontaneous communicative phrases" (APA, 2000) by age 3; whereas, those with autism often do not. Further, children with Asperger's typically have normal intellectual abilities. Children diagnosed with Asperger's have "clinically significant impairment in social, occupational, or other important areas of functioning" (APA, 2000, p. 84) which can manifest in a failure to develop peer relationships, in a lack of emotional or social reciprocity, and in a failure to develop appropriate nonverbal skills. Morrison (2009) provided the following recommendations for teachers to help students with Asperger's:

- *Use clear, concrete language.* While students with AS may have an impressive vocabulary about specific topics, they rarely understand jokes or sarcasm.

- *Help develop social skills.* Encourage partner or group work with assigned tasks. You will need to model appropriate behaviors or provide a written script for your students with AS.

- *Monitor peer relationships.* Many children with AS are bullied. If you sense students with AS are being intimidated or mistreated, step in and let those who are bothering the student know that teasing or harassing is not allowed in your classroom or in the school. (p. 154)

Emotional Disturbance

The behaviorally- based disability, *emotional disturbance*, is not a psychiatric disorder; rather, it is a term used in IDEA legislation to define and serve behavior disorders significantly impairing learning and academic achievement. This allows schools to serve a multitude of psychiatric behaviorally based disorders, such as, conduct disorders, oppositional defiant disorders, and disruptive behavior disorders. The diagnostic criteria depend on the state and school system, however, the prevailing diagnostic characteristic is the student's behaviors necessitate intervention and services in special education in order for the student to succeed in school. According to the IDEA 2004 legislation, emotional disturbance is defined as follows:

I. *Emotional disturbance* means a condition exhibiting one or more of the following characteristics over a long period of time and to a marked degree adversely affects a child's educational performance:

    a. An inability to learn that cannot be explained by intellectual, sensory, or health factors.

    b. An inability to build or maintain satisfactory interpersonal relationships with peers and teachers.

    c. Inappropriate types of behavior or feelings under normal circumstances.

    d. A general pervasive mood of unhappiness or depression.

    e. A tendency to develop physical symptoms or fears associated with personal or school problems.

II. Emotional disturbance includes *schizophrenia*. The term does not apply to children who are socially maladjusted, unless it is determined they have a serious emotional disturbance. (U.S. Department of Education, 2011).

Characteristics common in students with emotional disturbance indicate two patterns of behaviors: externalizing and internalized (Snowman, McCown, & Biehler, 2009).

- *Externalizing* students are often aggressive, uncooperative, restless, and negativistic. They tend to lie and steal, defy teachers, and be hostile to authority figures. Sometimes they are cruel and malicious.

- *Internalizing* students, by contrast, are typically shy, timid, anxious, and fearful. They are often depressed and lack self-confidence. (Snowman, McCown, & Biehler, 2009, pp. 204–205)

Teachers are more likely to identify students who display externalizing behaviors rather than internalizing. However, the student who is more withdrawn can be at greater risk for developing depression and for suicide

(Snowman, McCown, & Biehler, 2009). The following sections provide teaching strategies that have been shown successful with students who have behaviorally based disorders.

Teaching Alternatives for Students with Behaviorally Based Disorders

As Carri (1985) argued, the characteristics of students who have behavioral disorders present teachers with a different set of demands than those placed on teachers of students with other disabling conditions. One successful approach is teaching behaviorally disordered students to monitor their own behavior. Bender and Evans (1989) reported, "Research has demonstrated the effectiveness of self-monitoring with various types of secondary disabled students, including both students with learning disabilities and students with behavioral disorders" (p. 207). Other approaches include relaxation training and class meetings.

Self-Monitoring

McLaughlin, Krappman, and Welch (1985) studied the effects of self-monitoring on four students with behavioral disorders who demonstrated low levels of task-oriented behavior. Baseline observations of behavior demonstrated the range of **on-task behavior**—defined as 'students working on the currently assigned classroom activities-was between 24 and 60 percent before the intervention'. During self-monitoring intervention, students were instructed to mark a "+" column on a recording sheet if they were on-task, and a "−" column if they were off-task. They completed this procedure whenever they thought about paying attention during half-hour instructional lessons over a 30- to 40-day period. An aide observed the students during the intervention and for 60 days after the intervention. The intervention phase showed a 28 to 67 percent improvement in on-task behavior, and the follow-up phase showed on-task behavior of 90 percent or higher for all four students.

Although self-monitoring has many advantages, several cautions are in order. First, studies demonstrating the effectiveness of self-monitoring have used subjects who were hyperactive or distractible rather than defiant or aggressive. Therefore, caution should be used when implementing this intervention with the latter types of children who have behavioral disorders. Finally, the requirements for implementation suggest that the student must "buy into" the process. If students do not find success in schoolwork or teacher praise, other reinforcers should be used. (See Chapters 6 and 12.)

Relaxation Training

Another strategy that offers potential for teaching many students who are behaviorally disordered is *relaxation training* (monitoring students' involuntary

Programs requiring students with behaviorally based disabilities to monitor their own behavior are effective in keeping students on-task.

Student intervention programs are effective when students believe in them.

Relaxing exercises can reduce the misbehavior of behaviorally based disordered students.

physiological processes, such as muscle tensing, brain wave activity, heart rate, blood pressure, and breathing patterns). "This procedure can be very helpful for the typical behaviorally disordered student who demonstrates hyperactivity, impulsivity, and frequent out-seat behaviors" (Bender & Evans, 1989, p. 91). The school counselor, school psychologist, or medical staff should be able to advise if such services are available in your school district.

Class Meetings

Yet another strategy for working with students who have behaviorally based disorders is the use of *class meetings*. As early as 1965, William Glaser used this method in the development of **reality therapy**—a technique designed to focus on the specific behavior (rather than on the child) and to develop alternative behaviors to satisfy the student's needs. "This technique would be appropriate in a secondary civics class that included several non-disabled students as well as several students with moderate disabilities. Also, junior or senior high school classes that stress human relationships would be an appropriate mainstream setting for these meetings" (Bender & Evans, 1989, p. 93).

Effective use of class meetings for behavior control of students who have behavioral disorders requires the classroom teacher to have some understanding of reality therapy techniques. Both the teachers and students must know how to share power in discussions and be willing to participate in frank and open discussion. This requires a level of maturity some students don't have. Other classroom behavioral techniques for students who are behaviorally disordered are discussed in detail in Chapters 6 and 12.

Students Who Are Learning Disabled

Students with learning disabilities (LD) have average to above average intelligence but are unable to adequately process information, and learning is often hindered. LD results from a dysfunction of psychological processes other than intellectual disabilities, emotional disturbance, sensory deprivation, or sociocultural factors. Students with learning disabilities may be awkward, hyperkinetic, and impulsive; others may appear hypokinetic and uninterested in academic activities. Because many regular education school programs are not designed to accommodate this type of behavior, these students are frequently viewed as having behavior problems. Frustration resulting from an inability to perform classroom tasks may lead these students to act out in class or fail to display "teacher-pleasing behaviors," such as raising a hand to respond or staying in their seat. Very few students with learning disabilities are hostile or physically aggressive, but their disruptive behavior can be frustrating to their teachers and peers.

Often students with learning disabilities have impairments in the psycho-motor, visual, or auditory domain. Students who have *psychomotor disabilities* are likely to be in poor physical condition or exhibit awkwardness. Their written assignments can also provide clues—handwriting may be unusually large or small and written on one corner of the paper.

If the basis of the student's problem is visual, the teacher may notice that the student cannot follow visual directions, may tend to forget things seen, and may be easily distracted by surrounding activities. Furthermore, such students tend to move their eyes excessively or inappropriately. Auditory disabilities are characterized by students failing to follow oral directions, forgetting directions, and being easily distracted by noise and confusing similar sounds.

> The student with learning disabilities includes a broad range of neurological problems that are quite distinct from either retardation or emotional disturbances. The LD child is likely to have difficulty with reading, writing, spelling, and math. The LD child often has difficulties with attending, concentrating, remembering, organizing, sequencing, coordinating; and distinguishing right from left, letters, and numbers. (Wenar, 1994)

- According to the Learning Disabilities Association of America, 10 to 15 percent of students have learning disabilities. A child who demonstrates a number of the following may indicate a need for further testing:
- Is disorganized
- Is easily distracted
- Has a poor attention span
- Overreacts to noise
- Doesn't enjoy being read to
- Has poor hand-to-eye coordination
- Uses words inappropriately
- Is hyperactive
- Has limited vocabulary
- Is unable to follow directions
- Sometimes has poor emotional control
- Has difficulty remembering
- Chooses younger playmates or prefers solitary play
- (Wenar, 1994)

According to Wenar (1994), students diagnosed with learning disabilities need the opportunity to act and verbalize on what they learn. To help them, teachers should encourage students to verbalize what they have learned, construct models, draw pictures, and provide illustrations and pictures of what is to be learned.

Teaching Alternatives for Students Who Are Learning Disabled

Woodrich (1994) suggested that students who have learning disabilities and who were offered (1) immediacy cues (eye contact, forward leaning), and (2) focused immediacy cues plus modeling of exploration (drawing the child's attention to observations) often showed higher levels of exploration under both kinds of supportive conditions. The facilitative teacher must remember that any obstacles preventing success for these students, whether attitudinal, emotional, physical, or academic, need to be addressed.

Similar to Ms. Barnes's seventh-grade class Todd was fortunate to observe, many other approaches are available for reaching the reluctant student with learning disabilities. In Vancouver, British Columbia, nonproductive students are asked to draw a picture and then write a story below it. The teacher first discusses the content without referring to grammatical errors and later addresses grammatical errors. Lake Washington school district has volunteer tutors who keep daily progress charts. A New York inner-city teacher assigns students such complex topics as aerodynamics and rocket building. Students must read and work math and physics to build model rockets. The details of such techniques are discussed in Chapters 6 through 12.

STUDENTS WHO ARE SENSORY IMPAIRED

Teachers can help students develop confidence in themselves by demonstrating they have confidence in those students.

Students who are visually impaired and hearing impaired are referred to as *sensory impaired*. Visually impaired students include individuals who are partially sighted and who are blind; hearing-impaired students include those who are deaf or have partial hearing.

Visually disabled students vary in the extent of their disability; only about 10 percent of the legally blind are totally blind. Critical to teaching students with visual impairments is the *degree of the disability*. The *length of time* the student has had the visual impairment is also important. Those whose problems have been life-long often need additional help developing concepts of space and form; whereas, those whose blindness is recent often need more help adjusting to their loss of sight.

Students who have hearing problems range from those who can hear and understand speech by using such supports as hearing aids, to those who are classified as deaf, who at most are able to distinguish only amplified sounds. In considering the range of the hearing impairment, the primary task for the teacher is determining how the hearing loss affects the student's ability to do academic work. Again, how long the student has had the hearing loss is important, *whether the hearing loss occurred before or after the development of speech and language* is critical. A major problem of students who have been deaf since birth is the development of speech and language comprehension.

Teaching Alternatives for Students Who Are Sensory Impaired

When working with students who are visually and hearing impaired, a good beginning is accepting the students and believing in their ability to adjust to your classroom. Your confidence they will be productive students is essential. It is especially important to remember that a student who has a visual or hearing impairment does not necessarily have impaired intellectual functioning.

The teacher is responsible for creating a climate of acceptance among the student's peers. Because visually and/or hearing-impaired students are unable to pick up on all the stimuli providing clues as to how and when they should respond, they often respond inappropriately or not at all. Peers who are insensitive to these limitations may interpret their response (or absence of response) as unfriendly or antisocial. The limited vocabulary of some of these students may further restrict their responses. The teacher should make every effort to provide a positive climate focusing on the abilities and potentials of these students, rather than on their limitations. Suggestions for the classroom environment for students who are sensory impaired include the following:

- Seating the student(s) toward the front of the class or teacher
- Providing class assignments in bold, large print for students who are visually impaired
- Having all class assignments and class notes in print for students who are hearing impaired
- Using recorders for repeating academic information
- Working closely with families and school personnel who are knowledgeable in the area of the student's impairment, also taking advantage of sign-language interpreter if available in the classroom

Speech or Language Impairments

Speech and language are among the most complex behaviors that children learn. *Communication disorders* can be defined as a significant deviation in speech

or language from norms based on sex, age, and cultural, ethnic, or social expectations (Haring, 1982). Communication disorders among students can have a detrimental impact on their academic and social behavior, resulting in the following:

- Students having difficulty communicating what they have learned and understanding what is to be learned, and

- Poor self-concept often as a result of self-consciousness, reluctance to attempt communication, and stress.

A fundamental goal of educators should be to identify academic deficiencies of students.

Speech or language disorders include *speech impairments*, defined as the inability to produce sounds effectively; *articulation disorders*, characterized by substituting one sound for another, distorting sounds, and adding or omitting sounds; and stuttering and voicing problems, which includes inappropriate pitch, quality, or loudness (Woolfolk, 1995).

Adapting instruction often includes the guidance of a specialist, but the classroom teacher can work with students to improve their communication difficulties. Suggestions for teachers include:

- Encourage students to speak out in class, but do not force them to do so.

- Communicate with families of students about resources outside the classroom.

- Listen attentively with patience, and do not allow ridicule by other students. (Lewis & Doorlag, 1991; Wood, 1989)

In addition, teachers should avoid interrupting or attempting to finish sentences for students with speech or language disorders. The teacher needs to create a safe, classroom environment allowing these students the time they need to speak and complete their thoughts without concern that others will make fun or become impatient with them.

PROACTIVE EXERCISE

You have students who are physically impaired, as was Mario in Ms. Barnes's class, and one who is sensory impaired. How would you accommodate their physical and academic needs?

TODD WILLIAMS...

classroom was quiet for the first time in 2 weeks. Quiet in an academic sense-the only noises were from squeaky chairs, the rustle of paper, erasers rubbing out incorrect and correct answers, and an occasional sigh. Todd's students were taking their six-week's exam. Todd enjoyed giving exams. No lecturing or lesson plans, just pass out exams and monitor. Exams are a time for students, rather than the teacher, to perform.

As Todd scanned his class, he was sure he could predict with considerable accuracy his students' test scores. Amy would make a C+, mused Todd. Amy was very popular with the other students, a cheerleader but, like many of her peers, often more interested in members of the opposite sex than in school. Ferris would, at best, make a D or fail. He was not interested in social studies, and Todd was surprised and pleased to learn that Ferris played first chair trumpet in the school orchestra. Ferris was scheduled to play a solo for spring graduation ceremonies. Ferris had confided in Todd that he wanted to drop out of school and form a rock band. Tina would make an A. Tina always made A's in everything. She was bright and quiet and worked diligently,

an absolute delight for any teacher. She and Juan were competing for "highest academic honors" of their class. Theo, an exceptional athlete, would make an A or a B. Theo was the exception to the stereotype "dumb jock;" he made good grades. Al, the class clown, would make a C. Todd couldn't help but laugh at the stunts Al pulled in class, but he was still trying to figure out a way to get Al to study. "Maybe if I threatened to get him kicked off the debate team. No, I couldn't do that," thought Todd. "Or could I?" he mused.

Todd thought he would probably spend his teaching career trying to figure out the diversity of intelligence and talent among his students: Sherry, a C student who played classical piano; Steve, the B+ student who worked so hard to maintain his grades so he could get into a "good" university, whereas Tina and Juan made A's with seemingly little effort; and Stewart, confined to a wheelchair and who, despite being spoiled and obnoxious and a C– student, had the ambition and potential to be a sports commentator. "Assisting students to discover and capitalize on their talents is a special responsibility," Todd thought as Rick raised his hand for assistance.

> Programs for the gifted must address subject matter thoroughly.

> Most educators use the Wechsler Scales, the Kaufman Scales, or the Stanford-Binet to assist in identifying gifted students.

STUDENTS WHO ARE EXCEPTIONALLY GIFTED AND TALENTED

Thus far, we have provided information to help teachers plan for students with many types of disabilities. Another group of students who often need special educational opportunities is the group known as the *gifted* and *talented*. In the past, students who often have been the most neglected were too often those with exceptional gifts and talents. Such students, if appropriately challenged, have the potential to excel academically and socially. Attempts to reach these students have met with obstacles, including the lack of agreement on characteristics to be considered when defining this group. The next section we look at attempts to serve this special population of students.

Because the gifted and talented are not considered disabled, there is no federal interpretation of giftedness in IDEA nor are there federal mandates requiring special education services. Each state determines whether gifted students will be served, and schools must rely on local and state funding if serving these students. Currently, only 60 percent of states have legislation mandating services for gifted and talented (Gargiulo & Metcalf, 2012). However, these exceptional students need appropriate educational experiences to help them develop to their full potential. An abundance of materials and resources are available to challenge these students; yet, traditionally; the practice has been to give the gifted the same assignments-and, perhaps even worse, more of the same problems assigned in class. This practice should be replaced by activities capable of holding their interest and challenging their intellect. Many school systems have trained professionals to work in programs for the gifted and talented. Ask whether your school or school system has such resources and inquire about programs for identifying gifted students. The teacher's first responsibility to these students is to identify them.

Identifying Gifted and Talented Students

Originally passed in 1988, the **Jacob K. Javits Gifted and Talented Students Education Act of 2001** provides the following definition of gifted and talented:

Most programs for gifted students group them for part or all of the day.

Students, children, or youth who give evidence of high achievement capability in areas such as intellectual, creative, artistic, or leadership capacity, or in specific academic fields, and who need services and activities not ordinarily provided by the school in order to fully develop those capabilities. (National Association of Gifted Children, 2008 p, 10)

The determination of eligibility for services in gifted and talented programs varies in different states and in different school districts. However, a common criterion used for acceptance is obtaining an IQ of 130-135 or above on the Wechsler Scales, the Kaufman Scales, or the Stanford-Binet. Furthermore, most school systems do not use IQ exclusively, but consider teacher rating scales, student grades, scores on standardized tests, and/or tests of creative thinking when determining eligibility.

When you think of a gifted and talented student, what characteristics come to mind? Bohlin, Durwin, and Reese-Weber (2009) summarized research on the common traits of students who are gifted and talented:

> Many gifted students are self-conscious.

- Students who are gifted master knowledge or skills in a particular domain earlier than their peers (Steiner & Carr, 2003; Winner, 1996). They tend to have above-average ability in a particular subject, such as reading, mathematics, science, art, or music, or they have above-average ability overall (Renzull, 2002).

- These students process information more efficiently, learn at a faster pace, use more effective strategies, and monitor their understanding better than their non-gifted peers (Davidson & Davidson, 2004; Robinson, 2000; Steiner & Carr, 2003).

> Grouping gifted students can improve their self-images.

- These students are independent learners. They require less direct instruction and support from teachers than their non-gifted peers (Winner, 1996). They also make discoveries on their own and solve problems in unique ways, showing flexibility and creativity in the way they apply their knowledge to novel situations.

- Students who are gifted possess a high level of interest and intrinsic motivation, an internal drive to learn and master topics within their area of giftedness (Winner, 2000). As preschoolers, children who are gifted display unusual curiosity, a high level of questioning, and an intense desire to learn (Creel & Karnes, 1988; Gross, 1993). School-aged students who are gifted seek out challenging tasks, exhibit boredom at tasks they consider too easy, and have high personal standards for their performance, sometimes to the point of perfection (LoCicero & Ashbly, 2000; Parker, 1997).

Once gifted students are identified, most programs providing special services group these students for part or all of the day. According to Feldhusen (1989),

> Children who are gifted and talented complain a great deal about the boredom of their classroom experiences; they are forced to spend a lot of time being taught things they already know, doing repetitive drill sheets and activities, and receiving instruction on new material at too slow a pace. These experiences probably cause

gifted youth to lose motivation to learn, to get by with minimum effort, or to reject school as a worthwhile experience. (p. 6)

Grouping gifted and/or talented students for all or portions of the school day or week can serve as a motivator; interacting with other students who are also enthusiastic about astronomy, robotics, Shakespeare, or algebra can heighten enthusiasm for learning. In regular classes, gifted children often hide or suppress their talents or enthusiasm for academic topics because of the ridicule of peers such as being labeled a "nerd." In classes for the gifted and talented, the reverse is often true: mutual reinforcement and enthusiasm for academic interests can be very motivating.

A research study on grouping the gifted, Kulik and Kulik (1987) concluded that the most positive effects of grouping came from programs designed especially for talented students. Students in these programs gained more academically than they would have in heterogeneous classes. Special within-class grouping designed for talented students raised academic achievement substantially. The Kuliks (1987) concluded that grouping can be a powerful tool in the education of gifted and talented students.

Feldhusen (1989) presented the following highlights of research on gifted youths; the research provides several useful guidelines for serving this special population.

1. *Identification.* Schools are often ineffective in identifying gifted students, especially in finding talent among children from poverty and minority backgrounds, very young children, and underachievers. Identification is most often based on intelligence tests; use of creativity tests or achievement tests is rare. Multiple data sources should be used to identify types of giftedness and to specify appropriate program services.

2. *Acceleration.* Acceleration motivates gifted students by providing them with instruction that challenges. Accelerated students show superior achievement in school and beyond. Despite the fears of some educators, acceleration does not damage the social-emotional adjustment of gifted youths.

3. *Grouping.* Grouping gifted and talented youths for all or part of the school day can serve as a motivator. In special classes or cluster groups for the gifted, mutual reinforcement for academic interests prevails. Removing gifted students from regular classrooms does not deprive other students of role models; instead, it allows them to be leaders and top performers.

Removing gifted students from regular classrooms does not deprive other students; instead, it allows them to be leaders and top performers.

PROACTIVE TEACHING

CLASSROOM SITUATION	PROACTIVE ALTERNATIVES
1. You notice that a few of your better students with inadequate math backgrounds learn by rote to get correct answers, but they do poorly on written problems.	· When developing new academic material in math or any subject, identify the knowledge your students will need to accomplish the lesson's objectives. Take the appropriate measures to discover whether students have those skills. This might be accomplished with a pretest. Have remedial material prepared that can be used to review students on essential background material information. · Rote memory requirements for new academic material should be kept to a minimum. Successful cognitive growth among students is more likely when rote memorization requirements are infrequent (Glover & Bruning, 1990).
2. Earlier, Todd mused about the variety of academic skills among his students. Similarly, some articulate well, some read fluently, others appear to have good listening and note-taking skills. Some students work well independently, others are successful working in groups, and many prefer teacher-oriented lectures.	· Prepare a variety of methods to teach new information. Use visual aids such as PowerPoint, charts, diagrams, computers and iPads, if available. · Check your library or media center for videos on the subject. · Plan field trips and group work, and locate guest experts on current academic topics. If appropriate, provide the opportunity for students, especially elementary students, to handle objects related to new concepts. An example might be wooden or plastic geometric shapes (squares, triangles, balls, rectangles) used to teach the concepts of density, volume, area, length, and width.

Teaching Alternatives for Gifted and Talented Students

Once gifted and talented students are identified, how can teachers teach them? Let's follow the experiences of one new teacher thrust unprepared into a classroom of gifted students.

CASE STUDY

Gerald Lassiter was an outstanding student in elementary school, high school, and college. In his sophomore year of high school, he took the SATs and scored 1370. He was salutatorian of his high school class. When he enrolled in a major state university on the Atlantic coast, he surprised everyone, including his family, by deciding to become a social studies teacher. In large measure, this decision was sparked by Gerald's admiration for one of his high school teachers.

Two months prior to completing his final year of college, Gerald was selected by the School of Education faculty as the outstanding senior in teacher education. With a grade point average of 3.9 (4.0 = A), he graduated magna cum laude and landed a teaching position at one of the best schools in the state for student teaching, Benton's West High School.

West High School, serving an affluent area of the city, had won numerous citations for excellence. Gerald realized that Benton offered the social and cultural advantages of a major city, and West High School was a dream come true for a first-year teacher.

Gerald's assignment included teaching three sections of American History and two sections of Social Studies. However, two weeks before classes were to begin, Gerald's principal, Dr. Bradovich, informed him, "I have to make a minor change in your teaching assignment. We just had a late resignation from Ms. Eleanor Moody. She taught our section of social studies for gifted and talented students. I would like to give that class to you. You'll have four sections of history along with the gifted and talented class."

After a pause, Gerald responded, "I'm a little uncomfortable with having to take the class for gifted and talented. I don't have any special preparation in that area."

"Don't worry," the principal assured him. "We have a coordinator in the central office who will supply you with plenty of assistance. Her name is Dr. Turner. I'm going to have her send you some materials right now so you can look them over in the remaining weeks before school starts. I have a great deal of confidence in you. After all, you're a gifted person, yourself. I think this assignment will be challenging for you and for the students."

Gerald was unsure whether to be worried or honored by his new principal's decision. In reality, he felt both. Using the materials forwarded to him by Dr. Turner and two books he purchased from a university bookstore, Gerald spent the week before the start of school consuming information about teaching gifted students. His first official act when he got situated in Benton was to contact Dr. Turner and arrange an appointment. During the meeting, Dr. Turner gave Gerald a box of materials, including specific lesson plans for the first 10 classes. "I suggest you try to follow these plans as closely as possible," she urged him. Not knowing what was in the lesson plans, Gerald simply nodded and left.

The first day of classes was exciting. Gerald was especially anxious to meet his third-period class-the advanced section in social studies for the gifted and talented. The class had 10 students, all seniors.

When Gerald introduced himself, one young man in the front row immediately inquired, "What happened to Mrs. Moody? She was supposed to teach this class." "Mrs. Moody resigned and the class was assigned to me," Gerald responded. One female student asked, "Weren't you here student-teaching last spring? I think my sister was in your American history class."

For the most part, the students were pleasant. Gerald immediately sensed, however, that competition among the group was intense. These were the 18 brightest students he had ever encountered. He was thankful that Dr. Turner had provided him with the materials. He knew he would need all the help he could get.

On the third day of class, Gerald was surprised to find Dr. Turner sitting in the room at the beginning of the period. "Don't mind me," she said. "I just want to observe." Dr. Turner returned at least once a week for the next 3 weeks. She would sit silently and didn't' provide Gerald any feedback following her visits. At first, he didn't mind, but now the visits were becoming troublesome. In large measure, this was due to the fact things were not going as well as Gerald had hoped. The students exhibited little enthusiasm. They were overtly complaining about the class being "too routine;" and they kept asking when they would be doing things independently. Gerald decided it was time to talk to Dr. Bradovich.

> Effective programs for the gifted students must provide for in-depth, content-based learning while providing for exploratory learning as well.

The appointment took place in the principal's office after school. Gerald started by providing a brief summary of what had occurred in the class, up to that point. He was candid about the student dissatisfaction. "Dr. Bradovich, I'm convinced that these students want to work more independently. Dr. Turner's lesson plans, the ones she gave me and wants me to follow, are designed to have the entire class doing the same things."

"Have you tried talking to Dr. Turner?" Dr. Bradovich inquired. "Yes, very frequently. But I never get anything from her except more lesson plans. I really think these students want to compete academically against one another. I think they want to be turned loose on challenging projects."

"Well, she's the expert, Gerald," the principal responded. "She's pretty well respected in this school system."

"When I decided to become a teacher," Gerald stated, "I thought I would have the opportunity to use my talents to be creative. You know, that is true with regard to my American history classes. Yet, the gifted and talented class seems to be very confining. At times I feel like I'm just a robot in class. In this instance, I think the students are correct. The class is too confining."

"Gerald, you have a long and probably successful career ahead of you. Be patient. Schools require certain levels of structure. We cannot afford to have teachers doing 'their own thing.' Dr. Turner's paid to provide advice, and that's what she's doing."

Clearly, this is not the experience teachers or students want to have. In analyzing what went wrong here, address the following questions:

1. What criteria did the principal use to assign the gifted and talented class to Gerald? Is Gerald at a disadvantage because he is a first-year teacher? Why or why not?

2. Discuss the positive and negative ramifications of teachers being given lesson plans that they are directed to follow.

3. Should teachers have significant degrees of freedom to apply their professional skills? Should first-year teachers have any less freedom than their more experienced peers? Explain your answer.

4. Discuss the mistakes made by Gerald, Dr. Turner, and Dr. Bradovich.

5. What would be an appropriate curriculum for these students?

If the needs of gifted students are to be met, once they are identified and grouped, they must be provided with a special curriculum. A curriculum alternative for gifted students has three important dimensions:

1. A content-based mastery dimension that allows gifted learners to move more rapidly through the curriculum.

2. A process/product/research dimension that encourages in-depth and independent learning.

3. The freedom to explore issues, themes, and ideas across curriculum areas.

(Van Tassel-Baska et al., 1988).

Emphasis should be placed on both the written curriculum and instructional techniques (Table 5.3). A shift in instructional techniques and a procedure for reviewing and adopting text materials are needed.

PROACTIVE EXERCISE

You have two exceptionally gifted students in your class (IQs above 130). One earns excellent grades; the other earns only average grades. How would you address their academic needs?

TABLE 5.3

Appropriate Adaptations of Curriculum, Instruction, and Materials for Gifted Learners

Curriculum

Compression by using a diagnostic-prescriptive approach for basic skill learning	Development of advanced product related to the content area
Acceleration of content	Integration of content area by key ideas, issues, and themes
Reorganization of content according to higher-level skills and concepts	Integration of ideas across related content areas
Infusion of higher-order thinking skills into content	

Instruction

Faster-paced instructional pattern	Use of cooperative learning groups for problem solving and special projects (cluster by ability/interest)

More frequent use of inquiry techniques	More frequent use of discussion
Use of varied questioning strategies that include convergent, divergent, and evaluative	Greater use of independent contract work and study
Use of a variety of instructional strategies	

Materials

Advanced reading level	Problem sets, exercises, and activities organized from simple to complex and including examples that extend 2 to 4 years off level
Higher-level questions for discussion	Extension activities that allow students to pursue a topic in depth
Ideas for group and independent student investigation	Idea connections to multiple areas of curriculum

Many contemporary programs for gifted and talented students include nontraditional content. Basic research skills can be taught to gifted children of middle-school level and even younger. Scientific research methodology is being taught successfully in science classes. Junior high students are being employed by school districts to conduct workshops for teachers on the use of computers (Torrence, 1986, p. 640). In other classes for gifted students, such skills as inventing, logical reasoning creative writing, thinking and forecasting are being taught. See the Proactive Teaching box for other ideas on stimulating gifted students.

PROACTIVE TEACHING

CLASSROOM SITUATION	**PROACTIVE ALTERNATIVES**
You have several gifted students in your classes. You notice they are typically well behaved but some seem to be bored with the day-to-day assignments and some are not performing as well academically as they should.	· Prior to the start of the school year, prepare class assignments that are advanced for the grade level you are teaching. Also, prepare interesting and stimulating projects such as debates, oral presentations, simulations, and field projects designed for advanced students but can be used by any student who is willing and prepared.

· Confer with counselors, school psychologists, former teachers, and families to determine interests, ideas for academic projects, and other school services available for your gifted and talented students.

STUDENTS WHO ARE UNDERACHIEVERS

Underachievers are students with high intellectual or academic potential whose performance falls in the middle third **in** scholastic achievement-or worse, in the lowest third (Gowan, 1957). Most teachers realize that underachievement is a serious problem. Many students achieve far below their abilities. A second reason for concern is students who are achieving below their abilities academically are also contributing socially below their abilities (Henson, 2012). Further, once gifted students begin to perform below their ability, the trend is difficult to reverse.

More than half of all gifted students achieve well below their ability levels.

Identifying Underachievers

Underachievers, like all special students, must first be identified by the teacher before they can get help. You may find it more difficult to recognize underachievers because they are frequently mistaken for low-ability students (Spicker, 1992). Note the frequent characteristics of underachievers (Saljo, 1991):

Underachievers are often mistaken for low-ability students.

- Belligerent toward classmates and others
- Extremely defensive (given to rationalizing, ad-libbing, excusing failures, lying)
- Fearful of failure and of attempting new tasks because of the likelihood of failure
- Resentful of criticism, yet likely to be highly critical of others
- Prone to habitual procrastination, dawdling, daydreaming, sulking, brooding
- Frequently absent
- Inattentive (wriggling, doodling, whispering)
- Suspicious, distrustful of overtures of affection
- Rebellious
- Negative about own abilities

Often low performance is a result of expectations of the teacher, and/or parents, and/or the student herself

Perhaps no student would display all of these characteristics but any student who shows several should cause concern.

Some of the likely causes of underachievement are physical limitations (such as poor vision or hearing), learning disabilities, and even social maladjustment. Often performance below ability is a result of low expectations at home and school, which leads to low expectations by the student. But to be sure that a particular student is indeed performing well below ability, you must check previous performance records, report cards and standardized tests. For example, a student who is making C's but has stanine IQ scores of 8's and 9's, is clearly performing below ability. Stanine scores designate the particular one-ninth segment on the bell curve where the student scores compared to peers.

INTASC Standard 1   Learner development

Methods for Teaching Underachievers

Once you have identified underachievers in your class, you have alternatives to help them improve their academic and social performance. Consider using some of the following:

- Guidance or counseling to develop positive self-concepts
- Extensive use visual mediums instead of textbooks; use of computer recorded lessons to improve listening, thinking, and reading skills
- Firsthand experiences to stimulate and motivate, especially for students from disadvantaged backgrounds (remember, upper- and middle-class students, as well as poor and some minority students, may come from such backgrounds)
- Assignments and teaching methods adjusted to student interests and abilities relating to established goals, whether personal or academic
- Teacher-student sessions for planning and explaining classroom material to be covered
- Tutoring by willing volunteers or peers who can provide the warmth, understanding, and praise often missing at home
- Group therapy with a warm, understanding counselor or teacher to discuss freely any fears, frustrations, or angers
- A team approach to working with underachievers who are gifted or talented, including the teacher(s), family, a counselor, and student
- Grades and tests as measures of progress indicating areas needing additional work
- Instruction on concentration, remembering, understanding and following directions.
- Instruction in problem-solving and the inquiry method
- Informal grading such as conversations with students and observing their performance in the classroom.

TECHNOLOGY IN THE CLASSROOM

Technology plays an important role in the lives of individuals who have disabilities. Parette, Hourcade, and Vanbiervliet (1993) wrote that "the increasingly expanding possibilities of technologies to help children in academic settings will require educational and related services personnel to rethink the scope of instructional opportunities for students with disabilities" (p. 19). Establish a systemic procedure for assessing and purchasing appropriate technology for students with disabilities.

TABLE 5.4				
Assistive Technology Conferences				
Conference	**Date**	**Attendance**	**Target Audience**	**Contact**
Technology and Persons with Disabilities- Annual Conference on Contemporary Applications Of Technology	Spring	2,000	Mixed	Office of Disabled Student Services California State University-Northridge 1811 Nordhoff Street -DVSS Northridge, CA 91330. 818/885-2587
ConnSENSE	Summer	200-300	Mixed	UConn Special Education Technology Lab 249 Glenbrook Road, U-64 Storrs, CT 06269-2064. 860/486-0172
RESNA Annual Conference	Summer	1,000-2,000	Mixed	RESNA 1101 Connecticut Avenue NW, Suite 700 Washington, DC 20036. 202/857-1199

International Society for Augmentative and Alternative Communication	Summer	1,000	Mixed	Applied Science and Engineering Laboratories University of Delaware/ A. I. duPont Institute P. O. Box 269 Wilmington, DE 19899 · 302/651-6830
Annual Closing the Gap Conference	Fall	1,200	Mixed	Closing the Gap P.O. Box 68 Henderson, MN 56044 · 612/248-3294
International Technology and Media (TAM) Conference	Winter	400	Educators TAM	c/o The Council for Exceptional Children 1920 Association Drive Reston. VA 22091-1589 · 703/620-3660

Source: Parette. Hourcade, & Vanblervliet, 1993

- To match technology effectively with any student, there are two major considerations: characteristics of the student and characteristics of the technology.

- The characteristics of the student are of utmost importance. Concerning students with disabilities, an assessment should be made of students' present level of functioning academically, socially, and physically and also their preferences concerning technology.

- Once relevant characteristics have been identified and considered, the focus should be placed on the diversity and quality of technology available.

- Simplicity of operation is essential with students, especially those with mental or physical impairments.

- Technologies will be used for a long period of time, so adaptability and the potential for upgrading are very important.

- The reliability and repair record of the technology being considered is crucial. For example, students using wheelchairs daily will cause wear and tear on the seats and armrests, and equipment can become soiled and damaged. Therefore, reliability and performance are crucial. The best information about technology reliability can often be obtained from the students who use the technology.

- Many resources are available for those interested in technology for students with disabilities. Table 5.2 includes conferences that address the research, availability, costs, and variety of adaptive technology. ■

SURFING • THE • WEB

The National Association of School Psychologist provides a resource library that includes information pertaining to students with special needs: **http://www.nasponline.org/resources/index.aspx**

Web Sites of Professional Organizations Devoted to Specific Disabilities:

American Association on Intellectual Disabilities and Developmental Disabilities: **http://www.aamr.org/**

American Speech-Language-Hearing Association:**www.asha.org/**

National Association of the Deaf: **www.nad.org/**

National Association of Gifted Children: **http://www.nagc.org/**

National Autism Association: **www.nationalautismassociation.org/**

National Center for Learning Disabilities: **http://www.ncld.org/**

National Federation of the Blind:**www.nfb.org/**

U.S. Autism and Asperger's Association: **www.usautism.org/** ■

🍎 A Teacher's Class

NAME: Renée Hidgon Coward, former member of the North Carolina Teacher of the Year Team

I have a poster on my lab table of a huge orangutan slumped up against a tree trunk. His expression is 100 percent exasperation. The caption says, "Just when I figured out all the answers to life, they changed all the questions. That poster has become a symbol of my philosophy of teaching.

Eighteen years in the classroom has taught me that it is physically impossible for me to teach my students the answers to all the questions of life. Not only are those answers changing at this moment, but the questions in our culture, changes in our needs, and

expectations result in changes in our questions. The answers of today will not solve the questions of tomorrow.

I can, however, empower my students and help them determine their own questions; and I can help guide them in gaining the skills necessary for solving questions. This requires a tremendous leap of faith on the teacher's part because it involves giving up a position of ultimate authority and assuming the position of facilitator of learning.

To empower students means students assume responsibility and don't wait for an order, while the teacher relinquishes the giving-orders mode. Empowered students can use genetic engineering and DNA fingerprinting analysis as tools to solve classroom mysteries. Empowered students can convince county officials of the need to rebuild silt fences to better contain eroding streams' banks. Empowered students can build a half-scale model of the space shuttle and launch it from their classroom. Empowered students can reach for the stars. *(Asheville Citizen Times, 1997)* ■

RECAP OF MAJOR IDEAS

1. Today, when possible, students with disabilities attend classes with their nondisabled peers. This may require providing special instruction and activities for these students or adapting teaching materials and class activities.

2. Individuals who have no disabilities have a tendency to underestimate the mental ability of students with physical disabilities.

3. Federal law requires teachers to design an instructional program that meets the unique learning needs of each student with disabilities.

4. In working with students who have disabilities, teachers should always consider the degree of severity of the disability, the duration, and the level of stability.

5. Students with behavioral disorders need to experience success and should not be subjected to threats or ridicule.

6. Families of children with disabilities have the right to help plan educational programs for their children and a right to evaluate it and require changes to improve it.

7. Public Law 94-142, the Individuals with Disabilities Education Act of 1990 (amended from 1975), requires that students be placed in the environment that will least restrict their learning; for some students

this will require special classes, but for most it will mean placement in classes with peers who do not have disabilities.

8. All teachers have multiple responsibilities for meeting the educational needs of all students in their classes, including both students who are disabled and nondisabled.

9. The percentage of gifted students who perform poorly is too high.

10. Programs for gifted students must provide for in-depth, content-based learning and also for independent and exploratory learning.

11. Grouping gifted students removes them from much peer criticism and allows the other students to experience more success.

12. There are ways to identify underachievers and help them.

13. The earlier teachers begin seeking help for students with special needs, the more likely their efforts will succeed.

FURTHER APPLICATIONS

1. Because developing IEPs should be a cooperative effort, you can facilitate this process by developing a way to solicit the cooperation of parents and the student. When working with parents ,you should avoid using jargon. This is an excellent first step to improving your relationship with parents and the student. Identify two additional methods that might facilitate parent and student cooperation in developing an IEP.

2. Research studies have shown that exposure to disabled students improves teachers ' attitudes toward working with them. Increase your contacts with individuals who are disabled by seeking out individuals who are disabled at the university or at a local school. If your college has a special education department, ask for an appointment with a faculty member; or if you have an opportunity to visit a local school, make an appointment with the counselor who may wish to contact a district special educator. These educators may be able to give you helpful advice plus arrange opportunities for you to tutor a student who has a disabling condition.

3. Teachers can facilitate learning for students who are orthopedically disabled by providing a climate of success and by including them in the social activities of the class. Consider the following (which Ms. Barnes used with her seventh graders):

   a. Assign a student on a daily or weekly basis who functions as an assistant for students who are orthopedically impaired. Responsibilities might include (depending on the degree of disabling condition) turning textbook pages; assisting the students in getting to the lunchroom, playground, and bathroom and writing down assignments.

b. Provide a recorder or written instructions for students who cannot write because of a disabling condition. This allows them to keep up with class assignments, lectures, and homework requirements.

c. Locate orthopedically disabled students in the classroom in an area that allows for mobility. Often this is near the front of the class close to the doorway. Students who are in a wheelchair or who must use aids for mobility, such as crutches, are often very mobile if given space.

List two additional ways a teacher might facilitate social and academic success for the student with orthopedic disabilities. Compare and exchange your list with those of your classmates.

4. The serious student is sometimes challenged to find ways to succeed academically without alienating less-dedicated classmates. You can help. List two ways you could make academic success a rewarding endeavor for gifted students. Compare your list with those of your classmates.

KEY TERMS

mainstreaming
PL 94-142
American Disabilities Act
No Child Left Behind Act of 2001
Individuals with Disabilities Education
   Improvement Act of 2004
Elementary and Secondary
   Education Act Flexibility 2011
individualized education program (IEP)
inclusion
cooperative learning
orthopedic disabilities
intellectual disabilities
autism
Asperger's Syndrome

emotional disturbance
attention-deficit/hyperactivity
   disorder (ADHD)
speech impairments
articulation disorder
on-task behavior
relaxation training
class meetings
sensorily impaired
learning disability (LD)
gifted and talented
grouing
acceleration
underachiever
stanine score

LOOKING AHEAD

Educational psychologists believe both "good" and "bad" student behavior is learned. By understanding how students learn to behave, teachers can design and use activities leading to desirable social and academic behavior. The classroom environment dramatically influences student behavior and learning. Chapter 6 explains the many known classroom variables influencing such student behavior. ■

Part 3

Major Learning Theories and How They Are Used in Teaching

Chapter 6

Behavioral and Social Learning: Theories and Applications

LEARNING OBJECTIVES

Upon completing this chapter, you should be able to:

1 Define classical (respondent) conditioning in the classroom.

2 Explain why teachers should avoid using ridicule, threat, and sarcasm, and relate three alternative strategies for maintaining discipline.

3 Identify two major categories of reinforcers that can be used in the classroom.

4 Define and list three ways secondary reinforcers can be effective in the school environment.

5 Define and compare the effectiveness of ratio and interval scheduling of reinforcement.

6 Define shaping, modeling, and chaining, and explain how teachers can use these concepts to enhance student learning and social behavior.

7 State four basic rules for establishing and using a token economy in the classroom.

8 Compare and contrast traditional methods teachers have used to dissuade student misbehavior with more effective contemporary approaches.

9 Relate how teachers focusing their attention on inappropriate student behavior can sometimes adversely affect student behavior.

10 State two ways a teacher can involve students when developing class rules.

11 Explain the statement "all teachers are models," and identify two teacher qualities essential to effective modeling.

INTRODUCTION

Chapter 6 examines the question, what is **learning**? Obviously, learning is a primary concern of educational psychology and the proactive teacher. We will present the fundamentals of behavioral and social learning theories as they relate to student learning. Educators must be knowledgeable of the learning process and how to identify factors making learning more efficient. Teachers can use such information to significantly improve academic achievement in their classes (Oakes, 1992).

Students learn from more than the skills and academic content we teach them. For example, self-concept and the social aspects of personality are learned. How children feel about themselves depends on their experiences both inside and outside the classroom. Habits, attitudes, values, motives, and to some extent emotions are learned. Helping teachers understand the learning process is a major goal of educational psychology.

Consider the school-day experiences of Renee in terms of student learning, teacher impact on learning, and the relationship of both on her behavior, attitudes, and values.

CASE STUDY

Renee, a fifth grader, hurries into the schoolyard. The bell rings just as she reaches the school entrance. She's late. Rejecting her urge to go to her locker, she scurries down the hall toward her classroom. Already, she's beginning to feel nervous; she perspires and has difficulty with a lump in her throat. Why should Renee be experiencing such physiological reactions just because she heard a bell ring? She vividly remembers being late to class on two other occasions. On both occasions, her teacher reprimanded her in the presence of her peers and kept her after school to make up the missed time. The bell now symbolizes more than a bell to Renee. It is a "stimulus" so adverse that its sound generates several complex physiological and psychological reactions (slight trembling, fear, perspiration, and anxiety). Renee has no control over her physiological reactions. She has been **conditioned** to respond as she did. When Renee opens the classroom door, her teacher turns toward her. There's nervous laughter from the class.

"Well, Renee, you're late again. I'll see you after school!" More nervous laughter from the class follows Renee to her seat. Predictably, when the next bell rings, Renee jerks, glances toward the teacher, and thinks "I hate school."

An hour later, Renee's teacher announces it's time for the math lesson. For the first time in the school day, Renee smiles as she searches for her math homework in her notebook. "Math's easy and it's fun. I even made an A in math on my last report card," Renee recalls to herself. As she rechecks her homework, she smiles again because she knows it's correct. Her brother Jim checked it with her last night. "He's in the tenth grade and he's really smart, and he's even teaching me all about logarithms," she thinks to herself. "I'll bet nobody in class knows that logarithms are nothing but exponents. I bet they don't even know what exponents are. I'm going to make an A again next 6 weeks because Jim said he would help me in math every night. I wish Jim was our teacher instead of Ms. Mean."

During mid-afternoon, Renee repeatedly looks at the wall clock. At 1:55, she beams when the classroom door opens and the art teacher, Ms. Worley, enters. She instructs the class for a 45-minute period. "Ms. Worley is my favorite teacher," Renee muses, as she remembers the second-place blue ribbon she won 2 weeks ago in the fourth-grade art show and how Ms. Worley said she was proud of the winners. The winners had their picture taken as a group and it appeared in the school paper. "I love art; it's one of my favorite subjects," Renee thinks. Today the art session consists of sculpturing, and as Renee molds and kneads her clay into the model of a horse, she is unaware that Ms. Worley is standing in front of her desk smiling. "Renee, your art work is very good; I'm so proud of your progress." Ms. Worley couldn't help but notice the embarrassed smile and the quiet "thank you" of Renee's response.

LEARNING ABOUT LEARNING

Let us analyze Renee's classroom experiences. How many aspects of learning can you find illustrated in her day? Renee's day involved *classical conditioning, operant conditioning, punishment, positive reinforcement*, and *success*. These important terms are going to be defined and discussed and will be analyzed in terms of the responses Renee made to her classroom experiences. The incidents occurred in a background of learned values shared by Renee, her teachers, and her fellow students. However, the various incidents differed in the principles of learning involved.

What factors contributed to Renee's successes and failures? Did the results of being late (symbolized by the bell) "teach" Renee to "hate" school? Could Renee be taught to cope with adverse situations such as being late and her punishment? Did the 'A' on her report card and the attention of her brother reinforce or motivate Renee to continue to excel in math? What effect did the second-place ribbon in the art contest have on Renee's performance during art class? Why are there such dramatic differences between Renee's two teachers? Did they *learn* to behave toward Renee as they did? We leave Renee now, but we'll check with her later in the chapter. We're relieved that a frustrating day for her is ending with success.

> Learning is often defined as a change in knowledge, ability, and behavior resulting from being taught and/or experience.

Learning must be defined very carefully to differentiate from such concepts as behavior and development. Learning is inferred from behavior; hence, **learning** is often defined as a relatively permanent change in an individual and/or their behavior resulting from training, being taught or experience, as opposed to change that may be attributed to growth, maturation, or some temporary state of the individual (Mazur, 1990, Williams & Anandam, 1973). Can there be learning without some measured change in behavior? Continue to read.

Behavioral learning theory attempts to reduce the learning process into elementary components. Rather than working with complex patterns of responses such as those Renee experienced, early studies centered on changes in the frequency, magnitude, and speed of responses. Such understanding, it was hoped, could be used to predict learning in more complex situations. Let us begin with the basic assumptions of behavioral learning theory.

ASSUMPTIONS OF BEHAVIORAL LEARNING THEORY

> Behavioral learning theorists believe behavior is learned and consequences that follow behavior can either promote or deter the behavior.

First, behavioral learning theorists assume that behaviors, "good" and "bad," adaptive and maladaptive, are learned. Second, if behavior is learned, it follows that teachers can employ principles of learning to bring about changes in student behavior. General laws and principles of learning have emerged from the research in behavioral learning theory. In the simplest of terms, behavior followed by pleasant consequences tends to be strengthened and repeated, and thus learned. Behavior followed by unpleasant consequences tends not to be repeated and thus not to be learned (Alberto & Troutman, 1999; Charles, 1981).

Behavioral learning theorists assume that behavior—good and bad, is learned.

For generations, families and teachers have applied the principles of behavioral learning theory to teach and discipline children, as in "Eat all of your vegetables and you may have dessert." "When you finish your math assignment, you may be excused for play period," promises the teacher. The child who runs into the street is confined to her room. The student who makes good grades on his/her report card is given extra attention by the family. Most of us have heard "just ignore him and he'll stop; he's only doing that for attention." If he does stop the behavior, then we have an example of **extinction**-withholding reinforcement of a behavior to reduce its recurrence (Skinner, 1953). Conversely, as students observe their teachers cleaning the area around their desks or exhibiting appropriate behavior during emergency drills, these teachers are **modeling**—a procedure that demonstrates behavior to be imitated (Bandura, 1969).

Most learning theorists agree that regardless of grade and achievement level, students learn from teachers, peers, books, and even the physical layout of the classroom (Bullough, 1994). Part of what students learn is measurable as specific knowledge, but they also learn more complex things like attitudes and social behavior, and a host of other traits. An important part of the teacher's job is to formulate these complex situations into understandable principles of learning and motivation. Consider the comments of Dr. John Stone.

A VIEW FROM THE FIELD

PROFILE

J. E. Stone (Ed.D., University of Florida) is former professor of Human Learning and Development, East Tennessee State University. He taught graduate and undergraduate courses in child development, educational psychology, research, and statistics. Dr. Stone is a licensed educational psychologist and certified school psychologist, and he *serves* as a consultant to teachers, physicians, and parents on child learning, development, and behavior problems. Dr. Stone's research interests are behavioral teaching methods and the evaluation of teacher effectiveness. His articles on these topics have been published in a variety of publications, including *National Forum* and *CEOR Quarterly*. He's currently President of 'Education Consumer Foundation' (www.education-consumers.org). Dr. Stone consults nationally on testing and assessing student achievement.

QUESTION: What do behavioral scientists mean when they speak of "explaining" or "understanding?"

Dr. Stone: Scientific explanations are cause-and-effect explanations. Just as an environmental scientist might say that smog is caused by sunlight energizing a reaction between engine exhaust and atmospheric nitrogen, a behavioral scientist might say that the tantrums displayed by the young child are caused by parental response to the child's emerging expressions of emotion. Thus, when behavioral scientists speak of explaining or understanding something, they are referring to the relationship between the effect or phenomenon of interest they are attempting to explain and a condition(s) or *event(s)* that appears to control or "account for" the effect.

Because scientific understanding is based on fallible evidence rather than absolute truths, cause-effect relationships are *never* known with absolute certainty. Thus, cause-effect relationships are referred to as functional relationships, *even* when control of an effect has been demonstrated.

QUESTION: What types of evidence provide credible support for a "scientific" explanation?

Dr. Stone: Although the phenomena scientists seek to explain often involve complex causes and effects, credible explanations require evidence that the proposed cause or causes, in fact, control the effect. Until an explanation is supported by such evidence, it is technically called a hypothesis.

The most direct and credible *evidence* of cause-effect relationships is the demonstrated control of an effect through experimental manipulation of its cause(s). *However*, most explanations in the behavioral sciences are not supported by such evidence. Rather, they are often based on the less definitive finding that a naturally occurring effect can be predicted from observation of its cause. For example, the widely known hypothesis that student success in school can be enhanced by improving a student's self-esteem is based mainly on the finding that student performance in school can be predicted from measurements of student self-esteem.

Although it may be true that self-perceptions influence student performance, the evidence of a predictive relationship informs educators only that certain types of self-perception and certain levels of performance are typically found together. This finding is consistent with the expected causal relationship, but it may mean only that success in school and degree of self-esteem are both controlled by a third factor, such as parental support and encouragement. An equally credible interpretation is that success in school causes students to develop self-esteem. ■

HOW THE SCIENTIFIC STUDY OF LEARNING BEGAN

Crossman (1975, p. 348) writes of one of the first uses of behavioral learning theory.

There's a fascinating history behind the pretzel. About 610 A.D., an imaginative Alpine monk formed the ends of dough, left over from the baking of bread, into baked strips folded into a looped twist so as to represent the folded arms of children in prayer. This tasty treat was offered to children as they learned their prayers and thereby came to be called "Pretiola"—Latin for "little reward." (From the back of a Country Club Foods pretzel bag, Salt Lake City)

The well-known 1800s work of Jan Itard depicted in the book *The Wild Boy of the Aveyron* (Itard, 1962), presents one of the earliest documented uses of reinforcement in educational practice. Itard's work with Victor, a boy literally captured in the wild, is legendary. His use of reinforcement techniques are largely overlooked, but his work suggests that he employed such techniques in much the same way sophisticated researchers do presently.

Pavlov and Respondent Conditioning

Ivan Pavlov, the Russian physiologist, and his investigations of **classical conditioning** are familiar to students of psychology. Pavlov was the first to report scientifically on classical, or **respondent conditioning**, which uses stimulus relationships by scientifically examining the range and variety of *stimuli* (any physical event or object in the environment) that will elicit a particular response (Hill, 1970). **Respondent behavior** refers to behavior elicited automatically by a particular stimulus. An example would be Renee's physiological reactions (fear, perspiration, and anxiety) to the bell, indicating she was late again. Glandular activity such as salivation (when you smell cookies baking or bacon frying early in the morning, if such causes you to salivate), and becoming anxious when you are not prepared for an exam in one of your classes are examples of respondent behavior.

Originally, Pavlov was attempting to answer this question: If you give a dog food to eat, how soon will just the sight of food, acting as a stimulus, cause salivation and the secretion of the various digestive fluids?

In the course of his research on digestive glands, Pavlov began to notice an interesting phenomenon: As his dogs became familiar with the laboratory and the experiment, they would begin to salivate and secrete stomach acids as soon as Pavlov walked into the lab. He discovered that his dogs salivated when they merely saw food, just as a hungry person might salivate when smelling doughnuts in a bakery.

For classical conditioning to occur, there must be a stimulus (such as the presence of food) that regularly elicits a consistent response (such as salivation). The food is known as an **unconditioned stimulus (UCS)**, and the reaction to this stimulus (salivation) is called the **unconditioned response (UCR)**. A neutral stimulus (such as a tone), that originally has not elicited salivation, is now presented. If it is a stimulus that does not elicit the unconditioned response, it is called a **conditioned stimulus (CS)**. The CS (tone) may be presented simultaneously or immediately preceding the unconditioned stimulus (food), after which the unconditioned response (salivation) occurs. After repeated pairings of the CS (tone) with the UCS (food), the tone develops

The smell of freshly baked bread, cinnamon rolls, coffee brewing . . . If you're getting hungry, you are engaging in respondent behavior.

Pavlov was awarded a Nobel prize in 1904 and became internationally known for his work in the physiology of digestive glands.

Classical conditioning involves establishing a connection between a neutral stimulus and an existing response.

the capacity to evoke a response, like salivation, even in the absence of food. This salivating to the tone in the absence of food is called the **conditioned response (CR)**. Classical conditioning consists of substituting one stimulus for another and is often referred to as **stimulus substitution**.

Watson's Learned Habits

After becoming familiar with Pavlov's work, John B. Watson began to expand on his classical conditioning theory. In 1913, Watson published a very influential paper suggesting that many human activities could be explained as *learned habits. He argued that m*ost complex human activities are a result of respondent conditioning (see Table 6.1). His opinions conflicted with the beliefs of his peer psychologists. The work of Pavlov and Watson is considered by many as the cornerstone of contemporary behavioral learning theory.

THE CLASSROOM ENVIRONMENT

Many of you, after reading about Pavlov's dogs, are probably thinking, "In every psychology class I've taken, I've had to read about Pavlov's dogs. What does all this have to do with life or, more specifically, with teaching in the classroom?" Classical conditioning is as much a part of our everyday lives as the smell of apple pie, becoming "anxious" before a quiz, and that "queazy" feeling you experience when you see a police car's red lights flashing in your rearview mirror. All are examples of classical conditioning. When seeing a police officer or a person with wild, purple hair stirs feelings of resentment or admiration, this, too, can be the result of classical conditioning. Obviously, not all examples of classical conditioning are aversive. You can become nervous, have your pulse rate increase, perspire, and even cry when you anticipate seeing a close friend or relative you haven't seen in a long time. You may have the same experiences when you inadvertently notice your second graders collecting money to buy you a birthday present.

To illustrate conditioning in the classroom, let's revisit Renee in the fourth grade. Let us attempt to explain the relationship of classical conditioning and Renee's response to being late for class. As you recall, Renee experienced an unpleasant incident in class because she was late; she also had been late on two other occasions. Conditioning about school rules begins for Renee and other children as early as nursery school and kindergarten. Pupils are taught by their teachers and families that they have to be in school by a designated time. They are further instructed that to be late is undesirable, unacceptable, or even bad. This conditioning process is continued by each succeeding teacher, as illustrated by Renee's fourth-grade teacher. The consequence of being late can vary from understanding to chastisement. Obviously, most elementary students soon learn (or become conditioned) that being late is something to avoid; and, yes, some learn being late gets attention. Predictably, when these young students realize they are going to be late, many become anxious, nervous, and even cry. Others don't seem to mind at all; some may be late because they want the attention elicited by the tardiness.

	TABLE 6.1	
	The Basics of Classical or Respondent Conditioning	
Term	**Definition**	**Example**
Unconditioned stimulus (US)	A stimulus that automatically elicits an unconditioned response	If the smell of fresh bread and doughnuts in a bakery causes you to salivate, then the smell of bread can be defined as an unconditioned stimulus.
Stimulus	An object or *event* in the environment defined by our senses (Operant psychologists typically define stimulus as an object or *event* that occurs before or simultaneously with a response.)	Students scurry to their lockers after bells signal the end of a school day. The bell can be defined as a stimulus.
Neutral stimulus	A stimulus that has no recognizable effect on a defined behavior	If a teacher rewards students with candy as a reward for *improving* spelling quiz scores and the result is no improvement in scores, the free time could be defined as a neutral stimulus in relation to spelling quiz scores. (You should be very cautious about using eatables as a student reward. Health issues and allergies could pose serious problems.)
Unconditioned response	A response elicited by an unconditioned stimulus	If the smell of fresh bread and doughnuts causes you to salivate, then salivation can be defined as an unconditioned response.
Conditioned stimulus	A stimulus that has acquired the ability to elicit a conditioned response by consistent pairing with another stimulus that already evokes the response	When Renee jerked or gets anxious at the sound of a school bell because of her aversive experiences of being late, then the bell can be defined as a conditioned stimulus.
Conditioned response	A response that is elicited by a conditioned stimulus	In the example cited for a conditioned stimulus, the anxiousness of Renee is identified as the conditioned response.
Generalization	Generalization occurs when a student's capability of performance is elicited by stimuli or environments other than the stimulus or environment where the performance was originally learned	A fifth grader learns the concept of fractions in math class. As a result, in her social studies class she understands what one-third of eligible *voters* in the state voting in the last election means.

Once a response has been conditioned to a specific stimulus, a similar stimulus can produce the response. This process of substituting stimuli is called generalization.

Initially, the teacher's understanding or displeasure is the unconditioned stimulus, and the resulting student anxiousness, crying, or not caring is the unconditioned response. Teachers who understand the classical conditioning process understand why students such as Renee will exhibit such responses when they're going to be late.

Let's introduce an unrelated or conditioned stimulus, such as a tone, to our explanation. Under normal conditions, the sound of a bell to beginning first graders produces no anxiety or tears. But if the first graders learn (or are conditioned) that the sound of the bell means they're late, and as a result they will be the recipient of the teacher's wrath, then this sound may soon elicit anxiety, frustration, or even crying. Why did Renee become anxious with a lump in her throat, at the sound of a bell? It was the result of classical conditioning. The bell is the conditioned stimulus that elicits the conditioned responses of tears and trembling. Can you identify the unconditioned stimulus? If you say it is the teacher's displeasure, ridicule, or punishment, you are correct. Figure 6.1 illustrates the connection between Renee's response to being tardy and classical conditioning.

External Factors Affecting Student Behavior

Pavlov's continued work added to our understanding of classical conditioning in the school environment. For example, he experimented extensively with the processes of **generalization**. He found that once a response had been conditioned to a specific stimulus, it was not necessary to present the exact stimulus for the response to occur again—a similar stimulus would also evoke the response (Lazarus, 1976). This tendency to elicit the same response using similar stimuli was labeled **generalization**. For example, Renee might also become reluctant to answer questions during class for fear of ridicule or other unpleasant reactions from her teacher and fellow students. When teachers present fear-eliciting stimuli such as ridicule, contempt, or excessive criticism, the results can generalize to the extent that speaking in class elicits fear and anxiety, just as a tone elicited salivation with Pavlov's dogs.

Most students are able to discern among expectations of various teachers but for some students it is difficult.

Students' fear of teachers can generalize to other teachers and often to other stimuli in the school environment. Students are constantly required to make very subtle discriminations about situations in school that require very specific modes of responding. Unfortunately, sometimes young students (or even adults) are unable to discriminate between the expectations of various teachers (or of the same teachers in different situations at different times) and behave accordingly. Therefore, the classroom teacher should be aware of the potential dangers of aversive punishment. Psychologically, the potential harm is well defined in conditioning principles. (This is discussed in detail in Chapter 12.)

At the start of first grade, the ringing class bell produces no fear in Renee.

However, after Renee is late to class and is chastised for her tardiness, she associates the ringing bell with her teacher's wrath.

Now when the bell rings, Renee exhibits trembling and tearfulness—the result of classical conditioning.

Figure 6.1 Stimuli and responses in classical conditioning

Hopefully, when you become a teacher, you will behave in ways that enhance the likelihood of being regarded by your students as positive, understanding, and enjoyable. If so, students (especially elementary) will be more likely to generalize their positive feelings toward you and learning, to other teachers, and their peers. Can you identify examples of classical conditioning Renee experienced with Ms. Worley that were pleasant? The Proactive Teaching box looks at ways many students have been conditioned and suggests proactive alternatives for overcoming their learned behaviors.

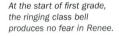

PROACTIVE TEACHING

As we have stressed in this chapter, learning theorists contend that a considerable amount of student behavior can be attributed to classical or respondent conditioning. As a result, you can expect the following or similar incidents to occur in your future elementary or secondary classroom.

CLASSROOM SITUATION

You have been cautioned by fellow teachers to expect the following behaviors:

1. Your students will rush from their seats to the next class or their lockers each time the school bell rings announcing lunch or the end of a class period.

PROACTIVE ALTERNATIVES

· During the first week of class, communicate verbally and in writing the conduct you expect from your students. This should include the behavior of students when a bell rings. For example, communicate to students that desks

2. During emergency drills, some elementary students will become loud and unruly.

3. During science lessons on reptiles, a few middle school students will want to leave the room.

4. Some high school transfer students will be quiet, sullen, and refuse to take part in class activities.

should be orderly and assignments turned in before they leave, and they are to leave class in an orderly manner (Chapter 12 discusses the specifics of classroom behavior).

· It is impossible for a teacher to know all the reasons and causes of student behavior. *However*, you can proactively prepare. Early in the school year, prepare students for such activities as emergency drills, field trips and class guests. For example, let students know in advance appropriate procedures for emergency situations, and discuss the reason for drills. Often discussion, your demeanor, and preparation can alleviate students' anxiety, especially among younger students.

· Preparation should also include communicating lesson plans. Make students aware of future lesson and curriculum content. This can prepare students for science lessons on such topics as reptiles or spiders.

· New students should be informed of counseling services and introductory information from their teacher(s). Try to make time to individually discuss class rules and school norms with new students, and a sincere welcome will often be modeled by other students.

WHY STUDENTS BEHAVE THE WAY THEY DO: OPERANT LEARNING AND BEHAVIOR

Most of the behavior and events occurring in the classroom do not fit the classical conditioning paradigm. This is true because there is generally no identifiable eliciting stimulus for the broad class of behavior that appears to be "voluntary." The operant model or **operant conditioning** paradigm provides an analysis of learning that appears to be *emitted* rather than elicited.

B. F. Skinner first distinguished operant from respondent conditioning. Skinner believed the vast majority of human behaviors are purposive and intentional, not responsive. His pioneering work in operant learning and behavior began with his publication of *The Behavior of Organisms* (1938), where he outlined the basic principles of operant conditioning.

In 1953 Skinner published *Science and Human Behavior*. In this book, he defined how behavioral principles, studied using animals, influence the behavior of people in society. Few data supporting Skinner's generalizations of animal behavior to human behavior existed in the early 1950's but his work influenced others to investigate operant conditioning in social settings.

During the 1970s the application of operant principles to a variety of fields, including education, clinical psychology, and social work "came of age." The work of Quay and Peterson (1975), Lindsley (1978), Lovaas and Newsom (1976), Azrin and Foxx (1971), Ayllon and Roberts (1974), and many others demonstrated how the principles of learning can be used in a variety of social and academic settings.

The distinctive characteristic of respondent behavior is that it is in response to stimuli and is involuntary, whereas the characteristic of operant behavior is that it operates on the environment. Operant behavior, in contrast to respondent behavior, is under voluntary control. Operant behavior includes all behavior that "operates on" changes, or affects the outside environment (Keller, 1969). Walking, talking, playing, finishing homework, taking a quiz, emailing, conversing with a friend, cutting class, driving a car, and texting are all examples of operant behavior, according to behavioral learning theory. When a student studies to do well on a quiz, calls the teacher a bad name, campaigns for class president, takes drugs, or drops out of school, that student is engaging in operant behavior. We trust you can begin to visualize the importance of operant behavior in the classroom. Because it is important to understand how operant behavior is maintained in the classroom, let us review the principles involved.

Environmental Determinants of Student Behavior

Operant behavior is determined by the conditions or consequences that follow it. That sounds simple, and occasionally it is, but often it is very complex (Phelps, 1991). This is because so many and varied consequences can follow operant behavior. Consider first, those consequences of a response that increase the probability of that response recurring. Any consequence that increases the probability a response it follows will occur is defined as

> Most human behavior is operant behavior—that is, behavior that is initiated to operate on or change the environment.

> Teachers can use positive reinforcers such as good grades, approving smiles, or verbal compliments to produce desired student behavior.

> Positive reinforcers are stimuli that are presented following behavior; whereas negative reinforcers are taken away following behavior.

a **reinforcer** (Skinner, 1938). A reinforcer may be as elementary as a smile or verbal compliment from the teacher. This might occur after a student has successfully completed a daily assignment, shared with a fellow student, or earned an academic honor.

Behavioral learning theory centers around the concept of reinforcement, and effective teachers understand how student behavior can be influenced in the classroom by reinforcers. However, to simply conclude reinforcement strengthens a response is not sufficient. Unfortunately, the learning process is not that simple. Effective use of reinforcers demands an awareness of reinforcement variables such as types of reinforcement, schedules of reinforcement, and behavior-eliciting techniques.

No teacher can control all the variables students bring to the classroom; however teachers have a significant impact on the way students perform academically and behave socially in the classroom.

Influencing Student Behavior through Reinforcement

INTASC Standard 8   **Instructional strategies**

Reinforcers are typically classified as either positive or negative. We will also discuss punishment, which is often confused with negative reinforcement.

POSITIVE REINFORCEMENT. A positive reinforcer is a stimulus (any physical event or object in the environment) that, when presented, increases the probability of the response or behavior it follows (Keller, 1969). Such stimuli are often called *rewards* and are often associated with pleasantness. Some positive reinforcers, such as food, water, and shelter, are biologically significant. Some, such as praise, affection, and approval, are considered to be socially significant (Moles, 1989). The realm of positive reinforcers in the classroom might include teacher praise, a smile, good grades, and tangible reinforcers, such as free time, storytelling, and games. In the classroom, these reinforcers might be earned by students for academic accomplishments and appropriate behavior. Teachers can and should be very imaginative in finding and using positive reinforcers in their classes. Imagine, if you can, a class with no positive reinforcers. Yuk! Does this sound like some of the classes you've had in the past? Surely none you're taking now!

Renee encountered a number of reinforcers. The second-place ribbon she won in the art contest, the 'A' on her report card, her brother's assistance with her math homework, and Ms. Worley's praise could be examples of positive reinforcers.

Notice that we said "could" be examples of positive reinforcers. Objects and events can be defined as positive reinforcers *only if they strengthen the behavior they follow*. If, for example, a middle school teacher having difficulty getting her students to complete homework uses candy to reward them for completing their homework, yet, fails to increase the number of students who complete their home-work, then the candy cannot be termed a positive reinforcer. If this same teacher states "every student who completes homework earns an extra 5 minutes free time" and, as a result, more students begin completing homework then the 'free time' can be defined as a positive reinforcer.

Positive reinforcers have three primary attributes: (1) they increase the future rate and strengthen or enhance the occurrence of the behavior; (2) they are administered contingently on the behavior occurring; and (3) they are adminis-tered following the behavior's occurrence (Williams & Anandam, 1973).

Reinforcement impacts both students and teachers. Consider the comments of Cynthia Lancaster, former Washington State Teacher of the Year.

> The qualities of teachers are as varied as our population, but certain qualities seem to make it much easier to be successful. No one should be surprised, but unfortunately many are, that one of the prerequisites should be intelligence. This is a demanding field that requires the ability to make long- and short-range plans for a diverse group while also implementing myriads of individual sub-plans. Teach-ers handle not only their subject matter but an incredible amount of paperwork and interpersonal relations. It is a job whose stress is rated with that of a surgeon or air traffic controller and whose pay is less than that of a garbage collector. To go beyond classroom survival to success takes a well-rounded person able to maintain a balance between his or her personal and professional life. The demands of the job require that teachers should work to maintain good personal health. This means, of course, both physical and mental health. An interest in the student, the curriculum, and the profession as a whole is even more vital as the world shrinks and our responsibilities expand. The teaching profession is at an exciting time. Teachers will need to be more flexible and open to changes and new ideas. The field of education is not a place for cowards. The next decade will be exciting, but I think incredibly difficult. It will help if those who are entering the profession bring with them a desire for adventure and a well-developed sense of humor.

NEGATIVE REINFORCEMENT. Like positive reinforcers, **negative reinforcers** strengthen behavior. A negative reinforcer is a stimulus event, when *removed*, increases the probability of the response it follows (Skinner, 1953). Negative reinforcement describes the relationship between a stimulus and a behavior

Unaware of how reinforcement works, teachers and families often give in to inappropriate student behavior; thus reinforcing the behavior.

it follows. The rate of the behavior's occurrence increases when some usually *aversive* environmental condition is removed or reduced in intensity. A parent may say to a child, "You may leave your room after you finish your homework". If escaping the aversive environment, in this case the room, enhances the likelihood of the child finishing homework, then the parent has used a negative reinforcer. In the school environment, a positive reinforcer is typically a "desired" stimulus presented to the student. Usually negative reinforcement implies that an **aversive stimulus** (something unpleasant) is removed from the student's environment, such as the example of leaving the room after completion of homework. If a teacher says, "Cornelius, before you join the rest of the class for play activities, you must finish your math assignment," that teacher is making use of negative reinforcement, but only if this contingency increases the likelihood Cornelius will finish math.

Families and teachers often misuse negative reinforcement. When students cry or throw temper tantrums over assignments or because they do not get their way and the family member or teacher allows the students to get their way, then the students quickly learn that crying and throwing temper tantrums will result in the termination of homework or getting their way.

How can negative reinforcement be used in such an example? Suppose you have just placed a third grader in **time-out** for throwing a temper tantrum during science. Time-out is defined as isolating a student from sources of reinforcement for a specified period of time but never isolated alone by themselves (Sherman, 1973). Time-out could be in a designated corner of the room or a seat facing the wall. After the third grader is in time-out, you respond to the temper tantrum by saying, "When you stop misbehaving, you may leave time-out and rejoin the class." If you allow the third grader to leave time-out upon cessation of the tantrum behavior, you have employed negative reinforcement. The response "not engaging in temper tantrums" has been strengthened. This is true because you have removed an aversive stimulus (being confined to time-out). Other examples of negative reinforcement might be:

- "You may leave your desk after finishing your assignment."
- "You must stay after class until you finish yesterday's homework."
- "Get control of your temper and you may leave your room."

PUNISHMENT. Negative reinforcement should not be confused with punishment. Punishment is defined as presenting, after the performance of a behavior, an aversive stimulus that *weakens* that behavior (Bandura, 1969). If you can remember that both positive and negative reinforcers strengthen behavior while punishment weakens behavior, the difference between reinforcers and punishment becomes evident.

Punishment has been a topic of considerable controversy in contemporary education and in educational psychology. Should teachers punish? If yes, under

> Both positive and negative reinforcers strengthen behavior, whereas punishment weakens behavior.

what circumstances and what type of punishment should teachers use? If no, what are appropriate effective alternatives to punishment? The punishments that Renee experienced (reprimanded in the presence of her peers and having to stay after school) are examples of misguided attempts at punishment with poor results (Renee deciding "I hate school"). Therefore, we will focus on punishment later in the chapter, emphasizing types, if it is appropriate, ramifications, and alternatives.

What were some of the positive experiences Renee fortunately encountered? What kind of reinforcers are available for classroom personnel?

Types of Reinforcers

Let's follow Todd as he tries a new experiment.

TODD WILLIAMS...

was trying to devise a plan for involving his students in the development of rules that would govern class conduct. Generally, he was proud of the fact that he was able to maintain fairly good class discipline. Lately, however, there seem to be too many exceptions.

Gino loved attention and too often found disruptive ways to get what he wanted. Faye was habitually late for class, while an increasing number of other students were late with assignments. Additionally, Todd was spending too much time repeatedly telling students, "Okay, settle down," "Get back to your seats," "No need for giggling," "Quiet, we're taking a test," and so on.

Todd tried to keep his class rules to a minimum, but he wanted student input for these changes. He thought it would be a good idea to ask the students what they enjoyed most and least about class. This would give him and the students a good starting point for establishing class rules. He followed up by asking the students for suggestions on rules they thought would make class more enjoyable. Next, he asked these two last questions:

1. What specific types of student academic and social conduct should be prohibited during class, and what should be done when inappropriate behavior occurs?

2. What types of student academic and social conduct should occur during class, and what should happen when appropriate behavior occurs?

Todd then categorized student input according to the following:

1. What students enjoy *most* about class

2. What students enjoy *least* about class

> Primary reinforcers are unlearned; secondary reinforcers are learned.

3. What would make class more enjoyable
4. Student behavior that should not be allowed
5. Suggestions for consequences of inappropriate student behavior
6. Appropriate student behavior for the classroom
7. Student suggestions for consequences of appropriate behavior

Todd is trying to discover which reinforcers his students will value enough to effect changes in their behavior. There are two major types of reinforcers, **primary reinforcers** and **secondary reinforcers** (Lundin, 1974; Skinner, 1953; Travers, 1977).

PRIMARY REINFORCERS. Primary reinforcers are those stimuli that are biologically important and significant to the student. Primary reinforcers are described as unlearned or **unconditioned reinforcers**. Primary reinforcers include food, water, shelter, sex, and sleep. The most common primary reinforcer for use in the classroom are edibles, generally used with younger or mentally impaired students. Such primary reinforcers can be very effective when presented with appropriate social behavior if the students value such reinforcers. However, problems with allergies, diabetes, and other health issues often limit the type of edibles teachers can use. Cookies might facilitate your 2nd grade students finishing their math assignments, but explaining to families why their son or daughter is ill because of an allergy to sugar or flour could be very embarrassing.

PROACTIVE EXERCISE

Todd thought he had followed a good plan for gathering data for establishing class rules. Do you agree? What answers do you suppose he got for the seven categories he listed? We will continue discussing Todd's findings later in the chapter.

SECONDARY REINFORCERS. As Todd's data gathering implies, proactive teachers should use secondary or conditioned reinforcers. Social stimuli or reinforcers, such as a smile, a good grade, or praise, are all examples of secondary reinforcers. Secondary reinforcers do not have a biological importance to students; however, they have reinforcement properties because they are associated or paired with primary reinforcers. For example, why are you reading this text? Is it because of your love of truth and wisdom? Could be, but we suspect you want to make a good grade on your next quiz and eventually make a decent grade in the course, earn your diploma, graduate, get a job, and earn money. If so, then you are reading this text because of secondary reinforcers (grade, diploma, graduation, money) and you want to earn money to by food, clothing and shelter (primary reinforcers).

Because secondary reinforcers do not have biological significance, their value has to be learned or conditioned. A first grader typically has to be taught to value an 'A' on his/her report card, but college students do not. They have been conditioned for years to value an 'A', the dean's list, graduation, diplomas, and a job.

Teachers cannot assume identifying a particular reinforcer or stimulus will be sufficient to get students to respond appropriately (Sulzer-Azaroff & Mayer, 1991). How can you teach your future students to value appropriate behavior, learning, and good grades? Consider the comments of Cynthia Lancaster, former Washington State Teacher of the Year, in the A Teacher's Class box.

> When attempting to identify secondary reinforcers, such as grades, teachers should first be sure students value these reinforcers.

A Teacher's Class

NAME: Cynthia C. Lancaster, Former Washington State Teacher of the Year

PROFILE: Ms. Lancaster's teaching techniques are an eclectic blend of things found to be *effective over* many years. Currently, she is struggling to integrate more whole language into her reading program without discarding other useful tools such as phonics, which is once again out of *favor*. A large part of her day is spent trying to build some sense of responsibility and self-respect in children who see neither at home.

ADVICE TO BEGINNING TEACHERS: My advice to those entering teaching would be to be *very* serious about their job and the profession—but not to take themselves too seriously. Enjoy what you do at least the majority of the time. Be *positive* about the contribution you are making and expect to get rich in your next lifetime.

QUESTION: A primary concern of current and future teachers is the behavior of students (both appropriate and inappropriate) and the effect student behavior has on academic achievement. What would you recommend to future teachers who want to enhance appropriate student behavior and decrease inappropriate student behavior?

Academic learning cannot and will not take place in a classroom that does not have an expectation of and insistence on appropriate classroom behavior. All teachers, new or experienced, must accept the responsibility for establishing a positive learning environment. Every year, every class period, students must know what the expectations are for their behavior, and they must also know the positive rewards for, or negative consequences of, their behavior.

Standards for your class must be attainable and in effect from the time they are stated until the end of the term or until new standards are put in place. This does not mean that students and teacher can't have fun. It is easier to create a positive learning environment when students don't have to keep testing your rules. The present environment outside of school has so little structure, we need to provide a place where students know that the guidelines are there. When very inappropriate behavior occurs, and it probably will, it is important to have administrative backing to follow through on your consequence. Students should also be sure of a positive reinforcement for appropriate behavior. Once established, this type of atmosphere gives teachers more time to teach and students more time to devote to learning. Students should be involved in developing rules, but they need to be rules you can all live with on a daily basis.

A new teacher recently watched his class tearing around the gym in total disarray. He complained to me that they were always "awful" in the gym. I asked him if he had gone over the class rules with them. He said he had done that the first week of school. I asked him if this was the behavior his rules had required of them. After he answered in the negative, I suggested he try going over the rules again. His look was pure shock as he said, "But I'll have to do it every day." This young man had let things go until he dreaded coming to school. He is trying to establish control very late in the year, with a sympathetic administrator. I hope it is not too late for him to regain his credibility and retain his contract. ■

> Teachers can influence the effectiveness of reinforcers by changing the time interval or the ratio of the reinforcement.

INTASC Standard 1   Learner development

Teaching Students to Value Academic Success

As emphasized by Cynthia Lancaster, many beginning and experienced teachers are puzzled to discover that some of their students do not share their love for learning; furthermore, the lowest achievers who have the greatest need for help are often the most reluctant to ask for it (Newmann & Wenlage, 1993). How does a beginning teacher "appropriately address the responsibility for establishing a positive learning environment in their classroom"? Can teachers teach children to enjoy the learning process? Let us continue by defining specific methods of addressing academic success and learning.

Reinforcement Schedules

Up to this point, the chapter has centered on the role of reinforcement in strengthening a response or making it more likely to occur in the future. One of the quickest ways to increase the frequency or strength of a response is to reinforce the response each time it is performed. This is called **continuous reinforcement**; that is, the response is reinforced continuously (each time it occurs). However, there also are many situations where responses are only occasionally or partially reinforced. A **reinforcement schedule**, on either occasional or partial reinforcement, is a method of arranging reinforcement contingencies with respect to the passage of time or to the number of responses (Sulzer-Azaroff & Mayer, 1991). If reinforcement is based on passage of time, it is called an **interval schedule of reinforcement** (Ferster & Skinner, 1957). If reinforcement is based on the number of responses, it is called a **ratio schedule of reinforcement**.

INTERVAL SCHEDULES. An interval schedule is based upon the time that must elapse before a response is followed by reinforcement. Interval schedules may be fixed or variable. On a **fixed interval schedule**, the desired response, after a defined amount of time has elapsed, is reinforced. This fixed interval may be so many seconds, minutes, hours, or whatever the conditions demand. For example, disruptive second graders may be rewarded every five minutes they sit working on their lessons without disrupting class.

A **variable interval schedule** is based on an average time interval. If a fixed interval schedule of five minutes with the disruptive second grader were converted to a variable interval schedule, reinforcement would be obtained every five minutes on the average. For example, on a fixed interval the second grader's teacher would reinforce the student four times every twenty minutes (once every five minutes). When using a variable interval schedule, the teacher might reinforce after two minutes, then ten minutes, then three minutes, then five minutes. The second grader is reinforced four times in twenty minutes but at *varying* time intervals.

RATIO SCHEDULES. When a reinforcement schedule is based on the number of responses instead of a time interval, it is called a **ratio schedule**. On a ratio schedule, reinforcement may be given after every response, every other response, every tenth response, or whatever is desired by the experimenter or teacher. When the **variable ratio schedule** is employed, responses are reinforced randomly around some average ratio. If a teacher reinforces a student every time the student performs a defined behavior, then the teacher is using a fixed ratio schedule of reinforcement. If the teacher reinforces a student, using a variable ratio schedule, the teacher reinforces the student randomly. The teacher might reinforce the first time the behavior occurs, then wait until the third time, then the fifth, then the first again. The variable ratio schedule is very powerful in eliciting behavior. The students don't know when they are going to be reinforced. Ever wonder why slot machines in casinos are so popular? The machines use a variable ratio of reinforcement.

Each of these schedules (ratio and interval) can be used in the classroom. In fact, they are all in effect in classrooms already, unfortunately, often without the awareness or comprehension of teachers, such as Ms. Lancaster's gym teacher. Most student progress reports are issued on a fixed interval basis.

Progress sheets and report cards are usually issued every 6 or 9 weeks. The teacher who walks about the room stopping occasionally to recognize a student's best efforts is usually administering reinforcement on a variable interval basis.

Ratio and interval reinforcement are also of interest to educators because of their relationship to the field of motivation. Motivating learners is a primary concern of teachers. We often define a well-motivated person as an individual who can produce large amounts of work with only occasional rewards. Is motivation something that comes from within (internal) or does it depend on external events and rewards? Or is it a combination of both? (Chapter 11 discusses the elements of motivation in detail.)

Student Study Guide

> For desired behaviors that are rarely demonstrated, teachers can reinforce approximate behaviors, thus shaping toward the target behavior.

> As a behavior is learned and practiced, teachers can gradually remove cues, prompts, and other helpful stimuli.

INTASC Standard 3   Learning environments

Eliciting Appropriate Student Behavior

Two proactive methods for eliciting and then reinforcing desired student behaviors are shaping, and chaining.

SHAPING A primary theme of operant conditioning is based on the principle of reinforcement of desired or appropriate responses. However, some behaviors are so complex or occur so infrequently they might not be reinforced often enough to be learned. Teachers can't always wait for desired responses by students to occur. Some behaviors are long sequences of responses and must be learned in small steps. Examples could be as elementary as learning multiplication skills and the alphabet or as complex as brain surgery. **Shaping** is a procedure whereby desired behavior is taught by reinforcing *successive approximations* of that behavior (Becker, Engelmann, & Thomas, 1975; Laud, 1998). The teacher begins by reinforcing any student response in the desired direction of target behavior and gradually, step-by-step, requiring a closer approximation of the desired behavior before administering reinforcement. Suppose a teacher wants to increase the number of social interactions of an extremely shy, withdrawn 9-year-old third grader. If the teacher decides to reinforce when an obvious social interaction occurs, the student may go for months without volunteering to answer a question or initiating a conversation, much less giving an oral presentation in class.

Although it appears to be simple, shaping is often complex and difficult to execute. To maximize the likelihood of success with our extremely shy and withdrawn third grader, a teacher could:

1. Define the target or desired behavior (perhaps an oral presentation in class).

2. Identify the successive approximation steps that are going to be reinforced such as: eye contact, responding orally to questions, asking questions, initiating conversation, and engaging in social interaction with more than one person.

3. Immediately reinforce approximations to target behavior (the oral presentation).

4. Communicate with your student what you are going to reinforce and try to get the student's suggestions concerning reinforcers.

CHAINING Behavior encountered in the classroom is usually much more complex than a simple response association. The learning of these more complex behaviors is called **chaining**.

Suppose a teacher has difficulty in getting students to proceed to the lunchroom quietly without disturbing others. This problem could be approached by teaching separate units or chain of behaviors. For example, the teacher might have the class practice:

- Lining up inside the classroom at lunchtime

- Leaving the classroom quietly

- Proceeding to the lunchroom without disturbing other classes in session

- Purchasing food and sitting down to eat in an orderly fashion

If lunchroom behavior is a problem, this chain could be extended to include:

- Eating lunch without throwing mashed potatoes and dipping Debbie's scarf in milk

- Leaving the lunchroom without disturbing others

- Proceeding back to class without disturbing others

- Entering the classroom and proceeding to desks

If any of the individual units are a problem, they can be worked on separately and put into the appropriate sequence or chain. However, the teacher must know whether a student can perform all of the units involved in the chain. The units involved in getting students to the lunchroom could be further broken into individual chains for learning.

Chaining provides the teacher with a technique to teach very complex behaviors. This is important because students must acquire literally thousands of response chains to acquire the skills demanded by academe. These chains may be elementary motor skills such as holding a pencil, buttoning a skirt, or printing their names; or they may be as complex as integral calculus and organic chemistry. Could you recommend to Cynthia Lancaster's gym teacher a "chain" of behaviors that would address the inappropriate behavior of the gym students?

> Complex behaviors can be taught by breaking down the act into small behaviors and teaching them in sequence.

The basics of operant conditioning are summarized with examples in Table 6.2.

	TABLE 6.2	
	The Basics of Operant Conditioning	
Term	**Definition**	**Example**
Positive reinforcer	The presentation of a stimulus following a response that increases the future rate or strength of the response	A teacher rewards students 5 minutes of free time for completed class assignments. If, as a result, the class assignment completion rate increases, then the 5 minutes of free time can be defined as a positive reinforcer.
Negative reinforcer	The removal of a stimulus (usually aversive) following a response that increases the future rate or strength of the response	The family of Brad, a sixth grader, requires him to stay in his room until he completes his homework. If Brad's homework completion rate increases because the requirement of staying in his room will be removed if he completes the work, then confinement to his room can be identified as a negative reinforcer.
Punishment	A stimulus (usually aversive) following a response that decreases the future rate of or weakens the response	A second-grade teacher decreases by 5 minutes the play period of a disruptive student for disturbing class. If, as a result, the number of disruptions by the student decreases, then the 5-minute penalty can be defined as punishment.
Primary reinforcer	A stimulus that can be defined as a reinforcer because it satisfies a physiological need	Food is an example of a primary reinforcer for people.
Secondary reinforcer	A stimulus that has acquired reinforcing properties because of being paired with a primary reinforcer(s)	Grades, popularity and money are common examples of secondary reinforcers.
Reinforcement schedules	The pattern of the delivery of reinforcers contingent upon the number of correct responses (ratio) and upon the occurrence of correct responses following a specified period of time (interval)	If a teacher rewards students after every fourth correct answer, the teacher is using a ratio schedule of reinforcement. If a teacher rewards a student for the first correct response after a specified time period, the teacher is using an interval schedule of reinforcement.

Term	Definition	Example
Shaping	The process of teaching new behaviors by rewarding successive approximations to the new behavior	Assume a teacher is concerned that Lani, who is extremely shy, never responds orally in class. The teacher might first reward Lani for eye contact, then for raising her hand, then for emitting a yes/no response, then for emitting a response of several words. Such a process is called shaping.
Chaining	An instructional technique that requires the teacher to reinforce appropriate or correct responses in a sequence that results in performing the target behavior	A mother is teaching her 3-year-old son how to put on a shirt. She might first reward him for placing his right arm in the right sleeve, then the left arm in the left sleeve, then buttoning the front of the shirt, then tucking the shirt into his pants.

PROACTIVE TEACHING

CLASSROOM SITUATION

You are concerned about the general environment and atmosphere of your classroom. You recognize the classroom environment has a dramatic impact on learning and social behavior.

PROACTIVE ALTERNATIVES

You can take a number of steps to enhance the social and academic climate of your classroom.

· Arrange your classroom to fit the academic needs of your students. This may mean arranging student desks, tables, and chairs in rows or semicircles. You may want to design the layout of your classroom to include "**Learning Centers**," which are defined as classroom areas focusing on a major academic or social topic such as science, math, or English; current *events;* depending on the topics and student/teacher interaction planned for the day. When direct instruction with student attention is required, arranging desks in a traditional (rows facing the teacher) is the most effective (Renne, 1997). For class discussion, interaction, and participation arranging in circles or semi-circles is most effective (Borden, 2003). Arranging the classroom environment for optimum learning and appropriate behavior is discussed in more detail in Chapters 6, 8, 9, and 12).

· Prepare your class to accommodate the needs of students with impairments, per-haps by placing furniture for students with physical impairments close to classroom doors and placing students with hearing and vision impairments toward the front of the room (discussed in detail in Chapter 5).

· Posters, prints, student displays, and internationally flavored art forms and plants can add ambience, color, and feelings of comfort to any academic setting. Such classroom decor can be costly, so involve students and parents and provide them the opportunity to add to the decor of their classroom setting. Remember that you and your students will be spending the major portion of the day in your class. Therefore, make your classroom a pleasant place to be.

Morrow and colleagues (2006) offer an excellent example of an exemplary 4th grade teacher arranging the class for optimum learning and appropriate behavior while integrating class subject matter. The class day is arranged as follows:

· When students enter the classroom in the morning, there is a "Do Now" message on the board.

· After students finish the "Do Now" assignment (approximately 15 minutes), they line up for Music.

· When students return from Music, the teacher discusses projects due, homework and "Do Now" assignment.

- Next on the agenda is the teacher reading aloud to students. Before reading, she leads a discussion on predictions of what is to be read from previous reading or story title.
- During her reading, teacher pauses and discusses important issues from reading, emphasizing connections to other subject matter such as social studies and math.
- The teacher uses vocal and facial expressions to express characters in story, stopping to emphasize connections of story to her students.
- After reading, social studies begins with a unit on regions of the U. S. The teacher assigns her students a book project choosing a state in the United States as the topic. She discusses what the finished product should look like and provides time for students to begin.
- When Social Studies ends, student work in progress is taken up and students are assigned to groups for the next subject—Math.

  This proactive scheduling of class activity and integration of subject matter continues throughout the class day.

> " Teachers may count themselves successful when their students become engrossed in their field, study conscientiously, and do more than is required of them, but the important thing is what they do when they are no longer being taught. "
>
> B. F. SKINNER

SOCIAL LEARNING THEORY

Social learning theory examines how children learn—by observing, modeling, and imitating others' behaviors. Social learning theory is often used to explain the acquisition of language and other complex behaviors (Eggen & Kauchak, 1992).

Beyond Reinforcement

Many view reinforcement in broader terms than we have defined in this chapter. As early as 1966 Rotter's research on the nature of effective reinforcement, argued that positive and negative reinforcement are effective only to the extent they are perceived by students to be contingent upon their behavior.

More researchers (Evertson & Harris, 1992; Fuhr, 1993; Lincoln, 1993; Tierno, 1991) also contend that students who are rewarded for good school performance (for example, receiving good grades) will respond with enhanced effort in school only to the extent they perceive and value the relationship between their behavior and the reward. Rotter further suggested that the ability to link behavior and rewards is determined by more than just a specific experience, such as experiences in other situations the student perceives as similar to the present situation.

Social Reinforcement

Past social learning theorists such as Zimmerman and Kleefield (1977) and Bandura (1986, 2001) acknowledge the value of reinforcement and, as a result, have expanded its definition to include the social aspects of the school environment. They contend that *social reinforcers* are prevalent in the classroom environment and include direct reinforcement, vicarious reinforcement, and self-reinforcement. Direct reinforcement occurs during the process of *modeling* (discussed later). A middle-school computer science teacher, for example, may demonstrate to a student the proper use of a keyboard. If the student is able to imitate the demonstration, and the teacher praises or rewards the student with a good grade, then direct reinforcement takes place.

Communicating to students through sources other than the teacher can be accomplished through vicarious reinforcement; this "happens when we see others being rewarded or punished for particular actions and then modify our behavior as if we had received the consequences ourselves" (Woolfolk, 1995, p. 221). For example, if the student sitting next to Renee heard her being praised by Ms. Worley for her artwork and as a result worked more diligently on his work, this would demonstrate vicarious reinforcement. It is very important for teachers to understand that reinforcement such as praise, a smile, or a good grade directed toward one student can impact other students. Vicarious reinforcement is also often the result of modeling. In this situation a student may observe how other students are treated in certain situations and, as a result, imitate their behavior. For example, a student observes a classmate being praised by the teacher for turning in math homework on time and, as a result, works hard to turn in the next math homework assignment in anticipation of receiving teacher praise and attention. Conversely, vicarious reinforcement can also result when students see others being ridiculed or criticized by teachers. Students who watch other students being criticized may react accordingly. Remember the "nervous laughter" of Renee's peers when she entered the classroom late? A teacher's expression of anger can obviously condition students that something unpleasant is likely to follow. Hence, recognition of teacher anger can trigger fearful reactions in the student. Remember Renee beaming and smiling when Ms. Worley came into her classroom? Hence, teacher praise and warmth can trigger pleasant reactions in students.

Self-reinforcement is one of the most important academic reinforcers. In self-reinforcement, students are reinforced by personal goals, standards, or criteria they have set for themselves; they do not depend on reinforcement from others. A major goal of education is facilitating student independence, self-reliance, and self-motivation. Self-reinforcement is critical to the educational process (Chance, 1992).

Secondary school students may read and learn English literature because they enjoy good reading, or because they have discovered that such reading is essential to earning a good grade. Therefore, for them, learning English literature is reinforcing because of their personal values and their desire to please a teacher or earn a good grade.

The "Model" Teacher

The process whereby students learn from imitating the behavior of another individual, such as another student or the teacher, is called *modeling*, or **social learning** (Bandura, 1977, 2000). Modeling is an important factor in the school environment because the behavior of an influential or prestigious person, such as a teacher, is more likely to be imitated by students. Streitmatter (1994) points out that teacher practices and behavior are often modeled by students at times when the teacher is unaware that modeling is taking place.

Social learning theorists such as Albert Bandura (1969, 1986, 2000, 2001) maintain that the concept of imitation, or modeling, is critical in explaining and expanding learning among students, particularly the learning of social behavior. Consequently, he began to study how teacher models could be used to enhance the academic and social behavior of students.

The majority of students, including those who are gifted and those who are physically or mentally impaired, respond to the behavior of a *model*. Models are observed in real life, or they can be portrayed in films, on TV, or in books. It is important, however, to point out that neither adults nor students imitate or model indiscriminately. Some models are more apt to be imitated than others, particularly those perceived to be warm and nurturing, popular and those in positions of status and power (Lewis & Watson, 1996). Additionally, they typically are in a position to give and withhold rewards and reinforcers.

Research by Alvord and O'Leary (1985), Bandura (2000), and Glasser (1990) demonstrated that modeling and imitation can have a dramatic effect on the behavior of students in the classroom. As models, teachers can influence the selection of standards of achievement, the bases for self-evaluation, and the development of moral judgment. As students come in contact with teachers and

The ways teachers treat students affects the behavior of other observing students.

Instructor Manual

Teachers are role models for students.

Bandura maintains that the behavior of one person is often influenced by the consequences of behavior observed in another person (vicarious reinforcement), as occurs with teacher and student.

peers, they observe their behavior and often adopt their language, mannerisms, and other types of social and academic behavior. The teacher is consistently in the presence of students during the school day and is typically in control of the dispensation of rewards such as smiles, verbal praise, and a host of others. These types of teacher behaviors also are apt to be imitated. Researchers at the Center for Research at Stanford University offer further evidence that students view teachers as models; students' repeat a recurring message-they want their teachers to care about them (Bosworth, 1995).

WHAT WOULD YOU DO?

In every state, education reform programs are increasing the pressure on teachers to increase the achievement scores of students. Suppose you have a student who is highly admired by his or her classmates and yet this student thinks it's cool to cruise along and earn Cs and Ds. One such student actually responded to just enough test items to earn a C or C minus, leaving the rest of the questions blank. He didn't want to be thought of as a 'nerd' by his peers. Is it feasible to use another student as a model to reverse the behavior of this student?

Ms. Susan C. Lloyd, former Alabama Teacher of the Year provides an Excellent Example of a 'Model' Teacher.

 A Teacher's Class

> In the past, teachers used aversive strategies to deter undesirable behavior. Skinner suggested that teachers should accentuate observed correct behavior rather than calling attention to misbehavior.

NAME: Susan C. Lloyd, former Alabama Teacher of the Year

PROFILE: Ms. Lloyd taught sixth grade (Language Arts and Social Studies).

ADVICE TO BEGINNING TEACHERS:

- Teachers must have an inherent, vibrant love of the learning process.

Discipline, motivation, and parent relationships become manageable in a classroom with this type of leadership at its heart.

The most significant evaluation of student achievement should be the extent to which they want to know more ■

PROMOTING APPROPRIATE STUDENT BEHAVIOR

Behavioral and social learning theorists suggest it is presumptuous to assume something magic happens to children when they reach school age, causing them to be willingly taken from their family; placed in a strange environment, a school; and forced to sit in a classroom with a teacher they've just met, and work for 7 to 8 hours a day for a "good grade" on a report card they see only once every 6 to 9 weeks. Additionally, those children who do not adjust to this sudden abridgement in their lives are often given labels, such as inattentive, difficult to manage, and even such as ADD (attention deficit disorder). Still, children must adjust and learn. How do we promote appropriate behavior in students and stimulate motivation and ability to learn?

The application of behavioral learning principles to the classroom environment has been fruitful. Students high in achievement motivation tend to achieve more (Stipek, 1993). Such applications have had two basic purposes: (1) to stimulate student academic achievement and (2) to reduce or eliminate inappropriate student behaviors incompatible with studying and learning (Jones, 1996). We define inappropriate behaviors in this context as those behaviors of students that reduce the likelihood learning will occur in the classroom.

Skinner suggested that teachers focus on appropriate student behavior. He argued that students receiving a correct response or a good grade on a paper or report card can become an insignificant event when compared with anxiety, fear, and aggression—the inevitable by-products of aversive control practiced in many schools. For example, Skinner noted, in grading a paper most teachers place red marks near the incorrect items and ignore those items the student answered correctly. A preferable method, he suggests, would be just the opposite, calling attention to the correct items and ignoring errors.

Alternatives to Failure

A fourth-grade teacher we know marks incorrect answers with a very small "x" while marking correct answers with a large check mark "✓". She has also developed a "positive" alternative plan for grading papers with many incorrect answers. An example is illustrated in Figure 6.2.

For students who produce failing papers, this creative teacher rewards for improvement. She does this by allowing students to earn 1 minute of "free time" for each correct answer exceeding the number correct from previous quiz or paper. Some of her spelling or math students began the school year by getting only 4 or 5 of 20 problems correct but when rewarded for improvement rather than punished with failing grades, these students worked to improve, rather than getting discouraged.

Other examples include rewarding and recognizing student academic achievement and appropriate classroom behavior with the examples illustrated in Figures 6.3, 6.4, and 6.5. Could you use such techniques when you teach?

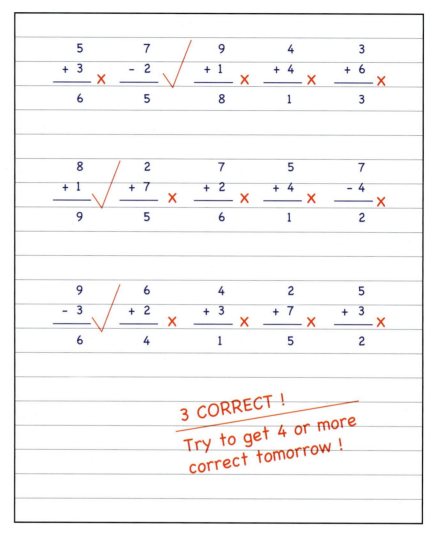

Figure 6.2 Sample of a positive grading technique

Figure 6.3 Awards to all students who completed homework every day this week with an 80% and above accuracy rate

Teacher Goals

Teachers' goals vary, but it has been our experience that goals of practicing teachers and prospective teachers are compatible. If you ask currently practicing teachers or a group of prospective teachers to state their goals for their classrooms, many will say they want their students to:

- Learn and to be well behaved in the classroom

- Feel free enough to ask and answer questions in the classroom (interact with the teacher and peers)

- Enjoy school while experiencing academic success
- Develop social skills that will enhance their ability to get along with their peers and with adults (Jones, 1996)

How have we traditionally accomplished these goals? Unfortunately, secondary and elementary schools have often depended on two methods—punishment, and/or the threat of punishment, and grades.

Consider a typical classroom environment where some students are quietly attending to academic tasks and behaving appropriately. Another group of students is misbehaving, talking out of turn, talking while the teacher is trying to teach, moving about the room without permission, and/or bothering other students. In such a classroom environment, which set of students gets the most of the teacher's attention? Typically, teachers will attend to those who are causing trouble, telling them to "Be quiet," "Sit down," and "Do your work," which are all examples of aversive control. Those students who are behaving appropriately and are involved in assigned academic tasks are often inadvertently ignored (Good & Brophy, 1997).

Figure 6.4 Class party for all students as a reward for excellent behavior while the substitute teacher was "pinch-hitting" for me last week

Behavioral and social learning theorists suggest reversing this scenario; students attending to their academic work and behaving should be getting the teacher's attention while those who are not should be ignored or punished.

How should a teacher respond in such situations? Let us begin by examining ways that *proactively* stimulate academic success. Remember that Todd was gathering data from his students earlier in the chapter? Let's revisit Todd's class for an update.

> Typically, teachers give much of their attention to disruptive students. Behavioral and social learning theorists suggest that teachers focus their attention on those students who are attending to the learning task at hand.

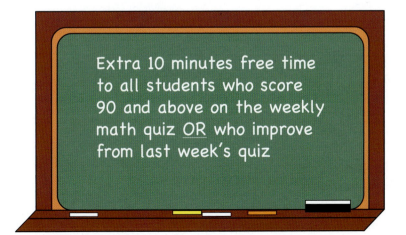

Extra 10 minutes free time to all students who score 90 and above on the weekly math quiz OR who improve from last week's quiz

Figure 6.5 Free time for test success and improvement

> Clear communication of teacher expectations is essential for student achievement.

TODD WILLIAMS...

had gathered his data for involving his students in establishing class rules. First, he asked for suggestions during a class discussion. A few students dominated that discussion, so Todd provided an opportunity for all students to submit suggestions for class rules through a written survey. His data gathering resulted in the following:

1. What students enjoyed most about class.
   a. Field trips
   b. Videos and TV specials
   c. Class parties
   d. Class debates
   e. Class discussions
   f. Guests who discuss contemporary issues in social studies
   g. When Brent and Dean (class members) compete in joke telling

2. What students enjoyed least about class.
   a. Exams and tests
   b. When class is boring
   c. Getting bad grades on exams and tests
   d. When class projects and papers are due
   e. When class is too noisy and Mr. Williams gets upset and I can't get my work done
   f. Substitute teachers
   g. When students are supposed to make oral presentations and no one is ready

3. What would make class more enjoyable?
   a. More field trips and TV specials concerning social studies
   b. Make everyone be quiet when we have work to do
   c. More interesting textbooks
   d. More class discussions
   e. No tests, serve pizza, let everyone sleep, and no class on Fridays

4. Concerning behavior and consequences, (we're discarding item e.), Todd's students seemed ambiguous. The overwhelming majority didn't like other students disrupting class. In fact, they were harsh with their recommendations on consequences for inappropriate student behavior. However, they had few suggestions for consequences of *appropriate* student behavior.

Todd felt he had the information he needed for implementing class rules. Do you agree? What would you recommend as a result of Todd's data?

INTASC Standard 8   Instructional strategies

Facilitating Academic Success

Promoting motivation and achievement requires putting in place a classroom setting and plan that reinforces desired behaviors. These include such behaviors as attending class, getting to class on time, and having appropriate materials (Ames,

1992; Jones, 1989). As mundane as these behaviors might appear, without them, it is difficult for students to accomplish academic tasks. When students routinely arrive late or fail to bring the classroom material they need, the teacher can waste a lot of classroom time attempting to get lessons underway. Behaviors such as "being prepared for class" should never be taken for granted.

The most important student behaviors are those demonstrating academic productivity (Phelps, 1991). You should specify the academic behavior expected from your students and the consequences of such behavior, namely reinforcers. Often students don't perform academically because they get confused about expectations. This is due to academic objectives being poorly defined or communicated.

Todd has an excellent format for getting his students involved in this process. They identified numerous potential reinforcers and academic activities (students quiet when work is due, class discussions, debates, guest lecturers).

Premack Principle

> "Finish your math and we will have 15 minutes of free time." (the Premack Principle)

Rewarding behavior demonstrating academic productivity should be an important feature of a classroom management program.

Another very effective way to enhance academic effort is through the use of the Premack principle. Premack (1959) proposed that a preferred activity (for example use of computer, free time, art or engaging in a discussion on a chosen topic) could be used to strengthen a less preferred activity (for example, completing an English assignment or working math problems) by making the preferred activity *contingent* upon completion of the less preferred. Privileges are thus used to strengthen appropriate academic behavior. Jones and Jones (1986) demonstrated

Identification of effective reinforcers are limited only by the imagination of teachers and their students.

Teachers should reinforce appropriate academic behavior with such as praise and approval.

Token economics uses tokens or check marks students can trade for tangible such as academic material or special privileges.

Tokens received for appropriate behavior can be taken away for inappropriate behavior. This concept is known as response cost.

that students may significantly increase academic productivity when the Premack principle is used appropriately.

For the Premack principle to work, students must find the preferred activity options reinforcing. How do you identify activities that reinforce students? You might simply ask your students to suggest what they would like to do during free time. Todd's discussion with his students is a good example. However, students' verbal reports of what they prefer may not always agree or include what they actually prefer (Jones & Jones, 1986). The teacher may suggest options to students. For example, there is evidence the study of Russian, using the computer, and art can be used as highly reinforcing activities for disadvantaged students (Kaufman, 1976), yet few students would initially list the study of Russian as a high-priority activity.

Imaginative, proactive teachers might begin with a list of events, activities, and tangibles as potential reinforcers. This list should be subject to modification depending upon observations of the teacher and suggestions from students. Table 6.3 offers examples and suggestions of such reinforcers, but it is important to remember that the list is not all-inclusive and is limited only by your and your students' imaginations.

The Token Economy

Behavioral and social learning theorists contend that a major component in any effective student behavioral management system is the use of immediate consequences for behavior. Traditionally, the major sources of reinforcement for appropriate academic and social behavior in an academic setting have been grades, promotion to the next grade, and graduation. Obviously, there are other types of reinforcement in such settings, such as teacher praise, family approval, peer recognition, and even such things as honor rolls and high ranking in the class. However, some of these reinforcers—grades, promotion, or graduation— either cannot be or are not used as *immediate* consequences for appropriate academic or social behavior in the classroom. Behavioral learning theorists contend reinforcement that can be immediately given or taken away (depending upon student behavior) can be very effective.

One alternative is a contingency management system—the **token economy**. Token economies involve the earning of tokens, points, check marks, or chips for appropriate student social and academic behaviors. Such tokens are later cashed in for backup reinforcers, such as grades, free-time activities, and tangible payoffs. Token economies have been found to be effective in working with almost all types of students-the learning impaired, typical students, gifted students, college students, elementary students, and secondary students (Hughes & Hendrickson, 1987; Alberto & Troutman, 2006). A typical token reinforcement system consists of two components: (1) tokens, points, or check marks and (2) some type of backup reinforcer (Table 6.3). Figure 6.6 illustrates an example of rules for a token economy.

Todd had an excellent start identifying possible reinforcers. His students suggested field trips, TV specials, and class discussions—all potential academic reinforcers they enjoy in class.

Obviously, tokens awarded for appropriate behavior can be taken away for inappropriate behaviors. The process of taking away tokens for inappropriate behavior is called **response cost** (Kazdin & Mascitelli, 1980).

Additionally, the more efficient token economies place a ceiling on the number of points a student can have taken away. The purpose of response cost should be to weaken inappropriate behavior. The purpose of putting a ceiling on the number of points students may lose is to retain the system's effectiveness. An alternative is to set limits on the number of points a student can lose in a day. If that limit is exceeded, then the student will be sent to the office, have a note sent home to the student's family, or be subject to some other defined punishment that is truly aversive to the student.

Both the teacher and the student should keep an accurate record of the number of tokens earned. When the token is in the form of objects, such as chips, a token box can be designated for storing in an assigned location or at the student's desk. When the token is in the form of points earned or check marks, a chart or some recording card similar to that displayed in Figure 6.6 can be used.

TABLE 6.3		
Menu of Reinforcers or Honors Activities		
ELEMENTARY STUDENTS		
Individual Activities	**Group Activities**	**Tangible Reinforcers'**
five minute use of iPOD, iPad, iTOUCH. Two minutes for texting class members	watching TV or video	pencils
free time	free time for learning	paper
teacher helper for the day	centers (study of foreign language, word-processing, *videos*, books, magazines, games, computer(s), aquarium, newspapers, music)	pen
time for computer games		magic markers
leader during play activity		glue
cleaning board		large erasers
errands to office		tape

(Continued)

TABLE 6.3 (CONTINUED)
Menu of Reinforcers or Honors Activities

ELEMENTARY STUDENTS

Individual Activities	Group Activities	Tangible Reinforcers'
tutoring other students	class bingo, class spelling bee	construction paper
sitting with a friend in class	trip to library	notebooks
taking care of class aquarium	class party art activities (coloring, painting, clay, finger painting)	crayons
first in line	time on computers	pencil sharpener
oral presentations to the class		rulers
passing or collecting assignments		play money
	students choosing class guest	toys
playing a game with a friend (chess, monopoly, puzzles, etc.)	ball games during play activities against other classes	games
writing on the board		art supplies
	producing a play	football, baseball, or basketball pictures
	teacher reading to the class	puzzles
working on models (planes, ships, cars, motorcycles, animals, etc.)		models of ships, planes, cars
		Nerf basketballs and footballs
		frisbees

SECONDARY STUDENTS

Individual Activities	Group Activities	Tangible Reinforcers
use of iPOD, iPAD, iPHONE time for texting	field trips (museums, historic sites, industry, plays, concerts)	academic material
free time for homework or individual research		paperback books
sitting with a friend	producing a play	videos
oral presentation	adopting an impoverished family	tickets to school *events*, magazines (sports, teen, *movie*, etc.)

SECONDARY STUDENTS		
Individual Activities	**Group Activities**	**Tangible Reinforcers**
creative writing and art projects	watching special *movies* or TV programs	
	class project for needy family	
listening to music	class conservation project (planting trees, shrubbery, flowers; cleaning up public area)	
reading teen magazines, books, newspaper, science, English, math, history projects	class debate	
	games (talent contests, painting a mural, etc.)	
	making a video	
word processing	class science project	
crafts	class involvement in local or national election	
grading papers		
games (chess & computer games)	class project for the elderly	posters (psychedelic, *movie* and TV stars, sports figures)
	adopting a student with an impairment	
	guest speaker for class	
T-shirt art	class discussion on topic of choice	
	family-student party	pen lights
	visiting an institution for mentally emotionally, physically impaired, guest speaker on drug and alcohol abuse	diaries
	visit art gallery or library	
	auction in class	
	TV/video during class	

'Be very cautious with edibles such as candy; while you might not be ethically opposed to such reinforcers, familiarity with the health problems of your students (allergies, diabetes, tooth decay) is essential. Tangible rewards can be expensive. The academic reinforcers we suggest have been found to be equally effective. Remember, the best source of ideas for reinforcers and/or honors activities is your students.

Alternatives for Minimizing Disruptive Behaviors

May we speculate as to why disruptive behaviors are of such paramount concern to teachers? First, some of these behaviors are personally irritating. Being hit in the posterior with an eraser, being called a disparaging name, having students talk and laugh while you are teaching, or having students refuse when you ask them to do something can leave you feeling unappreciated. Beyond the personal irritation, teachers recognize that disruptive behavior can nullify attempts to foster academic productivity. Disruptive behaviors prevent both the disruptive student and other students from attending to academic-related activities (Chandler, 1990).

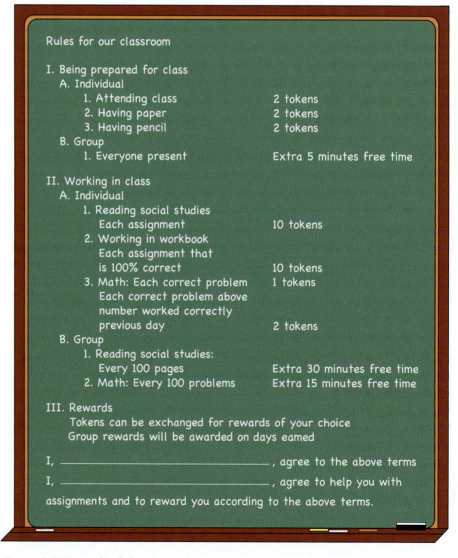

Rules for our classroom

I. Being prepared for class
　A. Individual
　　　1. Attending class   2 tokens
　　　2. Having paper   2 tokens
　　　3. Having pencil   2 tokens
　B. Group
　　　1. Everyone present   Extra 5 minutes free time

II. Working in class
　A. Individual
　　　1. Reading social studies
　　　　Each assignment   10 tokens
　　　2. Working in workbook
　　　　Each assignment that
　　　　is 100% correct   10 tokens
　　　3. Math: Each correct problem   1 tokens
　　　　Each correct problem above
　　　　number worked correctly
　　　　previous day   2 tokens
　B. Group
　　　1. Reading social studies:
　　　　Every 100 pages   Extra 30 minutes free time
　　　2. Math: Every 100 problems   Extra 15 minutes free time

III. Rewards
　　Tokens can be exchanged for rewards of your choice
　　Group rewards will be awarded on days earned

I, _____ , agree to the above terms

I, _____ , agree to help you with
assignments and to reward you according to the above terms.

Figure 6.6 Example of classroom token economy

One approach is to make no reference to disruptive behaviors, depriving the disruptive student the satisfaction of being the center of attention. A different strategy is to communicate to students, early in the school term, the consequences of disruptive behavior and follow through when such behavior occurs. Penalizing students for inappropriate behaviors ordinarily leads to a faster reduction of these behaviors than simply ignoring them.

However, a long list of negative behaviors gives the impression that your class is restrictive. A better approach is to keep the list of inappropriate behaviors very short and include only those that interfere with safety and/or the academic performance of other students. The best course of action may be just to list "disturbing others" as the only negative behavior and then provide several examples of disruptive behavior (for instance, talking while the teacher is giving instructions, throwing objects, or hitting other students).

Some students respond emotionally to repeated penalties. Because of their anger, they may emotionally react to the teacher and loss of privileges. Common reactions to penalties include, "He hit me first," "Everybody else has been doing it," "Go ahead and punish me; I don't care." Some students respond to penalties with profanity. If you can, you should initially ignore emotional outbursts and later deal with them in private conferences. You can also minimize emotional outbursts from students by administering penalties in a businesslike, unemotional fashion, as "DeWayne loses two points for hitting Pat" or "McKenzie loses a token for talking while I'm giving instructions." For further suggestions emphasizing teacher caring and reason, see Forest Gathercoal's (1993) book *Judicious Discipline*.

> When teachers identify inappropriate behaviors, they should include the behaviors that interfere with academic performance.

TECHNOLOGY IN THE CLASSROOM

Technology-based programs are making a dramatic impact in both school-based and other community programs. The Ford Foundation acknowledges the following:

Since 1986, the Ford Foundation and Harvard's Kennedy School of Government have given Innovations in American Government awards to programs that can serve as models. Here are 6 that stood out in a review of 95 past winners:

- *Community Voice Mail* (Seattle, WA): A telephone message system to reach homeless people. It has been adapted by many other cities.

- *Video Courts* (Kentucky): Replacing the court reporter with a video camera saves time and money and is now done in hundreds of courtrooms in many states.

- *Medical Care for Children* (Fairfax County, VA): Low-cost medical and dental care for the uninsured children of the working poor. It's now in many states.

- *One Church/One Child Minority Adoption Campaign* (Illinois): Helps predominately African American churches work with the state to encourage the adoption of minority children. ■

S U R F I N G • T H E • W E B

'Strengthening Teaching' is the major focus of a website furnished by the U.S. Department of Education. (**http://www.ed.gov/pubs/teaching**). A resource for student learning is the National Research Center on Student Learning at the University of Pittsburg (**http://www. lrdc.pitt.edu**).

The Department of Education also offers (**http://www.ed.gov/pubs/parents.html**). Another resource for teachers, counselors, and parents is the Administration for Children and Families website (**http://www.acf.dhhs.gov**). This is an excellent resource of vital information that brings together a range of federal programs, including Aid to Families with Dependent Children, At-Risk Child Care, Child Welfare *Services*, Community *Services* Block Grants, Foster Care and Adoption Assistance, Head Start, and the National Center on Child Abuse. ■

RECAP OF MAJOR IDEAS

1. Behavior that leads to pleasant consequences is usually repeated, whereas behavior that is followed by unpleasant experiences tends to be weakened.

2. Teachers who understand classical/respondent conditioning can use this process to promote learning in their classrooms.

3. Most human behavior is operant—that is, overt, purposeful, and self-initiated as compared with responsive behavior.

4. Secondary reinforcers work only if students understand the connection between the secondary reinforcers and their behavior.

5. Teachers can increase the success of reinforcers by understanding the relationship and importance of both internal and external reinforcers.

6. Reinforcers strengthen behavior while punishment weakens behavior.

7. A reinforcement schedule is a method of arranging reinforcement contingencies with respect to the passage of time or to the number of responses.

8. Complex behaviors can be taught by breaking them down into small units.

9. The ways teachers treat individual students affect other students in the class.

10. Intentionally and/or unintentionally, teachers are role models for their students.

11. Effective teaching requires effective classroom management skills.

12. Effective proactive teachers direct the majority of their attention to appropriate student behavior.

13. Rewarding appropriate student behavior is an effective deterrent to inappropriate behavior.

14. Teachers should communicate the desired and undesired behaviors expected of students and the rewards and penalties for each.

15. Teachers should involve students in the development of class rules by soliciting student input on identifying appropriate correct and inappropriate behaviors and consequences for each.

16. All teachers serve as models; those perceived by students as warm and nurturing generally exert more influence.

17. Popular classmates can become effective peer models.

FURTHER APPLICATIONS

1. Develop a daily lesson plan that includes a menu of both primary and secondary reinforcers.

2. For a lesson in your own chosen subject and grade level, choose between using ratio scheduling and interval scheduling. Write a rationale to defend your choice.

3. Choose a complex concept in your future teaching curriculum, and show how you can break it down into many simple parts, using shaping or chaining.

4. Behavioral learning theorists contend that considerable student behavior is a result of classical, or respondent conditioning. Consider the following incidents in a typical elementary and/or secondary classroom.

a. A class that has typically displayed an unusual amount of disruptive behavior is quiet and attentive as a visiting teacher discusses his tour of duty in Iraq.

b. During the school day, unexpected visitors arrive and students begin to be disruptive.

c. A student is creating havoc in your class and with your nerves by giggling and laughing at inappropriate times.

d. A small puppy on the school lawn causes a fourth grader to become fearful and anxious.

For each of these classroom incidents, list two reasons why the given reaction might occur and two options for addressing the situations. Be very specific and compare your answers with those of your fellow students.

KEY TERMS

learning	unconditioned reinforcer
behavioral learning theory	conditioned reinforcer
extinction	pairing
modeling	continuous reinforcement
classical conditioning	reinforcement schedule
stimuli	interval schedule
neutral stimulus	fixed interval schedule
unconditioned stimulus (UCS)	variable interval schedule
unconditioned response (UCR)	ratio schedule
conditioned stimulus (CS)	variable ratio schedule
conditioned response (CR)	shaping
stimulus substitution	fading
generalization	chaining
operant conditioning	social learning theory
operant behavior	direct reinforcement
reinforcer	vicarious reinforcement
law of effect	self-reinforcement
satisfier	social learning
positive reinforcer	observational learning
negative reinforcer	rehearsal
aversive stimulus	Premack Principle
punishment	token economy
primary reinforcer	response cost
secondary reinforcer	

LOOKING AHEAD

Chapter 6 emphasized how the teacher and the classroom environment affect the behavior of students. Behavioral approaches to teaching and learning is an extremely important topic and complements our next chapter topic, the cognitive development of students. Contemporary educational psychologists have long stressed the importance of student creativity, perception, memory, thinking, and problem solving. These mental or cognitive functions are the major topics of the next two chapters. ■

Chapter 7

Introduction to Cognitive Views of Learning

LEARNING OBJECTIVES

Upon completing this chapter, you should be able to:

1

Briefly outline the history of cognitive views of learning.

2

Define the terms working memory and long-term memory.

3

Explain the sensory relationship of *information processing* and cognitive development.

4

Define *metacognition*, and relate how students can use metacognitive processes to enhance their cognitive functioning.

5

List Flavell's three categories of metacognitive knowledge.

6

Relate the role of Gestalt psychology in contemporary learning views.

7

Define and compare insight, perception, and attribution.

8

Explain the neurological cognitive mechanisms of the information-processing model.

9

Explain *interference theory*, and relate two strategies teachers can use to reduce *forgetting* and loss of information by students.

10

Define *coding* and explain the role it plays in processing information.

INTRODUCTION

Ulrich Neisser's 1967 book Cognitive Psychology launched the era of cognitive learning and placed the learner in the center of an interactive environment.

"It is strange that we expect students to learn, yet seldom teach them anything about learning. We expect students to solve problems, yet seldom teach them about problem solving. And, similarly, we often require students to remember a considerable body of material, yet seldom teach them the art of memory. It is time we made up for this oversight, time that we developed the applied disciplines of learning, problem solving, and memory. We need to develop the general principles of how to learn, how to remember, how to solve problems, then to develop applied courses, and then to establish the place of these methods in an academic curriculum" (Norman, 1980).

More than three decades ago, D. A. Norman stressed the need for future teachers to become cognizant of how students acquire, store, retrieve, and use information and knowledge. The processes of the mind, mental activities, are referred to as **cognitive processes**. Cognitive processes include the fascinating functions of the mind; recognition, memory, thinking, problem solving, and creativity (Matlin, 1989). How students think, perceive, remember, and solve problems has been and continues to be of great concern to educators. Many educators maintain that developing students' cognitive processes should be a primary goal of teachers (Glover & Bruning, 1990).

During the last four decades, **cognitive learning theory**, the scientific study of the relationship of cognition and learning, has emerged as a major force in researching mental processes. Cognitive learning theorists, such as Glover and Ronning (1987), Matlin (1989), Mayer (1992), and Reed (1992), believe learning is fundamentally and primarily a cognitive process.

This is exemplified by statements of Mr. James E. Ellingson, former fourth grade teacher and Minnesota Teacher of the Year.

- Learning is personal and individualistic. We all construct our own meanings.

- Individuals move at different rates and by various means through similar stages of specific learnings.

- Learning requires risk taking and accepting approximations.

- Learning is active and integrative.

- Learning is the construction of meaning. Meaning generation is the essence of learning.

> By the time you reach the period at the end of this sentence, you will have engaged in several distinct cognitive processes. Without any particular strenuous effort on your part, you are grasping the meaning of this sentence right now, even as 'perhaps' your attention has begun to wander to an upcoming rendezvous, a test tomorrow, hunger pains, or whatever. However, the ease with which we engage in cognitive processes shouldn't blind us to their complexity.
>
> BEST & ORNSTEIN, 1986, P.4

Mr. Ellingson's comments imply that cognitive processes are imperative to the learning process. The term *cognitive* is derived from the Latin verb "cognoscere," which means "to know." The cognitive aspect of learning theory deals with how students come to understand themselves and their environments and using their cognitive abilities, they act on their environments (Bigge, 1981). Ulrich Neisser (1967), a pioneer in applying cognitive psychology to the learning environment, defined *cognitive psychology* as the processes used to transform, reduce, elaborate, store, recover, and use *sensory input*.

With the publication of *Cognitive Psychology* (1967), Ulrich Neisser, was one of the first to investigate student cognition and the learning environment. The learning environment, as defined by Neisser, encompasses the overall characteristics of the learner, including the purposes of the learner, the demands of what is to be learned, and how the learner interacts with the overall learning environment. As a result of Neisser's work, *thinking, memory*, and *problem solving* became the major foci of cognitive learning theory. For example, researchers learned that students were capable of learning and remembering much more information than was previously believed possible. This news was encouraging to teachers, many of whom already knew students have a wealth of untapped potential.

In Chapter 6, we looked at how behavioral learning theory focuses on *external* events and the environment to explain the behavior of students. Cognitive psychology emphasizes a different aspect of human activity, namely, *mental processes*. These include ways to enhance student memory, understanding the complexities of student perception, and teaching students the mechanisms of learning, thinking, creativity and problem solving.

THE EVOLUTION OF COGNITIVE LEARNING THEORIES

Beginning with World War II, a "cognitive revolution" was underway, radically changing the way student learning was addressed. Reed (1992) stated the ramifications of this cognitive movement.

> "The most exciting development in the field of cognitive psychology is not a particular theory or experimental finding but a general trend. Cognitive psychologists have demonstrated an increasing interest in studying complex, real-world tasks and are making significant progress in understanding how people perform these tasks."

Prior to World War II, the study of cognitive psychology was limited. John B. Watson, the American psychologist (discussed in Chapter 6), criticized those who studied thought processes, saying that to study how people think is impossible because you cannot get inside their heads. At best, you can only observe their behavior. Watson's reasoning seemed to make sense to many people; consequently, for generations the focus of American psychology was predominately behavioral rather than cognitive.

However, World War II brought a need for people to perform many skills faster and better. For example, many skilled pilots and radar technicians were needed; lives were being lost and planes were being destroyed by pilot errors. Seeking help with these problems, the U. S. military turned to psychologists, who were given the task of studying human performance and developing more efficient training programs. This work and the government's confidence in these programs caused people to accept for the first time the idea that human performance, decision making, and information processing could be scientifically investigated. The success of these military studies caused psychologists to think about mental structures and processes, giving rise to the beginnings of cognitive learning theory. The cognitive movement continued during the 1950s, with a number of psychologists challenging Skinner's behavioristic explanation of language development.

Other factors contributed to the cognitive revolution, including significant memory research. Cognitive psychologists began to investigate and speculate about different kinds of memory, exploring its organization and proposing memory models. Early contributions made to cognitive learning theory included Piaget's theory of cognitive development and Bruner's theory of discovery learning.

> Piaget and Bruner both argued that independent inquiry leads to students' understanding and increased application of academic content.

Discovery Approach to Learning

Students can be taught to become better problem solvers, and teachers can use well-defined procedures for getting students to develop learning strategies and think better.

Chinese Proverb

I hear . . . and I forget.

I see . . . and I remember.

I do . . . and I understand.

Similar to the teachings of this ancient Chinese proverb, Bruner (1956, 1966, 1971, 1978, 1982) emphasized inquiry as a learning process he called the **discovery approach to learning**. Differing with behaviorists, Bruner suggested that by helping students discover the context and information within the context of a field of study, teachers can facilitate student memory and their ability to apply what has been learned. Piaget and Bruner both argued that when students learn on their own, it is more meaningful than when they learn as a result of others. The discovery method is rooted in Piagetian theory, which maintains that students who discover information do not depend as much on the teacher to motivate them as do students relying on teacher direction.

Bruner encouraged teachers to teach students *how* to seek solutions to academic problems. Such teaching would help students develop problem-solving skills, promote students' confidence in their learning abilities, and prepare them to deal with the social and academic problems of their learning environment.

Guided Discovery Learning

Guided discovery learning is problem solving with the teacher providing step-by-step directions (Mayer, 2004), ensuring that learning takes place. *Open discovery* is problem solving without the teacher's close monitoring. However, problem solving is often more suited to guided discovery learning because it enables students to develop learning strategies. With guided discovery learning, teachers can explain materials to be learned. Guided discovery learning opened the door for more contemporary cognitive views on learning.

Piaget's Contributions

Two major contributors to the rise of cognitive psychology were Piaget's developmental work and the defining of **information processing** as a vehicle to explain the mechanisms allowing students to develop, think, and learn. Information processing, which had its origins in communication and computer science, suggests that mental processes can be interpreted as a flow of information through various stages (Matlin, 1989).

INFORMATION PROCESSING AND COGNITIVE DEVELOPMENT

Piaget's theory of cognitive development is recognized by some educational psychologists as the "most nearly complete systematization of how individuals develop cognitively" (Sternberg, 1984, p. viii). However, other educational psychologists contend his theory is incomplete because it does not provide details of how individuals develop, think, and learn. Information processing suggests that another way to study cognitive development is by investigating ways the brain deals with or processes information taken in by the senses. This is the focus of the information-processing model.

The Information Process Model

The information-processing model is based on the processing and interpreting of sensory data and the converting of such data into a form that can later be recalled. Interpreting sensory input includes determining whether or not it is to be remembered and its relationship to past knowledge, and then storing it in retrievable form.

Information-processing theorists believe that by studying the ways we process information we can gain an understanding of how people think.

Information-processing theorists contend that by studying how we process information we can gain insight into how people think, perceive, interpret, and believe. Information-processing theory has changed considerably over the past 30 years. During the 1960s, mathematicians attempted to define the concept of information. Many contended that the function of information was to reduce the uncertainty of future events. The development of the digital computer enhanced this idea. Computers demonstrated that complex actions could be broken down into a series of "yes" or "no" decisions, namely a *bit* of information. The adjective *binary* refers to information expressed by only two elements. Examples would be right/wrong, yes/no, correct! incorrect, and 0/1. If the computer could give correct feedback with this bit of information known as *binary code*, then a computing machine could theoretically duplicate the cognitive processes of an individual. This has evolved to IBM's development of "Watson"; a computer which is simulating human memory and problem solving dramatically demonstrated on the national TV program 'Jeopardy' in 2010.

> To enrich classroom learning opportunities, teachers must continue to search for activities that involve student creativity.

Neurological Cognitive Mechanisms

The off/on pattern of binary is analogous to the triggering of individual **neurons** within the human being. Neurons, or *nerve cells*, are defined as the elements of the nervous system that bring sensory information to the brain, store memories, reach decisions, and control the activity of the muscles. At birth, our brain contains between 100 and 200 billion neurons. These cells specialize in the process of regulating communication and behavior. Human learning depends on the speed of neural events. Neural action time takes only one-thousandth of a second, and billions can act simultaneously. In a sense, simple computer technology is based on the action of the human nervous system. This analogy has been very seductive to many cognitive learning theorists (Best & Ornstein, 1986).

Sensory Registers and Receptors: Receiving and Storing Information

Contemporary information-processing theorists study the process of learning as a system of brain functions (Reed, 1992). Students' primary contact with the information and knowledge they're expected to learn is through their **sense receptors**. Sense receptors are defined as those sense organs allowing us to make contact with our environment (Santrock, 1997). Students listen to their teachers (ears), read the texts (eyes), smell food in the school cafeteria (nose), and write or model with clay (hands).

Our sense receptors transmit information about stimuli in our environment to the information-processing system. We are defining a **stimulus** as a change in the environment that can be detected by the sense organs. The importance of how we perceive stimuli is dramatically illustrated in the following case study.

CASE STUDY

Mr. James, a 12th-grade history teacher, had assigned his Honors Class (HC) what he thought was a creative, challenging project. The students were to identify an event in history they perceived as having an impact on today's society and their personal lives. Each student was to prepare a 3-page paper for a 10-minute oral presentation in class. Following each topic presentation, class time was allotted for questions and class discussion.

When most of the students had finished their presentations, Mr. James was pleased and disappointed. For the most part, they had picked important dates in American history—the signing of the Declaration of Independence, the Gettysburg Address, Nixon's resignation as president. Mr. James' disappointment came in their inability to articulate how their topics impacted today's society and themselves, personally. Class discussions had been brief with very few responses from class members. Mr. James thought, "This is my Honors Class, but maybe I expect too much. They're still just high school students. Relating historical events to contemporary society and yourself can be difficult, even for educated adults."

It was almost lunchtime and Mr. James was thinking about pan pizza, when Charlie's turn came to present the last topic. Charlie was a C+ student who, like a few others in the class, always appeared to perform below his ability. He qualified for HC with high IQ and test scores. Charlie stood before the class and began to read his paper.

"Helping my grandfather clean out his attic last week, I found this old 1953 *"Harper Magazine."* Charlie opened the magazine. "There's an article in it entitled 'The Great Mokusatsu Mistake'. The article is about World War II. My grandfather told me his dad fought in that war. The article said that when Germany surrendered, Japan was left to fight alone, and the American forces were winning. Then there was this Potsdam Conference in Germany, where the United States, Britain, and China—demanded Japan surrender or be destroyed.

They waited for Japan's answer. Two days later, the word came that the Premier of Japan, Kantaro Suzuki and his cabinet had decided to 'ignore' the demands, but three weeks later the Japanese accepted the Potsdam terms. But what's interesting and terrible, is that during those three weeks, atomic bombs were dropped on the Japanese cities of Hiroshima and Nagasaki. The article says this gave birth to the nuclear weapons age. What the article says that is almost unbelievable is three weeks earlier the Japanese cabinet had decided to accept the Allied ultimatum, but by a mistake the prime minister made an announcement that was taken to mean the opposite. The premier told the Japanese newspaper reporters that his cabinet was holding an attitude of

Mokusatsu, a word difficult to translate directly into English. He meant his cabinet was withholding comment on the ultimatum, until their decision was ready to be announced. But an English news agency, in translating Suzuki's statement into English for broadcast to the West, put the wrong meaning on Mokusatsu and mistranslated it as 'ignore.' The United States, waiting for Japan's answer to Potsdam, was informed the Suzuki cabinet was 'ignoring' the surrender ultimatum. On the basis of this, the decision to drop atomic bombs to crush Japan was undertaken and Japan's surrender came 3 weeks later, after the bombs had been dropped."

Charlie paused then continued. "Sometimes it's not too difficult to see how writings in history relate to us. When people misinterpret, like the translation of 'mokusatsu,' terrible things can happen. This is important because it demonstrates how people's thinking and understanding can affect our lives today. I think we should remember that if national leaders can be wrong, so can we, and sometimes that can hurt other people and ourselves."

Charlie paused, and asked if there were any questions or comments.

The discussion that followed was lively, and Todd thought 'Finally'! He let class discussion continue for an extra ten minutes before calling class to order with the following assignment.

By tomorrow, turn in a paragraph-long answer to each of the following questions:

1. Is Charlie's story from *Harper's Magazine* true? (Problem solving)

2. Could there be other viewpoints to the story? (Creativity)

3. What other WWII historical facts can you find that relate to the story? (Thinking & Memory)

4. What insights does the story provide to understanding other cultures and languages? (Information Processing)

Mr. James once again thought, "Students never cease to amaze me with what is going on in their minds." The pan pizza tasted great that day.

As information is received through our sensory organs, our sensory registers prolong some of these stimuli long enough for perception to occur.

Perception: Interpreting Our Environment

As dramatically illustrated by the case study, our interpretations are based on our perceptions. **Perception** is defined as the process of determining the meaning of what is sensed. For example, perception occurs when students can give meaning to stimuli in their classroom environment such as writing a theme on "hot ice" (see p. 264). Perception goes beyond the mere process of sensing stimuli in the environment; perception implies the ability to give meaning to stimuli. In this age of instant information, a critically important quality of effective teachers is the ability to help students accurately process what they encounter (Mustacchi, 2011).

Research to date has focused on three components of sensing stimuli, as illustrated in Figure 7.1: (1) the **visual sensory register**, (2) the **auditory sensory register**, and (3) the **tactual sensory register** (Bower, 1989). Student perception begins with how they see the environment through these sensory registers. The importance and the physiology of the sensory registers cannot be overemphasized because they interpret those stimuli we experience in our environment long enough to allow us opportunity for perception.

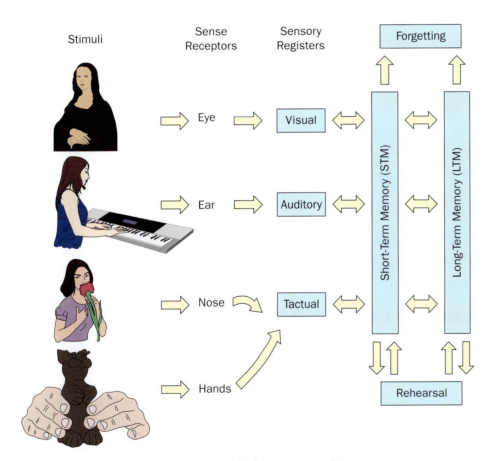

Figure 7.1 Information-Processing Model of Cognition and Learning

Eyes give students the opportunity to read and send information to the *visual sensory register.* Ears give them the opportunity to listen to teachers and send information to the *auditory sensory register. Tactual sensory registers* allow students the opportunity to experience our environment in many areas, such as sculpting or smelling, with their noses and hands serving as sensory organs.

Data gathered by seeing, listening, and touching are interpreted by our sensory registers, resulting in perception. Despite their differences, our sensory registers have some common characteristics:

- Information is stored in our sensory registers for an extremely brief time, varying from .25 second or less in the case of vision to perhaps 1 second for touch to 2 or even 4 seconds in the case of audition (Santrock, 1997).

- Subsequent stimuli presented to the same sensory organ interfere with previously perceived sensory information. For example, if you read a single word on a printed page and are asked to recall that word, you can. If you read 10 words on a page and you are asked to recall the third word read, it is more difficult. We tend to lose our memory of recurring information, such as dates or names, as we incorporate earlier information with the more recent.

- Sensory registers are outside the control of the individual. The individual can neither prolong the duration of sensory memory nor change its form.

- The properties of sensory storage, such as duration and capacity, appear to vary across individuals and at various developmental levels. Additionally, such sensory registers are physiologically related to memory (Flavell, Green, & Flavell, 1995).

Information-processing theory also includes the study of **memory** and **metacognition**.

PowerPoint

Short-term memory (holding information for about 20 seconds) mechanisms and long-term memory (permanently storing information and knowledge) impact student learning at all levels of development.

Short-Term Memory and Piaget's Developmental Levels

Recall that infants in the first months of the sensorimotor period do not have *object permanence*, or the knowledge an object exists when it is out of sight. According to Case (1984), infants' **short-term memory** (STM) allows them to recognize an object and perhaps even that the object is missing, but it will not allow them to perform the operation of searching for the object.

Additionally, children in Piaget's preoperational period (ages 2–7) lack **conservation skills**. When first shown two glasses of the same size containing the same amount of liquid and then shown the liquid of one glass poured into a taller, thinner glass, they will indicate that the taller, thinner glass contains more liquid. Their mental maturity does not allow them to accurately consider *both* qualities of height and diameter, so they ignore the quality of diameter. Recall James Ellingson's (Minnesota Teacher of the Year) observation that "Learning is developmental. Individuals move at different rates and by various means through similar stages of specific learnings."

Short-Term Memory and Classroom Learning

Often students fail to succeed on school tasks because of limited and inefficient short-term memory. Students may use reasonable strategies for solving complex mental problems, but may oversimplify problems or ignore important information because of limited short-term memory. Case presents the following guidelines for helping teachers teach problem solving.

1. Identify the errors in strategy used by students who are not succeeding. For example, students may be asked to solve this problem:

    Mike pours three glasses of juice and four glasses of water into a pitcher. Amy pours four glasses of juice and four glasses of water into a pitcher. Which pitcher will taste stronger of juice?

To correctly solve this problem, a student must determine the ratio of juice to water in each pitcher. A reasonable but incorrect strategy may be simply counting the number of glasses of juice poured into each pitcher.

2. *Highlight inadequate strategies and features the student is ignoring and demonstrate a better strategy.* In the preceding example, teach students that three pieces of information are necessary to solve the problem and demonstrate how to determine the ratio of juice to water. Students can then practice determining different ratios.

3. *Plan instruction to keep short-term memory requirements to a minimum.* Do not assign students problems with too many pieces of information or irrelevant details.

4. *Arrange instruction in small steps and allow opportunities for practice so problem solving operations become automatic.* Emphasize one new strategy at a time and require students to practice the strategy. Before moving on to new strategies, determine the strategy is being used efficiently.

STM is not limited to processing newly perceived information; it also can simultaneously process information recalled from LTM. This capability of STM has led many information-processing theorists to employ the term **working memory** (WM) rather than short-term memory. However, Gagné (1985) suggests that the two terms define different aspects of memory: STM emphasizes the duration or how long information is processed, whereas WM is the area where conscious mental tasks are completed. As you read this text or solve for x in the equation ($x + 10 = 20$), you hold the text or solve the equation in WM. We will use the term WM because of its application to education in that information in long-term memory can often be retrieved and utilized in working-memory (Martinez, 2010).

> Learning must be functional, meaningful, and relevant to be worthwhile and effective. (J. E. Ellingson, Minnesota Teacher of the Year)

> Learning requires risk taking and an acceptance of approximation. (J. E. Ellingson)

> Learning is active. (J. E. Ellingson)

Working memory (WM) combines information we have already learned with information in our current environment.

Long-Term Memory

Long-term memory (LTM) is the part of our brain that acts as a storehouse where large amounts of memory are stored for a long time, often throughout life. Some psychologists believe the storage is permanent; although we may not be able to retrieve some of this knowledge, they insist it remains and is ready to be used if we could retrieve it.

When information is received, through our sense receptors, some is discarded before storage, some is placed only in our short-term memory, and some is simultaneously placed in both our short-term and long-term memory. Unlike STM, which has only the capacity to store about seven chunks of information at once, our LTM has unlimited capacity.

Successful methods for storing information in these two systems differ. For example, rehearsal is essential to keep information in the STM, but *elaboration* is needed for LTM storage. Elaboration involves making broad generalizations about the information. Additionally, information can flow from long-term memory to working-memory (Mustacchi, 2011).

INTASC Standard 2 | Learning differences

Metacognition: Knowing Yourself

Students can be taught how to think better, solve problems more efficiently, and develop learning strategies; however, good thinking is not something that comes naturally (Perkins, 1988). Thinking requires developing tactics, strategies, techniques, and methods. Cognitive psychologists have developed interesting and insightful theories about how teachers can teach their students to more effectively think, problem solve, and develop learning strategies.

Metacognition can be defined as the mental activities individuals use to monitor, control, and plan problem solving, comprehension, memory, and other cognitive processes (Flavell, 1979, Metcalfe & Shimamura, 1994). Metacognition can be thought of as knowing *how* to learn and think. For example, when you study for an exam, you use strategies to learn the material; reading the textbook, underlining key points, and then reviewing major topics. You might use a strategy for learning concepts by reviewing and then having someone quiz you until you can answer correctly. These learning strategies are all examples of metacognition.

"Cramming" and pulling "all-nighters" are also learning strategies, and, candidly, although more effective strategies are available, cramming and all-nighters are sometimes effective, in the short term.

Similarly, you use metacognition while taking an exam or test. For example, if you analyze the tactics you use to solve problems, and when you have solved the problems you check your work, you are using knowledge about thinking and learning to improve your performance.

If teachers encourage students to experiment with a variety of strategies; students may find a strategy suitable to their learning style.

> Metacognition is the process of using cognitive processes to improve thinking skills.

PROACTIVE EXERCISE

A teacher explained the lack of metacognitive skills with some of her students:

"What I continually have to stress to my students is thinking and planning before they begin working on math problems. Some are so impulsive they jump right in and start working before even checking to see if the problem is addition, subtraction multiplication or division."

This is common among younger students because their metacognitive strategies are typically limited; however students, even younger ones, can be taught such skills. How would you teach such skills?

> Student metacognitive ability depends on mental ability, the nature of the task at hand, and knowledge of previously developed metacognitive strategies.

Metacognitive Knowledge

One of the most prominent pioneers of contemporary metacognitive phenomenon was J. H. Flavell (1979, 1985, 1995, 2002). Flavell defined **metacognitive knowledge** as the segment of our stored knowledge that indicates to us that we use different tasks, goals, actions, and experiences to process different types of information.

Flavell proposed three general categories of metacognitive knowledge. The first, **personal knowledge**, is the beliefs people have about their cognitive abilities in comparison with other people. For example, you may believe you study better late at night than early in the morning, that you are better at math than you are in English literature, or that Lo Suu has better social skills than you.

The second, **task knowledge**, is the understanding that, variations within a task have implications for how you go about solving the task. For example, task knowledge is recognizing that a word problem in math requires different strategies from those used in solving this equation for a: $5a + 6 = 26$. A word problem requires reading, understanding what is read, and formulating what is read into a solvable problem.

The third type of metacognitive knowledge, **strategy knowledge** is an awareness that certain strategies will be more effective than others in solving different problems. Strategy knowledge also implies the ability to choose the appropriate problem-solving strategy. When you read a few pages of text, and answer questions about those pages, you use certain strategies to comprehend and determine the main ideas. However, you probably would not use the same strategies to memorize a list of spelling words.

In summary, **metacognition** is defined as mental activities used to plan, monitor, and control problem solving, comprehension, memory, and other cognitive processes. Some describe this process as "*thinking about your own thinking.*" The components of metacognitive knowledge include:

- *Personal knowledge—our* beliefs about our cognitive skills
- *Task knowledge—our* ability to understand that different tasks require different strategies for solution
- *Strategy knowledge—our* ability to choose an appropriate strategy to solve a task because it is more effective than alternative strategies

Teaching Metacognitive Strategies

Metacognitive strategies can be introduced into the classroom in unique ways, as demonstrated by Brian Lawson.

CASE STUDY

Brian Lawson, a suburban high school teacher, related the following in an informal after-dinner conversation during a regional educational psychology conference. He was lecturing on the differences in democracy, communism, and socialism to his 12th-grade history class. It was obvious he was not communicating. Josh was asleep. Rita and Phil were engaged in giggling and flirting. Most of the others were staring out the window. Reminders to "pay attention . . . this material will be covered on the next quiz," and "Wake up, Josh!" were ignored. The end-of-class bell rang, and the students demonstrated enthusiasm for the first time as they loudly exited the room. "My only thought was, 'I have to do something. These students are bright, and the subject matter should be interesting. My students are getting cheated, and so am I."

Early the next morning, Mr. Lawson discussed in detail a new plan. His principal, Ms. Humphrey was skeptical but agreed to try his idea for two weeks. That day, Mr. Lawson explained to his twelfth graders, "Students, since the topic we have been covering in class, 'Forms of Government,' is not very interesting or relevant to you personally, I've decided to discontinue teaching in this area." Sighs of relief and murmurs of "great" and "super" echoed from the class. As he sat down at his desk and opened the morning paper, he said, "I think it would be appropriate for us to use this time to study, read, or do whatever." The students looked puzzled, glanced at each other, smiled, and waited as he became engrossed in his paper.

The students shrugged and began to read and chat with each other. Thirty minutes passed until Trish asked if "forms of government" would be covered on the six-weeks' exam. "Oh, I almost forgot about your grade," he responded. Mr. Lawson opened his desk drawer and withdrew a box filled with 28 small cloth bags and stated, "I have a bag of coins for each of you and an agreement for each of you to sign." He passed out a bag and a written agreement to each student and explained, "The bag of coins is your 'A' on the 6-weeks' exam. If you simply return the bag of coins to me at the end of the 6-weeks' period, you will receive an 'A'. The agreement is for you to sign if this plan is okay with you."

A bit bewildered and confused, the students passed the coins and agreement forward. Mr. Lawson announced that he was going to leave the coins and agreements in Ms. Humphrey's office.

Two days passed. The students grew more curious and edgy as Mr. Lawson continued to read his paper during class and totally ignore the students. Finally Trent asked, "When do we get our coins back from the principal's office for our 'A'?" Mr. Lawson responded, "That's your problem." Silence followed until Trent asked, "Whatta you mean? You took 'em! You have to give 'em back."

Coolly, Mr. Lawson, "Says who?"

"Well, if you don't give them back, we still get an 'A', right?"

"No," Mr. Lawson responded, "As our agreement you signed states, you must be in possession of your coins at the end of the six-weeks' period to receive an 'A'. Did you not read the agreement?" Trent retorted, "What are you going to do if we don't have the coins at the end of the six-weeks' period? Give everybody an 'F'?"

Icily, Lawson responded, "Yes, that's exactly what I'm going to do."

Silence, then snickers, then comments of, "Gimme a break," and "He's bluffing" followed. Mr. Lawson retreated to his paper.

The rest is history, or should we say politics. The students descended upon Ms. Humphrey's office and were rebuffed because they had no spokesperson. Max, a 200-pound, muscular student, demanded to be spokesperson for the class because he was tired of being pushed around. The class reluctantly agreed. The principal's office again refused to hear the class because their spokesperson was not elected and because they were not an "officially recognized body within the school." An attempt to steal the coins from Ms. Humphrey's office was thwarted, and a petition to force Mr. Lawson to begin teaching was ignored. Parents were informed by a few students, and after a meeting with Ms. Humphrey, they

> A positive, challenging, nonthreatening classroom environment is needed to stimulate students to the formal operations level.

informed their children "they couldn't help them, they were on their own." The students met again and elected Chen-Lou their spokesperson. The class elected a slate of officers who attempted to meet with Ms. Humphrey. The response was "all officially-recognized groups within the school must have a constitution." A hastily written document posing as a constitution was refused, forcing a major rewrite.

Finally, a meeting between Ms. Humphrey, the students, and Mr. Lawson was convened. The students presented their complaints in writing, documenting their teacher's actions. Mr. Lawson badgered the students with their signed documents and refused to budge. Ms. Humphrey, acting as an intermediary, interceded with a six-weeks' exam that read:

> You may earn the return of your coins by answering the following questions and submitting them by Friday of this week to Mr. Lawson.

1. During the past two weeks, how would you describe the behavior of Mr. Lawson? (a) dictatorial, (b) democratic, (c) socialistic. Explain your answer.

2. During the past two weeks, how would you describe the characteristics of the "revolution" that took place in your class: (a) communistic, (b) democratic, or (c) socialistic? Justify your answer.

3. It is the opinion of Mr. Lawson that the characteristics of communism, socialism, and democracy were evident in your class and the principal's office the past two weeks. Do you agree? State three reasons why or why not.

> Mr. Lawson agreed to teach class discussing these questions prior to the six-weeks' exam.

1. Can you identify the metacognitive aspects of Mr. Lawson's actions?

2. Does requiring students to understand concepts such as socialism and democracy require the cognitive skills discussed earlier?

3. Could you modify Mr. Lawson's actions to fit other classroom situations that might impact on the cognitive development of students?

Many educational psychologists agree that teaching metacognitive skills, as illustrated by Mr. Lawson, is one of the more important aspects of education Flavell, (2002), Sternberg (1985, 1988, 1990a, 1990b). Classroom problems often result from a lack of metacognitive skills. Proactive teachers do not have to be as dramatic as Mr. Lawson to facilitate metacognitive skills. Teachers can facilitate cognitive development by helping students define goals, structure problems and teach them how they can test themselves (Flavell, 2002).

The Proactive Teaching box offers additional ideas on teaching children how to learn and think.

PROACTIVE TEACHING

CLASSROOM SITUATION

You are aware that your students' educational success and academic interests will be significantly impacted by their cognitive processes and ability. Additionally, how well students learn, read, write, solve problems, perceive, and remember depends on the attributes of their educational background. Because of the diversity among today's students (as discussed in Chapter 1), there are vast differences in student cognitive abilities. However, you are aware that student cognitive skills can be taught, and you want your curriculum to include the enhancement of student cognitive functioning.

PROACTIVE ALTERNATIVES

· Be aware of school resources that provide information on a student's educational history. IQ and achievement scores, along with previous teacher reports, can be very important sources of information *if* used not to label but to *positively* address student curriculum content. Teacher pretesting, student interest inventories, student/teacher interaction, questioning and awareness of student interests via assignments, and family or caretaker information are vital to understanding individual student cognitive processes.

· Remember that skills such as reading, writing, creativity, and problem solving are cognitive tasks. Your approach to teaching these skills should include cognitive enhancing activities.

· For example, students will vary in information-processing abilities. Some students will grasp complex concepts and be unable to do (or be indifferent to) "rote" academic tasks.

· Cognitive psychologists are aware that teaching content is important, but stress on the importance of the "process of learning." Cognitive learning theorists argue that knowledge taught is often quickly outdated, but knowing how to learn can be used throughout life. Therefore, plan to use some curriculum time to teach students how to learn (detailed discussion in Chapter 8).

GESTALT INFLUENCE ON COGNITIVE LEARNING VIEWS

Gestalt psychologists believe individuals react to their total experiences, not just too present stimuli.

Our perceptions can be distorted by the arrangement of stimuli.

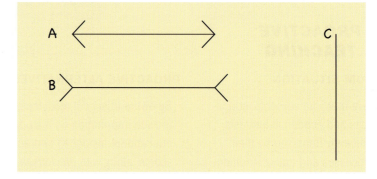

Figure 7.2 Which line is the longest?

Another primary contribution to the development of contemporary cognitive learning is the research of three German psychologists: Wolfgang Kohler, Kurt Koffka, and Max Wertheimer. Collectively, their work is known as **Gestalt psychology**, which means the scientific study of form, shape, or configuration. These Gestalt theorists disagreed with the behaviorists, who argued learning could be broken down into elements for study, contending that learning is more than the adding of associations. Gestalt theorists argue that individuals react more to total experiences than to individual elements in the environment.

Gestalt psychology has much to offer teachers. A major task of the proactive teacher is to discover ways of providing students opportunities to experience content. Gestaltists contend such "whole" experiences will lend a more thorough understanding of academic material. Human learning and perception, according to Gestalt psychologists, are influenced by the way stimuli are arranged, and their arrangement may hold more meaning than the stimuli, themselves. Figure 7.2 reflects the effect arrangement can have on perception. In Figure 7.2, can you determine which line is the longest? If you chose line A, B, or C as the longest line in Figure 7.2, you are incorrect; all the lines are the same length. As suggested by Gestaltists, our perceptions can be distorted or altered by the arrangement of stimuli. How does such information affect us in the real world? In Figure 7.3, which building wall is the tallest? Probably you can determine the answer because of your experience with Figure 7.2. The buildings are the same height. Now perhaps you can better understand the confusion that can occur when you ask a friend to meet you at the tallest building on the block. If people with "normal" vision can easily make perceptual errors, imagine the difficulty of the visually, learning, or mentally impaired.

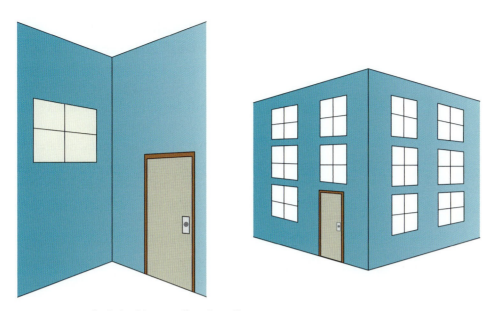

Figure 7.3 Which building wall is the tallest?

Now, imagine the complexity of sorting, interpreting, understanding, and learning among the diversity of stimuli students experience during childhood.

Insight and Perception

When you begin teaching, you will no doubt experience the satisfaction of students' reactions when they gain an **insight** into some part of the lesson. **Insight** is a word Gestalt psychologists define as 'learning that comes together instantaneously'.

> "An important contribution of the Gestaltists is the idea that people get stuck solving problems because they cannot change their problem-solving set—since they cannot look at the situation in a new way, they cannot see a new way to fit the elements together. For example, when trying to solve the six-stick problem (Figure 7.4), many people have trouble changing their problem-solving set from two dimensions to three. Giving a hint like this (or as some Gestaltists call it, giving direction) is important in problem solving because it helps people break out of their old ways of organizing the situation. The new way of looking at this problem afforded by thinking in three dimensions is called insight—the sudden flash that occurs when you finally see how to fit the sticks together" (Mayer, 1992, p. 40).

THE PROBLEM
Given six sticks, arrange them to form four triangles that are equilateral and with each side one-stick long.

THE SOLUTION
Some subjects take the six sticks

and form a square with an X in it, such as

However, this solution is not acceptable because the triangles are not equilateral—each has a 90-degree angle. To solve the problem, the solver must think in three dimensions, making a pyramid with a triangle base. For example, an overhead view is

with the middle point raised from the triangle base.

Figure 7.4 The Six-Stick Problem

The solution and flash of **insight** are often accompanied by the "aha!" exclamation. Still, some psychologists question the existence of insight (Weisberg, 1993). Their reasoning is that insight is arrived at differently by individuals and may not exist for some. However, knowing how individuals organize and interpret experiences differently can help teachers understand how students draw such different conclusions from similar experiences and, indeed, how two students, or, even two entire classes can respond so differently to the same instructional environment. Research suggests that creative classrooms can enhance the cognitive development of students. Note the experience of Mr. Jennings.

Mr. Jennings was discussing the topic of the next assignment with his 11th graders. The assignment was a two-page theme, "Hot Ice." The students were arguing over the meaning of the term *hot ice*. Jeff was scientific. He maintained that hot ice meant "dry ice" or frozen carbon dioxide. Rod was cool and stated that "hot ice is stolen diamonds looking for a fence." Andrea, an ice skater, disagreed. She insisted that hot ice was a slang ice-skating term that meant the skating ice was fast and good for precision skating. Mr. Jennings smiled and refused to take sides, insisting that students could define hot ice the way they wanted to for their themes.

Attribution

Cognitive learning theorists refer to these differences in perception as differences in **attribution**, meaning how and to what individuals attribute their experiences and perceive their present and past environments. Terrell fails a test and attributes his failure to not studying, or to the teacher not liking him, or to the test being too hard. Cognitive learning theorists suggest that a vital part of the educational process is teaching students how to appropriately cope with their environmental circumstances. Grades and achievement test scores are used to determine successful and failing students but analyzing students' perceptions, thinking, and self-concepts is more difficult because these behaviors are difficult to measure. However, they manifest themselves in the classroom and demonstrate how students process information.

Because of the vast number of stimuli in our environment, individuals must select information to process.

INTASC 7   Planning for instruction

Many students have difficulty simultaneously attending to all the stimuli they experience in their environment.

Enhancing Student Memory

In this section, we discuss factors impacting memory, including forgetting, and tools for using memory effectively.

Attention

How can understanding the information-processing model help you when you begin teaching? Can you use information-processing model to help your future students sort out relevant stimuli in the educational process? First, consider the process we commonly call **attention**. Attention may be defined as the concentration and focusing of mental activity (Matlin, 1988). The purpose of attention is to prevent overload. When new information is presented to a student, attention determines whether or not the information will be remembered. Our sensory system is capable of gathering more information from the environment than we are able to assimilate. Simply stated, our ability to think about events going on around us is limited; thus, students are limited in the number of environmental stimuli they can simultaneously focus.

For example, a student's sensory system may be informing her that the teacher is talking, DeWayne is wearing a red shirt, a friend is passing her a note, her book is open, the carpet is worn, the flag outside is still, and she is hungry. Even though our sensory system is extraordinarily efficient, there is a limit to the type and number of stimuli we can simultaneously process. Thus, students cannot concurrently read a book, take a quiz, answer a teacher's question, and talk with a friend. They must choose to *attend* to those stimuli they need to address.

Working memory (WM) - where conscious work is occurring, and long-term memory (LTM) - where information is stored for later use.

Attending focuses on the student's limited ability to cope with sensory input. As a future teacher, be aware of your students attending to the business at hand; the lesson. As you continue reading this chapter, think about methods you can use to get students to focus on academics. The final section of this chapter and Chapter 8 will offer suggestions.

Information stored in LTM must be retrieved before it can be used. The good news is that there are processes and techniques students can use to improve their ability to retrieve information.

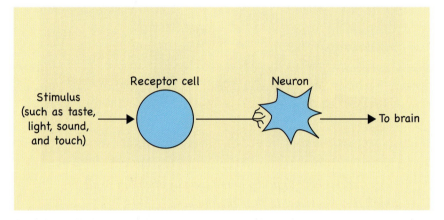

Figure 7.5 Our brain consists of 100 billion neurons all interacting. How we communicate and act depends on these interactions, which occur thousands of times a second.

Coding: "I Know That"

Working memory is defined as the area of the brain where work is being done (Figure 7.5). This suggests that WM includes such dimensions as problem solving, decision making, and creating new knowledge. Long-term memory is where information is stored for later use (Gagné, 1965). Coding is defined as the process whereby new information and working memory is integrated with known information (Reed, 1992). Information in WM mayor may not be coded. If coding occurs, then information may be stored in LTM for later use. Information stored in LTM may be recalled over a lifetime or, as many teachers are painfully aware, it can be forgotten after a short period of time.

There is controversy over whether or not everything we have ever stored in LTM stays there permanently, but information-processing theorists do agree much of what we have learned can stay with us for a long time (Kail, 1985; Perkins, 1989). However, information stored in LTM must be retrieved before it can be used again. If a person can retrieve (remember) a piece of information, such as a historical date, this information flows to WM for use. The information is then used to solve problems, make decisions, and/or respond. The study of LTM and WM help us understand learning and remembering can be improved.

How would you pronounce the following? Ba....seba....ll Did you pronounce it 'baseball'?

Why Students Forget: Decay and Interference Theories

How many times have we heard the concern of teachers echoed in statements like "I covered the material three times and still they forget" or "How could my students not remember?" The question of how and why students forget has been pondered for as long as there have been students around to remember and forget.

An early explanation for forgetting was decay theory; arguing people's memories fade (decay) with the passage of time (Ebbinghaus, 1913). To understand this theory, think about an ice cube in a warm place. With the passage of time, the ice cube will melt away until it is no longer discernible.

Decay theory has two parts. First, the more time that passes after learning, the less will be remembered. Second, if presentation rates of materials are accelerated, learning should result in better memory because there is less time to forget. For example, if you have 30 minutes to learn a passage of information you have 29 minutes to forget the first part of it. If this same information is presented in 15 minutes, you only have 14 minutes to forget the first part.

However, as logical as this theory sounds, contemporary educational psychologists believe it is wrong (Glover & Bruning, 1990). Haven't there been times when you could remember information you learned months or even years ago (LTM), and, yet, you couldn't remember what the teacher said at the beginning of the hour? Today, decay theory has been replaced generally by a more plausible explanation of forgetting, **interference theory**.

According to interference theory, the performance of one learning task can interfere with the performance of another. Contemporary researchers consider this a valid explanation for forgetting. Unlike decay theory, interference theory suggests that the passage of time is not the crucial factor in forgetting. Forgetting will occur as time passes, but the reason will be because of new conflicting information entering memory and interfering with previously learned information. Two types of interference affect our ability to remember: **retroactive interference** and **proactive interference**. Todd had experiences with each in his classroom.

> Research has found decay theory to be inaccurate and it has been replaced by interference theory, which holds that previous and subsequent learning can interfere with current learning.

Chapter Modules

> Teachers can help reduce the loss of retained information due to interference by planning shorter learning units and by reviewing each part of a unit as parts are completed.

TODD WILLIAMS...

had spent a week discussing the implications, causes, and ramifications, of the Afghan War, followed by a week discussing the Iraq war. Todd then administered an exam covering Afghan War material; 2 days later he gave an exam covering both the Afghan and Iraq conflicts. Students did much better on the first exam covering just the Afghan War than on the exam covering both. It appeared students had lapses of memory, confused and mixed the issues, facts, and ramifications of the conflicts on the second exam.

Teachers can address their students' forgetting by (1) teaching similar concepts at different times, (2) reviewing each lesson, and (3) making sure students understand current concepts before introducing new concepts.

"To enhance the likelihood that new information will be remembered, students should be active rather than passive." (Glover & Bruning, 1990).

INTASC Standard 8   Instructional strategies

Transfer and Rehearsal

Transfer is typically defined as the influence of prior knowledge and learning on the learning of new skills and information. It is important for teachers to understand there can be **positive transfer** (when previous learning facilitates understanding and mastery of new information) or **negative transfer** (when previous learning interferes with learning new subject matter or information). To minimize negative transfer, Todd might have prevented the poor grades on his second history test if he had divided the Afghan War and Iraq War materials into smaller segments and tested accordingly. Also, after covering the material on the Afghan War, he might have reviewed that material before giving the test. Alternatively, he might have covered some material after the Afghan material that was totally unrelated before going into the material on Iraq. Or, Todd might have taught about the two conflicts, using different teaching methodologies. The Afghan War could have been taught by independent study and oral reports, while the Iraq War could have been taught via lecture and class discussion.

We now know the greater the similarity of the learning task, the higher the likelihood either retroactive or proactive interference will occur (Dempster, 1985). Learning theorists agree that a total understanding of why students forget is yet to be determined; the research continues. However, to help your students minimize their forgetting:

- Review what you have taught them.

- Use rote memorization and/or phonics when appropriate, such as learning to spell words; try to make learning a pleasant experience.

- If you find yourself in the situation Todd had, teaching similar material—the histories of conflicts—teach such subjects independently.

- Also, make sure that your students have learned the topic before going on to similar material.

Also, 'remember' that **rehearsal** enhances the likelihood that information can be recalled. **Rehearsal** refers to using procedures that maintain the vitality of information in working memory (Berliner & Casanova, 1990). Glover and Bruning (1990) offer the following guidelines for minimizing forgetting:

1. *Learners should be active rather than passive*. To enhance the likelihood that new information will be remembered it should be rehearsed. For example, new learners should be actively involved in a task rather or in addition to passively listening or observing.

2. *Test frequently*. Testing gives students an opportunity to rehearse to-be-remembered information (Foos & Fisher, 1988).

3. *Avoid interference in your class*. Give tests at the beginning of the day. Covering new materials during the first part of the period and then quizzing on old information can result in both proactive and retroactive interference.

4. *Teach your students to "overlearn" information.* **Overlearning** is the continued practice of an errorless recitation and can be a great help in reducing interference effects. If learners practice until the first errorless recall and then practice the materials that many more times, overlearning is fairly well assured and interference is much less likely.

5. *Have students picture where and how they will have to remember information.* Pairing learning with the cues students will use to remember helps students organize their memory.

> Retrieval is the process of transferring information from LTM to WM for use. It can be improved through rehearsal.

TECHNOLOGY IN THE CLASSROOM

More than two generations ago the impact of technology on the cognitive functioning of students was dramatically articulated by Rickelman, Henk, and Melnick (1991, pp. 432–433):

> Because our knowledge base in all disciplines is expanding at a phenomenal rate, more efficient means of organizing and retrieving information are necessary. And with this explosion of knowledge comes a concomitant need to expand our definition of reading literacy. To cope with an abundance of information, readers will need to understand how to formulate and conduct systematic searches of available data, skim and scan text for relevance, and retrieve and comprehend pertinent content.

> Electronic data storage now provides children a way to meet these data management needs and to develop their literacy capabilities. As a result, in an age when access to information is becoming as important as firsthand personal knowledge, electronic encyclopedias and databases will play an increasingly prominent role in our children's education. As so aptly stated by (Boink, 2010), "a major role of today's teachers is that of the 'concierge' who helps students find educational resources as they need them." ■

R. J. Rickelman, W.A. Henk & S. A. Melnick, "Electronic Encyclopedias on Compact Disk," The Reading Teacher, 44(6), February 1991. Copyright @ 1991 by the International Reading Association (www.reading.org)

SURFING • THE • WEB

One of the best resources for teachers and families concerned with the cognitive development of their students and children is the National Endowment for the Humanities (NEH). The NEH sponsors programs and projects designed to enhance knowledge of and interest in all of the humanities—language, literature, philosophy, archaeology, comparative religion, and ethics (**http.//www.neh.fed.us**). Within the Department of Health and Human Resources is the National Institute of Mental Health (**http.//www.nimh.nih.gov**). The journal of 'Cognitive Development' website address is - **http://piaget.org/**.

RECAP OF MAJOR IDEAS

1. Research in cognitive learning theory has produced a wealth of information on student memory, and the process is of perception and thinking.

2. Piaget and Bruner believed students learning through guided discovery develop a clearer understanding and better application skills of what is learned.

3. Our brains are complex but computers such as IBM's 'Watson' are beginning to duplicate thought processes.

4. Teachers can enrich students' learning opportunities by activities involving the senses.

5. The degree students pay attention or attend to new information influences whether or not the information will be remembered.

6. Working memory (WM) is a part of the brain where conscious, current work is being done, whereas long-term memory (LTM) is a part of the brain where information is stored for later use.

7. Teachers can use such activities as re-reading material, reviewing and testing to help students retrieve stored information. This process is called rehearsal.

8. Decay theory—which holds that the longer the learning period and the longer since learning occurred, the less an individual will remember—has been replaced by interference theory, which says that the performance of one task can interfere with the performance of another.

9. Teachers can help students reduce the loss of learned and retained information by planning shorter learning units and by reviewing each part of the unit as it is completed.

10. Teachers can help their students minimize their forgetting by teaching enthusiastically, separating similar concepts, reviewing each lesson, and by ensuring that students understand a concept before progressing on to other concepts.

FURTHER APPLICATIONS

1. Make a list of the 'insights' you have gained from reading about cognitive theories, and for each insight, relate one way, you as a teacher, can apply this insight to improve your teaching.

2. Suppose computer scientists eventually achieve their goal of having computers, such as IBM's 'Watson' duplicate human thinking. Describe a project for the computer that would make a significant contribution to student learning.

3. For a learning unit in your teaching field, list four student activities involving a different sense.

4. Perception requires the ability to relate new information to stored information. Choose a lesson and list at least two ways teachers can help students relate new information to existing information.

5. Examine a lesson plan. Look for related items within the lesson. Describe two strategies for avoiding interference.

KEY TERMS

cognitive processes
cognitive learning theory
discovery approach to learning
guided discovery
open discovery
information processing
sense receptors
perception
memory
sensory memory
short-term memory (STM)
working memory
problem solving

long-term memory (LTM)
metacognition
metacognitive knowledge
personal knowledge
task knowledge
strategy knowledge
Gestalt psychology
insight
attribution
coding
decay theory
interference theory

LOOKING AHEAD

Chapter 8 focuses on *applying* cognitive learning theory to the classroom environment. Future teachers should be aware of how the classroom environment impacts the cognitive development of students. Chapter 8 presents alternatives for enhancing the cognitive functioning and abilities of students, with emphasis on problem solving, creativity, and thinking. ■

Cognitive Learning Strategies Applied to Teaching

LEARNING OBJECTIVES

Upon completing this chapter, you should be able to:

1

Define *metacognition* and explain how it relates to enhancing student memory.

2

Describe four *mnemonic* techniques that can help students recall academic content.

3

Define *advance* and *key word organizers* and explain their importance before and during lessons.

4

Describe the implications, differences and limitations of *preferred* learning style and *required* learning styles.

5

Relate two metacognitive strategies to improve a student's ability to process information.

6

List four qualities of a good thinker in the classroom environment.

7

Define two strategies for facilitating student thinking and learning skills.

INTRODUCTION

The explosion of research on cognitive approaches to learning during the past four decades has produced a wealth of strategies the classroom teacher can apply to teaching and learning. In this age of technology, teaching cognitive strategies, such as enhancing and making students aware of their mental capabilities, has become increasingly important. The comments of Nancy C. Townsend, former South Carolina Teacher of the Year, underscore this critical issue.

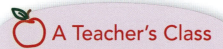 A Teacher's Class

NAME: Nancy C. Townsend, former South Carolina Teacher of the Year

TEACHING TECHNIQUES: I use a smorgasbord of teaching techniques: lecture, participatory learning, cooperative learning, games and simulations, and learning with technology. Very simply, I use whatever methods I feel will work best with the students in a given class.

ADVICE TO ASPIRING TEACHERS: Don't be lured into thinking that a license to teach is your appointment as a final, finished product. Instead, your license is a license to *practice* the art and science of teaching. Your license says that you have the basic knowledge, the basic tools, and the basic requirements to become a professional educator. How much you learn *after* receiving your teaching license depends on you, and you start that education in your first year in the classroom. Don't let anyone fool you—the first year is the hardest and the most critical.

Your first year of teaching is critical because everything else you do will be built upon that foundation. Remember when you were in college and you chose your professors by what the student grapevine said about whether they were easy or hard, good or bad? The tables are now turned. How you handle your classroom and how you handle relationships with students during this critical first year constructs what the student grapevine says about you.

You will begin your first year with nothing—no lesson plans, no worksheets, no activities, no tests—and you will build these from scratch. In later years, you will draw on and modify this material, discarding what didn't work and improving on what did. As you fine-tune your classroom instincts, you suddenly discover that what works well with one class won't work at all with another, and suddenly, you have discovered the one truth about teaching that the college of education forgot to tell you—that teaching is a profession of constant change.

To add the piece de resistance, you will be involved in a yearlong cat-and-mouse game with your students, where their behavior is concerned. They will test you. They will try you. All in their quest to answer two critical questions: How strictly will your enforce the rules, and how fairly will you do this?

Students want three things from a teacher, justice, fairness, and equity.

At the end of your first year, you'll be tempted to give up, but don't. A wise assistant principal, listening to my complaints about student tests my first year, told me that the difference between the first and second years of teaching was like the difference between night and day. Boldly and blindly, I trusted his advice and signed that contract for a second year. In September, I discovered he was right. Students knew who I was, what I stood for, and that my classes were disciplined, fair, and equitable. Make your first year—and every year—what it should be—the foundation of a lifelong career to practice the art and science of teaching.

QUESTION: What advice would you give aspiring teachers whose curriculum planning includes the enhancement of the cognitive functioning of students?

Cognitive development should be a primary concern to current and future teachers and curriculum planners. Students must be cognitively ready to handle the complexities of abstract and formal operational thinking. I teach the ninth grade, and the importance of cognitive readiness is readily apparent when students tell me they have studied clauses, participles, gerunds, and infinitives in eighth-grade English and "didn't understand any of it." Students at the eighth-grade level in my particular school situation are cognitively not ready for this at the eighth-grade level. In such instances, curriculum must be adjusted to accommodate student readiness.

In addition, much ado has been made recently about heterogeneous versus homogeneous grouping. A more appropriate discussion should revolve around grouping students by learning styles. When we finally match curriculum scope and sequence to cognitive development and group classrooms by learning styles, students will have much greater academic success. Current and future teachers must learn as much as possible about how the brain functions, how we learn, and how memory works. Teachers must also have access to learning style inventories on both the Dunn and Gregoric models. These models can be easily administered to their classes at the beginning of each year for grouping purposes. We must finally begin to tailor education to the student, not the student to education. ■

Nancy Townsend and other teachers agree: the cognitive abilities of students are critical to learning. Cognitive and neuro- scientists have begun to map the processes involved in problem solving (Mayer, 1992). However, many teachers are not adequately prepared to help students with their cognitive learning skills, and often teachers have limited time to collaborate and exchange their ideas with other teachers (Darling-Hammond & Sclan, 1996). Cognitive learning theorists are well aware of the problem of getting students to retain, understand, and apply academic information and curriculum content.

Heeding the advice of Ms. Townsend, this chapter will discuss techniques teachers can use to improve student memory, creativity, and problem-solving skills. The relationship of student cognition and self-reliance will also be discussed.

INTASC 8 — Instructional strategies

Enhancing Student Memory

Metacognitive Skills

Research related to the metacognitive views discussed in Chapter Seven has been fruitful in providing well-defined strategies for the classroom teacher. Teaching students *skill*s to enhance memory is critical to academic success (Kane & Kane, 1990). As Nancy Townsend noted, "curriculum must be adjusted to accommodate student readiness." A major contribution of the cognitive literature is the study of **metacognition**.

The term metacognition refers to individuals' awareness of their cognitive processes and capabilities. Metacognition involves problem solving, understanding and comprehension. A classroom example might be a tenth-grade chemistry student assessing the level of difficulty involved in learning the atomic weights of elements and developing a strategy for this learning task. Metacognition can and should be addressed by the proactive teacher (Bruning, Schraw, Norby, & Ronning, 2004, Mayer, 1992). Kane and Kane (1990) stress the importance for teachers to realize that older students often use appropriate strategies to understand and comprehend, while younger students often do not. Younger students often have difficulty defining and using strategies for higher-order thinking skills, but such strategies can be taught to students as young as four and five (Mayer, 1992).

Three related skills involved in metacognition are **awareness, diagnosis**, and **monitoring** (Kail, 1984). Awareness relates to students being aware of different learning strategies available and how strategies can vary with subject matter. This is especially true with younger students who must be reminded of how to approach learning tasks and what is to be learned. This is often true of students regardless of age and grade level.

Diagnosis is the ability of a student to assess the difficulty of the task at hand. The level of difficulty varies with students. Some students find the task of understanding exponents difficult, whereas others would find the task "no problem."

Monitoring is most often evident with skilled learners and consists of determining how well the learner is remembering. This can be accomplished by reviewing, self-testing, or getting someone to assess. Monitoring is critical to efficient memory because it allows the learner to determine what has been learned and what academic content requires additional work.

By improving the metacognitive processes of students, teachers can help their students improve problem-solving skills and comprehension

Using mnemonics assists students remembering by pairing new material with familiar material.

Mnemonics

One way to help students retain new information is a method called **mnemonics**, which may be defined as pairing something memorable, such as a word or object, with new information (Higbee & Kunihira, 1985). Most students, at sometime have used mnemonics as a device to help them remember. For example, if you use the phrase "fall backward and spring forward" to remember which way to set your clock, you are using a mnemonic device.

We will discuss several types of mnemonics, including *acronyms and acrostics*, the *link* and loci methods, and the *peg word* and *key word* techniques.

Acronyms and Acrostics

Teachers often use mnemonic devices, for example, reminding students *"i* comes before *e* except after *c";* a way to remember the title of a poem or book by a certain author is to remember the first initial of each word in the title, such as ROAM, for Rime of the Ancient Mariner; or FACE can assist students in recalling the spaces of a treble clef. Remembering a word (or **acronym**) formed from the first letters of other words can be a very useful mnemonic device.

Acrostics is defined as forming a sentence or phrase with each word corresponding to the first letter in the words that need to be remembered (Rothstein, 2001). An example would be elementary and middle school teachers using the letters in Roy G. Biv to help students remember the order of colors in the spectrum: Red, Orange, Yellow, Green, Blue, Indigo, and Violet. By instructing students in mnemonics, teachers provide a useful and powerful learning tool (Kilpatrick, 1985; Levine, 1985).

Link Method

The mnemonic **link** (or chain) method uses imagery in recalling a list of items to be learned. The link method is especially suited to younger students because of its simplicity. Suppose you are trying to teach third graders to bring their paper, pencil, books, and lunch money to class. You might suggest they bring their money to buy something to eat, their pencil and paper to write about what they ate, and their books to read about the nutritional value of the food they're eating.

Loci Method

Another very common mnemonic, similar to the link method, employs visual imagery and is called the **loci method**. Loci is Latin for "places or locations." For example, a teacher suggests his/her students think of well-known locations, such as the rooms in their homes or areas in their school. Students then place the items they are required to remember in the various familiar locations. If, for example, the teacher wants students to remember famous authors and poets, they might have a series of locations such as their driveway for Dickens, the front door for Frost, the living room for Longfellow, the dining room for Dickinson, the kitchen for Keats, the bedroom for Byron, and the hallway for Hemingway. A tour

Student Study
Guide

might continue until all of the poets and authors to be recalled have a location in the house.

Peg Word Technique

Another type of mnemonic, called the peg word technique, can help students remember lists of items in a particular sequence. The student memorizes a series of 'pegs' where items can be 'hung'; for example, A, B, and C, with 'A' for apple, 'B' for banana, and 'C' for cantaloupe. Often pegs have some sort of rhyme scheme, such as 1, 2, 3 with "1 - bun," "2 - shoe," and "3 - tree." Peg word techniques are more effective if they are easy to visualize.

Key Word Method

The key word method also uses imagery; however, rather than rhyming, a key word refers to objects that can be visualized. Developed to assist students memorize foreign language words, the key word method is suited for learning new vocabulary. For example, a sixth grader is attempting to learn to spell "encompasses." A key word for "encompasses" might be "compass," which will be flagged with compass directions. So, when required to define encompasses on a test, the student will envision compass directions and associate the picture with encompasses.

Students should be taught various strategies to learn and understand new information. Also, mnemonic schemes can be used to organize information to be learned into units that can facilitate learning and enhance recall.

PROACTIVE EXERCISE

Many students collect lessons and materials for use in their future classrooms. Suppose you want to collect a list of mnemonics. What two or three mnemonics would you find most useful?

RETENTION AND UNDERSTANDING

Remembering information is only one phase of learning. **Retention** and **understanding** are crucial to the learning process.

TODD WILLIAMS...

was halfway through the series of seminars on student problem solving. So far, he had been pleased with the progress the seminars had made. The panel had attempted to address relevant teacher concerns. However, during the afternoon break, some teachers were saying they wanted to see other types of problems addressed, such as, "How can I get my students to organize their thinking?" and "How can I get my students to conceptualize and better understand subject matter?" They further complained that teaching a concept to 30 students was difficult because there were 30 diverse interpretations of what was explained. Additionally, they asked, "how can I get my students to be more creative with problem solving and comprehension?" and "can we discuss alternatives for making students better readers and writers, and can we provide students better learning and studying strategies?" The next day's meeting began with the moderator saying it was time to move on to some of the more complex problems teachers encounter, and ask for suggestions. Several teachers raised their hands.

> Teachers' use of advance organizers prior to presenting academic content provides students a method of organizing new information.

Todd and his fellow teachers are concerned about making subject material more meaningful and easier to remember and understand. Learning can be facilitated by presenting words and/or organizers providing clues about new information, enabling students to organize their thinking. Two techniques for increasing the meaningfulness and retention of subject matter are known as **advance organizers** and **key word organizers**.

Advance Organizers

Advance organizers relate new material to what students already know (Ausubel, 1980). The purpose of advance organizers is to aid learners in assimilating new information into existing knowledge. When beginning a unit of study, the teacher should first provide the class with a list of learning objectives and concepts such as the 'objectives' at the beginning of each chapter in this text. This is a use of advance organizers. When teachers identify a lesson's major concepts *prior* to the lesson, students tend to remember more of the important concepts. If the teacher identifies the major concepts at the end of the lesson or *after* a video is shown, students tend to remember more content, but not necessarily the most important concepts (Ausubel, 1980).

Key Word Organizers

Examples of key word organizers are those words that we have put in **bold type** in this text. By putting our **key words** in bold type, we are identifying key concepts to help you process and organize material as you read. Once information is organized, and/or processed via meta-memory skills, or once mnemonics are used to enhance memory, how can students learn information to the extent it is understood *and* retrievable?

> Procedures such as re-reading material and outlining a chapter to assist learning are examples of rehearsal.

Rehearsal

Rehearsal is another very efficient process for improving both the understanding and memory skills of students. Rehearsal refers to procedures that maintain the vitality or usability of information in working memory (WM) (Matlin, 1989).

Rehearsal takes several forms in the classroom, including re-reading material, browsing through a chapter, outlining a chapter, or repeating aloud. You will use rehearsal at the end of this chapter if you read the recap of major ideas.

PQ4R

PQ4R is a mnemonic used to organize classroom activities to improve student retention.

Another very useful technique for enhancing the meaningfulness and retention of information was developed by Thomas and Robinson (1972). They used the acronym PQ4R as a mnemonic. PQ4R describes steps (P—preview, Q—question, 4R—read, recite, reflect, review) for teaching students to master or better understand information. It is useful to note that PQ4R can be used at any grade level. The PQ4R for studying this chapter might be defined as follows:

1. *Preview.* The first task of learners to better understand and learn new materials is *previewing*. This preview typically consists of leafing through the new materials, noting section headings, key word organizers, perhaps reading summaries, and noting other pertinent information. Such a preview provides learners with an *overview*, or a very general outline of the new material to be learned.

   At the beginning of this chapter, hopefully you noted the title as a key to content; Applying Cognitive Learning Strategies in the Classroom Environment. A scan of the major headings (Enhancing Student Memory, Remembering and Understanding, and Promoting Student Achievement) further shapes the view of how the material will be presented. The list of 'Key Terms' at the end of the chapter adds still more definition. The chapter 'Objectives' and 'Introduction' provide advance organizers for the previewing student. Other pertinent information can be found in the titles of boxes and 'What Would You Do?' exercises.

2. *Question.* After previewing material, learners might list questions they think should be answered by the information they are about to master. These questions might serve as the advance organizers we have just discussed.

   Could you provide questions students might list about this chapter?

3. *Read.* This next step involves learners in the reading of the text. The initial reading is typically undertaken at a rapid pace with learners looking for central and main ideas of the text. Chapter, headings, sidebars, and paragraph introductions should be noted in this phase.

4. *Reflect.* Having initially read the material, learners should think about content meaning and implications. During this stage, students

should outline the material, review the parts of information found to be difficult, and answer the questions listed in step 2.

The 'Recap of Major Ideas' at the end of this chapter is useful for reflection.

5. *Recite.* Learners should begin to determine how well they recall or have learned chapter material covered. This can be done by self-testing, communicating material to another person or by verbally recalling material from memory. Hopefully, during this stage, learners are storing the new information in long-term memory (LTM).

   'Objectives' and 'Key Terms' could be useful in this step.

6. *Review.* This is simply the process of reviewing the material once again, giving attention to material learners find difficult.

   For example, a student finds one section difficult to grasp. The student should re-read that section and any supporting material that might make the section more understandable.

The PQ4R method can assist students with new learning tasks and can serve as a guideline for teachers to follow as they plan and present new academic material to students.

INTASC Standard 5 | **Application of content**

Promoting Student Achievement

The application of cognitive learning strategies to contemporary classroom concerns of student achievement is often unique and should be characterized by student involvement (Pesut, 1990). Many teachers intuitively use strategies that promote achievement and cognitive growth of students. Mr. Whitson was one such teacher.

WHAT WOULD YOU DO?

1. What behaviors or qualities do you believe enabled Mr. Whitson to retain his credibility in the presence of a lie such as cattywampus?

2. Teachers who encourage students to question should be prepared for all types of student questions. How should a teacher respond when students question social norms?

3. How should teachers respond to student questions when they don't know or have an answer?

4. Some teachers respond to questions they cannot answer by assigning the question as a project for the student who asked the question. Do you agree with this practice?

5. One of the authors was asked the following question by one of his eighth-grade science students: "Mr. Henson, you said that the electron travels at the speed of light (186,000 miles per second). It must have a lot of energy to be able to move that fast. Where does it get all that energy?" Mr. Henson had never been confronted with this question, and he did not know the answer, so he wrote to the authors of the science textbook (who, incidentally also didn't know). What other options did Mr. Henson have?

Mr. Whitson intuitively used techniques influencing the cognitive abilities and therefore the real-world academic achievement of his students. He probably would have defined and justified his teaching techniques as a desire to have his students question and achieve. Perhaps Mr. Whitson taught the way he did because he wanted to foster the cognitive skills of his students.

Promoting student achievement requires focusing on many aspects of cognitive learning, including:

- Developing conceptualization skills.
- Maximizing schemata and transfer of learning skills.
- Enhancing student motivation.
- Instilling confidence in students.
- Challenging students.
- Identifying personal learning styles.
- Developing good thinking skills.

Developing Conceptualization Skills

A major teacher concern is students developing broad **content generalizations**—those major understandings essential to understanding subject material. **Concept development**, or the process of acquiring the ability to develop concepts (*conceptualization*), can be a slow process (King & Kitchener, 1994). Furthermore, the concepts of students are often not the concepts teachers think their students have (Heckman, Confer, & Hakim, 1994).

WHAT WOULD YOU DO?

Suppose you direct a question to a student who has no inkling of the correct answer. How could you handle the situation in a way that would not embarrass the student?

Suggestion:

"Maybe my question was not clear. Let me try this one . . ." Henson (1996, p. 146) suggests that you modify the student's answer until it is acceptable and, if necessary, provide hints. If the student's answer is still not correct, quickly ask for volunteers to answer, with such as 'Can anyone add something to our answer?'

Which of these suggestions do you prefer? Or, perhaps you can think of another way to respond to an incorrect answer.

Developing an understanding of a lesson's major concepts is facilitated when teachers implement a plan to make it happen. Harrison (1990, pp. 502–505) suggests the following steps for helping students learn major concepts:

- Present a nominal definition of a concept and give examples.
- Emphasize the common attributes and ask students to name further attributes.
- Ask students to provide examples.
- Have students search for opposite examples.
- Have students name metaphors and examples comparing and contrasting to the original idea or concept.
- Have students review contexts in which the concept might take place.
- Describe the concept's application to the real world.
- Identify environmental factors that facilitate or hinder the concept's application.

Cognitive theorists contend that a major factor in determining student beliefs, values, and behaviors is student cognition.

- Formulate an operational definition involving the last steps of this process.

- Discuss consequences of solutions to a given problem, idea or concept.

Using Schema Theory and Transfer of Learning

Assuming teachers like Mr. Whitson have done a good job and students have the cognitive strategies needed to organize, master, and remember information, the question then becomes, "Can students use learned material in a new environment or learning situation?"

Schemata (plural of *schema*) are contents of memory containing elements of related information. Schemata influence the gathering of new information (Mandler, 1984). This is closely related to **transfer of learning**, which refers to students' ability to apply one learning experience to another learning experience. For example, Mr. Whitson's students learned that questioning was okay, even in other classes, perhaps to the discomfort of some of their teachers and to the delight of others.

If students have learned to add and subtract, this basic information should provide schemata for learning and solving future division and multiplication problems. Schema theory suggests the more a student knows about a subject, the easier it is to learn more about the subject and the more motivated the student is to learn.

Enhancing Motivation

Both behavioral and cognitive learning theorists point out that student achievement is dependent on more than a student remembering, understanding, and even being able to apply information. The motivation and confidence of students are essential to academic achievement regardless of ability to recall, understand, and apply.

As stated previously in the text, motivating students has always been, and continues to, be a major challenge for teachers. Cognitive learning theorists contend that in addition to reinforcement, students' behavior and academic performance are influenced by the students' beliefs, values, and cognitions. In short, it is students' interpretations of their environment that determine much of their behavior (Stipek, 1993). This implies that the confidence students have in their abilities is a major factor influencing academic achievement.

Teachers should try to help students maintain a positive view of their competencies (Bandura, 1986; Hill, 1990). When students believe they possess the ability to master school-related material, their chances for success are enhanced. Additionally, students who are confident of their ability will attribute their failure to lack of effort as opposed to lack of ability.

Mastery learning programs do not treat errors as failures, assuming students will experiment and take risks without fear of failure.

Students who attribute their failure to lack of ability are unlikely to put forth as much effort or be motivated when given similar assignments in the future. Students who attribute their failure to lack of effort will likely put forth more effort when facing future assignments. Remember Terrell in Chapter Seven who attributed his failure to effort, hard test, and teacher.

Instilling Confidence in Students

Typically, students are taught to avoid errors. Consider what happens in the typical classroom when students respond incorrectly to teachers' questions. Unlike Mr. Whitson, often students giving incorrect answers are told they are wrong, or ignored, as the teacher quickly looks to a more informed student for a correct response. Most likely, you have felt the consequences of giving an incorrect answer.

Teachers should be tactful during question-and-answer periods because wrong answers are public and comparable. Incorrect answers need not be treated by the teacher as something to be avoided or embarrassed about.

Students who continually turn in papers with no mistakes are typically very proud and should be; however, such students should be challenged, as Mr. Whitson was aware. If teachers treat errors and mistakes as something to be totally avoided, then students run the risk of being upset by errors and avoid risk-taking, which is essential to problem solving and creativity. This can be avoided by sensitive teachers like Mr. Whitson who appropriately teach students to take risks, question, and not to fear being wrong.

This does not imply teachers should ignore errors and poor performance. Stipek (1993) suggests the following strategies:

- Evaluate on mastery, rather than on a normative, standard.
- Minimize the probability that students' individual performances become a public issue in the classroom.
- Teach students that errors are a normal aspect of mastering new academic skills.
- Provide the opportunity for students to demonstrate competence.

For example, with some assignments (such as homework, class assignments, and some tests) it might be appropriate to make a check mark beside all correct answers while placing no marks beside incorrect answers. Students could then be given the option of resubmitting the paper with corrections or errors. Mastery would be achieved when the required total number of check marks is earned over a defined period of time.

Stipek and Daniels (1988) suggest three ways to motivate and instill confidence in students.

- Be sure your classroom environment facilitates the cognitive skills of students such as questioning, understanding, and problem solving.

- Try to motivate students to continue to learn without extrinsic reinforcers, which are often unavailable or delayed.

- Encourage independent, self-directed student learning strategies that will benefit your students outside of the educational structure.

In the A View from the Field box, Dr. Li Cao demonstrates how the variables we have discussed can be used effectively to teach students.

A VIEW FROM THE FIELD
A VIEW FROM THE FIELD

PROFILE

Li Cao is an Associate Professor in the Department of Educational Innovation at the University of West Georgia. Since he earned his Ph.D. in Educational Psychology from McGill University, he has taught in Saint Mary's University in Minnesota and the University of West Georgia. He received Distinguished Paper Awards from the American Educational Research Association, Eastern Educational Research Association, and the American Institute of Higher Education. His articles appear in *The Journal of Experimental Education, Teaching Educational Psychology, Metacognition and Learning, Australian Journal of Educational and Developmental Psychology, and Current Issues of Education*. His current research interests include metacognition, self-regulated learning, and effective e-learning.

QUESTION: What can teachers do to ensure in-depth learning in an age of digital speed?

Recent advancement of educational technology has provided teachers and students with new e-learning tools of finding, analyzing, creating, assessing, and sharing information. A major impact of these technologies highlights the notion of teachers as facilitators and students as active learners, and the importance of promoting learning beyond basic knowledge consumption. This technological-pedagogical shift challenges teachers on how to promote deep and meaningful learning among students.

Teachers can address this challenge by creating an educational environment that offers personalized learning experiences through student-teacher, student-student, and student-content interactions. These interactions facilitate and inspire students' learning and creativity, and help students relate the subject matter to personal knowledge and apply the newly developed knowledge to problem solving. Rather than testing inert knowledge, teachers help students learn how to recognize and solve problems, comprehend new phenomena, construct mental models of those phenomena, set learning goals, and self-regulate their learning. When students are given opportunities to investigate relevant, interesting phenomena and use the information they gather to solve problems, answer their questions, or inform others, they engage in learning that has significance and value. Their learning exemplifies characteristics of the in-depth and meaningful learning that is authentic, constructive, intentional, active, and cooperative.

SYNTHESIS BASED ON THE FOLLOWING REFERENCES

Bekele, T. (2009). Cognitive skills in internet-supported learning environments in higher education: Research issues. *Scandinavian Journal of Educational Research, 53*(4), 397–419. doi:10.1080/00313830903043182

Bernard, R. M., Abrami, P. C., Borokhovski, E., Wade, C. A., Tamim, R. M., Surkes, M. A., Bethel, E. C. (2009). A meta-analysis of three types of interaction treatments in distance education. *Review of Educational Research, 79*(3), 1243–1289.

Bonk, C. J., & Zhang, K. (2008). Empowering online learning: 100+ activities for reading, reflecting, displaying, and doing. San Francisco, CA: Jossey-Bass.

Cennamo, K. S., Ross, J. D., & Ertmer, P. A. (2010). Digital tools that support learning. *Technology Integration for Meaningful Classroom Use: A Standards-based Approach*. Belmont, CA: Wadsworth, Cengage Learning.

Havard, B., Jianxia, D., & Olinzock, A. (2005). Deep learning: The knowledge, methods, and cognition process in instructor-led online discussion. *Quarterly Review of Distance Education, 6*(2), 125–135.

Howland, J. L., Jonassen, D., & Marra, R. M. (2008). *Meaningful learning with technology* (4th ed.). Pearson: Boston, MA.

International Society for Technology in Education (ISTE). (2008). *National educational technology standards for teachers (NETS.T)*. Eugene, OR: Author.

Mayer, R. (2001). *Multi-media learning*. Cambridge, UK: Cambridge University Press.

Tallen-Runnels, M. K., Thomas, J. A., Lan, W. Y., Cooper, S., Ahern, T. C., Shaw, S. M., and Liu, X. (2006). Teaching courses online: A review of the research. *Review of Educational Research, 76*(1), 93–135.

QUESTION: How can today's teachers take advantage of current research on the cognitive development and functioning of students?

Research on the cognitive development involves the regular, age-related changes in children's capabilities to acquire and manipulate knowledge over time. Cognitive development is a constructive process in which children build increasingly differentiated and comprehensive knowledge through interacting with their environment. In this process, a developing child is born prepared to learn, but whose mind is also shaped by forces in the physical and social environment.

To promote optimal learning, teachers need to recognize the milestones of development and create learning environments that complement physical, cognitive, and social/emotional characteristics of their students. More specifically, teachers can furnish young children with stimulating and inviting experiences that feed their inherent curiosity and desire to venture into the world of formal learning. Likewise, teachers can encourage middle-school children to look more deeply at the world around them and help their students hone the tools they will require for independence and self-determination. Further, teachers can help adolescents map their futures by identifying their unique abilities and interests and by encouraging them to make reasoned and thoughtful choices. Teachers also need to be sensitive in observing individual differences among students and differentiate instruction for students with varied levels of readiness and abilities. Finally, teachers need to continually assess students' existing knowledge and create a supportive social context to advance student learning through teacher scaffolding and cooperative learning activities that encourage students to learn from each other.

SYNTHESIS BASED ON THE FOLLOWING REFERENCES

Alexander, P. (2006). *Psychology in learning and instruction*. Upper Saddle River, NJ: Pearson.

Bergin, C. C., & Bergin, D. A. (2012). *Child and adolescent development in your classroom*. Belmont, CA: Wadsworth Publications.

Bjorklund, D. F. (2012). *Children's thinking: Cognitive development and individual differences* (5th ed.). Belmont, CA: Wadsworth Publications.

Bredekamp, S. (1987). *Developmentally appropriate practices in early childhood programs serving children from birth through age 8*. Washington, DC: National Association for the Education of Young Children.

Palincsar, A. S. (1998). Social constructivist perspectives on teaching and learning. *Annual Review of Psychology, 49*, 345–375.

Perkins, D. N. (1992). *Smart schools: Better thinking and learning for every child*. New York: Free Press.

Piaget, J. (1969). *Science of education and the psychology of the child*. (D. Coltman, trans.). New York: Viking, 1970.

Vygotsky, L. S. (1978). *Mind in society*. Cambridge, MA: Harvard University Press. ■

Cognitive learning theorists encourage teachers to challenge students to try without fear of failure, and such opportunities should be offered at an early age.

Cognitive learning theorists maintain that there are attractive ways to present tasks and academic assignments that will appeal to students and enhance motivation. By studying the processes of thinking and learning, cognitive psychologists have tested several strategies teachers can use to motivate students to learn. By understanding these processes, teachers can enhance the amount and quality of learning in their classes.

Challenging Students

Even highly-motivated, bright students can become accustomed to error-less papers and high grades and, as a result, avoid trying new situations suggesting the possibility of failure. Obviously, such students can be conditioned to avoid the more difficult academic tasks, selecting ones ensuring the best grades. This is one explanation why so many highly-competent students avoid science and math in their academic careers (Glover & Bruning, 1990). This reinforces the value of Mr. Whitson's technique of introducing creative, challenging, academic tasks very early in students' academic careers, teaching them that questioning and making errors are part of the learning process and part of life.

> ### PROACTIVE EXERCISE
>
> Suppose you have students who are so intent on earning top grades that they are very reluctant to take risks. For example, they are uncomfortable with group projects or any type of cooperative learning. What would you do?

Identifying Learning Styles

Unlike Mr. Whitson's class discussed earlier, schools often treat students as if they are all the same. Students on the same grade level read the same text. Most classrooms are furnished to accommodate 25 to 30 students, and all of the chairs are the same size. Teachers often deliver instruction as though all students think alike. But cognitive learning theorists inform us that students perceive and learn in different ways. This has led to considerable research designed to determine how people learn and ultimately to identify students' individual learning styles.

Learning style is defined as how elements from basic stimuli in the current and past environment affect an individual's ability to absorb and retain information (Dunn, Bruno, Sklar, Zenhausern, & Beaudry, 1990). Those who have researched learning style are interested in answering such questions as: Does the student prefer to learn independently? Does he/she prefer to learn with peers, or to learn from teachers? What are the preferences of the learner in terms of teaching aids? Does the learner prefer teaching aids that

Students have preferred learning styles; some prefer to learn alone while others prefer working in groups.

are auditory, visual or both? Learning style is the summary of the student's opinions about the way he or she learns best (Dunn et al., 1990).

Hunt (1978) cautioned that learning style often refers to what the learners *require* and not necessarily what they prefer. A senior-high student who says she intends to major in engineering in college may not want to study math, therefore guidance by school professionals is often necessary. Student input concerning learning style preferences may provide some useful information to the classroom teacher (Gordon & Rabianski-Carrivolo, 1989) but due to lack of conclusive research findings, teachers should be cautious.

Learning style research has provided key postulates for teacher consideration:

- Children in grades 3 through 12 can reveal their preferred learning styles through a "learning style inventory," developed by Dunn, Dunn, and Price (1989).

- However, learning style research has, to date, been inconclusive, and teachers should be cautious about attempting to personalize learning environments.

- Preferred learning styles should be considered but not imperative.

- Teachers should neither disparage nor begrudge a child's need for structure, and learning styles should not be allowed to defer the academic needs and achievement of students.

INTASC Standard 1   **Learner development**

Developing Thinking and Problem Solving Skills

Teachers, since Socrates, have aspired to teach students how to think intelligently and apply what they have learned. Unfortunately, many teachers lament that students lack this ability. Teachers are often heard giving such directions as, "Think about what you are doing!" or "Think before you act!" Teachers want students to proactively think about subject matter, about themselves and others. However, this assumes that sometime during their early academic careers, students have learned to think well enough to enhance their academic efforts.

The general attitude educators hold toward teaching students to think was expressed as early as 1989 by the following RSB (Research for Better Schools), a nonprofit educational research and development firm.

> The importance of higher order thinking ability in the classroom, in the workplace and in today's complex society also underlines the need to develop thinking as a central focus of curriculum and assessment in the school curriculum. This is as true for the at-risk student as it is for the gifted learner.

Although we agree that students should "think" about subject matter and teacher goals should include improving student thinking, cognitive researchers caution that assuming an innate thinking capability to academic content can be erroneous. Although teaching students thinking skills is a critical issue, it is often ignored by teachers. In your academic career, how many times have you had a teacher announce in class, "Today, I'm going to teach you how to think"?

But what do we mean or what should we mean by "good thinking"? According to (Mayer & Wittrock, 2006; Nickerson, 1988), the characteristics of a good thinker include the following:

- Approaches new academic material skillfully and organizes for learning
- Organizes thoughts and articulates them concisely and coherently
- Understands the difference between reasoning and rationalization
- Attempts to anticipate probable consequences of alternative actions before choosing
- Has a sense of the value and cost of information, knows how to seek the information, and does so when it makes sense
- Can learn independently and, and equally important, has abiding interest in doing so
- Listens carefully to others' ideas
- Understands the difference between winning an argument and being right
- Recognizes that most real-world problems have more than one possible solution
- Habitually questions one's own views

> Teachers, since Socrates, have aspired to teach students how to think intelligently and apply what they have learned.

- Can represent differing viewpoints without distortion, exaggeration, or caricaturization
- Recognizes the fallibility of one's own opinions, the probability of bias in those opinions, and the danger of differentially weighting evidence according to personal preferences

Contemporary cognitive learning research has given us considerable insight on how to aid "good thinking."

Enhancing Thinking Skills

In our discussion, *thinking* will be defined as "focusing on deciding what to believe or do" (Ennis, 1987). Theorists have offered suggestions for enhancing thinking skills. Ennis suggests using the following tools to help your students improve their thinking skills:

1. Make statements about things students should do.
2. When students express their opinions, provide them with criteria for evaluating the merits of their opinions.

This last step is invaluable in teaching students to critique their thinking, because they are required to substantiate their positions.

Thinking also can be taught through curriculum content (Perkins, 1988). Perkins suggests using four design questions within the context of the subject content:

1. What is the subject matter's purpose?
2. What is the subject matter's structure?
3. What are the model cases?
4. What arguments explain and evaluate the object?

Paul (1987, p. 133) gives a good example of how this could be done within a history lesson by listing the flagrant differences between the colonial and British perceptions of the Boston massacre.

1. A colonial onlooker, standing 20 yards from the colonists, gave sworn testimony to the justices of the peace on April 23, 1775, that the British fired the first shot.
2. A colonial Tory (a sympathizer with the British) wrote an account on May 4, 1775, to General Gage (the British commander in Boston) in which he said that the colonists fired the first shot.

> Teaching students how to think does not require additional materials. An example is exposing students to contrasting views about an issue.

3. A young British lieutenant wrote in his diary on April 19, 1775, that the colonists fired one or two shots, then the British returned the fire without any orders.

4. The commander of the colonial militia, John Parker, in an official deposition on April 25, 1775, stated that he ordered the militia to disperse and not to fire, but the British fired on them without any provocation.

5. The *London Gazette* wrote on June 10, 1775, to its British readers that the colonists fired on the British troops first.

INTASC Standard 8   Instructional strategies

Imagine dividing your class into five groups, giving each group one of the above statements and asking each group to write a two page paper defending the statement. Each paper could be presented orally in class and debated.

If students are exposed to alternative viewpoints as part of instruction, such as in the Boston Massacre illustration, they will be exposed to thinking more logically about the relationship of facts and opinions. Contrasting views will appear in the classroom, and teachers can take advantage.

In conclusion, "good thinkers not only have the right thought processes, but they know how to formulate workable strategies for solving problems" (Sternberg, 1987, p. 253). Teaching students the correct thought processes to form workable strategies for solving problems is easier said than done. However, cognitive learning theorists have some very intriguing suggestions for such tasks.

Metacognition and the Classroom

Metacognitive strategies are vital to curriculum planning because student thinking is such an important aspect of the educational process (Swanson, 1990). **Metacognition** can be defined as "thinking about thinking" (Glover & Bruning, 1990). Recall that metacognitive processes involve the conscious monitoring and regulation of environmental stimuli. This can be illustrated by identifying the differences between cognitive skills and metacognition. When a student summarizes a history chapter, that student is exercising cognitive skills. When writing a summary of the history chapter for the purpose of self-evaluating their understanding of the material, students are engaging in metacognition. Simply stated, the difference between cognition and metacognition is a difference in self-awareness and control; metacognitive processes involve conscious monitoring and regulation.

> Metacognition requires an awareness of how one learns and efforts to monitor and improve one's learning skills.

"Keeping a daily record of their reflections can help students become active monitors of their own learning." (Eggen & Kauchak, 1992)

Eggen and Kauchak (1992) suggest several activities teachers can use to enhance students' metacognitive skills.

- Have students keep a *daily learning log*. This can include keeping a daily record of their reflections or reactions to academic activities. By shifting the focus from academic products to cognitive processes, you can help students become active monitors of their own learning.

- Demonstrate and discuss an appropriate metacognitive activity. As discussed in previous chapters, you can influence student behavior through *modeling*. Additionally, focus class discussions on processes, such as estimating task difficulty, identifying goals, choosing strategies or a sequence of steps, and planning for evaluation.

- Provide opportunities for *feedback*. Provide your students with opportunities to receive feedback on their understanding of academic material. For example, students can adopt the role of teacher and present information to other students within the class to demonstrate their understanding and get feedback from their peers.

- Provide instruction and *self-questioning techniques*. Stimulate self-monitoring by students by training them to self-interrogate. Require students to ask of themselves, "Do I understand this?"

- Teach students to *summarize material*. This teaches them to critically analyze their understanding of subject matter. Summarizing can be used when preparing to take a test or carrying out a set of instructions.

- Teach students to rate their own *comprehension*. For effective learning to occur, students must be able to monitor their comprehension. This might be as elementary as teachers presenting students with varying amounts and kinds of information and having students rate their understanding ("I understand well"; "I sort of understand"; "I don't understand").

- As a teacher, consider the following when presenting students new learning situations and activities: (1) the nature of the materials to be learned; (2) the students' current skills and knowledge; (3) the activities students will be required to do when presented with materials; and (4) the criterion tasks, or "tests," used to evaluate the degree of learning.

- Adapt a *studying model*. Teach learners to identify the purposes and reasons for doing an assignment before they begin it. They can do such things as browse, skim, or survey the material and pose questions that may be answered during the course of completing a task. Learners should continuously pose such questions as, "Does this make sense?" and "Am I doing it correctly?" After the task has been completed, they should ask, "Did I accomplish my academic task? If not, where did I go wrong? What have I learned from this experience? Are there new or related areas I would like to look into?"

PowerPoint

Additionally, the following proactive alternatives may be helpful.

PROACTIVE TEACHING

CLASSROOM SITUATION

1. Elementary Students

Teaching elementary students specific strategies for remembering is a delicate task. However, the use of memory strategies by younger students can be developed through patient, appropriate instruction and practice.

PROACTIVE ALTERNATIVES

· Concentrate on creating *awareness* with your younger students. Elementary students have to be made aware and reminded that the content is being taught is to be remembered. This is especially true of younger elementary students.

· Involve your younger students by using hands-on experiences and

2. Older Elementary, Middle, and
   Secondary Students

Cognitive psychology offers numerous
alternatives for teaching older,
more mature students strategies for
remembering.

exercises, visual aids, demonstrations, field trips, and videos on subject content.

· Provide ample time for question and answer sessions with your students, and review, review, review. This can be included in your lesson plans via repeated practice and review sessions. Be careful not to bore your students; provide different and interesting examples and summaries.

· Early in the academic year, teach your students the process of breaking down assignments into smaller tasks. Younger students can understand and remember information better if it is divided and spaced over time as opposed to being presented as a single, large unit of information. Use examples, such as a daily diary, that can be developed into a short story; learning the capitols of states or countries can be simplified by requiring five c capitols a week be memorized until all are learned. This process of breaking down assignments provides time for retention and review. Break down reading assignments into fewer pages, providing time for discussion, reflection, and review.

· Teach your students the process and meaning of "overlearning." Do this by planning for reviews and practice sessions and repeated testing. An elementary way to communicate this to students is to teach them to review until they can perform without error the required academic task.

· Build into your lesson plans methods that relate new academic material that students are required to learn to information already learned and understood by students. Linking information with advanced outlines of lessons, organizers, and analogies is a good way to accomplish this task.

· Present academic content and lessons in a logical sequence. Students are active processors of information and they can assimilate new material better if it is presented in logical steps. An example would be

    a. Enter the lab.

    b. Check out a microscope and slides.

    c. Adjust the microscope to view the slide content.

    d. Review the chapter in the text and identify the slide content.

    e. Answer questions in the chapter after identifying the slides.

    f. Review your results with your lab partner.

    g. Turn in your results.

· As with younger students, get older students involved. The question-and-answer sessions, visual aids, and field trip suggested for younger students are very important for older students as well.

· When developing your lesson plan, allocate time for teaching students cognitive strategies, such as advanced organizers, rehearsal, metamemory, and mnemonics, including PQ4R. Include these topics in the first assignments of the school year, so that early in the academic year students can monitor and then identify the strategies that work for them.

Applying Cognitive Strategies to the 3 R's

Cognitive learning strategies are now well defined for specific subjects, such as reading, writing, and math.

Reading

- Identify interesting enjoyable reading material. Do not be limited by textbook material. Newspapers, magazines, novels, and other books *related* to subject matter can be interesting reading material. This is a good way to match reading material to students' reading levels.

- Early in the school year, screen for auditory, vision, and perceptual impairments. Often such screening is done with early elementary students but not so with older students. Students' records, families, the school counselor, and school psychologists are good sources for referrals. The ability to trace a lack of cognitive development among students to a sensory impairment is not uncommon. (Santrock, 1997)

- Praise and reward students' successes. Often teachers focus on students' errors and mistakes, especially when students are learning something new, such as reading, where errors occur frequently. It is important to emphasize success, through praise and recognition of accomplishment.

- Read, read, read. As with many other cognitive tasks the best way to improve reading skills is to practice. This is especially true of younger students learning to read. Simply stated, the more

"The more children read, the more they will enjoy, comprehend, and remember." (Anderson, Wilson, & Fielding, 1988)

students read, the more they will enjoy, comprehend, and remember. (Anderson, Wilson, & Fielding, 1988)

Writing

- Provide students detailed instructions and guidance on writing topic or assignment, suggestions for review, and a means for determining if topic or assignment has been completed.

- Teach students to approach writing assignments creatively. Encourage brainstorming for novel ideas and approaches for communicating and making the student assignment and final document writing interesting and stimulating. Require a variety of writing assignments, in history, social studies, science, art, math, and other academic areas.

- As suggested for reading (read, read, read), require students to write, write, write. Practice in writing can be accomplished through a variety of student writing assignments, requiring rewrites and corrections, and designing ongoing writing assignments such as adding the reconstruction of the South to a paper on the Civil War.

Math

- Provide opportunities for students to view math as a creative cognitive learning task. Although such rote memorizing tasks as the multiplication tables are important, teachers should emphasize understanding and use of math that stimulates student interests, problem-solving abilities and very important, how math is the primary 'language' in other fields of study.

- Therefore, engage students in math activities not relying on memorization or formulas, without understanding. This might be calculating batting averages, determining the amount of fuel used by rockets, variation in musical notes and pitch, figuring the pollution index in air and water samples, or determining the percentage of females in executive positions in business and government.

- As with writing and reading, teach students the importance and use of math in their lives. Classroom assignments and activities should include the use of computer technology, simulations, information retrieval and problem solving that relates the importance of math in today's world.

TECHNOLOGY IN THE CLASSROOM

Educational psychologists and technologists have maintained for the past three generations that technology can have a dramatic impact on the cognitive development of students. Imagine the following:

- A secondary chemistry teacher provides students with the most advanced chemistry lab in the world.

- A middle school teacher takes seventh-grade students on a field trip to Mars for hands-on exploration and research.

- A medical student *repeatedly* practices delicate heart surgery procedures on the same patient until the procedure is perfected.

- Elementary students routinely observe the inner workings of the human body from birth to death as the body ages.

- Any age student has the opportunity to visit the labs of Galileo, Albert Einstein, or Sigmund Freud.

Are such educational tools, via technology, impossible, too expensive, or just some fantasy? Imagine the impact of such tools on the cognitive development of students. Educational technologists are now claiming that such student learning experiences are possible. Consider the following:

- In Chicago "YOUmedia"—a digital library space for teens has become a magnet for your people, citywide. A large room filled with the latest digital media (laptop computers, music keyboards, recording equipment video cameras and gaming consoles) have attracted students citywide. YOUmedia has become so popular the Chicago library plans to replicate it citywide.

- In Potomac Maryland, a teacher of advanced calculus has digitally recorded her lessons with a tablet computer then uploaded them to iTunes. Students use iPads to complete homework and class assignments. The process is called 'Flipped' classrooms.

- Uses and suggested uses of virtual reality in the classroom are being reported. For example, a student studying the exploration of the *Titanic* might manipulate from the classroom a robot submarine or robotics arm being used at the site of the *Titanic*, a very exciting possibility. ■

In the future, virtual reality technology could be a valuable teaching tool.

S U R F I N G • T H E • W E B

The National Institute for Literacy (**http://novel.nifl.gov**) lets students, teachers, and parents join in several online forums discussing literacy issues. The Literacy Directory Home Page (**http://novel.nifl.gov/litdir/index.html**) provides a large and comprehensive listing of Internet sites that have literacy and education information.

In addition, the Publications for Parents page (**http://www.ed.gov/pubs/parents. html**) has a number of titles that are vital to cognitive learning. Examples include "Helping Your Child Learn Math," "Helping Your Child Learn Science," "Helping Your Child Learn History," and "Helping Your Child Learn Geography." ■

Others have envisioned further wide-ranging educational uses for virtual reality, such as duplicate experiences in another country so students can interact and learn customs, beliefs and language. Consider the possibility of using VR to allow students to participate in historical events and interact with simulated persons from those events. The idea of a virtual reality "History Room" to permit users (students) to design, construct, and interact with dynamic historic systems has been proposed such as a physics classroom use where students create alternate worlds that violate physical laws of our universe.

RECAP OF MAJOR IDEAS

1. Students can learn how to improve their ability to process information, improve memory, and understand.

2. A teacher's ability to meet student learning needs is enhanced by developing a repertoire of teaching styles.

3. When choosing teaching and learning styles, teachers should solicit input from students, but should not allow such input to interfere with the academic requirements and achievement of students.

4. Students should be taught methods to analyze their thought processes. Teaching students how to analyze their thought processes has become a recognized goal for schools and teachers.

5. The development of student conceptualization skills involves schema theory, enhancing student motivation and interest, and instilling confidence in students.

FURTHER APPLICATIONS

1. Design a lesson to reduce the loss of student attention. Include in your strategy designing shorter lessons and using the skill of review.

2. Choose two learning strategies such as problem solving, discussion, questioning, simulations, or the case study method. For each strategy, read two recent articles, list the strengths and limitations of the strategy, and describe the teacher's role when using this strategy.

3. Using the list of 12 qualities of good thinkers, explain what you, as a teacher, can do to help students acquire five of those qualities.

4. Effective teachers work to provide a nonthreatening environment. They know that success is the best preparation for handling failure. Think about ways you can establish a safe climate in your classroom. Consider the power peer pressure can have on students and the

importance of students showing respect for their classmates. List three constructive ways teachers can respond to incorrect student responses.

KEY TERMS

metamemory

awareness

diagnosis

monitoring

mnemonics

acrostics

link method

loci method

peg word technique

key word method

advance organizer

key word organizer

rehearsal

PQ4R

concept development

schemata

transfer of learning

learning style

meta cognition

daily learning log

feedback

virtual reality

LOOKING AHEAD

Chapters 5 through 8 addressed the behavioral and cognitive aspects of the learning environment. Chapter 9, Learning and Instructional Tactics, emphasizes teaching methods and strategies promoting the behavioral and cognitive development of students. How can teachers foster "student understanding, creativity, and curiosity, and teach higher level thinking skills? Chapter 9 addresses these issues. ■

Part 4

Instructional Methods for Effective Teaching

307

Learning and Instructional Tactics

LEARNING OBJECTIVES

Upon completing this chapter, you should be able to:

1

Describe a method for facilitating student listening skills.

2

Name two effective applications of lecture instruction, and list two characteristics of students who benefit from lectures.

3

Explain the advantages and the teacher's role in *inquiry learning*.

4

Relate three significant characteristics of simulations to the instructional process.

5

Describe how teachers can capitalize on student interest in electronic gaming.

6

List six guidelines for teachers to follow when developing simulation instruction.

7

Name two advantages of 'direct instruction'.

8

Differentiate between goals and objectives.

9

Define three major criteria for establishing an educational objective.

10

Relate two ways teachers can promote students' higher-level thinking skills.

INTRODUCTION

Throughout this text, we have repeatedly emphasized the impact teachers have on student learning. Chapter 8 noted that effective teachers have an attitude of "my students are capable of achieving and I, as their teacher, am capable and responsible for ensuring they do." Additionally, effective teachers clearly communicate these expectations to students. This chapter provides teaching strategies for such communication.

Effective teachers typically possess a **repertoire** (collection) of teaching methods and the ability to select appropriate methods. Stallworth (1998, p. 17) stresses the need for teachers to systematically review their teaching strategies:

"A teacher's greatest opportunity for growth is systematic inquiry into his or her own teaching and learning."

This chapter will present six of the more important methods used in today's schools—**direct instruction, lecture, inquiry, questioning, simulations**, and **case study**. Additionally, we will explain the classroom circumstances such methods are most effective.

As you examine each method, ask yourself the following questions: For what classroom situation and students is this method most suited and beneficial? Is this method appropriate or inappropriate for certain objectives, students, and subjects? Can methods be blended to enhance effect of each method, and what is the teacher's role?

TODD WILLIAMS...

and two of his fellow teachers were chatting in the teachers' lounge during lunch break. Todd was lamenting his student's lack of interest in "Contemporary governance," the current topic in his social studies class. "I can hardly keep them awake. They yawn and roll their eyes. Max and Yvonne are usually asleep. I thought they'd be interested in local elections, presidential debates, and the freedom movement in the Middle East; but honestly they're bored and have no reservations about letting me know. I want government to be interesting to them but when I discuss the topic in class. . . ." Todd sighs and shrugs.

Mr. Stunovich, a science teacher, joined in. "You should try to get them to learn the symbols of the periodic table. One of my objectives is that students will be able to list the symbols for the elements, with a minimum accuracy rate of 90 percent. I passed out the table in class, told them to learn the symbols for the elements, gave them two weeks to do so, and then gave a quiz. The class average was 60." Mr. Stunovich continued, "Now get this, I told them I would give them another try. A week later I gave the exact same quiz and sure enough the class improved, to 64! Can you imagine giving the same quiz, and 64 is still the average grade? All they had to do to make A's was memorize'. So much for that 90 percent objective," Mr. Stunovich muttered.

Ms. Paterno, a geography teacher who had been listening quietly, finally interjected. "I was having the same problem as you guys but I tried some-thing and it worked. Spring for lunch tomorrow and I might tell you what I did." Moans eluded from Todd and Mr. Stunovich. Ms. Paterno grinned and continued, "I wanted my students to learn the forms of government of South American countries. My objec-tive was 80 percent mastery or above. I provided handouts with countries listed with their forms of government. We discussed at length how each government came about and its current history. I then gave a quiz and 60 percent of the class failed." Mrs. Paterno paused.

Todd and Mr. Stunovich in unison asked, "Well, what did you do?"

Ms. Paterno continued, "Well, you know how crazy these students are about these electronic games, all their iPads, iPods, and smart phones they carry around. And you know how crazy they are about football. So, I divided the class into two groups and announced the 'superbowl' of govern-ments of South American countries. I simply drew a football field on the board and announced the rules of the game. Both teams started with the ball on the goal line. Then I ask the teams to state the form of government of a South American country and they could use any electronic device they wanted to find the answer. The first team to answer correctly would get its ball advanced. I would ask a question and they would go into a tech frenzy, looking for the answer. They could 'google', text each other . . . anything they wanted. If the answer they came up with was correct, that team's ball advanced 10 yards. The first team to advance the ball the length of the field, or 10 correct answers, scored. The team then got a bonus question for the extra point, then we started at the goal line again. First team to win three games got to text anyone they wanted for ten minutes while the other team did homework."

Mr. Stunovich stammered, "You mean that worked?"

Ms. Paterno replied, "Well, it got a bit more complicated. Turk and Nix, who are football players, had some good suggestions. For example, once a team got inside the 40-yard line, or answered six questions correctly, they could go for a field goal for three points. Also, we had 10-yard penalties for wrong answers and for students who blurted out answers without conferring with their team. I think the students called this a 'flag on the play' or something like that. We played for 30 minutes every day for a week, and then I gave a quiz. The class average was 91; the lowest grade was 80 and that was with-out the use of their pads and phones."

Todd puzzled, responded, "You're kidding."

"No, and the students loved it. It was fun. I'm going to do it with North American countries next," Mrs. Paterno responded. The students want to design games for math and science. I'm working on that."

Mr. Stunovich quietly confessed, "You know that football game is not a bad idea. I might try that with my chemistry tables. It sounds like fun and it's worth a shot."

INTASC Standard 8   Instructional strategies

Teaching Methods and Strategies

Direct Instruction

As Todd is experiencing, much can be gained through teacher interaction (Behrstock-Sheran & Coggshall, 2010). Addressing the concerns of teachers like Todd, Mr. Stunovich, and Ms. Paterno, what are the characteristics of teaching methods and strategies they can use? A consistent finding in Educational Psychology research is that higher student achievement is related to teachers' use of **direct** or **active instruction** (Good & Brophy, 1997). This is especially true of highly effective teachers in low-performing, urban schools (Poplin et. al., 2011). Direct instruction means students spend most of their time during the school day being taught or supervised by teachers, instead of working on their own. The teacher actively teaches content to students and follows up with assignments applying the concepts students have been taught, as in the following:

> After Ms. Frank teaches her fourth graders the concepts of decimals and percentages, she follows up by assigning her students a project requiring them to calculate the percent of the day (24 hours) they spend (1) in school, (2) sleeping, (3) watching TV, (4) completing homework, and (5) engaged in other activities.

Although direct instruction includes frequent lessons where the teacher presents information and develops concepts through demonstration and lectures, most of the lectures involve question and answer sessions, with students providing feedback. Ms. Frank might begin by asking Theo and Terrece the percent of time each day they spend sleeping. If they respond with different percentages, then Ms. Frank would pursue this discussion. She might want to compare males' and females' time spent sleeping, completing homework, and stimulating class discussion.

Another characteristic of direct instruction is that teachers assume considerable responsibility for the academic achievement of their students (Good, 1983). They expect students to master the curriculum, with instruction.

Effective teachers question students and respond with appropriate feedback.

PowerPoint

Other characteristics of direct instruction include:

- Teachers need to properly prepare students for assignments.

- Lessons should be well organized, beginning with an overview.

- Advanced organizers, a review of the objectives, and an outline of the content should be utilized.

- Students should be made aware of the main ideas in the content (discussed in Chapter 8).

- During instruction, parts of the lesson should be summarized as they are completed, and the main ideas of the lesson should be reviewed.

- Teachers should review frequently and continually monitor student progress. The Proactive Teaching box example suggests how direct instruction content can be integrated into lesson plans.

PROACTIVE TEACHING

CLASSROOM SITUATION

At the beginning of the school year, as a proactive teacher you have outlined the academic content of topics to be covered in class. However, you want to include in your instruction, organized systematic plans for 'direct' instruction.

PROACTIVE ALTERNATIVES

When planning the curriculum content of active instruction, your plans could include a well-formatted time interval schedule, such as the following:

- 9:00 am–9:20 am Review and checking of previous day's work

- 9:20 am–10:00 am Presentation of new material, which includes advance organizers coupled with briskly-paced instruction

- 10:00 am–10:20 am Preliminary evaluation of student understanding and assigning practice material (homework or classwork) relating to new subject matter. This can be accomplished through testing, a question-and-answer session, or group work requiring students to articulate their understanding of new subject matter. Often student responses and difficulty of subject matter require

Effective, facilitating teachers provides students opportunities to practice and review newly learned academic material.

modification of time intervals for review or evaluation. However, proactive planning, using time intervals, ensures integration of the elements of direct instruction into your lesson plan.

Steps for Direct Instruction

Rosenshine (1986) describes several steps for integrating direct instruction into the typical class day that are comparable to the suggestions offered in the Proactive Teaching box.

- Daily review and check the previous day's work. Reteach or review material if errors are found on students' previous day's assignments or homework.

- Present new concepts and content. Follow a sequential pattern by first providing an overview of content, similar to the 'advance organizers' discussed in Chapter 8. Then proceed in small steps through the content, giving detailed explanations or instructions and repeating only in the context of student questions and student responses to teacher questions. Finally, as content is being mastered, introduce new content.

- Determine whether students have mastered content materials. This can be done with the students "practicing" in a group. Yelon (1996, p. 3) suggests that teachers provide student practice during the learning process; ask questions, and give students an opportunity to articulate what they have learned. When appropriate, provide encouragement and prompts. By evaluating student responses while reviewing, determine whether students understand the material. Students should be able to answer teacher questions on content material with an 80 percent (*or higher*) success rate.

- Provide feedback and corrective information to students on their answers to questions and on written assignments. Use percentage of errors as an indicator that review is required. When reviewing, simplify subject content; provide clues to the students; explain and review, using smaller steps than were used in the initial presentation of material.

- Allow students to independently work on the material through assigned academic tasks. Require students to review and practice until they have a success rate of 95 percent or higher on teacher questions and written assignments.

- Review previous material on a weekly basis.

Lecturing

Lecture instruction is the oral presentation of material and is most appropriate when students are relatively homogeneous (have similar backgrounds and abilities) (Rothstein, 1990). If longevity were a test of effectiveness, without question, lecture would be the most important teaching method used to date. For centuries, the lecture has remained a popular teaching method. Good and Brophy (2008) point out that such direct teacher instruction is a common characteristic of classrooms where students excel academically.

One strength of the lecture is efficiency. By lecturing, teachers can cover material in defined periods of time and preparation is simplified. The lecture is also an effective method for covering material as a frame of reference. This means a lecture can effectively introduce topics and summarize major concepts. The lecture is also a good way to demonstrate models and clarify confusing academic material.

Emphasizing the advantages and appropriate use of lectures is critical. Because of the way some lecturers present data, information is often quickly forgotten. Further, the lecture depends on teacher mastery of lecture content and is dependent on teacher interpretation and understanding of content. Effective listening by students is equally important and requires motivation, good organizational and planning skills, note taking skills, and question and answer skills. Unfortunately, many students are poor at note taking, especially younger students. Lectures also can produce frustration among students who do not understand subjectcontent . . .

The lecture is more effective for students who are good listeners, note takers and are motivated.

Improving Lectures

Lectures can be too formal, too authoritative, and too structured. Effective lecturers prepare students for new academic material by presenting objectives prior to the lecture. These objectives can be used as advance organizers, providing learners cues to help them focus on major concepts (Chapter 8).

> " Uncertainty is an integral part of the business of solving problems. "
> MARTINEZ, 1998, P. 609

> The National Science Foundation sponsored many studies on student inquiry and autonomy that demonstrated giving students opportunities to manipulate science materials, to contract with teachers about what to learn, to inquire on their own, and to engage in activity-based curricula all had substantial positive effects.
>
> WALBERG, 1990, P. 473

Teachers can further improve lectures by varying their presentations by using gesturing, pausing, and visuals such as SMART Boards and PowerPoint. Humor can lower anxiety, enabling both students and teacher to relax and feel comfortable. Students limited by achievement level often cannot understand lecture content. Reviewing material and providing remedial material are alternatives for such students.

Inquiry Learning: Fostering Creativity and Curiosity

Often considered the opposite of lecturing is the teaching method called **inquiry learning**. Unlike the lecture, which places the student in a passive learning role, inquiry learning requires students to be active.. Inquiry learning emphasizes student involvement in learning academic subject matter via independent study, oral and written reports, library searches, lab experiments, and fieldwork (Henson, 2012). Inquiry learning is very popular in the university setting, especially in graduate school. The teacher serves primarily as a facilitator, organizer, and consultant to students engaged in inquiring about subject matter. Some teachers choose inquiry because this level of student involvement is motivating and fosters creativity and because it provides students the opportunity to learn the *process* of inquiry.

Inquiry learning changes the teacher's role; it is not conducive to teachers who constantly dispense information. Since academic content is not always factual, teacher expertise is critical, especially with upper grade-level students. Effective teachers of inquiry encourage students to question and be skeptical.

Questioning: Stimulating Academic Interests

Similar to inquiry is the 'art' of **questioning** . Since about 300 B.C., questioning in learning and teaching processes has been widely recognized and used. Socrates used questions so effectively, students and others gathered in masses to observe, question, and learn from his skills. An advantage of questioning in today's schools is providing teachers a method to enhance student thinking skills and determine if students are learning and understanding subject content. Questioning also provides students a means of expressing curiosity, understanding, confusion, agreement, and disagreement.

However, to derive such benefits, teachers must use questioning effectively. An effective time to question is when reviewing lessons or units. Also, questions can be advance organizers, helping students to focus on important content.

Henson (2012) provides 12 guidelines for using questions.

1. Avoid using a long series of questions to introduce lessons.
2. Delay questions about content until a student knowledge base has been established.
3. Use a combination of levels of questions, extending from recall to evaluation.

4. Pause for at least 3 seconds following each question.

5. Do not expect students to always understand what a question means.

6. Address questions to individual students by using student names.

7. Keep content-oriented questions specific.

8. Help students develop skills in answering questions.

9. Encourage students to ask questions.

10. Assist students to develop skills in asking questions.

11. Listen carefully to student questions and respond, using their content.

12. Prior to reading assignments, showing a video, or taking a field trip, pose questions relative to major concepts or objectives of the coming student experience.

An important step in using questioning effectively is to reinforce student responses.

Student Study Guide

When verbally questioning students, at least 75 percent of the questions should elicit correct answers (Good & Brophy, 1997). Complex questions requiring higher levels of thought should also elicit the same high level of correct responses. Asking questions that 75 percent or more of the students can answer correctly might accomplish two important goals: students become confident because they are successful, and the simpler questions can actually enhance the attainment of higher-level learning objectives (Brophy & Good, 1986).

Teachers should not hesitate to question younger elementary students. With consistent and extensive feedback, teachers can elicit student input and cohesive answers from elementary students (Good & Brophy, 1997). Feedback should include acknowledgment of a correct or partially correct response, and further questioning should attempt to elicit more accurate responses if needed.

Effective teachers ask both challenging and easy-to-answer questions.

Effective teachers probe their students for answers that reveal understanding.

Students should be encouraged to ask questions.

Nadeen's fourth-grade class is discussing the section from Mark Twain's *Tom Sawyer* where Tom shows up at his own funeral. She asks Aretha, "How did Tom's aunt feel when he came through the door?" When Aretha answers, "She was glad to see him," Phil raises his hand and Nadeen turns to him. "Although she was glad to see that he wasn't dead, she was also angry that he had put her through a lot of worry," Phil responds.

How could Nadeen have improved her interaction with Aretha and Phil? According to the research reviewed by Good and Brophy (1997), Nadeen should have given more elaborate feedback to Aretha and questioned her again before calling on Phil: "Yes, Aretha, she was glad, but do you think she felt anything else?"

A final suggestion for using questions is to remember that students should be encouraged to formulate questions about academic content. As Einstein noted; "The formulation of a problem is often more essential than its solution." When students question, raise new possibilities or regard old problems from a new perspective, this suggests a measure of success in realizing student imagination and problem-solving skills.

Enhancing Student Listening Skills

Effective listening is critical to learning, and questions can be used to hone student listening skills. Teachers should use different and innovative methods to teach listening skills (National Reading Panel, 2000). Benoit and Lee (1988) suggest that students be encouraged to focus on the message by asking themselves the following questions:

- Why is the person communicating with you?
- What is your communicator's purpose?
- What does this person expect you to understand?
- How can you weigh the details the communicator is presenting?
- How prejudiced or biased is your communicator?
- How opinionated or self-interested is your communicator?
- What sincere interest does your communicator have in relating this message to you?
- Do you understand the language of the message?
- Does the message contain material you already know, share, or can discuss?
- Can you read between the lines and know what subject or idea is being communicated?

- Does the message have merit even though you disagree with the point of view expressed?

- Are you really absorbing the content of the message? Are you listening to the facts, details, and opinions?

Can you formulate a method of integrating lecture, inquiry, and questioning? If some of your future students have poor listening skills, what are your options? Could you use students who have good listening skills as models? Consider the suggestions of Marilyn M. Grondel, former Utah Teacher of the Year.

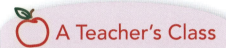 A Teacher's Class

NAME: Marilyn M. Grondel, former Utah Teacher of the Year

The following quote from Haim Ginott guides my actions in the classroom each day: "I've come to a frightening conclusion that I am the decisive element in the classroom. It's my personal approach that creates the climate. It's my daily mood that makes the weather. As a teacher, I possess a tremendous power to make a child's life miserable or joyous. I can be a tool of torture or an instrument of inspiration. I can humiliate or humor, hurt or heal. In all situations, it is my response that decides whether a crisis will be escalated or de-escalated and a child humanized or de-humanized."

I love and respect children. Each child that spends time in my classroom is a gift to me from his parents. It is my responsibility to cherish that gift, to dream for that child, to lift him to new heights, to help him be the best he can be.

I believe that wonder and joy are always in the attic of one's mind. However, in today's complex society, students enter the classroom with multiple problems and needs. Reaching all students and challenging them to grow requires using a variety of techniques.

Students have various levels of commitment to the learning process. There is not one program, one reform, or one method that will be the key to every student's learning opportunity. It is always necessary to explore new ideas and methods that will offer challenge, growth, and promise to every child.

A student's growth and success is an individual process rather than a competitive process. It is not the speed that a child learns at that is important but that they learn, no matter how long it takes. This statement guides the instructional method I use in my classroom.

I have developed units and activities to improve the learning process, to increase motivation of students, and to allow students to enjoy success at their *own* academic level. I believe curriculum goes beyond the basic program offered in the textbook. To be meaningful, students need to see how the curriculum fits in with their everyday experiences and interests.

Teaching in rural areas, I have found success in motivating students to read using a horse unit that encompasses nonfiction books to learn about the history and care of horses and fiction books to help students realize the enjoyment that comes from reading. This unit also provides for community members to share their knowledge of horses with the students and to bring horses to the school for a hands-on activity.

Another effective tool I use is modeling. Whatever the activity—silent reading, journal writing, reading with a partner, reading in a small group—I am an active participant. Before I ask students to give an oral book report, share their journal, or read a story they have written, I always do it first.

I use as many hands-on activities as possible. The value of helping others is fostered through working with first graders, the handicapped unit in our school, and their peers.

An ice cream day, in which small groups of students make freezers of ice cream to share with each other and the school staff, teaches responsibility and working together in a group to produce a successful product. There is always a feeling of pride in sharing a product with others.

I use community leaders and parents to expose students to various careers and the subject matter that they need to master to be successful in that career.

The instructional methods I have successfully used have often been developed with other teachers or have been an expansion of an idea presented by other teachers. I have presented my ideas and materials at various in-service workshops in our district and at the local school level.

I believe that a successful teacher does not keep ideas and materials secret. A successful teacher becomes more successful by dialoguing with colleagues and sharing ideas and materials. ■

As Marilyn Grondel states, "Reaching all students and challenging them to grow requires using a variety of teaching techniques."

Simulation

In an educational context, a **simulation** is a technique that teaches about some aspect of the world or environment by imitation or replication (Alessi & Trollip, 1991). Simulations can be motivating and interesting to students, but their major advantage is that students learn by interacting in a manner similar to the way they would react in real world situations. Examples for a history or social studies class might be simulating the United States Senate with students as senators of various states. Students might serve as representatives, simulate various senate committees, and elect students for minority and majority leaders. Example objectives of such a simulation could be (1) a better understanding of the relationship between the executive, legislative and judicial branches of our government; (2) the passing of laws; (3) international issues facing our government, such as conflict, pollution and use of natural resources; and (4) the meaning of the 'balance of power'.

Another example for an economics or business class might be simulating personnel who work in a bank. Class members could alternately serve as customers, investors, bank officers, tellers, and board members. Class objectives might include (1) understanding the processes of depositing and withdrawing money, debit and credit cards, calculating interest payments; (2) learning about the federal laws governing fraud and deposit insurance; and (3) examining the decision-making process involving investors, bank officers, and board members. As a teacher, if you are fortunate enough to have computer access for your students, computer simulation software is available in most, if not every subject.

> Simulation games can produce as much learning as lectures and significantly higher retention.

The advantages of simulation include;

- Involving students actively.
- Creating a high degree of interest and enthusiasm.
- Making abstract concepts meaningful to students.
- Providing immediate feedback to students.
- Allowing students to experiment with concepts and new skills without feeling the need to be correct at all times.
- Giving students the opportunity to evaluate their mistakes.
- Allowing students to practice communication skills.

Remember the words of Marilyn Grondel, "I am an active participant. Before I ask students to give an oral book report, share their journal, or read a story they have written, I always do it first."

Simulations and Electronic Gaming

Contemporary teachers recognize electronic games and gaming are an integral part of many of today's students daily environment but often fail to take advantage. Recently, video games surpassed Hollywood films in annual sales, becoming the most popular form of entertainment (Barab, Gresalfi, & Arici, 2009). Simulation gaming can have a significant impact on student retention (Marzano, 2009). One study compared the retention of students taught science using simulation gaming with traditional-taught science students. Both groups of students were tested two months later, and students taught using simulation games retained more science content (Barab et al., 2009). As stated earlier, many excellent computer simulation games are available from commercial publishers, and some of the best were developed by teachers.

Following are suggestions for teaching via classroom simulations (Alessi & Trollip, 1991):

- Identify your objectives.
- Decide on a problem or simulation.
- Define the scope of the simulation.
- Construct the rules.
- Identify students' goals.
- Write rules and teacher instructions.
- Design any additional parts.
- Develop a follow-up evaluation.

PowerPoint

CASE STUDY

Throughout this text, we continue to stress the theme of 'proactive teaching' and we hope as you are reading this text with a critical eye, asking yourself, "is the information in this book accurate? Are the authors' suggestions sound? Upon what do they base inferences and conclusions?"

Case study materials offer both you and your students a way to tie pro-action and practice together. The case study has proven effective in relating theory and practice by involving students in what they are studying (Kowalski, Weaver, & Henson, 1990). The case method refers to the use of cases as educational vehicles, giving students an opportunity to experience as they learn. Through discussion with others, definition of problems, identification of alternatives, statement of objectives and decision criteria, and choice of action and plan for implementation, the student gains an opportunity to develop analytical and planning skills. For example, in a medical laboratory analogy, the case provides the corpse for the medical student to practice and learn.

Naturally, the effectiveness of case study depends on the quality of cases used. Paget (1988) explains:

> A case report is a description of a factual situation that must be realistic and not obviously contrived or artificial. It must reflect the kind of situation encountered naturally in the conduct of the discipline concerned. It must be of practical and immediate importance to have relevance as an illustrative example.

Teachers can use case studies to teach students to identify important information, ask pertinent questions, and make judgments based on case information.

A sample case study follows.

CASE STUDY

Pat Ohlsen began her teaching career 17 years ago as a fourth-grade teacher at Rivera Elementary School. Her job has had its ups and downs, but Pat was happy as a teacher. Three years ago her colleagues elected her chair of grade four. She enjoys providing leadership, and since she became chair, several new programs have been introduced into the curriculum.

Due to budget cuts, the past year brought significant school reform mandates from the state legislature. One of the changes was combining kindergarten with grades 1 through 3. Pat predicts that the impact on teachers and students will be significant. She is especially concerned with providing a smooth transition for these students into grade four. In the last chair's meeting with the other fourth grade teachers, Pat expressed her concern. She proposed a strategy that included writing new goals and objectives and revising curriculum. But the other teachers were unenthusiastic about more planning and assignments.

Pat searched the Internet for materials that would stimulate her colleagues' interest in reshaping the curriculum to provide for the changes. She copied the following quotes, which she plans to use at her next meeting to garner more enthusiasm about the planning that she feels must be done.

- Take a second look at what happens to someone's "good luck." You'll find not luck, but preparation, planning, and success-producing thinking preceded his good fortune. Take a second look at what appears to be someone's bad luck. Look, and you'll discover certain specific reasons. (David Schwartz)

- Long-range planning does not deal with future decisions, but with the future of present decisions. (Peter Drucker)

- You can do what you want to do, accomplish what you want to accomplish, attain any reasonable objective you may have in mind. . . . Not all of a sudden, perhaps not in one swift and sweeping action of achievement. . . . But you can do it gradually—day by day and play by play—if you want to do it, you will do it, over a sufficiently long period of time. (William Holler)

Do you suppose Pat was successful in motivating her fellow teachers to get more involved? What else could she do to facilitate a smooth transition to the changes mandated?

PROACTIVE EXERCISE

Suppose you were a teacher at Rivera Elementary.

1. State one method for helping a class of incoming students make smooth transition into the fourth grade.

2. Write two goals you could share with families to help them with a new curriculum structure.

3. Write three methods teachers could use to minimize the difficulty experienced by students entering a new school.

In summary, recent research has produced considerable information about a variety of teaching methods including direct instruction, lecture, inquiry learning, questioning, simulation, and the case study. Prospective teachers should become aware of the strengths and limitations of each and the appropriate teacher's role when using each. Also, remember the advice of Marilyn Grondel, former Utah Teacher of the Year "The instructional methods I have used successfully have often been developed with other teachers or have been an expansion of an idea presented by other teachers."

Consider the following Proactive Teaching box which demonstrates how these multiple methods can be integrated to effectively teach students.

PROACTIVE TEACHING

CLASSROOM SITUATION

As a teacher, you want to take advantage of the various forms of instructional delivery of curriculum material.

PROACTIVE ALTERNATIVES

As part of your lesson planning, include various forms of instructional delivery. For example, consider the following variety of methodologies for teaching middle school mathematics.

· Lesson 1: *Lecture*—The relationship of sets and numbers

· Lessons 2 and 3: *Simulation*—Operations in addition and subtraction via computer-assisted instruction.

· Lesson 4: *Class Discussion*—Review with question-and-answer session on sets, numbers, addition and subtraction.

· Lesson 5: *Quiz*—*Sets*, numbers, addition and subtraction.

· Lesson 6: *Class Discussion and Lecture*—Review of quiz, introduction to multiplication and division

· Lesson 7: *Computer-Assisted Instruction*—Fundamentals of multiplication and division.

· Lesson 8: *Inquiry Learning*—Explanation of student independent study project entitled "Using Math Everyday", which entails a paper requiring the use of computer and/or hand-held computer device.

· Lesson 9: *Inquiry Learning*—Field trip to observe and participate in "district math contest," which involves participating in math and simulation competitions.

· Lesson 10: *Student Involvement in Preliminaries to Case Study*—Students begin presentation of independent study projects with each student required to complete a log of all topics presented with a brief description of each to be discussed in future classes.

These 10 lessons illustrate the variety of instructional methods available to teachers. Included in such methods will be homework, class assignments, review, testing and modifying curriculum content. Although you will probably have a favorite method for teaching, including the variety often needed to stimulate and interest students is not difficult.

ENHANCING STUDENT UNDERSTANDING OF ACADEMIC EXPECTATIONS

Student achievement is enhanced by teachers who use direct instruction, monitor student behavior, deal with transgressions quickly, clearly communicate academic behavior expected, and hold students responsible for such behavior by defining consequences, both positive and negative. Effective teachers

Establishing clear expectations of students is essential to good classroom management.

I believe curriculum goes beyond the basic program offered in the textbook. To be meaningful, students need to see how the curriculum fits in with their everyday experiences and interests. (Marilyn Grondel, former Utah Teacher of the Year)

communicate with their students verbally and in writing to ensure students understand expectations. Further, teachers clearly communicate to students goals of instruction.

Educational Goals

Teachers use two primary types of academic purpose statements; **goals** and **objectives** (Henson, 2011). *Educational goals* are expectations held for groups of students. They are specific and attainable. An example of an educational goal is "At the end of grade 8, students at Millersville Middle School will score in the seventy-fifth percentile or above on math and reading national achievement test." Notice this goal is group-defined (eighth-grade students at Millersville), and attainment is possible.

Educational Objectives

A student's growth and success is an individual process rather than a competitive process. It is not the speed that a child learns at that is important but that they learn. (Marilyn Grondel, former Utah Teacher of the Year)

Goals are needed to help a school, class, or other student(s) identify and achieve expectations. **Objectives are** needed to determine via measurement if goals have been obtained. According to Slavin (1990), objectives are statements of student expectations that are specific and measurable. Academically, educational objectives, often labeled *performance objectives* or *behavioral objectives*, and can be used for either student performance or teacher performance. By establishing objectives, teachers can accurately and clearly communicate expectations to students. Miserandino (1996, p. 210) reported, "Another way in which children develop perceived competence is through the expectations that teachers communicate to their students."

Setting objectives also allows teachers to measure whether specific competencies have been acquired. A major advantage of objectives is that they give direction to students, informing them of expectations and how such expectations will measured. When objectives are used "there are no unexpected or surprise results since both parties have agreed upon the end product" (Wulf & Schane, 1984, p. 117). Mastering the skills needed to write accurate objectives provides an accurate method for communicating and measuring the academic goals you set for your students.

Educational objectives should meet three basic criteria: defining student behavior, specifying conditions, and stating a minimal acceptance level.

It is critical for teachers to be accurate and clear when establishing objectives, especially with low-achieving students (Oakes, Quartz, Gong, Guiton, & Lipton, 1993). The following section relates suggestions for writing objectives.

Criteria for Writing Objectives

There are three essential criteria for writing objectives.

1. Objectives should be stated in terms of expected student academic and social behavior.

2. Objectives should specify the conditions of student performance.

3. Objectives should specify the minimum acceptable level of performance. (Slavin, 1990)

When a teacher states objectives in terms of desired student performance that are observable and measurable (note the objectives at the beginning of each chapter in this text), teacher and students understand what is expected and how these expectations will be measured. The lists of terms in Table 9.1 contains verbs that are specific, observable, and measurable and those that are too general and vague to be accurately observed and measured.

PROACTIVE EXERCISE

Suppose you are a tenth-grade English teacher who teaches composition writing. Select four of the most important ideas you want your students to learn. These will become the content for the first day's lesson in a unit entitled "Composition Writing."

Write three objectives in terms of desired student behavior. The emphasis should not be "Today I'll teach . . ." instead state "(As a result of the lesson,) each student will (be able to) . . ." Second, state the conditions students are expected to perform ("When given a list of adjectives . . ."). Third, state the expected level of performance ("Students will be able to identify and spell correctly with 80 percent accuracy" or "identify, without error, the subject of sentences."). Finally, avoid using verbs that cannot be observed or measured, such as *learn*, *know*, and *understand*. Instead, use such specific, action-oriented verbs as *identify*, *list*, *explain*, *name*, *describe*, and *compare*.

Instructor Test
Bank

TABLE 9.1
Performance Terms

Specific and Measurable	Vague and Not Measurable
Build	Appreciate
Classify	Consider
Contrast	Desire
Demonstrate	Feel
Distinguish	Find interesting
Evaluate	Have insight into
Identify	Know
Interpret	Learn
Label	Like to

(Continued)

TABLE 9.1 (CONTINUED)	
Performance Terms	
Specific and Measurable	**Vague and Not Measurable**
List	Love to
Match	Really like to
Measure	Recognize
Name	Remember
Remove	See that
Select	Think
State	Understand
Write	Want to

> Education objectives can be written in each of three major domains: cognitive, affective, and psychomotor.

WRITING PERFORMANCE OBJECTIVES

Many of the aims and goals of education deal with thinking (remembering the capitol of a state or solution to a math problem), others involve attitudes (development of appropriate social behavior), and still others focus on physical skills (running, sports). You can write performance objectives in each of these domains (cognitive, affective, and psychomotor). Let us examine writing objectives at varying levels of difficulty for the cognitive domain.

INTASC Standard 4   Content knowledge

Cognitive Development

One of the first systematic approaches to helping teachers write objectives at specified levels came in 1956, when Benjamin S. Bloom and a group of students at the University of Chicago developed a taxonomy of educational objectives in the cognitive domain (Bloom, 1956). Bloom's cognitive objectives included six levels:

- Level 1: Knowledge
- Level 2: Comprehension
- Level 3: Application
- Level 4: Analysis
- Level 5: Synthesis
- Level 6: Evaluation

LEVEL 1: Knowledge

The simplest and least demanding objectives are those requiring only memorization of facts; this requires meeting **knowledge-level objectives** . Before students can move on to more advanced levels of tasks, they must first learn certain basic facts. For example, balancing chemical equations requires students to know atomic symbols. Learning the atomic symbols can be done by rote memorization. An example of an objective written at the knowledge level for chemistry would be; "When given a list of ten elements and a list of atomic weights, students will be able to correctly match a minimum of eight of the ten elements with their atomic weights." Another example; "When given a list containing ten vertebrates and ten invertebrates, students will correctly identify a minimum of nine of the ten invertebrates."

These objectives contain the three essential criteria:

1. The conditions of the task students are expected to perform ("When given . . .").

2. Objectives are written in terms of desired student performance ("students will be able to . . .").

3. A statement of the minimum acceptable level of performance ("identify 8/9 of the 10 correctly"). Both objectives also contain action-oriented verbs that can be observed and measured ("match," "identify").

LEVEL 2: Comprehension

Comprehension-level objectives require students to translate, interpret, or predict a continuation of trends (Bloom, 1956, p. 149). For example, a social studies teacher who wants students to understand the differences between socialism and democracy may have the following objective for her students: "When given a paragraph containing distinct qualities for two political systems, students will correctly place an A or a D over each quality (A = Autocratic, D = democracy). Notice, this objective does not specify a minimum acceptable level of performance. When there is no mention of acceptable level, it should be assumed and communicated to students they are expected to perform with 100 percent accuracy.

LEVEL 3: Application

Application-level objectives require students to use principles or generalizations to solve a defined problem. For example, a music teacher might write the following objectives: "Given the lengths of two strings of equal diameter and equal tension, students will use their understanding of the effect of length on pitch to determine whether the longer or shorter string has the higher pitch." An English teacher might write the following objective: "Given the beats and measures in iambic pentameter, students will write a five-verse poem in iambic pentameter without missing more than one beat per verse." Notice that the depth of understanding and student ability to accomplish academic objectives increases at each level of Bloom's taxonomy. The ability to generalize and use principles enables students to apply their knowledge to solve many different academic tasks (Kutz, 1992).

Application- and analysis- level objectives require students to work with concepts, principles, and broad generalizations.

An instructor's attitude toward teaching responsibilities after class-room hours plays an important part in their effectiveness.

LEVEL 4: Analysis

Analysis-level objectives, like application objectives, also require students to work with principles, concepts, and broad generalizations. In addition, analysis-level objectives, requires students to break down the concepts and principles of the subject matter to understand better, and to do this they must understand both the content and its structural form. For example, a government teacher might write the following objective for a class studying how a bill becomes a law: "Given a proposed law, students will trace its development from the time it was introduced as a bill to its passage into law, explaining each major step."

LEVEL 5: Synthesis

The **synthesis-level objective** requires students to take several parts and put them together to form a *new* whole. Unlike the analysis-level objective, synthesis-level objectives require students to use divergent thinking and creativity. Synthesis requires experimentation and investigation. Ideally, synthesis-level objectives support students becoming more independent and needing less direction from their teachers. Students should learn and be exposed to problems having more than one possible correct solution; synthesis-level activities promote this concept.

For example, a history teacher who wants students to understand the problems faced by the settlers of this country might preface the unit with an assignment involving the following objective: "Suppose you are a member of a team of explorers who are going to start a new colony on an inhabited planet with the same atmosphere of earth. List 10 rules you would propose to guide the colonists. A minimum of five of the rules must serve to protect the interests of the native inhabitants."

> Evaluation, the highest level objective in Bloom's taxonomy, requires students to make judgments and offer evidence to support these judgments.

When you use synthesis-level objectives, give students enough direction to keep them making progress but not so much that they can avoid using divergent thinking skills.

LEVEL 6: Evaluation

Evaluation is the highest level in Bloom's cognitive domain. It is the highest because it is the only level requiring students to use defined criteria, not just opinions, to make judgments. Evaluation-level objectives contain various combinations of elements in the first five levels.

A speech teacher might use the following objective with students who are studying diplomatic and persuasive techniques: "While viewing a video recording of a president's two most recent public addresses, each student will rate the speeches in terms of tact and persuasion, stating three strengths and three weaknesss. After evaluation, propose two alternatives that would have made the speeches more persuasive."

Knowing how to write objectives at each of these cognitive levels can be an invaluable tool for the proactive teacher. With clearly written objectives, you and your students can understand academic and social expectations and how they will be measured.

PROACTIVE TEACHING

CLASSROOM SITUATION

You want to include in your lesson plans, requirements for your students involving the higher levels of learning: analysis, synthesis, and evaluation.

PROACTIVE ALTERNATIVES

Lesson planning requiring student analysis, synthesis, and evaluation can be difficult. However, with imagination and creativity, Bloom's higher levels of learning can be included in most lessons. For example, a spelling quiz might suggest only Level 1 (memorization), but to include higher levels of learning for a task as rudimentary as spelling consider the following:

· Level 1: *Knowledge*—Require students to *spell* words correctly (memorization of facts).

· Level 2: *Comprehension*—Require students to spell words correctly and to *define* words.

- Level 3: *Application*—Require students to spell, define, and use words appropriately in a sentence.
- Level 4: *Analysis*—In addition to Level 3 requirements, require students to *trace* the origin and derivation of a word, *provide* an antonym and synonym, and *identify* the part of speech of the word.
- Levels 5 and 6: *Synthesis and Evaluation*—In addition to Level 4 tasks, require students to *use* the words in a paper, a debate, a discussion, or writings such as a poem using various word meanings according to content and use. Additionally, require students to *suggest alternatives* to words that are more appropriate or that provide more clarity.

Affective Objectives

In the A View from the Field box, Dr. Jules A. Troyer discusses the relationship of student learning, teacher preparation, and curriculum objectives and the issue of teachers meeting state standards and objectives.

A VIEW FROM THE FIELD

PROFILE

Dr. Jules A. Troyer (Ph.D., Educational Psychology with an emphasis in Learning and Instruction and Quantitative Research Methods) is Assistant Professor of Psychology at Valdosta State University. She is former editor of the Delta Journal of Education. She has developed and validated a reliable new psychometric instrument to measure levels of consciousness and is currently testing it in a variety of research settings. She is also conducting research related to problem solving, literacy issues, and consciousness, and is actively pursuing grant funding related to learning and instruction programs in K-12 and higher education.

1. QUESTION: What is the relationship of student learning, teacher preparation, and curriculum objectives?

Dr. Troyer: The relationship between student learning, teacher preparation and curriculum objectives is reciprocal and interconnected. Teachers and administrators must carefully and precisely state curriculum objectives, in order to guide the design of instruction and the creation of reliable and valid methods of assessing student learning. Measures of student learning must be directly representational of the curriculum objectives. To make this happen, teachers must align the content of the course with the curriculum objectives and ensure the assessments are empirically reflective of those objectives. This is a synergistic and reflexive process, where each of the three elements influences the others. In addition to curriculum objectives influencing the way teachers prepare individual lessons and units, and the manner in which they construct assessments, teacher preparation and assessments inform the creation or modification of curriculum objectives. The mutual interdependence of measures of student learning, teacher preparation, and curriculum objectives sustains a system that is informed by data from all the existing parts.

2. QUESTION: How can beginning teachers ensure they are meeting state standards and objectives?

Dr. Troyer: Beginning teachers must use state standards—the comprehensive lists of content area standards that guide instruction and assessment from kindergarten through high school—to inform the goals, course content, and methods of assessment in their classes. These state standards delineate clear goals for specific grade levels in mathematics, writing, reading, science, social studies, and often in areas such as foreign languages, physical education, art and music. The selection of specific instructional strategies should be informed by the state standards for the grade level of the student, and the content area. One way new teachers can do this is to overtly include objectives and goals at differing levels of sophistication and difficulty. Teachers can use tools such as Blooms taxonomy, which is a hierarchy of six basic cognitive processes that range from simple to complex, to align instructional strategies with existing state standards. Beginning teachers should start their instructional planning by understanding what knowledge and skills the state expects students to acquire in the class and then match these goals with relevant instructional strategies and assessments. ■

TEACHING HIGHER-LEVEL THINKING SKILLS

Many contend the best way to educate students to perform higher-level operations is through the teaching of cognitive strategies (Pressley et al., 1990). A number of strategies and techniques have been used successfully to teach **higher-level thinking skills** . For example, after a review of some 50 studies, Rosenshine and Meister (1992) noted that many successful teachers use instructional procedures called scaffolds. **Scaffolds** are defined as "tools such as cue cards, or techniques, such as teacher modeling" designed to allow

The teaching of higher-order thinking skills is a topic of major concern with today's educators. These skills include comprehension and interpretation of text, scientific processes, and mathematical problem solving. While much has been written on the need for students to perform higher-level thinking operations in all subject areas, the teaching of these operations often fails, not because the idea is poor, but because the instruction is inadequate. (Rosenshine & Meister, 1992, p. 26) learners "to participate at an ever-increasing level of competence (Rosenshine & Meister, 1992, p. 27). For example, Scandamalia and Bereiter (1986) suggest students could be taught to use cues to write creative compositions, as in the following list.

Planning Cues Used for Opinion Essays	
New Idea	**Elaborate**
An even better idea is . . .	An example of this . . .
An important point I haven't considered yet is . . .	This is true, but it's not sufficient so . . .
A better argument might be . . .	My own feelings about this are . . .
A new way of thinking on this topic is . . .	I'll change this a little by . . .
No one will have thought of . . .	The reason I think so . . .
Improving	Another reason that's good . . .
I'm not being very clear about what I just said so . . .	I could develop this idea by adding . . .
A criticism I should deal with in my paper is . . .	Another way to put it would be . . .
I really think this isn't necessary because . . .	A good point on the other side of the argument is . . .
Putting It Together	**Goals**
If I want to start off with my strongest idea, I'll . . .	A goal I think I could write is . . .
I can tie this together by . . .	My purpose is . . .
My main point is . . .	

Anderson (1991) notes that some teachers use a procedure called *thinking aloud* when encouraging students to ask and generate questions.

- *For clarifying difficult statements or concepts*: I don't get this. It says, 'dark objects look smaller'. Does this mean a white elephant looks smaller than a black elephant? This rule must only apply to things that are about the same size. Maybe black shoes would make your feet look smaller than white ones.

- *For summarizing important information*: I'll summarize this part of the article where the Spanish started in North America. The title is "The Spanish in California," so the part about California must be important. I'll sum this up by saying that Spanish explorers from Mexico discovered California. They didn't stay in California but migrated to other parts of America. These are the most important ideas so far.

- *For thinking ahead*: So far this has told me that Columbus is poor, the trip will be expensive, and everyone's laughing at his plan. I'd predict Columbus will have trouble getting the money he needs for his exploration (Anderson, 1991).

The following case example (first discussed in Chapter 8) provides insight into ways teachers can teach high-level thinking skills in mathematics.

CASE STUDY

STUDENT: "Ms. Smith, I can't figure out the answer to this math puzzle."

TEACHER: "Which one, Finn?"

STUDENT: "The one that says, 'If you know there are six grapes and two plums for each person sitting at a table and there is a total of 24 pieces of fruit on the table, then you should know how many people are seated at the table", but I don't.

TEACHER: "Sure you do. Think a minute. Could there be only one person?"

STUDENT: "No."

TEACHER: "Why?"

STUDENT: "Because one person would get only six grapes and two plums and that's eight pieces of fruit, and there are more pieces than that."

TEACHER: "How many more?"

STUDENT: "Sixteen."

TEACHER: "And if each person gets eight pieces, how many more people could there be?"

STUDENT: "Two! So there must be three people seated at the table."

TEACHER: "See, I told you that you knew the answer! You just needed to think about the problem." (Phillips & Soltis, 1985, p. 12)

INTASC Standard 5   Application of content

Technology in the Classroom

What does technology offer in terms of teaching methodologies for the proactive teacher? Simulations imitate or create an analogy of real situations thus providing teachers the opportunity to offer students learning experiences that are otherwise too expensive, dangerous, or impractical.

Computer simulated software available for the classroom includes topics such as pollution control, African-American history, and freedom in the Mideast. Other contemporary topics technology can bring to the classroom include:

- Managing a nuclear reactor plant
- A volcanic eruption
- Flying an airplane
- The daily transactions of the stock market
- Fusion experiments and other physical science experiments
- Managing financial institutions

Such simulations require students to analyze, apply, and comprehend subject matter. These are the major objectives in Bloom's higher levels of learning. Simulations provide students the opportunity to integrate previously learned factual knowledge with abstract concepts.

Simulations respond based on the student's course of action, creating new decisions to be made based on previous and/or additional data. Therefore, many simulations require a high degree of student interaction, strategy, and decision making. Other factors making simulation an attractive teaching tool in the classroom include:

1. *There is no risk involved in simulation*. Simulation software can teach students to operate equipment that is potentially dangerous to a novice. Students can bring nuclear reactors to "critical mass" in a safe classroom environment.

2. *There is less expense involved in simulation*. Students can study and learn the results of their decision making by experimentally investing millions of dollars in the stock market, with the only cost to the school being the simulation software and hardware.

3. Simulated experiences are more realistic and convenient for students than real experiences. A student can sit in the cockpit of an airplane with simulated flight controls.

4. *Simulation overcomes the limitations of time*. Students do not have to wait for several generations to observe the effects of ocean pollution; or simulation software can give students a realistic picture of the environmental impact of a volcano eruption that occurred 100 or 10 thousand years ago.

5. *Simulation software makes it possible to focus on specific aspects of a topic or event*. A student can study the impact of pollution on specific topics such as drinking water, recreation, or property values.

6. *Simulated experiences can be repeated as many times as the user wants*. If a student misses a simulation because of absence, the simulation can be repeated with little teacher supervision. Also, often students can pursue "what if" questions and try different combinations of variable conditions.

SURFING • THE • WEB

The Department of Education has a website entitled, Teaching and Teacher Education (**http://www.ericsp.org**), which provides educational material related to student learning and instructional tactics. Additionally, "Helping Your Child Use the Library," located on the Publications for Parents Website (**http//www.ed.gov/pubs/ parents.html**) is an excellent resource.

RECAP OF MAJOR IDEAS

1. The lecture is a time-efficient, effective method for introducing lessons, videos, and other instructional material but its effectiveness depends on teacher skills and motivated students.

2. Inquiry learning involves students, is motivating, and teaches students to question and examine evidence before accepting information as truth.

3. Future teachers should learn how to use questions effectively, and students should be encouraged to ask questions.

4. Students can be taught to listen effectively.

5. Simulations can produce learning equal to that of lecturing and achieve a much higher rate of retention.

6. Educational objectives should be written in terms of expected student behavior, specifying a minimum acceptable level of performance, and the conditions students are expected to perform.

7. Educational goals should be written in terms of expected academic and social behavior.

8. The teaching of higher-level thinking skills should be a primary goal of teachers.

9. Social development of students is now considered imperative in today's educational environment.

FURTHER APPLICATIONS

1. The lecture is the teaching method often used for introducing a body of information, such as a lesson unit. To be effective, the lecture should be free of jargon and unfamiliar terms and, because some

students are basically visual learners, lectures should be supplemented by visual aids.

Choose a favorite unit that you will teach. Prepare a brief lecture to introduce this unit. Design a PowerPoint or other media instructional presentation.

2. You have learned that questions can be an effective way to involve students in classroom instruction. Questions are generally not an effective means of beginning the class, or teaching an entire lesson. It is better to build a knowledge base and then ask questions.

   Remember that students are often poor note takers. Expand your unit from question 1 to include handouts that capture the lesson's main ideas in notes.

3. Simulation games are effective for stimulating and actively involving students. Students enjoy simulation games, and are often motivated by them.

   One effective way to develop a simulation for the classroom is to pick a favorite TV game show, or if your students love sports, choose their favorite sport. Next, modify the game so that playing requires performing well academically. For example, you can divide your math or science class into two teams for a game of baseball. Make each question worth a single, double, triple, or home run, according to the level of difficulty of the question.

4. List two class academic objectives and explain how you would determine their effectiveness.

5. Objectives at the comprehension level require students to do more than just memorize. Students must translate, interpret, or predict a continuation of trends (Bloom, 1956).

   Write one comprehension-level objective in your teaching field that requires students to translate, one objective that requires them to interpret, and one that requires them to predict.

6. Suppose you are teaching the circulatory system to a biology class. Write an objective that will enable students to understand blood travel throughout the body. (*Hint*: You may want to designate one of the heart's chambers as a beginning point.)

7. Check your objective in item 6 to see whether it includes the three designated criteria: Is it written in terms of expected student performance? If so, underscore the part of the objective that identifies both the performer and the performance. Does the verb you used express action? Can your objective be observed and measured? Is your statement of conditions clear?

8. Because of their divergent and creative nature, synthesis-level questions are more difficult to write. You may need practice in writing objectives at this level.

    Suppose you are an art teacher. In your class, you have studied such concepts as cubism (using cubes to form objects) and pointism (using pencil points to form objects). Write an objective at the synthesis level that involves these concepts. (*Hint:* You might begin by identifying a particular effect you would like your students to achieve through the use of cubism and pointism; this might be a specific feeling or mood.)

9. Effective teachers know that students can be taught attention skills. Today, most college campuses have student developmental centers where students can get help improving their attention skills. If your college or university has a developmental center, arrange to visit the center. Ask about advice given students to improve their attention and listening skills. Make a list of the strategies appropriate for use with your future students.

KEY TERMS

repertoire
direct instruction
lecture instruction
inquiry learning
questioning
listening skills
simulation
simulation games
case study
objectives
educational goals
educational objectives

cognitive objectives
knowledge-level objectives
comprehension-level objectives
application-level objectives
analysis-level objectives
synthesis-level objectives
evaluation-level objectives
affective objectives
higher-level thinking skills
scaffolds
computer-assisted instruction (CAI)

LOOKING AHEAD

Chapter 9 recommended alternative teacher methodologies and strategies for enhancing student academic, behavioral, and cognitive development. Chapter 10 addresses the specific issues of student problem solving and creativity. Can student problem solving and creativity be facilitated by the teacher and attributes of the classroom environment? Chapter 10 examines those issues. ■

Chapter 10

Problem Solving, Creativity, and Constructivism

LEARNING OBJECTIVES

Upon completing this chapter, you should be able to:

1

Relate the historical roots of *problem solving* to the contemporary educational environment.

2

Describe the relationship of pragmatism and insight to problem solving.

3

Relate the contemporary views of problem solving to the classroom environment.

4

Differentiate and relate four different problem-solving techniques that can be taught to students.

5

Define *creativity* as it relates to students.

6

Identify three characteristics of creative students.

7

Describe three ways student creativity can be enhanced and encouraged within the school curriculum.

8

Differentiate among the terms *creativity, intelligence, knowledge,* and *motivation*.

9

List three creative classroom activities.

10

Define constructivism as it relates to learning theory and to the contemporary classroom environment.

Galileo formulated the problem of determining the velocity of light but did not solve it. The formulation of a problem is often more essential than its solution, which may be merely a matter of mathematical or experimental skills. To raise new questions, new possibilities, to regard old problems from a new angle, requires creative imagination and marks real advance in science (Einstein & Infeld, 1938).

INTRODUCTION

The search for teaching methods to helpt students become better problem solvers is a primary concern of the educational process. Providing students the opportunity to reach optimum academic levels requires opportunities to apply their knowledge to real-world situations (Winger, 2009). The same is true of enhancing and fostering the creative talents of students. Although educational psychologists sometimes disagree on how problem-solving skills and the creative talents of students should be taught, there is little disagreement on the importance of these issues (Glover & Bruning, 1990). Students are too often taught to simply master content (Perry, Vanderstoep, & Yu, 1993). While problem solving is not a substitute for acquiring knowledge, it can be a valuable tool in the process of understanding and enhancing learning (Knowles & Cole, (1994); with Presswood, 1994)

This chapter will focus on the influence of constructivism in today's classrooms and how the educational process can improve the problem-solving skills and creativity of students.

TODD WILLIAMS...

could sense that his students were getting a bit weary of day-to-day class activities and assignments, and frankly so was he. Both he and his students needed something different and more creative to stimulate class activities. Todd created the following 'creative' assignments.

1. If you were to start from this classroom and travel any way you wanted, how long would it take you to get to the top of Mount Everest? (Assume you have $10,000 in cash for travel and expenses.) Requirements for assignment: You must hand in a detailed log describing your method of travel, travel destinations, time taken, and costs incurred. You must also complete a written rationale of why you believe your route and plan is the fastest way to proceed.

2. You will be divided into five student teams. Each team is required to visit a landfill and report the following:
   a. Location and type of landfill
   b. Type of waste including hazardous materials deposited at landfill
   c. Surrounding environment (closest business and/or housing) and water (stream or lake)
   d. Permeability of soil in landfill
   e. Your opinion of immediate and future environmental consequences of landfill

3. Each student will be assigned a 2-hour time period during the next month working as an assistant on a crisis line at our local mental health center, VA hospital, or 911 number. You are to report in detail

your experiences and what you observed.

Todd announced to his class that they would be celebrating these new assignments with a 'wading party' on the school grounds the following day. His students were intrigued. Todd had a small wading pool inherited from previous renters of his apartment. The next day he took it to school and filled it with water. His students squealed as they took off their shoes and splashed in the pool.

Finally, one of his students noticed the equipment (hose, boards, chemicals, fish net, and one-gallon oil can) sitting off to the side. "Hey, Mr. Todd (name students like to call him), what's with all the stuff sitting over there?" asked

the student. The others stopped and listened.

Todd responded, "For the oil slick."

"What oil slick?" asked the student.

"The oil slick this class is going to have to clean up," answered Todd. Todd picked up the can and dumped a gallon of dirty oil into the wading pool. The students were stunned, especially the ones in the pool. Todd announced, "It is now your job to clean up the slick with the equipment sitting there."

After a moment, Josh said, "Let's skim it with the fish net."

"No," objected Sue, "block the oil off with the boards." Someone else wanted to pump it out with the hose.

Todd smiled and announced, "Better hurry, the slick is spreading."

HISTORICAL ROOTS OF PROBLEM SOLVING

Todd and his students were beginning their problem-solving exercises, but the process and study of problem solving have long historical roots in educational psychology. E. L. Thorndike (1879–1949) is considered by many as the father of contemporary views on problem solving. Thorndike's research was based on his observation of how long it took cats to free themselves from "puzzle boxes." Hungry cats were placed in boxes with food just outside the box. Thorndike studied the time and the methods the cats used to free themselves from the boxes to get to the food.

Pragmatism

Sixteenth century scientist and phologher Sir Francis Bacon gave the world the first pragmatic approach to problem solving, and variations on his approach are still used and advocated by educational researchers today. These steps are still used today:

1. *Problem definition.* Obviously, **problem definition** will determine the methodology or technique used to solve the problem. Therefore, teaching students alternative ways of defining and finding solutions to academic and social problems they encounter is critical for successful teaching (Cooper & Sweller, 1987).

The pragmatic approach advocated by John Dewey was one of the first systematic approaches to problem solving.

2. *Development of hypotheses.* After the problem has been defined, the next step is developing a hypothesis. **Hypotheses** are assumptions or predictions tested through research, or, more specifically related to problem solving, hypotheses are alternative ways of solving a problem. Generally, the more hypotheses generated, the more likely it is the problem will be solved (Rothstein, 1990).

An example might be comparing the effectiveness of two teaching methodologies (lecture vs. independent study). The example hypotheses could be, "A comparison of the student final exam scores will demonstrate significant differences in the two teaching methodologies—lecture and independent study."

3. *Testing hypotheses.* This is the process of testing and evaluating the hypotheses developed in step 2. For example, you could test lecture versus independent study teaching methods by comparing student final exam scores of classes taught via lecture and independent study.

4.   *Selection of best hypothesis.* Several hypotheses can normally be developed to solve a problem. Comparing the effectiveness of our two teaching methodologies might include comparing final exam scores, teacher and student attitudes toward the course, and achievement scores or report card grades. Educational psychologists emphasize using skills in decision making and problem solving to determine which hypothesis should be used to solve the defined problem (Dixon, 1987).

The importance of teaching problem-solving skills cannot be overemphasized in the educational process.

Psychologists have learned that problem solving is affected by the behavior of the classroom teacher (Knowles & Cole, 1994). Hayes (1989) notes that teachers should approach problem solving in a systematic way. The following is the methodology he suggests.

1. *Finding the problem*: recognizing there is a problem to be solved.
2. *Representing the problem*: understanding the nature of the problem to be solved.
3. *Planning the solution*: choosing a method for solving problem.
4. *Carrying out the plan for the solution.*
5. *Evaluating the solution*: asking "How valid and reliable is the result?"
6. *Consolidating gains*: learning from the experience of problem solving.

A classroom example of this sequence of actions as suggested by Hayes is illustrated in Table 10.1.

> Köhler disagreed with Thorndike concerning an individual's method of problem solving. Köhler believed "flashes of insight" provided solutions to problems.

Insight

Whereas Thorndike believed problem solving was a trial-and-error process, John Dewey advocated that efficient problem solvers follow well-defined basic steps. Wolfgang Kohler (1887–1967) believed problem solving was best accomplished through **insight**. Kohler, one of the founders of Gestalt psychology, argued that people "ponder and think" about problems. He believed proficient problem solvers examine, weigh, and consider parts of a problem until *flashes of insight* provide a solution. Although Kohler disagreed with Thorndike and Dewey's methods, his problem-solving procedures have similarities to steps recommended by Dewey.

TABLE 10.1	
Teacher Problem Solving	
Action	**Teacher Behavior Addressing the Problem**
1. Finding the problem	Teacher notices that Hewey has not turned in his homework for the past four days and he does not write down homework assignments when presented in class.
2. Representing the problem	Teacher concludes Hewey is not serious about completing and turning in homework.
3. Planning the solution	Teacher considers communication to Hewey's family or punishing Hewey when he fails to turn in homework but decides to first discuss with him the importance of homework and his grades. Teacher also offers assistance with homework if needed.
4. Carrying out the plan	Teacher assists with homework assignments when needed and praises Hewey when homework assignments are completed.
5. Evaluating the solution	Hewey begins to turn in homework, so teacher assumes problem is satisfactorily solved.
6. Consolidating gains	Teacher reviews with class the importance of homework in determining final grades.

1. *Identifying problem.* Kohler agreed with Dewey that a problem had to be defined and identified before it could be solved.

2. *Incubation period.* Kohler believed individuals, confronting a problem, take time to think about possible solutions. Kohler labeled this period the incubation period.

3. *Insight.* Kohler believed solutions to a problem occurred suddenly rather than incrementally. Kohler labeled sudden awareness to solutions to a problem as "insights."

4. *Memory of insightful solutions.* Once an individual solved a problem, Kohler believed he or she would remember the solution.

5. *Generalization of solutions.* Kohler believed problem solvers remembered solutions and also retained the ability to apply insightful solutions to future problems encountered.

Many aspects of Dewey's and Kohler's methods of problem solving are reflected in contemporary education and business research literature. Laudon and Laudon (1991), for example, suggest that "real life" problem solving can usually be seen as involving five stages (Figure 10.1).

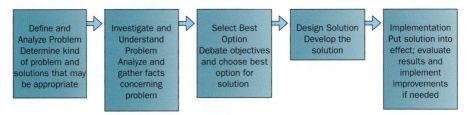

Figure 10.1 Solving "Real-Life" Problems

Problem Solving in Today's Classroom

Today, many educational psychologists recommend **information processing**, as discussed in Chapters 7 and 8, when addressing and defining the problem-solving process. As a teacher, you will encounter problems, such as deciding on exam format or the appropriate way to approach the family of a student who is misbehaving in class. Information-processing advocates that constructing a *problem representation* is crucial to solving problems. A problem representation includes the unique aspects of problem to be solved. These aspects include:

1. *The initial state.* This is the situation or environmental circumstance of the individual when a problem is identified. For example, a teacher, deciding between an objective or essay final exam (discussed in Chapter 14) or between a letter or conference with family of a student who is falling behind academically.

2. *The intermediate state.* This state begins when the individual starts the process of solving a problem. *Operators* are used in this state to bring

about a solution. Operators are defined as possible alternatives and actions an individual can take to solve problem. Often operators are limited because of unique aspects of the problem. A teacher who has 200 students might decide on objective tests rather than essay because of the number of students. A teacher might want to meet with the family of students who are excelling, rather than notifying via a note to personally review the student's superior scholarship.

3. *The goal state.* The goal state is the result or outcome the problem solver seeks. A teacher's goals in meeting with families about students who are failing might be communicating information prior to report card distribution to offer and solicit advice to help such students.

Table 10.2 illustrates the differences in operators as determined by the uniqueness of learning task and subject matter.

TABLE 10.2
Learning Tasks and Potential Student Operators

Subject	Problem or Learning Task	Operator Assigned to Students
Political Science	Students gain an understanding of the differences in family difficulties encountered by male vs. female veterans of the Iraq and Afghan wars.	Interview two male and two female veterans, of the Iraq and/or Afghan War. Compare and contrast the differences in their outlooks, opinions, and personal hardships concerning being separated from their families.
Science	Students need to understand the impact of pollution on a local lake or stream.	Identify stream or lake to be studied, pollution tests to be used and how tests will be conducted, recorded, and reported.
Social Studies	Students need to learn how to manage a family budget.	Construct mock families among class members. Make each family responsible for outlining a detailed family budget based on an annual income of $38,000 a year. The budget must include expenses for one child.

(Continued)

TABLE 10.2 (CONTINUED)		
Learning Tasks and Potential Student Operators		
Subject	**Problem or Learning Task**	**Operator Assigned to Students**
Finance & Business	Students need to understand bank statements, on-line banking, balancing of banking accounts, loan acquisition, payments and interest on credit cards and savings accounts (money market and CDs) and comparing interest rates.	Provide students a simulated bank account with checking and savings accounts, credit and debit card with balances. Visit local banking and/or savings institution.

Can you identify the operations, or actions, that students could take to solve the problems in Table 10.2?

> Contemporary cognitive psychologists suggest heuristics, (using knowledge to solve problems), is an excellent way to problem solve.

INSTAC Standard 1   **Learner development**

Problem-Solving Techniques: Searching for Solutions

Following are three major approaches to problem solving: (1) random search, (2) heuristics, and (3) algorithms (Rothstein, 1990).

Random Search

When using the **random search** method to solve problems, chance alone determines when a solution to a problem is reached. A student randomly looking for a particular book in the library without benefit of information or a computer search is an example of a random search. Randomly looking for a word or subject in a book without the use of the Table of Contents or Word Index is another example.

Randomly searching for the answer or solution to a problem is normally the least efficient way to find a satisfactory solution. The only advantage to random search problem solving is that it is a simple process and can be improved by systematically avoiding searching the same way twice. Because the random search method is highly inefficient, it is best avoided.

HEURISTICS

Heuristics is the application of knowledge to find solutions to problems. If a student knows the author of the book he/ she is looking for in the library and can use the library computer search, this knowledge greatly enhances the student's success in finding the book. Similarly, knowing how to use an index in a book could expedite the search for a word or subject topic. Heuristic approaches to problem solving include *proximity searches*, *means-ends analysis*, *brainstorming*, *analogies*, and *models*.

Proximity Searches are sometimes called *difference reduction*. A good example is the children's game of guessing a number between 1 and 100 in 10 guesses. The child guessing is given answers of "closer" or "farther away" when trying to guess the number. The purpose of the proximity search is to reduce the difference or gap between the problem state and goal state or, simply stated, to systematically eliminate the distance between the problem and the solution.

PROACTIVE EXERCISE

Suppose your class is preparing for a 'science fair'. Your students are planning for their entries but only two can be entered from each class. As their teacher, what planning and *brainstorming* techniques could you offer in deciding on the projects to be entered? Could you proactively have students first write a description of their ideas for projects? Could those student ideas be discussed in class? What evaluation procedures should be used? Should 'creativity', 'uniqueness' and 'originality' be used in evaluation? If so, how would they be defined? Should class members be part of the selection process? What would be the advantages of dividing the class into two or more groups to work on just two or more projects to be entered?

Means-Ends Analysis When using *means-ends analysis* heuristics, the problem is broken down into components or sub-problems. When each sub-problem is solved, the final solution is achieved. For example, let's return to the problem of choosing the two science fair projects from your class. The problem could be broken down into sub-problems as follows.

1. Proactive planning for project.

   - Class discussion of science project rules and regulations.

   - Having students submit written explanation of their ideas for science project.

   - Follow-up with suggestions for improvement of ideas, with possible class discussion.

   - Discussion of possible group projects, individual projects, or both.

2. Determine criteria for evaluation.

   - Class discussion of how projects will be evaluated.

   - Decision on class members or class committee being involved with evaluation.

3. Selection of winning projects.

4. Follow-up with perhaps a simulation of class science fair, with suggestions for two winners.

As a result of solving or answering the sub-problems of only two entries to the fair, the process of selection is solved.

Brainstorming

Brainstorming is a technique whereby a student, or a group of students, generates a large number of solutions to a problem (Butler, 2010). The potential solutions are then evaluated to determine the best alternative. You probably are familiar with brainstorming scenarios. When brainstorming is free of criticism, and students are encouraged to suggest imaginative alternatives, brainstorming can be fun and productive.

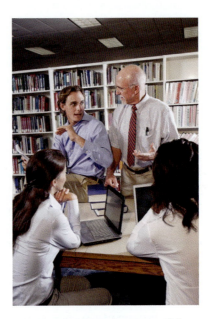

Brainstorming is often successful in producing an atmosphere eliciting unique, creative ideas.

Analogies

Analogies are used to provide direction of solutions to problems by using the knowledge of solutions to similar problems. You might encounter a class whose disruptions are interfering with academic productivity. Todd had this problem with his class and surveyed (Chapter 6) his students to identify an effective solution. You might perceive your problem as being analogous to his and decide to try a similar solution. The success of analogies typically depends on identifying and implementing appropriate components of a successful solution.

Models

The use of *models* can be very effective in certain problem-solving situations. Models of dams, building projects, weather patterns, and environmental pollution, are often used to assess such factors as benefits, costs, and environmental impact. Models are often used as an inexpensive way to study problems that can occur prior to and during construction or implementation.

Models in the classroom are often represented by **simulations** (Chapter 9). Simulations are methods of representing information and situations as they appear in the real world. As a teacher, you could provide a model dam for your students to use for studying electric power, and through simulation you could address such factors as population served, electric output, and water needed for generation of power and costs.

Algorithms

An *algorithm* is defined as a finite set of steps that, when executed, will consistently achieve specific goals (Troutman, White, & Breit, 1988). An example of an algorithm for solving the area of a rectangle would be;

1. Determine the height of the rectangle.
2. Determine the width of the rectangle.
3. Convert the height and the width to the same units of measure if needed.
4. Multiply the height by the width, which gives the area of the rectangle.

Solving problems using algorithms is similar to means-ends analysis problem solving. However, algorithms use precise rules to solve problems. If you are a computer whiz, you might be familiar with algorithms because they are frequently used to structure problems for computer programmers. Computer programmers can write the code required for each successive step in the algorithm, thereby solving the problem.

Summarizing, heuristics are methods that facilitate and simplify finding the solution to problems, whereas when properly used algorithms are specific procedures leading to the solution of problems. Heuristics, in comparison to algorithms, do not always provide a correct solution to a problem, but when heuristics work they typically provide a solution quicker than algorithms. The Proactive Teaching box offers further suggestions for incorporating problem-solving techniques into your curriculum.

PROACTIVE TEACHING

CLASSROOM SITUATION

You want your students to be comfortable with classroom problem-solving activities and assignments.

PROACTIVE ALTERNATIVES

· Design your lesson plans to include problem-solving activities. Do this prior to classes, beginning preferably early in the school year. Too often, teachers become occupied with conveying facts and information and either ignore problem solving

Instructor Manual

or provide problem-solving activities only as auxiliary assignments.

· We have discussed a number of problem solving strategies in this chapter. You might explain a problem in class then have some students brainstorm, some simulate, and others write an algorithm. Then have a class discussion comparing the results of each group.

· Address the anxiety level of students by starting with elementary problem-solving tasks. The major goal is teaching students the 'art' and techniques of problem solving. Expect application of problem-solving strategies after students have been taught and are comfortable with using the various techniques.

· Encourage students to ask questions about problem-solving activities. Encourage students to work in groups to share their ideas and strategies with their peers.

· Finally, relax and enjoy this part of your curriculum. Problem-solving activities can be a stimulating, active, enjoyable time.

INTASC Standard 9 & 10   Professional responsibility

PROACTIVE EXERCISE

Simulate a situation for your students, telling them they are serving on a school/community committee on the development of a community service program. They are to think about the needs of the local community. Is there adequate, alternative housing for the elderly? Are there adequate food banks and shelter for the indigent? Is there a need for a wildlife sanctuary? Is the landscape clean? Is the water safe? The students are to choose an area of need and devise a plan of sequenced steps (algorithm) to share and discuss in class.

1. How can you encourage your students to get involved with such projects?
2. How can you use this project to further develop student problem-solving skills?
3. What types of activities and groups can you initiate in your classes to ensure a variety of creative talents such as art, writing, and storytelling?

CREATIVITY

As we examine problem solving, it becomes evident that *creativity* can be a fascinating part of the process. This is true for both teacher and students. Some teachers seem to have a gift for devising creative activities for their classes, and some students appear to have a knack for finding unique and creative solutions to problems. Educational psychologists agree that creativity, like problem solving, is very important in the educational process, but most also agree that the concept and definition of creativity have been difficult to pin down (Kaplan, 1990). Berk (2005) defines creativity as "the ability to produce work that is original, yet appropriate and useful."

According to Sternberg (1985, 1988) we typically believe that creative individuals:

- Are willing to take chances
- Reject limitations and often try the impossible
- Appreciate the arts
- Have an unusual ability to make unique things
- Question social norms
- Are willing to actively address unpopular issues
- Are inquisitive and curious

> Creativity, like problem solving, is difficult to define but educational psychologists agree that it should be a primary concern in the educational process.

Glover and Bruning (1990) stated that defining creativity is no easy task but suggested creative problem solving has two aspects: **novelty** and **value**. Novelty refers to unusual or unique methods of solving a problem, and value means creative solutions are appropriate to the problem to be solved.

The assessment and testing of creativity was pioneered by J. Paul Guilford (1897–1987) and E. Paul Torrance (1915–2003). Many educational psychologists credit Guilford with pioneering creativity in education. During the 1950s and 1960s, Guilford defined creative thinking in terms of convergence and divergence. *Convergent thinking* implies deductive reasoning (going from general to specific). Convergent thinking leads to solutions generally accepted as correct, such as answers on a math or IQ test. *Divergent thinking* uses *inductive reasoning* (going from specific to general). Divergent thinking produces optional ways of solving a problem, some may be so unique or original they are not readily accepted.

By building on Guilford's work, Torrance provided a great deal of work influencing the contemporary study of creativity. Torrance developed one of the first recognized tests for creativity, the Torrance Tests of Creative Thinking (TTCT) (Torrance, Glover, Ronning, & Reynolds, 1989). According to Torrance, creativity is measured by four criteria:

1. *Fluency*. The ability of an individual to generate alternatives for a given problem. The more ideas or alternatives a person can generate, the higher the probability one will be an appropriate solution.

2. *Flexibility*. The ability to produce variation in ideas. Jason might state the only use he can think of for a brick is to build houses, buildings, apartments, and condos, whereas Trina can suggest using a brick for building, landscaping, serving as a paper weight or door stop, and placing in the tank of a commode for saving water. Trina gave the more flexible responses because her answers had variety, whereas Jason's were of the same nature and theme.

3. *Elaboration*. The ability to elaborate or develop and refine ideas to solve problems.

4. *Originality*. An individual's ability to generate original and inconspicuous solutions, and according to Torrance, the most important characteristic.

WHAT WOULD YOU DO?

Examine the Sternberg list on page 353. How will you encourage and foster a creative climate in your classroom and school?

Characteristics of Creative Students

The research on creativity suggests that intelligence, knowledge, and motivation are the key aspects in fostering creative behavior and can be enhanced by teachers in the classroom environment (Runco; Sternberg 2006).

"No matter how bright or hardworking an individual is, if opportunity to be creative is denied, there can be no creativity." (Hayes, 1989, p.322)

Intelligence and Creativity Intelligence and the creative behavior of students are often related. Except in rare circumstances, at least average intelligence appears to be necessary for individuals to exhibit exceptionally creative behavior (Rothstein, 1990). However, creative behavior is not limited to individuals with superior intelligence (Kershner & Ledger, 1985).

Additionally, creativity cannot be measured using intelligence tests or association with personality types, such as artists or musicians. Creativity can be found in almost all aspects of learning, vocations, and lifestyles.

Knowledge Exceptionally creative people typically spend a great deal of time learning and studying their fields and pursuing these talents. This pursuit appears to provide avenues and defines attributes for creative work. Typically, exceptionally creative people are very knowledgeable about the field of their creative efforts.

Motivation and Preparation Finally, similar to learning problem solving, creativity appears to require considerable effort and motivation. Chess masters require years of intensive training to master their game. Consider the time it takes violinists, pianists, artists, or mathematicians to master their creative talent.

Attempting to determine the relationship between creativity and preparation from a very extensive study of 76 internationally recognized composers, Hayes (1989, p. 297) found that very few of the great composers were able to produce master works with less than 10 years of preparation. "What composers need to write good music is not maturing but rather musical preparation."

Enhancing Creativity in the Classroom

PROACTIVE EXERCISE

As a future school professional how would you advise:

- Students who have exceptional creative talent in an academic area but are not motivated to study or pursue their talent?

- A student who wants to be a mathematician but has yet to demonstrate talent in that field?

- The families of the above students?

Our exercise expresses the potential impact teachers and the educational environment can have on the creative talents of students. The characteristics and potential of creative students emphasize the importance of efforts teachers should make to enhance the creative atmosphere of their classrooms. Kokot and Colman (1997, p. 224) caution teachers, ". . . teaching highly creative children requires more than a lesson plan. It means first recognizing and assessing their natural way of learning. By allowing them time to know by means of discovery through involvement and intuitive insight, learning can be a means of expression and wonderment for these children."

To enhance the creative atmosphere in their classrooms, teachers can provide opportunities for students to collaborate and discuss ideas for academic projects.

Methods teachers can use to encourage creativity among students include:

- *Model and demonstrate creativity yourself.* Once a month, an eighth-grade teacher in Knoxville, Tennessee, had students write on the things in class that "bugged" them the most. All responses were written on the board and students brainstormed to find solutions to each of the "bugging problems." The point of this example is that both teachers and students can be creative.

- *Provide opportunities for students to be creative and, like problem solving, allow students to work together on creative projects.* "Who in class would be interested in working on a mural for the wall?" Also, provide creative opportunities for students to work alone. "Marie is going to treat us tomorrow with a performance on her Cello."

- *When students are creative, be sure to recognize their efforts.* "I'm proud of your drawings. We will post them on the walls for families to see when they visit during our family-teacher meeting next week. I also want to discuss with you your preferences on field trips to the art gallery, community theater, and zoo."

- *Be very cautious about assigning grades to creativity.* Allow students to attempt creative expression without fear of failure. "If I were going to assign grades to your drawings, they would be all A's. I'm very proud of your efforts. With your next drawing, be thinking about how you can improve on color and texture."

Consider the comments of Dr. E. E. Thrower.

A VIEW FROM THE FIELD
A VIEW FROM THE FIELD

PROFILE

Dr. Thrower, a nationally certified school psychologist, earned her B.S. and M.A. degrees from the University of Tennessee and her Ph.D. in Educational Psychology/ Research from the University of Alabama. She has worked as a school psychologist in both the secondary school and university environment. She is currently associate professor at Montevallo University, Montevallo, Alabama. Dr. Thrower's research interests are with special needs students in higher education and creative uses of technology in education.

QUESTION: How can contemporary teachers facilitate creativity among their students?

Dr. Thrower: Creativity is a critical part of the learning environment with both teachers and students. Research on creativity in the learning environment has shown that given two students of equal intelligence, the more creative student will demonstrate higher levels of achievement. Concerning teachers, creativity is a behavior that can be facilitated and encouraged in the classroom. As with any learning activity, teachers need to provide time in the curriculum that is dedicated to student imagination and creativity. Therefore, a good place for teachers to begin is providing time for themselves and their students to be creative.

For fostering a creative classroom, I suggest the following:

- Provide lessons in which students are encouraged and feel secure taking risks. A "creative" teacher thrives in a classroom where students feel comfortable appropriately stating their opinions and asking questions.

- Periodically, provide students with problems to solve where creative answers and uniqueness are reinforced. A good example is challenging students to list as many ways as they can think of to survive a flood or how they would solve our country's pollution problems.

- Cooperative learning and group work lend themselves to creative thinking. Divide the students into groups and assign projects or a problem situation. Have the groups present their solutions and then discuss which was most creative and WHY?

- Deviate from the lecture format of teaching. Have students dramatize a history lesson with a skit or have them act out a character from history for a day and then see if students can identify each others' characters. In writing, a teacher can encourage creativity by having students word process at a computer with the screen turned off. This allows students to type anything they want without screen distraction.

Have the students discuss whether this made them feel more creative.

- Model creative behavior as a teacher. Be open to different types of answers and comments from your students. Recently, I observed an elementary teacher who was conducting a lesson on the vocabulary words for the week. She asked the definition of the word "subway." An eager excited student raised his hand and when called upon answered proudly "It's a place to buy sandwiches." Instead of telling the student he was incorrect, the insightful and creative teacher praised him for his correct answer and asked his classmates if they could think of other definitions.

Clearly, we want our students to build a good knowledge base, but it will be our more creative students who will invent cars that do not pollute, who will discover a cure for cancer, who will find solutions to poverty, and who will be future Nobel Prize winners. ■

Ms. Bea Volkman, former Alabama Teacher of the Year, provides a real-life example of how teachers can be creative with the events that happen in their classrooms.

🍎 A Teacher's Class

NAME: Bea Volkman, Ph.D., former Alabama Teacher of the Year

❝ It didn't creak or act at all as if it had been closed up in that humid portable all summer. It just pulled out, like any desk drawer might. With a glance inside, I called for Johnnie on the other side of the partition that divided our Learning Disabilities resource rooms. Together we sifted through the contents of the drawer: tiny teddy bears whose glass eyes only had been spared shredding, pencils that had been gnawed away until only the long slender graphite skeleton remained, and construction paper turned confetti. Then I pushed the intercom button and pleaded for help. By the time they got there, armed with mops and mousetraps, I had changed my mind. Johnnie and I had uncovered a nest of babies. No one around seemed to understand my logic that while, of course, "rats" are to be killed, newly born babies are to be protected. And besides that, in a couple of days all my students would be back to celebrate the beginning of a new school year, and would I have a surprise for them.

As fate would have it, things don't always go as planned. I tried to reconstruct the nest, and carefully closed the desk drawer, hoping the mother would never notice our intrusion. The next morning I tiptoed into the room, carefully pulled out the drawer and peeped in. Much to my chagrin, the newborns were gone; I obviously had not been as discreet as I thought. Later that morning, I opened the top drawer and discovered the mother had only moved her family upstairs. The next day she deserted, and by the third day I somehow felt responsible for finding the mother to nourish the babies who were as tiny and pink as the pencil eraser tips their mother had eaten from my desk drawer a few days earlier. In order not to break her neck or injure her in any way, I set out sticky paper mousetraps. Three times I captured mice, and each time Johnnie and I struggled to free the critter. I say struggle, for just as we'd get one appendage pulled free, another wriggling part would get stuck, and so it would go until finally the deed was done. We would drop the "mommy" into the nest, only to discover that the "mommy" was not the "mommy" at all; the babies continued to face starvation.

In the meantime, I scavenged an aquarium to create a glass house. The students were elated with the addition to our family, but the babies, in spite of my best efforts, were destined for an untimely end. I could not simply tell my children the babies had died; I had to turn this into a positive learning experience. We talked about growing up and going out into the world, you know, like the three pigs. For in all of nature, except for humans, babies mature quickly and get on with their successes. We remembered Dorothy's golden brick road and decided it was time to build our babies golden paths into the future.

Each member of our classroom took responsibility for one mouse and painted with words the most wonderful career for it we could imagine. We described each mouse as carefully and beautifully as we could. Together we wrote a poem, crafted a paper-mache house with as many gold brick paths flowing from it as we needed, and placed the clay adventurers we had made on their way. Eager to share the craft of our visions, we proudly took our conception downtown to Central Office for all the world to see." ■

PROACTIVE EXERCISE

- What problem-solving activities would you design for exceptionally creative students?

- What creative activities should be offered to such students?

CONSTRUCTIVISM

Beginnings

The constructivist approach to education attempts to shift education from a teacher-dominated focus to a student-centered one. The role of the teacher emphasizes assisting students in their learning and cognitive development to formulate new insights. Students are taught to assimilate experiences, knowledge, and insights with current knowledge and from this, *construct* new meanings to learned material. In this section, we examine constructivism's beginnings, the role of student experience in learning, and how such can be assimilated for understanding.

Constructivism is a learning theory with foundations in philosophy and anthropology as well as psychology (Brooks & Brooks, 1993). The philosophical foundations can be traced to fifth century B.C. when Socrates developed a systematic method of discovering 'truth' by combining questioning and logical reasoning. This new method was the foundation to advancing the problem-solving trait of constructivism.

Socrates' focus on developing better ways of understanding was advanced by his students, the most notable being Plato, who established an academy to teach others. Plato's most famous student, Aristotle, moved thinking from pure ideas to a focus on the universe. He believed the study of the physical environment (science) could clarify our understanding of how we think.

Experiential Education

Exploring or experiencing our physical surroundings (**experiential education**) is the focus of constructivism. During the sixteenth and seventeenth centuries, English philosopher Frances Bacon developed the *scientific method* to learn, explore and research the environment. Seventeenth-century British philosopher John Locke believed so much in experiential education that he labeled the mind a *tabula rasa*, or blank slate, and argued that the only way to learn or put information on the mind's blank slate was through experiences and reflecting on those experiences.

Proponents of constructivism (constructivists) believe that as we experience our environment, we tie information we get from experiences to our previous understandings and thus form new understandings. In other words, the process of learning creates knowledge. (For discussions on the teacher's role in aiding students understanding, see *ATE*, Henson, 1996.)

For constructivists, the act of teaching is the process of helping learners create knowledge. Constructivists believe in addition to discovery enabling us to understand, new information interacts with the learner's previous experiences and understandings. It is important to point out that constructivism is a learning theory that has gradually evolved over a period of approximately 2,500 years.

Another key element of constructivism is the realization that knowledge is temporary and fluid. Understanding is limited by individuals' capacity to understand and the new experiences they encounter. This component of constructivism took a quantum leap during the early twentieth century when American philosopher and psychologist John Dewey used the Chicago schools as a laboratory to study the learning process. Believing in the role direct experience has in learning, Dewey arranged for a school superintendent in Quincy, Massachusetts, Colonel Francis Parker, to employ experiential ideas Parker had learned in Europe. Later, while at the University of Chicago, Dewey developed the nation's first laboratory school. A century later, educational literature acknowledges the importance of such schools. "The teachers who are getting the greatest results treat their classrooms as laboratories" (Farr, 2011, p. 32).

The essence of Dewey's philosophy is reflected in his often-quoted phrase "learning by doing." This emphasis on doing should not be confused with American education's contemporary aim of preparing students for employment in the workplace. Constructivists recognize the vocational value of education, but also believe quality of life and learning to enjoy learning should be educational goals. Constructivists emphasize the motivational role of teachers in helping students learn to love learning. Unlike behaviorists, who sanction the use of tangible rewards, constructivists believe *internal motivation*, such as the joy of learning, is more effective than external rewards. Constructivism has been heavily influenced by the 1930s work of Russian psychologist L. S. Vygotsky (discussed in Chapter 2), who was intensely interested in the effects students' interactions have on learning. Jaramillo (1996, p. 136) explains, "Vygotsky noted that individuals interact with one another in social situations to socially negotiate meaning." Vygotsky also believed that the subject being studied influenced the learning process, thus various disciplines have their own learning methodologies.

Vygotsky believed teachers must consider a student's prior experiences when designing curricula, agreeing with Moore & Berry (2010) who stated that today's students have easy access to information, therefore delivery systems of the future will exacerbate the need for individualized learning.

Vygotsky's work formed the basis for the *cooperative learning programs* that have become popular in many contemporary schools. He recommended pairing more competent students with less capable students to elevate the latter's competence (Jaramillo, 1996). Meek (1998, p. 15) reported that "Nearly 100 percent of teachers reported using whole-group instruction at least once a week. More than 90 percent also reported working with individual students at least once a week; and at least 80 percent report on working with small groups that often." Sara Wessling (2010), the 2010 'National Teacher of the Year,' states, "We must commit to innovative teaching that will create opportunities to treat students as individuals (p. 16)."

Concepts and Learning

The emphasis constructivists place on experiential learning does not ignore the importance content has on learning. Constructivists' views on content emphasize the role **concept** plays in learning. A concept is a generalization about content giving meaning to similar events and ideas. Tyson and Carrol (1973, p. *25*) offered the following definition, "A concept is an inference based upon the notation of recurrence in the context of variance which enables one to order and organize experience." The importance of conceptual thinking is expressed by Winger (2009). "Today's tendency to focus only on standards, at the expense of concepts will fall short."

Too often, students deal with isolated facts, unaware of implied concepts. Even when focusing on concepts, teachers and students often are unable to understand their relationships to other concepts. Stefanich (1990, p. 48) explains:

> "Students tend to deal with concepts in isolation. They cannot effectively consider a number of isolated examples and apply these to general theory or principle. They cannot effectively apply a general principle to a number of instances or examples. They are unable to cognitively process variable time frames or situations which require simultaneous consideration of multiple characters or events."

Australian and Japanese teachers, whose students outscore U.S. students on the Trends in International Mathematics and Science Studies (TIMSS), (noted in Chapter 1), purposely limit each class session to one or two major concepts (Roth & Garnier, 2007).

Table 10.3 illustrates constructivist beliefs about (1) the purpose of schools, (2) the nature of learning, (3) motivation, and (4) the nature and organization of curriculum content. Table 10.4 suggests methods of constructivist teaching.

TABLE 10.3

Constructivist Education

The purpose of school	· School should promote creativity. · School should improve students' present and adult lives. · School should produce better thinkers. · Depth of understanding is most important. · Quality of learning is characterized by the learner's creative ability.
Learning	· Learning is creating new understanding. · Learning involves shaping information. · Success in learning any discipline requires discovering that discipline's unique structure.
Motivation	· Cooperation is a major motivating force. · Students learn information having personal value to them. · Discovering new relationships among concepts and developing new concepts is motivating. · The motivation required for learning is internal; therefore, good teachers arrange conditions to invite learning. · Interclass competition is important.
The nature of and organization of knowledge for curriculum content	· Content is built out of large understandings called content generalizations or concepts. · Knowledge is fluid. · Information should be organized to simplify and expedite its learning. · Student interests, current events, and ease of association should shape the curriculum.

TECHNOLOGY IN THE CLASSROOM

Educational psychologists agree that reading is one of the most creative student endeavors. Consider the following use of technology to facilitate reading related to problem solving and creativity.

"Technology is Causing Kids to Beg for Reading Time"

Of the 140 students who attend Pine Grove Elementary, a *K-5* school, set in the middle of apple and pear orchards in Hood River, Oregon, approximately *65* percent of them are children of migrant workers. Many of these children only attend school part of the year; many do not come from English-speaking families.

Despite the odds, the school is making great strides in engendering a love for reading in these children. Computer coordinator Sharlene Wilkin says that technology is the key to the children's enthusiasm. "Without the computer, most of these students—particularly the slow readers—would never read," says Wilkin. "Technology is causing kids to beg for reading time." ■

TABLE 10.4
Constructivist Teaching
· Invites students to discover information
· Invites students to identify academic content that interests them
· Helps students discover information
· Addresses discontinuity
· Encourages students to be creative while learning and considers a reasonable amount of noise and movement necessary and acceptable
· Strives to help students reach a deeper understanding of topics
· Uses students' personal interests to motivate
· Uses interclass competition to motivate

S U R F I N G • T H E • W E B

Excellent resources for problem solving, creativity, and constructivism include:
1. Center for the Future of Teaching and Learning, a resource on reading and reading-related issues (**http://www.cftl.org**)
2. Education Excellence Network-Thomas B. Fordham Foundation and the Hudson Institute (**http://www. edexcellence.net**) ■

RECAP OF MAJOR IDEAS

1. There is no universally accepted definition of problem solving or creativity. However, educational psychologists agree both are important in the educational process, and define qualities that proficient problem solvers and creative individuals share.

2. Problem solving and creativity can be taught in the educational process. Additionally, there are well-defined methods for teaching problem solving and enhancing the creative environment of the classroom.

3. Contemporary methods for classroom problem solving include:

   a. *Heuristics*: rules of thumb that can lead to the solution of a problem.

   b. *Random searches*: a way of problem solving that is highly inefficient because chance alone determines success.

   c. *Algorithms*: a procedure for solving a problem, using a finite set of steps.

4. Teachers can teach students problem solving through brainstorming, analogies, and models.

5. Creativity of students involves unique and novel responses to problems encountered. Creative individuals are characterized by intelligence, knowledge, and motivation in their fields or areas of creativity.

6. Teachers can develop a creative environment in their classrooms by modeling creative behavior, providing creative opportunities for students, and rewarding creative efforts.

FURTHER APPLICATIONS

1. Write three guidelines teachers can use when designing curriculum for developing student problem-solving skills and creativity. Compare your activities with those of your fellow students.

2. List three classroom activities you could use to enhance the creative behavior of your future students. Compare your activities with those of your fellow students.

3. Interview two classroom teachers to ascertain the methods and techniques they use to teach students problem solving and creativity. Compare your interviews with those of your fellow students.

4. Give one example of how you could use the three problem-solving approaches, random search, heuristics, and algorithms.

KEY TERMS

problem finding

problem definition

hypothesis

insight

problem representation

operators

random search

heuristics

proximity search

means-ends analysis

brainstorming

analogies

models

algorithms

creativity

Torrance Tests of Creative Thinking
  (TTCT)

constructivism

experiential education

concept

LOOKING AHEAD

Chapter 10 emphasized the importance of the teacher and the classroom environment in developing the problem-solving ability and creativity of students. However, teachers confronted with unmotivated students will find that teaching problem solving, creativity, learning, social and moral development is difficult. The next chapter focuses on motivation. Attributes of behavioral, and cognitive approaches to motivation are discussed, with an emphasis on methods and techniques classroom teachers can use to motivate students. ■

Part 5

Motivating Students and Managing the Classroom Environment

Chapter 11

Motivation

LEARNING OBJECTIVES

Upon completing this chapter, you should be able to:

1 Write and/or articulate a definition of *motivation*.

2 Analyze and evaluate three major theories of motivation, and list two classroom applications of each.

3 Explain three major implications of *Maslow's need theory* to classroom teaching and student motivation.

4 Explain two teacher options for high- and low-achievement motivated students.

5 Discuss the merits and limitations of *cooperative* and *competitive* goal systems.

6 Discuss the effects *goal structures* have on motivation.

7 Explain two alternative strategies teachers can use to assist students with low achievement motivation and high fear of failure.

8 Explain how teachers can use *metacognition* to impact student academic achievement and motivation.

9 Relate two alternatives teachers have in motivating *at-risk* students.

INTRODUCTION

Motivation is a way of explaining how people are aroused by an event, how they direct their behavior toward the event, and how they sustain that behavior for given lengths of time (Ball, 1982). In other words, motivation explains why individuals get interested and react to those events garnering their attention.

As a teacher, you will quickly become aware of the presence or absence of motivation among your students. Motivation is required to read this text-book, attend class, study for tests, clean your room, and get ready for a party. Motivation help students form an intention to learn (Pintrich & Garcia, 1992). Motivation is one of the many human characteristics affecting students' academic and social behavior and is related to other student characteristics, including curiosity, creativity, and self-concept.

TODD WILLIAMS...

and two teacher friends, Belinda and Brooks, had enjoyed a Saturday morning 'Waysider' breakfast, the best in town, maybe the best in the world. They were stuffed, and the coffee-sipping and conversation, as usual, found its way to their students. Belinda taught fourth grade, Brooks eleventh grade. "I really wish my students were more motivated," Belinda stated. "I don't necessarily mean for me as a teacher, although that would be nice, but I mean for the kids, themselves. Many simply don't seem to care."

Brooks, with a devil's advocate grin, countered, "Aw, come on Belinda, I have students, and so do you, who work hard, achieve, and are as moti-vated as they can be."

Belinda responded, "You're abso-lutely right. But when I give a test, students fail and don't seem to mind at all. If they don't have their homework assignments ready, they just shrug

it off. Sue Ella, one of my brightest students, is struggling to pass. You know why? She's convinced she's dumb, and those are her very words. 'I'm dumb; I can't do it.' She's afraid of failure and is convinced she can't do anything about it."

Brooks relented, "Yeah, I know, and believe me, the lack of motivation affects students in ways other than grades. I've had Ken in my office four times this month. He's so down he won't participate in class. He wouldn't even participate in our class party. He thinks nobody likes him and, of course, it's affecting his grades. But he's a bright, nice-looking kid. He's just not motivated to do anything in school. Then there are kids like Dexter. He's convinced he can't pass because I don't like him, and he's quit trying. His main goal is to disrupt class and get the attention of his buddies. I'm in the middle of explaining osmosis and out of nowhere he asks; 'Mr. Brooks don't you think smoking pot should be legal?'"

Belinda, hiding giggles, asked, "What are you doing about him?"

Brooks continued, "Well, I've talked with him about asking appropriate questions at the appropriate time, and I've gotten him involved in class, as my lab assistant. He finally agreed to talk with the school counselor next week. I also have an appointment with his mother on Monday. But I've got some who just can't seem to get enough. They want to learn, make good grades, the whole nine yards, but some . . . oh, boy. Valerie told me in class Tuesday she's not interested in science because next month she turns 16 and she's quitting school because school is boring. How do you motivate kids like that?"

Belinda quizzed, "Todd, you're awfully quiet. I suppose all your students are perfect?"

Todd responds, "Yes, they are. I have absolutely no problems. They're all model students. They work hard, behave themselves, and never give me a hassle. I suppose it's a result of my being such a masterful teacher."

Belinda stared at the ceiling and muttered, "I think I'm going to throw up."

Brooks, stuffing the bill for breakfast in Todd's shirt pocket asked, "Belinda, are you ready to go?"

With a slight grin, she responded, "Yes, I am." She and Brooks headed for the door.

Todd, still seated, protested, "Hey, I paid last time. Wait, you never did tell me if you think smoking pot should be legal."

> " Students who are academically unmotivated to learn . . . do not learn. "
> SLAVIN, 2012

> One problem teachers must address is finding effective ways to motivate students.

Perhaps, when you think about the time when you will teach, like Todd, you fantasize about having all model students, but if you teach longer than a few days, we're confident you'll experience students similar to those described by Belinda and Brooks. The importance of motivating students cannot be overemphasized. In this chapter, we'll discuss the theories of motivation as they relate to the classroom.

As Slavin's sidebar quote implies, one of a teacher's major tasks is to find ways to motivate students who seem to have little interest in classroom lessons and activities. As noted in Chapter 8, learning has the potential to fascinate students *if* the teacher has a repertoire of strategies making academic material interesting to students' (Rinne, 1998). This may be achieved in many ways, including explaining the importance of the topic to students and involving students in the discussion of topics, and by introducing interesting, motivating ways to engage students (Stipek, 1993; Williams 1998). For example, if a teacher asks students for the most interesting uses of computers they can think of and the result is a lively class discussion, the teacher has motivated students to engage. If a teacher reads from 'Tom Sawyer' or 'Harry Potter' and, as a result, students are motivated to check books from the library to read, this teacher has motivated these students.

However, student motivation must not be confused with classroom incentives (Slavin, 2012). *Motivation* is a student's interest in doing academic work and learning academic material. Classroom incentives are methods teachers *use* to motivate students; they include such activities as good grades, free time, and the awarding of stars or checks. For example, in attempting to motivate students who are not performing academically, Belinda might award free time in class for correct, completed assignments. Student motivation can be influenced by classroom incentives, but other factors, such as internal interest, family environment, interest in achievement, and students' perceptions of their abilities also play major roles in a student's level of motivation. For example, Brooks found that lack of motivation has affected both the social interaction and academic performance of one of his students. He has decided to motivate Ken by using the counselor and a meeting with Ken's mother.

There are many theories of motivation. This chapter will present three primary approaches to motivation: *behavioral*, *cognitive* (*attribution theory*, *achievement motivation theory*), and *social cognitive theory*). These theories are related, and they add to our understanding of what motivates students.

BEHAVIORAL APPROACHES TO MOTIVATION

As discussed in Chapter 6, behavioral and social learning theory emphasizes such concepts as reinforcement, conditioning, punishment, and alternatives to punishment. Using reinforcement to strengthen behavior, and removing reinforcement to extinguish behavior are applicable to motivation. Behaviorists contend motivation can be increased, decreased, maintained, and extinguished by external consequences. Students can be motivated to work and perform with reinforcement.

As explained in Chapter 6, there are two types of reinforcers: primary and secondary. Both primary and secondary reinforcers can strengthen behavior. Primary reinforcers, such as food and water, satisfy basic physiological needs. Secondary reinforcers, such as praise, grades, and money, become associated with primary reinforcers and, therefore, can be very motivating. Behavioral approaches to motivation contend that students can be motivated through reinforcement, which can include "the love of learning."

Motivation is often viewed along a continuum of *extrinsic* to *intrinsic* motivation. The behavioristic approach is often identified with extrinsic motivation. Extrinsic motivation depends on external rewards, such as grades or privileges. For example, Tina might be motivated to improve her grades as a result of her teacher rewarding improvement in her test performance with iPad time in class, or Austin might be extrinsically motivated to make the school honor roll because if he does, he earns the use of the family car. Some educators oppose the use of such rewards for fear they will reduce the level of intrinsic motivation (Kohn, 1993). If Tina and Austin are motivated by their love of learning or desire to be 'excellent students,' educational psychologists would say they are intrinsically motivated.

Alternatives for teachers facing such student motivational problems are suggested by Constance E. Cloonan, former New Jersey Teacher of the Year.

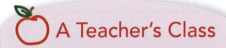 A Teacher's Class

NAME: Constance E. Cloonan, former New Jersey Teacher of the Year

In my experience as a teacher, I have found several effective ways to motivate students to learn. These approaches must be tailored to the developmental stages and needs of the particular students involved.

In motivating students, it is vital to create an academic environment that is highly challenging but within the intellectual reach of the students. For example, I try to have lots of manipulatives in my second-grade classroom that are just difficult enough to make my students "stretch" to do them. Students who learn in such an environment are stimulated by it and become more confident as they find themselves doing things they thought they never could. I always try to combine this challenging environment with lots of positive reinforcement for students whose effort and behavior are appropriately focused. This provides some of the motivation needed for students to work hard and continue in the learning process.

For students in need of special motivation, I set up a series of tangible rewards as external incentives. These incentives might be extra time at a learning center, extra project time to work with a partner, or some other classroom activity that we have established as being especially fun for the students. It also always includes praise and attention from me as well as any aides or volunteers in the classroom.

I use these rewards to spur my students to complete their assignments and to bring their assigned work up to the levels expected of the class. These incentives also serve to reinforce the standards and expectations established at the beginning of the school year.

Once these standards have been established and my students have developed good work habits, I try to move them away from external rewards and toward the more complex internal rewards. These internal rewards include pride in their own work and satisfaction in their own accomplishment. Moving

In attribution theory, the mainspring for motivation is the need to understand.

Three major attributions for causes of success and failure are a person's effort, a person's ability, and task difficulty.

students away from dependence on external rewards is always a difficult task. One way is to encourage students to share their completed work with classmates in pairs or in small groups. By providing time for this activity, students have the opportunity to informally enjoy a sense of success with one another and to experience the satisfaction that comes from success. As this happens, students begin to internalize the joy of discovery and learning, and motivation begins to become less dependent on the teacher. ■

INTASC Standard 2   Learning differences

Cognitive Approaches

As discussed in Chapters 7 and 8, cognitive approaches to motivation are based on the assumption that an individual's perceptions and thoughts about activities and events, or intrinsic sources, influence the way they respond. Recent work in educational psychology, particularly Bandura (1986, 2001, 2002), emphasizes the importance of factors such as perceptions and feelings and attempts to bridge the gap between behavioral and cognitive views of motivation. Bandura suggests several sources of student motivation, including **self-efficacy**, goals, and projections about outcomes of academic activity. Student motivation is affected by such thoughts as "Can I succeed?" or "What will happen if I fail?" These projections about outcomes are, in part, due to students' beliefs about their competency, or self-efficacy. In the Todd scenario, Sue Ella believes she is going to fail because "she's dumb". Ken is having difficulty passing because "nobody likes him." Dexter is convinced his teacher "doesn't like him" and Valerie is quitting school because "she's bored."

Cognitive approaches maintain that students can be motivated to perform well by rewards such as grades and praise, but in addition they can be motivated by factors such as interest, curiosity, and the desire to learn, solve problems and understand. Interestingly, female students are motivated to read by curiosity and aesthetics more than their male counterparts (Mucherah & Yoder, 2008).

A student exhibits *intrinsic motivation* by attempting to perform well on a test because of interest, the satisfaction of doing well, a sense of accomplishment, or other internal factors related to task or student. Miserandino (1996) found "children who were certain of their ability reported feeling curious . . . " (p. 208). The observant teacher is aware the classroom environment, student attitudes, peers and families all impact on a student's level of motivation to succeed academically and socially (Bandura, 2000). As noted in Chapter 8, it is important for teachers to be sensitive to students' feelings about themselves, what they care about, and what academic tasks will provide the success they need to feel capable (Darling-Hammond, 1998).

Attribution Theory

A major tenet for motivation is the search for understanding, or attempting to comprehend why events happen (Weiner, 2000). Weiner developed a theory labeled **attribution theory**, to explain how students reason and *attribute* causes of their successes and failures. An attribution question might be, "Why did I flunk this test?" or "Why did I get a good grade on this term paper?" Weiner argues that student answers to such questions are critical to a students' performance. For example, Francine may attribute her passing the geometry quiz because she studied, whereas Dexter believes he failed because the teacher is unfair. Understanding to what students attribute their successes and failures are critical factors in understanding their motivation.

Weiner believes students attribute four major causes to their successes and failures: their ability and *effort*, the *difficulty of task*, and *luck*. Other causes include mood, fatigue, illness, and bias on the part of the person evaluating their performance.

Weiner (2000) classified the causes into three dimensions, as noted in Table 11.1. The first dimension is **locus of control**. There are two types: *internal* and *external*. Students with internal locus of control believe they are responsible for their behavior and thus their successes and failures. They attribute success or failure to their ability and effort. If they do well on a test, they *attribute* it to studying for the test, trying hard, having the ability to grasp the material, or because they are 'good test-takers'. People with **external locus of control** believe their performance is due to *luck*, *difficulty of task*, or other circumstances beyond their control. We're sure you've heard comments such as, "I passed the test because it was easy" or "I don't know why I failed. I studied the wrong material. I don't have any luck on tests."

People with high internal locus of control tend to be more persistent on tasks and do not give up easily (Weiner, 2000). Students with either high external or high internal locus of control who experience too many failures may develop a posture known as **learned helplessness** (Maier & Seligman, 1976; Seligman, 2000). Students who experience learned helplessness might come to feel, regardless of how hard they try, they can't avoid failure, so they stop trying. For instance, a seventh-grade student exhibits low external locus of control if he says he didn't study for the test because "I'd fail anyway, so why should I study."

Research indicates that attributions to success and failure are often developmental in nature. Often attribution concepts are not understood by younger students, but older students (grades 5 through 12) typically understand the causes of their success and failure (Rubble, 1980). When students are asked to rate how important six causes (ability, paying attention, studying, luck, task difficulty, and assistance from others) are in their success or failure in the classroom, they rate studying and paying attention as particularly important (Hiebert, Winograd, & Danner, 1984).

Children with high internal locus of control do not give up easily.

TABLE 11.1

Causes of Success and Failure Classified According to Locus, Stability, and Controllability

Controllability	Internal		External	
	Stable	Unstable	Stable	Unstable
Uncontrollable	Ability	Mood	Task difficulty	Luck
Controllable	Typical effort	Immediate effort	Teacher bias	Unusual help from others

Adapted from Weiner (2000).

Attributions of success and failure typically develop during middle school and high school.

People with achievement motivation tend to be self-reliant and take responsibility for their behavior.

Failure often increases the motivation level of high achievers but often lowers that of low achievers.

INTASC Standard 1   Learner development.

Motivating Students to Achieve

Observe a group of students working in the classroom, and you will see that some are working hard and trying to do their best while others seem less motivated and are satisfied with borderline grades; Some don't seem to be motivated at all. **Achievement motivation theory** attempts to account for such differences in motivation among students. *Achievement motivation* is defined as actions and feelings related to achieving some internalized standard of excellence. Students with strong achievement motivation tend to be self-reliant, take responsibility for their actions, take calculated risks, plan prudently, and conserve time (Stepek, 1993).

Achievement motivation consists of a *tendency to approach an achievement goal* plus *past success* (Wigfield & Eccles, 2000). Accordingly, a student's tendency to approach an achievement goal is based on three aspects: the need for achievement, the probability of success on a task, and the value success on the task has for the student. A student's tendency to avoid failure is also based on three characteristics; the need to avoid failure, the probability of failure on the task, and the importance failure has for the student.

If Fletch, a ninth grader, faces the task of writing a term paper, his motivation for performing well might be his desire to succeed academically and the value performing well has for him (an excellent score for the school term and being an honor student). These three characteristics compose Fletch's tendency to approach the achievement goal of completing the term paper. As illustrated in Figure 11.1, Fletch will choose a fairly difficult topic for his term paper if his tendency to approach his achievement goal is greater than his tendency to avoid failure. If his tendency to avoid failure is greater than his tendency to approach the achievement goal, he will choose an easy topic.

As illustrated in Table 11.2, students who have high achievement motivation, failure on a task will increase their motivation because they want to improve.

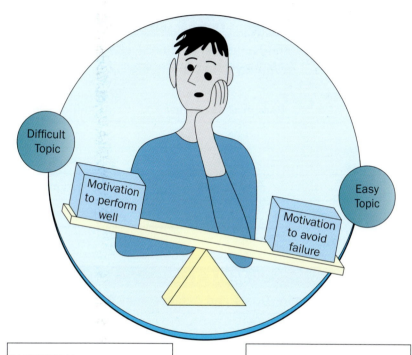

MOTIVATION TO PERFORM WELL Need to do well Probability of good grades Value of performing well (e.g., passing grades in class)	MOTIVATION TO AVOID FAILURE Need to avoide failure Probability of bad grades Value of failure (e.g., failing grade in class)
If the motivation to perform well is great, Fletcher will choose a difficult topic for his term paper.	If the motivation to aviod faflure is great, Fletcher will choose an easy topic for his term paper.

Figure 11.1 Fletch's Motivation for Choosing a Term Paper Topic

Social Cognitive Theory

Another theory of motivation, described by Dweck (1986, 2006) as a social cognitive approach, is related to both attribution theory and achievement motivation and focuses on students' beliefs about their intelligence (Table 11.3). Students may believe their intelligence is fixed, or cannot be changed, which describes the **entity theory of intelligence**. On the other hand, students may believe their intelligence is malleable, or can change, the basis of the **incremental theory**.

Students may have performance *goals*, seeking positive input from their teachers and/or avoiding negative evaluation of their performance. Students may

Mastery-oriented students thrive on difficult tasks; their counterparts often become anxious over difficult tasks.

have learning goals to increase their competence or understanding of subject matter.

TABLE 11.2
Effects of Success and Failure on Students with Different Levels of Achievement Motivation

Initial Achievement Motivation	Performance on Task	Effect on Achievement Motivation
High	Failure	Increases motivation
Low	Failure	Decreases motivation
High	Success	Increases motivation
Low	Success	Increases motivation

Adapted from Wemer (1979).

TABLE 11.3
Achievement Goals and Achievement Behavior

Theory of Intelligence	Goal Orientation	Confidence in Present Ability
Entity theory: Intelligence is fixed	Performance goal: To gain positive judgments	If high
	To avoid negative judgments of competence	If low
Incremental theory: Intelligence is malleable	Learning goal: To increase competence	If high or low

Adapted from Dweck (1986).

Students' confidence in their ability may range from high to low. Students may have **adaptive**, or **mastery-oriented** behavior patterns, characterized by challenge-seeking actions and persistence when faced with obstacles. Other students may have maladaptive, or helpless, behavior patterns, characterized by the avoidance of difficult tasks.

Dweck (1986) contends that the behavior patterns of students, mastery oriented or helpless, have profound effects on classroom performance. Her summary of research found that students with mastery-oriented behavior patterns were undaunted by obstacles; some even increased their performance when tackling challenging tasks. Students exhibiting helpless behavior patterns were often severely hampered by challenging academic tasks.

Maslow believed that people are motivated by the tension caused by unfilled needs.

According to Maslow, a person's physiological needs must be met before self-actualizing needs, such as learning, can be met.

Maslow's Need Theory

One of the most influential theories attempting to explain human motivation is **Maslow's need theory** (Maslow, 1968, 1970). According to Maslow's theory, if people experience unsatisfied needs, tension is created. This tension causes individuals attempting to achieve goals to reduce or remove the tension. Maslow (1968, p. 5) believed "the most important single principle underlying all development" is gratification of needs.

Maslow developed a hierarchy of seven basic human needs (Figure 11.2). **Physiological needs** include nourishment, sleep, and shelter. **Safety needs** consist of freedom from danger, anxiety, and threat. The third need is **love**—from families, teachers, and peers. Peers appear to have similar levels of motivation (Kinderman, 1993). **Esteem needs** consist of confidence and mastery of goals. The need for **knowledge** and **understanding** includes curiosity, exploration, and the desire to obtain knowledge. **Aesthetic needs** include the search for beauty. The seventh need, **self-actualization**, or self-fulfillment, consists of individuals developing and maintaining capacities serving to enhance themselves (Rogers & Freiberg, 1994).

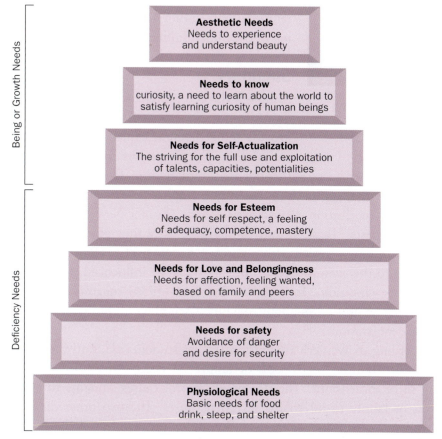

Adapted from Maslow (1970, p. 150).

Figure 11.2 Maslow's Hierarchy of Needs

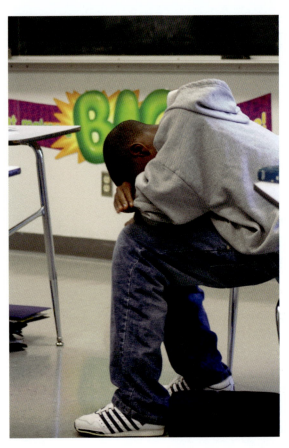

According to Maslow, a child whose deficiency needs are not met will not be motivated to meet being needs.

According to Maslow, people must satisfy physiological needs first. If this is not possible, then people will have no chance to satisfy higher-level needs. For example, if students are hungry and/or exhausted, they will not be motivated to fulfill the need for learning and understanding.

Maslow classified the first four needs (*physiological, safety, love*, and *esteem*) as **deficiency needs** and argued that all humans have these needs. If the first four needs are not met, motivation to learn will be dramatically limited. If students feel unloved and rejected by their families, this will negatively impact meeting the needs for knowledge, aesthetics, and self-actualization.

Maslow classified the last three needs as **being needs**. Like deficiency needs, motivation increases to satisfy being needs. However, being needs are never completely satisfied. When being needs are temporarily met, motivation continues in the seeking of continued fulfillment.

Summary

Although the behavioral and cognitive approaches to motivation have some aspects in common, they provide quite different explanations for causes of motivation. The key terms used in each of the theories are summarized in Table 11.4.

The behavioral approach to motivation emphasizes extrinsic reinforcement as sources of motivation. Constance Cloonan, former New Jersey Teacher of the Year, suggests "These incentives might be extra time at a learning center, extra project time to work with a partner, or some other classroom activity." According to this view, people's motivation can be influenced with reinforcement in the classroom. In addition, Bandura (1986) suggests that intrinsic factors such as projection about outcomes, self-efficacy, and goal setting also influence motivation.

According to Weiner's attribution theory, students are motivated because of their attributions for success or failure on tasks. Attributions are made along three dimensions. Their locus of control causes students to attribute success or failure to internal or external causes. The two other dimensions are student's perception of the stability and controllability of the causes for success and failure.

TABLE 11.4	
Key Terms Used in Theories of Motivation	
Theory	**Key Terms**
Behavioral theory	Reinforcement, punishment
Weiner's attribution theory	Locus of control: Internal, external
	Stability: Stable, unstable
	Controllability: Controllable, uncontrollable
Dweck's social cognitive theory	Theory of intelligence: Entity theory, incremental theory
	Goals: Performance goals, learning goals
	Confidence: High, low
	Behavior pattern: Mastery oriented, helpless
Maslow's need theory	Deficiency needs: Physiological, safety, love, esteem
	Being needs: Knowledge and understanding, aesthetic, self-actualization

Achievement motivation theory describes how students are motivated to achieve some internal standard of excellence. The need of students with high achievement motivation to approach an achievement goal is stronger than their need to avoid failure, and they will choose relatively difficult tasks. Students with low achievement motivation have a greater tendency to avoid failure than to approach an achievement goal, and they will choose relatively easy tasks.

Dweck's (1986, 2006) social cognitive theory suggests that motivation is influenced by an individual's belief that his or her intelligence is either fixed or malleable, whether individuals have performance or learning goals when approaching a task, and the amount of confidence individuals have in their ability. These three domains lead to two types of motivational behavior patterns: a mastery-oriented pattern, characterized by high persistence in the face of challenging tasks, and a helpless behavior pattern, characterized by a lack of persistence.

Maslow's need theory of motivation suggests people are motivated to achieve goals because of the tension created by unfulfilled needs. If people have physiological, safety, love, and esteem needs, they are motivated to engage in some activity to meet these needs. If these needs are met, then people become motivated to satisfy needs for knowledge, understanding, aesthetics, and self-actualization.

The A View from the Field box takes a practical look at what it really means to be motivated and how teachers can reach students who simply have not yet been "aroused" by the right motivation.

A VIEW FROM THE FIELD

A VIEW FROM THE FIELD

PROFILE

Steve Wininger is professor of psychology at Western Kentucky University. Steve earned his B.A. in psychology and philosophy at Georgetown College. He holds an M.A. in applied experimental psychology from Western Kentucky University. His Ph.D. is in educational psychology from Florida State University. Steve's research interests include learning, motivation, self-regulation, exercise, and sports.

QUESTION: If a learner gives up, saying, "I can't, how should a teacher respond?

Dr. Wininger: The first thing a teacher should do is assess the student's attributions. Why does the student think he or she can't do it? Attribution theory reveals that students who cite reasons for failure such as ability, the teacher, or subject difficulty do not believe they have control over learning outcomes and are more prone to giving up or developing maladaptive coping strategies such as task avoidance. Teachers should redirect these students to make more controllable attributions such as lack of attention, self-regulation, poor note taking, or ineffective study strategies. Once students' beliefs about why they are not succeeding are more controllable, then the teacher can work with the students to acquire new skills and better strategies that will positively impact their learning and subsequent motivation.

QUESTION: Many students are indifferent to grades, so what are some alternatives to using grades as motivation?

Dr. Wininger: The primary function of grades should be to provide feedback about learning progress. However, prior to any summative assessment, students need a reason to learn. The sub-types of regulation (i.e., motivation) from Self-Determination Theory are a great reference tool for discussing alternative forms of motivation. External forms of motivation such as rewards and punishment are the most commonly used "motivation strategies," however, research suggests they are not optimal and sometimes actually undermine enjoyment of learning. Another source of motivation consists of utilizing the emotions of guilt for sub-par learning behaviors and pride for exemplary behaviors. Research suggests that instilling guilt for underperformance prompts students to try harder. This is in contrast to saying it is "OK" when they under-perform, which may convey low achievement expectations.

A third motivation approach is working with students to set goals. Part of the goal-setting process involves the teacher articulating the value of learning the planned content; e.g., how does the material apply to students presently and how can they utilize it in the future? Once value is clearly established, specific and measurable goals should be identified that relate to both performance (knowledge to be acquired) and processes (learning methods or strategies).

Intrinsic motivation, designated as the optimal form of regulation, involves making learning fun or interesting. Research on interest development outlines a developmental sequence that starts with catching a student's attention with interesting activities. This is followed by more personal involvement or meaning, such as giving the students choices about what to study for papers or projects in order to take advantage of curiosity as a natural motivator. With encouragement from the teacher and continued opportunities to pursue similar content, the student develops a persistent or personal interest in the subject matter. In summary, in addition to grades, teachers could use emotions, meaningful goals, and interest to motivate their students. ■

APPLYING THEORIES OF MOTIVATION IN THE CLASSROOM

As Dr. Wininger implies, motivation has many dimensions, and it varies with grade level (Mucherah & Yoder, 2008). Teachers often have students, such as Dexter, who appear unmotivated to try even the most elementary academic tasks. Other students, such as Ken and Valerie, seem to have the ability to do well but don't appear to have much interest in learning and school. Even students who are highly motivated may show a lack of motivation for certain subjects or academic tasks. Unmotivated students can be a source of frustration for teachers, but there are numerous alternatives teachers can use to enhance student motivation.

Behavioral Approaches

The principles for applying behavioral learning theory to motivate students in the classroom were discussed in Chapter 5 and are addressed at length in Chapters 6 and 12.

Some behavioral alternatives teachers can use to enhance student motivation include:

- Establish classroom rules early in the year. The rules should include student input and should be clear and explicit. State rules positively, with consequences for adhering to and violating rules.

- Expect the best of students. Through explanation and modeling, teach students to strive for excellence.

Student Study Guide

- Construct your class to provide ample opportunity for student success, both socially and academically. Teacher attention to student success cannot be overemphasized and can be powerful motivators in the classroom setting.

- Students can make errors and still be successful and motivated but excessive failure can become self-perpetuating, resulting in low student motivation. Conversely, student success tends to increase motivation, producing a positive self-perpetuating cycle (Williams, 1997).

- Communicate regularly and positively with families of students.

Inform students you care, you want them to behave and learn. Inform families about school activities, expectations, and the successes of their children. Families of students should be an integral part of attempts by teachers to motivate students.

COGNITIVE APPROACHES

Attribution Theory

Some obstacles to academic performance are not within students' control.

Proactive teachers want students to learn to attribute their academic success and failure to individual effort. Weiner's attribution theory of motivation has many implications for classroom instruction. Several research studies support the assertion communication to students when failure is due to lack of effort rather than ability can produce significant changes in student effort (Dweck, 1986, 2006; Winfield & Lee, 1990). Furthermore, these changes can persist over time and can generalize to other academic tasks. Also, let students know you believe they will achieve. Williams (1997) reported when teachers express appreciation for students' work, students' feeling of belonging and academic achievement increased.

It is important to communicate to students when failure is due to lack of effort.

Stipek (1993) reported significant declines in students' perception of their self-competence as they move through elementary school. Research indicating that pre-school students have more confidence in their abilities than fourth graders illustrates the importance of students experiencing success throughout the elementary grades and, indeed, throughout their academic careers.

Another aspect of attribution theory that has implications for classroom teaching is the *controllability* of the causes for success and failure (Ball, 1982; Doebler & Eicke, 1979). If a teacher becomes aware that a student's failure is due to some reason the student can't control, such as a disruptive home environment, the teacher should intervene by seeking counseling and/or additional help. Teachers need to be alert to students not performing well academically because of reasons beyond the student's control (Phillips, 1998). The Proactive Teaching box offers further suggestions for enhancing the motivation of students.

PROACTIVE TEACHING

CLASSROOM SITUATION	PROACTIVE ALTERNATIVES
1. **Physiological needs of students:** Some of your students will come from impoverished family environments, and may come to school without breakfast and/or dinner the night before. As a result, they will be hungry, lethargic, and cannot perform academically.	· As stated in Chapter 1, acquaint yourself with school and community breakfast and lunch programs. On the first day of class, encourage eligible students to participate in such programs, which are often free to students from low-income families. Such facilities often provide clothing and transportation to and from their services. Disseminate this information to families prior to or early in the academic year.
2. **Feelings of success among students:** Some of your students seem to be defeated by school. They don't feel they can be successful academically, and as a result they perform poorly.	· As discussed in Chapters 6 and 12, plan to use reinforcement consistently and systematically. Many successful teachers plan activities in their classes, ensuring students some measure of success. Additionally, scheduling time to provide students with prompt, accurate, and personal feedback on good academic performance can promote students' feelings of success.
3. **Controllability:** You notice students' interests are often to the detriment of academics. Gavin is only interested in sports, Rivero is fascinated by sports car racing, and Julia is totally absorbed by dance.	· Knowledge of students' interests, gleaned from former teachers and families, can be an important source of motivation. Prepare lessons capitalizing on students' interests. Lessons for Gavin can include math (decimals and percentages via batting averages), geography (location of NFL and NBA teams), health, and PE (conditioning of athletes). Lessons for Rivero can include math and physics (speed, acceleration, and mechanics of cars). Dance can be used to teach Julia biology (the human body) and art (artistry of ballet).

Motivating Students to Achieve

CHALLENGING STUDENTS Atkinson's (1968) achievement motivation theory argues that altering classroom tasks for students, depending on their level of achievement motivation, is a necessity. Varying assignments is essential for achieving a positive match between each student's level of achievement motivation and classroom tasks. Teachers should attempt to foster challenge-seeking and persistent behavior in their students. In addition to providing students activities designed for student success and giving frequent praise, assist them in setting learning goals (Dweck, 1986).

High-interest activities designed to enhance interest in learning and performance cannot be overstated. Academic mastery-oriented patterns of behavior are facilitated by incorporating interesting, yet challenging, classroom activities.

> Teachers can assign different tasks to high-achievement—motivation students.

Physiological and Psychological Student Needs

Maslow's need theory contends higher-level needs cannot be met until the lower-level, or deficiency needs, are satisfied. Thus, students whose physiological needs are not met will not be motivated to acquire the higher-level needs of knowledge and understanding, aesthetic needs, and self-actualization. If students come to school anxious and fearful about their home environment, they can hardly be expected to be motivated to learn. However, teachers can be aware of the relationship between students' motivation, safety and physiological needs. Students are more likely to be motivated to learn in a physiologically and psychologically comfortable, secure environment.

> Learning is enhanced by a classroom climate where students feel secure.

Motivating At-Risk Students

Motivating low-achieving and/or at-risk students is a particular concern for teachers (Hodginson, 1985). **At-risk students** are those with a higher-than-average probability of failure and/or dropping out of school. (Manning & Baruth, 1996) maintain that most all students at sometime in their academic life may be at risk. Can teachers be successful in motivating such students? According to Alderman (1990, p. 28), "Teachers who are successful in reaching low-achieving students combine a high sense of their own efficacy with high, realistic expectations for student achievement."

Teachers with a high sense of **efficacy**, or confidence in their ability to influence student learning and motivation, are more likely to view low-achieving students as teachable (Ashton & Webb, 1986).

The following case study takes a look at how one teacher piqued the interest of her students.

> " When we teach students to take responsibility for their learning, we have taken a giant step in promoting motivational equality in the classroom. "
> ALDERMAN, 1990

CASE STUDY

Stonewall Middle School is located in the small rural community of Perry's Gap. The community is isolated by rugged, mountainous terrain. Rhonda Marshall is beginning her second year of teaching eighth grade science. Because she was single and just out of college when she accepted her first teaching position, she had serious reservations about living in a rural, isolated community but to her surprise, she fell in love with Stonewall Middle. The residents were concerned with education and with, their community; they supported their schools and teachers.

Initially, Rhonda was surprised with the varying levels of performance among the students in her classes. However, she soon accepted that some of her students were very bright and others were behind academically. Examples included Sharice who was an 'A+' student and Tyree who was three grade levels behind in reading and had no interest in school. The majority of her students performed academically but too many, like Tyree, were simply not motivated. Ms. Marshall pondered her problem. How could she reach those students who just didn't seem to care?

PROACTIVE EXERCISE

1. What do you suggest for Ms. Marshall?
2. How can Ms. Marshall plan future lessons that will be motivate her students?
3. What suggestions do you have for Sharice and Tyree?
4. Can Ms. Marshall capitalize on community interest and concern?
5. How could she best take advantage of 'The Incident'?
6. What other 'incidents' could you suggest?

The Incident

On Monday morning, Rhonda arrived at 7:15 to set up a distillery process for her first-period class. She purposely wanted all students to see this process as they entered class. She had the burner on and several tubes running across the long table at the front of the room. Jeff and Tyron, as usual, were first to enter, just as the tubes clouded with condensation. Tyron asked, "What's this, Ms. Marshall? What are you doing?"

"Good morning boys. It's a science demonstration. If you will take your seats, I'll show you as soon as everybody arrives."

When Johnna and Teresa walked in, their eyes went to the paraphernalia. "Wow. What's this?" Teresa blurted. Jeff signaled her to sit down. Other students began arriving in a steady stream. Rhonda worked quickly, making a few final adjustments. Finally, everyone had arrived. Ms. Marshall turned and faced the class. Every eye watched as the students waited for their teacher. Rhonda savored the moment. For the first time she could remember, she had all her students' undivided attention. Rhonda announced, "Today, I'm going to show you how to distill water. You'll learn about condensation, vapor, and steam."

Alderman (1990); Anderman & Maehr (1994) maintain that a prerequisite to student success is acquiring a high degree of motivation and student responsibility for their academic success. This can be addressed by teachers through *links* of communication to students, demonstrating the relationship of student effort and success (Alderman, 1990). *Links* are defined as follows.

- *Link* 1: *Proximal goals*. The first link to success is the setting of goals for performance. Goals play an important role in the cultivation of self-motivation by establishing a target or personal standard by which we can evaluate or monitor our performances (Bandura, 1986).

- *Link* 2: *Learning strategies*. Low-achieving students often fail to apply learning strategies that could be beneficial. In Link 2, students identify learning strategies to assist them accomplish their goals.

- *Link* 3: *Successful experience*. A learning goal, rather than a performance goal, is the key to success in Link 3 (Dweck, 1986). The focus in a learning goal is on "how much progress I made," not on "how smart I am."

- *Link* 4: *Attribution for success*. Students are encouraged to attribute success to their personal effort or abilities. The teacher's role is to assist students in making the appropriate attribution.

Links "only provide teachers and students with a framework for beginning the cycle of progress that fosters student responsibility for learning. When student's take responsibility for their learning, teachers have taken a giant step in promoting motivational equality in the classroom" (Alderman, 1990, p. 30).

OTHER METHODS FOR ENHANCING MOTIVATION

Competitive, Cooperative, and Individual Goal Structures

Goal structures specify the type of interdependence that exists among students as they attempt to meet learning goals (Johnson & Johnson, 1994). There are three such systems of student motivation, and each is associated with goal structures (Ames, 1992). The first motivation system, called **ability-evaluative**

motivation is defined by **competitive goal structures**. In competitive goal structures, rewards are given to students determined to be the best. Examples of this goal structure are grouping students by ability and calling attention to students who receive the highest grade. Motivation is assumed through limited attention to those few students who perform the best.

The second motivation system, **task mastery**, is elicited by **individualistic goal structures**. In this goal structure, rewards for one student are independent of rewards for other students. Students who operate under this structure attribute their success to effort and presume "I can if I try."

Teachers may choose to use competition, mastery, or cooperative goal structures. Each can have a different effect on student perceptions.

The third motivational system is **moral responsibility**, which is elicited by cooperative goal structures. In a cooperative goal structure, one goal is shared by a group of students, and the activities and efforts converge toward a common goal. This goal structure requires social interdependence, or sharing responsibility for achieving a goal, and invokes negative consequences for not doing one's part. This goal structure elicits affiliation and helping behaviors in students and results in increased peer interactions and more positive relations with others. A summary of the three types of goal structures follows:

- *Competitive:* Rewards are given to the best students.
- *Individual:* Rewards for a student are independent from rewards for other students.
- *Cooperative:* Students work in groups toward a common reward.

Differing goal structures in school elicit different motivational orientations in students. Competitive goal structures can result in negative interdependence among students; students could falsely perceive they can obtain their own goals only if other students do not obtain theirs (Johnson & Johnson, 1994). Williams (1997) reports that forcing low-achieving students to compete with high achievers made the low achievers feel detached from the class. Cooperative goal structures, on the other hand, result in interdependence; students can achieve their goals only if other students achieve theirs. Individual goal structures often result in little interdependence among students.

The three types of goal structures used in a classroom not only affect student motivation but also affect student achievement (Slavin, 2012). Competitive goal structures increase student achievement only for those students who have the ability to compete. Cooperative goal structures are designed to increase achievement for students of varying ability levels and to promote positive attitudes toward learning and increasing interpersonal skills.

> Cooperative goal structures elicit affiliation and helping behavior in students.

> Among individual students (competitive goal structures) competition increases student achievement for only the most capable students, whereas competition among groups of students (cooperative goal structures) increases achievement for all students.

Teachers need to develop the ability to determine which type is appropriate for each classroom activity. If goals are structured and determined by type of classroom activity, the following positive results are found. Students

- Achieve at a higher level
- Use more high-level reasoning strategies
- Have more internal locus of control
- Develop higher levels of achievement motivation
- Develop more interpersonal skills
- Value the classroom subject area more

(Johnson & Johnson, 2005)

Different classroom activities facilitate the three goal structures. Cooperative goal structures can be used with any type of classroom activity. Individual goal structures are appropriate when tasks require simple skill or knowledge acquisition, such as learning historical dates. Individual goal structures can also be used to supplement cooperative goal structures by assigning individual tasks within a group. Competitive goal structures can be used with activities requiring skill practice, knowledge recall, and review. Steps in designing cooperative, individual, and competitive goal structures in the classroom are listed in Table 11.5.

TABLE 11.5		
Steps for Designing Cooperative, Individual, and Competitive Goal Structures in the Classroom		
Cooperative Goal Structures	**Individualistic Goal Structures**	**Competitive Goal Structures**
1. Specify the academic and collaborative objectives for the groups.	Specify instructional objectives at the correct level for each student.	Specify instructional objectives at the correct level for each student.
2. Determine group size and members of each group. (Heterogeneous groups of high-, low-, and medium-ability students are usually best.)	Arrange the classroom to provide adequate space for each student to work uninterrupted.	Assign students to heterogeneous, cooperative learning teams. (The teams will prepare together and compete with each other in a tournament.)
3. Assign responsibilities to group members.	Plan activities that are self-contained and will foster independent work.	Plan the tournament by setting up an instructional game.
4. Explain academic task.	Explain the academic tasks to students.	Assign students and/or teams to compete with each other.

Cooperative Goal Structures	Individualistic Goal Structures	Competitive Goal Structures
5. Structure positive goal interdependence by asking the group to produce a single product and providing group rewards.	Communicate that students have individual goals and must work independently.	Prepare the materials necessary for the instructional game.
6. Structure individual accountability to ensure that all individuals in the group learn by giving practice tests and randomly selecting group members to answer questions.	Structure individual accountability by specifying that each student must master his or her assignment.	Arrange the classroom for the tournament.
7. Structure intergroup cooperation by encouraging groups to help other groups.	Explain the mastery criterion for each student	Explain the academic task and rules of the tournament
8. Explain the criteria for success. These criteria must be for acceptable work and may vary from group to group or individual to individual within a group.	Specify the desired behaviors that students must exhibit when working, such as working alone and pacing themselves.	Structure negative goal interdependence by explaining to students that their goal is to acquire more points for their team.
9. Specify the desired behaviors in the group, such as stay with the group, take turns, check to make sure everyone else in the group understands the material, and listen to what the other group members are saying.	Monitor students' behavior as they work.	Explain the criteria for success in the learning game.
10. Monitor students' behavior in the group.	Provide assistance with individual tasks when necessary.	Specify the desired behaviors. For example, students should seek fun and enjoyment, lose with dignity, and win with graciousness.
11. Provide assistance with group tasks, when necessary.	Intervene to teach students individual skills, when necessary.	Monitor students' behavior during the game to make sure rules are being followed and proper behavior exhibited.
12. Intervene to teach cooperative skills, when necessary.	Provide closure to the activity by summarizing major points or asking students to recall ideas.	Provide assistance with tasks, when necessary.

(Continued)

TABLE 11.5 (CONTINUED)		
Steps for Designing Cooperative, Individual, and Competitive Goal Structures in the Classroom		
Cooperative Goal Structures	**Individualistic Goal Structures**	**Competitive Goal Structures**
13. Provide closure to the activity by summarizing major points and asking students to recall ideas.	Evaluate the quality and quantity of students' learning independently of other students.	Intervene to teach students competitive skills, when necessary.
14. Evaluate the quality and quantity of students' learning and assess how well students function in groups.	Provide closure to the activity by summarizing major points or asking students to recall ideas.	Evaluate the quality and quantity of students' learning and discuss the competitive experience with them.

Qualitative Aspects of Motivation in the Classroom

Brophy (1987, p. 313) describes four types of strategies teachers can use for enhancing student motivation. **Task-exogenous, performance-focused strategies** stress offering incentives and rewards to students for successful performance. This strategy is an effective method for motivating students to perform. To minimize any undesirable effects of rewards, base the rewards on the quality of students' performance. Academic rewards can be powerful motivators (Chapter 12).

> Undesirable effects of rewards can be minimized by selecting academic rewards and stressing the quality of student performance.

The second type of strategy is **task-exogenous, value-focused strategies**. When teachers use these strategies, they are attempting to stimulate students to value an academic activity because the knowledge or skills acquired from the activity will be useful outside school and later in life.

Task-endogenous, performance-focused strategies, the third type of strategy, requires teachers to foster students' appreciation for learning and ability to apply what they have learned. Focus on concepts and labels to describe immediate learning outcomes, such as teaching them to think of a history assignment "in terms of 'understanding why slavery flourished in the South but not the North,' rather than 'studying history.'"

Motivation will increase if teachers help students take pride in being able to apply what they've learned.

The fourth type **is task-endogenous, value-focused strategies**. To use these strategies, teachers should attempt to increase student enjoyment of working on academic tasks. Brophy suggests metacognitive strategies are particularly relevant in using this approach. Teachers can enhance student motivation by helping their students learn, self-monitoring and other metacognitive skills discussed in Chapter 8. Class discussions, interesting material, and video presentations can be very interesting and motivating to students.

> Teachers should focus on specific concepts and immediate learning outcomes.

TECHNOLOGY IN THE CLASSROOM

As early as 1993, Alvestad and Wigfield suggested that student motivation can be accomplished through technology.

As many educators and psychologists have noted, some children are "intrinsically" motivated. These children do schoolwork by choice and for the sake of learning. Other children are extrinsically" motivated; they complete school tasks either because they have to or to get some type of reward.

Wondering how these two different groups of students are motivated in computer labs, these teachers compared a group of 5th grade mathematics students who worked in the school computer lab with a group who worked at home. The study showed that:

- Students who preferred challenging work achieved more than those who preferred easier work. They concluded that students who fail the difficult items can become debilitated, and may resort to daydreaming or even to deliberately making errors.

- Students motived by curiosity performed better than their counterparts who worked to please their teachers. Students who work to please their teachers are afraid of making errors and are likely to spend more time on each problem, run out of time, and end up scoring lower than their intrinsically-motivated counterparts.

- Intrinsically-motivated students don't need their teachers to confirm their success or failure. They feel more confident and are likely to work hard in their computer lab and persist until the problems are completed.

What are the implications of Alvestad and Wigfield's findings for motivating students in using technology?

S·U·R·F·I·N·G · T·H·E · W·E·B

Hats off to a remarkable program called the "Ask ERIC^{SM} Virtual Library" (**http://ericir.syr.edu/Virtual/**). In a partnership linking Syracuse University, the Department of Education, and Sun Microsystems, this virtual library features ERIC lesson plans for teachers. Also, the website at **http.//www.ed.gov/pubs/ TeachersGuide** is a teacher's guide to the Department of Education. ∎

RECAP OF MAJOR IDEAS

1. Classroom incentives are one of many factors that affect students' levels of motivation.

2. Students' levels of achievement can be enhanced by getting them to attribute their success or lack of success to their academic behavior.

3. The levels of achievement of students with high or low-achievement motivation can be influenced by beginning with easy tasks then assigning increasingly more difficult tasks.

4. According to Maslow's need theory, individuals' physiological needs must be met before their self-actualization needs can be satisfied.

5. Student motivation is often affected by factors outside the student's control.

6. Compared with competitive goal structures, cooperative goal structures increase achievement for more students and promote more positive attitudes and interpersonal skills development.

FURTHER APPLICATIONS

1. According to behavioral and cognitive theorists, negative factors in the classroom can contribute to student withdrawal, learned helplessness, and feelings of inadequacy. Additionally, students can become convinced they are academically inferior and cannot succeed because they have no "luck" or "teachers don't like them."

   List three factors in the classroom that could contribute to students' feelings of inferiority. List four teacher's actions that you think could contribute to students' feeling positive about themselves and their academic ability.

2. Consider the following:

Student	Problem
Renaldo—5th grade	Enjoys science to the exclusion of all other subjects. Only wants to study science and, as a result, earns superior grades in science and poor grades in other subjects.
Missy—7th grade	Is obsessed with making perfect grades. Constantly seeks teachers' approval, even on academic work she has been assured is outstanding.
Mark—2nd grade	Does not enjoy school. Cries and feigns illness in attempts to get to go home. Has high absentee rate.
Dewayne—11th grade	Disrupts class, is hostile and belligerent but very bright. Earns failing grades but is capable of doing much better. High probability of becoming a dropout.

Behavioral, and cognitive learning theorists suggest that motivation techniques are available to teachers who encounter such students. List one option that you would recommend to a teacher for each of the described students.

KEY TERMS

motivation
classroom incentives
behavioral approaches to motivation
extrinsic motivation
intrinsic motivation
cognitive approaches
attribution theory
locus of control
internal locus of control
external locus of control
learned helplessness
stability
controllability
achievement motivation theory
social cognitive approach
entity theory
incremental theory

performance goals
learning goals
mastery oriented
helplessness
Maslow's need theory
physiological needs
safety needs
knowledge and understanding needs
aesthetic needs
self-actualization
deficiency needs
being needs
links
ability-evaluative motivation
competitive goal structures
task mastery
individualistic goal structures

moral responsibility
cooperative goal structures
task-exogenous strategies

performance-focused strategies
task-endogenous strategies
value-focused strategies

LOOKING AHEAD

This chapter emphasized the importance of motivating students. Those who are unmotivated are rarely successful academically, whereas motivated students are typically the top performers, both academically and socially. How can prospective teachers and other school professionals maximize the likelihood students will be motivated? Additionally, what are the *proactive* alternatives for teachers to ensure a classroom of attentive, academically productive and socially adjusted students? Chapter 12 continues our discussion of these issues. ■

Chapter 12

Classroom Management

LEARNING OBJECTIVES

Upon completing this chapter, you should be able to:

1

List three characteristics of effective classroom management skills.

2

Explain two classroom management techniques teachers can proactively use to avoid classroom problems.

3

Explain how teachers can use *self-regulated learning* (SRL) strategies to facilitate students' disciplining themselves.

4

List three characteristics and advantages of *culturally responsive teaching* (CRT).

5

Define two strategies a teacher can use to involve students in selecting and implementing classroom rules.

6

Describe the four basic tenets of *student contracting*.

7

Define alternative ways with *ithiness*, overlapping, set induction, momentum, accountability, and proximity control can be used to enhance classroom management.

8

Explain the relationship of *time-on-task* and discipline problems in a classroom.

9

List three undesirable side effects of *corporal punishment*.

10

Relate two effective alternatives to *corporal punishment*.

INTRODUCTION

As a future teacher, how can you design your classroom environment to achieve the following:

- Your students learn and are successful, both academically and socially.

- Students stay on task and complete academic assignments.

- Students respect you, each other, and the racial, ethnic, and social differences among their classmates.

- Students feel safe and secure enough to freely express themselves, both socially and academically.

- You enjoy teaching and your students enjoy you as a teacher and the classroom environment you provide.

We suspect the overwhelming majority of our readers relish such a teaching environment. We ask the question because Educational Psychology research in **classroom management (CM)** offers proven options for maximizing the likelihood the above can be a reality in your classroom. We cannot overstress the importance of teacher skills in classroom management. As mentioned in Chapter 6, teachers can prevent certain behaviors by developing routines and arrangements (Landrum, Lingo, and Scott, 2011). Appropriate student behavior in the classroom is critical. If your students are disruptive, off task, disrespectful, and out of control, student learning, both socially and academically, will be compromised significantly if not impossible. As (Elias & Schwab, 2006) so perceptively stated:

> "Marzano' and Marzano's (2003) meta-analytic study suggests that classroom management is the single variable with the largest impact on student achievement. Why is that? Shouldn't the quality of math or language arts instruction make the biggest difference in terms of achievement? The most obvious reason for this influence is that effective classroom management sets the stage for learning. Without it, the classrooms are disorganized and chaotic, and very little academic learning can happen. Less obvious is that a teacher's classroom management practices are socializing influences on students. They communicate—subtly and not-so-subtly—messages about social norms and emotional behavior. Whether teachers are aware of it or not, students are constantly developing social and emotional skills (both good and bad) through modeling, experimentation, and reinforcement. Teachers' activities in the broad category called classroom management can help students develop healthy habits. However, they can also unintentionally encourage the learning of poor social and emotional skills."

Classroom management is defined as the ability of teachers and students to agree upon and carry forward a common framework for social and academic interactions, by creating an ethos of effort within a social fabric that is built over time, and ultimately leads to student self-discipline (Doyle, 1986; Rogers & Freiberg, 1994; Freiberg, 1999; Emmer & Stough, 2001).

We could not agree more with Elias and Schwab (2006) concerning the importance of teachers being capable of successfully managing their classrooms. Unfortunately, the assumption that beginning teachers, and even experienced teachers have sufficient classroom management skills is often incorrect.

> "Many beginning teachers express frustration and concern regarding their skills in the area of classroom management. They frequently comment about the lack of adequate classroom management coursework during their pre-service teacher education program, noting that what little information they received was too theoretical, too removed from their full-time field experiences. Perhaps, not surprisingly, over one-third of new teachers leave the profession by the end of third year of teaching, and many of these teachers list problems with student behavior as a significant factor influencing their decision to leave the profession" (Jones, 2006, p. 902).

Dr. Jones' statement implies that the inappropriate behavior of students and lack of teacher classroom management skills can have a devastating impact on the learning environment and on the most dedicated and well intended teachers. When the public and teachers are asked, 'What do you think are the biggest problems the schools of your community must deal with, 'lack of discipline' is topped only by 'lack of financial support' (Bushaw & Lopez, 2010). The above is unfortunate because educational research on classroom management provides a body of literature demonstrating successful classroom management techniques. Classroom management research, as early as the 1960s and 1970s include Kounin, Brophy, Doyle, and Glasser repeatedly demonstrated successful CM strategies. (Glasser 1969, 1990) was one of the first to provide very specific steps for teachers who face students who persistently violate rules. In 1977 he offered the following ten steps.

1. List typical teacher reactions to student disruptions.
2. Analyze the list and determine what techniques do and do not work and resolve not to repeat the latter.
3. With the disruptive student, improve your relationship by providing extra encouragement, asking the student to perform special errands, showing concern and reassuring that things will get better.
4. Focus attention on the students' disruptive behavior by requiring the students to accurately describe their inappropriate behavior. Once the behavior has been described, request that it stop.
5. If the disruptive behavior continues, call a brief conference and again have the student describe his or her behavior. Then have the student state whether the behavior is against the rules or expectations and ask what the student should be doing instead.

6. If necessary, repeat step 5. but this time ask the student to formulate a plan to resolve the problem. The plan must be more than a simple agreement to stop misbehaving. The plan must include commitment to positive actions designed to eliminate the problem.

7. If the problem still persists, isolate the student from class until he or she has devised a plan for ensuring that the rules will be followed in the future. Once approved, the student must make a commitment to follow it.

8. If this does not work, the next step is school suspension. Now the student must deal with the principal or someone other than the teacher, but this person will repeat earlier steps in the sequence and press the student to devise a plan that is acceptable. The student will either have to follow the reasonable rules in effect in the classroom or continue to be isolated outside of class.

9. If students remain out of control or do not comply with in-school suspension rules, their family is called to take them home for the day, and they assume in-school suspension the next day.

10. Students who do not respond to the previous steps are removed from school and referred to another agency.

During the 1970s Kounin (1970) identified teacher behaviors that could proactively prevent potential student behavioral problems. These teacher behaviors include:

- *Withitness*—The teacher is constantly aware of what is happening in all parts of the classroom by observing, moving about and having students work in small groups.

- *Overlapping*—Teacher is able to multi-task, such as using eye contact, and physical proximity (moving to area at the first sign of disruptive behavior) while continuing to teach.

- *Momentum during lessons*—Teacher is well prepared and lessons are briskly paced, providing students continuous academic stimuli more compelling than competing distractions.

- *Accountability during lessons*—Teacher lesson presentations include random questioning of students characterized by hesitation, looking about the classroom before calling on student to answer a question, interspersing student responses with class responses, requiring students to signal that they want to respond, and calling on students to comment on previous answers.

- *Challenge and variety of assignments*—Teacher provides varied, creative assignments at optimal levels of difficulty.

Glasser's, Kounin, and Doyle's contributions are provided to demonstrate the rich history of CM techniques and because application of their techniques have produced positive results on student behavior (Emmer & Stough, 2001; Brophy, 2006). The remainder of the chapter will focus on managing individual students and classrooms.

CONTEMPORARY CLASSROOM MANAGEMENT

Self-Regulated Learning

Student Study Guide

As our sidebar definition of classroom management implies, more recent classroom management techniques focus on student *self-regulation* and student *self-awareness*. As suggested by Glasser's ten steps, students can and should be taught to positively regulate and discipline their behavior and academic learning by focusing on self-discipline and self-regulation. If students can self-regulate, the classroom environment will be defined by appropriate academic and social behavior (McInerney & Van Etten, 2004; Mace, Belfiore, & Hutchinson, 2001). These internal student processes are defined as **self-regulated learning (SRL)**.

"Self-Regulated learning (SRL) refers to learning resulting from students' self-generated thoughts and behaviors that are systematically oriented toward the attainment of their learning goals . . . for example, attending to instruction, processing information, rehearsing and relating new learning to prior knowledge, believing that one is capable of learning and establishing productive social relationships and work environments" (Schunk, 2001).

(McCaslin et al., 2006) offers the following steps for establishing and supporting SRL.

1. Observe the student's behavior. Identify both the apparent needed skills and cause of the lack of SRL.

2. Make students aware of the problem and engage them as collaborators.

3. Work on students' internal dialogue. Teach them to replace "I don't care," or "I feel like giving up" with "I can learn this, if I try."

4. Students should be taught to proactively model feelings of "There I go, thinking I'm dumb. I need to think about what I need to do to get going on this . . ."; "There, I did try and it worked"; and "I did a good job on that".

5. Use rewards, if needed, to establish the initial behavior. Reinforcement should be linked to quality of performance.

6. Record proof of effectiveness.

More recent classroom management techniques emphasize managing the entire classroom while providing attention to individual students. Teachers may not be aware of all the variables involved in student behavior and learning. The teacher who sends students to the office because they disturbed class may not know that the students have not completed their homework assignments. Sending them to the office is teaching the students to disturb class whenever their homework has not been completed. Teaching self-discipline can be facilitated if teachers provide students with examples of desirable classroom behaviors and understandable reasons to engage in such behavior.

Culturally Responsive Teaching

Gay (2006) contends CM is more comprehensive than simply controlling student misbehavior. Because contemporary classrooms are now so diverse, current CM involves planning, facilitating and monitoring student learning experiences in the most diverse of classrooms. **Culturally Responsive Teaching (CRT)** blends such diversity with CM, providing alternatives for teachers. In planning classroom management, it is imperative classroom diversity be addressed as an important issue.

"Classroom management entails creating and sustaining classroom environments that are personally comfortable, racially and ethnically inclusive and intellectually stimulating." (Gay, 2006, p. 343).

Jones and Jones (2004) and Charles (1999) state that contemporary CM can be characterized by:

- Organizing physical spaces.
- Establishing student/teacher, student/student relationships through interaction.
- Planning and delivering instruction.
- Maintaining order and disciplining inappropriate behavior.
- Motivating students.
- Maximizing on-task learning.

Gay (2006) asserts, in addition to such characteristics, CM must be cognizant and inclusive of the diversity in today's classrooms. Weinstein et al. (2003) offers specific examples of how teachers can blend CRT with classroom management.

1. Become critically aware of personal cultural biases.
2. Become knowledgeable of the cultural heritages and ethnic diversity of their students.
3. Acquire an understanding of how the social, political and economic contexts of schools impact students.

4. Understand the academic and social importance of schools developing culturally responsive classroom management strategies.

5. Create a caring, learning classroom environment for all students.

CRT is not a simple task, but Gay (2006) offers the following advantages:

- Legitimizes the cultures and experiences of ethnically-diverse students.

- Contributes significant and accurate information about cultural diversity.

- Both teachers and students benefit through culturally-diverse curricula.

- Learning becomes an active, participatory endeavor, providing students personal meaning to academic content and learning.

- Promotes social justice and social transformation.

- Provides students comfort, skills and understanding of the cultural differences of home and school.

Summarizing, the primary goals of contemporary CM should include student self-regulation and recognition of student diversity. Student and teacher social and academic behaviors are the summation of the academic environment. Classroom management manifests itself in student learning, classroom behavior, in hallway conversations, on the school grounds, during home visits, in after-class conversations, and on field outings—whenever and wherever teachers and students interact, inside or outside the confines of the classroom. Appropriate, democratic management of these activities are essential for building the trust and confidence necessary for teachers and students to learn and assimilate academic and social information from each other.

> "If the classroom is a comfortable, caring, embracing, affirming, engaging, and facilitative place for students, then discipline is not likely to be much of an issue. It follows then that both classroom management and school achievement can be improved for students from different ethnic, racial, social, and linguistic backgrounds by ensuring that curriculum and instruction are culturally relevant and personally meaningful for them" (Gay 2006).

TODD WILLIAMS...

had arrived at the meeting a little early, and he was glad because the coffee was piping hot and the doughnuts were still warm. It was Tuesday evening, and Todd was attending the first in a series of what could be very interesting and relevant workshops. About a month before, Todd and his fellow teachers received an email with a survey explaining the agenda of the workshops.

The email announced that a series of sessions had been designed for the county's teachers. The workshops were voluntary. The survey was an attempt to elicit from teachers specific student problems they were having in their classrooms. The email and survey assured readers that the workshops would be very 'hands-on' and would address specific teachers' concerns noting that consultants and 'experts' from school systems and state universities would be involved. Each workshop would have structured discussions of the specific issues teachers listed in the survey, including the advice from the experts and input from participating teachers.

Todd thought the idea had merit and, in fact, was long overdue. He certainly had several issues he would like addressed by those who had been in the profession longer than he, and by the alleged experts. As he munched on warm doughnuts and sipped hot coffee, several fellow teachers filtered in. At precisely 7 o'clock the meeting began.

The experts included a panel of eight; members included a specialist in educational psychology, a school psychologist, a guidance counselor, a teacher in special education, and two peer teachers from the county and city. The meeting began with introductory remarks; "We're glad you're here," and "Be sure to sign up to get reimbursed for your travel expenses," and continued with an introduction of panel members and an explanation of the purpose of the meetings.

Each teacher was given a list of topics to be covered. The topics had been compiled from the surveys. Todd was pleased with the topics because they were practical and, in his opinion, dealt with the issues teachers encounter every day in their classes. Those issues included (1) promoting appropriate social and academic student behavior, (2) alternatives for managing inappropriate social and academic student behavior, (3) meeting the needs of exceptional students, and (4) enhancing social and interpersonal skills of students.

The meeting began with one of the panel members, acting as moderator, standing and announcing that the issues addressed during the workshop would be very specific to teachers' needs. She stressed there would be no platitudes, no generalizations, and no beating around the bush; the panel would, instead, be dealing with the hard, nitty-gritty problems of everyday teachers, like those present. They would begin with one of the more intriguing questions listed on the survey: A high school teacher had asked what he should have done when one of his ninth graders stood up in the middle of class, hit him in the rear with a piece of chalk, and proceeded to swear at him in the middle of a math quiz. This brought chuckles from the audience, and the meeting truly began.

> Schools mirror society. An increase in inappropriate behavior in society can be compared with an increase in school discipline problems.

Sometimes teachers and students see events differently, and differences in perceptions between teachers and students contribute to discipline problems (McCaslin & Good, 1996). For a reminder of the realities of teaching, compare the major classroom behavior concerns of today with those of 1986 and 1940 in Table 12.1. The concerns present a dramatic evolution of the generational changes in student behavior. For the last three generations, Americans have perceived discipline and drug abuse as the major problems in elementary and secondary schools (Bushaw & Lopez, 2010), the same problems as in society.

Teacher effectiveness rarely exceeds the teacher's ability to skillfully manage the academic and social climates of their classrooms. As stated earlier, CM skills are essential for effective instruction. The bottom line for teacher and student success; teachers must be proactive, facilitative, imaginative, cooperative classroom managers.

TABLE 12.1		
Major Classroom Behavior Concerns in 1940, 1986, and 2010		
1940	**1986**	**2010**
1. Talking	1. Use of drugs	1. Lack of financial support
2. Chewing gum	2. Lack of discipline	2. Lack of discipline
3. Making noise	3. Lack of financial support	3. Use of Drugs

'These were the top 3 discipline problems in public schools m 1940, 1986, and 2010.

Source: Johnston, W.J. (1985). *Education on Trial* (p. 20). San Francisco: 1(5 Press) and Phi Delta Kappa/Poll (2010).

Previous chapters have introduced many problems encountered by teachers. This chapter will go one step further and identify specific techniques teachers can use to address the academic and social problems they encounter. How can proactive teachers use the theories we have discussed in previous chapters to minimize and resolve real-disruptive classroom problems? We will look at the teacher's and student's role in creating a positive learning classroom environment. In the A View from the Field box, Dr. Jan Moore elaborates on teachers as effective classroom managers.

A VIEW FROM THE FIELD

A VIEW FROM THE FIELD

PROFILE

Dr. Jan Moore received her doctorate from Mississippi State University in Curriculum and Instruction. She is currently an associate professor at Eastern Kentucky University. She has 20 years experience in preparing and training pre-service teachers. Dr. Moore has taught courses in science methods, math methods, social studies methods, reading, classroom management, and educational foundation courses including undergraduate and graduate educational psychology. She strives to provide prospective teachers with an in-depth knowledge of the psychology of learning as well as skills to apply the concepts to their students. Dr. Moore

believes that competent teachers are aware of their students' developmental needs and expectations, and they make decisions accordingly to promote students' desire to learn.

1. QUESTION: What literature-based advice would you give to a new teacher wishing to establish a positive classroom environment?

Dr. Moore: As a new teacher, experience is lacking. So, my advice to a new teacher when deciding a strategy to create a positive classroom environment is to begin by analyzing and applying certain theories learned in your pre-service teacher preparation. For example, think of the three domains of development: cognitive, physical, and psychosocial. Ensure that students are physically comfortable in their environment. Try arranging desks and tables in a fashion where all students feel they can be seen and heard and have the attention of the teacher. The décor and literature on the walls should be uplifting, and rules and procedures stated in positive language. Students will perform better cognitively and behave more appropriately when they understand their teacher's expectations and their role in the learning process.

Finally, provide opportunities for students to work in groups that promote camaraderie by supporting learning efforts of all students, and teaching learners to accept and apply constructive criticism in the spirit intended. These are basic concepts that are not difficult to implement and should be of great assistance to beginning teachers. As you gain experience,

you will learn additional strategies that work best for you. Try new ideas to keep the environment interesting. Remember, the most important factor in creating and maintaining a positive, risk-free learning environment is you. Students will watch you closely and will follow your lead; therefore, check your attitude and disposition at the door and then proceed.

2. QUESTION: What steps can a teacher take to establish a climate ensuring fair treatment to all students?

Dr. Moore: Teachers who want to ensure fair treatment to all students must be willing to evaluate their classroom environment frequently, and must become cognizant of the common biases many teachers have but are unaware. Teachers may unknowingly treat students differently due to gender, race, religion, SES, and other attributions. Create a system of assigning students tasks, e.g., assisting the teacher with handing out supplies and being the leader of the line, so that all students have equal opportunities to participate in the classroom. Take time to become familiar with customs of students from diverse cultures. Accept that students have various learning preferences that may be influenced by culture.

Be consistent in how you reward and punish students. Have students keep a journal and, once a week, ask them what they enjoy most about class and what they would like to see changed. When addressing awkward topics, students may find it easier to be more forthcoming in journals.

Journal writing can be a valuable means for ensuring that all students have a voice. The most useful strategy for a new teacher is to be reflective and evaluate your classroom environment, often. Ask yourself, "Do all students have opportunity to participate?" Do I treat one or more students differently than others? If so, "how will I know?", and "Why?" "What can I do to ensure that all my students know they are valued?" ■

First-year teachers view classroom management and discipline as their greatest challenges.

INTASC Standard 3   Learning environments

The Teacher's Role in Classroom Management

Historically, teachers too often used a "hit-or-miss" approach to classroom management (Charles, 1989). Strategies used by teachers were often characterized by the use of force, punishment, and restraint. The following incident, in which Abraham Flexner, the father of modern medicine, recalls one of his early teaching experiences, reflects this early approach to discipline:

> "My first problem as a teacher was that of maintaining discipline among boys. . . . I recollect the fact that on the first or second day a boy by the name of Davis began an uproar in a beginning Latin class numbering about 50. I made a quick decision. I left the room and went to Professor [superintendent or principal] Kirby's office to ask his assistance in restoring order, promising if he helped me that I would never ask his aid again. . . . Entering the room, he raised his cane and with flashing eyes asked me to point out the culprit. When I pointed out Davis, he made for him . . . but taking discretion as the better part of valor, Davis made for an open window and jumped out. "Is there anyone else?" he asked.
> "No," I said. "The others will now behave themselves."
> (Manning, 1959)

Although this incident is antiquated and we do not recommend such classroom management techniques, it illustrates three important elements of classroom management. First, Flexner acknowledged the need teachers have for maintaining order in their classrooms. Second, discipline remains a major problem in our schools. The largest group of teachers in schools today has only one year of experience, compared with 15 years just 2 decades ago (Thornberg, 2010). As we have noted, studies of first-year teachers, indeed of all teachers, consistently reveal that discipline and classroom management are perceived to be one of the most difficult and problematic dimensions of classroom teaching (Emmer, 1994). Third, this incident is typical of how the potential involvement and cooperation of students are ignored. Unfortunately, instead of reinforcing desirable behavior, many teachers have depended on the use of punishment to deter unwanted behavior(Landrum, Lingo, & Scott, 2011.). In some states, corporal punishment is still a popular method of disciplining students in schools.

Research in CM suggests that today's prospective teachers can learn to "orchestrate smoothly operating classrooms," but success in achieving this goal requires preparation (Jones, 1996). As Phillips (1998) aptly remarked, "It is easier to predict and prevent than to react and repair."

Successful classroom managers prepare for classroom problems *before* they occur. Second, successful classroom managers have plans to *cope* with problems once they have occurred. Furthermore, the most successful classroom managers involve students when establishing rules to govern and/or manage the classroom. Finally, effective teachers plan and execute well-organized lessons. Typically, successful teachers spend most of their energy *preventing* problems as opposed to solving an endless litany of problems after they occur (Landrum, Lingo, & Scott, 2011).

Arrange your classroom to maximize communication with students.

Preventive Maintenance for Classroom Behavior Problems

Often teachers think they must choose between attending to students and attending to the lesson. To avoid this distracting sharing of attention and energy, the ideal approach is to get students to discipline themselves. This preventive approach to classroom management is based on two principles. First, emphasis must be placed on the student. Teachers should seek student input and then use their input to shape the classroom environment. Second, establishing a self-disciplining environment requires focusing on positive student behavior as opposed to negative or inappropriate student behavior (Emmer et al., 1989).

Setting Rules

Effective preventive management requires teachers to define and communicate social and behavioral expectations they hold for their students (Gathercoal, 1993). What may be interpreted as a serious breach of conduct in one classroom might not be considered an infraction in another teacher's room or by one student as compared to another. Therefore, clearly communicating expected social and academic student behaviors, preferably at the beginning of the school year, is essential. The following are guidelines for teachers beginning a dialogue with their students about classroom behavior and environment.

- Begin discussion with students during the first few class meetings.
- Keep list of rules short.
- State each rule simply.
- Include only those rules that you consider necessary. Be prepared to explain why each rule is needed.
- Focus on student behavior needed to achieve lesson goals.
- State consequences for breaking rules.
- State rewards for following rules.
- Make sure all class members have written access to the rules.

Although establishing rules is primarily the teacher's responsibility, students should be involved. Such involvement can motivate students to accept and abide by the rules. Involving students in the writing of policies addresses the roots of problems and the policies are more likely to be followed (Brasof, 2011). Begin by asking your students to identify behavior problems common in their classrooms. Ban (1994, p. 258) advises that you go further—"students should formulate a behavior statement or rule that deals with misbehavior." Such a system is based on the premise that the power of peer pressure can ensure students' compliance with the rules and is consistent with previously discussed SRL's goal of moving students from a state of imposed discipline to self-discipline.

> The best teachers spend more time preventing discipline problems than solving crises.

> Good disciplinarians have a few clear rules and communicate them to their students.

> Effective teachers are able to manage more than one class activity at a time and keep lessons moving at a brisk pace.

TECHNICAL TEACHING SKILLS

Because CM is so closely linked with instruction, and because 80 percent of all inappropriate behavior results from ineffective instruction (Phillips, 1998), we will review verbal and nonverbal skills teachers can use as they instruct.

Verbal Skills

Important teacher verbal skills for effective CM include **set induction, voice control**, and offering a variety of instructional methods shifting the level of teacher-dominated discussion.

Set Induction

Students often disrupt class because they do not understand the lesson. The beginning of each class period is crucial because this is the time when the foundation for understanding the rest of the lesson is established. Therefore, effective classroom managing teachers get the attention of students before proceeding into the lesson.

Techniques teachers use to get students' attention are collectively called *set induction* (Henson, 2011). Set induction can be accomplished in several ways. For example, teachers can begin lessons by telling high-interest stories related to the lesson (Henson, 2011). Teachers can use demonstrations to capture the interest of students. Teachers can simply wait until students settle down. We caution you against using this skill too often; students may learn that as long as they are noisy you will wait. Here's how one teacher effectively uses set induction.

> Jim Mosely's art students never knew what to expect on Mondays, other than it would be different than last week. To overcome the disruptions, the weekends bring to his classes, Mr. Mosely plans ways to recapture the students' attention on Monday mornings.
>
> Last Monday was typical. As students entered his class, they saw a large compressor, complete with a pressure control valve and a pressure gauge, sitting on his desk. They commented on the equipment, asking what it was and why it was on his desk. Jim did not respond. As the students began taking their seats and as the room began to fill, the discussions about the equipment grew. Only after the last student was seated did Jim offer an explanation. By this time, the suspense had every student waiting to hear his explanation.
>
> Jim reached into his desk drawer and, without saying a word, retrieved three brightly painted T-shirts. Pulling out an airbrush, he announced that today the class would begin a unit on airbrushing.

Jim Mosely had effectively used the skill of set induction to gain the attention of his students before beginning the lesson. Now he was ready to introduce principles of compression, air pressure, and painting.

Teachers tend to address most of their comments to high performers and fewest comments to low performers.

Voice Control

Verbal communication requires reception of vocal sounds, so teachers do not communicate verbally unless they are heard; thus sufficient volume is crucial. Unfortunately, many teachers find it difficult to overcome the noise pervading elementary and secondary classrooms. Physical limitations do present a problem for some teachers, but most can overcome noise issues by taking a few precautions.

Beginning teachers sometimes have a tendency to look only at the students in the front of the room, thus speaking only loudly enough for these students to hear. Furthermore, experienced teachers often direct most of their comments to the high-performing students (Good & Brophy, 1987, 1997), who tend to sit near the front of the room, so, again, teachers' comments are directed toward the front of the room. The result of these mistakes is teachers speak too softly for some of their students to hear their words. One obvious way to correct for this is to purposefully direct your comments to students in the back of the room, and ask students sitting farthest from you if they can hear. Often a simple rearrangement of student desks, such as placing them in semicircles, provides more access to students and to the teacher.

Another means of coping with volume-related problems is to reduce the interference. This may be as easy as closing a door or window, or it may be as complex as getting the attention of 30 or more students who have chosen talking over listening. Beginning teachers very quickly discover the difficulty of trying to shout over a classroom of disruptive students.

Varying Instructional Methods

Young students typically respond positively to stimulation and variety in the classroom curriculum. Developing a repertoire of instructional methods can lessen the level of teacher-dominated discussion, increasing student participation and verbal interactions. When proactively planning to avoid classroom problems, teachers have a choice. They can invest some time now and plan a variety of activities and alternatives into their lessons, or they can ignore the issue and pay later in terms of energy and time needed to subdue a room of disruptive students.

Ways teachers can plan variety into their lessons include using various instructional methods such as discussion, inquiry learning, questioning, simulations, lectures, games, and case studies. Student activities can be varied, including board work, individual and team projects, seatwork, discussion, role playing, guest speakers, and debates. A variety of media can also help, including TV, computers, CD players, smart phones, and PowerPoint presentations.

PowerPoint

Variety in lessons can help reduce discipline problems.

By keeping students "on task" teachers minimize discipline problems.

Nonverbal Skills

Nonverbal skills include managing *time-on-task* and using eye contact effectively.

TimeOn-task

An old adage states "Idle hands are the devil's workshop"; the adage could be changed to read, "An idle mind is the devil's workshop. "Students who are kept busy, both mentally and socially in constructive and challenging ways, do not cause as many disruptions as idle students. The difference in amount of time spent on instruction can vary extensively from one school to another. For example, Reinstein (1998) reported that one school where he taught provided 300 minutes of classroom instruction per week while another school where he taught provided only 200 minutes of instruction per week. A distinction should be made between assigned time and engaged time. For example, students could be assigned the last 15 minutes of the period to work math problems, yet they may actually stay engaged working the problems an average of 2 minutes; time-on-task should be the teacher's focus. Proactive classroom management requires, first, planning assigned time (here 15 minutes) and then supervising the engaged time to ensure students remain engaged on task for the duration of allotted time.

Eye Contact

Too often, when speaking, teachers focus their attention on their notes, board, or textbook, or they may look up toward the ceiling or to the side of the room to a window or wall. Direct eye contact with students communicates that the teacher is aware of their behavior and is interested in them.

One way to improve eye contact is to use fewer notes or substitute for the lesson plan a few very broad general statements. Another approach is to use PowerPoint. Unlike a chalkboard or flip chart, which forces the teacher to face away from the students, technology such as PowerPoint permits teachers to look directly at students throughout the lesson.

PROACTIVE EXERCISE

1. Perhaps the most common practice used by teachers to get initial classroom order is simply telling students in a loud voice to "be quiet," "settle down," and "take your seats"; however, this practice is seldom effective. An alternative is to speak softer in hopes students will ask their classmates to get quiet so they can hear. Another approach is to stand quietly and wait for the class to get quiet. Still another approach is **proximity control** or circulating among the noisy students. Think of the best teachers you've had in the past. Which of these methods did they use?

2. We have emphasized the need for clearly communicating behavioral expectations for students early in the year. Why is this necessary?

3. Reflect on your potential qualities as a teacher. What classroom management skills do you currently have that will be useful in the classroom? What uncertainties do you have about managing student behavior?

4. What are some student behaviors you find most distracting or disruptive? What student behaviors will you address in your classroom management plan?

The first part of this chapter emphasizes that effective teachers invest a substantial amount of energy in their efforts to proactively prevent classroom disruptions. Yet, the best preventive maintenance programs cannot ward off all student disruptions. Therefore, this part of the chapter will emphasize teacher management skills useful in addressing classroom disruptions. We will focus on strategies for solving immediate problems and alternatives to punishment.

SOLVING IMMEDIATE PROBLEMS

We again repeat a previous point worth remembering: teachers' time can be better spent on preventing problems than on solving problems. But there are times when teachers face disruptive situations occurring during class. Three approaches to solving classroom disruptions will be discussed: **silence, proximity control**, and **student conferences**.

Using Silence

On the average, teachers talk 75 percent of the class period (Goodlad, 1984). Although silence can be used effectively to discipline students, many teachers find using silence as a management technique very difficult. According to Dillon (1987), "It is the simplest yet the hardest to practice. . . . For many teachers, a period of silence seems to be awkward, perhaps wasteful."

Deliberate silence is difficult for teachers because most feel compelled to speak. This compulsion derives from a sense of responsibility, if not anxiety, for maintaining and directing classroom discourse. Consider the following example.

DeWayne brings to Ms. Thompson's sixth-grade homeroom numerous problems from home. He doesn't purposefully plan to cause trouble (although Ms. Thompson may question this position); it just happens. DeWayne's parents are going through a divorce. Ms. Thompson assigns daily homework, but DeWayne's home environment prevents him from completing these assignments. DeWayne lives with his mother and two sisters. His father is suing for custody.

Today's 8:30 period was a typical hour with DeWayne, whose attitude toward school, classmates, teacher, and himself was apparent. Without so much as a glance toward his teacher, DeWayne strolled to his chair and defiantly slammed his books down on his desk. His classmates have learned to give him space.

DeWayne immediately began his daily attempts to gain the attention of his peers. Ms. Thompson adjusts her routine, moving from behind her desk to gain an unobstructed view of DeWayne. He was predictable, and she didn't have a long wait. Rather indiscreetly, DeWayne began making a "psst" sound out of the corner of his mouth, attempting to get the attention of Teri sitting to his right. Ms. Thompson simply stopped talking and looked directly at him. The disruption momentarily stopped.

Once again Shirley had used silence to squelch a student's attempt to disrupt the lesson. But she knew that the results were only temporary. What other, more effective methods could she use to address DeWayne's behavior?

Proximity Control

Teacher nearness discourages disruptions.

The physical nearness (proximity) of a teacher to students can have considerable influence on student behavior. By moving closer to students, teachers communicate several messages. First, this says to students, "I'm standing close to you." Second, it says, "I don't dislike your company." Third, it says, "We have something in common." In fact, it communicates the positive message, "As your teacher, I want to work with you toward achieving the objectives of this class. In their book *Managing Secondary Classrooms*, Williams, Alley, and Henson (1999) stress the need to keep management systems positive. Let's return to Ms. Thompson, whom you'll recall we left in an unenviable situation realizing her attempts to address the disruptions of DeWayne were only temporary.

> As Ms. Thompson continued with the lesson, she continued to monitor classroom behavior, especially DeWayne's. The lesson underway, DeWayne's attempts to get the attention of his classmates resumed. As Ms. Thompson discussed fractions, without appearing to notice Billy's behavior, she slowly moved toward DeWayne until she stood near his desk. Once again, the unwanted behavior ceased. But, once again, Ms. Thompson knew her influence was temporary.

Ms. Shirley Thompson used a skill known as *proximity control*. She often uses this skill along with several other management techniques. With chronic discipline problems such as DeWayne's, proximity control should be paired with other teacher management options.

During conferences with disruptive students, teachers should remain firm yet calm, consistent, and positive.

Teacher-Student Conferences

Students, such as DeWayne, who are chronic disrupters of lessons and students who become violent in the classroom require different management strategies. For these students, a teacher/student/family conference is often a good alternative, and if the problem is persistent and serious the school counselor or other school professional should be present. The conduction of the conference is critical. The conference should never be used to attack the student; rather, it should focus on the student's behavior. The teacher should communicate a continued willingness to help the student make behavioral progress, but students must know they are responsible for their behavior. Glasser's ten steps offered at the beginning of the chapter provide a good outline and can be modified to fit specific student behavior, needs and family situation.

As a teacher, you have responsibility to provide a classroom climate conducive to learning. You, therefore, have a responsibility to prevent students from continually disrupting classroom learning. During conferences, teachers should remain firm and consistent, yet calm and positive. A good way to begin a conference might be "Denise, you're a nice young lady and I like you, but sometimes your behavior in class is way out of line and we need to talk about that. For example, . . . " For students like DeWayne, if teacher/student conference is ineffective, speak with school counselor, then if needed, a student/family/teacher/counselor conference.

PUNISHMENT AND DISCIPLINE

Another strategy used to solve discipline problems is punishment (Rich, 1989). **Punishment** is defined as the presentation of an aversive stimulus that weakens the behavior it follows (Skinner, 1953). Through the years, this approach has remained popular in American schools. Today many states prohibit the use of **corporal punishment** (punishment involving inflicting pain, such as slapping and spanking; Long & Frye, 1977). However, in twenty states corporal punishment is still legal and punishment has always been used extensively in American public and private schools.

Many educators contend that our educational system should not be characterized by aversive control (Johns & McNaughton, 1990) or making the school experience a determinant to a student's sense of self (Scott et al., 1996). Punishment and the threat of punishment often play a major role in the relationships of schools and the students they serve. Failing grades, spankings, detentions, threats, humiliations, and sarcasm all seem to mock the lament we have heard so many times from educators—"Won't they ever learn?" Many of our colleagues point out the adverse side effects (counter-aggression, social withdrawal, and anxiety) which can occur when punishment, especially corporal punishment, is used to control student behavior (Reis, 1988; Tauber, 1989). Millions of students have experienced our society's "educational process"; we challenge you to identify one who has escaped punishment.

"Common sense" would seem to indicate that student behavior leading to punishment would soon cease. However, early research (Azrin & Holz, 1966;

Corporal punishment has many negative side effects.

Dreikurs & Cassel, 1974) found that the subduing effects of punishment are often temporary. Therefore, the use of punishment cannot be defended on the grounds it will bring an end to disruptive student behavior.

The use of punishment in the classroom as the primary means of discipline is sufficient to elicit immediate protest and resistance by many educators. In many cases, such resistance is justified. Corporal punishment is administered to two hundred thousand students a year. However, many teachers are personally repulsed by the use of corporal punishment (slapping and spanking).

Following are several qualities deterring many teachers from using corporal punishment. Corporal punishment:

- Attacks the person, not the behavior.
- Addresses only undesirable behavior; it does not address desirable alternatives.
- Does not attempt to seek out the underlying cause(s) of inappropriate behavior.
- Can lower students' self-esteem, thus promoting further misbehavior.
- Can and at times does result in physical harm to student.
- Carries the subtle message that the best way to deal with life's problems is by using force.
- Is often used as a substitute for good planning.
- Corporal punishment establishes a barrier between teachers and students.
- Lowers other students' respect for the teacher and causes students to be fearful of teachers and school.
- Those teachers who use corporal punishment the most are apt to be the ones who have the least understanding of its ramifications.
- Perhaps most important, there are alternatives to corporal punishment that are more effective in reducing inappropriate behavior and do not have negative side effects.

> Locations for time out should be dull and isolated but free of frightening elements such as darkness.

Social Isolation

An alternative to corporal punishment for reducing inappropriate behavior is a procedure called **social isolation** or **time out**. Under this arrangement, the misbehaving student is removed for a short time from the environment where inappropriate behavior is being exhibited (Alberto & Troutman, 1986).

Social isolation should immediately follow the inappropriate behavior it is designed to weaken. The time-out space should be close to the regular classroom setting. Some teachers use a nearby coat room; others partition off a part of the regular classroom for a time-out space. Cold, damp, or dark rooms are to be avoided. The purpose of time out is not to frighten students. Likewise, cheerful TV, book, art and/or computer rooms are inappropriate. The isolation area is simply to be a dull space to locate a misbehaving student from whatever was reinforcing his or her disruptive behavior. Ideally, it should be an area where the student is visually and auditorily cut off from the reinforcing activities of the classroom. Otherwise, the student can still be reinforced for his disruptive behavior by what he/she sees and hears.

A student should take nothing, not even class material, to time out. Otherwise, time out may become a reinforcing activity, as in a computer or art room. For social isolation to be effective, a student need not stay isolated for long periods of time. (Walker et al., 2004) recommends one minute of time-out per year of age of student and should never be used for children younger than age 2. Usually the time needed for the student to settle down and begin to exhibit appropriate behavior, for example 6 minutes for a six-year-old, 10 minutes for a ten-year-old, is often sufficient for the teacher to reestablish a calm atmosphere in the classroom. Time out simply represents a way of minimizing the reinforcing effects of peer reactions on disruptive behavior (Corbett, 1990).

PROACTIVE EXERCISE

Suppose you accept a position at a school where corporal punishment is a primary strategy used to maintain classroom discipline. You may feel pressure from fellow teachers to use methods that you consider harmful. What kinds of actions can you use to persuade your colleagues to consider alternative approaches? What can you say or do to gain their support for using alternative strategies?

Response Cost

Another alternative to punishment is **response cost**, a reductive procedure consisting of the removal or withdrawal of reinforcers, contingent on a response (Sulzer-Azaroff & Mayer, 1991). Response cost differs from punishment in that punishment involves presenting an aversive stimulus contingent on a response, rather than withdrawing reinforcers as with response cost. For instance, a teacher may remove an elementary student's crayons from her desk, because of some misbehavior, such as throwing the crayons. For disruptive middle and high school students, a teacher may limit time with peers, sitting with peers in class or lunchroom or not allow student to attend the class party.

Within the school environment, typical response cost procedures are (1) removing points on a grade for unacceptable academic performance, (2) loss of class free time for disrupting class during a test, and (3) loss of privileges as part of a classroom management system (discussed later in chapter).

Research suggests response cost can reduce inappropriate student responses very effectively (Sullivan & O'Leary, 1990). Examples include aggression and classroom disruptions by elementary school students (Forman, 1980), and off-task and rule violations in classrooms (Rapport, Murphy, & Bailey, 1982).

The Proactive Teaching box discusses non-punitive measures for achieving appropriate student behavior.

PROACTIVE TEACHING

CLASSROOM SITUATION

Although you want a classroom atmosphere where student's enjoy learning and is characterized by well behaved students engaged in the learning process, you are realistic concerning discipline. You prefer a non-punitive, fair but effective approach to discipline.

PROACTIVE ALTERNATIVES

As we have discussed, there are CM techniques available to teachers who wish to be effective but non-punitive concerning student's inappropriate behavior. As part of your first discussion with your students concerning how class will be managed, be explicit about such issues as:

· Identifying behaviors of students that are not acceptable in class.

· What should and will happen when students misbehave.

· Identifying behaviors of students desired in class.

· What happens when students behave appropriately socially and academically.

Plan to discuss in detail with your students teacher responses to the above such as:

· Withdrawal of privileges (example: "Rob, you lose 5 minutes of free time for throwing chalk").

· Rewards for academic excellence (example: "Class party for all students who improve on their last math quiz.)

- Academic responsibilities (example: "Students who did not hand in their homework will be required to do so prior to extracurricular activities. Students who do hand in correct homework on time earn an extra five minutes free time").
- Student disciplinary limitations (example: "What happens if students continually misbehave? Should I write a note home to their families or send them to the office?").

Obviously, prior to classes beginning, you should talk with your school counselor, school psychologist, or administrator concerning school rules and disciplinary alternatives. Agreement between you and your students on how class will be managed can be very effective.

The first section of this chapter discussed skills that can be used to prevent behavioral problems in the classroom. The second section discussed skills useful in resolving present disruptions and behavioral problems. This next section will discuss strategies for shifting the responsibility for behavior to students through peer relationships and contingency contracting.

PEER RELATIONSHIPS

Peers play important roles in each other's behavior. Peers can serve as reinforcers by giving or withdrawing attention and approval. They also serve as models and a basis for social comparison (James & Egel, 1986; Strain & Fox, 1981). Often educators emphasize the relationship between teachers and students but overlook the importance of peer relationships. Peer relationships influence attitudes, values, and competencies of students and contribute to students' perceptions of their achievement. This is especially true for adolescents. Poor peer relationships during childhood can result in social misconduct and psychological problems during childhood, adolescence, and adulthood (Johnson et al., 1981). Peers can have a dramatic impact on problem behaviors. There is considerable evidence that using drugs, drinking, and sexual misconduct are related to peer influences and approval. The following are ways peer relationships can be used in CM.

Positive peer relationships are essential for socialization and achievement.

- Peer interaction can be used as reinforcers and/or rewards for appropriate social and academic behavior.

- Limiting peer interaction can be used to deter inappropriate social behavior.

- The consequences of appropriate and inappropriate peer relationships such as verbal interaction, bullying, teasing, friendship and 'clicks' can be directly addressed.

- Peer tutoring, or when one student assists another with academic tasks has been shown to benefit both participants (Good & Brophy, 1997). Therefore, tutoring can be used to enhance the academic, social and peer interaction of students.

Positive peer relationships can reduce social isolation and enhance social and academic competencies. Peer relationships can help students understand the perspectives of others.

PROACTIVE EXERCISE

Teachers should strive to promote constructive interactions between students.

Increasingly, teachers are being held accountable for the performance of their students on standardized tests (Henson, 2011). These conditions will require you to be effective in increasing the level of involvement of your students in their academic progress. Suppose you have students who are not keeping up with their classroom assignments. Suppose you have asked, "when will your assignment be completed?" and "what do you want to do?" but these questions get nowhere. What further non-punitive but effective measures can you take to motivate students to complete their assignments?

Positive peer relationships can enhance the social and academic success of students.

Rejection by Peers

Throughout school, peer pressure has significant influence on student behavior (Manning & Baruth, 1996). Students who perceive they are accepted by their peers are typically more willing to engage in classroom interactions and apply their academic abilities. Students who persistently feel rejected by their peers are often anxious, display more hostile behavior and tend to have negative attitudes toward school and other students (Brophy, 1985).

Teachers can foster peer relationships by promoting positive interactions between students during periods of class discussions, student interactions and controversy. Controversies occur when one student's ideas, attitudes, information, or conclusions are incompatible or disagree with those of other students. For example, Calvin, a student in Nadeen Frank's fourth-grade class, loudly announced he thinks that *The Adventures of Tom Sawyer* "is a stupid book" and he doesn't understand how anyone could enjoy it. Nat, a student who loves *Tom Sawyer*, responds "it's a great book" and he doesn't understand how Calvin can be so dumb.

Peer tutoring can produce positive results for both the tutor and the student being tutored.

Teachers can provide a cooperative climate for such controversies by requiring students to give accurate and complete information during disagreements and requiring each to listen. For example, Ms. Frank might give Calvin and Nat an opportunity to appropriately express their views on *Tom Sawyer* through critical essays, a debate, or oral presentations. One teacher we know would require Calvin to write five features of the book that he enjoyed, while requiring Nat to write five aspects of *Tom Sawyer* that he disliked. Calvin and Nat would then share their views in a discussion. Teachers should teach students to define controversies as problems to be jointly resolved by discussing their positions. Finally, teachers should foster the attitude among students that constructive disagreements can occur without attacks on each other's competence or values.

At this point you are probably thinking, "How can teachers plan their classrooms to be so precise and organized? After all, I will have 20 to 30 students in my class, and it will be difficult to praise, reinforce, ignore, be 'withit' while using peer tutoring." Can you suggest specific techniques that provide an 'umbrella' for a system of classroom management?

CONTINGENCY CONTRACTING

The development of a **contingency contract** system offers an efficient way to organize classroom proceedings (Jones & Jones, 1995). A classroom contingency contract is basically an agreement, preferably written, between teacher and students, as to how the classroom will be managed (Sulzer-Azaroff & Mayer, 1991). The word *contingency* implies that certain consequences will be dependent upon specified student behaviors both positive and negative.

> Contingency contracts should specify appropriate and inappropriate student behavior and describe the consequences of both types of behaviors.

When developing contingency contracts, students should be involved in the identification of appropriate and inappropriate behaviors and in identifying appropriate consequences to those behaviors.

The teacher is responsible for ensuring content in contracts is compatible with school policy.

Contracts can provide clear communication of teachers' expectations of their students.

Contracts should be administered on a voluntary basis. Individual students who oppose the contract option should not be forced to participate but are still required to complete academic assignments.

Contingency contracts usually provide three major types of information:

1. Specification of appropriate student behaviors.
2. Specification of inappropriate student behaviors.
3. Description of consequences for both appropriate and inappropriate behaviors.

Similar to self-regulated learning, discussed earlier in the chapter, a primary objective in developing a contract with students is to encourage students to monitor their own behavior (Carr & Ponzo, 1993; Cole, 1992); a secondary objective is to identify consequences for behavior having a productive effect on student academic performance and social behavior. The classroom contract should be the result of reasonable negotiations between the teacher and his/her student(s).

A first step might be to elicit students' agreement on what *they* perceive as appropriate and inappropriate behaviors and acceptable consequences for those behaviors. With young students, you might initially explain that you need their help in developing a good classroom. The discussion could be initiated by asking, "What are some things we could do to make this a really great class?" After fielding responses to this question, you might then ask, "What are some things students should not do while at school, things that could prevent us from having a good classroom?" A third question should be directed toward identifying reinforcing activities. You could explain to your students, "When students do good work, they sometimes earn special privileges. What kinds of special things would you like to earn for your good work and behavior at school?"

After each question, students' responses could be recorded on the board and evaluated by the class. Older students could be administered a brief questionnaire asking them to list behaviors they consider inappropriate, and activities they would like to engage in when they earn free time.

Although a classroom contingency contract should reflect students' recommendations, teacher ideas can and should be included. Students may make recommendations violating school regulations or are personally distasteful. For example, smoking or leaving school grounds might be listed as a high-priority activity by older students, but school regulations prohibit this behavior and you know such behaviors are harmful. Therefore, the tentative draft of contract can and should reflect both student and teacher input.

Explaining and discussing the contracting system to students is crucial to success. Once the contract has been finalized, discussed, and written, the teacher should answer questions from students (Figure 12.1). If you explain the purpose of contracting is rewarding appropriate academic and social behavior and the contract under consideration includes many of their recommendations, it is more likely students will perceive contracting as a worthwhile venture. In short, a primary objective of contracting is to make the classroom a more desirable academic and social situation for both the teacher and the students. A very important advantage of any contingency contract is the flexibility for changes and modification. Most likely there will be some classroom situations that both you and your students neglect in the initial development. For example, you and your students may have overlooked what happens when there's a substitute teacher, classroom visitors or field trips? We suggest a provision in the contract that provides time for updating and/or revisions. You might do this every Friday or when a classroom issue occurs' requiring discussion.

Learning theorists insist students enter any contract agreement voluntarily. Some students may not want to enter a contract agreement. Explain to such students they are still responsible for all class assignments but will not be privy to rewards defined in the contract. Often these students choose to enter the contract agreement during some period of the contract and should be allowed to do so.

Classroom contracts can be designed for an entire class, as illustrated in Figure 12.1, or for individual students, as illustrated in Figures 12.2 and 12.3. Figure 12.2 was designed for a fourth-grade student who was habitually late for class, typically did not come prepared with books and academic materials, and did not complete homework assignments. The contract shown in Figure 12.3 was designed for an eighth-grade student who was habitually truant from school and was failing academically.

Figure 12.1 Class Contingency Contract

I. Being Prepared for Class

   A. Attending class earns 2 points (To earn the 2 points you must be in class on time and in your seat when the class bell rings.)

   B. Bringing need school supplies (pencil, paper, and books) earns 2 points. Bonus: For not missing a day of class for an entire grading period (6 to 9 weeks)-14 points

II. Homework

   A. Homework completed

      1. 90–100% accurate—5 points

      2. 80–89% accurate—4 points

      3. 70–79% accurate—3 points

      4. 60–69% accurate—1 point

   B. Correcting Homework - After homework has been graded, you may correct errors and resubmit; if 100% correct—3 points

III. Class Work

   A. Finishing a daily learning activity in required time

      1. 90–100% accurate—10 points

      2. 80–89% accurate—7 points

(Continued)

Figure 12.1 Class Contingency Contract (Continued)

      3. 70–79% accurate—5 points

      4. 60–69% accurate—3 points

  B. Correcting learning activities - After learning activities have been graded, you may correct errors and resubmit; if 100% correct-4 points

  C. Weekly quizzes (given on Friday, made up of material covered that week in class)

      1. 90–100% accurate—20 points

      2. 80–89% accurate—15 points

      3. 70–79% accurate—10 points

      4. 60–69% accurate—5 points

  D. Unit exams given at the end of a grading period (usually six to nine weeks)

      1. 90–100% accurate—50 points

      2. 80–89% accurate—40 points

      3. 70–79% accurate—30 points

      4. 60–69% accurate—20 points

  E. Bonus class activities

  (There are numerous other ways to earn points in class.)

- Oral presentations: Choose a topic that relates to class material, research the topic, and present findings orally to class: 20 points

- Book report: A book report on a specified topic: 20 points

- Other creative academic activities such as:

      A. science or computer projects

      B. leading a class discussion

      C. art forms

      D. field projects or trips

IV. *Grades*

- Grades will be determined by the number of points achieved during the grading period (usually six to nine weeks).

  A = 350 to 450 points

  B = 250 to 349 points

  C = 150 to 249 points

D = 100 to 149 points

F = less than 100 points

- Points for grades should be modified for potential of students to earn points.

V. *Appropriate Behavior*

Every class member will earn an extra 10 minutes of free time for the following instances of appropriate class behavior:

A. When the class has visitors such as family member(s), teachers, or principal

B. During assembly

C. In the halls while leaving or entering school as a class

D. In the lunchroom

VI. *Inappropriate Behavior*

Class members will have to pay for the following behaviors:

A. Hitting others, throwing objects, absent without permission, off current academic assignment, loud talking or out of seat while the teacher is instructing: cost 10 points

B. Tardy, eating without permission, profanity and interrupting teacher vocally (does not include raising hand)-cost 6 points

C. Borrowing pencil, paper, or books; arguing: cost 4 points

After a student has been penalized three times (losing 25 points) during a school day (or class period) he/she will be sent to the assistant principal for the rest of the day (or class period). If a student receives eight penalties (losing 60 points) in class during a week, his or her family will be notified describing the student's misbehavior.

VII. *Report Card Grades* * *

A. Report card A's earns 75 points each.

B. Report card B's earns 50 points each.

C. Every C on your report card earns 25 points.

D. Report card D's earns 0 points.

E. Report card F's costs 50 points.

VIII. Privileges

In addition to grades, honors activities can be earned and will be based on points earned.

(Suggestions for honors activities are outlined in Chapter 6.)

(Continued)

> CM does not have to be as involved as Figure 12.1 example. Consider the following Case Study based on the experiences of an eighth grade teacher and friend.

Figure 12.1 Class Contingency Contract (Continued)

As your teacher, I agree to help you with your tasks and award grades and privileges according to the specifications of this contract.

*Consult with the teacher for guidelines on these projects.

**Report card points can be exchanged for free time and special privileges, as outlined in contract.

***Every Friday at 2:00 p.m., the contents of this contract will be discussed by students and teacher. At this time, new ideas and suggestions will be considered and agreed changes in the contract will be made to fit the needs of our class.

CASE STUDY

Ms. Batton had been teaching sixth grade for seven years and prided herself on maintaining a well-behaved, academically productive class but this group was different. She found herself spending an inordinate amount of time maintaining order. This group was talkative, loud, disruptive, and off task more than any class she had taught to date. At the beginning of the third week of class, Ms. Batton came up with a very simple but clever idea. At the beginning of class on a Monday morning, she wrote the number 15 on the board without explanation.

Class began and had not been going on very long when LaBron loudly interrupted as she was teaching. Without comment, Ms. Batton went to the board, erased the 15 and replaced it with 14. A student asked, "What's the 14 for?" Ms. Batton responded, "I was going to add 15 minutes of free time to the end of the day but since LaBron interrupted class we now have time for only 14 minutes. Ms. Spencer had to immediately replace the 14 with a 13 because Chris, sitting next to LaBron, punched LaBron on the shoulder. Later in the morning Ms. Batton replaced the 13 with 14. When asked why by a student she responded, "Because everyone is quietly working on our math assignment."

Over time, the number on the board was increased and decreased for a variety of different reasons. A minute was added because all students were in their seats when the bell rang, when an hour passed without disruptive behavior, 3 minutes was added for thirty minutes of group work without disruptive behavior, 5 minutes was added because the class behaved when there were class visitors. Minutes were deducted for talking out of turn, walking about without permission and whispering when Ms. Batton was teaching.

Ms. Batton reported, the time she saved in class from diminished interruptions greatly exceeded the rewarded free time. Often very simple CM techniques can be very effective.

Contracting between Students/Families/Teachers

Contracting techniques also can be used in situations involving families of students. Williams, Alley, and Henson (1999) advise teachers to involve families in CM programs. Scott et al. (1996) found it is crucial that both family and school be involved in helping students build self-esteem. Often family members of students ask teachers how they can foster and improve the academic and social behavior of their children. If such students are doing well in class and behaving themselves, the answer might be, "They are doing just fine; just continue what you're doing." However, if the student is having problems in school, such as behaving inappropriately or falling behind academically, a solution might be setting up a **home family-student contract** designed to address the needs of the student. The contract for home can be similar to the contracts discussed. Figure 12.4 is an example of a contract for a 10-year-old boy, and includes the activities, behaviors, and consequences; the number of points in each category, rewards that can be earned, and number of points required to earn each reward.

Home contracts are typically agreements between families and students involving achievement of goals or specification of behavior expected in the school environment. The effectiveness of family/son or daughter contracts has been demonstrated (Kazdin, 1985; Price & Marsh, 1985).

Effective home-based contracts are characterized by the following:

- Families, teacher, and student agree on the behaviors expected and on how the recording of behavior is to be determined.

- Families, teacher and student agree to the contingencies laid out in the contract as to academic or social tasks and how rewards are earned and administered. Also, a clear explanation of the level of academic and/or social performance of behaviors in question should be agreed upon.

- A method for modifying existing contract should be an integral part of the initial agreement. At least once per week, contract should be discussed by families, student and perhaps teacher as to effectiveness, modifications for improvement, and determination of points and rewards earned.

> Contracting can also involve agreements between students, student's families, and teachers.

Figure 12.2 Official Contract

TERMS OF CONTRACT

1. (Student name) will be in her seat when the 8: 15 a.m. bell rings. (5 points)

2. (Student name) will bring to class school supplies (paper, pencil or pen, and textbooks). (5 points)

(Continued)

Figure 12.2 Official Contract (*Continued*)

3. (Student name) will complete homework assignments—90% and above correct—and submit each day. (25 points per assignment)

4. (Student name) will ask permission to talk or leave seat by raising her hand. (10 points per hour)

REWARDS EARNED BY POINTS

25 points = 10 minutes free time:

50 points = Teacher assistant for one day

75 point = 15 minutes to TEXT friends

100 points = Work on computer for 20 minutes
Free time use:

- Read book from library or work on homework.
- Listen to music or use iPad
- Use computer for 15 minutes
- Choice of seat in class

Figure 12.3 Classroom Contract for Theo

METHODS FOR EARNING POINTS

By attending all classes at school each day and being on time to all classes, you can earn 5 points/day.

For each and every paper you bring home with a grade of 80 through 89, you earn 20 points.

For each and every paper you bring home with a grade of 90 or above, you earn 40 points.

For each and every paper you bring home that has a C grade, you earn 10 points; a B grade earns 20 points; and an A grade earns 40 points.

For each A you make on your report card, you earn 80 points.

For each B you make on your report card, you earn 50 points.

For each C you make on your report card, you earn 25 points.

No points are earned for D grades.

For each day you bring home your homework assignments (written), you earn 5 points. For each day you complete your homework assignments, you earn 20 points.

For a report card that has no F grades, you earn 500 points.

For a report card that has all A, B, and C grades, you earn 1000 points.

LOSING POINTS

For each F you make on your report card, you lose 100 points.

If you skip class or miss school without an excuse, you lose 300 points.

If a family member has to go to school to speak with the principal, your counselor, or your teacher about any "school disturbance" you are involved in, you lose 500 points.

PRIZES THAT CAN BE EARNED AS CHOSEN BY THEO

Prize	Point Value
Book of choice	400 points
Poster of choice	400 points
CD of choice	600 points
Friend overnight	800 points

> Home contracts should include extra rewards; privileges the student does not normally have.

The effectiveness and ultimate success of any home-based contract will depend on the willingness of the student's family to *follow through* on the contract, despite efforts on their son or daughter's to thwart, or abridge, the contract. Rewards earned by student should be extra; any privileges they have been privy to in the past should not be taken away and then earned as part of the contract system. The example contract (Figure 12.4, p. 435) for families was designed for a young person having difficulty with study habits and science.

Summarizing, the following are basic rules for implementing classroom contracts.

1. The contract payoff (rewards earned) should be immediate. This rule follows what has been stated as one of the essential elements of an effective reinforce and should be administered immediately upon performance of the target behavior.

2. Initial contracts should call for and reward small approximations. This form of *successive approximations-that* is, progressive steps toward the target behavior-is particularly useful for behaviors the

Involving families with the social and academic behavior of students can be accomplished with family-student-teacher contracting.

student has never performed before. A criterion level set too high, or a behavior category that is too broad (such as "clean your room") is not useful. A better alternative might be, "First, pick up all toys, books, and games from the floor and place them on shelves. Second, vacuum the floor. Third, make your bed. And, fourth, water plants."

3. Reward frequently with small amounts. Frequent delivery of reinforcement allows for closer monitoring of behavior change in progress by both teacher and student.

4. The contract should call for and reward accomplishment rather than obedience. Contracts that focus on accomplishments lead to independence. Therefore, appropriate wording is "If you accomplish . . . , you will earn . . . " as opposed to "If you do what I tell you to do, I will reward you with . . . "

5. Reward performance after it occurs. This rule restates an essential element of a reinforcer: It must be administered contingently. Inexperienced teachers sometimes state contingencies such as "If you get to go on the field trip today, you must complete all your homework next week." Teachers are usually disappointed with the outcomes of such statements.

6. The contract must be fair. The "weight" of the reinforcement should be in proportion to the amount of behavior required. The ratio set up in the contract should be fair to both the teacher and the student. Asking the student to finish 2 out of 20 problems correctly for 30 minutes free time is just as unfair as requiring students to correctly work 20 out of 20 problems to earn 2 minutes of free time.

7. The terms of the contract must be clear. Ambiguity causes disagreement and confusion. If the teacher and the student do not agree on the meaning of some item in contract, then teacher and student should communicate until meaning is clear.

8. The contract must be honest. An honest contract is one that is (a) "carried out immediately, and (b) carried out according to terms specified."

9. The contract must be positive.
   APPROPRIATE:
   "I will do _, if you do _."
   INAPPROPRIATE:
   "I will not do _, if you do _." "If you do not _, then I will_."
   "If you do not _, then I will not _."

home contract

POINT CHART

Task	Pts.	Mon.	Tues.	Wed.	Thurs.	Fri.	Sat.	Sun.
Has homework assignment requirements in writing	5							
Complete homework before 7.30 P.M.	5							
Completes homework at room desk	5							
Completes science homework 90% or above correct	10							
Receives B paper (any subject)	5							
Receives B paper (science)	10							
Receives A paper (any subject)	10							
Receives A paper (science)	20							
Is in bed by 11:00 P.M. (12:30 A.M on Fri. and Sat.)	5							
Extra								

PAYOFF

5 points: 1 hour of basketball _____

5 points: 1 hour with friends at pool _____

5 points: 1 hour of TV _____

10 points: Stay up 1/2 hour extra _____

15 points: Attend basketball or football game _____

20 points: Have friend stay overnight, or visit friend overnight _____

25 points: $2.00 to spend _____

Parents or Guardian's signature _____

Student's signature _____

Figure 12.4 Home Contract for Student and Parents

10. Contracting should be viewed as a method of enhancing the social and academic behavior of students. However, the primary goal of any CM methodology should be student-regulated learning and social behavior. Success of any CM methodology should be realized when students learn and behave for enjoyment of learning, good grades, and honors bestowed for such.

The Proactive Teaching box demonstrates steps you can take for establishing an effective contract with your class.

PROACTIVE TEACHING

CLASSROOM SITUATION

The first week of class you want to establish a classroom environment that promotes academic productivity and appropriate student behavior. Additionally, you want your students to become self-reliant, enjoy learning, and develop confidence in their abilities.

PROACTIVE ALTERNATIVES

Prepare to spend considerable time discussing with and getting input from your students about the kind of classroom you want to establish for you and your students.

· Prior to discussion with students, identify the academic and social behavior you want your students to exhibit. This should be in the form of a list that very specifically describes appropriate academic and social behavior.

Examples might include:

    a. Turning in classwork and homework on time

    b. Being on time for class (in seat when bell rings)

    c. Behaving when class has visitors

    d. Raising hand when needing assistance

Very specific goals provide clarity for both teacher and students and can serve as a starting point in discussions with your students.

· Identify numerous academic activities that you feel students would enjoy. Such activities as field trips, educational videos, guest speakers, class discussions, activities, parties, and free time can be suggested to students as reinforcing activities and can serve as prompts for their input.

· Identify problem-solving and creative academic tasks that serve to enhance cognitive skills.

Examples might include:

a. Debates

b. Simulation software (Chapter 9)

c. Oral presentations

d. Creative writing, storytelling (fiction, poetry, and critical analysis)

Give students the opportunity to add to your list. Often students have interests and talents for special projects, experiments, discussions, and papers.

TECHNOLOGY IN THE CLASSROOM

As a future proactive teacher, we trust you have been preparing and have given thought to the computer skills you will need as a teacher. Examine the following axioms (Henson, 2011), which addresses the computer knowledge you will need as a teaching professional.

- *Axiom 1: There is a definable body of computer knowledge that is indispensable for teachers.* Although the need for computer skills vary depending on subject matter taught, there are certain basic skills almost all teachers need. If you are lacking skills in word processing, Internet use and familiarity with such as smart phones, you should consider computer workshops for teachers.

- *Axiom 2: The computer needs of teachers vary, depending on subject content.* Some individuals have a natural aptitude for technology. You will notice among your future students, even younger elementary students, some with considerable computer skills. Teachers should encourage students who demonstrate such skills.

- *Axiom 3: Teachers should learn to operate the technology available in their schools.* As teachers begin preparing for their future technical responsibilities, one of the first questions is, "Once you learn to operate one system, can such skills transfer to other systems?" Usually, it is easier to learn other systems but do expect to spend considerable time learning any new computer system.

- *Axiom 4: An important criterion for selecting technology is intended use of the technology.* Two questions should be foremost in your mind as you begin the process of selecting technology. "What can I do with this technology that will assist in my teaching?" Also, "What is the quality of software the system offers?" Software limitations can place serious restrictions on the technology's ability to enhance classroom instruction.

- *Axiom 5: Teachers should use computers for the attainment of higher-order learning skills.* Many educational software programs require analysis, synthesis, and problem solving, and in doing so can help students develop problem-solving skills.

- *Axiom 6: Technology can be used to enhance learning in their classrooms.*

View technology as another tool you can use to help students attain course objectives.

- *Axiom 7: A proactive posture is essential for teacher success with technology.* Confidence is important in learning to use technology. Once you learn and understand the potential of educational technology, you'll probably find your concerns replaced by enthusiasm and interest. ■

S U R F I N G • T H E • W E B

Within the website Helping Your Child (**http://www.ed.gov/pubs/parents.html**) are the pamphlets "Helping Your Child Get Ready for School" and "Helping Your Child Improve in Test Taking." Also, we would like to mention the following as an example of "management" on the Web. Fed World (**http.//www. fedworld.gov**) boasts a site that is a gateway of in formation for numerous federal agencies.

Also **http://seab.envmed.rochester.edu/jaba/** is the site address for the Journal of Applied Behavior Analysis, a respected psychological journal, offering substantive articles on CM. ■

RECAP OF MAJOR IDEAS

1. When students are involved in making decisions about class rules, they tend to behave more responsibly, are self-motivated, and are more motivated to learn.

2. Although corporal punishment has many serious limitations and negative side effects, it continues to be widely used in American schools.

3. Effective classroom managers spend most of their time preventing discipline problems, not solving them.

4. Culturally Responsive Teaching (CRT) and Student-Regulated Learning (SRL) offer many advantages when designing any CM plan.

5. Effective teachers display withitness (an awareness of events throughout the classroom), overlapping (the ability to deal with several things at once), and proximity control (moving to potential problem areas), and they keep lesson momentum at a brisk pace.

6. Teachers should begin lessons when all students are attentive.

7. Teachers tend to address most of their comments to high-performing and most disruptive students.

8. The time assigned to study a topic affects level of mastery much less than time students actually spend on the subject (engaged time).

9. Student/teacher and student/teacher/family conferences can be effective if they focus on the behavior of student.

10. An important function of proactive classroom management is to teach students to discipline themselves.

11. Contingency contracting can provide the framework for systematic classroom management, both in classes and with parents.

FURTHER APPLICATIONS

1. Interview two elementary students, two junior high or middle school students, and two senior high students. Ask them what they perceive as the best and worst elements of their school. Compare the lists.

2. In two separate schools, interview a teacher who teaches at your preferred level. Ask how the teachers maintain discipline in their classrooms. Compare their techniques.

3. Read two or more recent articles on corporal punishment and make a list of its advantages and disadvantages. Next, interview two teachers who use corporal punishment, interview two who do not, and make a list of their reasons for using and not using this practice. Compare the two lists.

4. For further information on classroom management, see one of the author's new book, Methods for Teaching in Diverse Secondary and Middle Classrooms by Kenneth T. Henson: Dubuque, IA: Kendall Hunt, 2012.

KEY TERMS

classroom management

withitness

overlapping

set induction

volume

variety

nonverbal skills

time on task

assigned time

engaged time

proximity control

student regulated learning

culturally responsive teaching

punishment

time out

response cost

controversies

peer-tutoring

classroom contingency contracts

individual student contracts

family/teacher/student contracts

LOOKING AHEAD

This chapter examined the teacher's, student's and families' roles in classroom management. Chapter 13 addresses the grading and assessment of students and the use of standardized tests in the classroom environment. ■

Part 6

Grading and Assessing Student Performance

439

Chapter 13

Statistics and Evaluation in the Classroom

LEARNING OBJECTIVES

Upon completing this chapter, you should be able to:

1

Recognize graphs and tables purposefully designed to mislead the reader.

2

Develop a frequency polygon representing the performance of a class of students.

3

Name the three most commonly used measures of central tendency, and explain why the preferred measure of central tendency representing a set of data varies according to the data being interpreted.

4

Differentiate between measures of central tendency and measures of variability.

5

Define *normal curve*, and state conditions necessary to make it appropriate for classroom use.

6

Explain how the concept of *cause and effect* relates to correlations.

7

Compare and contrast various evaluation techniques available to classroom teachers.

INTRODUCTION

Critical to the role of proactive teaching is understanding basic educational research and statistics. **Statistics** are merely tools allowing teachers to describe a wide variety of characteristics of students, teachers, and schools; they help us develop and provide support for data gathering and evaluation.

Teachers' and students' attitudes toward statistics contain a mixture of understanding, awe, cynicism, suspicion, and contempt. The lack of understanding of statistics is unfortunate because, when used appropriately, statistics are essential to teachers in evaluating themselves and their students. Understanding statistics allows educators to make data-based decisions.

Statistics serve many valuable functions for teachers. They help teachers describe the many variables that are part of our profession, for example, student achievement. Statistics help teachers compare attributes or characteristics of students. They enable teachers to develop hypotheses, or tentative propositions, about the many problems in education. Statistics help teachers read and understand research articles related to the profession, and they can enable teachers to conduct their own research. Statistics allow us to be better informed citizens by evaluating the evidence news reporters, politicians, and advertisers use to support their claims, conclusions, and points of view. Finally, statistics help us communicate more honestly and accurately by providing quantitative evidence of student and teacher performance.

This chapter discusses the role of statistics in educational psychology. Methods of presenting data in tables and graphs are reviewed. Descriptive statistics, as related to the classroom, are explained.

> **INTASC Standard 6**   Assessment
>
> This entire chapter addresses INTASC Standard 6–Assessment.

STATISTICS AND TEACHER-CONDUCTED RESEARCH

Amy Brown, a fourth-grade teacher, is interested in how her students performed on their math quiz. She computes the average score and is surprised when it turns out to be 80 out of 100 points. "I thought most of my students made A's on the quiz," she says to herself. "Have I made a mistake in computing the average?" But, after re-computing the class average, she derives the same value.

Derrick Michaels is sitting in the teachers' lounge looking through the stack of journals. An article about a new reading program for first-grade students catches his interest. He comes across reports of correlations in the *Results* section of the article. "Ah, I understand this," he says to himself. "Correlations indicate relationships."

Trey Lang is worried about his fourth-period class at Jonesboro High School. It appears that his students spend most of their time talking to one another, instead of listening. He doesn't have this problem with other classes. "Maybe it's just me," he thinks. "Maybe I'm tired by fourth period and I just think this class is rowdy. How can I determine whether this class is as well behaved as my others?"

Angel Ramirez is the lead teacher in special education at King Middle School. She has been asked by the school district's coordinator of special education to determine whether a new math program for students with mental disabilities is as effective as the one currently used. Angel knows she probably should divide the students in her school into two groups and have one group participate in the new program and the other group participate in the current program. But, she doesn't know how to determine which students should be in each group or how to determine if the new program is as good as the old one.

What these teachers have in common is each can benefit from a better understanding of statistics. As you read this chapter, review the examples of Amy Brown, Derrick Michaels, Trey Lang, and Angel Ramirez, and consider how the information provided in each section will help them with their problems and with classroom problems you might encounter.

As early as 1980s, educators began to realize contemporary teaching often requires considerable research and statistical competence. The age-old practice of teachers being only the transporters of knowledge to pass on to their students would no longer be sufficient. Staying current and understanding today's professional responsibilities require teachers to understand educational research and statistics. As seen in an earlier chapter, the benefits of teacher-generated research are many and spill over to students who may become partners in classroom research. Through involvement with research projects, both teachers and students can develop a deeper understanding of their performance, learning environment and the tools needed for research and evaluation.

Supplementing this realization was a movement called **constructivism** (described in Chapter Ten).

"According to constructivist views, when presented with new information, individuals use their existing prior knowledge to help make sense of the new material" (King & Rosenshine, 1993, p. 127).

Believing students often understand better through generating their own knowledge, many educators began searching for ways to transition to more student-generated data and information. Some teachers began to respond to these concerns by learning how to conduct elementary studies in their classrooms. Because teachers are the essential determiners of achievement in their classrooms (Good & Brophy, 1887; Chimes & Schmidt, 1990; Bellon, Bellon & Blank, 1992; Gay, Mills, & Airasian, 2009; McMillan, 2012), we encourage teachers to conduct studies in their classrooms. As defined by McLaughlin, Hall, Earle, Miller, and Wheeler (1995), "**Action research** is a method for teachers to gather information about what is happening in their classrooms and throughout their school, and then to take action based on their analysis of that information" (p. 7).

Teacher-conducted research has many benefits. It has the obvious practical value of enabling teachers to find answers to nagging classroom problems. Through conducting their own studies, teachers become empowered with a sense of mission or purpose (Marriott, 1990) and a feeling of expertise (McMillan, 2012).

Involvement in research studies can have a positive effect on teachers. Sucher (1990) said that teachers find it 'invigorating'; and Chattin-McNichols and Loeffler (1989) called it 'mentally refreshing'. Teachers who conduct research often alter their attitudes toward the permanency of knowledge and learn to view knowledge as subject to change. As a result, researching teachers become lifelong learners (Boyer, 1990; Brownlie, 1990), better decision makers (McMillan, 2012), less defensive, more open, and more confident (Neilsen, 1990). Additionally, teachers who conduct research become more analytical (Goswami & Stillman, 1987; Neilsen, 1990), improve their educational practices (McMillan, 2012), and develop critical thinking and evaluation skills (McMillan, 2012).

However, the benefits from involvement in classroom research accrue only when teachers are involved either as the sole researcher or as a partner in the study—that is, in **identifying the problem, intepreting data**, and **drawing conclusions**. Partnerships can

Statistics help teachers communicate accurately about student performance by providing quantitative evidence.

develop among teachers or between teachers and other professionals (Henson, 1996; McMillan, 2012). Many contemporary teachers have extended these benefits to their students by involving them as partners in classroom research projects.

TABLING AND GRAPHING DATA

Teachers are confronted with the task of data manipulation on a daily basis. Whether it is reporting attendance, grading assignments, recording grades, or interpreting standardized test scores, teachers are statisticians. For example, if you were to administer a quiz to assess your students' mastery of a skill or topic, your goal would be to use the quiz results to provide information concerning your students' mastery. Casual observations allow you to make hypotheses, such as, "It appears a lot of my students flunked the quiz," but simply looking at the numbers can be misleading. Ms. Amy Brown, the fourth-grade teacher we discussed earlier, scanned her students' math scores and thought most of the students preformed well. The scores she observed are shown in Table 13.1. Computing the average score told her another story; it also raised questions. One method of answering questions about a set of data is through the use of a *table* or *graph*.

The most common way of tabling a set of numbers is to construct a *frequency distribution*. **Frequency distributions** are simple tables reporting the frequency, or the number of times, each number occurs in the set of data. There are two types of frequency distributions, ungrouped and grouped, as illustrated in Tables 13.2 and 13.3, respectively. These scores represent the math quiz scores in Ms. Brown's class.

In an **ungrouped frequency distribution**, every score is recorded, from high to low. As seen in Table 13.2, the scores in Ms. Brown's class ranged from 60 to 100. Next, the number of students who obtained each one of those scores is recorded in the Frequency column. For example, scores of 60, 80, and 100 were each achieved by two students. This type of information gives Ms. Brown a better idea of how the class performed on the quiz.

In an **grouped frequency distribution**, as seen in Table 13.3, the scores are not listed individually; rather they are arranged into groups, called intervals. Grouped frequency distributions provide a condensed table of the frequency of scores and should be used when you have a wide range of scores, as in the case of Ms. Brown's class. For example, in Table 13.3 we see that six students, or 60 percent of the class, scored 80 and above. Getting the right amount of intervals is important. If you have too many intervals, the grouped frequency distribution is going to be about as lengthy as the ungrouped distribution; yet, if you have too few intervals, the set of data can be masked, or difficult to interpret.

> Frequency distributions simplify large quantities of otherwise isolated information (such as test scores), enabling the teacher to generalize or understand the general level of performance of the class.

TABLE 13.1
Scores on Math Quiz for Ms. Brown's Fourth-Grade Class

Name	Score
1. Lo Chen	80
2. Gary	60
3. Juanita	100
4. Mishika	70
5. Michael	90
6. Angie	85
7. Debbie	75
8. Trent	80
9. Axel	100
10. Thurmond	60

TABLE 13.2
Ungrouped Frequency Distribution of Scores on Math Quiz

Score	Frequency	Percentage	Cumulative Percentage
100	2	20	100
90	1	10	80
85	1	10	70
80	2	20	60
75	1	10	40
70	1	10	30
60	2	20	20

TABLE 13.3
Grouped Frequency Distribution of Scores on Math Quiz

Score Interval	Frequency	Percentage	Cumulative Percentage
90–100	3	30	100
80–89	3	30	70
70–79	2	20	40
60–69	2	20	20

Percentages

Frequency distributions can provide additional information about a set of data. **Percentages**, or the portion of children who obtained each score or scored in each interval, can be computed as shown in Tables 13.2 and 13.3. Percentages are computed by dividing the frequency by the total number of children, then multiplying by 100. In Ms. Brown's class of 10 students, 2 students scored from 60 to 69; therefore, 20 percent of the children scored in this interval:

$$2 \div 10 = .2 \times 100 = 20\%$$

Cumulative Percentages

The **cumulative percentage** is another type of valuable information yielded by frequency distributions. Cumulative percentage indicates the percentage of children earning that score or below. For example, Table 13.3 indicates that 70% of the students obtained a score of 89 or less.

Histograms and Frequency Polygons

Often, pictorial representations of a set of data tell us more than tables and are useful for presenting data to others. Two typical types of graphs that provide "pictures" of data are the **histogram** and **frequency polygon**. A histogram is a series of columns with the base representing the score interval and the height representing the frequency, or number of students who scored in the interval.

> Converting the number of individuals in each group to percentages of the total population can further clarify the teacher's understanding of the levels of student performance.

TABLE 13.4					
Scores on Mr. Hanes's 20-Point Chemistry Quiz					
Name	**Score**	**Name**	**Score**	**Name**	**Score**
1. Tonya	1	9. Darrell	4	17. Tresh	13
2. Maurice	7	10. Beth	13	18. Yolanda	13
3. Tavar	13	11. Lo-Sung	16	19. Rosita	16
4. Lester	1	12. Damon	16	20. Chad	13
5. Reggie	10	13. Levon	13	21. Michael	13
6. Christi	16	14. Carmen	10	22. Joan	10
7. Latrez	19	15. Jerry	13	23. Ted	13
8. Rod	1	16. Matt	10	24. Sarah	16

Often trends in data can be determined more easily from a histogram than with tables. For example, Table 13.4 gives the chemistry quiz scores from Mr. Hanes's class; Figure 13.1 contains a histogram of the same scores. Although histograms are often constructed with the frequency representing

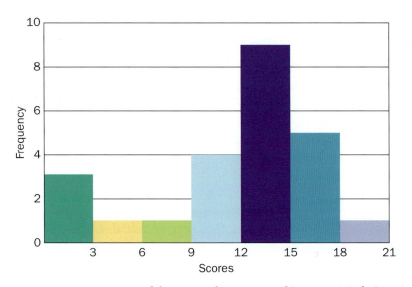

Figure 13.1 Histogram of the Grouped Frequency of Scores on Math Quiz

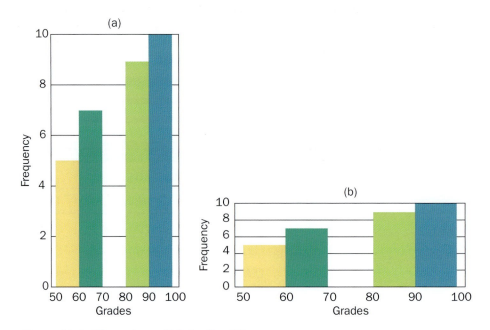

Figure 13.2 Illustrations of Misleading Histograms

the height of the columns, they also can be constructed with the percentages representing the columns.

Figure 13.2 presents two inappropriate histograms. Can you determine why? Figure 13.2 represents the class grades for Ms. Ruse, who is trying to convince her principal that she is a great high school teacher. She presents her students' final grades in the intervals of 90 to 100, or A's; 80 to 89, or B's; etc. Because the base of histogram (a) is too narrow in relation to its height, it appears that most of Ms. Ruse's students obtained A's and B's. This histogram did not convince the principal that Ms. Ruse was great, so she tried a different tactic. She gave about equal numbers of A's, B's, C's, D's, and F's and constructed a histogram with much too wide a base. The principal was not fooled by either trick.

We don't actually think teachers often follow Ms. Ruse's ruse, but, as you are aware, many advertisements on television and in magazines present purposefully misleading graphs. Pick up a magazine and see if you can find an ad that uses a misleading grade to portray something like "people who use our toothpaste have fewer cavities."

Another type of graph, called a **frequency polygon**, is very much like a histogram. But instead of columns representing the frequency of scores in an interval, a frequency polygon connects the midpoint of the top of the column with a series of lines. A frequency polygon is constructed by determining the midpoint of each score interval in the frequency distribution and plotting the midpoint against the frequency for the interval on the graph. Figure 13.3 shows an example of a frequency polygon based on Mr. Hanes's 20-point chemistry quiz scores. After the scores are indicated, straight lines connecting the dots are drawn. As with histograms, polygons can be constructed using percentages instead of frequencies.

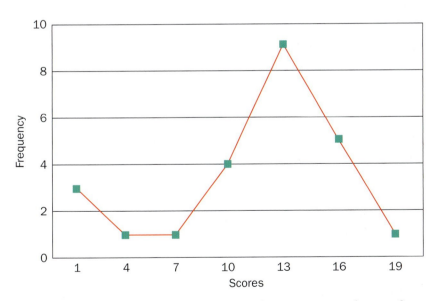

Figure 13.3 *Frequency Polygon of the Grouped Frequency Distribution of Scores on Mr. Hanes's Chemistry Quiz*

A normal distribution is always symmetrical, a bimodal distribution is one with two points with highest frequencies, and a skewed distribution is one in which a large number of scores is found on either end of the distribution.

Distributions

Distributions offer another pictorial aid for teachers. Teacher decisions can be aided by distributions. Was the test too difficult for the class? Too easy? Are there distinct populations in the class of which the teacher needs to be aware?

Distributions can be symmetrical or asymmetrical. **Symmetrical distributions** are those that, when divided in half by a vertical line down the middle of the distribution, have halves that form mirror images of each other. **Asymmetrical distributions** do not have halves that form mirror images. A **normal distribution** is always symmetrical, and the frequencies reach their peak at the middle of the distribution. A normal distribution is shown in Figure 13.4a. Many human abilities, such as intelligence, are assumed to have normal distributions.

Another type of distribution, shown in Figure 13.4b, is a **bimodal distribution**. Bimodal distributions can be symmetrical, as in Figure 13.4b, or they can be asymmetrical. The distinguishing characteristic of a bimodal distribution is there are two distinct points, or intervals, which have the highest frequencies in the distribution. Bimodal distributions are often caused by the inadvertent intermingling of two groups. Examples might include heavy mainstreaming, cultural differences, reading level, gender, and those who studied and those who did not.

Two types of asymmetrical distributions are positively and negatively skewed distributions, illustrated in Figure 13.4c and d. A **skewed distribution** is one in which a large number of scores is found in the lower or higher end of the distribution. In a **positively skewed** distribution, the frequency of higher scores occurs most in the lower end of the distribution and tapers off in the higher end. In a **negatively skewed distribution**, the frequency of higher scores occurs most in the upper end of the distribution. Look again at the

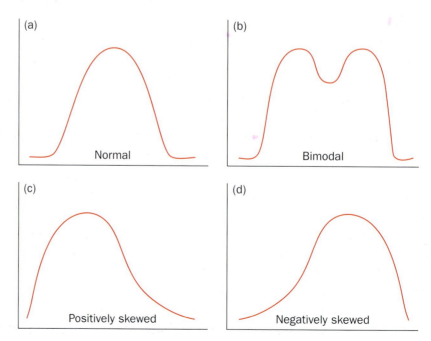

Figure 13.4 Types of Frequency Distributions

frequency polygon of Mr. Hanes's quiz scores in Figure 13.3. How would you describe the distribution of scores? If you answered negatively skewed, you are correct because the frequencies of scores are higher in the upper end of the distribution.

DESCRIPTIVE STATISTICS

The branch of statistics that serves to describe or summarize data is called **descriptive statistics**. Most research articles in education report some type of descriptive statistics. Often teachers use descriptive statistics to summarize classroom performance. For example, if your principal asked you how your students did on their math quiz, you would not begin reciting all the individual student scores on the quiz. Rather, you would probably tell the principal the average score on the quiz, thus making use of a descriptive statistic. This section of the chapter contains procedures for calculating the most common types of descriptive statistics: **measures of central tendency, measures of variability**, and **correlations**. This section also includes a discussion of the **normal curve**, which is necessary for understanding many types of descriptive statistics in education.

Measures of Central Tendency

Measures of central tendency describe average, representative, or typical values in a set of data by indicating where most of the values lie in the distribution. The three most common measures of central tendency are the **mean, median**, and **mode**.

The **mean** is the arithmetic average of a set of values. It is the most frequently used measure of central tendency. To calculate the mean, the numerical values are summed and then divided by the number of values. On Ms. Brown's math quiz, the sum of her students' scores was 800. This is divided by the number of students in Ms. Brown's class, 10, to yield a mean score of 80.

The **median** is the midpoint of a set of data, or the score with half of the values falling above it and half below it. To determine the midpoint, the scores are listed in numerical order from lowest to highest. If there is an odd number of scores, the median is the middle score. If there is an even number of scores, the two central scores are located and the median is the point halfway between these two scores. For example, with the scores 2, 3, 4, 6, and 7, the median is 4. With the scores 1, 2, 4, 5, 7, and 8, the two central scores are 4 and 5, so the median is 4.5. The ungrouped frequency distribution in Table 13.2 can be used to determine the median for Ms. Brown's class. The ten scores range from 60 to 100. The two central scores (mean and median) are both 80.

A third measure of central tendency is the **mode**, which indicates the value that occurs most frequently in a distribution. For example, in Ms. Brown's

---

Measures of central tendency (such as the mean, median, and mode) describe average or typical values in a set of data.

In a group of scores, the mean is the arithmetic average, the median is the midpoint between the two central scores in an even-numbered group or the central score in an odd-numbered group, and the mode is the score that appears most frequently in the group.

The best choice of central tendency to represent a group depends on whether the group data are skewed. The median is the best choice when the data are skewed.

class, the mode on the math quiz is 60, 80, and 100, with each score achieved by two students. The mode provides limited information about the central tendency of a distribution.

In **symmetrical distributions**, such as a normal distribution, the mean and median have the same value, as seen in Figure 13.5a. In **asymmetrical distributions**, the mean and median will never have the same value. In positively or negatively skewed distributions, the mean is affected more than the median.

As seen in Figure 13.5b, a positively skewed distribution, the mean is greater than the median because the few higher scores in the upper end of the distribution are pulling the mean toward the upper end. Similarly, in a negatively skewed distribution, shown in Figure 13.5c, the mean is less than the median because the few lower scores in the distribution are pulling the mean toward the lower end. Thus, the median is less affected by extreme scores and is the measure of central tendency that should be used when distributions are positively and negatively skewed. For example, in reports of family income in the United States, the median rather than the mean should be reported. Family income is negatively skewed because there are more people with low incomes than high incomes. If the mean were used, the billionaires and millionaires would pull the mean up and misrepresent the typical income.

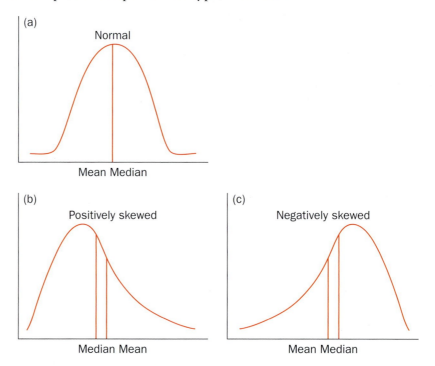

Figure 13.5 Location of the Mean and Median in Types of Frequency Distibutions

Measures of Variability

Although measures of central tendency provide a valuable description of a set of data, they do not indicate the different ways in which the values in the distribution are dispersed, or spread out. For example, 10 students in Class A all score 50 on an exam while in Class B five students score 100 and five score 0. The mean and median of both classes is 50. However, it is obvious that the students in the two classes did not perform equally: all the students in Class A scored 50, however the scores in Class B vary from 0 to 100. Measures of central tendency only tell us what the scores have in common, but nothing about how the scores vary. What types of measures do? **Measures of variability** provide information about the dispersion of data. Two measures of variability are the **range** and **standard deviation.**

The range is a quick and easy calculation to show the variation in data. It is simply the difference between the lowest and highest values in the distribution. On Ms. Brown's math quiz, the lowest score is 60 and the highest score is 100; therefore, the range in scores is 40 points ($100 - 60 = 40$). The range is a useful descriptive statistic, but it reflects only two values in the distribution. Thus, if a teacher had 100 scores, since only the lowest and highest scores are used in calculating the range, the other 98 scores would be ignored. Further, one extremely low or high score can affect the range and provide misleading information about the variability in a distribution.

> Unlike measures of central tendency, measures of variability indicate the different ways values in the distribution are dispersed.

PROACTIVE EXERCISE

Suppose in your first teaching position you are asked to integrate literature circles into your reading curriculum. If your students are like other students in schools across the country, the levels of reading ability will vary greatly from one student to another.

One of the joys of teaching is seeing how each student benefits from incorporating new teaching methods. It would be interesting to investigate whether literature circles would be more effective with your low ability readers, your grade level readers, or your gifted students. This knowledge could be shared with the other teachers in your school.

QUESTIONS

1. Which measure of central tendency would best represent a class of average size?
2. What variables would determine whether a particular measure would best represent a group?
3. Can you think of a situation where the mode would be useful to a teacher?

The standard deviation is a more precise measure of variability and is the most commonly used measure of variability. The **standard deviation** indicates how the values are dispersed around the mean and, thus, the degree scores or numbers are homogeneous or heterogeneous. **Homogeneous values** are a set of values that are all the same or approximately the same. **Heterogeneous values** are a set of values that are "spread out," some values are high, some are low, and some fall in the middle. If a distribution has a relatively small variance and standard deviation, more of the values are grouped around the mean of the distribution than toward the lower and upper extremes. Table 13.5 illustrates the computation of the standard deviation for Ms. Brown's math quiz.

The **standard deviation** gives an approximation of the amount the scores in a distribution deviate from the mean on the average. The scores on Ms. Brown's math quiz have a standard deviation of 14.3 (rounded). On the average, the children's scores deviated from the mean by about 14.3 points. Knowing this, we can take the mean of the quiz of 80 and add and subtract the standard deviation:

$$
\begin{array}{rr}
80.0 & 80.0 \\
-14.3 & +14.3 \\
\hline
65.7 & 94.3 \\
\end{array}
$$

This indicates that, on average, the children's scores on this quiz ranged from 65.7 to 94.3. The standard deviation is also useful for describing individual children's performance on the quiz. If Debbie, one of Ms. Brown's students, scored 65.7 on the quiz, we can interpret her score to mean that Debbie scored one standard deviation below the mean.

The Normal Curve

> Many human abilities, such as intelligence and psychomotor skills, form normal curves when performance in these areas is measured for a large number of people.

As noted in Figure 13.5, the **normal distribution** or the **normal curve**, has traditionally been an important part of statistics and testing. The concept of the normal curve was developed in the eighteenth century when someone discovered that if 10 coins were flipped many times, the frequency distribution of the number of heads formed a distinctive, symmetrical, bell-shaped curve, which came to be called the normal curve. Soon after, Francis Galton (1822–1911) found that many abilities, such as intelligence and psychomotor skills, also formed normal curves when performance in these areas was measured for a large number of people. The normal curve has been inappropriately used to distribute grades in classrooms and is unpopular among many college students.

Will intelligence and achievement be normally distributed among your future students?

TABLE 13.5

Computation of Variance and Standard Deviation of Scores on Ms. Brown's Math Quiz

Student	Xi	Xi − X	(Xi − X)′
1. Lo Chen	80	0	0
2. Gary	60	−20	400
3. Juanita	100	20	400
4. Mishika	70	−10	100
5. Michael	90	10	100
6. Angie	85	5	25
7. Debbie	75	−5	25
8. Trent	80	0	0
9. Axel	100	20	400
10. Thurman	60	−20	400
	$\Sigma X = 800$	0	1850

X_i = individual student score

$\bar{X}$ = mean score

ΣX = summation of scores

N = total number of students or raw scores

$E(X_i - \bar{X})^2$ = total of the square of each score minus the mean

$$\bar{X} = \frac{\Sigma X}{N} = \frac{800}{10} = 80$$

$$\text{Variance} = \frac{\Sigma(X_i - \bar{X})^2}{N-1} = \frac{1890}{9} = 205.6$$

$$\text{Standard deviation} = \sqrt{\text{variance}} = \sqrt{205.6} = 14.3$$

The steps for computation follow:

1. Calculate a deviation score (column 3) for each child. This is the child's score on the test minus the mean. For Angie, the deviation score is 5, or her test score of 85 minus the mean of 80.

2. Square each deviation score (column 4); in Angie's case, the square of 5 is 25.

3. Determine the sum of the squares for all of the students (column 4). In this case, it is 1850.

4. Divide this sum by the number of children minus 1, or 9. This yields the variance of 205.6 (rounded).

Will intelligence and achievement be normally distributed among your future students?

Although no distribution for a sample of people ever forms a perfect normal curve, we assume that distributions for a large number of variables would form normal curves if performance on these variables could be measured for all people. Intelligence and achievement are just a few of the many variables that educators assume are normally distributed. This assumption aids in the interpretation of many sets of data, especially in the interpretation of standardized test scores. The View from the Field box takes another view of what standardized test scores tell us.

A VIEW FROM THE FIELD
A VIEW FROM THE FIELD

PROFILE

Dr. Pemberton received her BS in Physical Education, MA in Guidance and Counseling and her Ed.S. degree from Tennessee Tech University. Dr. Pemberton currently works as a Special Education director for a public school system and is adjunct professor, Educational Psychology, Tennessee Tech University. Her areas of interest are evaluation, testing and assessment.

QUESTION: What does it mean when we say, "Eighty percent of the students in this school are above average?"

Dr. Pemberton: This statement is used often with administrators who want scores to "seem a little better" than they actually are. We assume the 50th percentile is average and any percent above this would constitute an above average score. However, one must realize that proficient does not, in any way, constitute high achievement.

Also, when we compare students with statements such as this, we are only describing a student's score when compared to the other students located at this school. We are comparing scores only. This statement does not, in any way, describe the actual strength/weakness/skill level of a student. This information would require that the scores be interpreted as criterion-reference. A **criterion-reference** score demonstrates mastery of very specific objectives.

If we use norm-referenced scores, then we are comparing an individual's raw score to a "norm" on a specific test. This type of assessment covers a wide range of general objectives. This is not a true picture of students' ability.

QUESTION: If we are to understand scores, we must understand their interpretation. What happens to the above-average student if we focus on the low achiever? Will average and above-average students be short-changed?

Dr. Pemberton: My answer would be "no". The above average student would not be neglected if the programs are designed appropriately. The effects of learning in a group vary, depending on what actually happens in the group, who is in it and what the teacher expects from the group.

Recent research has found that students in cooperative groups structured to require positive interdependence and mutual helping, learn more in the basic academic areas than students in unstructured groups.

One of the more positive cooperative learning precautions involving low achieving students would be to ensure that actual explaining and teaching are occurring, not just telling and giving. Cooperative learning is only as good as its design and implementation. Cooperative methods are both misused and underused in schools. The reason this happens is that a good amount of time must be invested in teaching students how to learn and be a contributing member of a cooperative group. ▪

Correlations

Correlations, one of the most popular types of descriptive statistics, indicate the degree two variables are *related,* or how the two variables "go together" or "vary together." Educators are often concerned with the association between two variables, for example, what is the relationship of socioeconomic status and school achievement, nutritional intake and attention span in the classroom, classroom size and performance on tests, and family's education and sibling intelligence. A **correlation coefficient** is an index or indicator of association. Correlation coefficients are also used for prediction. For example, the correlation between a kindergarten readiness test and performance in first grade allows us to predict how well children will do in first grade given their scores on the kindergarten readiness test. A common prediction made with correlations is college performance based on pre-entrance exams, such as the SAT and ACT.

> Correlations show the degree two variables are "related" or "vary."

PROACTIVE EXERCISE

Suppose you gave an exam and the overall class performance was poor. Under these conditions, would you consider using a normal curve distribution for grading? Why or why not?

Correlation coefficients range from −1.0 to + 1.0. A correlation of +1.0 indicates a perfect positive relationship between variables, a correlation of −1.0 indicates a perfect negative relationship, and a correlation of zero indicates that no relationship exists between the variables. The closer the correlation is to perfection of −1.0 or +1.0, the stronger the relationship between the two variables. Near zero correlations indicate weak relationships. Positive correlations, such as +.72 or +.68, indicate direct relationships, meaning the two variables vary in the same direction. For example, correlations between children's intelligence, their test scores, and school achievement tend to be about .70, meaning as intelligence test scores increase, achievement test scores increase in a similar fashion. Accordingly, as intelligence scores decrease, achievement scores decrease. Negative correlations, such as −.88 or −.67, indicate that as one variable increases, the other decreases, or the two variables vary in opposite directions. A negative correlation does not indicate a weak relationship between variables, rather it indicates an inverse relationship, which is expected for many variables. For example, the correlations between children's intelligence and misbehavior in the classroom are typically negative. As children's intelligence test scores increase, the number of times they misbehave in the classroom decreases. Near zero correlations indicate as one variable increases, the other variable may increase or decrease, with no predictability. For example, the correlation between intelligence and shoe size is near zero. Similarly, as children's intelligence test scores increase, their blood pressures may increase or decrease.

Table 13.6 shows the correlations from a study conducted by Harrison (1981). In this study, Harrison administered measures of cognitive, dental, social, and motor development to a group of 60 children in their first few weeks of the first grade. (Dental development, or teething, is a variable thought to be related to the physical development of children.) She then measured the achievement of the children in their last few weeks of the first grade to determine how well these developmental variables predicted the achievement of children at the end of the first grade.

> Negative correlations occur when one variable increases as the other variable decreases.

> Correlations indicate the degree of relationship between two variables, such as study time and grades on a quiz.

TABLE 13.6	
Correlations between Developmental Factors and School Achievement	
Measures	**Correlation**
Cognitive and achievement	.75
Motor and achievement	.53
Social and achievement	.32
Dental and achievement	−.09
Cognitive and motor	.65
Cognitive and dental	−.28
Cognitive and social	.47
Motor and dental	.02
Motor and social	.38
Social and dental	−.03

Source: Harrison (1981)

Let's examine and interpret some of Harrison's correlations. First, the measure having the strongest correlation (.75) with first-grade achievement is cognitive development. Thus, the more intelligent children were at the beginning of the first grade, the higher their achievement was at the end of the first grade. The other variables, dental and social development, did not predict achievement as well, having weak correlations of −.09 and .32, respectively. In fact, the relationship between dental development and achievement is almost zero, indicating virtually no relationship. Looking at the other correlations, we see that cognitive and motor development have a fairly high correlation of .65. The correlation between cognitive and dental development of −.28 is weak, however, indicating a slight tendency for intelligence to increase as teething decreases. What are the other correlations in Table 13.6 telling us about the relationships among these variables?

> Larger samples yield more stable correlations; therefore, correlations computed with small samples should be interpreted with caution.

When you interpret correlation coefficients, keep a few things in mind. First, the degree of confidence you can place in a correlation depends on the number of subjects used to compute the correlation. Larger samples yield more stable correlations, and correlations computed with small samples should be interpreted with caution. Second, correlations tell us nothing about cause and effect. Although there is a high correlation between cognitive development and first-grade achievement in Harrison's study, we cannot interpret this to mean that cognitive development **causes** achievement. Correlations simply indicate the degree of relationship between two variables. Although we can hypothesize that many of the variables having high correlations have a cause-and-effect relationship, we must never conclude cause and effect without first conducting an experimental study.

> High correlations, either positive or negative, cannot imply a cause-and-effect relationship.

Many variables having high correlations with each other obviously do not have a cause-and-effect relationship. A correlation of .95 between the number of storks sighted and increase in babies born clearly does not mean that storks cause population to increase.

Correlations indicate the degree of relationship between two variables, such as study time and grades on a quiz.

MEASUREMENT AND EVALUATION

The first part of this chapter focused on *measurement* and its use in the classroom. However, once student performance has been measured, the teacher's responsibility has only just begun; next, the teacher must *evaluate* overall performance and assign grades.

Measurement and **evaluation**, though frequently used interchangeably, have different meanings. **Measurement** means to ascertain the dimensions, quantity, or capacity. A carpenter measures the dimensions of a room without

PowerPoint

> The testing process should be conducted without any value judgments, but converting scores into grades requires the application of values.

passing judgment as to whether large is better than small, long is better than wide, or high ceilings are better than low ceilings.

At times, teachers also use measurement without regard to value. Teachers collect data on how groups and individual students are performing. By measuring the level of performance of individuals or groups, the teacher determines students' levels of performance. While using measurement, the teacher does not attempt to answer such important questions as: Is this current level of performance good or acceptable? Should it lead to retention or admission to a gifted program? Is the performance passing? A grade or C? These questions call for value judgments.

Evaluation means assigning value to something. When you see a Mustang convertible car or a pair of Reebok shoes, you automatically associate your opinion of their quality. Teachers also *evaluate* their students and classes when they determine whether students who perform at particular levels should pass or fail, receive A's or D's, or are overachievers or underachievers. Evaluation involves taking information about student performance and making value decisions about those levels of performance.

TODD WILLIAMS...

had just finished grading the midterm exam. As usual, he was not surprised by the grades of most of his students and, as usual, he was dumbfounded by the grades of others. Hank, Rip, and Carrie should have scored much higher, whereas Jerice, Wong, and Teresa, usually below-average students, made A's. Todd wondered about the relationship of IQ, achievement, and classroom test scores. He noticed that most of the time students' scores on classroom tests "correlated" with their performance on IQ and achievement tests, but sometimes they didn't.

As Todd thumbed through the midterm, he noted the types of questions he had used: multiple/choice, fill- in- the-blank, and matching. He often wondered about his exam question format. Should he use essay questions? What type of questions could best indicate what students have learned about the content? Todd even questioned paper-and-pencil tests. Some of his students did outstanding work on papers assigned, many could articulate answers to questions posed in classroom discussions and lectures, and others could make outstanding oral presentations on topics assigned. However, these same students often did not perform as well on written tests. Mr. Mueller, who taught English, advised Todd to examine the way he constructed his test questions. Mr. Mueller then began a long discussion about "stems," "distractors," and "holistic scoring" (see Chapter Fourteen for discussion of these terms), leaving Todd perplexed and puzzled.

As a teacher, one of your most important responsibilities will be evaluating student achievement. You may or may not be involved in developing your school's grading policy, but you will determine the evaluation procedures of your classroom. You will make decisions concerning when to evaluate your students, how many evaluations to administer, and what kind of evaluations to use. You will determine the factors constituting student grades. Such factors might include homework, periodic tests, midterm exams, finals, papers, classroom work, and student projects. Additionally, you will have to decide the percentage each factor counts toward the final grade. Consider the comments of Ms. Sandra P. Gifford, former Texas Teacher of the Year.

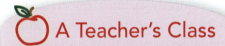

A Teacher's Class

NAME: Sandra Parks Gifford, former Texas Teacher of the Year

PROFILE: Ms. Gifford teaches regular, honors, and gifted English at Paris High School in Texas.

ADVICE TO ASPIRING TEACHERS: Aspiring teachers should truly wish to be teachers; therefore, teacher preparation should involve a period of internship in order for that person to decide his dedication to becoming an educator. A professional educator is one who is committed to service to and collaboration with others, to exemplary work, and to an ethic of caring.

QUESTION: What are your preferred teaching strategies?

My teaching strategies combine techniques appealing to auditory, visual, and tactile learners. Learning is not just the acquisition of data; it's the use of data in critical and creative thinking and in problem solving. Maximum learning occurs when the approach is thematic and interdisciplinary.

QUESTION: What is your opinion on student evaluation?

Evaluation is necessary for growth of both students and educators, but a test is not the most appropriate instrument for evaluation. A portfolio of student work or teacher accomplishments has more validity. Evaluation should encourage improvement, so educators should establish self-improvement goals and be held accountable for the completion of these self-directed objectives. ■

EVALUATING STUDENT ACHIEVEMENT

Let's examine **evaluation** in the classroom. Some types of evaluation teachers find useful include **summative, formative, diagnostic, performance, norm-referenced** and **criterion referenced evaluation** . . . We will also examine **grading** because it is the most recognized form of student evaluation.

Summative Evaluation

Most teachers are familiar with summative evaluation since it is used to derive grades. Summative evaluation occurs after instruction is completed, which may be at times or intervals during a grading period or at the end of the course or class, but always after the material being tested has been covered in class. Weekly exams given throughout a 6- or 8-week-grading period are summative exams if their purpose is to determine student grades.

Formative Evaluation

Formative evaluation is used by teachers to improve quality of instruction or to help students improve their learning skills. Formative evaluation occurs during the instructional unit, typically at close intervals. For example, if the biology teacher gives a weekly short-answer quiz to gather feedback on how well students are learning material presented, and uses the quiz results to improve teacher instruction, the teacher has used formative measurement. Later, if the teacher decides to "count" the scores as part of the students' grades, then this formative evaluation becomes a summative evaluation use of the exams.

Ian McLean thought formative evaluation might be just the solution he's been looking for to take the sting out of evaluating students.

> Historically, teachers have made little use of formative evaluation; yet, formative evaluation can be an important tool for improving instructional methods and strategies.

CASE STUDY

Ian McLean is a veteran teacher who has remained young at heart. To him, every day is a new experience, an opportunity to experiment with new approaches to instruction. He'll tell you in a minute that if he had his life to live over, he'd become a teacher all over again. "Where else can you experiment every day? What other profession would put you in the middle of the confrontation of so many minds? What other profession puts learning as its number one goal?"

Mr. McLean loves to learn, and he loves to help others discover new knowledge. Over the years, he has accumulated a large repertoire of teaching strategies, and he has used them all. If he uses a board assignment in his class one day, you can bet he will have a game, or film, or some entirely different type of lesson tomorrow.

When he began teaching, Mr. McLean hated testing. He remembers telling his colleagues that having to give out grades is the worst part of teaching. He detested giving F's, yet, he knew that he must issue grades reflecting the students' level of achievement; and each class, year after year, contained some students who did not achieve.

Recently, Mr. McLean has changed his mind about evaluation. He discovered a type of evaluation that doesn't have anything to do with grading. This newest discovery is formative evaluation. He was eager to begin trying this approach in his classes.

Ian's first approach to using formative evaluation was to set up his classes so that one day each week was earmarked as "pop quiz" day. But unlike those pop quizzes students hate, his pop quizzes would carry no credit. Instead, Mr. McLean would use these quizzes to determine potential areas of student misunderstandings. Surely the students would appreciate the opportunity to test their knowledge each week and discover areas in which they were confused.

But his anticipation was wrong. His students showed little interest in these opportunities. Instead, they complained about having to take tests that don't "count." Was Mr. McLean's idea to give a weekly formative exam a bad one?

WHAT WOULD YOU DO?

1. Why do you suppose Mr. McLean's students resented taking formative tests?

2. What types of follow-up do you think are required to make formative testing work?

3. Should Mr. McLean try to change his students' opinions about the relationship between grades and learning?

4. Is there evidence that contemporary educators place too much emphasis on scores and grades, as do McLean's students?

5. What do you think Mr. McLean should do next with formative evaluation?

Diagnostic Evaluation

Diagnostic evaluation is aimed at locating students' specific learning strengths and weaknesses. Once identified, the results can be used to make adjustments in both teacher and student activities.

Performance Evaluation

Performance evaluation requires students to apply the information they have learned to solve a practical problem (Mertler, 2003; Green & Johnson, 2010; Nitko & Brookhard, 2011). Performance evaluation became popular in the late 1980s and early 1990s when people became disenchanted with the testing programs several states used to make teachers accountable. Parents began demanding that their children be taught how to apply facts to solve problems. Performance evaluations ensure that students have the depth of understanding essential to apply information and solve problems.

"Accountability means that students or teachers must exhibit some standard of competency or performance, and schools must devise methods for relating expenditures to outcomes" (Ornstein, 1990, p. 51). Performance evaluation can be further defined by focusing on a process, a product, or both (Mertler, 2003).

Process Evaluation

Sometimes teachers are interested more in *how* students perform than in the results of the performance. For example, a physical education teacher might videotape students learning to golf, bowl, or dance. The replay can be used to help the student improve on driving a golf ball, bowling ball delivery, or dance step. Evaluation focusing only on the process is called **process evaluation**.

Proactive teachers might turn the cameras on themselves to study their classroom management styles or to study their instructional methods and strategies. Such practice would be an example of process evaluation and also an example of formative evaluation.

Product Evaluation

Product evaluation is the evaluation of some type of product the student has produced; it is the counterpart of process evaluation.

Norm-Referenced Evaluation

Norm-referenced evaluation is evaluation whereby success is determined by how the student performs compared with how all other students in class perform. For example, a reported norm-referenced score of the 90th percentile would mean the student scored as well as or better than 90% of those in a comparison group. The comparison group is termed the **norm group**. This type of evaluation is most frequently used in the scoring of standardized tests, such as the SAT. Before the No Child Left Behind Law (2002), it is applied less frequently in the K-12 classroom, but when teachers rank the scores on a particular test and assign the top group A's, the next group B's, and so on, until assigning the lowest group F's, they are using norm-referenced evaluation. When using this method, the teacher ensures all possible letter grades will be earned in the class; however, it also means that not all the students can earn top grades, despite how well each student performs (Mertler, 2003).

Criterion-Referenced Evaluation

Unlike norm-referenced evaluation, **criterion-referenced evaluation** bases success on criteria specified before evaluation occurs. Most teachers prefer criterion-referenced evaluation because they believe that these tests are fairer to students because all students are afforded the chance to earn top grades. Using criterion-referenced evaluation removes the need of forcing students to compete with others. Instead, students have the opportunity to succeed by fulfilling defined criteria.

Other proponents of criterion-referenced evaluation point out that when on real jobs in later life most students' success will be measured according to quality of work they perform compared with the level of performance expected by employers.

> Criterion-referenced evaluation frees students from having to compete with their classmates and bases success on the quality of the student's work.

Grading

Most teachers have little knowledge of various grading methods, the advantages and limitations of each, and the effect of grading on students (Guskey, Swan, & Jung, 2011). Often beginning teachers, and sometimes experienced teachers, think of tests and grades as though they are one and the same. They are not. Tests are only one of many ways to gather information on student learning. Other commonly used sources of testing include homework, term projects, written reports, and class presentations. By using the grades on a combination of such activities, teachers provide students opportunities to use a variety of their talents, providing a stimulus for growth in the skills required by each.

> Grades should be based on a variety of sources of information; tests are only one of the sources.

Opportunities to earn additional credit can enrich class offerings but only when students plan for such opportunities. Extra credit projects often backfire when students ask to do them near the end of the grading period. Most teachers agree that letting students copy reports verbatim from the Internet, books, or other online resources does little more than teach students to procrastinate and dislike report writing. The basis for deciding whether to permit students to do extra work for extra credit is whether you think the experience will result in additional student learning.

Some teachers keep a list of project topics from which students can choose. Other teachers offer their students the option of identifying extra credit opportunities and worthwhile projects.

After evaluating assigned activities, including extra credit, is it right to give students exactly what they earn for a grade, even if they only earned 10 or 20 out of 100 points? This question illustrates the dilemmas occurring when students are graded. After the fourth of six grading periods, suppose a student has a 60 average, which is the lowest passing average. In the fifth period, the student fails to make up missing work and has a computed average of 20. To pass, this student must earn a perfect score on the last grading period; virtually ensuring failure for the term.

If the purpose of grading is to determine which students will be promoted, then the 20 will be assigned. If the purpose of objective testing is to encourage the student to work harder, then some predetermined minimum grade such as 40 or 50 may be assigned. However, it is important for teachers to identify possible failing students in the first grading period. Family and/or student conferences concerning causes and solutions should be explored **before** the next grading period.

WHAT WOULD YOU DO?

1. Some teachers rank all scores for each class and assign grades to the major cluster (for example, first major cluster = A, second major cluster = B). Individual scores and small groups falling between clusters are assigned pluses and minuses. What are some advantages and disadvantages of this system?

2. How should teachers grade those students who are so academically challenged or behind they won't earn a passing grade?

3. Should effort be counted when assigning a grade?

4. What advantages can you see in teaching to the test?

5. Would you assign a failing grade to a student who has been present every day, attempted all classwork and homework assignments, and in general has worked up to his or her potential?

An additional consideration is that all grading systems involve error. Some students may get higher and others may get lower grades than they deserve. Although it is impossible to eliminate all such errors, it is possible to influence the type of error made. In this case, assigning the 20 increases the chances of failing a student who should pass and lowers the chances of passing a student who should fail. Similarly, assigning some predetermined minimum grade increases the chances of passing someone who should fail but lowers the chances of failing someone who should pass.

Clearly, there is no simple answer to the question of assigning the actual computed grade or a predetermined minimum grade. However, research has consistently shown that retaining students in a grade can have more negative than positive effects on students.

TECHNOLOGY IN THE CLASSROOM

Today the use of technology pervades all areas of statistical and mathematical calculation in the classroom.

Technology can be a tremendous asset when used to assist instruction in such courses as statistics and math. Until recently, using computers and hand-held devices in math classes was considered cheating. But that's when math education meant memorizing formulas and performing basic computations. The National Council of Teachers of Mathematics put an end to thinking about math as simply a rote skill. New math curriculum standards call for math education to stress analytic, problem-solving, and even creative aspects of mathematical thinking. Preparing students to meet that challenge requires technology. Additionally, teachers must be able to interpret and use test data to improve instruction, inform families, and respond to state and local student achievement requirements. The following provides excellent resources to assessment and statistical techniques.

- An article describing traditional and alternative assessment by Cole, Hulley, and Quarles (2009) is an excellent resource. The authors offer advice on how much assessment is necessary and when it is limited. They also describe how to use and implement alternative assessment methodologies. Cole, H., Hulley, K., & Quarles, P. (2009). "Does assessment have to drive the curriculum? *Forum on Public Policy Online, 2009*, 1–15. Retrieved from ERIC database.

- In an article by Shepherd and Mullane (2006), rubrics are presented as an effective method for the grading of performance-based assessment. Teachers are presented an effective method for the grading of performance based assessment. Teachers are presented with methodologies to effectively implement authentic assessment and how to use rubrics as scoring instruments. Shepherd, C. M., & Mullane, A. M. (2008). Rubrics: The key to fairness in performance based assessment. *Journal of College Teaching and Learning.* 5, 27–32. Retrieved from ERIC database.

- In a book authored by Suskie and Banta (2009), the reader is provided with information on what constitutes assessment, how to use assessments to measure students' learning, how to create and score alternative assessments, and how to share the assessment results with others. Suskie, L., & Banta, T. W. (2009). *Assessing student learning: a common sense guide (The Jossey-Bass Higher and Adult Education Series).* San Francisco, CA: Wiley, John, & Sons Incorporated.

- In Carroll and Carroll's (2003) book, the reader is presented with an easy to use guide to statistics as it relates to the K-12 classroom. The information on statistics is presented in a clear, concise easy to understand format, leaving the reader with an increased confidence on how to use and communicate with statistics. Carroll, S. L., & Carroll, D. J. (2003). *Statistics made simple for school leaders: Data driven decision making.* Rowman & Littlefield Education.

- Huff (1993) authored an informative book on how the media can and does "lie" with statistics. Huff presents the methods used by newspapers, magazines, books, and advertisements to mislead the public. His straightforward and reader friendly approach to explaining statistics make learning statistics simple and uncomplicated. Huff, D. (1993). *How to lie with statistics.* New York: Norton & Company, Incorporated. ■

SURFING · THE · WEB

A website published by Teacher Planet provides a number of rubrics in 18 different subject areas at five different educational levels. **www.rubrics4teachers.com**

Rubistar's website is another great resource for finding rubrics to use in a variety of subject areas. The site also provides the user with template to create rubrics. **Rubistar.4teachers.org/**

Elementary and Secondary Statistics at a Glance (**http://edreform.com/pubs/ edstats.htm**) offers a useful snapshot of public education in America. Want to compare your school or district with the national average? This is the place to come. U.S. information on schools, enrollment, teachers, student-teacher ratios, expenditures, salaries and wages, and overall funding is readily available.

The National Center for Education Statistics website address is **http://www. ed.gov/NCES**. ■

Resources

National Council of Teachers of Mathematics

Reston, VA information, (703) 620-9840; to order, (800) 235-7566 NCTM's two main publications are *Curriculum and Evaluation Standards for School Mathematics* and *Professional Standards for Teaching Mathematics*, both making recommendations for teaching problem solving and critical thinking.

Urban Mathematics Collaboratives

Education Development Center

55 Chapel St., Newton, MA 02160 Attn: Mark Driscoll

A group of 16 national sites established to implement the NCTM standards, using a variety of technologies. EDC is a research and development organization that provides technical assistance and outreach services to the collaboratives.

RECAP OF MAJOR IDEAS

1. In the past, teachers have made little use of formative evaluation; yet, formative evaluation offers important opportunities to improve instruction and learning.

2. Understanding measures of central tendency, variability, and correlation are fundamental to teachers involved in assessing student achievement.

3. Though used in many classes, the normal curve is often inappropriate for use in measuring student achievement.

4. Assignments permitting students to earn extra credit should be made early in the term and should involve activities that will result in learning.

5. By designing and conducting research studies in their classroom, teachers can empower themselves and their students.

6. Measurement and evaluation have different meanings. Measurement ascertains dimensions, quantity, and capacity. Evaluation involves

taking information about performance and making value decisions about those levels of performance.

7. Involvement with research makes teachers less defensive and more critical of their and others' behavior.

FURTHER APPLICATIONS

1. Read at least three articles on performance evaluation and write five performance questions in your major content area.

2. Interview two teachers, asking them to identify some ongoing problems in their classrooms. Choose one of these problems as a topic to research. Ask a research professor to help you design a study of this problem to be conducted by a teacher in that teacher's classroom.

3. Read and abstract three or more recent articles on performance evaluation. Make a table, logging in the purposes or advantages of performance evaluation and the suggested methodology for implementing performance evaluation, as given in each article.

KEY TERMS

statistics constructivism
action research frequency
  distribution ungrouped frequency
distribution
grouped frequency distribution
  percentages
cumulative percentage histogram
frequency polygon
symmetrical distribution asymmetrical
  distribution normal distribution
bimodal distribution
skewed distribution
positively skewed distribution
  negatively skewed distribution
  descriptive statistics
measures of central tendency mean

median
mode
measures of variability range
variance
standard deviation homogeneous
  values heterogenous values
  deviation score
normal curve correlation correlation
  coefficient measurement evaluation
summative evaluation formative
  evaluation diagnostic evaluation
process evaluation
product evaluation performance
  evaluation accountability
  norm-referenced evaluation
  criterion-referenced evaluation

LOOKING AHEAD

This chapter discussed statistics and evaluation and their use in the classroom; the next chapter emphasizes tests and other assessment instruments. ■

Chapter 14

Tests and Other Assessment Instruments

LEARNING OBJECTIVES

Upon completing this chapter, you should be able to:

1

Describe the strengths and weaknesses of objective tests, and construct a test reflecting two of these strengths and avoids two of the weaknesses.

2

Construct an essay test and an appropriate method to score this test.

3

Write a test item for each level of the cognitive domain.

4

Name six types of tests, and give a major purpose for each.

5

Explain three rules teachers should follow to write clear, concise test questions.

6

Write a test item for each level of the affective domain.

7

Create and describe a use for tables of specifications.

8

Relate two advantages of including both objective and essay items on a test.

9

Devise and describe a plan for removing ambiguity from matching and multiple-choice test questions.

10

Explain how you can minimize writing test items your students might interpret as tricky and/or insignificant.

INTRODUCTION

In recent years, political and social pressure for accountability have led school systems to rely more on standardized achievement tests to measure student progress. However, the most extensively used type of student achievement tests is still **teacher-made tests**.

Because most teachers use their tests on a weekly or other scheduled basis, this chapter will give particular attention to effective uses, construction, administration, and scoring of teacher-made tests.

This chapter is important because it answers critical questions often missing from other texts. For example, what is a table of specifications? And how can teachers use this tool to improve classroom testing? How can teachers design tests to avoid ambiguous and confusing items? How can teachers ensure that every item on their tests is a good question? How can teachers convince their students that they strive to make test questions fair? These questions and other important issues pertaining to testing and assessment are addressed in this chapter.

Perhaps you can remember having a test scored and returned and feeling cheated because you were unduly punished for missing some trivial question(s). Perhaps the test did not allow you to demonstrate what you understood about the important concepts. This chapter will prepare you to avoid making this mistake in the classes you teach.

INTASC – Standard 6   Assessment

Teacher-Made Tests

Teachers construct, administer, and score tests primarily to measure student achievement. **Teacher-made tests** are used for five major purposes. The most common purpose is to measure achievement of individual students and/or groups of students. With such tests, teachers, students, and families attempt to determine how well the learning of individual students is progressing. Families and teachers need to determine if individual students are appropriately using study time and putting forth the effort needed to progress academically. Teachers also need to determine if and how particular groups of students are progressing. For example, is the sixth-period class making continuous progress? A second purpose of teacher-made tests is to provide feedback to students.

A third function of teacher-made tests is determining how well students are progressing in defined content areas. Students and teachers often need to know whether individual students have disabling impairments in some defined area. In this context, teacher-made tests are commonly used as **diagnostic instruments** to identify defined strengths and weaknesses in student learning. For example, Nan may be weak in defining abstract concepts, or Juan may have an imagined weakness or mental block toward mathematics. Identifying such weaknesses can lead to remediation or need for tutorial assistance.

Fourth, teachers use teacher-made tests to analyze their teaching effectiveness. For example, by analyzing the results and feedback of weekly tests, the teacher might detect subject matter inadvertently omitted and/or content students found confusing or difficult. Unfortunately, neither teachers nor students typically make a practice of capitalizing on such potential.

"The gap between the potential of testing as a teaching-learning tool and the reality of current practice is wide" (Fielding & Shaughnessy, 1990, p. 90).

Finally, teachers can use teacher-made tests diagnostically to determine whether the test truly measures mastery of content. This practice will be explained in detail later in this chapter.

Knowing the uses for which tests are intended can provide a guide in test construction and administration. For example, a teacher suspecting an academic weakness within a group of students' might include specific types of questions to measure this weakness. A mathematics teacher who notices that a group generally performs poorly on written problems might construct a test to access students' reading level. Similar adjustments can be made in administering tests. A teacher who suspects that low performance results from students' lack of speed could increase the time allotted to take the test and see if improvement is realized.

The most time-consuming parts of testing for teachers are test creation and grading.

Testing Students

Traditionally, teachers have had considerable freedom in determining how often they test, what type of tests they use, and how they use test scores. But, recent demands for educational accountability have led to attempts to better define student achievement. Many educators are concerned that such pressures from reform groups and legislators coerce teachers to "teach to the test." Indeed, this is already happening in many school districts. The next 'A View from the Field' box offers commentary on this practice.

Instructor Test Bank

The major guide for constructing and administering tests should be the tests' intended purpose.

A VIEW FROM THE FIELD
A VIEW FROM THE FIELD

PROFILE

Gregory J. Marchant earned his Ph.D. in teaching-learning processes from Northwestern University. Prior to earning his doctorate, Dr. Marchant was a special education teacher. He is currently a Professor of Educational Psychology at Ball State University. His research involves the role of demographics in national and international standardized achievement test data.

QUESTION: Isn't "teaching to the test" wrong?

Dr. Marchant: The better assessments can resemble larger learning experiences with authentic (real-life) connections, the more valid they are. A test, however, is designed to provide only a snapshot of a larger learning experience. Teaching to the test shortcuts the experience of learning. It would be like having people pose for a photograph after a white water rafting excursion without ever having gone on the trip. A test is meant to encapsulate the learning experience, not be it. That being said, the unfortunate reality is that lives and livelihoods depend on test scores. To ignore their significance does a disservice to those most affected, whether it is a student being retained, a teacher being let go, or a school being closed.

QUESTION: How can teachers best involve their students in testing?

Dr. Marchant: Whether from teachers, families or by figuring it out on their own, some students have learned the tricks of the trade of taking tests. They are choosing the longest choice, answering "C", and bluffing their way through an essay, while students equal in content knowledge fail. To level the playing field for all students, teachers should teach test-taking skills, logic, and reasoning as it applies to test-taking. Ideally, students should not get an item wrong if they know the material, likewise, they should not get an item right if they do not know the material. In my undergraduate educational psychology course, I have students make up a multiple-choice quiz about themselves, where no one else in the class should know the answers. After exchanging quizzes, we analyze the clues that allowed other students to "guess" some of the items correctly. At any grade level, teachers can have their students make up quiz items to improve their understanding of the test items and to improve their understanding of content. ■

Finally, even with pressures to prepare students to perform well on achievement tests, future teachers should recognize they will spend considerable time on tests they construct. Future school professionals need to be prepared to construct, administer, and score a variety of tests; and they need to know how to choose among several types of tests. Choice should be based on the purpose for testing.

Table of Specifications

A good testing program reflects both the desired behaviors (reflected in test objectives) and content covered by the tests; therefore, test development should begin with examining the objectives and content covered during the time period. **A table of specifications** can be used to ensure that no objective or important content is inadvertently being omitted. A table of specifications is a chart listing objectives or behaviors on one axis and content generalizations (concepts, principles, theorems, axioms, etc.) on the other axis. See Figure 14.1a and Figure 14.1b

Tables of specifications can be as sophisticated as the one shown in Figure 14.1a. This table could be used by a school district to ensure the curriculum has objectives covering all levels of cognitive domains. Or, a less complex table of specifications can be created by a teacher to ensure the coverage of all content objectives on a unit test. This table would include the number of items per objective the teacher intends to use and identify the cognitive domain being assessed by the objective. Figure 14.1b illustrates a table of specifications a teacher might create to assess student knowledge of the book, *Charlotte's Web*.

Another prerequisite to test construction is deciding what type(s) of questions to ask. Fortunately, teachers have many types of questions they can choose, and they can also choose to use combinations of question types. The choices include objective and subjective test items (Mertler, 2003; Popham, 2011). Teachers should be aware of the strengths and limitations of each.

Objective Tests

Objective test items are those having a single correct answer (Mertler, 2003; Popham, 2011). Further, objective test items only require students to recognize the correct answer rather than formulate the answer, themselves. Objective items are also referred to as *structured-response* or *selected-response* items. There are several types of objective test items. Some of the more familiar objective test items include multiple-choice, matching, and alternative choice. Alternative choice items are those providing the student with two choices; true-false are the most popular type of alternative choice. Many teachers like to use objective tests items because of they are easy to administer, score, and interpret. The scoring of these items can be made even simpler if the teacher has access to scanning and scoring technology. Teachers with up to 150 or 200 students a day must economize testing time. Can you imagine how long it would take you to score 150 to 200 essay exams? Therefore, most teachers with so many students use objective tests.

> Objective tests are easily and quickly scored, and they enable the teacher to measure a broad range of content.

> Objective tests focus on what students recognize to be correct but are limited in providing students options for demonstrating all they know about content.

OBJECTIVES	Cognitive						Affective					Psychomotor						
	Knowledge	Comprehension	Application	Analysis	Synthesis	Evaluation	Receiving	Responding	Valuing	Organization	Characterization	Perception	Set	Guided Response	Mecahanism	Compared Overt Response	Adaption	Origination
1. Apply symbols	✓																	
2. Identify terms	✓																	
3. Write paragraph			✓															
4. Record weather		✓																
5. List effects	✓																	
6. Identify clouds			✓					✓					✓					
7. Design mural			✓					✓					✓					
8. Research climate			✓				✓											
9. Complete activities			✓															
10. Apply symbols		✓																
11. Complete evaluation			✓													✓		
12. Resupply center									✓									
13. Perform in groups									✓									
14. Label measure		✓																
15. Interview			✓					✓										
16. Record forecast		✓						✓						✓				
17. List machines		✓																
18. Construct instruction				✓														✓
19. Write question	✓																	
20. List rules	✓																	
21. List services		✓																
22. List variables		✓																
23. Make graph	✓													✓				
24. Make Puppets			✓													✓		
25. Write letter			✓															
26. Write story				✓														
27. Create game				✓												✓		
28. Write review		✓																
29. Develop problem				✓												✓		
30. Construct satellite				✓												✓		

Figure 14.1a   Table of Specifications on Curriculum

Another advantage of objective tests is they require less time to answer because students are only asked to *recognize* what is correct rather than being required to *create* answers. Therefore, teachers can test more material in a shorter amount of time than they can with other types of assessment techniques, such as essay teats. A final advantage of objective items is their high reliability, when compared to other types of tests (Johnson & Johnson, 2002; Mertler, 2003; Popham, 2011).

Objectives:	Recall of Information Read	Application of the Information Read	Analysis of the Information Read
1. The student will (TSW) identify main characters of the book, *Charlotte's Web*	5 Items	0 Items	0 Items
2. TSW identify the main plot of the book, *Charlotte's Web*	5 Items	0 Items	0 Items
3. TSW identify the setting of the book, *Charlotte's Web*	2 Items	0 Items	0 Items
4. TSW describe ending of the book, *Charlotte's Web*	2 Items	4 Items	0 Items
5. TSW critique the book, *Charlotte's Web*	0 Items	2 Items	3 Items

Figure 14.1b   Table of Specifications on Charlotte's Web

Limitations of Objective Tests

Some educational psychologists argue objective items only measure recall of knowledge rather than application. American schools are often criticized for failure to teach students how to think. Although some objective questions require higher levels of thinking, these questions are more difficult to write. Harris and Longstreet (1990) explain this shortcoming of objective tests:

Essay questions provide students opportunities to express their views.

> Furthermore, the advantage of their objectivity and easily accomplished scoring leads to one of the major limitations of these instruments, that is, the trivialization of the knowledge tested. The concise, clearly delimited response is emphasized; critical thinking, analytical skills, and conceptualization are all but ignored. Multiple-choice and fill-in responses are preferred; exposition and creativity are penalized. Thus, short-term objectives dependent on memorization are most likely to be measured; the long-term goals of reflective thought and understanding are bypassed. Ultimately, what is measured is what is convenient to measure but not necessarily what is most significant (p. 90).

Another limitation of objective tests is the considerable time and effort required to construct a quality objective test. In order for a test item to accurately measure a teacher's intended objective, effort and time are required in the writing of objective test items. Creating a quality multiple-choice test takes more time than other types of test items (Mertler, 2003; Popham, 2011). Objective test writing techniques will be explained later in the chapter under the heading *Test Construction*.

A final limitation of the objective test item is student guessing. Because the correct answer is provided, students can correctly guess the answer without actually knowing the material. If a teacher creates multiple- choice items with four options, the student has a 25% chance of correctly answering the item regardless of student's knowledge level. **Alternative choice tests** are affected the most by guessing, because these items provide the student with just two options. The lowest average grade on a true/false test tends to be 80% (Mertler, 2003) because students will correctly answer 50% of the items they do not know.

SUBJECTIVE TESTS

Unlike objective items, which only require recognition of the correct answer, subjective questions ask students to demonstrate what they know. With a subjective item, the teacher provides some type of prompt and the students are required to respond to the prompt. These items are also referred to as *supply-type, free-response*, and *constructed-response* items (Mertler, 2003). Subjective test items include short answer items and essay items.

Short Answer Test Items

Short answer items are self-explanatory: they require a brief response to a question or to an incomplete statement. The incomplete statement items are *completion items* and are commonly referred to as *fill-in-blank*. Typically, items asking a question are labeled as *short answer* and incomplete statements are labeled as fill-in-the-blank (Mertler, 2003). These items can be used to measure basic student knowledge, but they can be written to measure application of knowledge (Mertler, 2003; Popham, 2011; Tanner, 2001). Teachers like short answer items because they are easy to construct and relatively easy to score. These items also considerably reduce the chance of students correctly guessing answers. Another advantage to short answer items is they tend to be reliable (Mertler, 2003).

Short-answer items have limitations. They usually measure basic knowledge. Creating short answer items to measure higher level cognitive skills takes time and expertise. Further, student handwriting and spelling can make scoring difficult. A teacher will need to determine and communicate to

Most objective tests measure only simple recall of facts

students *before* the test is administered, how spelling and handwriting will be factored into scoring.

Essay Items

An **essay item** is one providing students with a prompt or question with the expectation of the students responding by writing paragraphs or developing themes (Mertler, 2003; Popham, 2011). Sometimes teachers need to test students' ability to compose their thoughts and express themselves in writing. Essay items are the best method for the assessment of writing skills. Essay items require students to process information, determine what information is vital, organize that information, and express what they have learned, in their own words. Essay questions also provide teachers a format to measure student values and attitudes. Additionally, by allowing students to express themselves, essay questions can encourage creativity. Another advantage to essay items is they provide the teacher an opportunity to understand the student's line of thought (Mertler, 2003).

However, as with other types of items, essay items have limitations. The scoring of essay tests is difficult and time-consuming. Because there is usually not one, single correct answer, scorers must use their professional judgment. Determining how an essay item will be scored, creating a rating scale to be used while scoring, developing a model response, and factoring in sentence formation, handwriting, and spelling require considerable time (Mertler, 2003). In addition to their time-consuming nature, essay items are notoriously unreliable (Johnson & Johnson, 2002).

Teachers' needs for understanding more about testing and for appropriate application of this understanding are clear. Popham and Hambleton (1990) attribute such needs to several causes. Until recently, tests were used chiefly as a method of assigning grades and were otherwise of little concern to teachers and administrators. But contemporary, proactive teachers can and, indeed, must become knowledgeable and proficient in test construction, administration, and scoring.

TEST CONSTRUCTION

From your experience as a student, no doubt you have felt the frustration of having to respond to poorly-constructed test items that you considered ambiguous: true-false items, partially true and partially false, multiple-choice items having more than one correct response, and fill-in-the-blank items with two or three correct answers. This results in student complaints such as "I know the material but this test doesn't let me demonstrate what I know." Quality tests have several characteristics. First, they are easily understood by students

Instructor Test Bank

Clarity and well-written directions are paramount qualities of all good tests.

The value of test items should be proportional to the emphasis given the item in instruction, importance, and academic assignments.

taking the test. Clear directions should be provided at the beginning of the test. For example,

> The value of each item on this test is shown in parentheses next to the item. There is no penalty for guessing. You will receive a 10-minute warning prior to the end of the test. When testing time is up, you must promptly turn your paper face down. If you have questions, please raise your hand. When you finish your test, please begin working quietly on tomorrow's assignment, Exercise 6-2.

Giving written directions on the test is important, in addition to providing directions orally. Some students get anxious over tests; others are eager to begin the test because they are afraid they may run short on time. Other students try to get last-minute information fixed in their minds. These students may not focus on oral directions. They will benefit from having directions in writing.

Other directions may be needed on specific parts of the test. For example, teachers may want to inform students that a matching item may be paired with more than one statement. Such specific directions should be written at the beginning of each section of the test.

Other critical factors involved in constructing tests include assigning value to questions, choosing type of questions, and using a variety of questions.

ASSIGNING VALUE TO QUESTIONS

At least two important factors should be considered in determining how much value to assign to test items. First, consider the amount of time and emphasis given to each item in class and on student assignments. Does this item reflect one or more lesson objectives? "The items on the test should be similar to the instructional objectives" (Griswold, 1990, p. 19). Test items should be weighted (or assigned a value) according to the importance of the content being measured.

Second, consider the amount of time required to respond to each item. The value assigned to items should reflect the percent of time required to answer the question. Once you have decided how many points to assign each question, sequence the items so the ones counting the most are nearer the front of the test. If you place these items near the end of the test, some students might run short of time before getting to them. Further, your directions should indicate the time a student should devote to items counting the most, and you should announce during the test when students should begin working on these items.

CHOOSING THE RIGHT TYPE OF QUESTIONS

Generally, it is best to begin the test with the easiest questions and sequence them so the items become increasingly more difficult. Providing the opportunity for students to begin the test successfully can give students the confidence needed to perform their best. Savitz (1985) found that this practice increases students' test scores by about 10 percent. Attempting to place the most valuable questions near the beginning of the test while attempting to place the easiest questions at the beginning may prove to be a challenge, but accurately measuring student achievement is always a challenge.

Using a Variety of Questions

Because different types of questions have varying strengths and weaknesses, teachers should always consider using a variety of question types for tests. As teachers create tests, they should consider objectives being measured and what types of items would best assess their objectives. Teachers should consider whether they are measuring basic knowledge or assessing more advanced cognitive skills. Consider the amount of time allotted for the test. Consider how the information was presented in class and the types of exercises used to gauge student learning. Once teachers have determined the types of questions to use, clarity is essential. The intent of most tests is to measure the degree of purposeful learning that has occurred. Ambiguous and vague questions prevent teachers from accurately measuring student achievement. If your students earn top grades on your test, you are going to assume they understand the material and are ready for more advanced topics. If your students do poorly on a test, you should design instruction to address topics not mastered. Teachers place a lot of faith in tests; therefore, you will want your tests to provide accurate information about your students.

Instructor Test
Bank

Writing Multiple-Choice Items

Multiple-choice tests account for 70 percent of all tests given in academic programs (Henson, 1996). To construct multiple-choice test items, begin by considering the purpose of the test and the strengths of this type of question.

To measure learning that has occurred, each test item should help discriminate between those students who have mastered class objectives and those who have not.

A major strength of multiple-choice items is they offer the teacher an opportunity to test a large amount of content. They can also measure degrees of judgment. Multiple-choice items seem best suited to bring out the finer distinctions between what is correct and what is incorrect.

To begin writing multiple-choice questions

- Decide on the number of alternatives needed in each question.
- Make sure the questions discriminate mastery from non-mastery of the content.
- Write clear, concise questions.
- State the test items positively.
- Avoid obvious answers.

However, like other types of objective tests, multiple-choice tests do not permit students to express themselves; therefore, they do not promote either creativity or communication skills. The ability of multiple-choice tests to provide students opportunity to apply knowledge to solve problems is very limited. Because of these limitations, teachers should consider using subjective test items in their assessment rather than only limiting themselves to multiple-choice tests. Consider the comments of Mr. John Snyder, former Nevada Teacher of the Year.

A Teacher's Class

NAME: John Snyder, former Nevada Teacher of the Year

PROFILE: Mr. Snyder teaches computer programming at Cimarron-Memorial High School in Las Vegas, Nevada.

QUESTION: What techniques do you use to teach problem-solving skills to your students?

The key, it seems to me, is to introduce a subject and make an assignment that will cause the student to ask the question that will require the instructional objective as an answer. Fall too far short with your information, and the student gets frustrated. Give too much, and it is not internalized. ■

> "All of the above" and "none of the above" are weak responses because they are poor measures of the level of content mastery

Deciding How Many Alternatives To Use

To reduce the margin of guessing, each multiple-choice question or stem should have at least four possible answers. Avoid "none of the above" and "all of the above" (Ellsworth, Dunnell, & Duell, 1990; Mertler, 2003; Popham, 2011). The familiar "none of the above" is often included because it is easy and quick to write, yet this choice contributes nothing to two major goals of testing: to measure the students' mastery of the material and to teach unlearned material to students. The equally common choice "all of the above" also does little to assess content mastery.

Making Questions Discriminate

A major strength of multiple-choice tests is their ability to determine which students have mastered the material, so each question should address this goal. The ability of a question to determine who has and who has not mastered content is called **discriminatory power.**

To discriminate best, each question should provide at least two or three viable distractors (answers that are attractive choices to students who have not mastered the material). A study of 32 educational psychology textbooks found all 32 recommending teachers make all distractors plausible (Ellsworth et al., 1990). Ideally, items should be written at a level of difficulty that requires students to think. Attractive alternative choices requiring students to think also raise the cognitive level of the test beyond simple recall.

Andrew Porterhouse is getting a much-needed lesson in the discriminatory power of test items.

CASE STUDY

Andrew Porterhouse was excited about his first year of teaching. The first 6-week grading period was almost over, yet it seemed he had just started yesterday. Andy was relieved to discover that he could handle his classes, but he would be the first to admit that he had some major concerns.

To start his career, Andy chose an inner-city school. He knew he had taken on a challenge by teaching middle-level grades (sixth, seventh, and eighth). He had forgotten how much energy preadolescents have and how awkward this age is for many youngsters. But Andy felt good about choosing this grade level because he thought he could provide badly-needed guidance.

But what Andy wasn't prepared for was the level of apathy of many of the students' families. Most of his students were growing up as "latchkey" children, many were from one-parent families, and some lived with relatives. When the school had its first family' night, only one of his 160 students' parents came to Andy's room.

The lack of concern for school also manifested itself in the classroom. In his methods classes, Andy was forewarned about students of this age group's tendency to "test" the teacher's management skills but he was prepared for the test. What worried him was the students' total lack of concern for learning. Andy first tried a couple of weekly quizzes to "wake them up." This tactic had worked well for some of his college teachers. However, most of his students failed the quizzes, and many of his students didn't seem to care.

He gave the first major test at the end of the third week. The test was a comprehensive, multiple-choice test. The scores were so poor he dreaded returning the papers. Some of the older students complained, saying the test was ambiguous and unfair. They argued that Andy should "scale" the grades. Andy didn't make any promises because he had serious reservations, and he wanted to think about it before making a decision.

Over the next few days, Andy pondered this problem. He decided to talk to Ms. King, the school counselor, who was in charge of administering the achievement tests to students. Ms. King pointed out to Andy that scaling the grades would not improve the students' poor attitudes toward learning. She suggested a way he could determine whether his test was really unfair, as several of the students had claimed. The method she suggested was called **item analysis**, and here's how it works.

After administering and scoring the exam, place the highest one-third of the papers in one group and the lowest one-third in a second group. For classes with 40 or more students, use 20 percent instead of one-third. Beginning with item **1**, compute the discriminatory power of this item, using the following formula:

$$DP = \frac{Hc - Lc}{T}$$

DP stands for discriminatory power, or the ability of this Item to discriminate between those who mastered the content in this question and those who had not.

Hc equals the number of students in the high one-third group who scored item 1 correctly;

Lc equals the number of students in the low one-third group (or 20 percent for large classes) who scored item 1 correctly;

T equals the total number of students taking the test.

Ms. King informed Andy that if the discriminatory power is positive, the item is valid, but if the discriminatory power is negative, the item is invalid and should be removed from the test. Ms. King said that a positive discriminatory power is valid because this provides evidence the students who displayed the highest mastery of the material were the ones more likely to get the item correct, and evidence that the students who knew the least about the material were the ones more likely to incorrectly answer the item. In other words, if a student knew the material, the student was more likely to get the right answer; and, if the student did not know the material, the student was more likely to answer incorrectly. A negative discriminatory power is invalid because it provides evidence that if a student knows the material, the student was more likely to answer incorrectly, and if a student does not know the material, the student was more likely to answer correctly. Just the opposite of what Andy or any teacher wants. Andy thanked Ms. King for her advice. He was eager to get home, have a bite of dinner, and put Ms. King's test to the test.

Counting the test papers, Andy found that 31 first-period students had taken the test. So he located the 10 papers with the highest total scores and the 10 with the lowest scores (see Table 41.1). On Item 1, he saw that 8 of the high-scoring group had scored this item correctly and that only 2 of the lower group had scored this item correctly, so he computed the results:

$$\text{Item 1: } DP = \frac{Hc - Lc}{T} = \frac{8 - 2}{10} = \frac{6}{10} = .6$$

Since .6 is a positive number, the item does discriminate in favor of those who understand the content that this item measures. Andy felt relieved that his test started with a valid question. He proceeded to analyze the rest of the test.

WHAT WOULD YOU DO?

1. What disadvantages could you find in using unannounced (or pop) quizzes?

2. What criticisms could you offer regarding Andy's concern over the low test scores? What should be his major concern?

3. What advantages and disadvantages are associated with the practice of scaling grades?

4. What advantages can you identify associated with computing the discriminatory power of every test item?

5. Some critics say that teachers should start from the beginning when constructing a test, never using questions that have been used before. Do you think this is right? Why? Why not?

> Item clarity can be enhanced by keeping the responses short and by avoiding redundancy among the responses.

On Item 2, six students in the high group scored it correctly and eight students in the low groups scored it correctly. Andy's computation was as follows:

$$\text{Item 2: } DP = \frac{Hc - Lc}{T} = \frac{6 - 8}{10} = \frac{-2}{10} = -.2$$

Andy's winning streak was short-lived. He wondered how students in the low group had outscored those in the high group. Perhaps they had just guessed better. Or maybe he had miss-keyed the test or inadvertently had two correct answers. Or, maybe there was something misleading in how the question was worded that only the high group understood well enough to be misled.

On Item 3, all students in both groups scored this item correctly, so Andy plugged their information into his formula:

$$\text{Item 3: } DP = \frac{Hc - Lc}{T} = \frac{10}{10} = 1.0$$

He thought, "this is certainly different. Ms. King had not mentioned this possibility. She said all items with positive discriminatory powers were valid and all items with negative discriminatory powers were invalid and should be thrown out, but she didn't say what should be done with items with no discriminatory power." Having remembered from an educational psychology class that tests should begin with some easy items, Andy decided to keep this item because everyone had passed it. Had fewer than half in each group passed it, he would have discarded the item.

As Andy continued analyzing the rest of his test, he realized he still had much to learn about testing and grading. But he felt good knowing he had taken the first step to begin learning more about this important role of a proactivce teacher.

Writing Clear, Concise Questions

Attributes of good test items:

- Good test questions don't require students to expend unnecessary energy to figure out what the question is asking.

- Avoid jargon and use common vocabulary all students understand.

- Keep each item short.

- Achieving clarity often requires rewriting your test items. For guidelines to creating test items, see Figure 14.2 on page 492. As you rewrite, you may discover that your item has redundancy, interfering with the meaning.

Examine the following examples:

1. Writing can be made more forceful by
   a. eliminating positive verbs
   b. avoiding simple words
   c. avoiding superfluous words
   d. avoiding use of the present tense

This item could be simplified as follows:

1. Writing can be made more forceful by avoiding elementary words that are

    a. positive

    b. simple

    c. superfluous

    d. written in the present tense

> Clarity can be enhanced by writing test items positively

Writing Positive Test Items

Positive statements are easier to understand than negative statements. Asking students to choose an answer that is "not" correct doesn't measure your intended objective. It measures the students' ability to ignore your directions! Most likely, your multiple-choice directions will include "choose the correct answer." Consider the first example below. In order for students to get the correct answer, they must ignore your directions and choose the option that isn't correct. Some students will miss this item simply because it will not make sense to them to choose an option that isn't correct. The second example below allows students to better show mastery/non-mastery of the objective while also providing valid information about the student.

> Multiple-choice test items should avoid obvious responses.

1. Which of the following is not a state capitol?

    a. Annapolis

    b. Boston

    c. Carson City

    d. Philadelphia

By writing this item more positively, it can be altered to read:

1. Which of the following is a state capitol?

    a. Birmingham

    b. Boston

    c. Las Vegas

    d. Philadelphia

Avoiding Obvious Test Responses

Previously, you were advised to include at least two or three viable choices, or choices that students will find attractive. This will help avoid obvious choices, but sometimes teachers unwittingly make the correct answer obvious. Examine the following test items to see if you can identify any obvious responses.

1. A well-known Swiss/French psychologist is

    a. James Smith

    b. Donald Jones

     c. Jean Piaget

     d. Robert Williams

2. The pretest can be used as an

     a. advance organizer

     b. review

     c. reinforce

     d. stimulus

3. The Civil War began in the year

     a. 1215

     b. 1666

     c. 1705

     d. 1861

In Question 1, choice (c) can be identified as the correct answer by recognizing a Swiss/French name. Choice (a) in Question 2 requires only the ability to recognize proper article usage, and Question 3 should include nineteenth-century choices other than correct answer (d).

Writing Matching Test Items

Matching test items require students to make associations. Frequently, teachers use matching questions along with other types of questions. When including a matching section along with other types of questions, provide specific directions for this part of the test.

The writing of good matching tests requires the following general guidelines. Begin by informing students whether a choice can be used only once or it may be used more than once. Otherwise, students may automatically eliminate those choices for which they have already found a match. Likewise, if some choices possibly have no matches, inform students. To dissuade students from guessing and using the process of elimination, a third important guideline is to include more choices than items.

Examine the list below; it is confusing because it has too many matches. For Item 1, (c) is obviously the preferred response, but (e) is also partially correct because the weight of water and later deposits of sediment produce heat and pressure. For Item 2, the obvious preferred response is (d), but because the process used to form metamorphic rocks uses heat and pressure, items (a) and (e) are also

> The matching section of a test requires its own set of directions, which should be written at the beginning of the section.

Students find ambiguous questions frustrating.

partially correct. For Item 3 both (a) and (e) are correct. Response (b) is correct for both Items 4 and 5.

Tests such as this can be confusing and frustrating to students. Justifying grades on such tests is equally unpleasant for the teacher. You can improve such items by having only one correct response for each statement and by adding an extra response, one that has no match.

> Specificity increases the power of essay questions to discriminate between those students who have mastered content and those who have not.

Statement	Response
1. Sedimentary rocks	a. Formed by heat
2. Metamorphic rocks	b. Formed by volcanoes
3. Igneous rocks	c. Formed by deposits in water
4. Obsidian	d. Formed by existing rocks
5. Pumice	e. Formed by pressure

Writing Essay Questions

Discussion questions, (questions beginning with the verb "discuss") invite students to respond by saying anything they want, even though they may possess little or no understanding of the topic. But, correctly written, essay items focus or channel student responses, requiring students to address the answer needed. The first step in writing essay questions is to identify issues you want students to address. Specifically, identify the concepts you want students to develop or address in their responses.

For example, suppose you have just taught a unit on economic impact of the Gulf War. You have chosen a discussion test to measure what your students understand or learned about this war. You could simply write an item that says, "Discuss the economic impact of the Gulf War." But such items often do little to measure what students understand; furthermore, they can leave students frustrated, wondering, how does my teacher really want me to respond? How will this item be graded?

Rather than risking student confusion and not soliciting correct responses, as a proactive teacher you can place some boundaries on student responses. For example, you might write the following essay item, "Name and discuss three economic consequences of the Persian Gulf War."

Suppose, during previous class time a student had presented a report comparing two of these strategies. Then you might want to pursue this item even further by requiring students to include this information. The revised item might be as follows: "Name three economic ramifications of the Persian Gulf War, and evaluate the effects of two of these ramifications."

By being specific, you have removed the ambiguity of this question. Your students will appreciate clarity. Those students who have mastered subject content can respond with confidence to questions. How do essay questions test those students who have not mastered the content? For them, you have removed the option to "talk about" the war. By tightening the focus of essay questions, you improve the item's ability to discriminate between those students who have mastered content and those students who have not. This should be a primary goal of test construction.

Developing Test Items
General Guidelines

1. Test items should cover important content and skills.
2. The reading level and vocabulary of each item should be as simple as possible.
3. Each item should be stated in an unambiguous manner, confusing sentence structure and wording should be avoided.
4. Items should not consist of verbatim statements or phrases lifted from the text.
5. Clues to the correct answer should not be provided.
6. Vary the types of items that appear on classroom tests.
7. Group items similar in format together so that each type appears in a separate section (e.g., all multiple-choice items should be grouped together).
8. Each section should be preceded by clear directions.
9. Within each section, order the items from easiest to most difficult.
10. Although all items types will not appear on every test, a good order of items is: true-false, matching, short answer, multiple-choice, and essay.
11. Provide adequate space for students to respond to each item.
12. Avoid splitting items between two pages.

Adapted from: Mertler, C. A.(2003). *Classroom assessment. A practical guide for educators*. Los Angeles: Pyrczak Publishing.

Figure 14.2 General Guidelines for Developing Test Items

OVERCOMING THE LIMITATIONS OF OBJECTIVE TESTS

Objective tests are criticized for failing to stimulate higher-order thinking (cognitive domain) and for failing to shape sound social attitudes in students (affective domain). Both limitations can be addressed.

Using Objective Tests to Measure Student Achievement

Objective test items are also criticized (and accurately so) for only testing simple recall. But proactive teachers who plan ahead can devise objective tests to measure higher levels of thinking and problem solving. Let's consider the cognitive domain of Bloom's Educational Taxonomy with methods that can be used to construct test items to measure at each level.

Level 1: *Knowledge.* Items measuring only the retention of facts.

Level 2: *Comprehension.* When students comprehend information, they do more than just remember; they understand information well enough to translate, interpret, or even predict future trends. For example, students can be asked to explain the differences between theocracy, democracy, and a dictatorship. Additionally, students can be asked to predict future types of governments represented at the United Nations, basing each prediction on current trends in world governments.

Level 3: *Application.* Application-level questions require students to apply abstractions to solve problems. For example, in a biology class students studying body organs learn that organs work together to achieve results that could not be achieved by only one organ. This principle is called *synergism*. Then students are given an imaginary problem-solving situation. For example, they are given the task of loading a refrigerator onto a flatbed truck. They have a pulley, but the pulley was made for smaller jobs and is not capable of lifting the refrigerator. They also have a half-dozen pieces of hardwood lumber that measure $2'' \times 6'' \times 10''$. Applying the principle of synergism, students could use the pulley along with an inclined plane made from the lumber and perhaps would also use some of the lumber as fulcrums to pry the refrigerator as they slid it up the ramp. Thus, applying the concept behind the process of synergism, they would combine more than one simple machine to achieve a goal.

Another approach to the application level is to ask students to restate a scientific principle applied under varying conditions. When studying Boyle's law, which says that pressure and volume are inversely related, students might be asked what would happen to the pressure on the wall of a canal when the width of the canal was reduced by half to accommodate a barge.

Level 4: *Analysis.* Analysis-level thinking requires the breaking down of generalizations, concepts, and principles to understand the lesson. For example, an English teacher may require students to read the poem "Richard Corey" and explain the moral of the poem. Or a physics teacher studying the workings

PROACTIVE EXERCISE

Cheryl Glasscoe's physical science classes are a mess, or are they? Throughout the classroom and the adjoining lab, are piles of debris. In one corner is a stack of gutter and downspouts. Another corner has long, narrow strips of plywood.

Some student stations in the lab have piles of plastic materials of various sizes and shapes. For the next three days groups of 10th, 11th, and 12th graders will enter the room, sign in with Ms. Glasscoe, and proceed to assigned workstations, where each student, and a partner, will design and build a racetrack. Next Tuesday will be NASCAR race day, and each team (pair of students) will enter its final product in the NASCAR competition.

   a. What level(s) of thinking are promoted with this assignment?
   b. What problem-solving skills does such a project potentially teach?
   c. What criteria should a teacher use to evaluate this project?
   d. How might a teacher involve students in the evaluation of their own projects?

of a computer might ask a group of students to suggest ideas for future software to address global pollution.

Level 5: Synthesis. Synthesis-level questions require students to combine several concepts to communicate a different idea; students must be creative. This level of thinking requires divergent thinking or inductive thinking, beginning with specifics and generalizing to a broader application. For example, having studied the effects of temperature and sugar on texture, chemistry students might be asked to examine two pieces of cake baked at different temperatures and determine which was baked at the higher temperature. The process could be repeated using different amounts of sugar and asking students to examine samples and ascertain which has more sugar. To void guessing, each question should be followed by the statement "Justify your answer."

Level 6: Evaluation. Evaluation-level questions require students to make judgments based on logic and consistency. For example, in your methods classes you may be required to perform peer evaluations. Each of your critiques of peer lessons might include an explanation of why you gave your fellow student a high, average, or low score. You might use criteria provided by your professor, and other accepted generalizations on teaching found in your textbooks and in journals.

Writing Affective Test Items

> Higher-order affective questions and higher-order cognitive questions are more difficult to write but address both student achievement and student creativity.

Traditionally, the impact of emotions on learning has been ignored. While the relationship between cognition and emotions is still being researched, the importance of this relationship is recognized. Ninety-three percent of the remembered messages teachers leave with their students are emotional (Phillips, 1998).

Growth in students affective domain is typically slower than growth in their cognitive domain. Helping students develop a sound value system is an important goal for teachers. A widely recognized source for studying the *affective domain*, or attitudes, is the *Taxonomy of Educational Objectives Handbook II: The Classification of Educational Goals: Affective Domain* by Krathwohl, Bloom, and Masia (1964). These educators present five levels in the affective domain:

Level	Development
1—Receiving	A willingness to tolerate a phenomenon
2—Responding	Voluntarily using the phenomenon
3—Valuing	Prizing and acting on the phenomenon
4—Organizing	Using values to determine interrelationships between the phenomena
5—Characterizing	Organizing values, beliefs, ideas, and attitudes into an internally consistent system

Following is an example of a question written at each level:

Level	Question
1—Receiving	A social studies teacher asks a small group of students, "Would you mind if Eric joins your group?"
2—Responding	A physical education teacher might ask, "Would you like to join the after-school softball team?"
3—Valuing	A school psychologist asks, "What kinds of posters do you display on your walls in your room?"
4—Organizing	A health teacher might have students consider the pros and cons of moving a victim with a neck injury and then have them vote for or against a state law preventing unauthorized people from moving injured people.
5—Characterizing	A science teacher might ask students to develop a matrix illustrating daily behaviors that conserve natural resources, placing the natural resources on the Y axis and the behaviors on the X axis.

Testing these levels can contribute to affective growth and, in addition, a teacher might enrich the affective dimension of the curriculum by using values clarification activities. Commercially produced simulations and games are available, but you might also want to develop your own.

TEST ADMINISTRATION

Several years ago, a terrible story was told of some graduate students in Alaska who, while taking standardized tests, became so cold they experienced frostbite. The story illustrates a responsibility shared by teachers who give exams. The teacher's first responsibility is to make students comfortable. This means controlling the temperature, lighting, and noise level, preventing your own students and others from becoming disruptive, making efforts to relax students before the test begins, and preventing students from cheating.

Anxiety is often a distractor to students taking exams. Some anxiety can be helpful but too much can negatively affect student performance. When this happens, test scores can present a distorted view of student learning. Fielding and Shaughnessy (1990) recommend lowering student anxiety by explaining the purpose of tests and by providing students opportunities to become familiar with the test format. For example, students often ask certain questions about a forthcoming test: How much will it count toward the overall grade? How many questions will it have? Will there be problems to work? Will it be multiple-choice? True/false? Essay? As a proactive teacher, when you inform

Student Study
Guide

your students that a test is forthcoming, even before they ask, provide answers to these questions.

Finally, do not leave the room during the test, except for emergencies. Be systematic. Have students begin at the same time. When the allotted time expires, ask students to turn their papers face down, and collect them immediately. Don't make the common mistake of walking around the room during the test. This can distract and frustrate students.

WHAT WOULD YOU DO?

Noticing that a colleague is administering a test, some teachers consider this a perfect time to socialize. Suppose your students are quietly taking an exam, and a fellow teacher comes to your doorway and motions for you to come to the door to chat during the test. How would you respond?

> When administering tests, teachers are responsible for student comfort and freedom from distractions.

Giving Appropriate Oral Directions

Before distributing exam papers, preview the directions written on the test. Tell students what to do if they have questions and what to do when they complete the test. A quiet, raised hand for a question can be unobtrusive. If you or your students discover an error on the exam, wait and see if there are others. Once two or three errors are detected, you may decide to get all students' attention and correct all errors with a single disruption.

> Testing is a responsibility that should be conducted in a systematic and organized manner.

SCORING TESTS

To make your scoring as objective as possible, conceal the students' names. A way to handle this is to ask students to print their names only on the back side of the last page. Although you might recognize some of the papers, most teachers find while scoring tests, their attention is focused on scoring items accurately, and typically don't match handwriting with students.

Scoring Objective Tests

When scoring objective tests, the general guideline of 'concealing the students' names is applicable. If you notice an unusually large number of students chose the same wrong answer, read this question again to see if the wording was confusing or misleading. Perhaps the item contained a double negative, or the item may have been mistyped. Misleading or confusing items should be discarded and errors resulting from mistyping should be corrected.

Scoring Essay Items

By making essay questions specific, teachers can make the evaluation task easier. General discussion responses are difficult to score, but specifically-stated items produce responses more easily and accurately scored.

The procedures used to score essay items should reflect the purposes of the test. Because a major purpose of most tests is to measure student attainment of class objectives, take care to specify the academic content and ideas stressed in class and to assign points to content according to their importance. Begin the scoring process by making a key, such as the one shown in Figure 14.3.

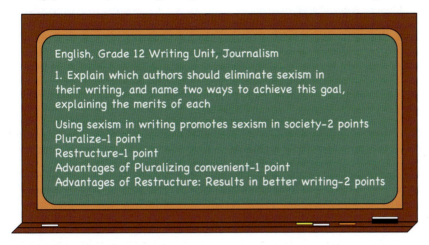

Figure 14.3 *Test Scoring Key*

Notice that the test item in Figure 14.3 has been broken down into three major parts. First, a compound question was asked because the teacher wanted to test for several objectives. Because essay items limit the range of content covered, teachers often choose to expand the amount of content covered by the exam.

Second, the teacher stressed the obligation writers have to avoid sexism in their writing because sexist writing fuels the continuation of sexist practices in society. Because this idea is considered important by this teacher, and it was stressed in class, the teacher assigned it two points.

Third, students were required to discuss two ways to avoid sexism: pluralizing and restructuring. Listing these strategies earns the students one point each. But knowing the advantage(s) of each earns additional points. How many? Knowing the advantages of pluralizing is worth one point, but knowing the one advantage of restructuring is worth two points. Why? The reasoning for assigning the restructuring advantage more points is that restructuring requires the writer to rethink what is being said, and, hopefully, this rethinking process improves the quality of the student's writing. Because the teacher endorsed the frequent use of this process, the teacher correctly assigned it more points.

PERFORMANCE ASSESSMENT INSTRUMENTS

Increasingly, through standardized testing and portfolio evaluation, students *and* teachers are being held accountable to higher-level, performance-based assessments.

Standardized Tests

In recent years, teachers have had an increasing responsibility for administering standardized tests. **Standardized tests** are tests that have been **normed**; this means average scores have been computed for large populations of students taking these exams. Traditionally, most norm scores have resulted from nation-wide administering of the exams; recently, because of concern for the U.S. students' inability to compete well with other nations, an increasing number of standardized exams have international norms.

Standardized tests have become statewide requirements for high school graduation in many states. Typically, college students pursuing teaching careers are being required to pass standardized exams. Some colleges require students to make minimum scores for admission to their teacher education programs; others require passing scores for graduation. Some state depart-ments of education require passing scores for certification. Some colleges use nationally-normed tests such as the National Teachers Examination, some use locally-developed basic skills tests, and some require a combination of the two. Most tests used in teacher education programs measure both con-tent knowledge (knowledge in the student's chosen teaching field(s)) and knowledge about teaching and learning. Some states are requiring *experienced* teachers to take standardized tests to ensure minimum levels of competency (Ornstein, 1990).

When you begin teaching, you may hear some of your colleagues criticize the use of standardized testing. Some school reformers have proposed the use of tests to weed out incompetent teachers and reward master teachers. The success of schools with local school-based school management teams is often determined by student achievement test scores, and the results may range from increased revenues for those schools whose students exceed expected levels of scoring to school takeovers by state government because student scores are below the minimum acceptable levels.

Such use of test scores implies that tests are capable of identifying suc-cessful teachers, unsuccessful teachers, successful schools, and failing schools. Furthermore, it is implying that student academic achievement is the purpose of schools. Do you agree or disagree with the following?

> Any society—be it a democracy, an autocracy, or a collectivist one—that insists on viewing children as a resource or a weapon, or a tool, or an instrument will end up by treating them as such, and no more. (Stinnett & Henson, 1982, p. 292).

Some states have come to realize the types of tests that have become traditions in American schools, such as true-false, multiple choice, matching, and fill-in-the-blank are sometimes inadequate in measuring student learning

Proactive teachers must view testing for what it is—an important tool that can be either misused or used appropriately to significantly improve the educational opportunities of students in our schools.

on demanding assignments. Consequently, these states are changing to performance-based assessments.

Although testing cannot be a cure for all educational shortcomings, proactive teachers must recognize that testing is a valuable tool. We caution you to recognize both the limitations and potentials of testing.

Cizek (1991) offers a good summary on the use of standardized tests:

> We should all recognize that we have not achieved technical perfection in assessment; we must also admit that existing instruments address only a portion of what is useful for both our students and ourselves. But we should not jettison the tests we have because they don't do everything we wish they could. At a minimum, tests do provide important information about *some* aspects of learning, as everyone should acknowledge. And we should develop new devices to assess other facets of students' intellectual growth (p. 58).

Authentic Assessment

In describing **authentic assessment** as it relates to teachers, Tellez (1996) stated, "Assessments are authentic according to the degree to which they are meaningful to and helpful for teachers in the exploration of their practice" (p. 707).

In the context of elementary and secondary classrooms, authentic assessment means assessment aimed at preparing students for life, assessment measuring skills citizens need to perform tasks common in daily living. For example, if a teacher wishes to determine if students can orally present on a selected topic, the teacher isn't going to give a multiple choice test. The teacher will design an assignment involving students' ability to effectively present orally; a skill useful in many arenas of life. Authentic assessment often involves solving problems individuals and groups commonly face. Herman, Aschbacher, and Winters (1992) state that authentic assessment "requires learners to actively accomplish complex and significant tasks, while bringing to bear prior knowledge, recent learning, and relevant skills to solve realistic problems" (p. 2).

Portfolio Assessment

Portfolio assessment requires a purposeful collection of tangible products providing evidence of a student's skills. By the early 1990s, portfolios had become a required part of many teacher education programs. Portfolios provide a means for students to demonstrate their abilities to perform a varied range of skills. Important to teacher portfolio development are lesson and unit planning, assessing student progress, and clarifying the teacher's philosophy so teacher and student activities are coordinated. Two important issues in the use of portfolios are the student's ability to understand and articulate the purpose and use of portfolios and the personal ownership that can develop as students and teachers use the portfolio to grow professionally (Miller & Tellez, 1993; Tellez, 1996).

Effective use of portfolios requires continuous reflection by their owners (Mertler, 2003; Popham, 2011; Van Wagenen & Hibbard, 1998). Portfolio builders should include examples of academic work and they must also include examples of the owner's "bad" and/or "ugly" work, so students can see the progress they have made (Wilcox, 1998). Improvement is enhanced by continuous reflection and assessment.

Autobiographical stories can generate insightful conversations among teachers and become good reflective tools for teachers (Clandinin, Davies, Hogan, & Kennard, 1993; Knowles, 1993). Experienced educators can help beginning teachers draw insights and meaning from these stories (Tellez, 1996).

In summary, when using any assessment procedures, the teacher should keep several points in mind:

- Tasks presented to students should be realistic, and the assessment device should reflect higher-level skills, not more trivial learning that could be assessed better in other ways.

- Teachers can question student responses orally by asking for clarification and evidence. These interactive procedures allow the teacher to develop a more comprehensive picture of a student's higher-level skills.

- Combine both traditional paper-and-pencil tests—which are most often best suited for recall, comprehension, and possibly application-with higher-level assessment devices and procedures to increase the reliability and validity of educational decisions.

TODD WILLIAMS'...

students were restless and festive, as was he. It was the last few minutes of the last class day of the year. His first year had been memorable with successes, failures, and everything in between, and he would never forget this first group of students. Five minutes before the final bell, Terrell asked through the clamor of checking in books and cleaning desks, "Last chance Mr. Williams . . . anything you want to lay on us?" Todd smiled, "Yes there is, Terrell, glad you asked. It is something my father shared with me when I was seriously considering dropping out of college and giving up on my career as a teacher." Todd hesitated as the class grew curious and quiet. Then he read from the 1994 Inaugural Address of Nelson Mandela.

"Our deepest fear is not that we are inadequate.

Our deepest fear is that we are powerful beyond measure.
It is our light, not our darkness, that most frightens us.
We ask ourselves who am I to be brilliant, gorgeous, talented and fabulous?
Actually, who am I not to be! Your playing small doesn't serve the world.
There is nothing enlightened about shrinking so that other people won't feel insecure around you.
We were born to manifest the glory that is within us.
It is not just in some of us; it's in everyone.
As we let our own light shine, we unconsciously give other people permission to do the same.
As we are liberated from our own fear, our presence automatically liberates others."

Todd paused and looked about this class for the last time. "You could say that these words and my father are the reasons I was your teacher this year." Todd stared at the floor for a moment, gathered himself, then asked his class, "Would anyone like a copy of what I just read?"

The students, not accustomed to such candor from a teacher, hesitated a moment, then a hand raised, then another and another until Todd stood before a class of raised hands. As he passed out copies of Nelson Mandela's words, the successes of the year loomed larger and the failures and all in between faded for a time.

TECHNOLOGY IN THE CLASSROOM

This is the last chapter, so we feel we would be remiss if we did not cover the very important topic of *Computer Ethics*. How does the subject of computer ethics relate to the classroom environment? If our educational system is successful in making U.S. students computer literate, then computer ethics will become a social and personal issue. On a social scale loom such issues as the following:

- Should we sell computers to countries supporting terrorism?

- Is it right to replace unskilled workers with computer-guided robots?

- What are the health consequences of using video-display terminals? (Gotterbarn, 1991, p. 26)

- How does online learning differ from the traditional classroom?

Personally, computer ethics involves such issues as software piracy, gambling, pornographic material on the Internet, and hacking into secured databases. The computer impacts on almost every aspect of our lives. If the educational environment continues to stress the importance of technology in the classroom, then addressing such issues will become imperative. Additionally, how can we measure success and/or failure in addressing such issues? ▪

SURFING • THE • WEB

At the website "Office of Educational Research and Improvement" (**http://www.ed.gov/pubs/TeachersGuide/oeri.html**) students and teachers can learn about 24 research and development centers. Within ERIC, the "Assessment and Evaluation" address is **http://ericae.net**.

On the website, "**Goodcharter.com**," Charis Denison presents ethical dilemmas for classroom discussion. This is a wonderful website to use with your students to address moral development. Students can log on and reply the presented dilemmas and view what other students have posted. Denison (n.d.). **Goodcharter.com**. Retrieved from: **http://www.goodcharacter.com/dilemma/archive.html** ▪

Additional Reading

In order to be competent, teachers need to be skillful in interpreting research and having a basic understanding of statistics. Further, teachers are ethically bound to be able to appropriately evaluate students and interpret test results. Available is a wealth of resources to assist teachers in the evaluation of tests and statistics:

- Two articles describing the use and interpretation of standardized tests include one written by Buddy (2009) and one by Ballard and Bates (2008). Buddy provides the reader with information on how to interpret and share test data. She also provides strategies and resources for the reader to use to increase competence in test data. Ballard and Bates examined the relationship between standardized tests and classroom teaching. They provide the reader with both the benefits and the shortcomings of standardized tests.

- In Kohn's (2000) book, *The Case Against Standardized Testing*, an informed look is presented on the overuse and overemphasis of standardized tests in the U.S. He also presents the reader with alternatives to standardized testing that are available to measure student learning.

RECAP OF MAJOR IDEAS

1. Objective tests enable teachers to measure over a broad body of content; essay tests restrict the teacher to measuring over a small body of content.

2. Essay test answers should be determined before the test is given so that specific concepts can be identified and assigned values.

3. Test item values should be proportional to the emphasis and time afforded the item in class and on homework assignments.

4. Of the types of objective tests, multiple-choice tests are preferred because, correctly written, they can require students to engage in higher order thinking.

5. Objective questions can be written to test higher levels of thinking and problem solving, but, in the past, teachers have used mostly simple recall questions.

6. Tests should be administered in a very serious, organized manner. The teacher is responsible to guard against disturbances, which students often find annoying and frustrating.

7. Clarity is an important objective in the construction of all types of tests.

FURTHER APPLICATIONS

1. Construct an essay test. Then rewrite each question, making questions more precise. Be sure to add a statement of directions at the beginning of the test to guide students' behavior during the test and immediately after they take the test.

2. Interview at least two teachers and ask each the following questions:

   a. Do you prefer to give objective or essay tests? Why?

   b. Along with tests, what additional criteria do you use to determine grades?

   c. Do you use the normal curve? Why or why not?

   d. What advice can you give to help a new teacher do a better job with testing?

3. Anticipating the time that you will have a guest visit your classroom during an exam, write a response that you would give to an unannounced visit by

   a. A student family member

   b. A fellow teacher

   c. Your principal

4. Ask a classmate to discuss and interpret with you the statement, "Essay tests measure what a student knows, and objective tests measure what a student does not know." From your discussion, write a one- to three-page paper in support of essay tests.

KEY TERMS

teacher-made tests
diagnostic instruments
table of specifications
objective tests
reliability
essay questions
weighted
stem
discriminatory power
distractors

item analysis
discussion questions
delimitations
divergent thinking
inductive thinking
standardized test
normed test
authentic assessment
portfolio assessment

Glossary

The numbers in parentheses indicate in which chapter(s) the terms are discussed.

ability-evaluative motivation One of three types of student motivation; elicited by *competitive goal structures* (11)

abstract Nonconcrete; the ability to consider concepts apart from a particular application (2)

acceleration A speeded-up or more intensive educational program; recommended as a means of motivating gifted students by providing them challenging instruction (5)

accommodation According to Piaget, altering *schemata* to be consistent with the environment (2)

accountability Students and teachers have to meet some standard of competence or pass a *performance evaluation* (13)

achievement The fourth of Marcia's four periods; at this point teens have passed through crisis, exploration, and questioning and have made a commitment (3)

achievement motivation theory Attempts to explain varying levels of effort among students; actions and feelings related to achieving some internalized standard of excellence (11)

acquired immunodeficiency syndrome (AIDS) A disease of the immune system, resulting in progressively debilitating opportunistic infections (1)

acrostics A technique for remembering; forming a sentence or phrase with each word corresponding to the first letter in the words that need to be remembered (8)

action research A method for teachers to gather information about what is happening in their class-rooms and to take action based on the results (13)

adaptation According to Piaget, changing a response to the environment or changing the *schemata* to reconcile it to one's existing schemata (2)

advance organizer An aid for helping students learn new material by associating it with what they already know (8)

aesthetic needs The search for beauty; sixth in *Maslow's need theory* hierarchy (11)

affective education Curriculum designed to teach students skills in building self-esteem (3)

affective objectives Foundations that teachers hope to develop in students' character, such as attitudes, values, and beliefs (9)

algorithms A finite set of steps that when executed will consistently achieve defined goals (10)

American Disabilities Act (ADA PL 101-336) Signed into law by George W. Bush in 1990, ADA prohibits discrimination against persons with disabilities (5)

analogies Use the knowledge of solutions to similar problems to provide direction to solutions to a targeted problem (10)

analysis-level objectives Require students to work with principles, concepts, and broad generalizations and to break down a subject matter to its structural form to understand it (9)

application-level objectives Require students to use principles or generalizations to solve a defined problem (9)

articulation disorder A type of speech and communication disorder, characterized by substituting one sound for another, distorting sounds, and adding or omitting sounds (5)

Asperger's Syndrome (AS) A disorder marked by severe and sustained impairments in a child's social interactions different from autism due to differences in speech and language development (5)

assigned time The duration students are provided to accomplish assigned work or tasks (see also *time on task, engaged time*) (12)

assimilation According to Piaget, altering responses to the environment to be consistent with the *schemata*; also, the process whereby those of different cultures learn how to adjust to another culture (2, 4)

asymmetrical distributions When divided in half vertically, these *frequency distribution* halves do not form mirror images (13)

at-risk'students Students with a higher-than-average probability of dropping out of school or failing academically (11)

attention deficit/hyperactivity disorder (ADHD) A set of symptoms reflecting excessive inattention or hyperactivity and impulsivity within the context of what is developmentally appropriate for the child's age and gender (5)

attribution According to *cognitive learning theorists*, the differences in the way individuals perceive their past and present environments (7)

attribution theory Weiner's theory that attempts to explain how students think about causes of their successes and failures (11)

auditory content Information cued from the ear; part of Guilford's content dimension (5)

authentic assessment Measures those skills students will need to perform tasks common in daily life; aimed at preparing students for life (14)

autism Individual's diagnosed with autism display markedly abnormal or impaired development in social interaction and communication and a markedly restricted repertoire of activity and interests (5)

autonomy versus shame Erikson's second crisis; toddlers leave this stage with the *psychosocial value* of *will* and achieve independence (3)

aversive stimulus An object or event experienced as something unpleasant (6)

awareness One of the skills involved in *metamemory*; alertness in drawing inferences from what one experiences (8)

behavioral approach A method of studying human behavior that focuses on observable events and the predictions and control of human behavior (11)

behavioral content Information about feelings and behaviors of people as seen through their body language; part of Guilford's content dimension (5)

behavioral disorders Students who are behaviorally confused or bewildered; many do not understand social stresses and feel unaccepted in their efforts to resolve them and may react hostilely or apathetically (5)

behavioral learning theory Scientific explanation of learning that focuses on the behavior of learners and attempts to reduce the learning process into elementary components (6)

behavior pattern The fourth domain of the *social cognitive approach*; includes *mastery oriented* and *helpless* patterns (11)

being needs Maslow's last three needs (*knowledge and understanding, aesthetic*, and *self-actualization*); these are never completely satisfied (11)

bimodal distribution A distribution that has two distinct points, or intervals, with the highest frequency in the distribution (13)

Bioecological Model of Development Urie Bronfenbrenner offers a model of human development that includes the hereditary and biological traits of an individual such as inherited ability, race and intelligence (3)

brainstorming A technique in which an individual or a group generates a large number of solutions to a problem without censoring them before a period of evaluating them; the best are used to address the problem (10)

case studies Examples of actual classroom experiences teachers have encountered; method that uses real classroom experiences as a means to tie theory and practice (9)

centration Children's inability to focus on more than one dimension of a problem; characterizes Piaget's second, or *preoperational*, period (2)

chaining Learning more complex behaviors through engaging in a series of connected stimulus-response behaviors sequenced (6)

classical conditioning A process furthered by Pavlov that examined which *stimuli* would evoke particular responses; the process of establishing a connection between a *neutral stimulus* and an existing reflex; *also known as respondant conditioning* (6)

class meetings Structured meetings with teachers, students, and sometimes parents/guardians that are held to discuss class environment and rules (5)

classroom contingency contract An agreement (generally written) between a teacher and students about how the classroom will be managed (12)

classroom incentives Methods teachers use to motivate students, including grades (11)

classroom management The teacher's ability to cooperatively manage time, space, resources, and student behavior to provide a climate that encourages learning (12)

coding A process in which new information in *working memory* is integrated with known information (7)

cognition One of Guilford's five operations; involves discovering, knowing, or comprehending (5)

cognitive approaches An approach to studying mental processes that assumes people's perceptions and thoughts influence the way they respond to *stimuli* (11)

cognitive development Mental processes by which individuals acquire a more sophisticated and complex understanding of the world around them (2)

cognitive learning theory The scientific study of the relationship of *cognition* and *learning* (7)

cognitive objectives Bloom's six levels (*knowledge, comprehension, application, analysis, synthesis, evaluation*) for measuring cognitive performance (9)

cognitive processes The functions of the mind including creativity, memory, thinking, problem solving, and attention (7)

commitment According to Marcia, personal investment in an occupation or belief (3)

communication disorders Defined as a significant deviation in speech and language from norms based on sex, age, and cultural, ethnic or social expectations (5)

competence The *psychosocial value* achieved through resolving the *crisis* of *industry versus inferiority* in Erikson's fourth stage of development (3)

competitive goal structure A reward system that generally only acknowledges the best (11)

componential intelligence *Intelligence* of the internal world of the individual, characterized by high test scores and other measures of analytical thinking (5)

comprehension-level objectives Bloom's second *objective*; requires students to translate, interpret, or predict a continuation of trends that demonstrates they understand the logic that leads to those trends (9)

computer-assisted instruction (CAI) Use of the computer to teach or train; allows students to learn at their own pace (9)

concept A *generalization* about content that gives meaning to otherwise seemingly unrelated facts (10)

concept development Process of acquiring the ability to form concepts (8)

concrete operations Piaget's third level of development (ages 8 to 11); can perform first-order operations and think deductively (2)

conditioned reinforcer Learned *reinforcers*, which have reinforcement power because they are paired with *primary reinforcers* (6)

conditioned response (CR) The response evoked by a *conditioned stimulus* (6)

conditioned stimulus (CS) An event or object paired with an *unconditioned stimulus* to eventually evoke a particular response (6)

confidence The third domain of the *social cognitive approach;* people may have strong or little belief in their own abilities (11)

confluent education Interaction between the cognitive and affective variables in the learning process (3)

conservation An aspect of *centration;* children's inability to recognize that when one dimension of a problem changes, others may or may not remain constant (2)

constructivism A learning theory with roots in philosophy, anthropology, and psychology that says students use their existing knowledge to help them make sense of new material; a movement to shift education from a teacher-dominated focus to a student-centered one (10, 13)

contextual intelligence Wisdom about the external world; street smart (5)

contingency contracting system A written agreement specifying desired student behaviors or actions and the consequences for both appropriate and inappropriate behaviors (12)

continuous reinforcement The practice of reinforcing a response each time it is performed to strengthen it (6)

controllability Weiner's third dimension of causality; controllable causes include effort and bias; uncontrollable include ability and luck (11)

controversies Arise when one student's ideas or conclusions differ from those of another, and each wants to push his or her views (12)

conventional morality Second of Kohlberg's three levels of morality; comprises two stages, mutual interpersonal expectations and social conscience (3)

convergent production Using information stored in *memory* to generate the one correct solution to a problem; contrasted with Guilford's *divergent production* (5)

cooperative goal structure One goal is shared by a group of students, and their activities and efforts converge toward a common goal **(II)**

cooperative learning Teaching that facilitates students working together to achieve a common goal (5)

correlation A *descriptive statistic;* indicates the degree to which two variables are related (13)

correlation coefficient An index of association, used for making predictions about how variables interrelate; variables can be positively or negatively related (13)

creativity Part of *problem solving;* using inventive, novel, or refined solutions to address issues or needs (10)

crisis According to Marcia, those times in adolescence when teenagers are actively involved in choosing among alternatives leading to stress based on the need to make decisions (3)

criterion-referenced evaluation A *measurement* of achievement of previously announced specific criteria or skills in terms of absolute levels of mastery; focuses on performance of an individual as measured against a standard or criteria rather than against others' performance, as with *norm-referenced tests* (13)

cultural discontinuity The clash of two cultures; people with one set of values and norms find themselves at odds with a society with different values and norms (4)

culturally compatible classrooms Classrooms in which an environment has been created that stresses respecting and learning about the cultures of the various attending children (4)

culturally responsive teaching (CRT) The process of planning, facilitation and monitoring student learning experiences in the most diverse of classrooms (12)

culture The attitudes, behaviors, and values of a group; includes one's nationality, ethnicity, race, gender, socioeconomic background, and age (4)

cumulative percentages The portion of students who obtained a particular score or below it (13)

cyber-bullying The use of technology to intimidate and humiliate (3)

daily learning log A daily record kept by students of their reactions to their academic activities (8)

decay theory An explanation for why we forget that argues that memory fades with the passage of time; replaced by *interference theory* (7)

deficiency needs Physiological, safety, love, and esteem, according to Maslow; when not met, *motivation* to find ways to meet these needs increases (11)

delimitation Setting boundaries on students' responses to questions to avoid inappropriate classroom responses (14)

descriptive statistics The branch of statistics that describes or summarizes data; includes *measures of central tendency, variability* and *correlations* (13)

developmental learning stages According to Piaget, the four periods children pass through during their early formative years: *sensorimotor, preoperations, concrete operations,* and *formal operations* (2)

deviation score A score minus the *mean* in a distribution; used to calculate *variance* (13)

diagnosis The ability to assess the difficulty of a memory task at hand; a component of *metamemory* (8)

diagnostic evaluation Testing aimed at identifying specific student strengths and weaknesses in learning (13)

diagnostic instrument Used by teachers to detect students' strengths and weaknesses in learning (14)

dialect A variation of standard English that is notable in vocabulary, grammar, or pronunciation (2)

diffusion The first of Marcia's four periods; during this period adolescents lack *commitment* to their future occupation or current beliefs (3)

direct instruction A method of learning in which students spend most of their school day being taught by teachers instead of working on their own (9)

direct reinforcement Occurs during *modeling*, when the pupil is able to emulate what the model has demonstrated (6)

discovery approach to learning Process developed by Bruner, that attempts to help students discover information within the context of a field of study as a means of helping them remember and apply what they have learned (7)

discriminatory power The ability of each item to distinguish between those who mastered the content in the question and those who did not (14)

discussion questions Test items that begin with the verb "discuss"; inadequate for measuring students' knowledge about the subject (14)

disequilibrium Occurs when current *schemata* are inadequate or unclear to the individual, requiring adjustment to the schemata (2)

distractors Answers in multiple-choice tests that provide attractive alternatives to the correct response (14)

divergent production Producing a wide variety of items from information stored in *memory* to solve a specific problem or answer a specific question; contrast with *convergent production* (5)

divergent thinking Beginning with specifics and generalizing to a broader application (14)

diversity Human characteristics in individuals or groups that have the potential to either enrich or limit a student's capacity to learn from the school environment (4)

educational goals Expectations held for groups of students; specific and attainable (9)

educationally at-risk Children whose chances for graduation from high school are small (1)

educational objectives Performance, or behavioral, *objectives* that emphasize student rather than teacher performance (9)

educational psychology Applying the principles of psychology to education, addressing the learning process and instructional strategies that impact learning (1)

effective schools Schools that are successful in educating and socializing students while maintaining high morale among teachers, staff, and administrators (1)

effective teachers Teachers who can facilitate academic development and nurture social development among their students (1)

efficacy The extent to which teachers believe they and their students can succeed (1)

egocentrism Children's belief that the world revolves around them; characterizes Piaget's second, or *preoperational*, period (2)

ego integrity versus despair The *crisis* during Erikson's eighth stage (maturity); resolution leads to *wisdom* (3)

Elementary and Secondary Education Act Flexibility 2011 (ESEA flexibility) ESEA flexibility allows state's education agencies to request flexibility in meeting the requirements of NCLB (No Child Left Behind) (5)

engaged time The duration spent focused on accomplishing a task (12)

entity theory Belief that *intelligence* is fixed and unchangeable; part of the theory of intelligence, or first domain in the *social cognitive approach* (11)

equilibrium According to Piaget, the process of maintaining balance, or an understanding of

the environment consistent with current *schemata* (2)

essay questions Measure students' knowledge by allowing them to write in-depth about the subject matter (14)

esteem needs *Confidence* and mastery of goals; fourth in *Maslow's need theory* hierarchy (11)

ethnicity A cultural heritage shared by a group of people (4)

evaluation Determining whether a piece of information satisfies logical criteria; assigning a value to something (5, 13)

evaluation-level objectives The highest of Bloom's objective levels; requires students to define criteria and then assess how well they were met (9)

experiential education A key method of *constructivism;* learning by exploring or experiencing one's physical surroundings (10)

experiential intelligence The mediation of experience on the internal and external world of the individual (5)

external locus of control Belief that behaviors are caused by factors beyond one's control, such as luck, the difficulty of the task, and so on (11)

extinction Withholding reinforcement of a behavior to reduce its recurrence (6)

extrinsic motivation Incentive that depends solely on external rewards, such as grades; associated with *behavioral learning theory* (11)

fading Gradually removing prompts, cues, or other helpful *stimuli* as a means of prompting desired behavior (6)

feedback Presenting information to students that helps them gauge the success of activities they have completed (8)

first-order operations Operations on objects; part of Piaget's third, or *concrete operations*, period (2)

fixed interval schedule A *reinforcement schedule* that continually reinforces a response whenever a predetermined time interval has elapsed (6)

flexible Adaptable thinking (2)

foreclosure The second of Marcia's four periods; adolescents accept their parents' values and occupational choices and have not yet experienced an identity crisis (3)

formal operations Piaget's fourth level of development (ages 11 to 15 and older), during which adolescents perform second-order operations and use *flexible* thinking (2)

formative evaluation Testing used by teachers to improve the quality of instruction; occurs during the instructional unit and is given in small doses at close intervals (weekly, short-answer tests) (13)

formative measurement Testing that occurs before instruction, used to develop needed instruction as determined by the results of the test (13)

frequency distribution Tables that report the frequency that a number, or event, occurs in a set of data (13)

frequency polygon A graph similar to a *histogram;* connects the midpoint of each interval in a *frequency distribution* and plots each against its corresponding frequency (13)

friendship Having close, personal relationships with others (3)

generalization A process whereby once a response has been conditioned to a particular stimulus, a similar stimulus can be used to evoke the same response (6)

generativity versus stagnation The *crisis* during Erikson's seventh stage (middle adulthood); resolution leads to care (3)

Gestalt psychology The scientific study of form, shape, or configuration; proponents argued that individuals react to their total experiences rather than to individual elements as postulated by behaviorists (7)

gifted and talented Students, children, or youth who give evidence of high achievement capability in areas such as intellectual, creative, artistic, or leadership capacity, or in specific academic fields, and who need services and activities not ordinarily provided by the school in order to fully develop those capabilities (5)

grouped frequency distribution Arranging scores into intervals to provide a condensed view of how often a range of scores occurs (13)

grouping Placing students with similar talents together for all or portions of the school day to heighten their learning experiences (5)

guided discovery Problem solving with the teacher providing step-by-step directions (7)

helpless A maladaptive *behavior pattern,* characterized by avoidance of difficult tasks (11)

heterogeneous values A set of values that are spread out in a distribution, some low, some high, some in the middle (13)

heteronomous morality Part of Kohlberg's first, or *preconventional morality* stage; children are egocentric and do what is right to avoid being punished (3)

heuristics Applying what one already knows to help find solutions to problems (10)

higher-level thinking skills Operations that include comprehension and interpretation of information and problem solving (9)

histogram A pictorial representation of a *frequency distribution* (13)

holistic academic atmosphere A learning environment that encourages group work (4)

home parent-student contract An agreement between parents and a student specifying goals and behaviors expected of the student in the school environment (12)

homogeneous values A set of values in a distribution that are the same or approximately the same (13)

humanistic approach Focuses on the *intrinsic motivation* of students; developed as a reaction to behaviorism (11)

hypothesis An assumption or prediction tested through research; alternative ways of viewing the solution to a problem (10)

identity confusion Results from a negative resolution of the *identity versus role confusion* crisis in Erikson's fifth, or adolescence, stage (3)

identity crisis According to Erikson, a period of time (fifth, or adolescence, stage) when teenagers are confused about their roles (3)

identity versus role confusion The *crisis* in Erikson's fifth stage (adolescence); resolution leads to fidelity (3)

inclusion The practice of placing physically or mentally challenged children in regular classrooms (5)

incremental theory A belief that *intelligence* can change; part of the theory of intelligence, or first, domain in the *social cognitive approach* (11)

individualistic goal structure Rewards for one student are independent of others' efforts (11)

individualized education program (IEP) Educational plans designed to meet the unique needs of individual students (5)

Individuals with Disabilities Education Improvement Act of 2004 (IDEA) IDEA requires written Individual Education Plans (IEPs) for students with special needs to address students 'educational process' (5)

inductive thinking See *divergent thinking* (14)

industry versus inferiority The *crisis* in Erikson's fourth (elementary school) stage; resolution leads to *competence* (3)

information processing A vehicle to explain the mechanisms that allow individuals to develop, think, and learn (7)

initiative versus guilt The *crisis* in Erikson's third stage of development (preschool); resolution leads to purpose (3)

inner speech The process of children using language to guide themselves through learning tasks (2)

inquiry learning A teaching method that requires students to take an active role in the learning process; emphasizes investigation by students of subject matter via independent study, oral and written reports, library searches, lab experiments, and fieldwork (9)

insight According to Gestaltists, learning that comes together instantaneously; a means of accomplishing *Problem solving* (7, 10)

instrumental purpose Part of Kohlberg's first, or *preconventional morality* stage; children do what's right because it's fair (3)

intellectually disabled Students who are intellectually disabled have significantly sub-average intellectual functioning and adaptive behavior when compared to their chronological or grade-age peers (5)

intelligence A measure of the range of an individual's intellectual abilities (5)

interference theory Replaced *decay theory;* argues that we forget because new conflicting information enters *memory* and interferes with what has been previously learned (7)

internal locus of control Belief that behaviors are contingent on relatively permanent characteristics, such as ability; belief that we are responsible for our own successes and failures (11)

interval schedule A *reinforcement schedule* based on passage of time (6)

intimacy versus isolation According to Erikson, the first *crisis* of young adulthood (sixth stage); resolution leads to love, or mutual devotion (3)

intrinsic motivation Incentive that comes from within or one's own values; associated with *humanistic* and *cognitive approaches* (11)

irreversibility Children's inability to retrace their steps when trying to solve a problem; characterizes Piaget's second, or *preoperational*, period (2)

item analysis A means of determining whether a test is fair by measuring its *discriminatory power*, or the ability of each item to discriminate between those who mastered the content in the question and those who did not (14)

key word method A learning aid that associates words to be learned with words that can be visualized as a means of remembering them (8)

key word organizer Words used to identify key concepts and organize information for readers; often set in boldface type (8)

knowledge and understanding needs Curiosity and the desire to *learn;* fifth in *Maslow's need theory* hierarchy (11)

knowledge base The body of known information in a field, such as *educational Psychology* (1)

knowledge-level objectives Bloom's first *objective;* before students tackle advanced levels of tasks, they must first master a primary *knowledge base* (9)

Kohlberg's theory of moral development Kohlberg's theory that there are six stages of moral development *(heteronomous, instrumental purpose*, mutual interpersonal expectations, social conscience, *social contract*, and *universal and ethical principles)* contained within three levels of morality *(preconventional, conventional*, and *postconventional)* (3)

language acquisition Developing speech (about ages 2 to 3); a major component in *cognitive development (2)*

latchkey children Children who are at home alone before and/or after school with no adults present (1)

law of effect Thorndike's law, which says that if a *stimulus* is followed by a response and then a *satisfier*, the stimulus-response connection is strengthened (6)

learned helplessness Individuals belief that no matter how hard they try, their success depends on outside factors, or *external locus of control* (II)

learning A generally permanent change in behavior that results from training or experience (6)

learning disability (LD) Students who have average to above-average intelligence but are unable to adequately process information to the extent that it hinders their learning (5)

learning goals Students' desire to increase their competence or to master a new skill; part of the goal, or second, domain in the *social cognitive approach* (11)

learning style How elements from basic *stimuli* in the current and past environment affect an individual's ability to absorb and retain information (8)

lecture instruction Oral presentation of material to students; most appropriate when students are homogeneous in their abilities (9)

link method Uses imagery to help remember a list of items (8)

links Ways to communicate to students the relationship between effort and success; includes goals, learning strategies, successful experiences, and how success is attributed or viewed (11)

listening skills The ability to focus on another person's communications and decipher purpose, expectations, biases, sincerity, and other characteristics of the message (9)

loci method Mentally placing items in a room or other location as a means of remembering the items by associating them with the location (8)

locus of control Weiner's first dimension of causality; consists of *external locus of control* and *internal locus of control* (11)

logic and objectivity Thinking deductively when solving problems; characterizes Piaget's third, or *concrete operations*, period (2)

long-term memory (LTM) The part of the brain that acts as a storehouse where large amounts of *memory* are stored for a long time, perhaps throughout life (7)

love To be cherished by one's family, friends, and peers; third in *Maslow's need theory* hierarchy (11)

main streaming Placing students with disabilities in classes with nondisabled students (5)

Maslow's need theory Used to explain human *motivation;* contains a hierarchy of seven levels of need, in which lower-level needs must be satisfied before higher-level needs; includes: *physiological, safety, love, esteem, knowledge and understanding, aesthetic,* and *self-actualization needs* (11)

mastery oriented An adaptive *behavior pattern,* characterized by challenge-seeking actions and persistence (11)

maturation Physiological changes that result from heredity and minimal nutrition but that do not require learning or exercise (2)

mean The arithmetic average of a set of values, generated by summing the values and then dividing by the number of values included (13)

means-ends analysis A form of *heuristics;* solving a problem by subdividing its elements and solving those (10)

measurement A value-free term that means to ascertain the dimensions, quantity, or capacity of (13)

measures of central tendency Describe average values in a set of data by indicating where most of the values lie in a *frequency distribution; mean, median,* and *mode* (13)

measures of variability Describe how numbers are dispersed, or spread out, in a *frequency distribution;* includes *range, variance,* and *standard deviation* (13)

median The midpoint of a set of data; the score in which half the values fall below and half above (13)

memory Storing information for later use; one of Guilford's operations; the store of things learned and retained from one's experiences (5, 7)

menarche The beginning of menstruation in adolescent females (3)

mentally retarded Students who have learning rates that are slightly to considerably lower than those of their chronological or grade-age peers (5)

metacognition "Thinking about one's own *thinking*"; the conscious *monitoring* and regulation of one's thoughts; the mental activities used to plan, monitor, and control *problem solving, comprehension, memory,* and other *cognitive processes* (7, 8)

metacognitive knowledge The segment of our stored knowledge that indicates to us that we use different tasks, goals, actions, and experiences to process differing types of information (7)

metamemory Individuals' awareness of their own memory processes and capabilities (8)

mildly retarded Students who are similar to their normal classmates in height and weight but lacking in strength, speed, and coordination; many have short attention spans and may display disruptive behavior in the classroom (5)

minority group A group of people who have been socially disadvantaged based on race or ethnicity (4)

mnemonics A technique for remembering; pairing something memorable, such as a word or an object, with new information (8)

mode The value that occurs most frequently in a set of data (13)

modeling A procedure that demonstrates behavior to be imitated (6)

models Using replicas (physical or *simulations)* as an inexpensive way to study problems and seek their solution (10)

monitoring Process where the teacher assesses how well learners are remembering; one of the components of *metamemory* (8)

moral responsibility Third of three *motivation* systems; elicited by *cooperative goal structures* (11)

moratorium The third of Marcia's four periods, during which teenagers are experiencing a *crisis* but have yet to make a *commitment* (3)

morphology Smallest units of meaning of any language; one or more phonemes, or basic sounds, such as prefixes, suffixes, verb tenses (2)

motivation According to Piaget, the result of *disequilibrium;* a desire to learn to acquire methods to handle the disequilibrium; a hypothetical construct that explains why people get interested and how they react to the events that get their attention (2, 11)

multicultural materials Learning resources, including textbooks, designed to reverse students' negative images of minorities and replace them with positive, balanced images (4)

negatively skewed distribution The frequency of scores congregates in the upper, or left, end of a *frequency distribution* (13)

negative reinforcer A stimulus event that, when removed, increases the probability of the response it follows (6)

neutral stimulus Something that does not evoke a particular response prior to conditioning (6)

No Child Left Behind (NCLB) Signed into law by President George W. Bush in 2002. NCLB required all students grades 3 through 8 to take yearly standardized achievement tests in math, reading, and in 2007 science was added and all students grades 3 through 5, 6 through 9 and 10 through 12 were required to take tests (1)

nonverbal skills Managing students' activities or focus without speaking; includes *time on task* and using eye contact effectively (12)

normal curve See *normal distribution*

normal distribution A *frequency distribution* that is always symmetrical and reaches its peak at the middle; the form most distributions of data will tend to when samples are sufficiently large-generally, at least 100 (13)

normed test A test rated for average scores based on large populations scores; see *standardized tests* (14)

norm-referenced evaluation An objective test that is standardized on a group of individuals whose performance is evaluated in relation to the performance of others; contrasted with *criterion referenced test* (13)

objectives Statements of student activity that are specific enough to be measurable (9)

objective tests Those tests whose items have a single correct answer such as multiple choice, matching, true-false, fill in the blank; attempts to remove the potential for teacher bias (14)

object permanence The knowledge that objects exist even though they are out of sight; part of Piaget's first, or *sensorimotor*, stage (2)

observational learning *Modeling;* the process of learning from observing others' behavior (6)

on-task behavior Students actually working on currently assigned classroom activities (5)

open discovery *Problem solving* without the teacher's close monitoring (7)

operant behavior Behavior that changes or affects the outside environment (6)

operant conditioning Learning that is strengthened by the consequences it produces (6)

operations According to Piaget, the strategies and rules used to solve problems (2)

operators Part of the process of solving a problem; the alternatives reexamined and then the actions taken to solve the problem (10)

orthopedic disabilities Impairments that interfere with the normal functions of bones, joints, or muscles, including organs and systemic malfunctions (5)

overlapping The teacher's ability to manage more than one classroom activity at a time (12)

pairing Combining *primary* and *secondary reinforcers* to strengthen the effectiveness of the secondary reinforcer (6)

peer tutoring One student assisting another in learning academic tasks or skills (12)

peg word technique A technique for remembering items in a particular sequence, involving hanging items on an easily associated peg; for example, "A" is for "apple" (8)

percentages The portion of students who obtain a score, or who scored within an interval of scores (13)

perception The process of determining the meaning of what is sensed (7)

performance evaluation Requires students to apply information they have learned to solve a problem; an outgrowth of the new emphasis on *accountability* (13)

performance-focused strategies Stress the performance as the end goal; offer rewards to achieve the best performance (11)

performance goals Students' attempts to gain positive judgments of their competence; part of the goal, or second, domain in the *social cognitive approach* (11)

personal knowledge Beliefs people have about their own cognitive abilities in comparison with those of others; one of Flavell's three categories of *metacognitive knowledge* (7)

phonology The science of speech sounds; the study of the approximately forty phonemes, or basic sounds, in English (2)

physiological needs Nourishment, sleep, and shelter; first in *Maslow's need theory* hierarchy (11)

PL 94-142 The public law titled Individuals with Disabilities in Education Act (IDEA); passed in 1975 (as the Education for All Disabled Children Act) and amended in 1990, it requires that children with special needs be placed in the "least restrictive environment" that will facilitate their learning (5)

portfolio assessment A collection of tangible student products examined for evidence of the student's skills (14)

positively skewed distribution The frequency of scores congregates in the lower, or right, end of a distribution (13)

positive reinforcer A *stimulus* presented subsequent to behavior that strengthens the behavior (6)

postconventional morality Third of Kohlberg's three levels of morality; at this level, comprising *social contracts* and *universal and ethical principles*, people must understand how others are affected (3)

PQ4R *Mnemonic* (Preview, Question, Read, Reflect, Recite, Review) for a series of steps used to teach students to master information (8)

preconventional morality First of Kohlberg's three levels of morality; comprises *heteronomous* and *instrumental purpose* stages (3)

Premack principle Premack's theory that a preferred activity could be used to strengthen a less preferred activity by making the former contingent on completing the latter (6)

preoperational period Piaget's second level of development (ages 2 to 7), during which children develop symbolic modes of representation (2)

primary reinforcer *Stimuli* that are biologically, or physiologically, important (food, water, shelter, sex, sleep); *unconditioned reinforcers* (6, 11)

proactive alternatives Options for teachers when preparing for future educational decisions (1)

proactive teachers Teachers who plan ahead and prepare for the time when classroom decisions have to be made (1)

problem definition Explaining a dilemma or issue in a manner that helps determine the method or technique for addressing it (10)

problem finding Problem formulation; an important aspect of scientific discovery (10)

problem representation A means of including all of the unique aspects of the problem to be solved, including its initial, intermediate, and goal states (10)

problem solving Using learning processes to answer inquiries or academic questions; a process of creating knowledge (7)

process evaluation Focuses only on how students perform, or the process they use (13)

product evaluation Assesses a product the student has produced; counterpart of *process evaluation* (13)

Programs for International Student Assessment (PISA) An international evaluation of 15-year-old student achievement in reading, math and science (1)

proximity control Standing near misbehaving students until the misbehavior subsides (1, 12)

proximity search A difference reduction; reduces the available choices when solving a problem (10)

psychosocial value Positive behavioral values, such as hope, *will*, and fidelity, developed through resolving the crises in each of Erikson's eight stages of development (3)

puberty One of the two periods of adolescence, distinguished by the marks of sexual maturity; typified by growth, high energy, and maturation of nerve and muscle tissue (3)

pubescence Preadolescence; one of the two stages of adolescence, consisting of the two years preceding puberty and the beginning of the adolescence growth spurt (3)

punishment Presenting a stimulus after the performance of a behavior (usually aversive) that weakens that behavior (6, 12)

questioning A teaching method that allows introduction of lessons or new units, is an effective complement to videotaped lessons, acts as an *advance organizer*, and is an aid to help students focus on the most important content (9)

race A group of people who share common biological traits that are seen as self-defining by the people of the group (4)

Race to the Top (R2T, RTT) RTT is a United States Department of Education program, announced by President Barack Obama, designed to address the needs of teacher and school effectiveness and student learning (1)

racial prejudice Unreasonable bias toward a group of individuals based on race (1)

random search Solving a problem by chance (10)

range The difference between the lowest and the highest values in a distribution (13)

ratio schedule A *reinforcement schedule* based on number of responses (6)

reactive teachers Teachers who respond to present conditions in the classroom (1)

readiness The level of mental development necessary to benefit from experiences (2)

reflective Reacting to one's own thinking (2)

reflexive Reacting to one's own environment (2)

rehearsal Teaching desired behavior through combining modeling with training sessions that include prompting of the behavior and praise when it is enacted; procedures used to retain information in *working memory*, including re-reading, browsing, outlining, or repeating material (6, 8)

reinforcement schedule A method of arranging the use of *reinforcers* based on passage of time or number of responses (6)

reinforcer Any consequence that increases the probability that a response will occur again (6)

relaxation training Monitoring the involuntary physiological processes, such as muscle tensing, brain wave activity, heart rate, blood pressure, and breathing patterns, of behaviorally disordered students to help them relax and focus on classroom activities (5)

reliability The extent to which a test is dependable and consistent when administered to the same individuals on different occasions (14)

repertoire A collection of teaching methods and the ability to select the one appropriate to a particular student need (9)

resolution Resolving the *crisis* involved at each stage of Erikson's theory; prerequisite for advancing to the next stage (3)

response cost Taking away tokens, or rewards, from students for inappropriate behavior (6, 12)

role and perspective taking Understanding others' intentions, motives, thoughts, and emotions (3)

Rosa's Law Signed into law by President Barack Obama in 2010. Rosa's Law replaces the term "mental retardation" with "intellectual disabilities" in all federal articles related to education (1)

safety needs Freedom from danger, anxiety, and threat; second in *Maslow's need theory* hierarchy (11)

satisfier A result that is positive, or pleasurable, enough to strengthen a connection between *stimuli* and the responses that follow (6)

scaffolds Tools or techniques that form the instructional procedures for teaching *higher-level thinking skills* (9)

schemata According to Piaget, the thoughts, memories, and understandings gained by children through experience; contents of *memory* that contain elements of related information and influence the gathering of new information (2, 8)

school reform reports Various local, state, and national reports that recommend change in our nation's schools (1)

secondary reinforcer *Conditioned reinforcer;* nonbiological reinforcers (praise, grades, money) that gain their effectiveness through *pairing* with *primary reinforcers* (6, 11)

second-order operations Children can use concepts never before encountered and objects they can't manipulate (2)

self-actualization Self-fulfillment; seventh in *Maslow's need theory* hierarchy (11)

self-concept Individuals' perceptions of themselves; how they feel about themselves and their abilities; self-esteem (3)

self-esteem See *self-concept* (3)

self-regulated learning (SRL) Teaching students to positively regulate and discipline their behavior and academic learning by focusing on self-discipline and self-regulation (12)

self-reinforcement Augmentation through personal goals, standards, or criteria set by the individual (6)

self-understanding An aspect of social cognition; understanding one's self is necessary to understanding others in social situations (3)

semantic content Meanings; part of Guilford's content dimension (5)

semantics The study of meanings of words and groups of words (2)

sense receptors Sense organs that allow us to interpret our environment (7)

sensorily impaired Students who are visually or hearing impaired (5)

sensorimotor period Piaget's first level of development (birth to age 2), during which infants develop the ability to use symbolic thought (2)

sensory impaired Students who are visually impaired and/or hearing impaired are referred to as sensory impaired (5)

sensory memory According to Atkinson and Shiffrin's later discounted theory, a large storage system that could record information from the senses with considerable accuracy; *stimuli* from the environment first entered here (7)

set induction Techniques (telling stories, speaking softly, doing demonstrations) teachers use to get students' attention (12)

sex discrimination Prejudice based on gender (1)

shaping A procedure that teaches desired behavior by reinforcing successive approximations of that behavior (6)

short-term memory (STM) *Working memory;* the *memory* we have in our consciousness, allowing us to deal with our current experiences and solve problems (7)

simulation A technique that teaches about some aspect of the world by imitation or replication (9)

simulation games Enactments that place students in lifelike roles; results in higher learning retention rates for students (9)

skewed distribution A distribution that concentrates a large number of scores in its lower (right) or upper (left) end (13)

social cognition The way that people reason about themselves and others in social situations (3)

social cognitive approach Students' beliefs about their own *intelligence* and includes four domains: theory of intelligence, goals, *confidence,* and *behavior patterns* (11)

social contract Utility and individual rights; people should obey laws to protect the rights of all (3)

social convention A general and shared knowledge determined by the social systems in which people participate (3)

social interaction Having bonding relationships with others; according to Piaget, a critical factor in *cognitive development* (2)

social knowledge Interpersonal understanding, including knowledge of other people, friendships and peer groups, and social roles and situations (3)

social learning *Modeling;* learning through observing and modeling others' behavior (6)

social learning theory The theory that children learn through observing and *modeling* others' behaviors and rewards (6)

socially gifted Those individuals who, because of their environment and innate ability, are popular and often perceived as leaders among their peers (4)

speech impairments A type of speech and communication disorder; the inability to produce sounds effectively (5)

stability Weiner's second dimension of causality; stable causes include ability and effort; unstable include mood and luck (11)

standard deviation The square root of the *variance* which demonstrates the amount the scores in a *frequency distribution* deviate from the *mean* on average (13)

standardized tests Exams that have been *normed,* or rated for average scores based on large populations of students taking the tests; now required for high school graduation in many states (14)

stanine score Nine classes into which normalized test scores are divided along a bell curve (5)

statistics Tools that allow teachers to describe a variety of student characteristics and provide quantifiable measures for supporting or refuting hypotheses (13)

stem A multiple-choice question set up to lead to several possible answers (14)

stimuli Any physical events or objects in the environment that evoke an activity (6)

stimulus substitution Substituting one stimulus for another as in *classical conditioning* (6)

strategy knowledge Awareness that certain strategies will be more effective than others in solving different problems; one of Flavell's three categories of *metacognitive knowledge* (7)

structure of intellect model Theory by Guilford that assumes three dimensions of intelligence (content, operation, and product) that form a systematic collection of abilities used for various forms of information (5)

summative evaluation Testing that occurs after instruction is complete and is used to arrive at a grade (13)

symbolic content Items that represent other items, such as numbers or letters; part of Guilford's content dimension (5)

symbolic modes The ability to use representations of objects, rather than needing the objects present to understand them; occurs during Piaget's second, or *preoperational*, period (2)

symmetrical distribution A *frequency distribution* that when divided in half by a vertical line forms mirror images of each half (13)

synthesis-level objectives Bloom's fifth *objective;* requires students to take parts and make them into a whole; requires divergent thinking and creativity (9)

systematic Methodical thinking; organized according to a system (2)

table of specifications A chart that lists *objectives* or behaviors on one axis and content *generalizations* (concepts, principles, theorems, axioms) on the other (14)

task-endogenous strategies Focus on working on a task for the enjoyment of the process (11)

task-exogenous strategies Focus on working on a task for the rewards to be gained (11)

task knowledge Understanding that variations in a task have implications for how to go about solving it; one of Flavell's three categories of *meta cognitive knowledge* (7)

task mastery Second of three motivation systems; elicited by *individualistic goal structures* (11)

teacher-made tests Exams constructed by teachers to measure achievement, provide feedback, determine student progress, analyze their own teaching effectiveness, and diagnose whether content mastery is being measured (14)

theories of intelligence Theories that focus on individuals' cognitive abilities and their structures, including Guilford's *structure of intellect* model, Sternberg's *triarchic* model, and Jensen's Level I and Level II model (5)

theory of psychosocial development Theory by Erikson that concentrates on the development of healthy, positive *behavior patterns* (3)

thinking Reasoning; considering; developing tactics, strategies, techniques, and methods by design or thought (7)

time on task The duration students actually devote to doing work assigned by the teacher (12)

time out An alternative to corporal punishment that involves isolating a misbehaving student from a situation for a short time (12)

token economy A contingency management system espoused by behavioral and social learning theorists, designed to evoke desired behaviors; systems consist of a token used as a reward and a backup *reinforcer* (grades, free time, and so on) (6)

Torrance Tests of Creative Thinking (TTCT) A test for creativity created by Paul Torrance; looks for four criteria: fluency, *flexibility*, elaboration, and originality (10)

trainable retarded Students who are typically 25 to 53 percent lower than those of average intelligence in their level of intellectual development; many can be educated for jobs requiring exceptional skills (5)

transfer of learning Students' ability to apply one learning experience to another (8)

triarchic theory of intelligence Sternberg's theory that there are three types of intelligence: *componential, contextual*, and *experiential* (5)

trust versus mistrust First *crisis* in Erikson's theory; children leave this stage (infancy) with the value of hope and achieve identity (3)

unconditioned reinforcer Unlearned, or naturally occurring, *reinforcers; primary reinforcers* (6)

unconditioned response (UCR) The reaction to an unconditioned stimulus (6)

unconditioned stimulus (UCS) An object or event that naturally evokes a particular, or *unconditioned, response* (6)

underachiever Students who have high intellectual potential whose performance fails to reflect their potential (5)

ungrouped frequency distribution Recording scores, or numbers, from highest to lowest without placing the numbers into intervals, or ranges, of scores (13)

universal and ethical principles Last of Kohlberg's six stages; judgment of what is right is based on self-chosen ethical principles, which may conflict with laws (3)

value-focused strategies Concentrating on learning or completing tasks because the experience will continue to benefit the doer (11)

values clarification A teaching approach in which students learn to choose their values, celebrate those values and act upon them by incorporating them into their daily lives (3)

variable interval schedule A *reinforcement schedule* that reinforces responses on a variable interval of time elapsed (6)

variable ratio schedule A *reinforcement schedule* that reinforces responses randomly around some average ratio (6)

variance An indicator of how the values in a distribution are dispersed around the *mean;* suggests the degree to which the numbers are *homogeneous* or *heterogeneous* (13)

variety Using a *repertoire* of instructional methods lessens the level of teacher-dominated discussion and increases student participation (12)

vicarious reinforcement Occurs when an individual modifies his or her behavior to emulate that of someone else who has been rewarded for that behavior (6)

virtual reality A technology that uses computers to simulate an alternate world; an interactive tool, it allows users to engage in the simulated environment using their senses (8)

visual content Information cued from the eye; part of Guilford's content dimension (5)

volume An attribute of voice control; raising this attribute can ensure the teacher is heard or lowering it can force students to listen more attentively (12)

weighted Assigning value to test items based on the importance of the content being measured, the time spent in class on homework, or a combination of these variables (14)

will *Psychosocial value* achieved through resolution of Erikson's second *crisis, autonomy versus shame* (3)

wisdom *Psychosocial value* achieved through resolution of Erikson's eighth crisis, ego integrity versus despair (3)

withitness The teacher's ability to be aware of events occurring simultaneously in the classroom (12)

working memory (WM) Area of the brain where work is being done; *short-term memory;* can simultaneously process newly perceived information and information that is recalled from *long-term memory* (7)

zone of proximal development The degree or amount that students can and have learned on their own compared with their potential for learning when assisted by an adult (2)

References

CHAPTER ONE

Armstrong, D. G., Henson, K. T., & Savage, T. V. (2009). *Teaching Today* (8th ed.). Upper River, NJ: Pearson.

Armstrong, D. G., Henson, K. T., & Savage, T. V. (1989). *Education: An introduction* (3rd ed.). New York: Macmillan.

Ball, D. L., & Farzani, F. M. (2011). Teaching skillful teaching. *Educational Leadership, 67*(3), 40–45.

Banks, R., Kopassi, R., & Wilson, A. M. (1991). In R. C. Morris (Ed.), *At risk students.* Lancaster, PA: Technomic.

Berliner, D. (1990, March). Creating the right environment for learning. *Instructor, 99,* 16–17.

Berliner, D., & Biddle, B. J. (1997). *The manufactured crisis.* New York: Longman.

Biddle, B., Good, T., & Goodson, I. (1996). *The international handbook of teachers and teaching.* New York: Kluwer.

Blake, B. (1996, December 1). Faces of AIDS. *Ashville Citizen Times,* B1.

Bryant Jr., J. (2011). Dismantling rural stereotypes. *Educational Leadership, 68*(3), 54–58.

Bushaw, W. J., & McNee, J. A. (2009). Americans speak out. The 41st Annual Phi Delta Kappa/Gallup Poll of the Public's Attitudes Toward the Public Schools. *Phi Delta Kappan, 91*(1), 9–23.

Carson, M. D., & Badarack, G. (1989). *How changing class size affects classrooms and students.* Riverside, CA: University of California at Riverside, California Educational Research Cooperative.

Carter, K., & Doyle, W. (1996). Personal narrative and life history in learning to teach. In J. Sikula, T. Buttery & E. Guyton (Eds.), *Handbook of research on teacher education* (2nd ed.). New York: Macmillan.

Christensen, D. (1996). The professional knowledge research base for teacher education. In J. Sikula, T. Buttery & E. Guyton (Eds.), *Handbook of research on teacher education* (2nd ed.) New York: Macmillan.

Clark, R. W., Hong, L. K., & Schoeppach, M. R. (1996). Teacher empowerment and site-based management. In J. Sikula, T. Buttery & E. Guyton (Eds.), *Handbook of research on teacher education* (2nd ed.). New York: Macmillan.

Clifford, M. M. (1984). Educational psychology. In *Encyclopedia of education.* New York: Macmillan.

DuFour, R. (2011). Work together, but only if you want to. *Phi Delta Kappan.*

Duke, D. L., & Jacobson, M. (2011). Tackling the toughest turn-around: Low-performing high schools. *Kappan, 92*(5), 34–38.

Elam, S. M., Rose, L., & Gallup, A. (1996). The 28th Gallup/Phi Delta Kappa Poll of teachers' attitudes toward the public schools. *Phi Delta Kappan, 78*(1), 41–59.

Erasmus, C. C. (1989). Ways with stories: Listening to the stories aboriginal people tell. *Language Arts, 66*(3), 267–275.

Farr, S. (2011). Leadership: Not magic. *Educational Leadership, 68*(4), 28–33.

Ferguson, D. L., & Halle, J. W. (1995, Spring). Editorial: Considerations for readers of qualitative research. *Journal for the Association for Persons with Severe Handicaps, 20,* 1–2.

Flanders, N. A. (1990). Honor becomes effective teaching. In M. L. Kysilka (Ed.), *Honor in teaching* (pp. 84–90). West Lafayette, IN: Kappa Delta Pi Publications.

Friday, W. (1990). Professional renewal and restoring honor to the profession of teaching. In M. L. Kysilka (Ed.), *Honor in teaching* (pp. 99–102). West Lafayette, IN: Kappa Delta Pi Publications.

Glover, J. A., & Bruning, R. H. (1990). *Educational psychology principles and applications* (3rd ed.). Glenville, IL: Scott, Foresman.

Grinder, R. E. (1981). The "new" science of education: Educational psychology in search of a mission. In F. H. Farley & N. J. Gordon (Eds.), *Psychology and education: The state of the union*. Berkeley, CA: McCutchan.

Gronlund, N. E., & Waugh, C. K. (2009). *Assessment of student achievement* (9th ed.) Upper Saddle River, NJ: Pearson.

Guyton, J. M., & Fielstein, L. L. (1991, January/February). A classroom activity to increase student awareness of racial prejudice. *Clearing House, 64*(3), 207–209.

Hanny, R. J. (1994). Don't let them take you to the barn. *Clearing House, 67*(5), 172–181.

Henson, K. T. (2010). *Supervision for instructional improvement*. Long Grove, IL: Waveland Press.

Henson, K. T. (2011). *Methods and strategies for teaching in secondary and middle schools* (6th ed.). White Plains, NY: Longman.

Hersh, R. H. (2009). A well-rounded education for a flat world. *Educational Leadership, 67*(3), 50–53.

Horton, L. (1988, March). The education of most worth: Preventing drug and alcohol abuse. *Educational Leadership, 45*, 4–8.

Ingersoll, R., & Merrill, L. (2010). Who's teaching our children? *Educational Leadership, 67*(8), 15–20.

Johnston, J. M. (1990). *What are teachers' perceptions of teaching in different classroom contexts?* Paper presented at the annual convention of the American Educational Research Association, Boston, MA.

Jones, M. (1990, October). Actions on theory and target students in science classrooms. *Journal of Research in Science Teaching, 27*, 651–660.

King, P. M., & Kitchener, K. S. (1994). *Developing reflective judgment thinking in adolescents and adults*. San Francisco: Jossey-Bass.

Kochan, F. K., & Herrington, C. D. (1992, Fall). Restructuring for today's children and strengthening schools by strengthening families. *Educational Forum, 57*, 42–49.

Meier, D. (1995). *The power of their ideas: Lessons for America from a small school in Harlem*. Boston: Beacon Press.

Nye, B. A., Achilles, C. M., Boyd-Zaharias, J., Fulton, B. D., & Wallenhorst, M. P. (1994). Small is far better. *Research in the Schools, 1*(1), 9–20.

Provasnik, S., Kewal Ramani, A., Coleman, M. M., Gilbertson, L., Herring, W., & Xie, Q. (2007). Statistics of education in rural America. Retrieved from the National Center for Education Statistics at http://nces.ed.gov/pubs2007/2007040.pdf.

Reames, E. (2010). Creating personal learning sebs: The pover of reflection in mentoring. In K. T. Henson, *Curriculum planning: Integrating multiculturalism, constructivism, and education reform*, 4th ed. Long Grove, IL: Waveland Press.

Reed, S., & Sautter, R. C. (1990). Children of poverty. *Phi Delta Kappan, 71*(10), K4.

Redman, G. L. & Redman, A. R. (2011). *A casebook for exploring diversity*. Boston: Pearson.

Ripley, A. (2010). What makes a great teacher? *The Atlantic, 305*(1), 58–66.

Rothman, R. (2009). Improving student learning requires district learning. *Phi Delta Kappan, 91*(1), 44–50.

Rutter, M. (1983). Stress, coping and development; Some issues and some questions. In N. Garmezy & M. Rutter (Eds.), *Stress, coping, and development in children.* New York: McGraw-Hill.

Silva, E. (2010). Rebuild and they will come. *Educational Leadership, 67*(8), 60–65.

U. S. Department of Education. (1994). *Digest of education statistics,* 1994–95. Washington, DC: National Center for Education Statistics. U. S. Government Printing Office.

U. S. Department of Education. (2010). *Digest of education statistics,* 2010–11. Washington, DC: National Center for Educational Statistics. U. S. Government Printing Office.

U. S. Department of Health and Human Services, Administration on Children, Youth, and Families. (2006). *Child maltreatment: Reports from states to National Child Abuse and Neglect Data System.* Washington, DC.

U. S. Department of Health and Human Services, Administration Children, Youth and Families. (2010). Retrieved January 27, 2011, from http://www.acf..hhs.gov/acf_services.html.

Woodring, T. (1995). *Effects of peer education programs on sexual behavior, AIDS knowledge and attitudes:* Paper presented at the annual meeting of the Eastern Psychological Association, Boston.

Yelon, S. L. (1996). *Powerful principles of instruction.* White Plains, NY: Longman.

CHAPTER TWO

Armstrong, D. G., Henson, K. T., & Savage, T. V. (1997). *Teaching today: An introduction* (5th ed.). New York: Merrill.

Berk, L. E., (2001). *Awakening children's minds: How parents and teachers can make a difference.* New York: Oxford University Press.

Berlinger, W. W., & Yates, C. M. (1993). Formal operational thought in the gifted: A post-Piagetian perspective. *Roeper Review, 15*(4), 220–224.

Braine, M. D. S. (1987). What is learned in acquiring word glasses? A step toward an acquisition theory. In B. MacWhinney (Ed.), *Mechanisms of language acquisition* (pp. 51–76). Hillsdale, NJ: Erlbaum.

Bruder, I., Buchsbaum, H., Hill, M., & Orlando, L. C. (1992). School reform: Why you need technology to get there. *Electronic Learning, 11*(3), 22–28.

Capon, N., & Kuhn, D. (1979). Logical reasoning in the supermarket: Adult females' use of a proportional reasoning strategy in an everyday context. *Developmental Psychology, 15*(4), 450–452.

Case, R. (1984). The process of stage transition: A neo-Piagetian view. In R. J. Starnberg (Ed.), *Mechanisms of cognitive development* (pp. 19–44). New York: W. H. Freeman.

Cooledge, E., Bishop, D. V. M., Koppen-Schomerus, G., Price, T. S., Happe, F., & Eley, T., et al. (2002). The structure of language abilities at 4 years: A twin study. *Developmental Psychology, 36,* 749–757.

Coltheart, M. (1987). Functional architecture of the language-processing system. In M. Coltheart, R. Job & G. Sartori (Eds.), *The neuropsychology of language* (pp. 3–26). Hillsdale, NJ: Erlbaum.

Crago, M. (1992). Communication interaction and second language acquisition: The inuit example. *Tesol Quarterly, 26,* 487–505.

Diaz, R. M. (1983). Thought and two languages: The impact of bilingualism on cognitive development. *Review of Research in Education, 10*, 23–54.

Eggen, P. D., & Kauchak, D. (1992). *Educational psychology: Classroom connections*. New York: Macmillan.

Eimas, P. D. (1985, January). The perception of speech in early infancy. *Scientific American, 252*, 46–52.

Fabes, R. A., & Martin, C. L. (2000). *Exploring Child Development*. Boston: Allyn & Bacon.

Gagnon, E. (1996). *What's on the Web?* Fairfax, VA: Internet Media Corporation.

Gardner, H. (1982). *Developmental psychology: An introduction* (5th ed.). Boston: Little, Brown.

Genesee, F., Paradis, J., & Crago, M. (2004). *Dual language development & disorders: A handbook on bilingualism & second language learning*. Baltimore: Paul H. Brooks.

Glassman, M. (2001). Dewey and Vygotsky: Society, experience, and inquiry in educational practice. *Educational Researcher, 30*(4), 3–14.

Gleason, J. B. (1989). *The development of language* (2nd ed.). Columbus: OH: Merrill.

Glover, J., & Bruning, R. H. (1990). *Educational psychology: Principles and applications* (3rd ed.). New York: Addison-Wesley.

Goetz, G. T., Alexander, P. A., & Ash, M. J. (1992). *Educational psychology: A classroom perspective*. New York: Macmillan.

Graseck, S. (2009). Teaching with Controversy. *Educational Leadership, 67*(3), 45–49.

Grinder, R. E. (Ed.). (1975). *Studies in adolescence* (3rd ed.). New York: Macmillan.

Henson, K. T. (2010). *Supervision for instructional improvement*. Long Grove IL: Waveland Press.

Hetherington, E. M., & Parke, R. D. (1986). *Child psychology: A contemporary viewpoint* (3rd ed.). New York: McGraw-Hill.

Klausmeier, H. J. (1988, Summer). The future of educational psychology and the content of the graduate programs in educational psychology. *Educational Psychologist, 23*, 203–220.

Klausmeier, H. J., & Sipple, T. S. (1982, April). Factor structure of the Piagetian stage of concrete operations. *Contemporary Educational Psychology, 7*, 161–180.

Knovac, J. D. (1993). How do we learn our lessons (Helping students learn how to learn)? *Science Teacher, 60*(3), 50–55.

Kowalski, T. J., Weaver, R. A., & Henson, K. T. (1994). *Case studies on beginning teachers*. White Plains, NY: Longman.

Martinez, M. E. (1998). What is problem solving? *Phi Delta Kappan, 79*(8), 605–609.

Matlin, M. W. (1989). *Cognition*. Fort Worth, TX: Holt, Rinehart & Winston.

Miller, S. A., & Brownell, C. A. (1975, December). Peers, persuasion, and Piaget: Dyadic interactions between conservers and non-conservers. *Child Development, 46*, 992–997.

Murray, F. B. (1979). *The conservation paradigm: The conservation of conservation research* (Tech. Rep. No.2). Newark, DE: University of Delaware Studies in Education.

Pearson, B. (1998). Assessing levical development in bilingual babies and toddlers. *International Journal of Bilingualism, 2*(3), 347–372.

Piaget, J. (1952). *The origins of intelligence in children*. New York: International Universities Press.

Piaget, J. (1960). *The child's conception of the world*. London: Routledge.

Piaget, J. (1963). *The child's conception of the world*. Paterson, NJ: Littlefield, Adams.

Piaget, J. (1964). *Judgment and reasoning in the child* (Marjorie Warden, Trans.). Paterson, NJ: Littlefield, Adams. (Originally published in translation, 1928, Harcourt, Brace & Co.)

Piaget, J. (1969). *The mechanisms of perception.* New York: Basic Books.

Piaget, J. (1970). *Science of education and the psychology of the child.* New York: Viking.

Piaget, J. (1972). Intellectual evaluation from adolescence to adulthood. *Human Development, 15*(1), 1–12.

Rathus, S. A. (1990). *Psychology.* Fort Worth, TX: Holt, Rinehart & Winston.

Rebok, G. (1987). *Life-span cognitive development.* New York: Holt, Rinehart & Winston.

Rodda, M., & Grove, C. (1987). *Language, cognition, and deafness.* Hillsdale, NJ: Erlbaum.

Ross, D. D., Bondy, E., & Kyle, D. W. (1993). *Reflective teaching for student improvement.* New York: Macmillan.

Selekman, H. (2012). In Henson, K. T. (2012). *Methods for teaching in diverse middle-level and secondary classrooms, 2nd ed.* Dubuque, IA: Kendall Hunt.

Teale, W. H., & Sulzby, E. (1986). *Emergent literacy.* Norwood, NJ: Ablex.

Vygotsky, L. S. (1962). *Thought and language.* Cambridge, MA: MIT Press.

Vygotsky, L. S. (1978). *Mind in society: The development of higher psychological processes* (M. Cole, V. John-Steiner, S. Scribner & E. Souberman, Eds. and Trans.). Cambridge, MA: Harvard University Press.

Wadsworth, B. J. (1978). *Piaget for the classroom teacher.* New York: Longman.

Wertsch, J. V. (Ed.). (1985). *Culture, communication, and cognition: Vygotskian perspectives.* Cambridge: Cambridge University Press.

CHAPTER THREE

Amato, P. R. (2006). Marital discord, divorce, and children's well-being. In A. Clarke-Stewart & J. Dunn (Eds.), *Families count: Effects on child and adolescent development* (pp. 179–202). New York: Cambridge University Press.

Apple, M. W. (1990). Is there a curriculum voice to reclaim? *Phi Delta Kappan, 71*(7), 526–530.

Beane, J. A. (1982, May). Self-concept and selfesteem as curriculum issues. *Educational Leadership, 39*, 504–506.

Bronfenbrenner, U. (1989). Ecological systems theory. In R, Vasta (Ed.), *Annals of Child Development* (Vol. 6, pp. 187-249). Boston: JAI Press, Inc.

Bronfenbrenner, U., & Evans, G. W. (2000). Developmental science in the 21st century: Emerging theoretical models, research designs, and empirical findings. *Social Development, 9,* 115–125.

Bronfenbrenner, U. (2005). *Making human beings human: Bioecological perspectives on human development.* Thousand Oaks, CA: Sage.

Bushaw, W. J. & McNee, J. A. (2009). "Americans speak out. The 41st annual Phi Delta/Gallup Poll of the public's attitudes toward the public schools." *Phi Delta Kappan 91*(1) 9–23.

Byrne, B. M., & Gavin, D. A. (1996). The Shavelson Model revisited: Testing for the structure of academic self-concept across pre-, early, and late adolescents. *Journal of Educational Psychology, 88*(2), 215–228.

Carr, M., & Kurtz-Costes, B. (1994, June). Is being smart everything? The influence of student achievement on teacher's perceptions. *British Journal of Educational Psychology, 64,* 263–276.

Cook, J. L., & Cook, G. (2005). *Child Development: Principles and perspectives.* Boston: Allyn & Bacon.

Damon, W., & Hart, D. (1982). The development of self-understanding from infancy through adolescence, *Child Development, 53,* 841–864.

Eisenberg, N., & Harris, J. D. (1984). Social competence: A developmental perspective.

The School Psychology Review, 13(3), 267–277.

Erikson, E. H. (1959). *Identity and the life cycle: Selected papers.* Psychological issues, Monograph (No.1, Vol. 1). New York: Norton.

Erikson, E. H. (1968). *Identity: Youth and crisis.* New York: Norton.

Erikson, E. H. (1963). *Childhood and society* (2nd ed.). New York: Norton.

Feather Jr., R. M. (2012). Frontloading: A solution for shy or disengaged students? A case study in Henson, K. T. Methods for Teaching in Diverse Middle-level and Secondary Classrooms, (2nd ed.). Dubuque, IA: Kendall Hunt.

Flavell, J. H. (1979). Metacognition and cognitive monitoring: A new area of cognitive developmental inquiry. *American Psychologist, 34*(10), 906–911.

Garbarino, J., & deLara, E. (2002). *And words can hurt forever: How to protect adolescents from bullying, hassassment, and emotional violence.* New York: Free Press.

Gilligan, C. (1982). *In a different voice: Psychological theory and women's development.* Cambridge, MA: Harvard University Press.

Henson, K. T. (2010). *Supervision for instructional improvement.* Long Grove IL: Waveland press.

Hersh, R. H., Paolitto, D. P., & Reimer, J. (1979). *Promoting moral growth: From Piaget to Kohlberg.* New York: Longman.

Hoffman, M. L. (2001). A comprehensive theory of prosocial moral development. In A. Bohart & D. Stipe & (Eds.), *Constructive and destructive behavior* (pp. 61–86). Washington, DC: American Psychological Association.

Josephson Institute of Ethics (2010). From josephsoninstitute.org.

Kohlberg, L. (1958). *The development of modes of moral thinking and choice in the years ten to sixteen.* Unpublished Ph.D. dissertation, University of Chicago.

Kohlberg, L. (1969). Stage and sequence: The cognitive developmental approach to socialization. In D. A. Goslin (Ed.), *Handbook of socialization theory and research.* Chicago: Rand McNally.

Kohlberg, L. (1978). Revisions in the theory and practice of moral development. In W. Damon (Ed.), *Moral development: New directions for child development* (No.2, Vol. 10, pp. 83–88). San Francisco: Jossey-Bass.

Kohlberg, L. (1981). *The Philosophy of Moral Development.* New York: Harper & Row.

Kohlberg, L. (1984). *The psychology of moral development.* San Francisco: Harper & Row.

Landrum, T. Lingo, A, Scott, T. (2011). "Classroom misbehavior is predictable and preventable", *Phi Delta Kappan 93*(2) 30–34.

Lerner, R. M., Theokas, C., & Bobek, D. L. (2005). Concepts and theories of human development: Historical and contemporary dimensions. In M. H. Bornstein & M. E. Lamb (Eds.), *Developmental science: An advanced textbook* (5th ed. pp. 3–43). Mahwah, NJ: Erlbaum.

Lounsbury, J. H. (1991). A fresh start for the middle school curriculum. *Middle School Journal, 23*(2), 3–7.

Mack, J. E., & Ablon, S. L. (Eds.). (1983). *The development and sustenance of self-esteem in childhood.* New York: International Universities Press.

Marcia, J. E. (1966). Development and validation of ego identity status. *Journal of Personality and Social Psychology, 3*(5), 551–558.

Marcia, J. E. (1967). Ego identity status: Relationship to change in self-esteem "general adjustment" and authoritarianism. *Journal of Personality, 35*(1), 119–133.

Marcia, J. E. (1980). Identity in adolescence. In J. Adelson (Ed.), *Handbook of adolescent psychology*. New York: Wiley-Interscience.

Marlowe, H. A., Jr. (1986). Social intelligence: Evidence for multidimensionality and construct independence. *Journal of Educational Psychology, 78*(1), 52–58.

Minuchin, P. (1982). Middle years development. In H. E. Mitzel, J. H. Best & W. Rabinowitz (Eds.), *EncyclopJedia of Educational Research*, (5th ed., Vol. 3, pp. 1229–1236). New York: The Free Press.

Miserandino, M. (1996). Children who do well in school: Individual differences in perceived confidence and autonomy in above average children. *Journal of Educational Psychology, 88*(2), 203–214.

Nucci, L. P. (2006). Education for moral development. In M. Killen & J. Smetana (Eds.), *Handbook of moral development*. Mahwah, NJ: Erlbaum.

Nucci, L. P. (2001). *Education on the Moral Domain*. New York: Cambridge Press.

Oana, R. G. (1993). *Changes in teacher education: Reform, renewal, reorganization*. Professional development leave report. Bowling Green, Ohio: Bowling Green University.

Pellegrini, D. S. (1985). Social cognition and competence in middle childhood. *Child Development, 56*, 253–264.

The Pew Internet and American Life Project (2007). From pewinternet.org.

Rogers, D. (1982). *Adolescent development*. In H. E. Mitzel, J. H. Best & W. Rabinowitz (Eds.), *Encyclopedia of Educational Research*, (5th ed., Vol. 1, pp. 67–76). New York: The Free Press.

Scott, C. G., Murray, G. C., Mertins, c., & Dustin, E. R. (1996). Student self-esteem and the school system: Perceptions and implications. *Journal of Educational Psychology, 89*(5), 286–293.

Sebald, H. (1986). *Adolescence: A social psychological analysis*. (3rd ed.). Englewood Cliffs, NJ: Prentice-Hall.

Selekman, M. D. (2009/2010). "Helping self-harming students." *Educational Leadership, 67*(4), 48–53.

U. S. Department of Education. (2010). *Digest of education statistics, 2010-11*. Washington, DC: National Center for Educational Statistics. U. S. Government Printing Office.

U. S. Department of Health and Human Services (2009). Frequently Asked Questions: Administration for Children and Families. Retrieved November 2010 from http://www.acf.hhs.gov/acf_services.html#CDan.

U. S. Department of Health and Human Services, Administration, Children, Youth, and Families, (2010). Retrieved Jan 27, 2011, from http://www.acf.hhs.gov/acf_services.html.

Walker, L. J. (1984). Sex differences in the development of moral reasoning: A critical review. *Child Development, 55*, 677–691.

Weinstein, C. S. (2007). *Middle and secondary classroom management: Lessons from research and practice* (3rd. ed.). New York: McGraw-Hill.

Woolfolk, A. (1987). *Educational psychology* (3rd ed.). Englewood Cliffs, NJ: Prentice-Hall.

CHAPTER FOUR

Antin, M. (1912). *The promised land*. Boston: Houghton-Mifflin.

Ball, D. L. & Ferzani, F. M. (2011). *Educational Leadership, 68*(4), 40–45.

Bandura, A. (1986). *Social foundations of thought and action.* Englewood Cliffs, NJ: Prentice-Hall.

Banks, J. A. (1994). *An introduction to multicultural education.* Boston: Allyn & Bacon.

Barton, P. E., & Coley, R. J. (2009/2010). Those persistent gaps. *Educational Leadership. 67*(4), 18–23.

Berends, M. & Penaloza, R. (2010). Increasing racial isolation and test score gaps in mathematics. *Teachers College Record, 112*(4), 978–1007.

Betancourt, H. & Lobez, S. R. (1993). "The study of culture, ethnicity, and race in American Psychology." *American Psychologist, 48,* 629–637.

Bialystok, E., Majumder, S., & Martin, M. M. (2003). Developing phonological awareness: Is there a bilingual advantage? *Applied Linguistics, 24,* 27–44.

Biemiller, A. (1993). Lake Wobegon revisited: On diversity and education, *Educational Researcher, 22*(9), 7–12.

Black, L. J., & Toreilo, J. (2012). Three strikes and you're out! A case study in Henson, K. T. Methods for Teaching in Diverse Middle-level & Secondary Classrooms, (2nd Ed.). Dubuque, IA: Kendall Hunt.

Blake, S. (1993). Are you turning female and minority students away from science? *Science and Children, 30*(4), 32–35.

Bode, P., & Fenner, D. (2010). Incarcerated youth and integrated arts education. Paper presented at the annual convention of the National Art Education Association, Baltimore.

Boutte, G. S., & McCormick, C. B. (1992). Authentic multicultural activities. *Childhood Education, 68*(3), 140–144.

Boyd, R. S. (1996, November). New discoveries lead scientists to rethink racial differences. *Ashville Citizen Times.*

Bruder, I., Buchsbaum, H., Hill, M., & Orlando, L. C. (1992, May–June). School reform: Why you need technology to get there. *Electronic Learning, 11,* 22–28.

Caplan, N., Choy, M. H., & Whitmore, J. K. (1992). Indochinese refugee families and academic achievement. *Scientific American, 266*(2), 36–42.

Carter, D., & Wilson, R. (1991). *Minorities in higher education: Ninth annual status report.* Washington, DC: American Council on Education.

Chen, C. & Stevenson, H. W. (1995). "Motivation and mathematical achievement: A comparative study of Asian-American, Caucasian-American, and East Asian high school students. *Child Development, 66,* 215–234.

Children's Defense Fund. (2010). *Child Poverty.* Available online: http://www.childrendefense.org/familyincome/childpoverty/default.aspx.

Chudowsky, N., & Chudowsky, V. (2010). *State test score trends 2007-2008, Part 5: Are there gender differences between boys and girls?* Washington, DC: Center on Education Policy.

Davidson, A. L., & Phelan, P. (1993). Cultural diversity and its implications. In P. Phelan & A. L. Davidson (Eds.), *Renegotiating cultural diversity in American schools.* New York: Teachers College Press.

Deaux, K. (1993). Commentary: Sorry, wrong number: A reply to gentile's call. *Psychological Science, 4*(2), 125–126.

DeGennaro, D. (2010). Opening digital doors. *Educational Leadership, 68*(3), 73–76.

Divan, K. (1994, 5 December). Chart of kindergarten awards. *Wall Street Journal,* B1.

Drake, D. D. (1993). Student diversity: Implications for classroom teachers. *Clearing House, 66*(3) 264–266.

Ducette, J. P., Sewell, T. E., & Shapiro, J. P. (1996). Chapter 5: Diversity in education: Problems and possibilities. In F. B. Murray (Ed.), *The teacher educator's handbook: Building a knowledge base for the preparation of teachers.* San Francisco: Jossey-Bass.

Duplechain, R., Reigner, R., & Packard, A. (2008). Striking differences: The impact of moderate and high trauma on reading achievement. *Reading Psychology, 29*(2), 117–136.

Ebron, A., & Lamb, Y. R. (1995). Race in America report: Beyond boundaries. *Family Circle, 108*(14) 90–93.

Eliot, L. (2010). The myth of pink and blue brains. *Educational Leadership, 68*(3), 32–37.

(ETS) Educational Testing Service (2008). *Technology in Classrooms: The state of technology in U. S. classrooms.* Princeton, NJ.

Ferriter, W. M. (2010). How flat is your classroom? *Educational Leadership, 67*(7), 86–87.

Freeman, N. K., & Boutte, G. S. (1996) Eliminating gender bias in the classroom. *Kappa Delta Pi 33*(1) 24–27.

Gandara, P. (2011). Overcoming triple segregation. *Educational Leadership, 68*(3), 60–63.

Garcia, E. (1993). Language, culture, and education. In L. Darling-Hammond (Ed.), *Review of Educational Research*, (Vol. 19, pp. 51–100).

Garcia, J., & Garcia, R. (1980). Selecting ethnic materials. *Social Studies, 44*, 232–234.

Garibaldi, A. M. (1992). Educating and motivating African American males to succeed. *Journal of Negro Education, 61*(1), 4–11.

Glatthorn, A. (1993). *Learning twice.* New York: HarperCollins.

Gleitman, H. (1991). *Psychology* (3rd ed.). New York: Norton.

Gomez, M. L., & Smith, R. J. (1991, January/February). Building interactive reading and writing curricula with diverse learners. *Clearing House, 64*(3), 147–151.

Gullnick, D. M., & Chinn, P. C. (1994). *Multicultural education in a pluralistic society.* Columbus, OH: Merrill.

Harris, C. R. (1991). Identifying and serving the gifted new immigrant. *Teaching Exceptional Children, 23*(4), 26–30.

Hawley, W. D. & Nieto, S. (2010). Another inconvenient truth: Race and ethnicity matter. *Educational Leadership, 68*(3), 66–72.

Haycock, K. (2001). Closing the achievement gap. *Educational Leadership, 58*(6), 6–11.

Janzen, R. (1994). Melting pot or mosaic? *Educational Leadership, 51*(8), 9–11.

Jewett, T. O. (1996). Gender and the sciences. *Kappa Delta Pi, 33*(1), 16–19.

Krugman, P., (2008, Feb. 18). Poverty is poison. Retrieved June 18, 2009 from http://www.nytimes.com/2008/2/18/opinion/18krugman.html.

Lemke, C., & Coughlin, E. (2009). The change agents. *Educational Leadership, 67*(1), 54–59.

Leroy, C., & Symes, B. (2001). Teachers' perspectives on the family backgrounds of children at risk. *McGill Journal of Education, 36*(1), 45–60.

NEA Today. (1990). People-and the winners are . . . , 2.

Orfield, G., & Frankenberg, E. (2005). Where are we now? In F. Shultz (Ed.), *Annual Editions: Multicultural Education* (pp. 10–12). Dubuque, IA: McGraw-Hill/Dushkin.

Orfield, G. & Frankenberg, E. (2008). *The last have become first.* UCLA Civil Rights Projects. Proyecto Derechos Civiles.

Ovando, C. (1994, March 18). *Curriculum reform and language minority students.* Presentation delivered at the 1999 Professors of Curriculum Meeting. Chicago. People-and the Winners are . . . (1990, March). *NEA Today, 21.*

Poplin, M., Rivera, J., Durish, D., Hoff, L., Kawell, S., Pawlak, P., Soto Hinman, I., Straus, L., & Veney, C. (2011). Highly effective teachers in low-performing urban schools. *Phi Delta Kappan, 92*(5), 39–43.

Pressley, M., Raphael, L., Gallagher, J. D., & DiBella, J. (2004). Providence St. Mel School: How a school that works for African American students works. *Journal of Educational Psychology, 96*(2), 216–235.

Quest, N. M., Hyde, J. S., & Linn, M. C. (2010). Cross-national patterns of gender differences in mathematics: A meta-analysis. *Psychological Bulletin, 136*(2), 103–137.

Rebell, M. A. (2008). Equal opportunity and the courts. *Phi Delta Kappan, 89*(6), 432–439.

Renzulli,J. S., & Reis, S. M. (1991). The reform movement and the quiet crisis in gifted education. *Gifted Child Quarterly, 55*(1), 26–35.

Schofield, J. W. (1991). School desegregation and intergroup relations. *Review of Research in Education, 17*, 235–412.

Sears, J. (1993). Responding to the sexual diversity of faculty and students: Sexual praxis and critical reflective administrator. In C. A. Copper (Ed.), *Educational administration in a pluralistic society.* Albany: State University of New York Press.

Sizer, T. R. (1992). *Horace's compromise: The dilemma of the American high school.* Boston: Houghton-Mifflin.

Slavin, R. E. (1998). Can education reduce social inequity? *Educational Leadership, 55*(4), 6–10.

Springer, M. (2009). Focusing the digital brain. *Educational Leadership, 67*(3), 34–39.

Steinberg, L. (2005). *Adolescence* (7th ed.). New York: McGraw-Hill.

Streitmatter, J. (1994). *Toward gender equity in the classroom: Everyday teachers' beliefs and practices.* Albany: State University of New York Press.

U. S. Census Bureau (2010). Available online: http://www.census.gov.

U. S. Department of Health and Human Services. (2010). *Frequently Asked Questions: Administration for Children and Families.* Retrieved March 25th, 2011, from http://www.acf.hhs.gov/acf_services. html#caan.

Vasquez, J. A. (1990). Teaching to the distinctive traits of minority students. *Clearing House, 63*(7), 299–304.

Woolfolk, A. E. (1995). *Educational psychology* (6th ed.). Needham Heights, MA: Allyn & Bacon.

Yee, A. H. (1992). Asians as stereotypes and students: Misperceptions that persist. *Educational Psychology Review, 4*, 95–132.

CHAPTER FIVE

American Psychiatric Association. (2000). *Diagnostic and statistical manual of mental disorders* (4th ed., Text Revisions). Arlington, VA: American Psychiatric Association.

Barkley, R. A. (1990). *Attention-deficit hyperactivity disorder: A handbook for diagnosis and treatment.* New York: Guilford.

Bender, W. N., & Evans, N. (1989, December/ January). Mainstream and special class strategies for managing behaviorally disordered students in secondary classes. *High School Journal, 72*, 89–96.

Bohlin, L., Durwin, C. C., Reese-Weber, M. (2009). *Edpsych modules.* Boston: McGraw-Hill Companies Inc.

Campbell, S. (1988). *Longitudinal studies of active and aggressive preschoolers: Individual differences in early behavior and in outcome*. Paper presented at the 2nd Rochester Symposium on Developmental Psychopathology, Rochester, NY.

Carri, L. (1985). Inservice teachers' assessed needs in behavioral disorders, mental retardation, and learning disabilities: Are they similar? *Exceptional Children, 5*(1), 411–416.

Creel, C., & Karnes, F. A. (1988). Parental expectations and young gifted children. *Roeper Review, 11*, 48–50.

Davidson, J., & Davidson, B. (2004). *Genius denied: How to stop wasting our brightest young minds*. New York: Simon & Schuster.

Feldhusen, J. F. (1989, March). Synthesis of research on gifted youth. *Educational Leadership, 46*, 6–11.

Gargialo, R. M., & Kilgo, J. L. (2011). *An Introduction to young children with special needs birth through age eight*. Belmont, CA: Wadsworth Cengage Learning.

Gargialo, R. M., & Metcalf, D. (2010). *Teaching in today's inclusive classroom*. Belmont, CA: Wadsworth Cengage Learning.

Gargialo, R. M. & Metcalf, D. (2012). *Teaching in today's inclusive classroom, 2nd ed.* Belmont, CA: Wadsworth.

George Bush Presidential Library and Museum. (2011). *Americans with Disabilities Act 20th anniversary:* Retrieved from http://bushlibrary.tamu.edu/features/2010-adal.

Goodenow, C. (1993, Fall). Classroom belonging among early adolescent students: Relationships to motivation and achievement. *Journal of Early Adolescence, 13*, 21–43.

Goodenow, C., & Grady, K. (1994, Fall). The relationship of school belonging and friends' values to academic motivation among urban adolescent students. *Journal of Experimental Education, 62*, 60–71.

Gowan, J. C. (1957, November). Dynamics of the underachievement of gifted children. *Exceptional Children, 24*, 98–101.

Gross, M. (1993). *Exceptionally Gifted Children*. London: Routledge.

Haring, N. G. (Ed.). (1982). *Exceptional children and youth* (3rd ed.). Columbus, OH: Merrill.

Henson, K. T. (1996). *Methods and strategies for teaching in secondary and middle schools* (3rd ed). New York: Longman.

Henson, K. T. (2012). *Methods for teaching in diverse middle-level and secondary classrooms, 2nd ed.* Dubuque, IA: Kendall Hunt.

Janney, R., & Snell, M. (1996, Summer). How teachers use peer interactions to include students with moderate and severe disabilities in elementary general education classes. *Journal of the Association for Persons with Severe Handicaps, 21*, 72–80.

Kulik, J. A., & Kulik, C. C. (1987, July). Effects of ability grouping on student achievement. *Equity and Excellence, 23*(1–2), 22–30.

Landau, S., & McAninch, C. (1993). Young children with attention deficits. *Young Children, 48*(4), 49–58.

Lewis, R. B., & Doorlag, D. H. (1991). *Teaching exceptional children in the mainstream* (3rd ed.). New York: Macmillan (Merrill).

LoCicero, K. A., & Ashbly, J. S. (2000). Multidimensional perfectionism in middle school age gifted students: A comparison to peers from the general cohort. *Roeper Review, 22*(3), 182–185.

Love, H. D. (1974). *Educating exceptional children in a changing society*. Springfield, IL: Thomas.

McGee, R., & Share, D. L. (1988, May). Attention deficit hyperactivity disorder and academic failure: Which comes first and what should be treated? *Journal of the American Academy of Child and Adolescent Psychiatry, 27*, 318–325.

McLaughlin, T. E, Krappman, V. E, & Welch, J. M. (1985, July/August). The effects of self-recording for on-task behavior of behaviorally disordered special education students. *Remedial and Special Educatigon, 6*, 42–45.

McNamara, B. E. (1986). Parents as partners in the I.E.P. process. *Academic Therapy, 21*(3), 309–319.

Morrison, G. S. (2009). *Teaching in America* (5th ed.). Upper Saddle River, NJ: Pearson Education Inc.

National Association of Gifted Children. (2008). *Javits Program Description*. Retrieved from http://www.nagc.org/index.aspx?id=572.

National Association of School Psychologists. (1992, May) Position statement on students with attention deficits. *Communique, 20*, 5.

Parette, H. P., Hourcade, H. P., & Vanbiervliet, A. (1993, Spring). Selection of appropriate technology for children with disabilities. *Teaching Exceptional Children, 4*, 18–22.

Parker, W. D. (1997). "An empirical typology of perfectionism in academically talented children." *American Educational Research Journal, 34*, 542–562.

Renzulli, J. S. (2002). Emerging conceptions of giftedness: Building a bridge to the new century. *Exceptionality, 10*(2), 67–75.

Robinson, N. M. (2000). Giftedness in very young children: How seriously should it be taken? In R. C. Friedman & B. M. Shore (Eds.), *Talents unfolding: Cognition and development* (pp. 7–26). Washington, DC: American Psychological Association.

Saljo, R. (Ed.). (1991). *Learning and Instruction, 1*(3). [Special issue on culture and learning].

Savich, C. (2008). *Inclusion:* The pros and cons-A critical review. *Outline submission.* Retrieved from ERIC Database (501775).

Snowman, J., McCown, R., & Biehler, R. (2009). *Psychology Applied to Teaching.* Boston: Houghton Mifflin Company.

Spicker, H. H. (1992). Identifying and enriching rural gifted children. *Educational Horizons, 70*(2), 60–65.

Steiner, H. H., & Carr, M. (2003). Cognitive development in gifted children: Toward a more precise understanding of emerging differences in intelligence. *Educational Psychology Review, 15*(3), 215–246.

Stern, J. D. (1992, Winter). How demographic trends for the eighties affect rural and small-town schools. *Educational Horizons, 70*, 71–77.

Torrence, E. P. (1986). Teaching creative and gifted learners. In M. C. Whittrock (Ed.), *Handbook of research on teaching* (3rd ed.). New York: Macmillan.

U. S. Department of Education. (2008). 28th Annual report to Congress on the implementation of the Individuals with Disabilities Act 2005, Washington DC: Office of Special Education and Rehabilitative Services.

U. S. Department of Education. (2011). 31st Annual report to Congress on the implementation of the individuals with Disabilities Act 2005, Washington DC: Office of Special Education and Rehabilitative Services.

U. S. Department of Education. (2011b). *ESEA Flexibility.* Retrieved from http://www.ed.gov/esea/flexibility.

U. S. Department of Education. (2011c). *What ESEA Flexibility means for students, teachers, and parents:Answering the public's questions.* Retrieved from http://www.ed.gov/esea/flexibility.

VanTassel-Baska, J., Feldhusen, J., Seeley, K., Wheatley, G., Silverman, L., & Foster, W. (1988). *Comprehensive curriculum for gifted learners*. Boston: Allyn & Bacon.

Wenar, C. (1994). *Developmental psychopathology* (3rd ed.). New York: McGraw-Hill.

The White House (2011). *Remarks made by the President on No Child Left Behind Flexibility*. Retrieved from http://www.whitehouse. gov/the-press-office/2011/09/23/ remarks-president-no-child-left-behind-flexibility.

Williams, L. J. (1997). *Membership in inclusive classrooms: Middle school students' perceptions*. Doctoral dissertation, University of Arizona.

Winner, E. (1996). *Gifted Children: Myths and Realities*. New York: Basic Books.

Winner, E. (2000). The origins and ends of giftedness. *American Psychologist, 55*(1), 159–169.

Wodrich, D. L. (1994). *Attention deficit hyperactivity disorder and your child*. Baltimore, MD: Paul H. Brookes.

Wolfberg, P. J., & Schuler, A. L. (1999). Fostering Peer Interaction, imaginative play and spontaneous language in children with autism. *Child Language Teaching and Therapy, 15*, 41–52.

Wolfberg, P. J. (2010). Play! A portal to new worlds. *Inclusive Play, 2*, 5–10.

Woolfolk, A. E. (1995). *Educational Psychology* (6th ed.). Boston: Allyn & Bacon.

Wood, J. W. (1989). *Mainstreaming: A practical approach for teachers*. Columbus, OH: Merrill.

CHAPTER SIX

Alberto, P. A., & Troutman, A. C. (2006). *Applied behavior analysis for teachers: Influencing student performance (7th ed.)*. Upper Saddle River, NJ: Prentice Hall/Merrill.

Alvestad, K. A., & Wigfield, A. L. (1993). A matter of motivation. *Executive Educator, 15*(1), 12–13.

Alvord, M. K., & O'Leary, K. D. (1985, July). Teaching children to share through stories. *Psychology in the Schools, 22*, 323–330.

Ames, C. (1992). Classrooms: Goals, structure, and student motivation. *Journal of Educational Psychology, 84*(3), 261–271.

Ayllon, T., & Roberts, M. D. (1974). Eliminating discipline problems by strengthening academic performance. *Journal of Applied Behavior Analysis, 7*(1), 71–76.

Azrin, N. H., & Foxx, R. M. (1971). A rapid method of toilet training the institutional retarded. *Journal of Applied Behavior Analysis, 4*(2), 89–99.

Bandura, A. (1969). *Principles of behavior modification*. New York: Holt, Rinehart & Winston.

Bandura, A. (1977). *Social learning theory*. Englewood Cliffs, NJ: Prentice-Hall.

Bandura, A. (1986). *Social foundations of thought and action: A social cognitive theory*. Englewood Cliffs, NJ: Prentice-Hall.

Bandura, A. (2000). Exercise of human agency through collective efficacy. *Current Directions in Psychology Science, 9*, 75–78.

Bandura, A. (2001). Social cognitive theory: An agentic perspective. *An annual review of psychology* (Vol. 52, pp. 1–26). Palo Alto: Annual Reviews, Inc.

Becker, W., Engelmann, S., & Thomas, D. (1975). *Teaching I: Classroom Management*. Champaign, IL: Research Press.

Bruder, I., Buchsbaum, H., Hill, M., & Orlando, L. C. (1992, May-June). School reform: Why you need technology to get there. *Electronic Learning, 11*, 22–28.

Bullough, R. J. (1994). Digging at the roots: Discipline, management, and metaphor. *Action in Teacher Education, 16*(1), 1–10.

Chance, P. (1992, November). The rewards of learning. *Phi Delta Kappan, 74*(3), 200–207.

Chandler, T. A. (1990). Why discipline strategies are bound to fail. *Clearing House, 64*(2), 124–126.

Charles, C. M. (1981). *Building classroom discipline*. New York: Longman.

Crossman, E. (1975). Communication. *Journal of Applied Behavior Analysis, 8*(3), 348.

Eggen, P. D., & Kauchak, D. (1992). *Educational psychology classroom connections*. New York: Macmillan.

Evertson, C. M., & Harris, A. H. (1992). What we know about managing classrooms. *Educational Leadership, 49*(2), 74–78.

Ferster, C. B., & Skinner, B. F. (1957). *Schedules of reinforcement*. New York: Appleton-Century-Crofts.

Fisher, S. (1993). *Riding the Internet highway*. Indianapolis: New Riders Publishing.

Fuhr, D. (1993). Effective classroom discipline: Advice for educators. *NAASP Bulletin, 76*(1), 82–86.

Gathercoal, F. (1993). *Judicious discipline* (3rd ed.). San Francisco: Caddo Gap Press.

Glasser, W. (1990). *The quality school: Managing students without coercion*. New York: Harper & Row.

Good, T. L., & Brophy, J. E. (1997). *Looking in classrooms* (7th ed.). New York: Longman.

Hill, W. F. (1970). *Psychology: Principles and problems*. Philadelphia: J. B. Lippincott.

Hughes, C. A., & Hendrickson, J. M. (1987, August). Self-monitoring with at-risk students in the regular class setting. *Education and Treatment of Children, 10*, 225–236.

Itard, J. M. G. (1962). *The wild boy of Aveyron*. New York: Appleton-Century-Crofts.

Jones; V. F. (1989). Classroom management: Clarifying theory and improving practice. *Education, 109*(3), 330–339.

Jones, V.F. (1996). Classroom management. In J. Sikula, T. Buttery, & E. Guyton (Eds.), *Handbook of research on teacher education* (2nd ed.). New York: Macmillan.

Jones, V. F., & Jones, L. S. (1986). *Comprehensive classroom management: Creating positive learning environments* (2nd ed.). Boston: Allyn & Bacon.

Kaufman, R. A. (1976). *Identifying and solving problems: A systems approach*. La Jolla, CA: University Associates.

Kazdin, A. E., & Mascitelli, S. (1980). The opportunity to earn oneself off a token system as a reinforcer for attentive behavior. *Behavior Therapy, 11*, 68–78.

Keller, F. S. (1969). *Learning: Reinforcement theory* (2nd ed.). New York: Random House.

Laud, L. E. (1998). Changing the way we communicate. *Educational Leadership, 55*(7), 23–25.

Lazarus, A. A. (1976). *Multimodal behavior therapy*. New York: Springer.

Lewis, C. C., Schaps, E., & Watson, M. S. (September 1996). The caring classroom's academic edge. *Educational Leadership, 54*(1), 16–21.

Lincoln, W. (1993). Helping students develop self-discipline. *Learning, 93*(3), 38–41.

Lindsley, O. (1978). Teaching parents to modify their children's behavior. In L. E. Arnold (Ed.), *Helping parents help their children*. New York: Brunner/Mazel.

Lovaas, O. I., & Newsom, C. D. (1976). Behavior modification with psychotic children. In H. Leitenberg (Ed.), *Handbook of behavior modification and behavior therapy* (pp. 303–360). Englewood Cliffs, NJ: Prentice-Hall.

Lundin, R. W. (1974). *Personality: A behavioral analysis* (2nd ed.). New York: Macmillan.

Moles, O. C. (Ed.). (1989). *Strategies to reduce student misbehavior*. Washington, DC: Office of Educational Research and Improvement, U.S. Department of Education.

Morrow, L. M., Reutzel, D. R. & Casey, H. (2006). Organization and management of language arts teaching: Classroom environments, grouping practices, and exemplary instruction. In C. M. Everston & C. S. Weinstein, *Handbook of classroom management: Research, practice, and contemporary issues* (pp. 559–581). Mahwah, New Jersey: Lawrence Erlbaum Associates publishers.

Newmann, F. M., & Wehlage, G. G. (1993). Five standards of authentic instruction. *Educational Leadership, 50*(7), 8–12.

Oakes, J. (1992). Can tracking research reform practice? Technical, normative, and political considerations. *Educational Researcher, 21*(4), 12–21.

Phelps, P. H. (1991, March/April). Helping teachers excel as classroom managers. *Clearing House, 64,* 241–242.

Premack, D. (1959). Toward empirical behavior laws: I. Positive reinforcement. *Psychological Review, 66,* 219–233.

Quay, H. c., & Peterson, D. R. (1975). *Manual for the behavior problem checklist*. Champaign, IL: Children's Research Center, University of Illinois.

Rotter, J. B. (1966). Generalized expectancies for internal versus external control of reinforcement. *Psychological Monographs, 80,* 1–28.

Sherman, A. R. (1973). *Behavior modification: Theory and practice*. Belmont, CA: Wadsworth.

Skinner, B. F. (1938). *The behavior of organisms*. New York: Appleton-Century-Crofts.

Skinner, B. F. (1953). *Science and human behavior*. New York: Macmillan.

Stipek, D. J. (1993). *Motivation to learn: From theory to practice* (2nd ed.). Boston: Allyn & Bacon.

Streitmatter, J. (1994). *Toward gender equity in the classroom: Everyday teachers' beliefs and practices*. New York: State University of New York Press.

Sulzer-Azaroff, B., & Mayer, G. R. (1991). *Behavior analysis for lasting change*. Fort Worth, TX: Holt, Rinehart & Winston, Inc.

Tierno, M. J. (1991). Responding to the socially motivated behaviors of early adolescents: Recommendations for classroom management. *Adolescence, 2,* 569–577.

Travers, R. W. M. (1977). *Essentials of learning*. New York: Macmillan.

Williams, R. L., & Anandam, K. (1973). *Cooperative' classroom management*. Columbus, OH: Merrill.

Woolfolk, A. (1995). *Educational Psychology* (6th ed.). Needham Heights, MA: Allyn & Bacon.

Zimmerman, B., & Kleefield, C. (1977). Toward a theory of teaching: A social learning view. *Contemporary Educational Psychology, 2,* 158–171.

CHAPTER SEVEN

Berliner, D., & Casanova, U. (1990, May). Helping kids learn how to learn. *Instructor, 99,* 16–17.

Best, D. L., & Ornstein, P. A. (1986). Children's generation and communication of mnemonic organizational strategies. *Developmental Psychology, 22*(6), 845–853.

Bigge, M. L. (1981). *Learning theories for teachers* (4th ed.). New York: Harper & Row.

Boink, C. J. (2010). "For openers: How technology is changing school." *Educational Leadership, 37*(7) 60–65.

Bower, T. G. R. (1989). *The rational infant*. New York: Freeman.

Bruner, J. (1966). *Toward a theory of instruction*. Cambridge, MA: Belknap Press.

Bruner, J. S. (1971). *The relevance of education*. New York: Norton.

Bruner, J. S. (1978). From communication to language: A psychological perspective. In I. Markova (Ed.), *The social context of language* (pp. 84–97). New York: Wiley.

Bruner, J. S., Goodnow, J. J., & Austin, G. A. (1956). *A study of thinking*. New York: Wiley.

Bruner, J. S. (1982). The organization of action and the nature of adult-infant transaction. In M. Cranach & R. Harre (Eds.), *The analysis of action* (pp. 93–110). New York: Cambridge University Press.

Case, R. (1984). The process of stage transition: A neo-Piagetian view. In R. J. Sternberg (Ed.), *Mechanisms of cognitive development* (pp. 19–44). New York: Freeman.

Dempster, F. N. (1985). Proactive interference in sentence recall: Topic-similarity effects and individual differences. *Memory & Cognition, 13*(1), 81–89.

Ebbinghaus, H. (1913). Uber das gedachtnis. In H. A. Roger & C. Bossinger (Trans.), *On memory* (pp. 2–81). New York: Teachers College. (Original work published 1885)

Flavell, J. H. (1979). Metacognition and cognitive monitoring: A new area of cognitivedevelopmental inquiry. *American Psychologist, 34*(10), 906–911.

Flavell, J. H. (1985). *Cognitive development*. Englewood Cliffs, NJ: Prentice-Hall.

Flavell, J. H., Green, F. L., & Flavell, E. R. (1995, March). Young children's knowledge about thinking. *Monographs of the Society for Research in Child Development, 1*, (Serial No. 143).

Flavell, J. H., Miller, P. H., & Miller, S. A. (2002). *Cognitive development* (4th ed.). Upper Saddle River, NJ; Prentice-Hall.

Foos, P. W., & Fisher, R. P. (1988, June). Using tests as learning opportunities. *Journal of Educational Psychology, 80*, 129–183.

Gagné, R. M. (1965). The analysis of instructional objectives for the design of instruction. In R. Glaser (Ed.), *Teaching machines and programmed learning, II: Data and direction* (pp. 32–41). Washington, DC: National Education Association.

Gagné R. M. (1985). *The conditions of learning and theory of instruction* (4th ed.). New York: Holt, Rinehart & Winston.

Glover, J. A., & Bruning, R. H. (1990). *Educational psychology principles and applications*. Glenville, IL: Scott Foresman.

Glover, J. A., & Ronning, R. R. (1987). About educational psychology. In J. A. Glover & R. R. Ronning (Eds.), *Historical foundations of educational psychology*. New York: Plenum.

Kail, R., & Pellegrino, J. (1985). *Human intelligence: Perspectives and prospects*. San Francisco: Freeman.

Martinez, M. E. (2010). Muman Memory: The basics. *Phi Delta Kappan 91*(8), 62–65.

Martinez, M. (2010). Does group IQ trump individual IQ? *Phi Delta Kappan 92*(1), 72–73.

Matlin, M. W. (1988). *Sensation and perception* (2nd ed.). Boston: Allyn & Bacon.

Matlin, M. W. (1989). *Cognition* (2nd ed.). New York: Holt, Rinehart & Winston.

Mayer, R. E. (1992). *Thinking, problem solving, cognition* (2nd ed.). New York: Freeman.

Mayer, R. E. (2004). Should there be a three-strikes rule against pure discovery learning? The case for guided methods of instruction. *American Psychologist, 59*(1), 14–19.

Metcalf, J., & Shimamura, A. P. (Eds.). (1994). *Metacognition: Knowledge about knowing*. Cambridge, MA: MIT Press.

Mustacchi, J. (2011). Making meaning. *Educational Leadership*, *68*(4), 75.

Neisser, U. (1967). *Cognitive psychology*. New York: Appleton-Century-Crofts.

Norman, D. A. (1980). Cognitive engineering and education. In D. T. Tuma & F. Reif (Eds.), *Problem solving and education: Issues in teaching and research*. Hillsdale, NJ: Erlbaum.

Perkins, D. N. (1988). Creativity and the quest for mechanism. In R. J. Sternberg & E. E. Smith (Eds.), *The nature of creativity* (pp. 305–336). New York: Cambridge.

Perkins, D. N., & Salomon, G. (1989, January/February). Are cognitive skills context-bound? *Educational Researcher, 18*, 16–25.

Reed, S. K. (1992). *Cognition* (3rd ed.). Pacific Grove, CA: Brooks/Cole.

Rickelman, R. J., Henk, W. A., & Melnick, S. A. (1991). Electronic encyclopedias on the compact disk. *The Reading Teacher, 44*(6), 432–434.

Santrock, J. W. (1997) *Life-span development*. Dubuque, IA: Brown & Benchmark.

Sternberg, R. J. (Ed.). (1984). *Human abilities: An information-processing approach*. New York: Freeman.

Sternberg, R. J. (1985). *Beyond IQ: A triarchic theory of intelligence*. New York: Cambridge University Press.

Sternberg, R. J. (1988). *The triarchic mind: A new theory of human intelligence*. New York: Viking.

Sternberg, R. J. (1990a, January). Thinking styles: Keys to understanding student performance. *Phi Delta Kappan, 71*, 366–371.

Sternberg, R. J. (1990b). *Metaphors of mind: Conceptions of the nature of intelligence*. Cambridge, England: Cambridge University Press.

Tulving, E. (1985). How many memory systems are there? *American Psychologist, 40*(4), 385–398.

Weisberg, R. W. (1993). *Creativity: Beyond the myth of genius*. New York: W. H. Freeman.

CHAPTER EIGHT

Anderson, R. C., Wilson, P. T., & Fielding, L. G. (1988, Summer). Growth in reading and how children spend their time outside school. *Reading Research Quarterly, 23*, 263–284.

Ausubel, D. P. (1980, Fall). Schemata, cognitive structure, and advance organizers: A reply to Anderson, Spiro, and Anderson. *American Educational Research Journal, 17*, 400–404.

Bandura, A. (1986). *Social foundations of thought and action: A social cognitive theory*. Englewood Cliffs, NJ: Prentice-Hall.

Bruning, R. H., Schraw, G. J., Norby, M. M., & Ronning, R. R. (2004). *Cognitive psychology and instruction* (4th ed.). Columbus, OH: Merrill.

Darling-Hammond, L., & Sclan, E. M. (1996). Who teaches and why: Dilemmas of building a profession for twenty-first-century schools. In J. Sikula, T. Buttery, & E. Guyton, *Handbook of research on teacher education* (2nd ed., pp. 67–102). New York: Macmillan.

Dunn, R., Bruno, J., Sklar, R. l., Zenhausern, R., & Beaudry, J. (1990). Effects of matching and mismatching minority developmental college students' hemispheric preferences on mathematics scores. *Journal of Educational Research, 83*(5), 283–288.

Dunn, R., Dunn K., & Price, G. E. (1989). *Learning Styles Inventory (LSI): An inventory for indentification of how individuals in grades 3 through 12 prefer to learn*. Lawrence, KS: Price Systems.

Eggen, P. D., & Kauchak, D. (1992). *Educational psychology: Classroom connections*. New York: Macmillan.

Ennis, R. (1987). A taxonomy of critical thinking dispositions and abilities. In J. Baron & R. Sternberg (Eds.), *Teaching thinking skills*. New York: Freeman.

Glover, J., & Bruning, R. H. (1990). *Educational psychology: Principles and applications* (3rd ed.). New York: Addison-Wesley.

Gordon, E. W., & Rabianski-Carrivolo, N. (1989). Learning styles: An interview with Edmund W. Gordon and N. Rabianski-Carrivolo. *Journal of Developmental Education 13*(1), 20.

Harrison, C. J. (1990). Concepts, operational definitions, and case studies in instruction. *Education, 110*(4), 502–505.

Heckman, P. E., Confer, C. B., & Hakim, D. (1994). Planting seeds: Understanding through investigation. *Educational Leadership, 51*(5), 36–30.

Henson, K. T. (1996). *Methods and strategies for teaching in secondary and middle schools* (3rd ed.). New York: Longman.

Higbee, K. L., & Kunihara, S. (1985, Spring). Cross-cultural applications of Yodai mnemonics in education. *Educational Psychologists, 20*, 57–64.

Hill, W. E. (1990). *Learning: A survey of Psychological interpretations* (5th ed.). New York: Harper & Row.

Hunt, E. (1978). Mechanics of verbal ability. *Psychological Review, 85*(2), 109–130.

Kail, R. (1984). *The development of memory in children* (2nd ed.). San Francisco: Freeman.

Kane, M., & Kane, D. (1990). Right or left: Which is the right cognitive style for quality teaching? *American Secondary Education, 18*(3), 12–16.

Kilpatrick, J. (1985, Spring). Doing mathematics without understanding it: A commentary on Higbee and Kunihara. *Educational Psychologist, 20*, 65–68.

King, P. M., & Kitchener, K. S. (1994). *Developing reflective judgement: Understanding and promoting intellectual growth and critical thinking in adolescents and adults.* San Francisco: Jossey-Bass.

Levin, J. R. (1985, Spring). Yodai features = mnemonic procedures: A commentary on Higbee and Kunihara. *Educational Psychologist, 20*, 73–76.

Mandler, J. M. (1984). *Stories, scripts, and scenes: Aspects of schema theory.* Hillsdale, NJ: Erlbaum.

Matlin, M. W. (1989). *Cognition* (2nd ed.). New York: Holt, Rinehart & Winston.

Mayer, R. E. (1992). *Thinking, problem solving, cognition* (2nd ed.). New York: Freeman.

Mayer, R. E., & Wittrock, M. C. (2006). Problem Solving. In P. A. Alexander & P. H. Winne (Eds.), *Handbook of educational psychology* (2nd ed., pp.287–303). Mahwah, NJ: Erlbaum.

Nickerson, R. (1988). On improving thinking through instruction. In E. Rothkopf (Ed.), *Review of research in education* (pp. 3–57). Washington, DC: American Educational Research Association.

Owen, D. (1990, September). The best teacher I ever had. *Life Magazine, 70.*

Paul, A. (1987). The Language of language: Looking outward for practical applications and inward for keys to the mind. *Chronicle of Higher Education, 33*(44), 4–9.

Perkins, D. N. (1988). Creativity and the quest of mechanism. In R. J. Sternberg & E. E. Smith (Eds.), *The nature of creativity* (pp. 305–336). New York: Cambridge.

Pesut, D.J. (1990). Creative thinking as a selfregulatory metacognitive process-a model for education, training, and further research. *Journal of Creative Behavior, 2*(24), 105–110.

Rothstein, R. (2001). Improving education and achievement: A volume exploring the role of investments in schools and other supports and services for families and communities. Washington, DC: The Finance Project.

Santrock, J. W. (1997). *Life-span development.* Madison, WI: Brown & Benchmark.

Sternberg, R. J. (1987). *Advances in the psychology of human intelligence*. Hillsdale, NJ: Erlbaum.

Stipek, D. J. (1993). *Motivation to learn* (2nd ed.). Boston: Allyn & Bacon.

Stipek, D. J., & Daniels, D. H. (1988). Declining perceptions of competence: A consequence of changes in the child or in the educational environment? *Journal of Educational Psychology, 80*(5), 352–356.

Stuart, R., & Thomas, J. C. (1991). The implications of education in cyberspace. *Multimedia Review, 2*, 10–17.

Swanson, H. L. (1990, June). Influence of metacognitive knowledge and aptitudes on problem solving. *Journal of Educational Psychology, 82*, 306–314.

Thomas, E. L., & Robinson, H. A. (1972). *Improving reading in every class: A source book for teachers*. Boston: Allyn & Bacon.

CHAPTER NINE

Alessi, S. M., & Trollip, S. R. (1991). *Computer based instruction, methods, and development*. Englewood Cliffs, NJ: Prentice-Hall.

Anderson, V. (1991). *Training teachers to foster active reading strategies in reading-disabled adolescents*. Paper presented at the annual meeting of the American Educational Research Association, Chicago, IL.

Barab, S. A., Gresalfi, M., & Arici, A. (2009). Why educators should care about games. *Educational Leadership, 67*(1), 76–80.

Behrstock-Sherratt, E. & Coggshall, J. G. (2010). *Educational Leadership, 67*(8), 28–34.

Benoit, S. S., & Lee, L. W. (1988). Listening: It can be taught. *Journal of Education for Business, 63*(5), 229–232.

Bloom, B. S. (1956). *Taxonomy of educational objectives: The classification of educational goals, Handbook I: Cognitive domain*. New York: McKay.

Brophy, J. E., & Good, T. L. (1986). Teacher behavior and student achievemgent. In M. Wittrock (Ed.) *Handbook of research on teaching* (3rd ed.). New York: Macmillan.

Good, T. L. (1983, Fall). Classroom research: A decade of progress. *Educational Psychologist, 18*, 127–144.

Good, T. L., & Brophy, J. E. (1997). *Looking in classrooms* (7th ed.). New York: Longman.

Good, T. L. & Brophy, J. E. (2008). *Looking in classrooms* (10th ed.). Upper Saddle River, NJ: Pearson/Allyn & Bacon.

Henson, K. T. (1996). *Methods and strategies for teaching in secondary and middle schools* (3rd ed.). White Plains, NY: Longman.

Kowalski, T. J., Weaver, R. A., & Henson, K. T. *(1990). Case studies on teaching*. White Plains, NY: Longman.

Kutz, E. (1992). Teacher research: Myths and realities. *Language Arts, 69*(3), 193–197.

Martinez, M. E. (1998). What is problem solving? *Phi Delta Kappan, 79*(8), 605–609.

Marzano, R. J. (2009). Six steps to better vocabulary instruction. *Educational Leadership*, 67(1), 83–84.

Mayer, R. E., & Fay, A. L. (1987). A chain of cognitive changes with learning to program in logo. *Journal of Educational Psychology, 79*(5), 269–279.

Moore, R. & Berry, B. (2010). The teachers of 2030. *Educational Leadership, 67*(8), 36–39.

National Reading Panel. (2000). *Teaching Children to read: An evidence-based assessment of the scientific research literature on reading and its implications for reading instruction* (NIH Pub. No. 00-4769). Washington, DC: National Institutes of Health.

Oakes, J., Quartz, K., Gong, J., Guiton, G., & Lipton, M. (1993, May). Creating middle schools: Technical, normative, and political considerations. *Elementary School Journal, 93,* 461–480.

Paget, N. (1988). Using case methods effectively. *Journal of Education for Business, 63*(4), 175–180.

Phillips, D. C. & Soltis, J. F. (1985). *Perspectives on learning.* Columbia: Teachers College Press.

Poplin, M., Rivera, J., Druish, D., Hoff, L., Kawell, S., Pawlak, P., Hinman, I., Straus, L., & Veney, C. (2011). She's strict for a good reason: Highly effective teachers in low-performing urban schools. *Phi Delta Kappan, 92*(5), 34–38.

Pressley, M. J., Burkell, T., Cariglia-Bull, L., Lysynchuk, J. A., McGoldrick, B., Schneider, S., Symons M., & Woloshyn, V. E. (1990). *Cognitive strategy instruction.* Cambridge, MA: Brookline Books.

Rosenshine, B., & Meister, C. (1992, April). The use of scaffolds for teaching higher-level cognitive strategies. *Educational Leadership, 49,* 26–33.

Rothstein, P. R. (1990). *Educational psychology.* New York: McGraw-Hill.

Slavin, R. E. (1990). *Cooperative learning theory, research, and practice.* Englewood Cliffs, NJ: Prentice-Hall.

Stallworth, B. J. (1998). Practicing what we teach. *Educational Leadership, 55*(5), 77–79.

Walberg, H. (1990). Productive teaching and instruction: Assessing the knowledge base. *Phi Delta Kappan, 71*(6), 470–478.

Wulf, K. M., & Schane, B. (1984). *Curriculum design.* Glenview, IL: Scott, Foresman.

Yelon, S. L. (1996) *Powerful principles of instruction.* New York: Longman.

CHAPTER TEN

Berk, L. E. (2005). *Infants, children and adolescents* (5th ed.). Boston: Allyn & Bacon.

Brooks, J. G., & Brooks, M. G. (1993). *The case for constructivist classrooms.* New York: Grossman.

Butler, J. (2010). Selecting activities to personalize the curriculum. In Henson, K.T. Curriculum planning: Integrating multiculturalism, constructivism, and education reform, 4th ed. Long Grove, IL: Waveland Press.

Cooper, G., & Sweller, J. (1987, December). Effects of schema acquisition and rule automation on mathematical problem-solving transfer. *Journal of Educational Psychology, 79,* 347–362.

Dixon, D. N. (1987). A history of counseling psychology. In J. A. Glover & R. R. Ronning (Eds.), *Historical Foundations of Educational Psychology* (pp. 62–73). New York: Plenum.

Einstein, A., & Infeld, L. (1938). *The evolution of physics: The growth of ideas from early concepts to relativity and quanta.* New York: Simon & Schuster.

Farr, S. (2011). Leadership: Not magic. *Educational Leadership, 68*(4), 28–33.

Glover, J. A., & Bruning, R. H. (1990). *Educational psychology principles and applications,* (3rd ed.). Glenville, IL: Scott, Foresman/ Little Brown.

Hayes, R. A. (1989). *The complete problem solver* (2nd ed.). Hillsdale, NJ: Erlbaum.

Henson, K. T. (1996). Teachers as researchers. In J. Sikula, T. Buttery & E. Guyton (Eds.), *Association of Teacher Educators: Handbook of Research on Teaching* (2nd ed.). New York: Macmillan.

Jaramillo, J. A. (1996). Vygotsky's sociocultural theory and contributions to the development of constructivist curricula. *Education, 117*(1), 133–140.

Kaplan, P. S. (1990). *Educational psychology for tomorrow's teacher*. St. Paul, MN: West.

Kershner, J. R., & Ledger, G. (1985). Effect of sex, intelligence, and style of thinking on creativity: A comparison of gifted and average IQ children. *Journal of Personality and Social Psychology, 48*, 1033–1040.

Knowles, J. G., & Cole, A. L. with Presswood, (1994, Spring). We're just like the beginning teachers we study: Letters and reflections on our first year as beginning professors. *Curriculum Inquiry, 24*, 27–52.

Kokot, S. J., & Colman, J. (1997). The creative mode of being. *Journal of Creative Behavior, 31*(3), 212–226.

Laudon, K. C., & Laudon, J. P. (1991). *Business information systems: A problem-solving approach*. Chicago, IL: Dryden.

Meek, A. (1998). America's teachers: Much to celebrate. *Educational Leadership, 55*(5), 12–16.

Perry, M., Vanderstoep, S., & Yu, S. (1993). Asking questions in first-grade mathematics classes: Potential influences on mathematical thought. *Journal of Educational Psychology, 85*, 31–40.

Roth, K. J. & Garnier, H. J. (2007). How five countries teach science. *Educational Leadership, 64*(4), 16–23.

Rothstein, P. R. (1990). *Educational psychology*. New York: McGraw-Hill.

Runco, M. A. (Ed.). (2006). Creativity theories and themes: Research, development, and practice. Burlington, MA: Elsevier Press.

Stefanich, G. P. (1990, November). Cycles of cognition. *Middle School Journal, 22*, 47–52.

Sternberg, R. J. (1985). *Beyond IQ: A triarchic theory of human intelligence*. New York: Cambridge University Press.

Sternberg, R. J. (Ed.). (1988). *The nature of creativity*. New York: Cambridge.

Sternberg, R. J. (2006). Creating a vision of creativity. The first 25 years. *Psychology of Aesthetics, Creativity and the Arts, 5*(1), 2–12.

Torrance, E. P., Glover, J. A., Ronning, R. R., & Reynolds, C. R. (Eds.). (1989). *Handbook of creativity: Perspectives on individual differences*. New York: Plenum Press.

Troutman, A. P., White, J. A., & Breit, F. D. (1988). *The micro goes to school: Instructional applications of microcomputer technology*. Pacific Grove, CA: Brooks/Cole.

Tyson, J. C., & Carroll, M. A. (1973). *Conceptual tools for teaching in secondary schools*. Boston: Houghton Mifflin.

Wessling, S. (2010). "Teachers make the difference." *Phi Delta Kappan, 92*(1), 16.

Winger, T. (2009). Grading what matters. *Educational Leadership, 67*(3), 73–75.

CHAPTER ELEVEN

Alderman, M. K. (1990). Motivation for at-risk students. *Educational Leadership, 48*(1), 27–30.

Alvestad, K. A., & Wigfield, A. L. (1993, January). A matter of motivation. *Executive Educator, 1*, 12–13.

Ames, C. (1992, September). Classrooms: Goals, structures, and student motivation. *Journal of Educational Psychology, 84*, 261–271.

Anderman, E. M., & Maehr, M. L. (1994, Summer). Motivation and schooling in the middle grades. *Review of Educational Research, 64*, 287–309.

Ashton, P. T., & Webb, R. B. (1986). *Making a difference: Teachers' sense of efficacy and student achievement*. New York: Longman.

Atkinson, R. C. & Shiffrin, R. M. (1968). Human memory: A proposed system and its control process. In K. W. Spence & J. T. Spence

(Eds.), *The psychology of learning and motivation: Advances in research and theory (Vol. 2)*. SanDiego, CA: Academic Press.

Ball, S. (1982). Motivation. In H. E. Mitzel, J. H. Best & W. Rabinowitz (Eds.), *Encyclopedia of Educational Research* (Vol. 3, 5th ed., pp. 1256–1263). New York: Free Press.

Bandura, A. (1986). *Social foundations of thought and action*. Englewood Cliffs, NJ: Prentice-Hall.

Bandura, A. (2000). Exercise of human agency through collective efficacy. *Current Directional in Psychological Science, 9,* 75–78.

Bandura, A. (2001). Social cognitive theory: An agentic perspective. *Annual Review of Psychology, 52,* 1–26.

Brophy, J. (1987, October). Synthesis on research strategies for motivating students to learn. *Educational Leadership, 45*(2), 40–49.

Darling-Hammond, L. (1998). Teacher learning that supports student learning. *Educational Leadership, 55*(5), 6–11.

Doebler, L. K., & Eicke, F. J. (1979). Effects of teacher awareness of the educational implications of field dependent & field independent cognitive style on selected classroom variables. *Journal of Educational Psychology, 71,* 226–232.

Dweck, C. S. (1986). Motivational processes affecting learning. *American Psychologist, 41,* 1040–1048.

Dweck, C. S. (2006). *Mindset. The new psychology of success*. New York: Random House.

Hiebert, E. H., Winograd, P. N. & Danner, F. W. (1984). Children's attributions for failure and success in different aspects of reading. *Journal of Educational Psychology, 76*(6), 1139–1148.

Hodgkinson, H. L. (1985, June). *All one system: Demographics of education-kindergarten through graduate school*. Washington, DC: Institute for Educational Leadership.

Johnson, D., & Johnson, R. (1994). *Learning together and alone: Cooperation, competition, and individualization* (4th ed.). Boston: Allyn & Bacon.

Johnson, D. W. & Johnson, R. T. (2005). Cooperative learning in S. W. Lee (Ed.), *Encyclopedia of school psychology*. Thousand Oaks, CA: Sange.

Kinderman, T. A. (1993, November). Natural peer groups as contexts for individual development: The case of children's motivation in school. *Developmental Psychology, 29,* 970–977.

Kohn, A. (1993, September). Choices for children: Why and how to let students decide. *Phi Delta Kappan, 74,* 783–787.

Maier, S. F., & Seligman, M. E. (1976). Learned helplessness: Theory and evidence. *Journal of Experimental Psychology: General, 105*(1), 3–46.

Manning, M. L., & Baruth, L. G. (1996). Learners at risk: Three issues for educators. *Clearing House, 69*(4), 239–241.

Maslow, A. H. (1968). *Toward a psychology of being* (2nd ed.). New York: Van Nostrand.

Maslow, A. H. (1970). *Motivation and personality* (2nd ed.). New York: Harper & Row.

Miserandino, M. (1996, June). Children who do well in school: Individual differences in perceived competence and autonomy in aboveaverage children. *Journal of Educational Psychology, 88,* 203–204.

Mucherah, W. & Yoder, A. (2008). Motivation for reading and middle school students performance on standardized testing in reading. *Reading Psychology, 29*(3), 214–235.

Phillips, G. (1998, July 6). *Leadership in a synergestic culture*. Fourth Annual Principals Academy Retreat: Making a difference in student behavior. Lexington, KY.

Pintrich, P. R., & Garcia, T. (1992, April). *An annotated model of motivation and selfregulated learning*. Paper presented at the annual meeting of the American Educational Research Association, San Francisco.

Rinne, C. H. (1998). Motivating students is a percentage game. *Phi Delta Kappan, 79*(8), 620–628.

Rogers, C. R., & Freiberg, H. J. (1994). *Freedom to learn* (3rd ed.). Columbus, OH: Merrill.

Rubble, D. N. (1980). A developmental perspective on theories of achievement motivation. In L. J. Fyans (Ed.), *Achievement motivation: Recent trends in theory and research.* New York: Plenum.

Seligman, M. E. P. (2006). *Learned optimism: How to change your mind and your life (2nd ed.).* New York: Pocket Books.

Slavin, R. E. (2012). *Educational Psychology* (10th ed.). Upper Saddle River, NJ: Pearson.

Stipek, D. J. (1993). *Motivation to learn* (2nd ed.). Boston: Allyn & Bacon.

Weiner, B. (2000). Interpersonal and intrapersonal theories of motivation from an attributional perspective. *Educational Psychology Review, 12,* 1–14.

Wigfield, A. & Eccles, J. S. (2000). Expectancy value theory of achievement motivation. *Contemporary Educational Psychology, 25,* 68–81

Williams, L. J. (1997). *Membership in inclusive classrooms: Middle school students' perceptions.* Unpublished Ph.D. dissertation, University of Arizona.

Williams, L. J., & Downing, J. E. (1998). Membership and belonging in inclusive classrooms: What do middle school students have to say? *The Journal of the Association for Persons with Severe Handicaps, 23*(2), 98–110.

Winfield, L. F., & Lee, V. E. (1990). *Gender differences in reading proficiency: Are they consistent across racial groups?* Baltimore, MD: Johns Hopkins University Center for Research on Effective Schooling for Disadvantaged Students.

CHAPTER TWELVE

Alberto, P. A., & Troutman, A. C. (1986). *Applied behavior analysis for teachers.* Columbus, Ohio: Merrill.

Azrin, N. H., & Holz, W. C. (1966). Punishment. In W. A. Honig (Ed.), *Operant behavior: Areas of research and application* (pp. 380–447). New York: Appleton.

Ban, J. R. (1994, May/June). A lesson plan approach for dealing with school discipline. *Clearing House, 67,* 257–260.

Brasof, M. (2011). Student input improves behavior, fosters leadership. *Phi Delta Kappan, 93*(2), 20–24.

Brophy, J. (1985). Classroom management as instruction: Socializing self-guidance in students. *Theory into Practice, 24*(4), 233–240.

Brophy, J. (2006). History of research on classroom management. In C. M. Everston & C. S. Weinstein (Eds.), *Handbook of classroom management: Research, practice, and contemporary issues* (pp. 3–43). Mahwah, New Jersey: Erlbaum.

Bushaw, W. J. & Lopez, S. J. (2010). A time for change: 42nd Annual Phi Delta Kappa/Gallop Poll of the Public's Attitudes Toward the Public Schools. *Phi Delta Kappan, 92*(1), 8–27.

Carr, S., & Punzo, R. (1993). The effects of selfmonitoring of academic accuracy and productivity on the performance of students with behavioral disorders. *Behavioral Disorders, 18*(4), 241–250.

Charles, C. M. (1989). *Building classroom discipline: From models to practice* (3rd ed.). New York: Longman.

Charles, C. M. (1999). *Building classroom discipline* (6th ed.). New York: Longman.

Cole, C. (1992). Self-management interventions in the schools. *School Psychology Review, 21*(2), 188–192.

Corbett, W. T. (1990). The time-room: A key component of a total school discipline program. *Clearing House, 63*(6), 280–281.

Dillon, J. T. (1987). Teaching and the art of questioning. *Phi Delta Kappa Fastback, 194,* 38.

Doyle, W. (1986). Classroom organization and management. In M. C. Wittrock (Ed.), *Handbook of research on teaching* (pp. 392–431). New York: Macmillan.

Dreikurs, R., & Cassel, P. (1974). *Discipline without tears.* New York: Hawthorne.

Elias, M. J. & Schwab, Y. (2006). From compliance to responsibility: Social and emotional learning and classroom management. In C. Everston & C. S. Weinstein (Eds.), *Handbook for classroom management: Research, practice, and contemporary issues.* Mahwah, NJ: Erlbaum.

Emmer, E. (1994, April). *Teacher emotions and classroom management.* Paper presented at the annual meeting of the American Educational Research Association, New Orleans.

Emmer, E., Evertson, C., Sanford, J., Clements, B., & Worksham, M. (1989). *Classroom management for secondary teachers* (2nd ed.). Englewood Cliffs, NJ: Prentice-Hall.

Emmer, E. T. & Stough, L. M. (2001). Classroom management: A critical part of educational psychology with implications for teacher education. *Educational Psychologist, 36,* 103–112.

Forman, S. G. (1980). A comparison of cognitive training and response cost procedures in modifying aggressive behaviors of elementary school children. *Behavior Therapy, 11,* 594–600.

Freiberg, H. J. (Ed.). (1999). *Beyond behaviorism: Changing the classroom management.* Boston: Allyn & Bacon.

Gathercoal, F. (1993). *Judicious discipline* (3rd ed.). San Francisco: Caddo Gap.

Gay, G. (2006). Connection between classroom management and culturally responsive teaching. In C. M. Everston & C. S. Weinstein *Handbook of classroom management: Research, practice, and contemporary issues* (pp. 343–372): Mahwah, NJ: Erlbaum.

Glasser, W. (1969). *Schools without failure.* New York: Harper & Row.

Glasser, W. (1990). *The quality school: Managing students without coercion.* New York: Harper & Row.

Good, T. L., & Brophy, J. E. (1987). *Looking in classrooms* (4th ed.). New York: Harper & Row.

Good, T. L., & Brophy, J. E. (1997). *Looking in classrooms* (7th ed.). New York: Harper & Row.

Goodlad, J. I. (1984). *A place called school: Prospects for the future.* New York: McGraw-Hill.

Henson, K. T. (2011). *Methods and strategies for teaching in secondary and middle schools* (6th ed.). White Plains, NY: Longman.

James, S. D., & Egel, A. L. (1986). A direct prompting strategy for increasing reciprocal interactions between handicapped and nonhandicapped siblings. *Journal of Applied Behavior Analysis, 19,* 173–186.

Johns, F. A., & McNaughton, R. H. (1990, May). Spare the rod: A continuing controversy. *Clearing House,* 388–392.

Johnson, D. W., Maruyama, G., Johnson, R., Nelson, D., & Skon, L. (1981). Effects of cooperative, competitive, and individualistic goal structures on achievement: A meta-analysis. *Psychological Bulletin, 89,* 47–62.

Johnston, W. J. (1985). *Education on trial*. San Francisco: ICS Press.

Jones, V. (1996). Classroom management. In J. Sikula (Ed.), *Handbook of research on teacher education* (2nd ed., pp. 503–521). New York: Macmillan.

Jones, V. (2006). How do teachers learn to be effective classroom managers? In C. M. Everston & C. S. Weinstein (Eds.), *Handbook of classroom management: Research, practice, and contemporary issues* (p. 902). Mahwas, New Jersey: Lawrence Erlbaum.

Jones, V., & Jones, L. (1995). *Comprehensive classroom management*. Boston: Allyn & Bacon.

Jones, V., & Jones, L. (2004). *Comprehensive classroom management: Creating communities of support and solving problems* (7th ed.). Boston: Allyn & Bacon.

Kazdin, A. E. (1985). Selection of target behaviors: The relationship of the treatment focus to clinical dysfunction. *Behavioral Assessment, 7*, 33–47.

Kounin, J. (1970). *Discipline and group management in classrooms*. New York: Holt, Rinehart & Winston.

Landrum, T. J., Scott, T. M., & Lingo, A. S. (2011). Classsroom misbehaviour is predictable and preventable. *Phi Delta Kappan, 93*(2), 30–34

Long, J. D., & Frye, V. H. (1977). *Making it till Friday: A guide to successful classroom management*. Princeton, NJ: Princeton Book Company.

Mace, C. F., Belfiore, P. J., & Hutchinson, J. M. (2001). Operant theory and research on self-regulation. In B. J. Zimmerman and D. H. Schunk (Eds.), *Self-regulated learning and academic achievement: Theoretical perspectives* (2nd ed., pp. 39–66). Mahwah, NJ: Erlbaum.

Manning, J. (1959). Discipline in the good old days. *Phi Delta Kappan, 41*(3), 87–91.

Manning, M. L., & Baruth, L. G. (1996). Learners at risk: Three issues for educators. *Clearing House, 69*(4), 239–241.

Marzano, R. J. & Marzano, J. S. (2003, September). The key to classroom management. *Educational Leadership, 61*(1), 6–13.

McCaslin, M., & Good, T. L. (1996). *Listening in classrooms*. New York: HarperCollins.

McCaslin, M., Bozack, A. R., Napoleon, L., Thomas, A., Vasquez, V., Wayman, V. & Zhang, J. (2006). Self-regulated learning and classroom management: Theory, research, and considerations for classroom practice. In C. M. Everston & C. S. Weinstein, *Handbook of classroom management: Research, practice, and contemporary issues* (pp. 223–252). Mawah, NJ: Erlbaum.

McInerney, D. M., & Van Etten, S. (Eds.). (2004). *Big theories revisited*. Greenwich, CT: Information Age Publishing.

Phillips, G. (1998, July 6). Leadership in a synergistic culture. *Making a difference in student behavior*. 1998 Principals' Academy Retreat, Lexington, KY.

Price, B. J., & Marsh, G. E., II. (1985). Practical suggestions for planning and conducting parent conferences. *Teaching Exceptional Children, 17*, 274–278.

Rapport, M. D., Murphy, H. A., & Bailey, J. S. (1982). Ritalin vs. response cost in the control of hyperactive children: A within-subject comparison. *Journal of Applied Behavior Analysis, 15*, 205–216.

Reinstein, D. (1998). Crossing the economic divide. *Educational Leadership, 55*(4), 28–29.

Reis, E. M. (1988). Effective teacher techniques: Implications for better discipline. *Clearing House, 61*, 356–357.

Rich, J. M. (1989). The use of corporal punishment. *Clearing House, 63*(4), 149–152.

Rogers, C. & Freiberg, H. J. (1994). *Freedom to learn* (3rd ed.). New York: Merrill.

Scott, C. G., Murray, G. C., Martins, C., & Dustin, E. R. (1996). Student self-esteem and the school system: Perceptions and implications. *Journal of Educational Research, 89*(5), 286–293.

Schunk, D. H. (2001). Social cognitive theory and self-regulated learning. In B. J. Zimmerman & D. H. Schunk (Eds.), *Self-regulated learning and academic achievement: Theoretical perspectives* (2nd ed. pp. 125–152). Mahwah, NJ: Erlbaum.

Skinner, B. F. (1953). *Science and human behavior.* New York: Macmillan.

Strain, P. S., & Fox, J. E. (1981). Peers as therapeutic agents for isolate classmates. In A. E. Kazdin (Eds.), *Advances in clinical child psychology* (Vol. 4, pp. 167–197). New York: Plenum.

Sullivan, M. A. & O'Leary, S. G. (1990). Maintenance following reward and cost token programs. *Behavior Therapy, 21*, 139–149

Sulzer-Azaroff, B., & Mayer, R. G. (1991). *Behavior analysis for lasting change.* Fort Worth: Holt, Rinehart & Winston.

Tauber, R. T. (1989). Discipline theory: Making the most of what works now. *NASSP Bulletin, 73*, 1–4.

Thornberg, R. (2010). A study of children's conceptions of school rules by investigating their judgments of transgressions in the absence of rules. *Educational Psychology, 30*, 583–603.

Walker, J. E., Shea, T. M. & Bauer, A. M. (2004). *Behavior management: A practical approach for educators* (8th ed.). New Jersey, Pearson.

Weinstein, C. S., Curran, M., & Tomlinson-Clarke, S. (2003). Culturally responsive classroom management: Awareness into action. *Theory into practice, 42*(4), 269–276.

Williams, P. A., Alley, R., & Henson, K. T. (1999). *Managing secondary classrooms: Principles and strategies to effective discipline and instruction.* Needham Heights, MA: Allyn & Bacon.

CHAPTER THIRTEEN

Bellon, J. J., Bellon, E. C., & Blank, M. A. (1992). *Teaching from a research knowledge base.* New York: Macmillan.

Boyer, E. (1990). *Scholarship reconsidered: Priorities of the professorate.* Princeton, NJ: Carnegie Foundation for Advancement of Teaching.

Brownlie, F. (1990). The door is open. Won't you come in? In M. W. Olson (Ed.), *Opening the door to educational research* (pp. 21–31). Newark, DE: International Reading Association.

Bruder, I., Buchsbaum, H., Hill, M., & Orlando, L. C. (1992). School reform: Why you need technology to get there. *Electronic Learning, II*(8), 22–28.

Chattin-McNichols, J., & Loeffler, M. H. (1989). Teachers as researchers: The first cycle of the teachers' research network. *Young Children, 44*(5), 20–27.

Chimes, M., & Schmidt, P. (1990). What I read over my summer vacation: Readings on cultural diversity. *Clearing House, 64*(1), 44–46.

Gay, L. R., Mills, G. E. & Airasian, P. (2009). *Educational Research: Competencies for analysis and applications.* Boston: Pearson Education.

Good, T. L., & Brophy, J. E. (1987). *Looking in classrooms* (4th ed.). New York: Harper & Row.

Goswami, D., & Stillman, P. (1987). *Reclaiming the classroom: Teacher research as an agency for change.* Portsmouth, NH: Bovnton Cook.

Green, S. K. & Johnson, R. L. (2010). *Assessment is essential.* Boston: McGraw-Hill.

Harrison, P. L. (1981). Mercer's adaptive behavior inventory, the McCarthy scales, and dental development as predictors of first-grade achievement. *Journal of Educational Psychology, 73*(1), 78–82.

Henson, K. T. (1996). *Methods and strategies for teaching in secondary and middle schools* (3rd ed.). New York: Longman.

King, A., and Rosenshine, B. (1993). Effects of guided cooperative questioning on children's knowledge construction. *Journal of Experimental Education, 61*(2), 127–148.

Marriott, V. (1990). *Transition*. Unpublished paper.

McLaughlin, H. J., Hall, M., Earle, K., Miller, v., & Wheeler, M. (1995). Hearing our students: Team action research in a middle school. *Middle School Journal, 26*(3), 7–12.

McMillan, J. H. (2012). *Educational research: Fundamentals for the consumer* (6th ed.). Boston: Pearson Education Inc.

Mertler, C. A. (2003). *Classroom assessment: A practical guide for the educators.* Los Angeles: Pyrczak Publishing.

Neilsen, L. (1990). Research comes home. *Reading Teacher, 44*(1), 248–250.

Nitko, A. J., & Brookhart, S. M. (2011). *Educational assessment of students* (6th ed.). Boston: Pearson Education, Inc.

Ornstein, A. C. (1990, October/November). National reform and instructional accountability. *High School Journal, 74*, 51–56.

Sucher, F. (1990). Involving school administrators in classroom research. In M. W. Olson (Ed.), *Opening the door to classroom research* (pp. 112–125). Newark, DE: International Reading Association.

CHAPTER FOURTEEN

Ballard, K., & Bates, A. (2008). *Making a connection between student achievement, teacher accountability, and quality classroom instruction.* Qualitative Report, *13*, 560–580.

Buddy, J. (2009). *Standardized test review 101.* School Library Monthly, *23*(4), 18–21

Cizek, G. J. (1991, January). Reasoning about testing. *Education Digest, 56*, 56–58.

Clandinin, D. J., Davies, A., Hogan, P., & Kennard, B. (1993). *Learning to teach, teaching to learn.* New York: Teachers College Press.

Ellsworth, R. A., Dunnell, P., & Duell, O. A. (1990, May/June). *Journal of Educational Research, 83*(5), 290–293.

Fielding, G., & Shaughnessy, J. (1990, November). Improving student assessment: Overcoming the obstacles. *NASSP Bulletin, 74*, 90–98.

Gotterbarn, D. (1991). Computer ethics responsibility regained. *National Forum, 61*(3), 26–31.

Griswold, P. A. (1990, February). Assessing relevance and reliability to improve the quality of teacher-made tests. *NASSP Bulletin, 74*, 18–24.

Harris, K. H., & Longstreet, W. S. (1990, November/ December). Alternative testing and the national agenda for control. *Clearing House, 64*, 90–93.

Henson, K. T. (1996). *Methods and strategies for teaching in secondary and middle schools* (3rd ed.). New York: Longman.

Herman, J., Aschbacher, P., & Winters, L. (1992). *A practical guide to alternative assessment.* Alexandria, VA: Association for Supervision and Curriculum Development.

Johnson, D. W. & Johnson, R. T. (2002). *Meaningful assessment: A manageable and cooperative process.* Boston: Allyn & Bacon.

Knowles, J. G. (1993). Life history accounts as mirrors: A practical avenue for the conceptualization of reflection in teacher education. In J. Calderhead & P. Gates (Eds.), *Conceptualizing reflection in teacher development.* Washington, DC: Falmers Press.

Kohn, A. (2000). *The case against standardized testing. Raising scores, ruining the schools.* Portsmouth, NH: Heinemann.

Krathwohl, D. R., Bloom, B., & Masia, B. (1964). *Taxonomy of educational objectives Handbook II: The classification of educational goals: Affective domain.* New York: McKay.

Mertler, C. A. (2003). *Classroom assessment: A practical guide for educators.* Los Angeles: Pyrczak Publishing.

Miller, A., & Tellez, K. (1993). *Innovative use of teaching portfolios in a professional development school.* Paper presented at the annual meeting of the Association for Teacher Educators, Los Angeles.

Ornstein, A. C. (1990, October/November). National reform and instructional accountability. *High School Journal, 74*, 51–56.

Phillips, G. (1998, July 6). *Leadership in a synergestic culture.* 1998 Principal's Academy Retreat: Making a difference in student behavior, Lexington, KY.

Popham, W. J., & Hambleton, R. K. (1990). Can you pass the test on testing? *Principal, 69*(3), 38–39.

Popham, W. J. (2011). *Classroom assessment: What teachers need to know* (6th ed.). Upper Saddle River, NJ: Prentice Hall.

Savitz, F. R. (1985). Effects of easy questions placed at the beginning of science multiple-choice examinations. *Journal of Instructional Psychology, 12*, 6–10.

Stinnett, T. M., & Henson K. T. (1982). *America's public schools in transition: Future trends and issues.* New York: Columbia University Teachers College Press.

Tanner, D. E. (2001). *Assessing academic achievement.* Boston: Allyn & Bacon.

Tellez, K. (1996). Authentic assessment. In J. Sikula, T. Buttery & Guyton, E. (Eds.), *Association of Teacher Educators Handbook of Research on Teacher Education* (2nd ed., pp. 704–721). New York: Macmillan.

Van Wagenen, L., & Hibbard, K. M. (1998). Building teacher portfolios. *Educational Leadership, 55*(5), 26–29.

Wilcox , B. (1998, June 26–27). Writing for publication workshop. Pittsburgh, PA: Duquesne University.

Name Index

Subject Index